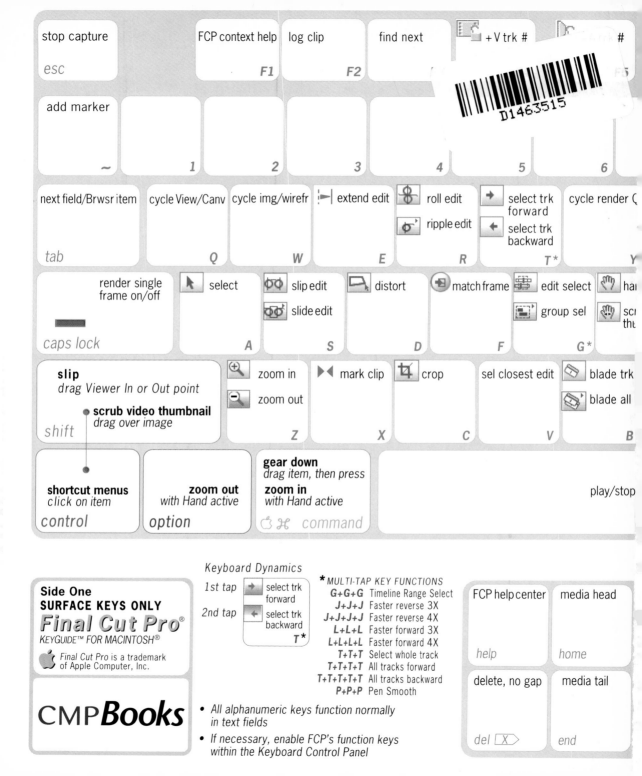

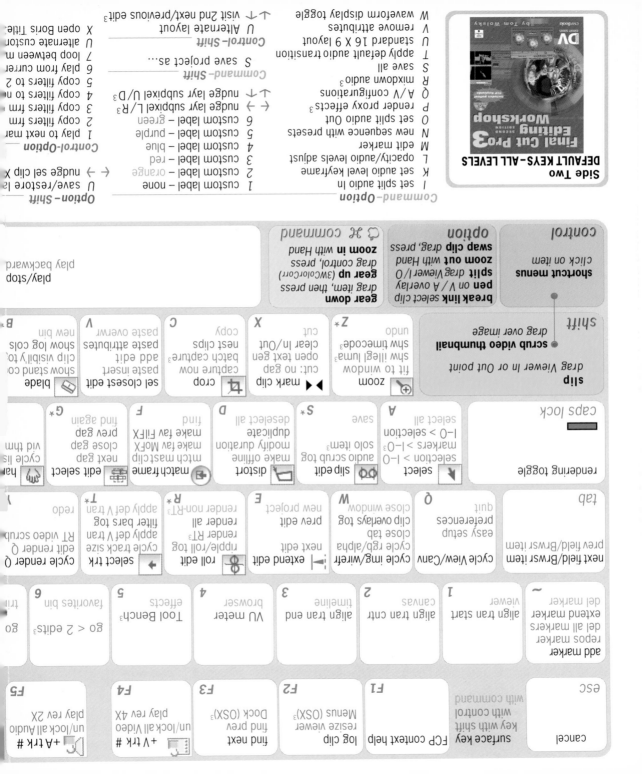

FINAL CUT PRO 3 EDITING WORKSHOP

Second Edition

Tom Wolsky

CMP **Books**

CMP Books
CMP Media LLC
1601 West 23rd Street, Suite 200
Lawrence, Kansas 66046
USA
www.cmpbooks.com

Technical Editor: Jeff Greenberg
Editor and layout design: Madeleine Reardon Dimond
Managing Editor: Michelle O'Neal
Cover layout design: Damien Castaneda

Distributed in the U.S. by:
Publishers Group West
1700 Fourth Street
Berkeley, California 94710
1-800-788-3123
www.pgw.com

Distributed in Canada by:
Jaguar Book Group
100 Armstrong Avenue
Georgetown, Ontario M6K 3E7 Canada
905-877-4483

ISBN: 1-57820-118-7

CMP**Books**

For B.T.
With All My Love

Reviewers' Comments

"It takes a pro to teach Final Cut Pro, and Tom Wolsky delivers. His years of TV and film experience make him uniquely qualified to demystify Final Cut Pro and teach good editing techniques. Every editor needs this book."

— Jim Heid, 'Mac Focus' columnist, *Los Angeles Times*

"If you want to learn editing with Final Cut Pro, look no further. Tom Wolsky brings a depth of experience to digital editing that few others share. He has proven himself an excellent teacher at Stanford University's Academy for New Media, and I will encourage, if not require, future students of the Academy to read this book."

— Phil Gibson, Executive Director, Digital Media Academy

"Tom has done a terrific job of putting it all together here — editing, compositing, effects, compression — and even better, he tosses in liberal doses of solid craft advice that can come only from a seasoned pro."

— Ralph Fairweather, Final Cut Pro development team member and 2-pop.com Final Cut Pro forum co-developer

"Tom Wolsky's longtime professional career with ABC News in London — and his later teaching position and full-time studio work in California — takes this work far beyond the simple "how to" books that address Final Cut. In Tom's hands, the subject becomes a look into the process of professional editing and project management as well. Because of this, we believe that he knows Final Cut in many ways better than the people that write the program."

— Ron and Kathlyn Lindeboom, founders, creativecow.net

"I have been reading Tom's post at 2-pop for years and I have learned a great deal from him at the Boards. He always writes clearly, his instructions are detailed and thorough."

— Ken Stone, photographer and FCP web host

"Easy reading, well-organized, thoughtful, and incisive. If you want to edit with Final Cut Pro, this is the book to get. With his years of experience on the network frontlines at ABC, Tom Wolsky gives readers not only the basics of Final Cut Pro, but also the insights and finer points of technique that differentiate the good editor from the great one. A superb way to learn today the new media tools we'll all be using to communicate tomorrow."

— Jack Smith, former ABC News correspondent and managing director, Burson Marsteller

Table of Contents

Introduction

The first movies were single, static shots of everyday events. The Lumière brothers' screening of a train pulling into a Paris station was a sensation. They followed this with a staged comic scene. Georges Méliès expanded this into staging complex tableaux. It wasn't until Edwin H. Porter and D. W. Griffith in the United States discovered the power of editing one shot next to another that the movies were really born. Griffith also introduced such innovations as the flashback, the first real use of film to manipulate time. Close-ups were used to emphasize the moment of impact; wide shots to establish context. The real discovery was that the shot is the fundamental building block of film, and that the film is built one shot at a time, one after the other.

Films and videos are made in the moments when one shot changes into another, when one image is replaced by the next, when one point of view becomes someone else's point of view. Without the image changing, you just have moving pictures. The idea of changing from one angle to another or from one scene to another, quickly leads to the concept of juxtaposing one idea against another. It soon becomes apparent that the impact of storytelling lies in the way in which the shots are ordered. Putting a certain shot after another shot has a different meaning if it is placed before the other shot. The classic example is the three shots of the burning building:

A. The building on fire

B. The building exploding

C. Three men running away

In this order the audience sees it as three men escaping the exploding building. If you see A, then C, followed by B, you might think the men are trying to escape the fire and are caught by the explosion. If you see C, then B, then A, you will probably think the men set the explosion that causes the fire.

The editor's first decisions are:

1. Which shot to use

2. In what order the shots will appear

3. How long each shot will be seen

Whether the editing takes place when the writer scripts one shot and then another, or the director stages a scene to be shot in a certain continuity, or in some moment of serendipity in the cutting room when one shot is placed next to another, that is where movies are made. Editing is about selection, arrangement, and timing. Editing creates the visual and aural juxtaposition between shots.

Editors like to think they can make or break a project. They most certainly can break one, and they can certainly rescue one, but for a project to be really good requires not only that it be edited well, but that it be shot in such a way that it *can* be edited well. This doesn't only mean that it is beautifully photographed; the most beautiful shots that can't be edited together effectively are pointless. That long, slow, lingering zoom out becomes an anchor that drags down the pace of the video. That perfectly smooth pan along the treeline down to the shore brings the video to a grinding halt. Do you know what the viewer looks at when he or she watches this type of pan? They're staring at the leading edge of the screen, watching what's coming around the corner. It isn't only slow movement that will destroy a sequence, but the very camera angles chosen to show the scene. Poorly placed cameras, poorly composed shots, and ineffective staging will do more to kill a video beyond what even the finest editor can resurrect.

Editing is an art and a craft, and like any craft it has to be learned. Simply possessing the tools is not enough. Anyone, even I, can buy a tool belt with a hammer and all the electric tools I could ask for, but I would still not be a carpenter, let alone an artist in wood. The same is true of editing. Acquiring and learning how to use the tools is only part of the process. You have to also learn the craft of using the tools. There are many ways to do this. I would like to think this book is one of the steps in the process. Another might be a course or the traditional method of apprenticeship, which was the way I learned both the art and the craft, in Stan Hawks's and Arthur Solomon's cutting rooms and at ABC with its many talented editors.

With the advancement in recent years of desktop video production, the editor has come to do more and more of what used to be separate crafts. The editor is more and more being called upon to create graphics, animation, and various special effects. Because of FCP's capabilities in these areas, I have laid considerable emphasis on these parts of the application. Now everything is a trick of light and magical software engineering that allows you to create a visual and aural experience for your audience. This video medium is now infinitely malleable, and FCP provides you the tool to control the medium with freedom, flexibility, and precision.

I am often asked how long it takes to edit something. The only answer I can usually find is that it takes as much time as you have. The constraints of time can have several causes:

- Deadline, as in broadcast airtime

- Cost, because of limitations of budget

- A combination of the two

I have worked on news pieces that should have taken an hour to edit that have been cut for air in less than ten minutes. And I have worked on pieces that could have been cut in an hour that took weeks. An edit can go on endlessly. It never really finishes; it simply stops. Painters often talk about painting in this way, that you just reach a point where the work stops and you say that is it. Eventually you reach a point at which all your additional effort isn't making it better, simply making it different, rearranging the shots, making subtle adjustments that can only be seen on the 20th viewing. It's often better to stop earlier rather than later.

Every editor comes out of a movie saying he could take ten minutes out of it. Often the picture would probably be improved by the trims, but then often enough it would be ruined. There is a danger in chipping away too much, in too finely honing a piece, eventually cutting into the core and damaging the material. As the editor you get used to seeing the pictures again and again. You see the content more quickly. You understand the flow of the shots more quickly, and then the danger is that you mistake your understanding and comprehension of the material for that of the audience, an audience who has never seen the film before. This happens less often when a director has a clear vision of the picture and has been able to convey that vision. The greater danger comes when the director's concept is unclear both to him or her and to you: then the risk of over cutting increases. Directors confident in their ideas, who know clearly what they want, tend to shoot less, with little extra cover. Sometimes this will get them and you as the editor into trouble in the cutting room. But when it works, when the director's vision is clear and well executed, the work can be very, very good. When it doesn't, the work tends to be very, very mediocre. Uncertain directors tend to overshoot, giving editors a vast range of choices and angles, more than they probably want, and certainly more than they need. This is where the greatest danger comes in overcutting: putting in too many angles to fit in every vision — a bit of this, a bit of that, and in the end, not much of anything.

This is a book about editing with the Final Cut Pro application. It is not a manual and is not intended to supersede or replace the FCP manual. If you want to know how every control, slider, and button in FCP functions, the manual supplied with the application is voluminous enough. This book is intended to be about editing.

The structure of this book follows that of the earlier edition, *Final Cut Pro 2 Editing Workshop*, but is significantly different in two main areas:

- The operating system, of course, which is completely new

- The enhancements and modifications that have been made to the application in the new version

This book is organized as a series of tutorials and lessons that I hope have been written in a logical order to lead the reader from one topic to a more advanced topic. The nature of your work with Final Cut Pro, however, may require the information for example in Lesson 7 right away. You can read that lesson by itself and get to make that scroll you need right now. There may, however, be elements in Lesson 7 that presuppose that you know something about using the **Viewer** in conjunction with the **Canvas**. This is where a good index comes in. If there's something in Lesson 7 that you don't understand, some term or procedure, try looking in the index.

The book can also be read in the more traditional manner, from start to finish, simply absorbing the lessons and the tips, without doing the lessons. Nor does the book need to be read in the traditional linear fashion beginning with this page, though this might be better for a new user to Final Cut Pro. If you've set up your system and perhaps have done the tutorial that comes with the application, you might want to skip the first couple of lessons. That said, there is much that is new in the operating system that all Macintosh users should be aware of. On the other hand, if there's some specific technique you'd like to learn about, go ahead and get right to it. There is also a lot that is new in this version of Final Cut Pro from earlier versions, great new **Color Correction** tools, real-time effects, the new **QuickView** window, new video scopes, and a host of other improvements. I hope there's enough in here to make all the lessons interesting reading for any FCP user.

The CD included with this book carries some of the lessons, project, and clips used in the book. Not all of the lessons require materials from the CD. For some, such as the first couple of lessons, you don't need any at all. For others you may want to substitute your own material, clips you want to work with or are more familiar with. I hope you find this book useful, informative, and fun. I think it's a good way to learn this kind of application.

In this book I offer a good many opinions on how I like to work with the application. I want to emphasize that these are only a single individual's views and are not necessarily the best way to work or the best way for you to work. Everybody has different experiences, especially working with an application as complex as Final Cut Pro. How you work depends on many factors, not least of which is your experience and the types of projects you're working on. These latter often dictate your workflow. I'm only offering suggestions for a variety of work scenarios. I hope you find one that's beneficial for you. Or better still, create your own.

Acknowledgments

I would guess most people think of writing as a solitary occupation, and by and large it is. Book production, on the other hand, is the result of a team effort, perhaps as large a team as for a film or video production. First of this team is Paul Temme, associate publisher for CMP Books, for his steady and thoughtful advice that again painlessly guided this project through to completion. Next in line must be Jeff Greenberg of Future Media Concepts, who gracefully took on the chore of being my technical editor. The book could well have been a disaster without his input. Any errors that remain are the results of my oversights or misunderstandings, not his. Many thanks are due to Michelle O'Neal and Madeleine Reardon Dimond for painlessly guiding me through the copyediting and layout process and to Damien Castaneda for his work on the covers.

So many helped in making this book possible: Lanny Cotler and Cotler Brothers Productions, for allowing me to use material from their wonderful 1997 independent film *Heartwood* with Hilary Swank, Eddie Mills, and the late Jason Robards; Sidney Kramer, for his expert advice; Ralph Fairweather, for his continuing advice and help to the community of FCP users; Tim Wilson of BorisFX, for always coming up with the answers to my questions; Shawn Bockoven and Hiroshi Kumatani, for their film look technique; Nathan Lewis Collett and Victoria Szabo of Stanford University; Jim Heid, for his advice, Toby Malina, for her gracious assistance, and Steve Broback, all of Avondale Media. To the creative software engineers who allowed me to put samples of their work on the CD, especially Klaus Eiperle, whose work is now included in the Final Cut Pro package and who patiently reworked FXScript features as I threw ever more demands at him. We've included samples of his latest work on the CD as well as updates for the existing plugins that come with FCP3. Mattias Sandström of Sweden, for his elegant Convolution film effect and TMTSfree filters; David Clark at Gideon Softworks, for letting us include GetInfo; Mike Bombich, for Carbon Copy Cloner; and Eric Fry, for his Timecode Calculator. Finally, many thanks to the many hardware manufacturers such as Aurora and Datacom and Sonnet and FirmTek and Griffin, and software producers like Adobe and Automatic Duck and Boris and Profound Effects, who allowed me to experiment and test and try out and poke around in their creations without let or hindrance.

A great many thanks are due to my partner B. T. Corwin for her insights, her endless encouragement, her engineering technical support, and for her patience with me. Without her, none of this would have been possible. Finally, again my thanks the wonderful people of Damine, Japan, who welcomed us into their homes and whose lives provided the source material for many of these lessons.

Lesson 1

Installing Final Cut Pro 3

Congratulations! You're about to install one of the most creative video tools available on a desktop computer, running on one of the most elegant, efficient, and stable operating systems yet devised. Welcome to Final Cut Pro 3, Apple's professional video editing software for use with its Macintosh computers. This wonderful application has brought affordable desktop video production to the reach of most people. I'm sure you want to dive right into it, but the application first must be installed properly on a properly functioning system. Video editing software is not a simple piece of shareware that you can install onto your computer and hope it will run without problems. Video editing software requires your system to be running in optimal condition, with all the correct system software and only the correct system software. Your hard drives must be clean and running properly, ready for moving large amounts of data at high speed.

Though FCP3 works equally well on both Mac OS 9.2.2 and OS X 10.1.1 and higher, I think many users will take this opportunity to migrate to Apple's new operating system. So for many FCP users, either first time or experienced, this version will present a new challenge, a new and very different operating system to run it.

In many ways, this is much more than a new operating system; it is a fundamentally new platform, a Unix-based platform running inside a Macintosh operating system's GUI (graphical user interface) shell.

What You Really Need

Let's first look at Apple's Minimum System Requirements for its new operating system. The Apple website gives a detailed list of the computers it supports. Basically it includes these machines: PowerMac G3, G4, or G4 Cube; iMac or eMac; PowerBook G3 or G4 (except the original PowerBook G3); or iBook.

This list of hardware is identical for OS 9.2.2 and OS X. So if you can run FCP3 on one, you can run it on the other.

In addition to the actual computer you will need at least 256MB of RAM as well as at least 1.5 Gigabytes available for installing the operating system. We'll talk more about RAM and drive space in a moment.

Apple's requirements for Final Cut Pro 3 are in Table 1.1.

> ✏️ **Note**
> **No Upgrade Cards?** The Apple website also says that the operating system does not support processor upgrade cards. In this Apple tends to err on the side of caution, for many people are running systems with various processor upgrade cards quite successfully. These cards serve to enhance render capabilities and speeds.

Table 1.1   Apple's Suggested Minimum System Requirements for Final Cut Pro

Computer	300-MHz Power Macintosh G3/350 megahertz (MHz) or faster with built-in FireWire PowerBook G3/400 MHz or faster with built-in FireWire iMac 350 MHz or faster with built-in FireWire iBook (Dual USB) 500 MHz or faster with built-in FireWire All with CD or DVD drive for installation
Real-time Requirements	500-MHz or faster single, or dual processor Power Mac G4 or PowerBook G4 required for G4 real-time effects 667-MHz PowerBook G4 required for mobile G4 real-time effects in DV format
Operating system	Mac OS 9.2.2 or later Mac OS X v10.1.1 or later
QuickTime	5.0.4 or later
RAM	256MB of RAM (384MB recommended for G4 real-time effects)
Hard drives	40MB of available disk space required for installation Recommended: 20G or greater Audio/Video-rated hard disk drive

Built-in FireWire is available on all the specified models except the older Beige G3s, which may be Apple's way of saying these legacy machines are still excluded from newer versions of FCP.

In reality, a dual processor 450MHz machine will get the same level of real-time performance as a single processor 500MHz G4.

Though the operating system can be either 9.2.2 or OS X 10.1.1 or later, we will concentrate on the OS X version, because it will probably be the one most used by those working with the application. For those who waited to switch to this system because their editing software was not compatible, this will perhaps be their first step into it.

Apple has also considerably raised the minimum RAM requirements from its original 105MB to 256MB minimum and a whopping third of a gigabyte of installed RAM to do real-time effects.

Apple has dropped its previously stated requirements for high-performance SCSI media drives because these have largely been superseded, except at the highest data rates, by fast and cheap IDE drives.

Which computer you purchase to run your editing suite is almost invariably dictated by your finances. My recommendation is always to get the biggest, fastest, most powerful computer you can afford. If you have budget constraints, get started on an iMac. If you need to be on the road a lot, get a PowerBook. If you have a larger budget, go for it: a multiprocessor G4, loaded with lots of RAM. To achieve real-time systems, Apple recommends at least a G4/500, but this is no guarantee that you will achieve the type of performance you would like. The faster the computer you have, the greater your real-time capabilities will be. Apple has published a graph that charts computer performance against application performance.

Loading What You Need

I think most experts would advise anyone installing video editing software to start with a clean installation of the operating system.

Note

A/V drive: An A/V-rated hard drive is one that is capable of sustained read/write speeds sufficient to support your video content. For DV material this would be a minimum of 15MB per second. Most 7,200rpm IDE drives can achieve this and more easily.

Real-time and OfflineRT

With version 3 of Final Cut Pro Apple introduces processor based real-time transitions, graphics, and motion. Prior to this version, real-time editing required hardware assistance through a PCI processor card. Computers are now fast enough — and getting faster every day — to achieve this with their own processor speed. FCP's real time is only with DV material and only displays on the computer monitor. It is for preview purposes only and will not output through the FireWire port to a camera or deck.

OfflineRT (real-time) is the ability of the application to capture DV material at low resolution using the Photo-JPEG codec. This allows the user to capture great amounts of material to relatively little hard drive space, about 40 minutes of offline material per gigabyte of drive space, compared to about five minutes for full-resolution DV. Capturing OfflineRT material requires a computer with a fast processor, a 500MHz or higher. However, it is possible, as we shall see, to capture at full resolution on a slower computer, then export to OfflineRT to conserve drive space, and work in real-time mode with draft-quality material on a computer that isn't the latest and fastest model.

The first difference a new user to OS X will probably encounter is that there no longer is a startup CD as such, not one which contains the operating system together with utilities such as **Drive Setup** and **Disk First Aid**. Now there is only the OS X installer CD. Loading the CD while already booted will bring up the window in Figure 1.1.

Double-clicking the **Install Mac OS X** icon will bring up the window in Figure 1.2, which will force you to restart the computer. By restarting from this button, the computer will boot off the OS X installer CD.

If you're already working in OS X and preparing for a clean system installation, you will probably also get a demand for an administrator's password, as in Figure 1.3.

Figure 1.1   Mac OS X CD Window

Figure 1.2   OS X Restart Window

📌 *Note*

Before Installation: If you already have material on your internal hard drive, before you begin the installation process, I would suggest you copy everything — system, applications, and any files you have — onto another hard drive as backup. OS9 isn't a problem because you can dump the whole thing — OS, applications, and all — into a folder somewhere and bring it back fully restored. If you already have OS X installed, this is more of a problem. You can't copy this operating system from drive to drive; it just doesn't work, because there are hidden files that the normal copying process ignores. As the system can't normally be backed up in this way, the essential things to move over are the OS X applications, which should always be in one folder. While running under OS9, move over the *Users* and the *Library*. And of course, also move over all the other files you want to keep: text, e-mail, Quicken, Contacts, etc. You are then ready to proceed with a proper installation. It is possible to back up the entire OS X partition by creating a disk image with Disk Copy and then using **Apple Software Restore** to recreate the partition. There are also great new shareware tools to help ease copying OS X partitions. Mike Bombich's Carbon Copy Cloner 1.2 is shareware, and it's available in the *Extras* folder on this book's CD. Shareware is a wonderful creation of the new digital age; if you use shareware, please support it.

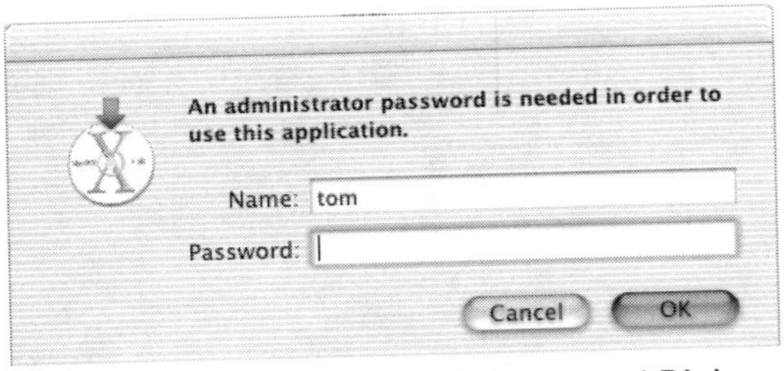

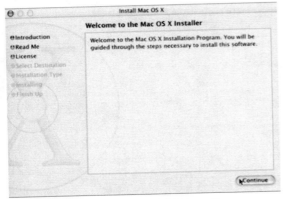

Figure 1.3   Administrator's Password Dialog

Figure 1.4   Welcome to OS X Installer

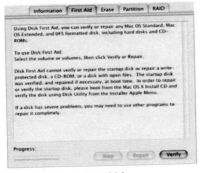

Figure 1.5   Installer>DiskUtilities

Figure 1.6   First Aid

The first screen after startup (Figure 1.4) will welcome you to the OS X installer, but before you begin the actual installation process, you should set up your system properly for operating with two systems, OS9 and OS X. This works best if your internal hard drive, the one used to store the operating system and applications, is divided into two partitions. One partition is for OS9 and all its applications, while the other is for OS X and all its applications. This drive should be separate from your high-speed media drives, not just be a separate partition.

Before you partition your system drive and install your systems, you'll need to run the new **Disk Utilities**, which combines the old **Drive Setup** and **Disk First Aid** into one. This is accessed on the OS X Installer CD from the **Installer** menu (Figure 1.5).

One of the first steps you should probably take is to select **First Aid** from the **Disk Utilities** screen (Figure 1.6). This will let you check through your drives to verify and repair them, always a good practice before system installation on a new drive.

Tip

Reset Password: In *Disk Utility* you'll also have access to the application **Reset Password**. This is the only place where this application is located. If you ever lose your OS X password, Reset Password will allow you to create a new password without actually installing the whole system. Guard your install CD, because this little application will let anyone crack into any part of your computer. They can even create a root password, so if they have Unix knowledge, they can enter even the most secure areas of the system.

Notice the other functions in the **Disk Utility** window. **Erase** used to be under the **Special** menu in earlier OSs. Notice also the **RAID** panel. **Disk Utility** allows you to create stripped arrays of hard drives for very high-speed performance for high data rate standard definition or high definition work. I would advise against using this RAID software because the drives will not be recognized when you are booted in OS9. Rather, use RAID software recognized by both OS9 and OS X, such as ATTO ExpressStripe, or those from SoftRAID or CharisMac RAID X which should be available soon.

Partition the Drive

One step in the **Disk Utility** you will want to do to your system drive is to partition it. I strongly advise doing this. It is likely that for some while, you will be switching back and forth between operating systems. Having two partitions allows you to create

RAID

Though DV is probably the most commonly used video format with Final Cut Pro, it is by no means the only format available. Many users work very successfully with video systems that can use much higher data rates than DV. They're using video capture cards such as the Aurora Igniter card. Many also are using uncompressed video with the Igniter or the Pinnacle CinéWave card, or Digital Voodoo or the Kona card from AJA. For these systems, you need faster IDE drives or even very fast SCSI drives. Fast IDE controller cards such as the Sonnet Tempo ATA133 have made it possible to capture and edit even uncompressed video using a pair of IDE drives that have been stripped together as a RAID.

RAID stands for Redundant Array of Inexpensive Drives, as opposed to a SLED, Single Large Expensive Drive. RAIDs are used for backup purposes, as well as for splitting high speed data streams between multiple drives for greater throughout than could be achieved on a single drive. A RAID used for video purposes is an array usually made up of two or more identical drives that are stripped with software to act as a single drive, though the CharisMac RAID X software allows for the first time the ability to strip together drives of different sizes.

For the highest data rates, you will need to have multiple drives stripped together as a RAID. Data can spread across these drives simultaneously, a bit here, a byte there. Because more heads are writing and reading data simultaneously, quicker access is achieved, and more data can be pumped through the system. This is necessary for high data rate media, particularly for uncompressed media.

A downside of multiple drive arrays is that if one of your RAID drives fails, everything is gone because the recorded material is stripped equally over all the drives as if they were a single unit. That said, RAID systems have been getting more and more reliable over the years. Medéa makes boxes containing four, eight, and sixteen IDE drives stripped together. This is just one solution for creating pristine, uncompressed video images. The comparatively low cost of these massive storage systems make uncompressed video a viable editing solution.

Figure 1.7   Start-up Dialog

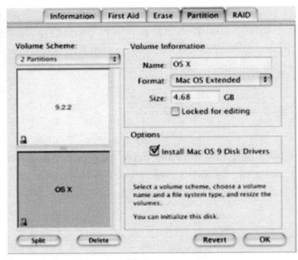

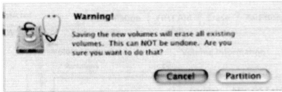

Figure 1.9   Partition

Figure 1.8   Warning Dialog

one system partition for each operating system. On each partition should be loaded the operating system and all the applications that work with it. So OS9 applications are loaded on the OS9 partition and OS X applications, as we shall do in a few minutes, are loaded on the OS X partition.

👉 Tip

Separate OS: One of the advantages of having separate operating systems on separate partitions is that on startup, if you hold down the **Option** key, you get a screen that allows you to chose which operating system you want to boot into (Figure 1.7). This does not work reliably if both operating systems are on the same partition.

1. To partition the drive, select the **Partition** window from the **Disk Utility** (Figure 1.8).

2. From the **Volume Scheme** popup, select two partitions.

3. Select each partition in the window and name it.

4. Make sure the **Install Mac OS9 Disk Drivers** box is checked. This ensures that the partitions will be visible to both OS9 and OS X. Click **OK**.

You will get a warning dialog (Figure 1.9) that cautions you that you are about to erase the drive and lose all the data on it.

Once the drives are partitioned, you are ready to begin system installation. After the OS X **Welcome** screen, you will next get the **Language Selection** screen (Figure 1.10).

After language selection, you will have to go through the legal rigmarole before you can begin.

5. One of the next prompts in the sequence will be to choose the drive on which to install the operating system. If you partitioned the internal drive of your computer correctly, you should be able to select the OS X partition for the installation (Figure 1.11).

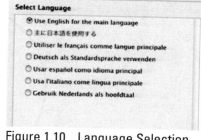

Figure 1.10   Language Selection

6. After selecting the partition for installation, but before you begin the actual OS X installation, click on the button marked **Custom**, which will bring up the window in Figure 1.12.

Here you will be allowed to deselect the language installations you do not require, which can save both hard drive space and installation time.

7. After you press the **Install** button, the installation process will begin.

This can take quite some time, depending on the speed of your computer and the amount of material you requested for installation. Once completed, the computer will automatically restart itself, booting off your newly installed operating system. The first screen that greets you on startup is Apple's new Aqua welcome screen (Figure 1.13).

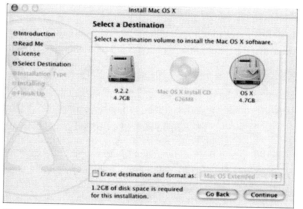

Figure 1.11   Destination Selection

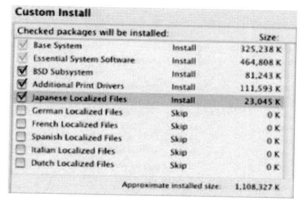

Figure 1.12   Language Selection Window

Figure 1.13 Apple Welcome Screen

Create Your Account

With Mac OS X, everyone who uses the computer can have an account with their own settings and a place to keep their documents.

Set up your account now. You can add accounts for others later.

Name: Tom Wolsky
Example: Mary Jones

Short Name: Tom
Example: mjones
An alternate name for your account, used by some network services. Enter 8 lowercase characters or fewer, with no spaces.

Password: ••••••••
The password for this account.

Verify: ••••••••
Enter your password again, exactly as you typed it.

Password Hint (optional):
Enter something that will help you remember your password.

Go Back   Continue

Figure 1.14 Creating User Account

8. As part of the registration process, you will be asked to create a new account (Figure 1.14).

This is an essential part of the OS X process. The new operating system is based upon secure, segregated users. At least one user must have administration privileges. This will allow you to perform functions such as installing software. We'll look at OS X operations and at **Users** after we've finished installing and configuring the systems.

9. After completing registration and setting your clock, time zone, Internet connection, and various other system preferences, you'll finally arrive at the new OS X desktop.

Before you go any farther, now would be the time to reinstall or restore your OS9 material.

10. If you've backed it up onto a separate hard drive, then simply drag all your OS9 material back onto your OS9 partition.

11. When that is done, reboot into OS9.

You can now restore any previously saved OS X material into your OS X partition, replacing some of what may have been created with the new installation.

12. If you do not have OS9 saved on another drive, now reinstall OS9 from an install CD.

13. After installation is completed, boot on your OS9 partition and check which operating system you have. If you are not using OS9.2.2, load your Final Cut Pro 3 Install or Upgrade CD and use the OS9 upgrades that are provided.

This will upgrade your OS9 system to OS9.2.2, which is minimum system requirement for FCP3.

14. Once these installations are completed, reboot into OS X. When the system is back up and running, one of the first things you should do is to check that you have the right operating system. Under the **Apple** menu you will find **About This Mac** (Figure 1.15).

The **About This Mac** window will tell you which operating system you're using. It needs to be Mac OS X 10.1.1 or later.

Updating the OS

If it isn't, you'll need to update the operating system. Unfortunately, the updates for OS X are not available on the FCP3 CDs. You will need to connect to the Internet to get these.

1. Again from the **Apple** menu, select **System Preferences**.

This is actually an OS X application, which holds an enormous number of user configurable preferences (Figure 1.16).

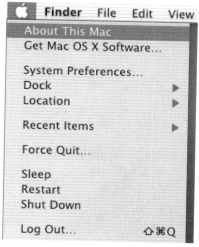

Figure 1.15   About This Mac

Note

RAM: Notice that the **About This Mac** window also tells you how much installed RAM you have in your system. As we saw, FCP3 requires a healthy amount of RAM and even more if you want to have real-time capabilities.

2. Before you get to the Internet, you'll probably need to go into the **Network** pane of **System Preferences** and configure your connection.

3. Once that's done, you can then select the **Software Update** pane (Figure 1.17) from the bottom row in **System Preferences**.

This may take some time, both to download the material, to install it, and to allow the system to optimize itself. It may also require one or more restarts of the system and reconnections to

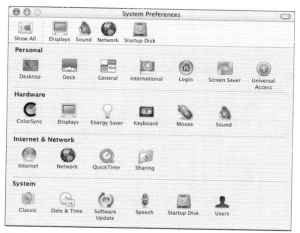

Figure 1.16   System Preferences

Figure 1.17   Software Update

the Internet to rerun **Software Update**, but keep going until you have the latest versions of the Apple system and basic install of applications, such as Internet Explorer, iTunes, iMovie, and others.

Optimizing your Computer for FCP

There are other things you can do in **System Preferences** to optimize your computer for video editing with Final Cut, mostly switching off things that might interfere with its operations while its running, such as that **Software Update** you just ran.

- Make sure **Software Update** is set to connect **Manually** and not on **Automatic,** so there is no chance it will take off and try to run while you're working in FCP.

- The **Displays** should be set so that your computer monitor is running in **Millions of colors** and at a recommended resolution.

- The **Energy Saver** should be set so that the system never goes to sleep. It's less critical that the monitor doesn't go to sleep. I usually set it around 10 minutes, but the system and the hard drive should never shut down. This can cause havoc with slow renders.

- One last step I would recommend is to switch off **Apple-Talk**. This is simplest to do in OS X by going to **Network Preferences** and creating a new **Location** called **None**. Set up your **None** location without any active connections — no Internal Modem, no Airport, no Ethernet — everything unavailable and shut off. To reconnect to the network, simply change back to a location from the **Apple** menu that allows access to whatever connection you want to use.

Note

QuickTime: Version 5.0.4 installs only some new elements into the array of QuickTime elements. This has led to some confusion because some items, such as the QuickTime Player, remain as QT5.0.2 items.

Installing Final Cut Pro 3 for Mac OS X

After you've made sure that you have the latest version of the operating system installed, you will need to install at least the version of QuickTime that comes on your FCP3 CD. This is Quick-Time 5.0.4. There may be updated versions available.

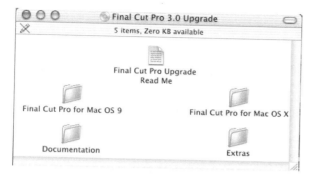

Figure 1.18   FCP3 Upgrade CD

Figure 1.19   Final Cut Pro for Mac OS X folder

1. Begin by loading the Final Cut Pro 3 Install or Upgrade CD. It should open with the window in Figure 1.18.

The items for FCP installation and QT upgrade are inside the *Final Cut Pro for Mac OS X* folder (Figure 1.19). QuickTime 5.0.4 is inside the *QuickTime Installer* folder (Figure 1.20).

Installers in OS X look very different from those in earlier operating systems.

2. Double-click on the QuickTime package. The installer will run, opening up the window in Figure 1.21.

3. You will have to click on the little lock in the lower left of the pane.

This is necessary to verify that you have administration privileges in OS X allowing you to install software. It will call up the dialog in Figure 1.22, asking for your user name and password.

4. You will then be called on to select the system you want to install to (Figure 1.23). Select your OS X partition and press **Continue**.

5. After the software is installed and optimized, as always with the installation of system level software, you will need to restart the computer.

There is one more step we want to take before we begin the Final Cut Pro 3 installation itself. While in OS X we should run the Classic OS9 startup. This is important when doing an upgrade because the CD needs to see the older application and its registration, which will be part of the OS9 system.

Figure 1.20   QuickTime Installer folder

Figure 1.21 QuickTime Install Window

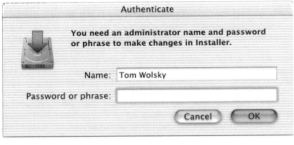

Figure 1.22 Administrator Password Dialog

6. You can start up OS9 Classic from the **System Preferences** application, from the Classic pane opened with the button in the bottom left corner (Figure 1.24).

Notice that in this pane you can start up the Classic system, restart it, or force quit it. By checking the box for **Start up Classic** on login, OS9 will automatically launch every time you restart the computer or log in as a new user. If you're doing a lot of work that takes you back and forth between systems, I'd have it set to launch automatically.

Finally you're ready to run your Final Cut Pro 3 application installer or upgrade software to get your video editing software ready to go.

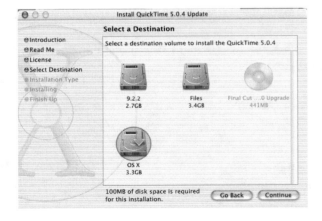

Figure 1.23 Partition Selection Window

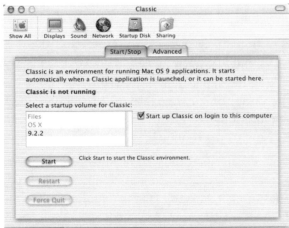

Figure 1.24 Classic Pane

Figure 1.25   FCP3 Updater Window

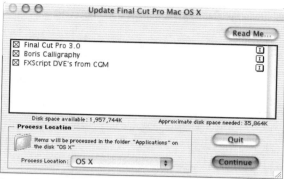

Figure 1.26   FCP3 Installation Window

Begin by double-clicking on the updater or the installer in the Final Cut Pro 3 for *Mac OS X* folder as in Figure 1.19. The FCP3 installer will bring up the window in Figure 1.25.

:Note

Updater: Though this is called an updater, it will really perform the installation of an entirely new piece of software. The only difference between the updater version and the full-install version is that the former will look to see if there an FCP system ID already loaded on your computer from the installation of a previous version of the software.

The installer will open up a simple window that lets you configure the installation and assign where to install the software (Figure 1.26).

For some reason, the default settings are to have Boris Calligraphy and FXScript DVEs from CGM switched off. You'll want these. Switch them on. Also notice that the default setting is to install the application inside the *Applications* folder on the OS X partition. This is a good idea and the best place for any OS X applications.

When installation is completed, Final Cut Pro 3 appears in the folder with its new icon (Figure 1.27) all by itself. There is no folder for additional items like plugins such as the Calligraphy generators and the CGM DVEs that you just installed. In the new OS, these are located elsewhere. They are now in the *Library*, inside *Application Support*, inside the *Final Cut Pro System Support* folder (Figure 1.28).

Name: Final Cut Pro
Kind: Application
Size: 22.1 MB
Created: 12/11/01
Modified: 12/20/01
Version: 3.0

Figure 1.27   New FCP3
Application Icon

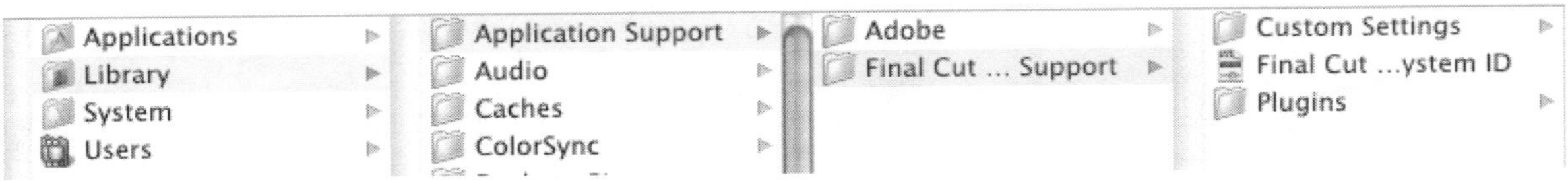

Figure 1.28 *Final Cut Pro System Support Folder*

👍 Tip _____

Get the Update: After you've installed the application or upgraded it from the CD Apple provides, it's probably a good idea to go to Apple's Final Cut website http://www.apple.com/finalcutpro to find the latest updates and maintenance releases available for the application. As of this writing FCP is in version 3.0.2, but by the time you read these words, this may well have changed. If you update to 3.0.2, Apple will give you a new Film Look filter from CGM.

👍Tip _____

Dock Shorthand: When an application opens, it appears in the **Dock**. To distinguish it from aliases of other applications, active applications have a small, black triangle next to their icons. And here's a handy way to navigate between open applications, **Command-Tab** will take you to the next open application in the **Dock**; **Command-Shift-Tab** will take you to the previous application in the **Dock**.

Welcome to Mac OS X

I know it's really tempting to get Final Cut going right away, but before you start it up, let's take a look around this new operating system. There is a lot that is very different here, starting with the **Desktop** and the **Dock** (Figure 1.29).

The **Dock** is similar to Apple's old **Launcher** application. It contains applications that are running as well as aliases of items. Anything can be placed in the **Dock** as an alias: files, folders, hard drive partitions, and aliases of applications. Some will be there by default already. Notice in Figure 1.29 that I've added an alias for Final Cut Pro. The alias was created simply by dragging the application icon from the *Application* folder into the **Dock**. The **Dock** is divided into two sections, one section of aliases of applications and the other of aliases of folders, files, drives, etc.

The **Dock** obviously takes up quite a bit of room and would be cumbersome when working in Final Cut, so I prefer to work with it hidden, or very reduced in size, on the right side of the screen. You can change the **Dock** settings either from the **Apple** menu or by contextual menu that is called up by **Control**-clicking on the join between the two sections in the **Dock** (Figure 1.30).

In addition to hiding the **Dock**, you can also reposition it from the bottom to the left or right of the screen. You can also turn on magnification, which is useful if you like to keep a lot of items in the **Dock** (Figure 1.31).

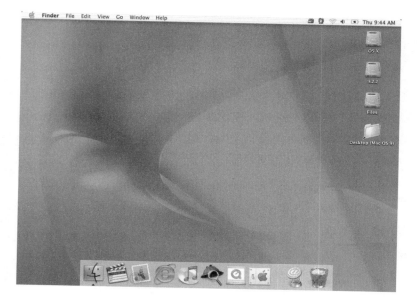

Figure 1.29   Mac OS X Desktop

Figure 1.30   Dock Preferences

While we're in the **Dock,** you might want to launch the Quick-Time Player and put in the registration number that was supplied with your copy of FCP3. This will give the QuickTime Player added functionality, including the ability to export, which can prove invaluable. When the Player launches, ignore the Quick-Time upgrade prompt by clicking on **Later** (Figure 1.32).

Instead, after the Player is fully launched, go to the new **Quick-Time Player** menu and from **Preferences** select **Registration** (Figure 1.33). Enter the name and serial number supplied on your software registration card.

Figure 1.31   Dock Magnification

Figure 1.32   QuickTime Upgrade Prompt

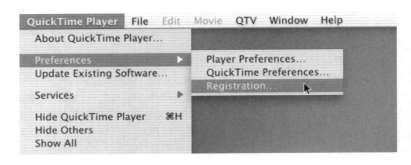

Figure 1.33   QuickTime Player
             Registration

One of the functions in the new Mac OS X is its ability to have multiple **Finder** windows open simultaneously. A new **Finder** is called up with the keyboard shortcut **Command-N**. This used to create a new folder. New folders are now created with the short-cut **Command-Shift-N**.

In the previous Figure 1.28, notice the new **Columns** arrangement in Mac OS X. This allows you to see the hierarchical arrangement of items in a folder and to move quickly from folder to folder. With multiple **Finder** windows open, it is simple to locate files and move them directly from one embedded folder into another.

An item in the *Applications* folder worth noting is the *Utilities* folder. This now contains many of the applications such as the Apple System Profiler that were available in Mac OS9. It also includes a number of applications unique to a Unix-based envi-ronment, applications such as Terminal, which opens a command line–driven interface allowing you to access the underlying core structure of the system.

Also in **Utilities** is the **Disk Utility** application that we saw earlier. It includes **First Aid, Erase, Partition,** and **RAID**. One of the more useful **Utilities** is the **Process Viewer**, which has a hidden function. Occasionally you may find that the **Dock** freezes or doesn't func-tion properly. You cannot force quit the **Dock** as you can with **Command-Option-Escape,** but you can with the **Process Viewer**. If you open the utility and select the **Dock** in the window, from the **Processes** menu you can choose **Quit Process** to force quit the **Dock** (Figure 1.34). After quitting, the **Dock** will return and be available again to you.

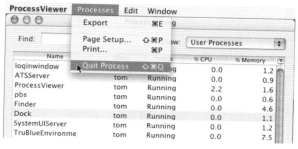 

Figure 1.34   Quit Process

Figure 1.35   Users Pane

Users

The ability of OS X to have multiple users is especially useful in an environment like a school or a production house with a number of projects running at the same time. Each project can be kept in a separate user environment that only an administrator can access. Users can be controlled from the **User** pane of **System Preferences** (Figure 1.35).

Notice that you can delete a User. This doesn't actually remove the user from the hard drive. The name will remain as **UserName Deleted**. To actually trash users and their files, you'll need to either do it while in OS9 or use more powerful utilities such as NetInfo Manager.

The **Desktop** you see in OS X is your desktop. Here all Users have their own desktops and their own preferences. The **Finder** has its preferences (Figure 1.36) called up from the **Finder** menu.

Notice that you can hide your hard drives so that they do not appear on the desktop at all.

Because each environment, including the **Desktop**, is unique to each user, there are separate application preferences for each user, including FCP's. These individual preferences are inside the user's *Library* folder, where there is a *Preferences* folder that holds two separate FCP folders, the Final Cut Pro User Data folder and below it the *Final Cut Pro User Settings* folder (Figure 1.37). The second folder only appears in secondary user's preferences, not the owner's, where only the first folder appears.

Tip

Shortcuts: You can call up the *Applications* folder from the **Finder** at any time with the keyboard shortcut **Command-Option-A**. Likewise you can bring up your *Home* folders with **Command-Option-H**, and your *Favorites* folder with **Command-Option-F**. To bring up a window with your partitions and drives displayed use **Command-Option-C** (C for computer).

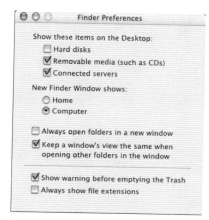

Figure 1.36   Finder Preferences

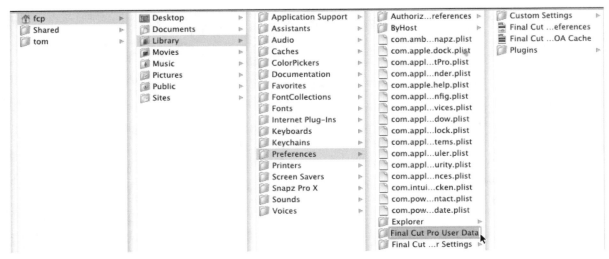

Figure 1.37 FCP User Preferences

Hidden Drives: If you do keep your drives hidden, try dragging them into the **Dock** as aliases. By mousing down on one of the drive icons you'll bring up a contextual menu that allows you to scroll through and select from the contents of the drive (Figure 1.38)

Notice that the *Final Cut Pro User Data* folder contains the *FCP Preferences* as well as the *FCP MOA Cache*. Custom Settings are also stored here, as well as plugins. Plugins can be loaded in the user's preferences, making them available to only a single user. They will not be seen by other users who launch the application.

Or plugins can be loaded into the system *Library* folder we saw earlier. In this case the plugins will be available to anybody starting up the application.

User capabilities in OS X create security and customizing abilities. But with these benefits come some important constraints. Users not only have individual workspace, but also have individual ownership of any documents or files they create. This means that only an individual user can modify or change a document such as

Figure 1.38 Contextual Menu from the Dock

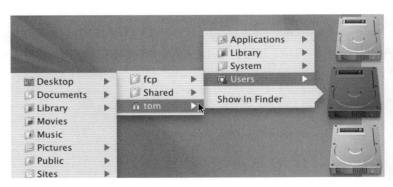

a Final Cut Pro project file. Others users do not have the necessary privileges to write to the file.

This can lead to some wonderful Catch-22 anomalies, which is why the CD that accompanies this book includes a wonderful piece of shareware called FileXaminer, which can be a lifesaver. This neat little application allows you to go to a file and change the user and the privileges from **Read Only** to **Read and Write** (Figure 1.39).

This is only a little of what this incredibly useful application can do. One of the neat things about FileXaminer is that it can be added to the **Finder** contextual menu, so you simply have to **Control**-click on an item or folder to call it up.

Users' Home folders are secure, and no one but the user can access them, so if you're going to have multiple users working on a single project, it would be best to store the project file in the *Shared* folder. Then all can access it, though the problem of ownership still remains. If you try to save an FCP project file to which you don't have user privileges, you'll get the error message in Figure 1.40.

If you are the owner of the file, after you save it into the *Shared* folder, you can use the file's **Information** window (**Command-I**) and change the privileges to give everybody **Read and Write** access (Figure 1.41). Or use FileXaminer to fix the problem if you're not the user. You will, however, still need an administrator's password to do this, even in the FileXaminer application.

Notice that in the **File Information** window, you can also change the application that will launch a file, which can be very useful indeed. You can for instance switch a QuickTime file to launch FCP rather than the QT Player.

Memory: How Much and What Kind

Video editing is memory intensive, both in terms of computational memory such as RAM and in terms of storage memory such as hard drive space. You can't get enough of either.

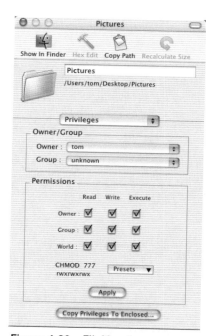

Figure 1.39 FileXaminer Privileges Window

Figure 1.40 File Error: Access Denied

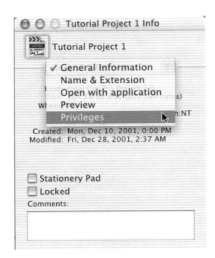

Figure 1.41   File Information
                    Window

Figure 1.42   Force Quit Window

RAM works very differently in OS X than in earlier OSs. First of all, **Virtual Memory** is always on in OS X. It cannot be switched off. The system allocates memory requirements as needed. The RAM requirements specified by Apple are for a minimum configuration and should be used as the minimum available for the applications. So if 256MB is all the memory you have, I would advise against trying to run any other applications simultaneously.

In OS X memory is allocated, segregated, and assigned to each application as needed in a remarkably complex fashion. Because of the segregation, no one application can crash and bring down other applications or the system itself. Someone described it as each application having its own sandbox to play in. It can mess up its play area as much as it wants without affecting any of the other sandboxes. Because of this, OS X has the ability to force quit any application, including relaunching the **Finder** without trashing the rest of the sandboxes. You can force quit from anywhere in the operating system, including from inside an application, by pressing **Command-Option-Escape**, which will call up the window in Figure 1.42. This will even work if you are inside a Classic application running under OS X.

Final Cut Pro likes to work with a lot of RAM, the more the better, especially for circumstances such as real-time capabilities or very large projects with lots of graphics work. Moreover, if you want more than one application open at a time, such as Adobe's Photoshop and After Effects, Discreet's Cleaner, Pinnacle's Commotion software or others, you're going to need lots more RAM. Amounts such as 765MB or even 1.5G of installed RAM are getting to be quite common.

Storage memory is the other essential part of any video system. DV in its simplest form consumes about 3.6MB per second of storage space. That translates to 216MB a minute, approximately 1G for five minutes, and almost 13G for an hour. Fortunately, cheap IDE hard drives for Macs are now available in ever-increasing sizes, with platter speeds and seek times ample for working with DV-quality material.

Multiple Drives

Because a digital video editing system needs to access and move large amounts of data at high speed, you need separate drives purely for storing video data. You should have one internal hard drive dedicated to your operating system and applications, such as Final Cut Pro, Photoshop, After Effects, Commotion, iMovie2, and everything else from Internet access software to word processing and spreadsheets. All of these should be on one drive. Those that work with OS X should be on its partition, and those that work with OS9 should be on that separate partition. Unlike video media, they usually don't take up a lot of space, so this drive doesn't need to be either exceptionally large or even exceptionally fast. You should also have at least one other hard drive, one that's large and fast. This drive — better still, drives — should carry only your media. I often put my Final Cut Pro project files on the same drive or folder as the media, though I think most experts would advise you against this. Most would tell you to keep your FCP project files on your system drive, or some other hard drive, separate from your media. This is probably good practice.

Your media drives should be used for nothing but video media. Erase them periodically to avoid fragmentation.

Real-time Editing

Real-time editing is wonderful for the flow of creativity. When you're editing, you want your concentration unbroken, the mechanics as transparent as possible. You want to try dissolves and simple titles with different small adjustments, a little earlier, a little later. You can't do this easily with a render-based system, no matter how fast. Watching the render indicator rolling across the computer screen takes your mind and your eye off the material you're editing. So if you can afford it and have the system capabilities, RAM, and processor speed to support it, I strongly recommend a real time–capable system. It is important to realize that in FCP a real-time system will provide real-time preview only, and only on the computer screen. To see your output on a video monitor, you will need an additional PCI card, such as an

Memory and Memory

Applications have to deal with two distinct types of memory: RAM and storage. They perform quite distinct functions. RAM (Random Access Memory) are the chips on your computer's motherboard that hold the system and applications while they are running. FCP is stored in RAM while it's open, as is the operating system.

The other type of memory is storage. The platters of the hard drive store your data. In the case of media drives for your video, these are often very big—and very fast—hard drives. They can store huge quantities of data and access them very quickly.

Drive Fragmentation

Hard drives become fragmented as more and more and smaller and smaller pieces of data get written to them. As you write data on the drive, it starts to fill up. If material is thrown away, the drive doesn't immediately start writing over the trashed material. It first writes onto empty drive space. This is why it's sometimes possible to recover material even after it's been put in the trash and the trash emptied. It really hasn't gone until something has been written over it. Eventually, though, all the drive space will fill up. At that point the drive starts writing over old, trashed material. If you throw more material away and record new material, you can see that it won't take long before your hard drive has little fragments of information scattered all over it. It gets harder for the drive to play back these fragments quickly enough to produce clean video performance without skipping and dropping frames as it goes.

Software applications such as Norton Disk Doctor have defragmentation routines. I would not really recommend them for video drives, especially very full drives. The simplest, most efficient way to defragment a drive is to erase it. It is also fatal — pretty much irrevocable — to any material. Do not perform this unless you no longer need any of the data on the drive. That said, erasing a drive or partition is quick and easy. Start up *Disk Utility* from inside the *Utilities* folder, and go to the *Erase* pan. Select the partition and click *Erase*. This will wipe the partition's directory. It effectively means that any new information written to the drive will start as if though it were completely blank. When you erase the disk, it's probably best to select **Mac OS Extended**, also known as HFS+. This allows you to write very large files to the hard drive, a very useful thing for video in which single clips can be gigabytes in size.

Some experts would suggest that you go even further and reinitialize your media drives, but I don't think this is really necessary. I have had media drives that went for years on their original initialization.

I like to partition my drives into separate volumes. The advantage of partitioning a single drive into separate volumes is that they're easier to wipe clean that way. I can move all the data off one partition, erase it, and move it back onto the drive. This will write the data cleanly and continuously without fragmentation. I also use partitioned drives to keep separate project media on separate volumes. The disadvantage is that you lose some drive space. Because some directory information needs to be written for each partition, and because you shouldn't fill each partition right up to the brim, partitioning wastes some space.

ATI Radeon card which will feed a S-video signal to your monitor. When you are using FCP's real-time mode, you must switch off output to your FireWire cable in **Preferences**. We'll look at **Preferences** in the next lesson.

Monitors

You should have a video monitor. It reproduces images differently than a computer monitor, which has much greater color depth, resolution, and contrast range, and does not have interlaced scan lines. These are all critical to how your video will finally look. If your project will be shown on a television set, you must edit with a video monitor that shows true output. You may also want a second computer display for the large number of windows that video editing applications need.

Speakers

Good quality speakers are really important. They should be connected to the same source as the video you're monitoring. If you are looking at your video on a television monitor, you should listen to your audio from the same source. So if you have a deck or a DV camera that is feeding the signal from your computer to your TV monitor, then that should also be feeding your audio speakers. Switchable speakers would be ideal, with two inputs to monitor either the video source or the computer output.

Firing Up the Application

Now it's time to launch that program. In this version of Final Cut Pro, when you first launch the application, you need to have your install CD loaded in your computer. It's part of Apple's software security. After you start up the application, the first window that greets you is one asking you to enter your name, organization, and serial number.

After a new installation, or after you have trashed your *Final Cut Preferences* file, you will first be greeted with the preferences screen in Figure 1.43.

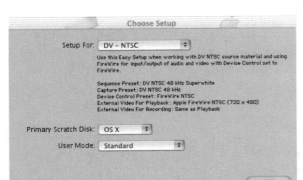

Figure 1.43   Start-up Dialogue

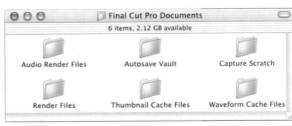

Figure 1.44   Scratch Disk Subfolders

This was introduced in Final Cut Pro 2 and is, I think, one of the few unfortunate things the application engineers have done to the program.

The default setting is DV-NTSC with audio at 48kHz. In FCP3 you have a DV-PAL option as well as the two OfflineRT options, which are used to capture material at low resolution to conserve drive space. Few other choices are available at this stage. I don't think this is the time to make these choices, but you have to.

Note _____

Autosave Vault: Notice the _Autosave Vault_ folder that is new to FCP3. This is also saved in the assigned scratch disk area. We'll look at this again in the next lesson on preferences.

The second popup makes you choose a scratch disk. The popup defaults to your system partition and offers you the choice of any hard drives on your system. Unfortunately, it forces you to assign a drive for your media, while not allowing you to create an internal folder for an individual project nor offering the option of skipping this step until you're ready to do setup procedures. Since you're forced to make a decision, leave it where it is for now. We'll change it in the next lesson. Selecting the drive and starting the application will actually create a folder called _Final Cut Pro Documents_ that will be inside the _Documents_ folder of your _Home_ folder. This folder will contain the subfolders in Figure 1.44. Live with it for now; we'll rearrange things in the next lesson on preferences.

Figure 1.45   User Mode Popup

The third popup, **User Mode** (Figure 1.45), lets you choose your workspace. Select **Standard** for now. We'll look at this in a bit more detail when we talk about preferences in the next lesson, beginning on page 58.

Understanding the Interface

Launching a new application for the first time is always an adventure, especially when it's as complex as Final Cut Pro and in a new operating system. Some software can be intimidating; some can be downright head scratching. I particularly love those applications that open with the standard **Application** menu, **File**, **Edit**, a few other things, and nothing else. You're staring at your computer screen wondering where to start or what to do.

That's certainly not the case with Final Cut Pro, which immediately fills your screen with windows, buttons, and tools to explore. Figure 1.46 shows what greets you when FCP is fully launched.

The Primary Windows

The screen is divided into four primary windows, with two large empty screens as your principal monitors:

- The **Viewer**, on the left, allows you to look at individual video clips.

- The **Canvas**, on the right, is the output of your material as you edit it together. The **Canvas** is linked directly to the **Timeline**.

- The **Timeline** for your video is the window with the horizontal bar below the **Canvas**. This is where you lay out your video and audio material in the order you want it.

- The **Browser** is the fourth window at the bottom left.

Though the **Viewer** is your primary editor in traditional three-point editing, you can also edit in the **Timeline** window, as well as control transitions and other effects. The project materials are listed in the **Browser**.

Think of the **Browser** as a giant folder. You can nest folders within folders, just like you can on a Mac desktop. This is not where your clips are stored; it is only a list. Your clips are physically stored on your media hard drives.

You'll also notice vertical bars that contain the **Tools** and **Audio Meters**.

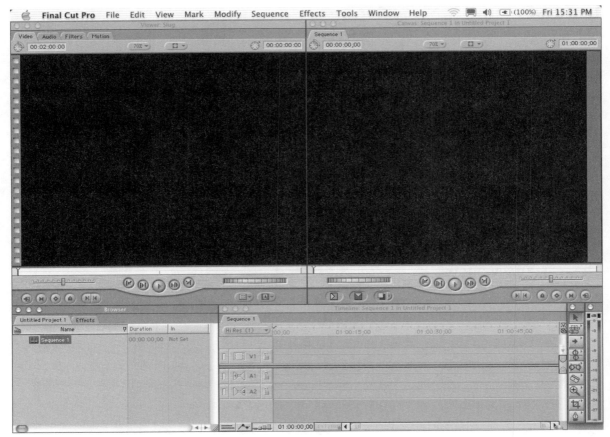

Figure 1.46   The Final Cut Pro Interface

Open Sequence: Should your project ever open and you don't see any **Canvas** or **Timeline**, it simply means that there is no sequence open. There needs to be at least one sequence in a project. Simply double-click the sequence in the **Browser** and it will open the **Timeline** together with its **Canvas**.

Figure 1.46 shows the default configuration, called **Standard**. It is ideal for working on PowerBooks, or when working with real-time capabilities or OfflineRT, where the primary viewing screen is the computer monitor. I think most editors, however, would prefer a video monitor to be their primary viewing screen. The video monitor is very different in color space, resolution, and contrast than a computer monitor, which is why it is important to check your material on a video monitor. To avoid having the computer spend a great of deal of time and processing power creating the image on the computer screen, I think many people still work with a smaller **Viewer** and **Canvas** and leave more space for the **Browser** and the **Timeline** windows. In the **Window** menu, select **Arrange>Wide** (Figure 1.47).

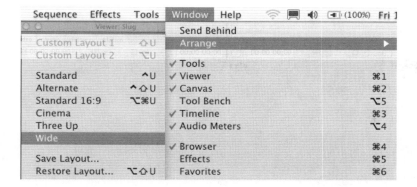

Figure 1.47 Window>Arrange>
Wide

This will bring up the arrangement in Figure 1.48. I find this a more convenient way to work, with smaller **Viewer** and **Canvas,** space for the **Browser,** and a nice long sweep of the **Timeline** window.

 Note

Sequence: You'll notice that the **Browser** is not empty. When you create a new project, FCP creates a new sequence called *Sequence 1.* You can rename sequences just like you would any file in the Mac **Finder**. Click on the name to highlight it, and type in a new name. You can have as many sequences as you want in a project, and you can place, or nest, sequences within sequences. We'll look at nesting later (page 334 in Lesson 8).

Note

Custom Screen Setting: You can set the screen anyway you like and save it as a custom setting. When you've arranged the screen to your taste, hold down the **Option** key. From the **Window** menu, select **Arrange>Set Custom Layout 1** or **Set Custom Layout 2,** shown in Figure 1.47. Quickly return to these settings at any time using keyboard shortcuts (**Shift-U** for **Custom Layout 1** and **Option-U** for **Custom Layout 2**) or by choosing them from the **Windows>Arrange** menu.

Tip

Save Custom Setting: You can also use **Save Layout,** which will bring up the dialog box in Figure 1.49. This will allow you to save a custom window setting, which will be stored in the *Window Settings* folder of your *Preferences* folder. **Restore Layout** will open a dialog box that will let you select from your stored custom settings. Remember, if you save to your *User Preferences* folder, the custom settings will only be available to you and not to other users you might log in.

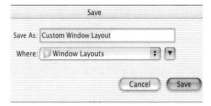

Figure 1.49 Custom Window
Settings

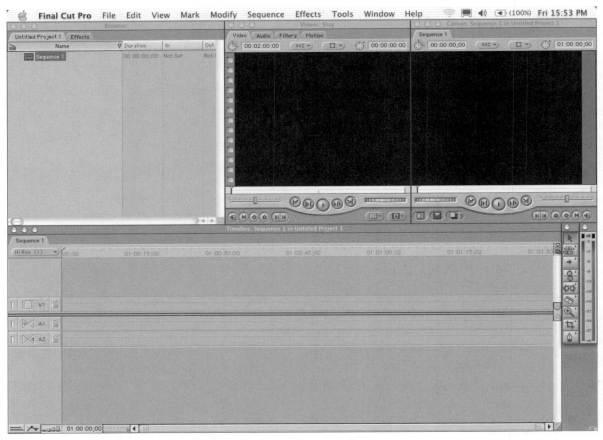

Figure 1.48   FCP Wide Arrangement

Tabbed Palettes

You've probably also noticed that most of these windows have tabbed palettes with other windows behind them. Let's take a quick look at what's back there. Tabbed in the **Browser** is the **Effects** window. Video and audio effects, transitions, and generators are stored here, including any favorites you want to access frequently.

The **Viewer** has tabs behind it as well:

- **Audio** lets you see a video clip's audio waveform and manipulate the sound by raising and lowering the levels or panning the stereo from left to right.

- **Filters** lets you control and animate effects applied to clips over time.

- **Motion** lets you animate the image with keyframes to move it about the screen by animating the center point.

In the **Motion** window, most of the properties can be animated — scale, rotation, cropping edges of the frame, and distortion of the image, which will change its shape. You can change the image's opacity, making it more transparent. At zero opacity it will be invisible. You can add a drop shadow that will appear on any underlying layers, and you can add a motion blur, which simulates the amount of smearing created by movement across the screen. We will look at these animation tools in later lessons (see Lessons 8 and 9).

The **Canvas** and the **Timeline** window also have tabs. If you have more than one sequence open at a time, they will appear as tabs in the **Timeline** window and in the **Canvas**.

 Tip _____

Tab Display: Tabs can be pulled apart and docked into another window. You could pull out the **Audio** tab from the **Viewer** and dock it into the **Timeline** window or separate the **Video** into a different window from the **Audio**, displaying both simultaneously. Any combination of **Viewer** and **Timeline** combinations can be docked together. Tabs in the **Browser** and the **Canvas** can be pulled apart as well, but they cannot be docked in other windows. However, you can have more than one **Canvas** open at a time. Even though multiple **Canvases** can be open, they cannot be gang-synced. They wouldn't play together at the same time even if they contain the same material. Nor can multiple **Viewers** be played at the same time. Perhaps in later versions.

_____

Browser

Now let's bring some material into the project so that we can look at each window in greater detail. For this lesson, we'll use the material that Apple supplied on the Tutorial CD that came with your copy of Final Cut Pro 3. Insert the Tutorial CD into your CD drive and drag the *NTSC Tutorial* folder from the CD to one of your media hard drives. Don't put it on the same drive as your system or your Final Cut Pro application. Most of the tutorial files are in DV format and will not play properly off the CD, but only from your media drive.

Once you have the material on your hard drive, you need to bring it into your project. The easiest way to do this is to close the **Canvas**, which also closes the **Timeline**. You can also minimize the **Canvas** from the middle or yellow of the three balls, in the upper left corner of the **Canvas**. This will suck the window into the **Dock**. You can also do this by double-clicking on the dark bar at the top of the window — a bit clumsy, I find, and not as good as the old Window Shade behavior. Find the *NTSC Tutorial* folder you just put on your hard drive and drag the whole folder straight into the **Browser**.

The reason we're using the Final Cut tutorial folder rather than material on the book's CD is because the tutorial material has already been edited into shots. For this lesson, that's the best way to see the **Browser** at work. The material on the book's CD is unedited, raw footage. This book is about editing, after all, so it will be best to learn using the type of raw material you might have to work with.

The process of dragging from the **Finder** into the **Browser** is called importing and can be used for any material FCP uses — QuickTime movies, sound files, still images, etc. This is the simplest, quickest way to bring lots of material into your project. You can also use **Command-I** to import single items or the **File** menu under **Import>Folder** to bring a folder full of clips or other material.

The *NTSC Tutorial* folder contains two Final Cut project files. You can't import a FCP project into another FCP project, which is why you got an error message after you finished importing the *NTSC Tutorial* folder. Though you can't import another FCP project, you can have two projects open at the same time. You can use **Command-O** to open a project as you would to open a document in a word processing application. Each project will appear as a separate tab in the **Browser** window.

Importing Music

Importing from a music CD is slightly different from importing video. Audio files on music CDs are not standard AIFF sound files used by FCP. This version of FCP can work with files in the audio CD format, but it does raise some problems. To import an audio

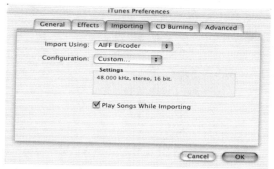

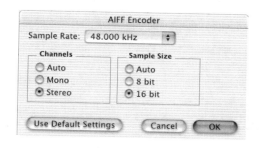

Figure 1.50   iTunes Importing Preference

Figure 1.51   iTunes Custom Settings

CD, you'll first need to copy it from the CD disk itself onto one of your media drives. Simply drag it from the CD to the media drive. After the file has been copied to your hard drive, then either drag it directly to the **Browser** as we did before or use **Command-I** to import it. It will appear in the **Browser** as a file appended with the suffix *cdda*.

Here's the problem: the audio CD format is at a sampling rate of 44.1kHz. This is not normally the sampling rate used by the DV format or by other video formats, which are more often either 32kHz or more commonly 48kHz. While FCP3 can deal with resampling the audio while it plays it back, this requires processor power and may limit your ability to do real-time effects or to play back video without dropping frames, i.e., the video stuttering. To avoid this, I would recommend resampling the audio to the correct sampling rate you want to use before importing it into FCP. Apple has already provided you with a simple tool to do this. It's called iTunes. This application may already have launched automatically when you loaded your audio CD. If it didn't, start it up.

1. Under the **iTunes** menu, go to **Preferences**, and in the **Preferences** window, select the **Importing** tab.

2. From the **Import Using** popup, select **AIFF Encoding**.

3. From the second popup, select **Custom**.

4. This will bring up the window in Figure 1.50.

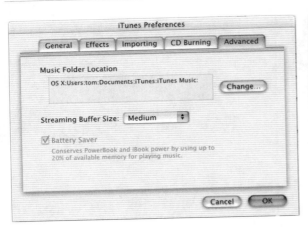

Figure 1.52 iTunes Advanced Window

Figure 1.53 iTunes Window

5. Set the sampling rate to 48,000Hz or whatever sampling rate you're working with.

6. Set the **Channels** to **Stereo** and the **Sample Size** to **16 bit,** as in Figure 1.51.

Once you've set this preference, you shouldn't have to change it again. One more item in the **iTunes Preferences** that you will want to set is in the **Advanced** tab (Figure 1.52).

7. Click on the **Change** button and navigate to the media drive where you want to save your music. Again, you may only have to do this once for a project.

Now you're ready to import the music.

8. In the **iTunes** window, **Command**-click on one of the checked track boxes. This will deselect all the tracks.

9. Now check the tracks you want, and then click the **Import** button on the upper right corner of the window (Figure 1.53).

iTunes will then copy the track from the CD to your designated hard drive location and will resample and convert it to an AIFF file as it does so.

The track you copied onto your hard drive will be inside a folder with the artist's name. If there was no name listed in iTunes, it will be inside a folder called **Unknown Artist,** inside a folder called *Unknown Album.* Now when you drag the track into your **Browser** or use **Command-I** to import it, the track will appear in the **Browser** appended with the suffix *aif* and will also be in the correct sampling rate that you chose in iTunes. Your system will be happy that you did this.

Note

Autosave: At some point in the process while you're working with FCP, you may get the dialog box in Figure 1.54. This is FCP's **Autosave** feature trying to create an archive copy of your project in its vault. We'll look at this more closely in the next lesson, but for now save your project. I'd suggest saving it in the *Shared* folder of the *Users* folder. Also note that projects created in OS X will not launch the application if you're running OS9. Rather, you have to start the OS9 version of FCP3 and then use **Cmd-O** to open the project file.

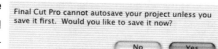

Figure 1.54   Autosave Warning

Bin Contents and Detail

In the **Browser,** open the *NTSC Tutorial* folder by:

- Clicking the twirly triangle to expand the folder view *or*
- Double-clicking on the folder icon

If you double-click, the folder will open in a new window. Though it uses a folder icon, which probably wasn't a good idea, in Final Cut–speak this folder is called a *bin,* an old film term. Think of long bits of processed film hanging from pins into a large, cloth-lined bin. Whatever you call it, it behaves like a folder.

Inside the **NTSC Tutorial** folder — now a bin— are two other bins, **Compositing Pieces** and **Dance Shots.** Open them by clicking the little twirly triangles to expand the folder view. Inside **Compositing Pieces** are *Blue Dance, Composited Text End,* and *Triangle,* which are video clips, and *Dances.psd, FCP Names.psd,* and *Title.psd,* which have sequence icons. This is because FCP imports Photoshop files as layered sequences; each of the layers in the PSD file appears as a separate video layer in the Final Cut sequence, one stacked on top of the other. The final item in

Tip

In v3.0.2, holding down the **Option** key while double-clicking a bin in the **Browser,** opens that bin as a tab in the **Browser** window. If more than one **Browser** window is open, the tab is attached to the window the bin came from.

Compositing Pieces is *background*, a graphic image file in PICT format. You'll notice the icon is different from the others in the bin.

The clips in the **Dance Shots** bin are pieces of video, except for *Jumptown.aiff*, which has the **Loudspeaker** icon and is a piece of swing music.

👉 *Tip*

Long Names: New to FCP3 is the ability to have the long names of clips in the **Browser** appear in **Tooltips**, which can be very useful if you have a number of clips that have the same beginning, as in Figure 1.55.

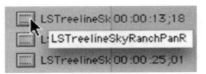

Figure 1.55 Long names

Stretch out the **NTSC Tutorial** bin window, and you'll see just some of the many things the **Browser** displays in List mode (see Figure 1.56).

The **Browser** shows the duration of clips, the In and Out points, which are probably marked **Not Set** at this stage. You also see track types, whether video and/or audio and how many audio tracks. Note that the Photoshop sequences tell you how many layers there are in the sequence. Clips can be marked as **Good**. This harks back to film days where good takes were placed in a separate bin for first consideration. Similarly in FCP, marking a

Figure 1.56 Browser List View

Name	Duration	In	Out	Media Start	Media End	Tracks	Good	Log Note	Label	Label 2
▽ ☐ Compositing Pieces									None	
background	00:00:10:00	00:01:00:00	00:01:09:29	00:00:00:00	00:02:09:29	1V			None	
Blue Dance	00:00:05:06	Not Set	Not Set	00:03:02:23	00:03:07:28	1V			None	
Composited Text End	00:00:03:15	Not Set	Not Set	00:00:00:00	00:00:03:14	1V			None	
Dances.psd	00:00:10;00	Not Set	Not Set	01:00:00;00	01:00:09;29	4V			None	
FCP Names.psd	00:00:10;00	Not Set	Not Set	01:00:00;00	01:00:09;29	10V			None	
Title.psd	00:00:10;00	Not Set	Not Set	01:00:00;00	01:00:09;29	3V			None	
Triangle	00:00:07:10	Not Set	Not Set	00:00:00:27	00:00:08:06	1V			None	
▽ ☐ Dance Shots									None	
Bloomies	00:00:08;08	Not Set	Not Set	02:12:02;17	02:12:10;24	1V			None	
Jeremy Solo	00:00:06;08	Not Set	Not Set	02:42:35;14	02:42:41;21	1V			None	
Johnny n Carl	00:00:04;28	Not Set	Not Set	02:41:42;10	02:41:47;07	1V			None	
Jumptown.aif	00:00:41:26	Not Set	Not Set	00:00:00:00	00:00:41:25	2A			None	
Overhead	00:00:10;21	Not Set	Not Set	02:39:26;28	02:39:37;18	1V			None	
Rob Dialog	00:00:25;01	Not Set	Not Set	00:05:06;26	00:05:31;26	1V, 2A			None	
Round n Round	00:00:10;08	Not Set	Not Set	02:12:18;07	02:12:28;14	1V			None	

clip **Good** lets you designate it for special attention. Comments
can be added to clips in the **Log Note** box or the **Label** box. You
just click in the box and type.

 Note _____

The FCP Facade: FCP and its entire interface is a facade. The whole structure is there simply to pass instructions to the computer about which pieces of video and audio to play when and what to do with them. The conveniences created for you in the **Browser** and in the **Timeline** are simply a very elaborate way of telling the computer what to do with the media on your hard drives and how to play it back. All the clips in the project, either in the **Browser** or in the **Timeline,** are simply pointers to the media on the hard drive. This is a nondestructive, completely nonlinear artifice. The clips are not "brought" into the **Browser** or placed on the **Timeline.** They never leave their place on the hard drives. They're never "in" the project at all except as a list. You can change the names in the list to anything more convenient that you like, and it has no effect at all on the data stored on your hard drive. All you're doing is changing how you give instructions to the data; you're not changing the data at all. On the other hand, if you change the names of the clips on your hard drive, that will throw FCP into confusion, and you'll have to reconnect each clip to establish the links between the two.

The **Browser** also shows the type of audio, presence of stereo,
frame size, and frame rate (in the case of these clips, 29.97 frames
a second, the standard frame rate for all NTSC video).

Other information displayed in the **Browser** is:

- Type of video compression used (in this case, DV-NTSC)

- Data rate

- Audio sampling rate

- Audio format

- Whether or not there is an alpha channel

- Checkbox for reversing the alpha channel

- Compositing mode applied to the clip
  (You can change it here as well by **Control**-clicking it.)

- Pixel aspect ratio
  (CCIR601 or nonsquare pixels, as is the case most types of
  digital video)

- Anamorphic status
  (displayed in the 16:9 frame aspect ratio)

As you scroll right along the window, you get more columns where you can type labels such as **Description**, as well as the **Scene, Shot/Take**, and **Comments 1** and **2**. You will also see **Offline**, and **Last Modified**. I'll go into detail about the differences between pixel aspect ratios, frame aspect ratios, and frame sizes in the next lesson.

Only the **Name** column cannot be moved. It stays displayed on the left side of the window. You can move any of the other columns by grabbing the header at the top of the column and pulling it to wherever you want the column to appear.

 Tip _____

Ordering: You can arrange the order in which clips are shown in List view by selecting the column header. By clicking the green arrow that appears in the header, you can change the order from descending to ascending. Also, if you **Shift**-click on the header of other columns, a little blue arrow will appear and will be added as secondary ordering lists.

Note _____

Sorting: Occasionally users are puzzled by FCP's sorting order. The sorting is alphanumeric, but even in OS X numbers do not maintain their natural order. That is, 1 is followed by 10, 11, 12, and 2 is followed by 20, 21, 22, and so on. The operating system itself uses natural ordering, but not the application. So to get numbers correctly ordered, it's a good idea to start numbers with leading zeros, so 01 is followed by 02, 03, and then 09 is followed by 10. Another feature that can cause confusion is that ordering extends to each bin separately. So, for instance, if you use name ordering for the **Browser** and then twirl open a bin, you'll see the contents of the bin stretching down the **Browser**, but the contents will not necessarily be in name order. To get naming ordering for the bin, you'll have to double-click it to open it into a separate window and click on the **Name** column. This feature allows you to maintain different sort orders for different bins.

NTSC vs. PAL

NTSC, which some wags say stands for Never Twice the Same Color, is actually the now-defunct National Television Standards Committee, which established the format used by television broadcasting in the United States. All of North America and Japan use this format as well. Europe and most of the rest of the world use PAL, for Phase Alternating Lines, which refers to the way color is handled. PAL uses a frame rate of 25fps. It's becoming increasingly popular in the United States as a format for digital video production destined for film. The PAL frame rate is very close to the standard film frame rate of 24fps, making it a good choice for budding filmmakers working with digital video who aim to distribute their projects in traditional film formats.

Using Contextual Menus

Even more information can be displayed in the **Browser** with the **Control** key, one of the most powerful tools in the application. Throughout Final Cut Pro, the **Control** key gives you access to contextual menus. These menus change depending on where your cursor is. If your cursor is above the column headers in the **Browser** and you press the **Control** key while clicking the mouse, you get a contextual menu (Figure 1.57).

Notice that in this version of FCP you can save and restore bin settings similar to the way you can save and restore window arrangements. These will be saved in a separate folder of your *Preferences* folder called *Column Layouts*.

The contextual menu in the **Browser** header lets you hide a column. It also lets you add even more columns to your **Browser**. You can change the columns from the default **Standard** columns to **Logging** columns, which show:

- Media Start and End times
- In and Out points
- Duration
- Good
- Description
- Scene, Shot, Take, and Reel
- Log Notes
- Four **Comments** columns, and a lot more

To any of the column sets, you can add auxiliary timecode columns, length, capture, and an important item called *Source*. This tells you the file path to the clip's location on your hard drive.

Another item hidden in the contextual menu is **Show Thumbnail**. This cool feature brings up a thumbnail that shows the first frame of the video. Grab the thumbnail and drag the mouse. This is called *scrubbing*, and what you're doing is dragging through the video clip itself so you can actually see what's in it. Viewing media like this in the **Browser** can save time. You can quickly scan through a shot to see if it's really the one you're looking for.

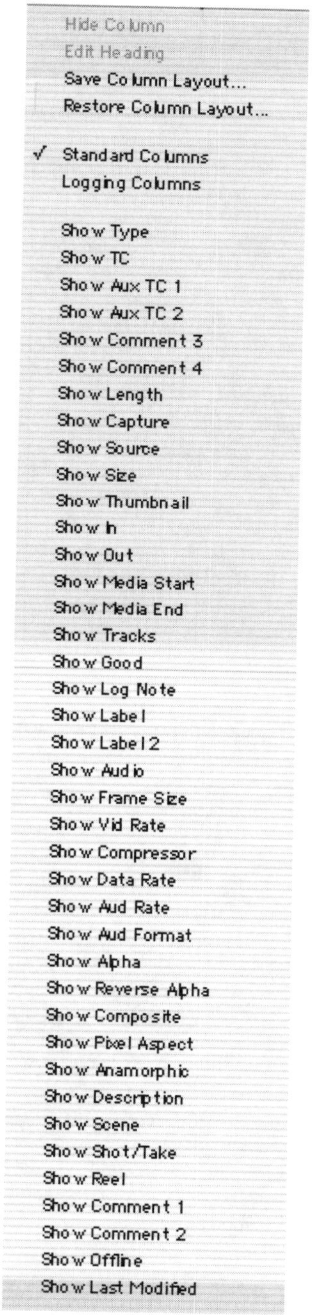

Hide Column
Edit Heading
Save Column Layout...
Restore Column Layout...

✓ Standard Columns
Logging Columns

Show Type
Show TC
Show Aux TC 1
Show Aux TC 2
Show Comment 3
Show Comment 4
Show Length
Show Capture
Show Source
Show Size
Show Thumbnail
Show In
Show Out
Show Media Start
Show Media End
Show Tracks
Show Good
Show Log Note
Show Label
Show Label 2
Show Audio
Show Frame Size
Show Vid Rate
Show Compressor
Show Data Rate
Show Aud Rate
Show Aud Format
Show Alpha
Show Reverse Alpha
Show Composite
Show Pixel Aspect
Show Anamorphic
Show Description
Show Scene
Show Shot/Take
Show Reel
Show Comment 1
Show Comment 2
Show Offline
Show Last Modified

Figure 1.57 List of Browser Contextual Menu Items

You can also change the Poster frame, the frame that appears in the thumbnail. The default is the first frame of the video (or the In point), but if you scrub through the video and find a new frame you would like to set as the thumbnail, press the **Control** key and release the mouse. A new Poster frame has been set. If you change the Poster frame for a clip here or in any other **Browser** window, the poster will change for each instance of that clip anywhere in the **Browser** and will also display as the poster when the **Browser** is set to Icon view.

Figure 1.58 Log Note Contextual Menu

> 👉 **Tip**
>
> **Contextual Menus:** Using contextual menus in List view lets you change items for multiple clips with a few clicks of the mouse. For instance, to add a comment to the **Log Note,** I simply select a number of clips. Then I use the contextual menu in the same column, the **Log Note** column. This will bring up a contextual menu with all my recent notes in that column. I select the one I want, and all the selected clips will have their log notes changed (Figure 1.58).

Figure 1.59 Bin in Icon View

In addition to List view, the **Browser** can also be seen in Icon view. Open the **Dance Shots** bin in a new window by double-clicking on it. Go up to **View** in the menus and drop down to **Browser Items>Medium Icons** (Figure 1.59). In FCP3 there is also a **Large Icons** view. **Small Icons** is pretty useless unless your eyesight is exceptional. In the **Browser, Shift-H** will toggle through the various icon sizes settings as well as list view.

All the clips turn into icons that show the Poster frame of the video. Though FCP calls these icons, they are thumbnails, just as the thumbnails we saw earlier in List view, with the same scrubbable property.

You can also set the Poster frame as before by tapping the **Control** key when you're over the frame you want to set.

You can call up the **Scrub** tool in other windows with the keyboard shortcut **HH**. In the **Browser**, though, the letter shortcuts will select only a clip or bin based on alphanumeric ordering.

Tip

Scrubbing: You can also use the scrub tool to run through the thumbnail at the head of each clip when it's laid out in the **Timeline** window. You might want to change from the normal track size to the largest one, or the thumbnails will be rather small.

 Tip

Copying: In Medium or Large Icon view, if you hold down **Control-Shift**, the cursor will change to the **Hand** tool with forward and reverse arrows that will let you scrub the thumbnails just like the thumbnails in List view (Figure 1.60).

Figure 1.60   Hand Tool

In the **Browser,** the **Control** key again provides a useful contextual menu. In the window it lets you change the views, make new bins and sequences, as well as import and arrange the material (Figure 1.61).

Clips themselves hold a contextual menu that can do a variety of useful things (Figure 1.62).

With the clip contextual menu open, a whole array of options is available. Two very useful ones are **Item Properties** and **Make Offline.**

Item Properties calls up an information window that tells you everything about a clip (Figure 1.63).

The popups allow you to change properties such as pixel aspect ratio and field dominance. It also lets you change properties such as composite mode and alpha interpretation. "What in the world is he talking about?" you're thinking. They're all great tools that you'll soon learn about. Notice also the two panels in the back, **Timing** and **Logging Info. Timing** (Figure 1.64) allows you to change duration and actually set In and Out points, start and end points for the clip, though it would be very unusual to actually do it in this window.

Figure 1.61   Browser Contextual Menu

Logging Info (Figure 1.65) gives you access to all the comments and notes for a clip. It's also a convenient place to add this material, especially if you're writing longer notes than just a few words.

Figure 1.62   Clip Contextual Menu

Selecting **Make Offline** from the clip's contextual menu evokes the dialog box in Figure 1.66. Here you can actually delete media from your hard drive. It is a powerful tool, but because of its power it is also dangerous. It's easy to inadvertently delete the media for another clip. Clips you see in bins may only be parts of longer pieces of media or they may be subclips. If you use **Move** or **Delete**, this media may be lost to other clips.

I seldom use **Delete Them from Disk**. At least from the **Trash** you have another chance to take it back before you empty the trash.

One of the other items that the clip's contextual menu brings up is **Labels**. These will tint the clip icon to colors, making different types of shots easier to identify in bins. Because these color labels carry over to sequences, clips in the timeline will appear with their label tint. New to version 3 is the ability to use the contextual menu to add **Labels** to **Sequences** and **Bins**, which can be very handy.

Tip

Label in Timeline: You can still change the clip label when it's in a **Timeline** with the **Modify>Labels** menu. You cannot simply change the label with a contextual menu without going through **Properties** and a more convoluted path than it's worth.

As you can see, the **Browser** window is not only full of important information about your video project, but its contextual menu is actually a powerful tool for manipulating the clips and graphics you're working with.

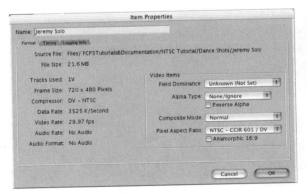

Figure 1.63   Item Properties

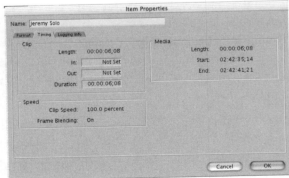

Figure 1.64   Timing Panel

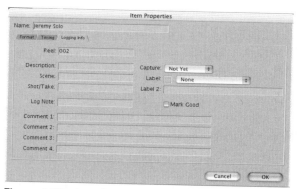

Figure 1.65   Logging Info

Figure 1.66   Making Offline

Viewer

The **Viewer** is one of the primary editing tools within Final Cut Pro. This is where you manipulate your clips, mark them and prepare them for insertion into your timeline. To load a clip into the **Viewer,** just double-click on it. Start by double-clicking on the clip *Bloomies* in the **Dancing Shots** bin (Figure 1.67).

Figure 1.67   The Viewer

Playing Clips

There are a number of different ways of playing a clip to look at your video. The most apparent is the big **Play** button in the middle of the **Viewer** controls.

There are other ways to view your video besides at real speed. Buttons on the **Viewer** do this, but learn the keyboard. It's your friend, and it's really a much simpler, easier way to control your editing than the mouse.

Spacebar

Press the spacebar to play the clip. To pause, press the spacebar again. Spacebar to start, spacebar to stop. To play the clip backwards, press **Shift**-spacebar. This method is much quicker and keeps your hands on the keyboard and off the mouse. You can play and manipulate clips in the **Viewer** with great efficiency using only the keyboard.

Keyboard Shortcuts

Another common way to play the clip is with the **L** key.

- **L** is play forward.
- **K** is pause.
- **J** is play backwards.

On your keyboard they're clustered together, but you're probably thinking, Why not comma, period, and slash? There is reason to the madness. **J**, **K**, and **L** were chosen because they're directly below **I** and **O**. **I** and **O** are used to mark the In and Out points on clips and in sequences. They are probably the most commonly used keys on the editing keyboard. Hence **J**, **K**, and **L**, positioned conveniently for the fingers of your right hand with the **I** and **O** keys directly above them.

You can view your video at other speeds. You can play your clip fast forward by repeatedly hitting the **L** key. The more times you hit **L**, the faster the clip will play. Similarly, hitting the **J** key a few times will make the clip play backwards at high speed.

To play a clip one frame at a time, tap the **Right** arrow key. To play it slowly, hold down the key. To play slowly backwards, hold down the **Left** arrow key. Pressing **K** and **L** together will give you slow forward, and **K** and **J** together, slow backwards. To go back to the previous edit — the cut prior to the point where you are currently — use the **Up** arrow key. To go to the next edit event, use the **Down** arrow key. To go to the beginning of the clip, press the **Home** key; to go to the end press the **End** key.

Table 1.2   **Some Principal Keyboard Shortcuts**

Play	L
Pause	K
Play backwards	J
Fast forward	Repeat L
Slow forward	L + K
Fast backwards	Repeat J
Slow backwards	J + K
Go to previous edit	Up Arrow
Go to next edit	Down Arrow
Go to beginning	Home
Go to end	End
Mark the In point	I
Mark the Out point	O
Go to In point	Shift-I
Go to Out point	Shift-O
Play Around Current Point	\
Play from In point to Out point	Shift-\
Match Frame	F
Mark Clip	X
Add Marker	M

Tip

Shortcut Help: If trying to remember all the keyboard shortcuts is shorting out your brain, you can get color-coded special keyboards with keys that display the shortcuts. Or you can use the stick-on overlays that come with FCP3. Some people swear by them, but I'm not a big fan. I guess it comes from typing a lot with real letters, but if you have a dedicated edit system, it might well be worth having a dedicated keyboard. A great tool I find is the KeyGuide™ which accompanies this book. No FCP editor should be without one.

Viewer Buttons

Let's now take a look at that array of buttons clustered around the bottom of the **Viewer** so that you are familiar with them and what they do (Figure 1.68).

The **Shuttle** tab, on the left just below the video display in the **Viewer,** lets you shuttle the clip forwards and backwards. Grab it with the mouse and move right and left.

Starting from the left in the group around the central **Play** button, the first button is **Go to Previous Edit** (**Up** arrow). The next button is quite useful — it lets you play from your In point to your Out point. The keyboard shortcut is **Shift-\.**

The next button to the right of the central **Play** button is **Play Around Current Point** (\). The default is for playback to start five seconds before where the playhead is, and play for two seconds past where the playhead is. You can change the default times in your preferences. We'll get to preferences on page 58 in Lesson 2.

The last button is **Go to Next Edit** (**Down** arrow).

Another cluster of smaller buttons sits at the bottom left of **Viewer.** From the left, the first button is **Match Frame** (**F**). This is a very useful tool, though it won't work for you at the moment. If you open a clip that's in a timeline, it allows you to match back to the same frame in the **Canvas.**

Figure 1.68   Viewer Buttons

> ☞ **Tip**
> _____
>
> **Match Frame Variation:** Another useful tool to remember is **Shift-F.** This is a variation of **Match Frame**. It matches you back to the same frame of the original clip in the **Browser**. This is very useful if you've opened a clip from the Timeline and you want to find the original in the **Browser**.

The next button is **Mark Clip (X)**, which selects as the In and Out points the entire length of the clip. This can be useful in the **Time-line** window, but isn't of much value in the **Viewer**.

The next button, the diamond shape, adds a keyframe, which you need when creating animation.

The next button adds a marker to the clip (**M**). Markers are useful. They let you set visible marks on clips that appear in the **Timeline** window. You can mark the beat of a piece of music, where a phrase appears in dialog, where a pan or zoom starts or ends. Practically anything you can imagine noting about a clip can be made to appear on the screen.

Next to the **Marker** button is a group of two buttons, first **Mark In (I)** and then **Mark Out (O)**.

There are two more buttons at the bottom right of the **Viewer**. The one with the **Clip** icon lets you load recently opened clips. Next to that is a button with a large **A**. This opens a menu that accesses the **Generators**, such as **Bars and Tone, Render Gradients, Color Mattes, Slug, Text, Title 3D**, and the **Title Crawl** tool. We'll delve into this button in Lesson 12.

Now we'll put some of what you've just learned into practice. Put your cursor in the white bar directly below the video image. As you mouse down, the playhead will jump to where you are. The playhead is the little yellow triangle with a line hanging from it. There are playheads all over Final Cut Pro. In addition to the **Viewer** they're in the **Canvas** and the **Timeline** window as well in the **Motion** window and every other place you can play video.

You could use the curved thumbwheel, the **Jog** control, to the right (below the video image) to scrub through the video as you scrubbed the thumbnails in the **Browser**. Don't bother with it. For now, scrub in the white bar, and you'll move the video backward and forward to your heart's content. Try navigating around the clip using the keyboard. Use the spacebar or the J, K, L keys. Mark in and out points on the clips using the I and O keys. Change them. Go forward. Go backwards. Scrub up and down. Get a feel of maneuvering through your digital material.

Figure 1.69 Top of the Viewer

Top of the Viewer

Let's look at the top portion of the **Viewer** for a moment (Figure 1.69). In the center are two buttons, actually popup menus. The one on the left, the **Zoom** popup menu, adjusts the size of the image displayed in the **Viewer**. You can set to **Fit to Window,** or to a percentage from very small to so large that you can see all the pixels at their blocky best.

The other button, the **View** popup menu, changes the view from Image mode to **Image+Wireframe,** or just **Wireframe** (Figure 1.70). You need this mode especially for compositing. Wireframes let you see the shape and size of an image. You have to be in **Image+Wireframe** or **Wireframe** mode if you want to resize a clip or rotate or move it around the screen. It also lets you look at the alpha channel of a clip and lets you set the background color or checkerboard pattern, as well as placing overlays.

Figure 1.70 View Popup Menu

👉 **Tip**
Alpha Channel: An alpha channel is a representation of an image that defines its transparency. A title for instance, has an alpha channel that defines the text as opaque and everything around it as transparent.

Notice the new option for **Timecode Overlay** in the **View** menu. This will show the current timecode together with the In and Out points as an overlay in the **Viewer** (Figure 1.71).

Viewer Time Displays

At the top of the **Viewer** are two sets of numbers. On the left is the duration of the clip from its marked In point to its marked Out point. If the In and Out are not set, it will show the duration of the media from start to finish. This is different from the duration of a clip, which is the distance from its In point to its Out point.

The time display on the right shows the timecode for the frame where its playhead is sitting. Timecode is crucial to video editing. It is a frame-counting system that is now almost universal to video cameras. Some cameras or decks simply begin recording timecode starting at 0; others can be set to begin at specified times. Either way, a number is assigned to every frame of video and is physically recorded on the tape. We'll look at timecode more closely in "Device Control" on page 87 in the next lesson on preferences.

The **Timecode** window in the **Viewer** can be used to go to specific points in the clip just by typing in the appropriate number. Like the **Duration** window, you can use it to add and subtract time.

This is just the surface of the **Viewer**. We'll be visiting it again and again in the lessons to come, especially the tabbed windows behind the video window.

Figure 1.71   Timecode Overlay

Exploring the Canvas

You'll probably first notice that the **Canvas** window (Figure 1.72) is very similar to the **Viewer**.

Most controls are duplicated. Some have been placed in mirrored positions, such as the cluster in the lower right corner, which mirrors the cluster in the lower left of the **Viewer**. The **Shuttle** and the **Jog** are also in mirrored positions in **Canvas**, but they function the same.

Changing Clip Duration

You can change the duration simply by typing in a new number. The change will be based on the in point. You can also add or subtract in the duration display. If you want to add three frames to a clip, type in *+3*. If you want to subtract six frames, type in *–6*. If you want to add or subtract seconds or minutes, type in the number of seconds followed by one period. The period stands for zero frames. So if you want to add in two minutes, you type *+2..*, which means two minutes, zero seconds and zero frames. So, to add one second and twenty frames to a clip, you'd type in *+120*.

You can also change the duration of a clip in the **Browser** by typing in a new duration in the **Duration** column. And, as we saw, you can change the duration in the **Timing** panel of the **Item Properties** window.

The time displays at the top function the same as in the **Viewer**. The two popup menus in the top center are the same also.

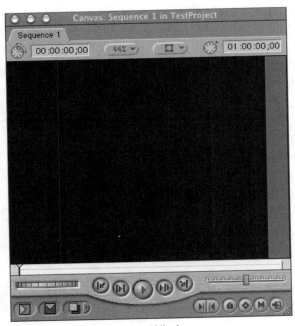

Figure 1.72   The Canvas Window

The only real difference is the cluster of colored buttons in the lower left corner. These are **Edit** buttons. Table 1.3 shows their functions and keyboard shortcuts starting from the left.

Table 1.3   Edit Buttons in Canvas

Color	Function	Keyboard Shortcut
Yellow	Insert	F9
Red	Overwrite	F10
Blue	Replace	F11

Inside these, as we shall see, are other edit functions that we'll get to later:

- **Replace**
- **Fit to Fill**

- Overwrite with Transition

- Insert with Transition

Timeline Window

Let's look at the **Timeline** window, which, being empty at this stage, isn't much to look at (Figure 1.73).

Tip

Shortcuts: There are simple keyboard shortcuts to select each of FCP's windows. The principal windows are shown in Table 1.4.

It's made up of tracks. Above the horizontal central double bar is the video track with the **Filmstrip** icon. Only **V1** is showing at the moment. Below the horizontal bar are the audio tracks with the **Loudspeaker** icons. The two showing, **A1** and **A2,** are awaiting a stereo pair of audio clips. Most of the controls for the **Timeline** windows are along the bottom and the left edge of the window.

The **Track** icons are highlighted in yellow because they are active, targeted tracks. We'll talk about targeting in later lessons. For the moment, you can untarget a track by clicking the yellow icon. Retarget it by clicking it again.

Table 1.4   Shortcuts

Viewer	Command-1
Canvas	Command-2
Timeline	Command-3
Browser	Command-4

Figure 1.73   The Timeline Window

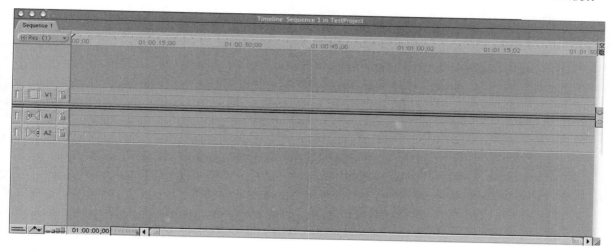

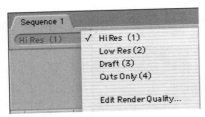

Figure 1.74   **Render Resolution Button**

The little button in the upper left corner of the **Timeline** window defaults to **Hi Res** (Figure 1.74).

When you need to render a clip, use this button/popup menu to set the render resolution. The lower the resolution, the faster the rendering process will be, but the image quality will be correspondingly poorer. Always switch back to **Hi Res** and render before you record to tape or render your sequence to a digital format for CD or DVD or the web.

The three little buttons in the lower left corner of the **Timeline** window change the window display (Figure 1.75). The first from the left displays keyframes that have been applied to clips. The second shows **Overlays**, which allow you to adjust the clip's audio levels and video opacity. The third button sets the track height. There are four settings of track height. Choose whichever is comfortable for you and your monitor's resolution.

Figure 1.75   **Timeline Buttons**

Next to these buttons is the **Current Time Display**. That's not the time on your watch; it's where you are in your sequence. Like all time displays in Final Cut Pro, it's addressable. Click in it to type a new number, or add and subtract a value, just as you did in the **Viewer**. When you change the time in the current time display, the playhead immediately jumps to that time.

The slider next to the **Time Display** lets you change the horizontal scale at which your clips are displayed in the **Timeline** window. With a blank window, it's useless.

The **Track Mover** tool lets you change the proportions of the video and audio panels, by moving the so-called **Static Display Line**. This can also be split to show different sections of the video and audio panels simultaneously, which can be very useful when you're working with multiple tracks of video or audio (Figure 1.76).

In the upper right corner of the **Timeline** window are two little icons that tell you whether **Snapping** and **Linking** are turned on (Figure 1.77).

If **Snapping** is on, the playhead, clips, and anything you move in the **Timeline** will want to butt up against each other as if they had magnetic attraction.

Turn on **Linking** if you want the sound and the picture together when you grab a sync clip. With **Linking** on, they'll move in unison. With it off, the two elements can be moved separately. I recommend leaving **Linking** on at all times, bypassing it only when necessary.

Figure 1.76   Track Mover and Static Display Line

Summary

So ends Lesson One. We've covered a lot of ground, worked our way into this new operating system and across this complex interface, and seen just the tip of the iceberg that lies under its deep waters. Spend some time clicking around in the Final Cut Pro windows. You can't hurt it. And remember to try the **Control** key to bring up contextual menus.

In the next lesson you'll to learn how to set up your system so that it works properly and how to get your own material into the Final Cut Pro edit suite.

Figure 1.77   Left: Snapping and Linking On
Right: Snapping and Linking Off

Lesson 2

Getting Your Material into Final Cut Pro

Digital video editing is divided into three phases:

- Getting your material into the computer

- Editing it, which is the fun part

- Getting it back out of your computer

Unfortunately, the first part is often the hardest and trickiest. It gets easier and more fun as you go. The last phase is the simplest.

This lesson is about the first part, getting your material into your computer. First you have to set up your application correctly. In Final Cut Pro, as in most video editing programs, that means setting up your preferences — lots of preferences and settings for video and audio.

After setting preferences, we'll go into logging and capturing your media. These fundamentals are absolutely necessary for Final Cut Pro to function properly. Set it up right, get your material into your project properly, and you're halfway home. You cannot overestimate how important this is. Many preferences can be set in the Final Cut interface. Preferences have been moved in OS X. In every OS X application **Preferences** are now under the ApplicationName menu. Some of the prefs may seem to be duplicates; some of them only appear in one location. What's important is to get them right.

To get them right, you need to understand something about the workflow of video editing and to make some decisions about how you want to work. You have to make a fundamental choice before you start: do you want to work online or offline?

At its simplest level, offline is working with a copy of your material that is never intended to be seen by anyone but the editor, producer, director, and those working on the project. It's the equivalent of a work print in film cutting, which used be to mostly in black and white, full of china graph marks, dust, scratches, and tape joins. The online version is what is intended to be seen by your audience. Because of the high cost of online equipment, editing a program at finished online quality was cost prohibitive, so most productions were first edited in offline quality. Traditionally the offline was done on a cheap editing system, perhaps even VHS, or at very low quality. This offline produced an Edit Decision List (EDL), which is a list of every single edit, video and audio, and the timecode which defined which tapes and which frames on that tape each edit came from. So offlining is a process of working at low quality on cheap machines, while onlining is the part of the process that changes the quality of the product to its final, finished version. In film days, this was the negative cutter's job; in tape production, it happened in an online edit suite with expensive videotape decks, controllers, mixers, and video engineering equipment.

In nonlinear editing, *offline* has come to mean the process of digitizing your video material at low resolution, thereby conserving drive space, while allowing the editor access to a huge amount of material. After editing the offline material, an EDL is again produced, which is used to redigitize the material in an edit suite capable of the finished resolution quality. In Final Cut Pro, the process remains within one edit suite. FCP is both the offline and the online suite. This simplifies the process and allows greater capabilities because you have the full resources of the application available to you, which you don't when exporting to an EDL. After the material has been redigitized at its high, final resolution, the finish work is done, tweaking the color and effects so every shot is as perfect as can be.

So this is the decision you have to make when you first set up your preferences: will you start by working in offline, capturing your material at low resolution first and then recapturing at high resolution, or will you capture at your final resolution from the beginning?

Setting Up a New Project

Let's begin by creating a new project.

1. Start by double-clicking the **Final Cut Pro** icon in the *Applications* folder. Or better yet, if you've created a **Dock** alias for FCP, simply click on the icon in the **Dock**.

FCP will launch the last project that was open. If a previous project does open up, close the **Browser**, which will close the project.

2. Go up to **File>New>New Project (Command-E)**.

Yes, it's **Command-E**, not the more customary **Command-N**, which is used to create a new sequence.

You get a new project called **Untitled Project** with the empty sequence in the **Browser** called *Sequence 1*.

Because FCP uses your project name to create folders inside designated folders such as the *Capture Scratch* folder, it's a good idea to give your project a name right away. At this stage you can't save the project because there's nothing to save. However, you can use **Save Project As** to save it with a name. FCP will use that name to create files in designated places on your hard drive.

Note _____

Offline Confusion: Confusion about the term *offline* has been compounded because FCP often uses the word to mean a clip that's in your **Browser** or **Timeline**, but whose source file is missing or deleted from your hard drive. When I speak of *offline* and of *OfflineRT,* I mean the workflow and not the missing media.

Tip _____

New Project: Actually if you have the **Browser** closed and press **Command-N**, it will create a new project, because there has to be a project for the new sequence to be in.

3. Go to your *User folder* and save the project inside as *PrefsProject*.

4. Go up to the **Final Cut Pro** menu and select **Preferences** (**Option-Q**).

It's an unfortunate choice of keyboard shortcut, I think. Just too darn close to **Command-Q**, the **Quit Application** shortcut. As soon as you open **Preferences**, this is what you see (Figure 2.1).

General Preferences

This is the **General Preferences** panel. In Final Cut Pro 3, there are two separate preference panels:

- One for user preferences

- Another specifically for audio/video preferences

The **User Preferences** are daunting, made up of no less than six tabbed windows, each full of potential booby traps. We'll work through it, starting with **General**, the first window. Fortunately, most of the items here can be left at their default setting.

Levels of Undo defaults to 10 actions, which seems to me a pretty good number. If you need to backtrack through more than 10 items, it's probably easier to fix the problem manually. You can make the number of actions up to 99, but the higher you make it, the slower your system will get. The application will have to keep more stored in memory, making its performance sluggish.

For **List of Recent Clips**, 10 seems like a good number also. This is the number of clips retained for the popup at the bottom of the **Viewer**. Again, a higher number means slower performance.

Multi-Frame Trim Size sets the number of frames that slip in the trim window. Five is the default. I prefer three. Pick what suits you. We'll look at items like multi-frame trimming in closer detail in Lessons 4–6.

Sync Adjust Movies Over allows you to let the application make sync adjustments for long DV clips. This was included in the original version of FCP because of problems with early model Canon DV cameras, specifically the XL1, Eluras, and Opturas. It's still in

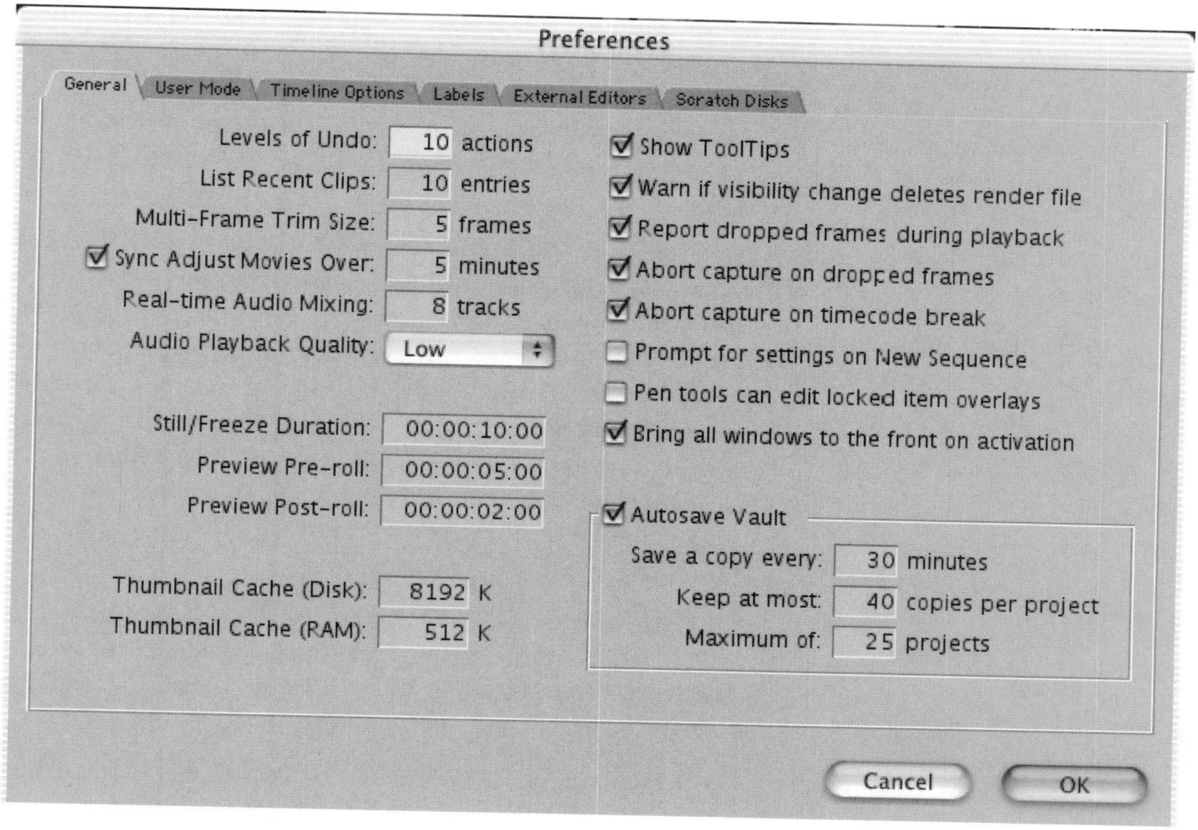

Figure 2.1   General Preferences Panel

here because some cameras are still having similar problems, mainly that its sampling rate is not precisely 48,000 or 32,000 samples per second.

It's almost impossible for a camera, a mechanical device, to be that precise. What's remarkable is that most DV cameras are extraordinarily accurate and will maintain sync over an hour of play time down to a quarter of a frame. Still, the **Sync Adjust** is there, just in case. It defaults to being checked on with five minutes. Unless you're working with one of the earlier Canons (before the GL1) or some specific camera that may have this problem, it's probably best to switch this off. If you are having sync problems, you can switch it back on and reimport your material. **Sync Adjust** only affects your clips on import, not on capture. With the cameras mentioned, you definitely must have it on. Switch it off if you are working with non-DV material or if you have clips with timecode breaks. TC breaks will adversely affect the synchronization adjustment and will throw your material badly out of sync. For these lessons, you should switch it off. We will be working with non-DV material (Photo-JPEG, in this case).

Real-time Audio Mixing determines how many tracks the application will play back in real time before it requires rendering, or the maximum number of audio tracks FCP will try to do in real time. This is no guarantee that it will be able to do it, but it will try. The default is fine. If you add more tracks to the sequence than the **Preference** setting, it will immediately want to render them. It might still play the tracks, but you'll hear an annoying beeping sound during playback. How many tracks your system can mix in real time depends on the speed of your system, CPU, drives, and RAM.

If you have problems with dropping frames, it might be wise to reduce the number of real-time tracks. Audio renders very quickly, so we're not talking about long waits for your sequence to play.

The default setting for the **Audio Playback Quality** popup menu is **Low**. This is a slight misnomer because it only affects playback for audio that needs to be resampled in the **Timeline**. Though audio resampling has been improved in FCP3, it's probably best to resample audio to the correct rate before placing in the **Timeline**. It's fine to work in **Low**; it will allow a greater number of real-time tracks for playback. When you're doing audio mixing, it's probably best to switch to **High**. On output to tape, export, or audio mixdown, this is automatically switched to **High**.

Still Image Duration sets the length of imported single-frame graphics and freeze frames made in FCP. You can change them once they're in FCP, but they'll appear at this length in the **Browser**. The default setting of 10 seconds seems long to me, so I set it to five seconds, a reasonable length for most stills or graphics from applications like Photoshop. Just type in the time you want. If you're doing training or other videos that require many full-screen graphics, leaving it at 10 seconds might be better for you. Though stills and freeze frames have a default duration of 10 seconds, that can be changed to any length you want. At this time, however, the implementation does not seem to be quite what it should be. You have to set the maximum duration for the still before it is placed inside a sequence. After that, the still cannot be extended beyond its designated duration. It can be made shorter, but not longer. There is also a sequence time limit of four hours which you still cannot exceed.

In the previous lesson we talked about playing around the current time. If you hit the **Play Around** button or use the keyboard shortcut \, playback will begin a defined amount of time before the playhead and play for a defined amount of time past it. You define those times here. The default **Preview Pre-roll** is five seconds, a traditional pre-roll time for VTR machines. The default **Preview Post-roll** is two seconds. Five seconds for a pre-roll always feel long to me, so I set it down to three seconds. I leave the post-roll at two seconds. Play with it and see what feels right for you.

Thumbnail Cache (Disk) and **Thumbnail Cache (RAM)** values have been raised considerably in this version of Final Cut, though still relatively small. I'd keep at the default values of 8,192k and 512k, unless you like to work in the **Browser** with lots of bins in Icon view or like to keep thumbnails open in List view. If you do, you may want to raise these values from the default. Make sure you have extra RAM available. Some people make these numbers quite high, 30MB or more. I don't use icons much, so I leave it low.

On the right side of this window is a list of checkboxes that have been changed somewhat from previous versions. The default for the first five is checked on, and I leave them that way.

With **Show Tooltips** on, a tool tip will appear when you hold the cursor over an icon for a moment. If you don't know what the tool is for, it's useful. If you do know, you're probably not lingering long enough for the tip to appear.

Visibility Warning throws up a warning message if you click to make invisible a track with rendered material. It warns you that making the track invisible will unrender the clips and gives you a chance to avoid that.

The next preference has proponents for and against it. **Report Drops** throws up a warning dialog whenever the application drops frames during playback. If you have a good, clean system with plenty of power and fast drives, you're probably not going to get this message often. If you're having problems, or if your system is marginal, it can be annoying when this message pops up and stops your workflow. My advice is to leave it on. If you get the warning often, try to deal with it. If it gets bothersome and you'd rather push on with your work, switch it off and live with occasional video stuttering during playback.

I'm not quite sure why **Abort capture on dropped frames** was put here. It seems more like an AV preference, really a capture preference. There were problems with this setting in the previous version of FCP, which have apparently been fixed in v3. It's probably wise to leave this checked on.

This is followed by a new setting, **Abort capture on timecode break**. This can be a bit of a nuisance, but necessary if you're working with tapes with timecode breaks in them. If you are having trouble capturing, you might want to switch off the two **Abort** settings as there have been instances where they are upsetting capture.

Prompt for Settings on New Sequence is self-explanatory. Leave it off once you've established your sequence presets. Some people, especially in multiuser environments, with different people working on different types of projects, prefer to have this checked on so that a reminder appears each time a sequence is created to tell you what type of sequence you're creating and to allow you to change it.

Pen Tools Can Edit Locked Item Overlay should definitely be left off. It's easy enough to unlock a track to edit and then relock it, but making adjustments to locked tracks can be dangerous.

Bring all windows to the front on activation is new to OS X. This system has a "feature" that allows you to have windows from different applications in the foreground, overlapping each other. If this preference was not checked on, and while I was in another application I clicked on the **Timeline** to switch to FCP, only the **Timeline** window would come to the fore. Generally this is not very useful, hence the need for this preference, which I would advise leaving on.

Also new to FCP 3 is *Autosave Vault*. Autosaving was available in previous versions of the application, but now the program actually saves your project incrementally with a date-and-time stamp. This section in the lower right corner of the **General** preferences panel is where you assign how often you want the project saved, how many copies to keep, and how many projects you want to be held. Saving a project to disk can take a moment or two. The larger the project gets, the greater the number of clips and sequences, and the longer the save will take. So interrupting your work flow by setting the **Save a copy** box too small might be counterproductive.

I find the default of 30 minutes a good number. You probably won't lose too much if the application does crash, plus you'll save a couple of days worth of work in the vault. If you make the save time to quick — say 10 minutes or less — you may want to increase the copies per project that's saved. The **Autosave** function has changed in this version of FCP. It no longer maintains a separate file while you work. (If you crashed, it asked you if you wanted to open it.) Now the only files saved are in the *Autosave Vault* and are called up from the **File** menu by selecting **Restore Project.** You'll be given a dialog that offers you a list of time stamped copies of that project (Figure 2.2).

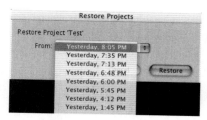

Figure 2.2   Restore Project Dialog

New to FCP3 is the **Revert Project,** which as in other applications will take you back to the last saved state. Note that neither **Restore** nor **Revert** will bring back arrangements. These are in your preferences and will not be restored.

The *Autosave Vault* is by default located wherever your *Scratch Disk* is set. This is unfortunate because projects files are ideally not placed on the same drive as the media. There is a preference for where the vault is set; unfortunately it's not here. It's in the **Scratch Disks** panel, which we'll get to on page 68.

That's it for the first window of **Preferences,** the easy part. Open up the next tab, **User Mode** (Figure 2.3).

Tip

Back Up! Remember the vault is constantly emptying itself of older saved projects, so as an extra back up, at the end of each day, or after a substantial revision, save a copy of the project into a separate folder. Hold down the Option key drag one of the project files from the vault and pull it into another folder to save it separately.

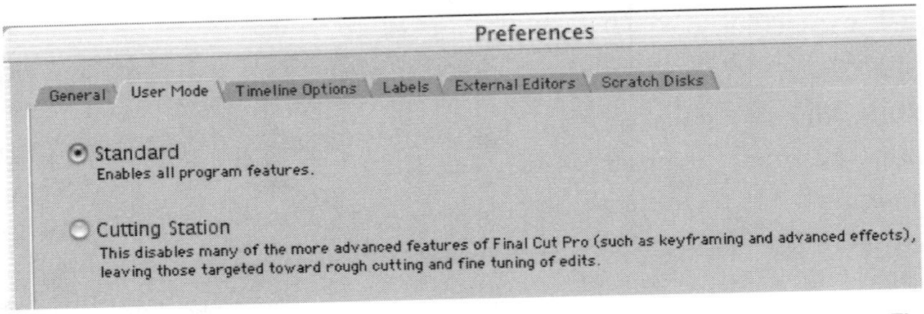

Figure 2.3   User Mode Preferences Panel

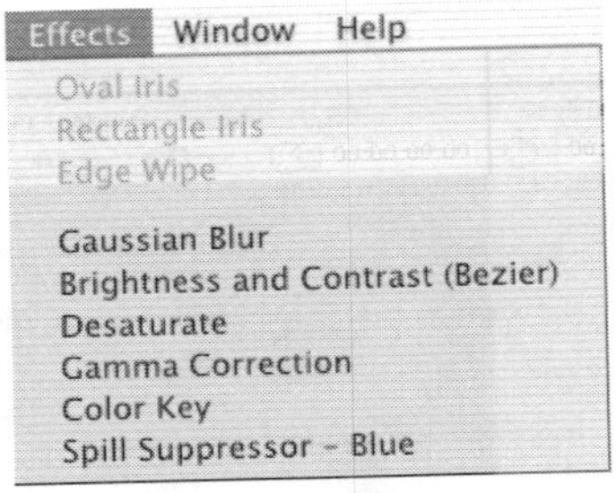

Figure 2.4   Cutting Station Effects and Transitions

User Mode

User Mode offers two options:

- **Standard**

- **Cutting Station**

For these lessons and probably for most users, the default **Standard** mode will be correct. **Cutting Station** gives you limited tools, few effects, few transitions, and no motion keyframing. The **Browser** doesn't have an **Effects** tab, and the **Effects** menu limits effects and transitions those shown in Figure 2.4. Though the new **Tool Bench** is available in **Cutting Station**, it would be nice if the new **Color Correction** tools were available as well, to go along with the few legacy color tools still available.

I think the intent of **Cutting Station** mode is primarily for working offline when you intend to export an Edit Decision List (EDL) to an online or linear editing system. Because EDLs can only pass on a limited amount of information, it is useful to work in an environment limited mostly to what EDLs can handle. Though **Cutting Station** mode removes **Insert** and **Delete Tracks** from the **Sequence** menu, it does not limit the number of tracks you can have. It does, however, greatly limit the number of effects and transitions you can do. Multiple tracks, some effects, and some transitions do not translate to EDLs, so **Cutting Station** isn't only for EDL users. It's really a simplified version of FCP. If you want to change from one mode to the other, you have to close the application before the change takes effect.

Note

Missing Cross Dissolve: For some reason, **Cross Dissolve** is missing from the Transitions list in **Cutting Station** mode, though it can be called up with **Command-T**. If you have selected **Cross Dissolve** as your default transition, you can still apply it with the **Control** key contextual menu on the edit point. It will also appear as the default transition using the **Canvas Edit Overlay**, all of which we'll discuss later.

Timeline Options

Timeline Options is the next tab in the **User Preferences** setting. (Figure 2.5).

Non-Drop Frame Vs. Drop Frame

Drop Frame and Non-Drop Frame have nothing to do with whether or not your system will drop frames when it plays back, and no actual frames are dropped in Drop Frame. These are only counting methods for dealing with NTSC's bizarre frame rate of 29.97 frames per second. Non-Drop Frame is the simpler method, displaying numbers based on the frame rate as if it were actually 30 frames per second. The problem with this is that when your timecode gets to the one-hour mark, one hour of real world time has already gone by almost four seconds earlier. If you're not working to a specified time constraint, or a short time constraint, it's simpler to work in NDF, though the default for most DV cameras is DF.

Drop Frame uses a complex method of counting which compensates for the difference between 29.97 and 30 frames per second. DF drops two frames a minute, except for every tenth minute. This means that at the one-minute mark, your drop-frame video will go from 59:29 to 1:00:02. There is no 1:00:00 or 1:00:01. It should be noted that the mini-DV format uses Drop Frame as its counting method. DVCAM and DVCPro can use either. The convention is that DF is written with semicolons, or at least one semicolon, as in 2:29;15, while NDF is written only with colons, 2:29:15.

Figure 2.6   Name Style

Figure 2.7   Name Plus Thumbnail Style

Figure 2.8   Filmstrip Style

Here you define your personal preferences for your sequence timeline layout. You can set:

- The time at which your timeline starts. It defaults to begin at one hour, but it can be set to zero if you wish. You can check if you want your timeline to count in **Drop** or **Non-Drop Frame** mode. The default is **Drop Frame**, because mini-DV counts in drop frame mode.

- The track size

- The default number of tracks a new **Timeline** opens with

- The style the tracks are displayed in: **Name**, **Name Plus Thumbnail**, or **Filmstrip** (Figures 2.6–2.8).

Note

Remember: Using **Filmstrip** will require considerably more system overhead and a larger **Thumbnail Cache** size.

Figure 2.9   Sequential Audio Tracks

Figure 2.10   Paired Audio Tracks

Audio tracks can use one of two naming conventions, **Sequential** or **Paired**; the default is **Sequential** (Figures 2.9–2.10). To be honest, I can't see much advantage to using **Paired** instead of **Sequential**, but it's there if you want it.

I leave the next three checkboxes off (**Show Filter and Motion**, **Show Keyframe Overlays**, **Show Audio Waveforms**). They're more conveniently toggled on and off in the **Timeline** as needed.

The next item, **Show Through Edits,** is new to FCP3. It places triangular marks on clips that have been cut but have contiguous timecode on either sides of the edit point (Figure 2.11). They allow you to easily see where these points are and remove them if you want. If you don't like the marks, switch them off here.

Labels

Introduced in Final Cut Pro 2 were the colored labels we saw in the first lesson. You can define the labels' names in the **Labels** tab (Figure 2.12).

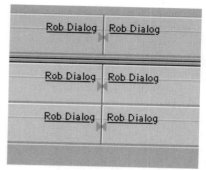

Figure 2.11   Through Edit Marks

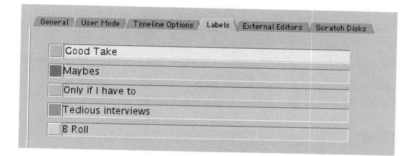

Figure 2.12   Labels Preference Tab

Your label names will appear in the clip contextual menus. The label colors, however, are fixed. You can't select your own color from a color picker.

External Editors

New to Final Cut Pro 3 is the **External Editors** tab. Here you can define which applications are use to work on different types of files outside of FCP (Figure 2.13).

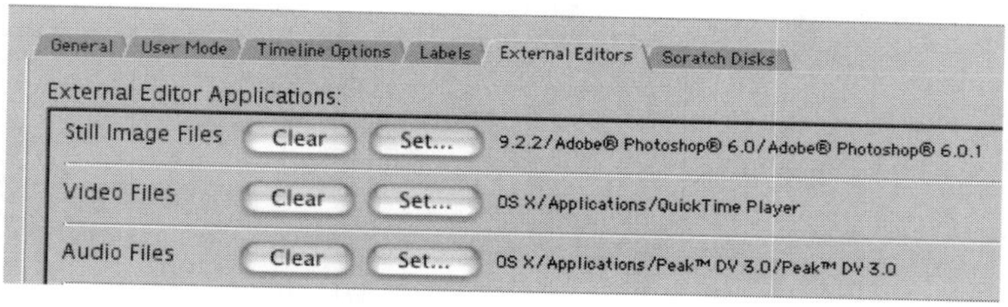

Figure 2.13   External Editors Tab

Figure 2.14   Open in Editor

This allows you to launch an application to alter a clip in either the **Browser** or the **Timeline**. Select a clip and hold down the **Control** key for the contextual menu choice **Open in Editor** (Figure 2.14).

This will launch the application that you specify in this preferences panel. After you edit the clip — such as a still image in Photoshop — those changes will be reflected in FCP.

You can set **External Editors** for **Stills**, **Video**, and for **Audio**. Be aware, though, that if you set the QuickTime Player as your editor for video files and choose Peak DV as your editor for audio files, then if you select **External Editor** for the audio portion of a sync sound clip, FCP will open the QuickTime Player, not Peak DV. FCP thinks of the audio track as part of a single video clip and so uses the QT Player. Single audio files, even if the creator type is QuickTime, will still open with the separate audio editor, such as Peak DV.

Note

Changes in Photoshop: Sometimes changes made to a file in Photoshop, particularly to the layer structure and opacity, will cause the file to appear to be Offline, bringing up the dialog in Figure 2.15. Select **Reconnect** and navigate to the PS file on your hard drive. If the dialog does not come up and the file still appears to be offline, select it in the **Browser**, and from the contextual menu chose **Reconnect Media** (Figure 2.16).

Scratch Disks

Next in the tabbed window is **Scratch Disks** (Figure 2.17). I would have thought this was another AV preference, but it's here.

Let's look at the lower portion of the window before we tackle setting the disks.Except for some specialist systems, make sure that the **Capture Audio and Video to Separate Files** box is left unchecked. This box is primarily a legacy of older systems that

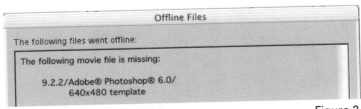

Figure 2.15   Reconnect Dialog

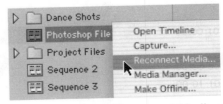

Figure 2.16   Contextual Menu>Reconnect Media

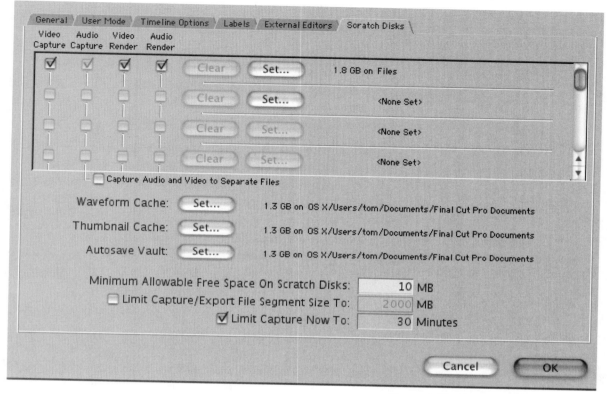

Figure 2.17   Scratch Disks
Preferences Panel

worked better with separate files on separate drives. If yours is one of the few capture cards that prefers this option, check this box. In all other cases, particularly for DV, leave it unchecked. For most applications the default settings work well.

The *Waveform Cache*, the *Thumbnail Cache* and *Autosave Vault* all default to the drive that you set when you first launched the application. The first two can remain where they are, but *Autosave Vault* should probably be changed to the *Shared* folder. Leaving it where it is means only the current user has access to the vault. In the *Shared* folder, all users can access it.

Minimum Allowable Free Space On Scratch Disks defaults to 10MB. Many people feel that the hard drive will fragment heavily and slow down at this level. Some go so far as to say that you should leave 25% of your drive free. For large drives, this seems a bit excessive. I leave it at about 100MB and have not had prob-

 Note

OS X Users: Because every user is OS X is unique, each user will get the startup dialog asking to set **Scratch Disks** location when the application starts. Each user will have to change these preferences when first coming to the application.

lems. If you have a large single partition above 50GB, perhaps you could set this number to 1G.

Unless you have a particular reason, you should leave **Limit capture/export segment size to** unchecked. This feature limits the size of segments FCP can capture or export. If your drives have been initialized as HFS+, this should not be a problem. FCP should capture large size clips without segmentation.

The **Limit Capture Now To** box makes it easier to use **Capture Now** by improving the application's performance. Without it FCP would check the available hard drive space before it started **Capture Now**. This could take a long time while the application rummaged through your assigned drives. This box allows you to limit the amount of space FCP will search for. It will stop searching either when it runs out of drive space or reaches the limit you designate. The default is 30 minutes, or about 6G of file space at DV settings. FCP can search through this space quickly.

Let's get back to the main body of the **Scratch Disks** window. Here you assign scratch disks for your captured material and for your render files. Normally you set your project's video, audio, and render files in the same location. You can set them to separate locations, but this practice is largely a legacy from slower machines and slower drives. For high resolution work at high data rates, setting audio to a different disk drive helps achieve better performance because the heads only need to serve video or audio, not both. With multiple tracks of audio in a sequence, the drive-handling audio has a great deal of work to do. Having a separate drive deal slowly with the high data rate video portion of the signal makes it easier on the system to achieve playback without dropping frames. For DV material, however, the same drive should always be used for both video and audio. Set each drive you want to capture to, and the application will fill that drive and then move onto the next.

By default, FCP3 assigns separate render folders for audio and video. When you click the **Set** button, a navigation window allows you to select the location for these files. Usually I go to the drive I want to use for a project and create a new folder (Figure 2.18).

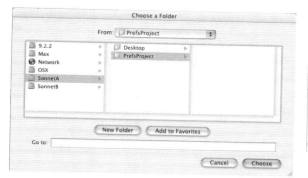

Figure 2.18   Scratch Disk Navigation Window

Figure 2.19   Project Folder

In this case, I created a folder called *PrefsProject*. At the bottom of the window, a button marked **Choose** allows you to choose that folder for your captured material and for your render files. When you press the button, FCP automatically creates three new folders inside your project folder (Figure 2.19).

These folders are the *Capture Scratch* folder, the *Render Files* folder, and the *Audio Render Files* folder. *Render Files* contains the video renders; *Audio*, the audio renders. As you capture or digitize material, it is stored in *Capture Scratch*.

If you have more than one hard drive or partition, you can set multiple locations in the **Scratch Disks Preferences** window. In FCP3 you can set up to 12 drives or partitions. The application automatically switches from one partition to another as they fill.

This is the end of the first panel of **Preferences** for Final Cut Pro 3. So far this has been the easy stuff. The other panel is **Audio/Video Settings**.

Audio/Video Settings

From the **Final Cut Pro** menu, select **Audio/Video Settings**, or use the keyboard shortcut **Command-Option-Q**. Like the shortcut for **General Preferences**, this one is really too close to **Command-Q**, used for quitting the application. A different combination for both would be better. However, when you open the **Audio/Video Settings**, it brings up the **Summary** tab (Figure 2.20).

Note

Naming Drives and Partitions: It is generally considered not a good idea to use a numbering scheme like 1, 2, and 3. Nor is it a good idea to name drives or partitions Blue, Blue 1, Blue 2, etc. Some FCP users seem to have trouble with drives that use a name that is included in part of another name. The application seems to be much happier with unique drive names such as Larry, Mo, and Curly.

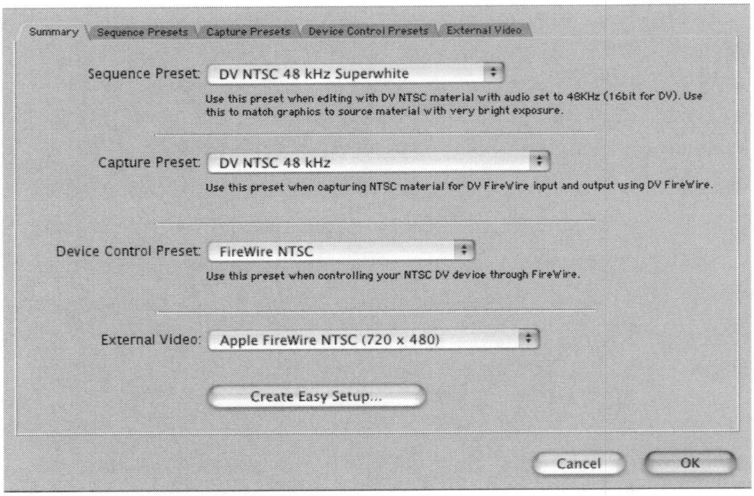

Figure 2.20   Audio/Video Summary
             Tab

As the name indicates, this window summarizes the other four tabbed windows. Each popup gives the settings for that window, settings you define in the other windows. The names you assign appear here. You can change easily from one preset to another.

The **Summary** panel lets you create your preferred setup. After you've made your selections, press the **Easy Setup** button at the bottom of the panel. The dialog box in Figure 2.21 appears.

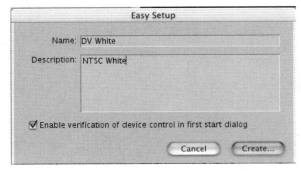

Figure 2.21   Easy Setup Dialog

These preferences are saved in the *Customs Settings* folder in your system's *Library,* inside *Application Support,* inside *Final Cut Pro System Support.* Placing it here means that it will be available to all OS X users.

Note the checkbox for **Enable Verification of Device Control in First Start Dialog.** Unchecking this will stop FCP from looking for a device to control when the application is launched. It seems strange that it's buried at the stage when you're saving the preset. It's a useful preference, and I would have expected it to appear in the **Device Control** panel.

Custom Settings: As you noticed, FCP has four standard locked settings: **DV-NTSC48kHz Superwhite**, **DV-PAL 48kHz Superwhite**, **OfflineRT-NTSC** (Photo-JPEG), and **OfflineRT-PAL** (Photo-JPEG). To lock your own custom selections, move them from their current location to a special location is inside the application package. It's best to do this with the application closed. The default location is inside the system *Library*. Go to *Library>Application Support>Final Cut Pro System Support> Custom Settings*. In this folder you'll find your **Easy Setup** saved settings. To lock it you want to move it to a folder inside the application. **Control**-click on the *Final Cut Pro* application in the *Applications* folder (Figure 2.22). From the contextual menu, select *Show Package Contents*. This will open a folder containing one item: *Contents*. The folder you're looking for is *Contents>Resources>English.lproj>Final Cut Pro Settings>Hardware Settings*. The sequence preset that you created for the custom **Easy Setup** will now appear in the **Sequence Preset** window as locked. If you reinstall the software, these will be lost, of course.

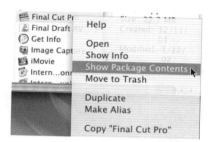

Figure 2.22 Final Cut Pro>Show Package Contents

You can evoke **Easy Setup** quickly from the **Final Cut Pro** menu or with the keyboard shortcut **Control-Q**. The dialog box summarizes your settings and allows you to switch between presets (Figure 2.23).

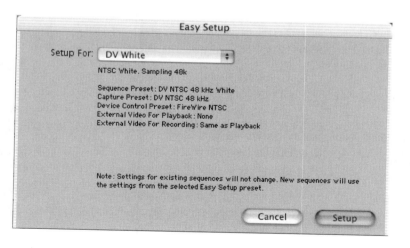

Figure 2.23 Easy Setup Popup and Summary

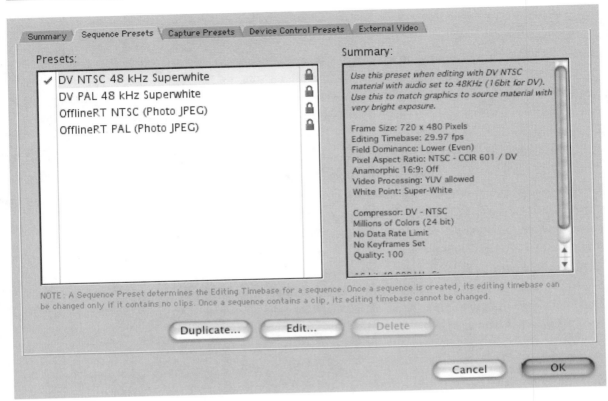

Figure 2.24   Sequence Presets Panel

Sequence Presets

Sequence Presets looks limited when you first open it up (Figure 2.24). FCP3 gives you just four default presets. The four are those you were asked to choose from when you first started the application:

- DV-NTSC 48kHz Superwhite
- DV-PAL 48kHz Superwhite
- OfflineRT NTSC (Photo-JPEG)
- OfflineRT PAL (Photo-JPEG)

The lessons in this book are based primarily on Photo JPEG NTSC. If you want to use a preset other than what you have from Apple you can create your own. Hardware manufacturers often

OfflineRT

This is new to FCP3. Normally DV material is captured at its full resolution, 3.6MB per second, less than five minutes per gigabyte. OfflineRT allows an editor to capture DV material at low resolution first, saving drive space. The material is captured using the DV format, but the computer transcodes it to Photo-JPEG as it captures. It requires a fast computer to do this, a G4/500 or better. The material has a frame size of 320x240 and is quite heavily compressed, down to 660k per second. It looks like VHS material, quite soft and not too blocky and pixilated as you might expect. Working in OfflineRT allows you to have nearly ten times as much material on your hard drive, 40 minutes per gigabyte.

There are two ways to get to work with OfflineRT. If you're computer is fast enough, you can capture directly to OfflineRT from tape, which of course will save you a great deal of drive space. If your computer isn't fast to capture the DV material and convert it to Photo-JPEG on the fly, which is what the OfflineRT process does, then you have to capture in DV and use **Media Manager** to recompress to OfflineRT. We'll look at how to work with **Media Manager** on page 138 in Lesson 3. After the material has been reduced in size, the DV media can be thrown away to recover the drive space. You may have to do this in chunks if you're pressed for drive space. Next you edit in OfflineRT. Once you've got you're material cut down, you go to **Media Manager** and make everything offline. That frees up your drive space again. You now have to recapture everything that you need for your final edit from the original DV tapes, based on your offline sequence. That's the process of offlining. Obviously, if you have the drive space, it's much easier to simply work with the original DV material and not bother with the whole offline process at all.

create their own presets, which may be installed for you when you install the software that goes with your specific hardware.

☞ Tip

Presets: If you try to edit a locked preset (and the four supplied by Apple are all locked), you will get the warning box in Figure 2.25, which will lead to the **Preset Editor**. The basic presets cannot be unlocked or changed.

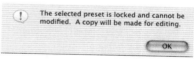

Figure 2.25   Preset Warning Box

To create your own custom preset, start off by duplicating either the existing DV-NTSC or the DV-PAL preset.

When the preset has been duplicated, the preset editor opens up. (Figure 2.26). As it opens, the **Name** panel is highlighted for you to rename your preset. You can also edit the description for the **Summary** panel.

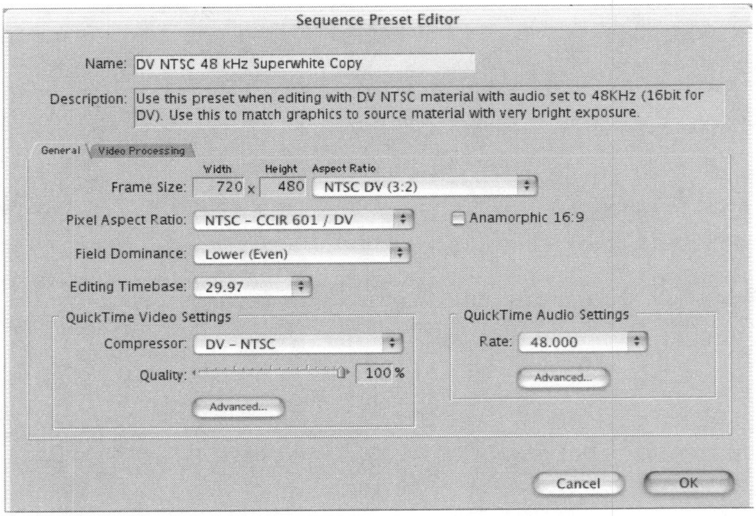

Figure 2.26   Sequence Preset Editor

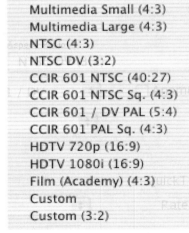

Below that are the real settings controls:

- **Frame Size**

- Its partner **Pixel Aspect Ratio**, the relation of the width of the frame to its height

The standard television set has an aspect ratio of 4:3. Right away you see a problem. Figure 2.27 shows an aspect ratio for NTSC DV of 3:2. That's because we're about to enter the wonderful world of rectangular pixels.

The **Frame Size** input boxes and the **Aspect Ratio** popup (Figure 2.28) offers a plethora of standard choices. When you select an aspect ratio, one of the standard frame sizes will automatically load as well.

The three most common NTSC frame sizes are:

- Traditional desktop video format NTSC 4:3 with a frame size of 640×480

- DV format NTSC DV 3:2 with a frame size of 720×480

- CCIR601 NTSC 40:27 with a frame size of 720×486

For these lessons, the **Frame Size** popup should be set to **Multimedia Large 4:3**, which creates a frame size of 320×240.

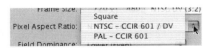

Figure 2.27   Frame Size Popup

Figure 2.28   Pixel Aspect Ratios Field

Note

No Sequence Preset for CD Projects: For the projects that accompany this book on the CD, it is not necessary to create a **Sequence Preset** that match the material. Sequences are already provided in the project with the correct preset. If others are needed, you can create them simply by copying the sequence that's already in the project.

Below the **Frame Size and Aspect Ratio** popup is **Pixel Aspect Ratio** with a popup (Figure 2.28) that allows you to select one of three types of pixels, two rectangular and one square. This is where you define whether your system is using square pixels or the CCIR601 pixel. These two items should really be hardwired to each other. Once you've chosen your frame size and aspect ratio, your pixel aspect ratio is predetermined. Letting you choose something different here is a recipe for trouble.

Next to the **Pixel Aspect Ratio** popup is a box that lets you set a flag telling your computer that your material is in widescreen aspect ratio. Only check this box if you're shooting and editing in 16:9.

Field Dominance is next (Figure 2.29). FCP uses the term *field dominance*, but it should more properly be *field order*. For consistency, we'll use the term FCP uses. It determines which field of video is scanned first, upper or lower, or if there is no field dominance at all. For these lessons we are using **None** because the

---

CCIR

CCIR stands for yet another committee, the former Comité Consultatif International des Radiocommunications (International Radio Consultative Committee), now the International Telecommunication Union. Their 601st recommendation created the so-called D1 pixel, the tall, narrow pixel that is the bane of present-day desktop digital video. High Definition formats have gone to using square pixels, which will simplify the desktop work environment considerably.

Square Vs. Rectangular Pixels

Computer screens like the one you're using with FCP use tiny little square pixels to represent information. When video was first created on desktop computers, systems used the square pixels of the computer screen. The standard television screen's 4:3 aspect ratio was translated into 640 horizontal pixels by 480 vertical pixels. The analog video world, of course, had no pixels to start with and entirely different issues to deal with, mainly that the system was based on horizontal, interlaced lines of information. To maximize the horizontal resolution, the powers that be in the world of digital video decided to create pixels that were narrower than they were tall, making little rectangular boxes. When the desktop converged with video, as it does with everything, a major pain was created. Little rectangular pixels didn't fit the square pixel world.

What is 16:9 anyway?

16:9 is widescreen video. Though they have not caught on much yet in the United States, widescreen televisions are fairly common throughout Japan. Consequently, Japanese manufacturers have added this capability to many DV camcorders. The camera squeezes the pixels anamorphically (so everything looks squashed, as if it's tall and narrow) to fit into a 4:3 frame and then unsqueezes them for playback on a widescreen TV. This is a bit of a kludge. True widescreen is done with an anamorphic lens that distorts the image that's recorded onto the tape.

The problem is that many people want to do 16:9 but don't have the equipment to do it properly. To monitor it, you need a widescreen monitor or one can switch between 4:3 and 16:9. FCP will output the correct 16:9 display if the presets are correct, but you won't see it correctly without the right monitor. You will not see a letterboxed version. Some fairly expensive decks will take a 16:9 image and output it as letterboxed 4:3. You can also place your 16:9 material in a 4:3 sequence and force it to render out the whole thing. You'll then have letterboxed 4:3.

Most DV camcorders will flag 16:9 material as such. FCP will read this regardless of whether the 16:9 checkbox is applied. If you are shooting true 16:9 with an anamorphic lens, the checkbox will force FCP to treat it as widescreen material, even though it doesn't get the DV flag. So be careful. Don't check this box when your material is not 16:9, though it can be undone in the clip's **Item Properties** panel.

Photo-JPEG material is not interlaced. The default DV uses **Lower/Even** first.

Below **Field Dominance** is a popup which allows you to set the **Editing Timebase** — that is, frame rate of your sequence (Figure 2.30).

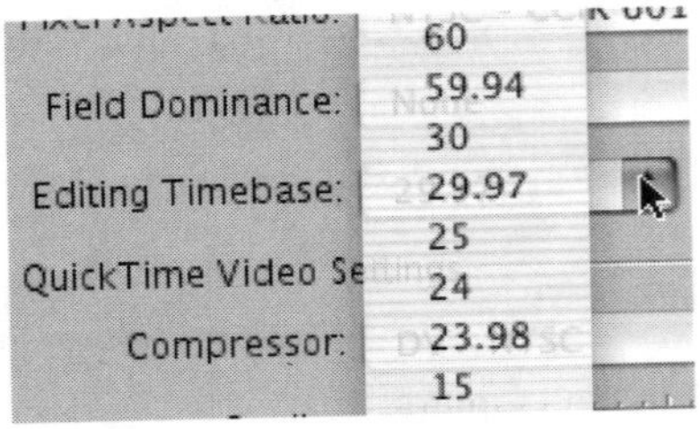

Notice that possible frame rates include the NTSC standard of 29.97 and its double, 59.94, which is used with applications such as After Effects that can create a separate frame for each field of video. New to FCP3 is the frame rate standard of 23.98 (really 23.976) used for film transfers.

Below **Editing Timebase** are two sections that you use to set the type of video and audio you're working with, video on the left, audio on the right.

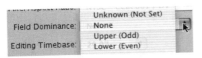

Figure 2.29   Field Dominance Popup

Figure 2.30   Editing Timebase

Note _____

Frame Rate: The sequence frame rate must be set here in **Sequence Presets** or in the **Sequence Settings** window before any clips are placed in the sequence. Once there are clips in the sequence, the timebase is locked and can no longer be changed. If you do want to change the timebase of a sequence after you've begun editing, simply select everything in the sequence (**Command-A**), and then cut the clips out of the sequence with **Command-X**. From the **Sequence** menu, you can select **Settings (Command-Zero)** and change the timebase. Then paste all the clips back into the sequence.

Final Cut Pro is a native QuickTime application, which is why you see QuickTime video and audio settings. The first popup here allows you to set the compressor that you are working with. The default is DV-NTSC, but you can choose from any number of other presets (Figure 2.31) as long as they actually match your material.

Below the **Compressor** popup is a **Quality** slider, which controls the render quality in the sequence. The **Edit Render Qualities**, which we saw earlier, only sets the resolution through frame size, while the slider sets the compression quality. For DV this means one of four quality settings for encoding compression:

- Low

- Medium

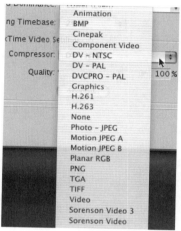

Figure 2.31   Compressor Presets

Interlacing

NTSC video is made up of 525 electronically scanned lines of information. (PAL is 625 lines.) To make up the full frame of video, each line has to be scanned once. Rather than scanning all 525 sequentially, the format scans alternative lines, the odd numbered lines 1, 3, 5, 7, etc., in one pass and the even numbered lines, 2, 4, 6, 8, etc., in another pass. Each pass makes up one field of video, and the two fields make up the full frame. Of course, if the camera is shooting a moving object, especially a fast moving object, the object's position when the second field is scanned will be different from when the first field was scanned. That's why it's important to know which set of lines is being scanned first, the even lines or the odd lines. Just to make this interesting, not all systems scan the same lines first. Also some systems give them different names. Instead of **Odd** and **Even**, they might call them **Upper** and **Lower**. **Upper** is **Odd**, and **Lower** is **Even**. Note that the field dominance for DV is set to **Lower**. DV is always **Lower/Even**, while the Aurora Igniter video card has a field dominance that is **Upper/Odd**. If you swap the field order of your video, any movement on the screen will produce a very peculiar fluttering, a rapid two steps forward, one step back look.

- High

- Best

Tip

Render Speed: The slider can be used to speed up rendering. Set the slider to **Medium**, and render times will be substantially faster while not make much apparent difference to the picture quality. You can always go back and change the slider to **Best** before doing your final output.

To get standard DV compression, the slider needs to be left at **Best**. These settings only affect render output and will have no effect on the capture quality.

Quite a few formats would prefer having specifications that set data rates rather than settings from a slider. Fortunately FCP provides the **Advanced** button for both video and audio. If you need to alter settings from presets to specialized settings for video and audio, use the **Advanced** button for these. The **Advanced Video** button brings up the box in Figure 2.32.

Here you can access the same compressors or codecs as in the **Video** popup. *Codec* stands for compressor/decompressor. Uncompressed video is approximately 900k per frame or 27MB per second. Almost all digital video is compressed to some extent. Some codecs, such as DV, are heavily compressed, usually considered 5:1, though on a single-frame basis, its compression would actually be about 7.5:1. You can also select the color depth for codecs that allow it, such as Animation.

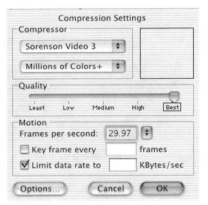

Figure 2.32 Advanced Video Button

Some codecs allow for variable compression, ranging from uncompressed or lightly compressed 1.5 or 2:1 all the way to heavily compressed, 20:1 for offline editing. You set the amount of compression with either the **Quality** slider or with the **Limit** box at the bottom of the window. The more you limit the maximum number of kilobytes per second — that is, the smaller the number you enter in **Limit** box — the more heavily compressed your material will be. The settings here should match those you put in the next window, **Capture Presets**.

The **Frame Rate** popup in this panel has limited choices. You should use the **Editing Timebase** popup on the main **Sequence Preset** panel.

Sampling Rate

The **Advanced** button (Figure 2.33) on the **Audio** side lets you select:

- Sampling rate

- Use or bit rate

- Stereo or mono

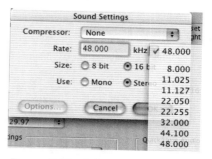

Figure 2.33 Advanced Audio Settings

The popup at the bottom of the **Sequence Preset** window limits you to three common sampling rates, 32kHz, 44.1kHz, and 48kHz, but the **Advanced Audio** button gives you more options.

Unlike video, where the sequence preset only affects render, this button will affect all audio because FCP changes the sampling rate in real-time, based on these settings.

Some digitizing boards use a sampling rate of 44,100Hz (44.1), which coincidentally and conveniently is the same sampling rate used by audio CDs. Yet another committee, this time the consortium of manufacturers who created the DV standard, thought it best to give the user a choice of sampling rates. Unfortunately, they didn't see fit to make one of those sampling rates 44.1. Instead they chose two different ones: 32,000Hz and 48,000Hz.

When you're working with DV in Final Cut, the choice has already been made for you. It was made in the camera. If the camera was set to 12-bit, it recorded at 32kHz; if it was set to 16-bit, it recorded at 48kHz. You get to choose in the camera before you start shooting. If you change it with the preset, FCP will try to change the sampling rate in real time, but you'll be able to do fewer tracks in real time.

So you should set the sampling rate in Final Cut to match the camera's sampling rate. It is best to avoid mixing sampling rates. What you should do is set your camera to 16-bit recording and leave it there. Set all your DV settings to 48,000 to match. Unfortunately, some cameras, even some expensive three-chip cameras, can only record in 12-bit. In that case, it's probably best to work only in 32kHz. If you are shooting in 32kHz, leave the radio box set to 16-bit, but change the popup to 32kHz.

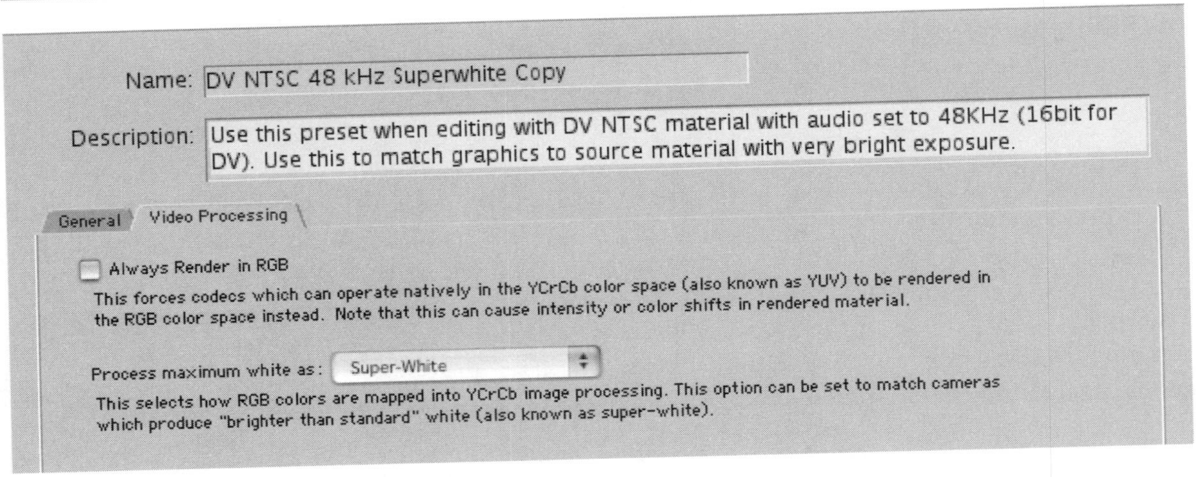

Figure 2.34 Video Processing Preset Editor

You could convert the sampling rate with the QuickTime Player, exporting your video and resampling it to 48kHz, but this would take a lot of time and drive space. It probably wouldn't be worth the effort. Only consider doing it if you have mixed material that uses different sampling rates. Resample the material with the QuickTime Player so that it's all at the same sampling rate. Open the clips in the QT Player and then export, making the sampling rate uniform throughout your project.

Video Processing Preset Editor

Notice back in Figure 2.26 on page 76 that the **Sequence Preset Editor** has a tab behind it. This is the only panel with a tabbed window, and it can be easy to miss. Bringing it to the front opens the window in Figure 2.34.

The only two items here are:

- A checkbox noting if your system allows processing video in RGB
  For most DV applications, leave it unchecked.

- A popup for setting the maximum luminance value
  For most DV applications, set **Process Maximum White** to **Superwhite**.

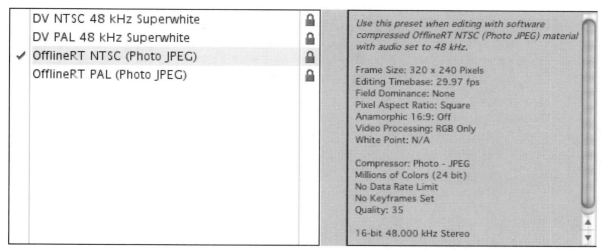

Figure 2.35 Summary Information for OfflineRT Photo-JPEG

Setting the popup to **White** will clamp the maximum luminance level to broadcast specifications. Unfortunately, most DV cameras record with a white level that exceeds broadcast standard. The problem is that if rendered luminance is clamped to the broadcast levels, then the white levels will change between what was shot in the camera and what was created in FCP, particularly noticeable during rendered transitions.

That's it for the **Sequence Preset** window. Once you've created your preset, gone through all the buttons, and changed everything to your needs, the right column displays the summary information (Figure 2.35).

Notice the check mark in the left column. Setting the check with a click in the column will designate the default sequence preset for each new sequence you create. The description in italics at the top of the summary will be the description that appears under the **Sequence Preset** popup on the **Summary** page.

Capture Presets

The next tab in the **Audio/Video** panel is **Capture Presets**, which opens with a set of options (Figure 2.36) similar to those in the **Sequence Preset** panel.

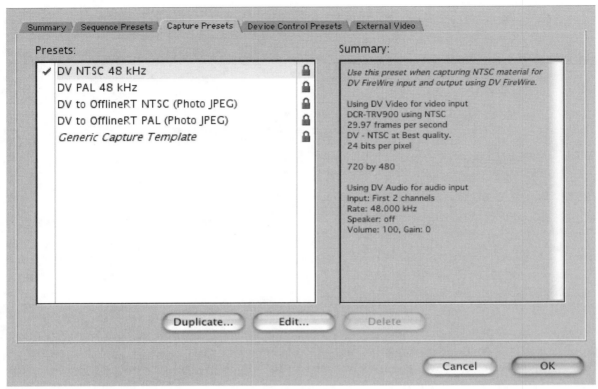

Figure 2.36   Capture Presets

Again, if you want something other than the standard presets, you'll have to start by duplicating one of the locked items, probably the DV-NTSC preset (Figure 2.36).

Like in the **Sequence Preset**, you can give a name and description to your new settings. Like in the **Sequence** tab, you set the frame size and flag whether your material is in 16:9 format. Below that are **Video** and **Audio** sections.

The standard DV preset (Figure 2.37) brings up all the usual suspects. The **Digitizer** popup lets you select the system you're using, for instance:

- DV

- A digitizing card such as the Aurora Igniter

- An uncompressed capture card such as the Kona card from AJA

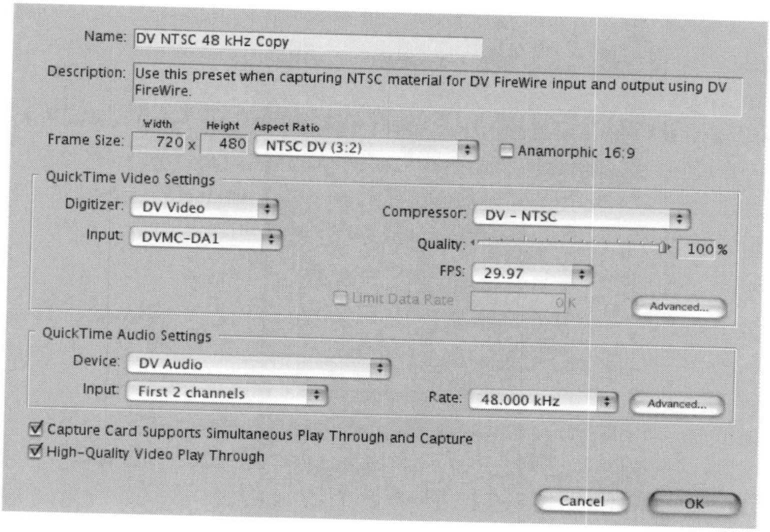

Figure 2.37   DV Capture Preset

Input lets you select where your material comes from if you have multiple sources feeding in, for instance:

- A digitizing card with multiple inputs, such as component, S-video, and composite

- A digitizing card and a DV input that you're switching between

- New in FCP3 is the ability of the application to sense the device that is plugged into the computer. The device's model number appears in the **Input** popup.

On the right, the **Compressor** popup offers the list of codecs we saw earlier in **Sequence Presets**. Again there is a **Quality** slider, but this one has no effect on the DV material. Why? Because your video has already been digitized, turned into a digital format inside your camera. All you are doing here is copying the digital information your camera recorded from the DV tape into your computer hard drive.

There is a popup to set the frame rate as well as a box to set the data rate for digitizing.

Lower in the window are the **Audio Settings**. **Device** lets you set the capture source, while the **Input** popup give you the option of choosing which tracks of audio to capture. Some cameras are capable of recording four tracks at 32kHz, 12-bit, but QuickTime is limited to capturing only two tracks at a time. The popup lets you set either the first two tracks, the second two tracks, or to mix the four together. To capture all four tracks, you'll need to make two separate captures passes.

The sampling rate is keyed to the **Device** popup, but it offers the odd choice of 44.1kHz under DV. Do not use it. Set it to the sampling rate of the material you're capturing. Unlike video, the audio sampling rate can be changed during capture. FCP pulls the audio out of the DV stream and creates a new AIFF track based on the sampling rate you select here.

The **Advanced** button has one important feature that you need to be careful about. You need to make sure the **Speaker** popup is set to **Off** or **Off While Recording** (Figure 2.38).

Leaving the **Speaker** on has caused sync problems in the past. The Mac tried to do double duty: create the AIFF at one sampling rate, while trying to send sound out the speaker at 44.1kHz through the computer's audio card.

The only additional item you can access here is the **Gain** slider, which you shouldn't be controlling here anyway. If you need to control the gain, you should do that in the **Log and Capture** window, which we shall get to on page 91.

The one checkbox at the bottom of the **Capture** window is self-explanatory. (The **Abort on dropped frames** checkbox used to be here, but it's now on the front **General Preferences** panel.) Check **Capture Card Supports Simultaneous Play Through and Capture** if your card does. Most do. DV does as well.

New in v3 is the checkbox for **High Quality Video Through**. In most cases this should be left on, though.

Again, when you're done creating your preset, the **Summary** appears on the right hand side, and again the italic description at the top is used in the **Summary** panel.

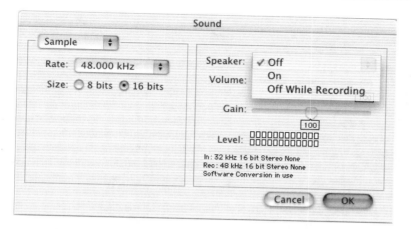

Figure 2.38   Advanced Dialog Box with Speaker Popup

It would be nice if you could create your **Capture Preset** and then press a button to make the **Sequence Preset** match the **Capture**. For now the onus is on you to make them match. It's not hard. Just be careful.

Device Control

This panel opens with another stark set of options. Most users will want to have device control, which is pretty simple to set up. To set up a new device control preference, start by duplicating one of the locked presets. Duplicating the **FireWire** preset will bring up the window in Figure 2.39.

Here again you can name and set the description for your preset. You use five popups to define the type of device control you're using and how you're connecting to your deck. One is dimmed in the **FireWire Device Control Preset**.

The first popup sets the **Protocol** (Figure 2.40). If you're working in DV, use **Apple FireWire**. If you're having difficulty communicating with your deck or camera, try **FireWire Basic**. RS-422 and RS-232 are Sony protocols that have been adopted by other manufacturers. For many years, RS-422 was the standard for device control. Provided your deck is capable of it, it will be absolutely frame accurate. The others are somewhat less reliable.

👍Tip

Third Party: Final Cut works with a great many devices from a number of manufacturers, all of whose equipment has different performance and specifications. Every camera or deck will handle device control different and will have different requirements for setup. Check the Apple Final Cut Pro website at **www.apple.com/finalcutpro/qualification.html** for FCP's requirements for working with different pieces of equipment.

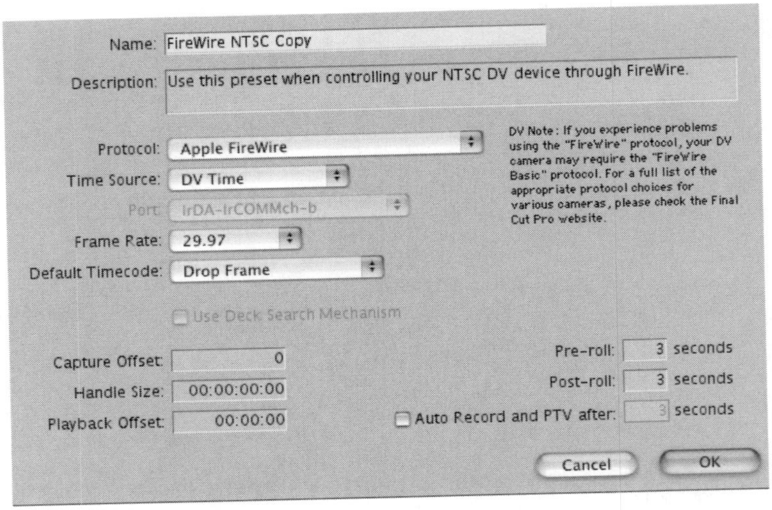

Figure 2.39 **FireWire Device Control Preset**

The next popup sets the source for your timecode (Figure 2.41). If you're working in DV, of course you set it to **DV Time**. If you're working with one of the other formats such as Betacam, Digibeta, or HD, you select **LTC**, **VITC**, or **LTC+VITC**, depending on where your TC is physically located on the tape. Sometimes it's recorded as a separate track called Longitudinal Timecode (LTC). Sometimes it's recorded as a part of the video signal, Vertical Interval Timecode, VITC. If you're working with Betacam and don't know which to use, usually the safest is **LTC+VITC**. The device control will look to either. Rarely does a tape have a different TC on LTC and VITC, though it can happen. The third popup sets the port that you're using to connect to the deck. With FireWire, the **Port** popup is dimmed. You can select a USB connection or serial port, if your computer has one.

Figure 2.40 **Device Control Protocol**

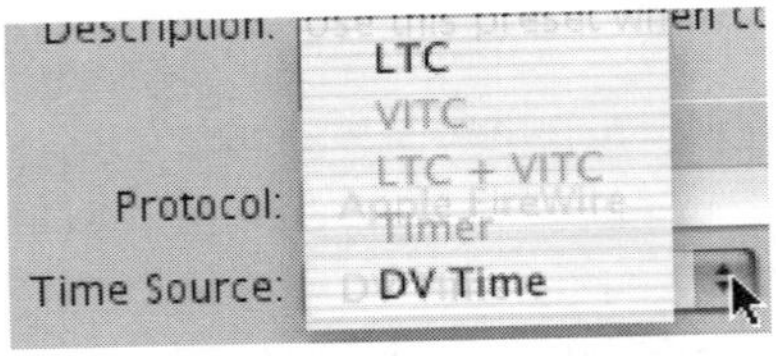

Figure 2.41 **Time Source Popup**

The fourth popup sets the frame rate, which should match your material, 29.97 for NTSC.

The fifth popup for **Default Timecode** is new to FCP3. Normally this is set to **Drop Frame** because this is the standard for DV. However, there are now cameras such as the Sony PD150 that allow you to set either **Drop Frame** or **Non-Drop Frame** when you are shooting. Hence the need for this popup. You should set it to whatever your source material is.

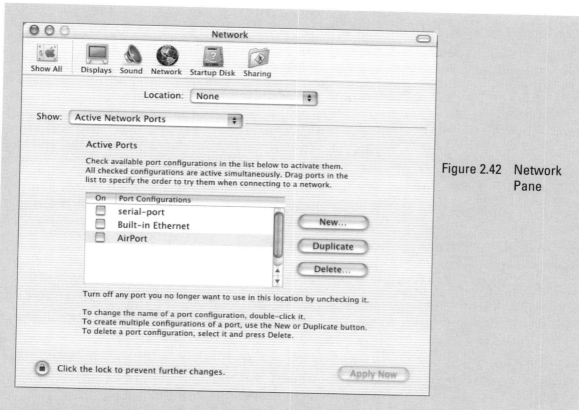

Figure 2.42　Network Pane

AppleTalk and Capturing

One checkbox that would be useful here be **Always Turn Off AppleTalk When Capturing**. You do not want AppleTalk suddenly polling your drives in the middle of a capture. In Final Cut you have to switch off AppleTalk manually. There is a fairly painless method of doing this in OS X. First you need to set up a new network preference. Launch **System Preferences** and select the **Network** pane. From the **Location** popup, create a **New Location** and name it **None.** From the **Show** popup, select **Active Network Ports**. Switch them all off as in Figure 2.42.

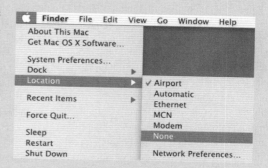

Figure 2.43　Location>None

Now whenever you want to turn off **AppleTalk**, go to the **Apple** menu and from **Locations** select **None** (Figure 2.43). That will turn off **AppleTalk** and all network connections. Don't forget to change back after you've finished capturing your material.

FireWire Frame Accuracy

Though FireWire will provide deck control, its performance in FCP has proven to be not always frame accurate. The FireWire protocols used in some devices do not consistently take the deck to the right frame. The DV timecode itself is always accurate, but the timecode doesn't always arrive accurately in the application; it's liable to be off by a frame or two. Most FireWire devices are DV decks and cameras, and for most uses with DV video, frame accuracy is not an issue. You're capturing your video at its final resolution. So it's not a big deal if the TC is off a frame or two. If you need to recapture your material after your media has been erased, work with extra media to ensure you get at least what you need, or work with a deck that supports the RS-422 protocol. Some DV decks have this capability. They are reliably frame accurate and will send accurate timecode to the application through the RS-422 connection while sending the video and audio through the FireWire connection.

The checkbox for **Use Deck Mechanism** is dimmed when you're working in DV. If you're using RS-422 or another protocol, this checkbox allows the deck to take control of the search routines. Many professional decks do this well, using timing and high-speed shuttle to get quickly from point to point on the tape. If your deck has this capability, by all means check the box.

Capture Offset allows you to calibrate the accuracy of your deck. This only works if the deck is consistently ahead or behind the capture point you specify and is used to calibrate frame accurate decks.

Handle Size lets you set how much extra material you capture before and after your marked In and Out points. If your deck is not frame accurate, you should probably set a handle size of at least one second. It's not a bad idea to set handles anyway so that you have extra material for transitions.

Playback Offset is similar to **Timecode Offset,** but it compensates for any delay when editing to tape. If you have decks capable of precise insert editing, be sure to calibrate them and see if any playback offset is necessary when editing from a sequence to tape. If you get duplicates of your first frame when you edit to tape, you can compensate for this here by entering the number of duplicate frames in **Playback Offset.** If the playback is coming in early, you can enter a negative number of frames.

The **Pre-roll** and **Post-roll** windows work similarly to the settings in the first window for **Preview Pre-roll,** except here it sets how far ahead of your capture point your deck will back up. Three seconds is a reasonable number for most decks. Don't set it to zero; no VTR can get up to speed instantly. Even three seconds is risky for some slow-responding DV camcorders. Five seconds would be safer, and some require seven seconds.

New to FCP3 is the **Autorecord and PTV** box. **PTV** stands for **Print to Video.** This feature will automatically put your recording device like a camcorder into record after a specified number of seconds.

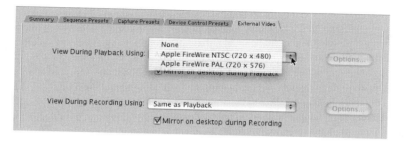

Figure 2.44 External Video Panel

External Video

The last tab in **AV Settings, External Video,** is almost bare (Figure 2.44). The popups let you set the way you view material during playback and while recording. If you're working in DV, select the default **FireWire** option. If you're working in other formats with a third-party board, other options will also appear here.

The **Option** button tells third-party boards to decompress and recompress video as required.

For **View During Recording,** it's simplest to set it to **Same as Playback.**

Once this last window is done, your preferences are set. Go back to the **Summary** window and see what your settings look like. If everything is okay, save it as an **Easy Setup** setting in your *Custom Settings* folder of the system, *Library>Application Support>Final Cut Pro System Support>Custom Settings.* It's placed here so that it's accessible to all users.

Log and Capture

So now you've set up your preferences, and you're ready to get your video material into your computer. Go to **File>Log and Capture (Command-8).** This brings up the **Log and Capture** window (Figure 2.46).

The window is divided in two. On the left is a **Viewer** like the standard FCP **Viewer,** but this is a viewer for your tape deck or camera. The control buttons — **J, K, L, I,** and **O** keys and spacebar —

Tip

Disabling Device Control: Though no checkbox enables or disables **Device Control** in Final Cut Pro, you can switch it off by choosing **Non-Controllable Device.** If you are working in DV with DV presets, switching will not stop FCP from asking for the FireWire device at startup, but if you create an **Easy Setup** which is made up of DV parameters but has **Non-Controllable Device** assigned, the application will not check for a drive at launch.

Preferences Folder

Once you've worked with your system a little bit and decided you really do like these preferences, it's a good idea to save them. This also saves any **Favorites** you create. So after you've made a few transitions or effects settings that you like, back up your prefs again. If you have problems with FCP, one of the first remedies anyone will suggest is to trash your *Preferences* file. If there is a problem with your system it's often your preferences that will corrupt. It's easy enough to back up the prefs file. Go into your *User Home* folder, **Command-Option-H** from the **Finder**. Go to your *Library*, choose *Preferences*, and find the folder called *Final Cut Pro User Data* (Figure 2.45).

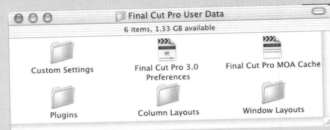

Figure 2.45   **Final Cut Pro User Data Folder**

Inside you can find six items, including two folders, *Custom Settings* and *Plugins*.

The other items should be your *Final Cut Pro 3.0 Preferences*, *Final Cut Pro MOA Cache*, and *Custom Layouts* and *Window Layouts*, if you've created any. The *Final Cut Pro User ID*, which under OS9 was in this folder, is in OS X in the *Final Cut Pro System Support* folder. Back up all of your *Preferences* folder. If you do need to trash your preferences, the only files you should remove are *Final Cut Pro 3.0 Preferences* and *Final Cut Pro MOA Cache*. You should also delete the *com.apple.finalcutpro.plist* file from the *Preferences* folder.

With these backed up and safe, whenever you do need to trash your preferences, simply replace them with your saved set. Do this with the application closed.

work exactly the same as in the FCP **Viewer** except that they control your deck either through the FireWire cable or the device control you assigned in your preferences.

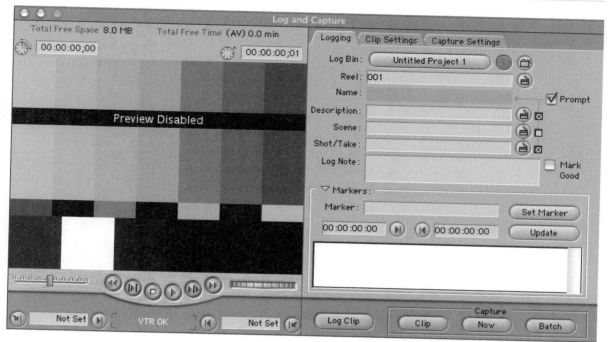

Figure 2.46   Log and Capture Window

Tip

L&C Size: The size of the *Log& Capture* window is determined by your window arrangement. If you want a large display for L&C, set your arrangement to **Standard** before you start up L&C. If you want a smaller screen on your computer monitor, set the arrangement to **Wide** before you launch the capture window.

The **Timecode** in the upper right of the **Viewer** is your current timecode on your tape, and the **Duration** on the upper left is the duration you set with your In and Out points as you mark the tape. A nice feature would be the ability to display a running duration after you enter an In point, so that the farther you played the tape, the greater the duration would get until you actually entered an Out point. Then the duration would simply display In to Out.

In addition to your keyboard shortcuts for **Mark In** and **Mark Out,** you also have buttons and timecode displays at the bottom of the viewer for these functions (Figure 2.47).

Figure 2.47   Log Window Controls

The two inner buttons mark the In and Out points, **In** on the left, **Out** on the right. The **Timecode** on the left is the In point, and the **Timecode** on the right is the Out point. Of the buttons on the far outside, the left one will take the tape deck to the assigned In point, and the far right one to the assigned Out point.

On the right of the **Log and Capture** window is another tabbed window (Figure 2.48). The farthest on the right is the **Capture Settings** tab (Figure 2.49). Two popups and a button access the preference settings you have already created. **Device Control** and **Capture Settings** let you set the preferences based on your names. The **Scratch Disks** button takes you directly to the **Scratch Disks Preferences** window so that you can change the assigned drives if you wish.

Let's now take a look at the middle tab in the window, **Clip Settings** (Figure 2.50). The top part of the panel allows you to change settings for your clip, to alter the **Hue**, **Saturation**, **Brightness**, **Contrast**, **Black Level**, and **White Level** of your clip as it is being digitized. This gives you useful control for images that have not been shot well or shot under less than ideal conditions. Fixing the levels here means that you won't have to fix them later and consequently have to rerender all your material.

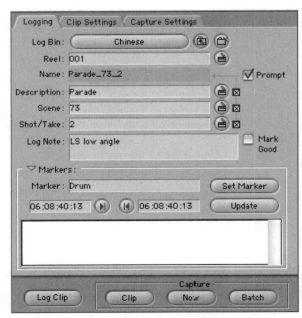

Figure 2.48   Logging Information Window

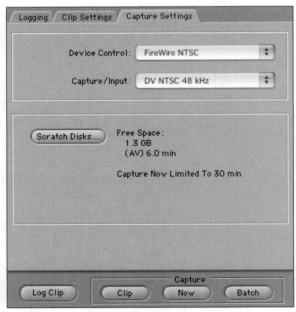

Figure 2.49   Capture Settings Panel

However, if you are working in DV, this entire top part of the window will be grayed out. Why? Because your material has already been digitized. It happened when the camera was recording. All you can do now is capture your material, which is basically copying the digital information off the tape and onto your hard drive. You are making a clone of your tape material, and if you don't process it any further with effects and record it back into the tape, it will be an exact copy of the original material.

Below the video controls is the **Gain** slider that allows you to control the audio levels of your material. You should check for every series of shots in which the audio levels change. Digital audio is completely unforgiving; there is no headroom. If you hit the red, the audio will immediately and very obviously distort. Analog audio is far more forgiving, allowing a fair amount of headroom. Watch the meters carefully and keep the levels within the green range of the meters. Unfortunately, the metering is not active during capture.

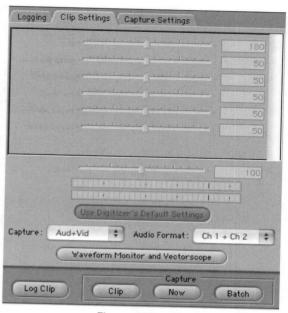

Figure 2.50   Clip Settings Panel

Obviously a reset button, the **Use Digitizer's Default Settings** button (below the meters) returns the capture levels to their standard settings.

Below the audio meters are two popups (Figures 2.51–2.52) that let you set the tracks you want to record:

- Video

- Audio

- Which audio tracks in what combination

For DV your choices are **CH1 + CH2** or **Stereo**. No selective channel recording or mixdown is possible during capture. Generally **Stereo** is easier to work with. It gives you two tracks that function in unison.

Figure 2.51   Capture Select Popup

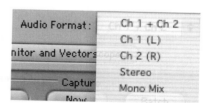

Figure 2.52   Audio Format Popup

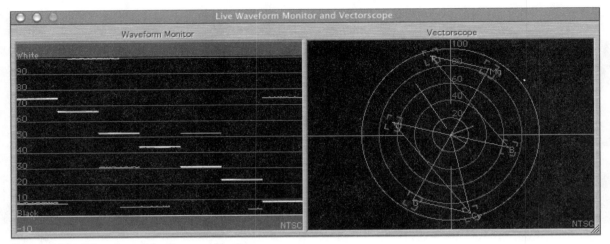

Figure 2.53   Waveform Monitor and Vectorscope

CH1 + CH2 allows you to record separate channels and discard one if they are identical to save track space, as has been done with the material used in these tutorials. With an analog digitizing card, you have the option of selecting channels individually as well as doing a **Mono Mix**.

Below that is a button that calls up FCP's **Waveform Monitor and Vectorscope** (Figure 2.53). These allow you to ensure that your video levels are correctly set.

Figure 2.54   Audio Meters

Note

Audio Displays: While you're looking at your tape and playing it using the **Log and Capture** window, you get two audio displays. Not only does the horizontal **Gain** display in the **Clip Settings** panel show the audio level, but so do the normal **Audio Meters** (Figure 2.54). Because these meters are peak program, you get a rapid response to the sound. A small red line shows the peak reading, and the little color boxes at the top indicate if the sound is too hot. If the little boxes go red you need to bring the level down. Unfortunately, during capture or digitizing, you do not have gain control, nor does metering work.

The **Vectorscope** works with color bars as seen here. If the video is correctly set, each bar will point to a corresponding target box on the scope.

The **Waveform Monitor** lets you set your video levels. Peak white should not exceed 100 IRE units if you are working in NTSC. In analog NTSC, black level should not fall below 7.5IRE. IRE stands for Institute of Radio Engineers. Their standards are used as a scale for measuring small amounts of voltage, as tiny as one volt, as in the case of a video signal.

Most camcorders and cameras using digital video record black at zero. However, DV material cannot be adjusted during capture. For analog material digitized through a video card, you can use the sliders in the **Clip Settings** window to adjust the levels. As I've said before, in DV you can't adjust anything here because you're simply copying the digital material, but you can monitor so that later you can make corrections in the software using video filters.

Strategies for Capturing

There are basically three strategies for capturing or digitizing material, and you choose the one you want to use with the buttons at the bottom of the **Logging** window (Figure 2.55).

The options you have are:

- **Clip**
- **Now**
- **Batch**

Note

Video Scopes: The new Video Scopes that appear in FCP3's **Tool Bench** are not active with the **Log and Capture** window. Only the original WFM and vectorscope appear beneath the **L&C** window during logging. Also note that at this time, there can be loss of the use of the J, K, L keys if the **Waveform Monitor** or **Vectorscope** are called up. If this happens, simply close and reopen the **Log & Capture** window.

Figure 2.55   Capture Buttons

Capture Now

This is the simplest way to work, but it gives you least control. It also requires that your material is properly shot without timecode breaks. These can cause havoc with any capture, particularly a **Now** capture.

Capturing large chunks of video with **Now** is a common work strategy. To use **Now,** you simply put the deck in play and click the **Now** button. A **Capture** screen comes up and begins recording as soon as it's checked your drives and found a video signal from your camera or deck.

FCP records the clip on your designated scratch disk until one of three events occur:

- It runs out of hard drive space.
- It hits your preference time limit.
- You hit the **Escape** key and stop the process.

If the capture stops because of the time limit, the deck also stops. The message in Figure 2.56 appears on the computer screen.

Capture Now has reached the user specified time limit.

OK

Figure 2.56   Capture Now Time Limit Message

After your capture is complete, the video appears in an untitled **Viewer.** Just drag the clip into a bin in your **Browser.** A dialog box will appear asking if you want to save the clip. Name it and save it into the folder you assigned for the scratch disk. With this method, you bring all your video material into your computer for editing into smaller subclips rather than using your deck to select clips.

Camcorders and FireWire-controlled DV decks are not very responsive to the control commands — start, stop, fast forward, rewind — nor are many of these devices really designed to shuttle and jog tape. This places great wear and tear on your deck's drive mechanisms, and if you're working off DV with a camcorder, you're putting a lot of strain on these tiny tapes and small mechanisms. They wear out quickly under this heavy use. What tape can't do quickly, i.e., move large amounts of data, computers are specifically designed to do. With **Capture Now** you're working to the computer's strength, using nonlinear, nondestructive editing to its fullest. Also, working with large chunks of video lets you do what NLE and computers do best: move big chunks of information quickly with a great deal of freedom.

FCP 3 has a wonderful tool for those working in DV with the **Capture Now** option. This is the ability to automatically mark up shot changes with **DV Start/Stop Shot Detection.** We'll look at it in "DV Start/Stop Detection" on page 122 in **Lesson 3.**

Batch Capture

For a variety of reasons — because it's a traditional work method, because of available drive space — the more commonly used work method is the batch strategy. This involves logging your tape and selecting the shots you want to capture. Look back at Figure 2.46. On the left side is the **Viewer** where you select shots by marking In and Out points. On the right is the **Logging** window (Figure 2.48) where you can enter a whole array of information about your clip.

Every clip must have a reel number assigned. This is so important that FCP starts with a reel assigned as 001. Every time you change a tape in a deck that is device controlled, the application will sense it and put up the warning in Figure 2.57.

The clip name is made up of a number of elements that you can choose with the **Prompt** checkboxes. Any checked item will be added to the name. You can make up a name that includes a label, a scene number, and a shot/take number. This is the standard feature film format for logging film clips. Much of FCP's interface draws from that model. Of course, you can name the clip anything that's useful to you. You can also add notes and **Mark Good,** another film term, which refers to marking the takes that looked good to the director. In the **Logging** window, you can even add markers and marker comments before your material is captured.

Tip

Relogging Clips: If you ever need to relog a clip, use this simple method. Open the original clip in the **Viewer** and then open the **Log and Capture** window. **Option**-click in the **Timecode Display** of the **Viewer** and you'll get a marquee with a plus sign around the number. Holding down the **Option** key, drag the number to the **In Point** box in the **Log and Capture** window. Then just type in a new Out point.

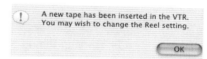

Figure 2.57   Tape Change Warning

Note

EDL Names: If you're going to be working toward creating an EDL (an Edit Decision List), it's important that you confine yourself to using reel naming conventions that EDLs understand. These conventions include using names with no more than eight characters, without spaces, and only capital letters. Different formats have different requirements, and it's best to check the naming convention for the system you're using before you assign reel names and numbers.

Once you've set an In and Out point for your clip and entered the logging information, you then press the **Log Clip** button. The clip immediately appears in your browser or a designated bin with a bright red diagonal line through it. The red line indicates that the clip has not been captured.

Tip —————————

Logging Bin: To assign a bin in your **Browser** as your **Logging** bin, simply **Control**-click on the bin you want to log into and from the contextual menu choose **Set Logging Bin**. A little **Clapperboard** icon will appear next to the designated bin.

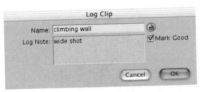

Figure 2.58   Clip Naming Dialog

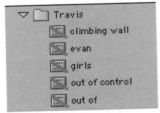

Figure 2.59   Offline Clips in Browser

Rather than hitting the **Log Clip** button, you could also press **F2**. If the tape is rolling while you're playing, that is you entered the **Out** point on the fly, something interesting happens. The deck stops and you get a dialog box to confirm the clip name (Figure 2.58). As soon as you click **OK** to accept the dialog, the frame after the previous Out point will enter as the new In point, and the deck will be put into play. The clip will appear in your designated logging bin with a diagonal red line through it (Figure 2.59). The clip is, in FCP terminology, considered offline, ready to be batch captured. The **F2** method can be very fast and efficient, if you want to batch capture.

The problem with this method of working is that you're putting the onus of the work on the log and capture process. It doesn't take advantage of nonlinear editing's real strengths. I feel that using **Capture Now** makes the whole organizing process much quicker and simpler.

If you do use **Log and Capture** to either conserve hard drive space or because you prefer to work that way, you will then need to complete the process by batch capturing your material:

1. Select the clips in your bin with the red diagonal bar through them, or simply select the bin itself.

2. Then press the **Batch** button, which brings up the window in Figure 2.60.

3. You can also select the clips and choose **Batch Capture** from the **File** menu (**Control-C**).

The popup at the top allows you to select which clips you want to batch capture. There is also a window for setting handles and a checkbox for coalescing clips. If you set handles, coalescing clips can save drive space and time. However, it's dangerous. It combines adjacent clips into one piece of media. You will now have created a single source file that supplies media for two or more clips. You may remove the source file and find you've unintentionally wiped out the media for a clip you still want. It's safest to leave **Coalesce** off. Clicking **OK** will automatically set the deck off, capturing from your tape the clips you've logging into your **Browser**.

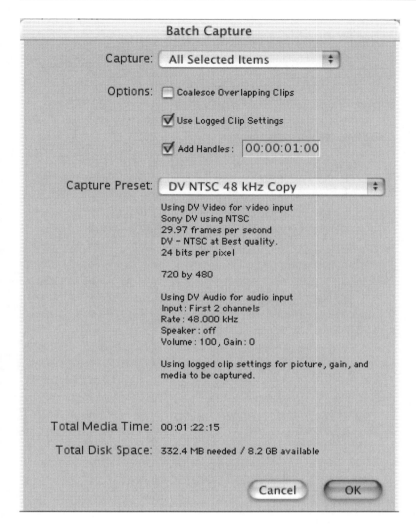

Figure 2.60   Batch Capture Dialog
Window

Notice the **Total Media Time** and **Total Disk Space** needed information at the bottom of the box. It's useful to double check your batch request, that you are capturing what you think you're capturing, as well as having the needed drive space. If something looks odd in the total time, check that you haven't selected more or fewer clips than you intended.

The popup in the middle of the **Batch Capture** dialog lets you select any one of your preset preferences. This is handy if you've captured at low resolution and want to quickly change to capture at high resolution. If you have these different preferences set up ahead of time, you can simply choose the preference in this popup.

Another method I like is to use an abridged form of logging on tape before batch capture. Here you quickly select In and Out points for large chunks of video on your tape, whole scenes or sections of material, dividing your tape up into four or five pieces, before you perform batch capture.

👆 *Tip*

Changing Clip Settings: If you ever log your material with the wrong settings — for instance, video only, when you wanted both video and audio — it's easy enough to change your offline clip settings. Just select all the offline clips in the **Browser** while it's in List view. In the **Tracks** column, **Control-**click on settings for any of the clips. From the contextual menu choose whatever settings you want (Figure 2.61). All the selected clips will change to the same settings.

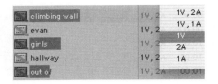

Figure 2.61   Track Settings Contextual Menu

🖈 *Note*

Segregated Memory: One of the nice aspects of working in OS X is that its applications are kept in segregated memory, so if you have plenty of RAM — 700MB or more — and a fast computer like a dual-processor G4/800, you can easily run multiple applications at the same time. You could, for instance, answer your e-mail and surf the net while the computer is doing that tedious batch capturing in the background. I would only suggest doing this on the very fastest of systems.

Clip

The third option in the **Log and Capture** window is the **Clip** button. This functions in the same way as the **Batch** button, except it captures an individual clip immediately after you enter its In, Out, and naming information. Many people use this as a controlled form of **Capture Now.**

1. Mark an In point near the beginning of the reel and then an Out point near the end.

2. Click **Clip** and let the deck and the computer do its thing.

3. Once the clip is captured, drag it into your **Browser** to make it available for your project.

Once you've set up your system and captured your material, you are ready to edit. Close the **Log and Capture** window before you start, however. You should not try to play video while **L&C** is open. **Log and Capture** is trying to suck in through the FireWire cable while the **Viewer** is trying to feed out through the same cable. This is the equivalent of northbound 580 being routed into southbound 580 in the middle of rush hour. So shut down **Log and Capture** before you begin editing.

Once you've captured your material, you'll notice that it appears in the **Browser** as a clip with a duration but with no In or Out points defined. **Capture** only sets the media limit, and FCP assumes you will want to edit the material further, so no In or Out points are designated. The clip has the *de facto* In and Out points marked by the limits of the media; they're simply not displayed in the **Browser** in the **In** and **Out** columns. If you capture with handles, however, the clips do come in with your designated In and Out points marked and the extra media beyond it.

Tools

There are some tools that will help you after you've captured your material, some of them new to FCP3. After you've captured a few clips, it's probably a good idea to analyze them to make sure everything is all right. Select the clip and from the **Tools** menu choose **Analyze Movie Clip** (Figure 2.62). If you choose **Analyze Movie File** you will get the navigation service dialog window to select a piece of media on your hard drive. This will bring up a window that gives you its clips technical details, frame size, data rate, video and audio track information, etc. (Figure 2.63). If there is something amiss here, the data rate is too low, or you have odd audio sampling rates, an odd data rate, or odd frames rates, you'll know something is wrong with your captured material.

Tip

Selecting for Batch Capture: You don't actually have to select each red-lined clip separately. You can just select the whole contents of the **Browser** for batch capture. FCP will then bring up a dialog box asking whether you want to capture all the clips, or just those offline. If you select offline clips only, it will batch capture all the material that is not already on your hard drive.

Figure 2.62   Tools>Analyze Movie Clip

Figure 2.63   Movie Analysis Window

Timecode Breaks

Timecode breaks or control track breaks have been the bane of video editors since tape machines were invented. Many an editor have cursed many a cameraperson for their failure to keep good TC on their tapes. This cursing has not stopped with the widespread use of nonlinear editing systems. Tapes are still being brought into edit rooms with breaks or discontinuities in timecode. These days, most consumer and pro-sumer cameras are designed to generate frame accurate timecode, and that's the way tape should be delivered. FireWire uses the TC recorded on tape when the video was shot to find your clips and control the deck during capture. This timecode information is passed on to the application and remains with the clip throughout the editing process. It's important to understand what happens in the camera while you're shooting.

There are a number of ways to ensure that there are no breaks in your DV TC. The simplest way, which I recommend for beginners and students in particular, is to prestripe your tapes, that is, record black and timecode on your tape before you shoot. You can do this in any camera or VCR: simply put the device in VCR mode and press the record button. With some cameras you might have to do it in camera mode; just put a lens cap on it or point it at a wall. Now whenever you shoot, your tape will have TC written on it. The camera will then read the TC and start writing from whatever it reads. No breaks.

If you don't want to prestripe the tape, you then just have to be careful when you shoot. After you shut off the camera to change batteries, for instance, not simply stop it after a shot, it's a good idea to back up the tape just a second to get back into the area of timecoded material. This is why it's always a good idea when shooting to let the camera run for a few moments after the action you're shooting is complete, before you stop the recording. That way you will have that moment or two of unnecessary material to back up into.

Prestriping is not a good idea for professional cameras. Many professional cameras using Record Run time-code must have the **Return Video** button pressed for the camera to seek the end of the written TC. If the cameraperson doesn't do this, you will get discontinuities in the TC, numbers that skip time, which are almost as bad as a timecode break that resets to zero.

Any timecode break is liable to cause a sudden loss of AV sync when you capture across it. So if you do have a tape with TC breaks in it, one of the simplest ways to get around the problem is to dub the tape. By dubbing it from one deck or one camera to another, the video and audio portion of the tape is copied exactly as it was on the original while at the same time, the recording deck is creating new, unbroken timecode.

Aside from shooting carefully, or prestriping the tape, another way around the problem is to log carefully and use **Clip** to capture so that the deck doesn't have to search through any of these timecode breaks. You can also log your clips, changing the reel name with each timecode break. When you go to **Batch Capture**, FCP will prompt you for the reel change. You then move the tape into the right area and tell FCP that you're on the new reel.

A fairly common occurrence when capturing or digitizing video is that the first frame appears as a freeze, producing what FCP calls a long frame. This occasionally happens in the middle of a clip or at a shot change. One of the **Tools** new to FCP 3 is the ability to find these long frames in clips. From the **Tools** menu, select **Mark Long Frames**. This will scan the clips and place a marker at each long frame. If there are no long frames, you'll see the message in Figure 2.63. In the **Tools** menu, there is also an item that will remove the long frame markers for you, **Clear Long Marks**.

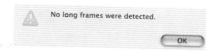

Figure 2.64   No Long Frames Detected

If there are long frames in your clip, you can twirl open the clip in the **Browser** and see exactly where the long frames are (Figure 2.65).

Notice that the Long Marks on the clip have timecode In and Out points and a duration, for how many frames the long frame extends. It is possible with care to cut these out to patch together your video. You'll also have to adjust the audio to keep it in sync with the picture, which may be more problematic and not always possible.

Figure 2.65   Long Marks in the Browser

Summary

With these two lessons we have just about completed step one of the three steps of digital, nonlinear editing. We have moved our video material from the recording medium into the computer. Additional material, such as graphics and audio, can be imported into the project. Most bitmapped image formats such as Photoshop, PICT, and JPEG can be dragged into the **Browser.** We'll look at this in more detail in later lessons. As we have seen, audio from CDs can also be imported and dropped directly into your sequences.

With your material in your computer, you're now ready to begin the second part of editing, the fun part.

Lesson 3

Cutting Up Those Shots

There is no right way to edit a scene or a sequence or even a whole film or video; there are only bad ways, good ways, and better ways. In this lesson we're going to look at some video and edit it. I'm going to give you a number of different ways of working with it and a few different ways to cut it up — I call them Slice and Dice.

Loading the Lesson

1. Start by loading the CD that came with this book into your CD drive. Open the CD.

You'll see two folders, one called *Media1* and another called *Projects*. Inside *Media1* is a QuickTime file and inside *Projects* are numbered Lesson folders. You'll notice that some of the lessons don't have folders, such as Lessons 1 and 2.

2. To start, drag the folder called *Media1* onto your media drive.

This may take a while. It contains the video material used in this book. When you begin any lesson that needs material from the

CD, the first step you should take is to drag the media folder onto the media drive of your computer. The clips included there will play much better and more smoothly from your high-speed drive than from any CD drive.

3. When that's finished, drag the folder *Lesson 3* from the *Projects* folder on the CD onto the system hard drive of your computer. You should probably place it in the *Shared* folder inside your system's *Users* folder. This way the material will be available no matter who logs onto the computer. You could also put it inside your own *Documents* folder if you want to keep it only available to yourself.

4. Before we start editing, look inside the folder *Media1* on your media hard drive. Double-click the QuickTime file called *Damine.mov* to open it.

This will launch your QuickTime Player and open the video clip. You'll be using this material for the most of lessons. Though the material was originally shot on DVCAM, to conserve space on the CD, the video has been compressed using the Photo-JPEG codec and reduced to a frame size of 320×240 pixels using the square-pixel aspect ratio. You know all about that now, right?

Note

Playing in Column View: In OS X, if your **Finder** is in Column view, you will get an icon with your video clip (Figure 3.1) that allows you to play through the video. This will work for any video or audio clip. It will not work if you use navigation services from inside the application — that is, try to import with **Command-I.** You will only get a QuickTime movie icon in the right column.

Figure 3.1 Playing Video Clip in Column View

Look through the video. It was shot in the tiny Japanese mountain village of Damine (pronounced Dameenay) during the annual Shinto festival called Dengaku. Now we're ready to begin editing.

5. Open the *Lesson 3* folder you dragged onto your system hard drive.

Inside you'll find an FCP project file called *L3*.

6. Open *L3* by double-clicking it, which will launch the Final Cut Pro 3 application.

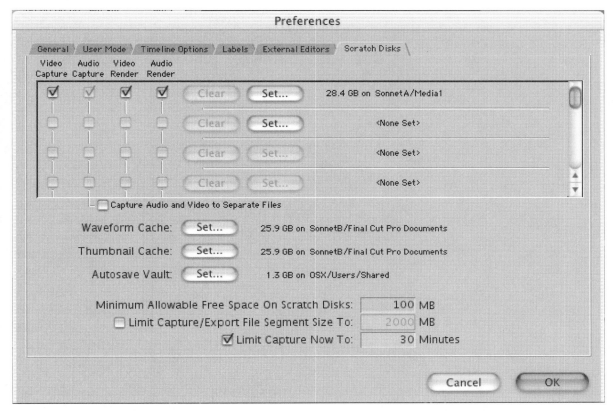

Figure 3.2   Scratch Disks
Preferences

The project is empty except for one sequence that is also blank.

Setting the Scratch Disk

Before you do anything else, you should set your scratch disk. Whenever you start a new project or open a project you haven't worked on in a while, assign the *Scratch Disk* and the *Autosave Vault*.

1. Go to the **Final Cut Pro** menu, select **Preferences (Option-Q)** and click on the **Scratch Disk**s tab (Figure 3.2).

2. To set the scratch disk, click on the top **Set** button and navigate to your media hard drive that holds the *Media1* folder.

3. Click on the *Media1* folder to highlight it, and click **Enter** or click on button marked **Choose,** as in Figure 3.3.

Figure 3.3   Settings Scratch
Disks

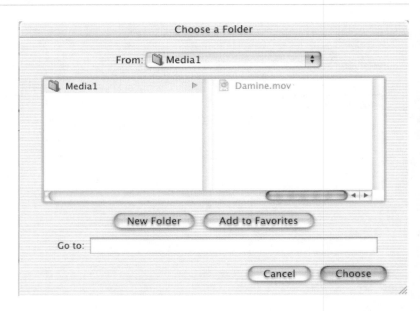

Selecting the *Media1* folder for your scratch disk will create inside it separate *Audio Renders Files*, *Capture Scratch*, and *Render Files* folders.

Setting the Autosave Vault

Next, set your *Autosave Vault*. Click the **Set** button opposite **AutoSave Vault** and find the *Shared folder*. You should do this every time you start a new project.

You need to do this each time you move between projects. The reason is that the FCP preference for scratch disks is not tied to a specific project, as I think it should be, but is tied to the application as a whole. Do it every time you open the application and you can't go wrong. With this housekeeping done, we're now ready to begin.

Importing the movie

1. Use **File>Import** (**Command-I**) to import the *Damine.mov* file from the folder inside the *Media1* folder on your hard drive. Or you can drag the clip directly from the *Media1* folder into your **Browser**.

✎ Note _____

Wide Window: Before we begin, let's set up the window arrangement. For this material, I'd suggest changing to **Wide**. Go to the **Window** menu **Arrange>Wide**. You probably don't want to use **Standard** because with material that has a frame size of 320x240, the standard screens will be scaling the image up, making it very pixilated.

2. After it's imported, double-click the *Damine.mov* in your **Browser** to open it in a **Viewer**.

You'll notice that no In or Out points have been set, and in the upper left corner, the duration of the clip shows 7:23:19. This is the material we're going to cut up in these lessons. This is the master clip.

Slice and Dice

We have basically two strategies for cutting up a long stretch of video such as this, which might be from the capture of a reel of tape.

1. The first is to create short clips while leaving the whole material intact in each clip. I call this the Slice method.

2. The second is to make subclips, which divide the master clip into shorter sections, each only the length of the selection. We'll call this the Dice or Subclip method.

They both have advantages and disadvantages. It's important to understand the distinction between different types of clips.

1. The source media is the actual digital material on your hard drive. The master clip, *Damine.mov* in this case, is the clip in your **Browser** that points directly to the media on your hard drive. It contains every frame of the source media.

2. A sliced clip is the same as the master clip it's taken from, except that a start point and an end point are defined for a particular shot.

3. In a diced clip, not only are the start and end points defined, but also the media that the clip can use is limited. The clip does not have all the media available to it that's in the original.

We'll look at this more closely later in the lesson on page 119, but first let's start with slicing.

Slice 1

Let's look at one of the three methods of slicing up your material.

1. Make a new bin in the **Browser** from the **File** menu: **File> New>Bin,** or more easily with the keyboard command **Command-B.**

2. Name the new bin **Clips.**

3. Now double-click *Damine.mov* to open it in the **Viewer.**

In this method, you can work either in the **Viewer** or in the **Time-line.** We'll start in the **Viewer** by looking at the material, selecting the pieces we want, and marking them with In and Out points.

4. Play the clip in the **Viewer** and stop when you get to the shot of a stone water basin with a bronze dragon's head spout. (It's the third shot in.)

5. Use the **Left** and **Right** arrow keys to find the first frame of this shot and press **I** to mark the In point.

6. Play the clip and find the end of that shot. It's fairly short, about five seconds.

7. When you've found the end, press **O** for Out point.

8. Grab the picture in the **Viewer,** drag it into the **Browser,** and drop it on the **Clips** bin.

You've now made a new clip in the **Browser.** You need to rename this clip something appropriate.

9. Twirl open **Clips** and double-click on the name *Damine.mov,* which will highlight it and open a renaming box. Type in a new name, *StoneBasin.*

10. Double-click the clip *StoneBasin* in your **Browser** to bring it back into the **Viewer.**

At this stage the **Browser** in List view and the **Viewer** should look something like Figure 3.4.

Figure 3.4   Browser and Viewer with
the Master Clip

 Note _____

Renaming Clips: You can rename your clips anything you want, move them around to various bins, place bins within bins, and arrange your material any way you like, but be aware that the underlying media that remains on your hard drive is unchanged in any way. Most importantly, its name is not changed. So if you ever need to reconnect the media or recapture it, FCP will always want to do it under its original naming convention and not change it to anything you do in the **Browser**.

Notice *StoneBasin* comes in with an In and Out point marked, and notice also that the clip contains all the video that's in *Damine.mov*. The upside of this is obvious. The master clip is made up of a long length of material, perhaps even a whole reel of film or a roll of videotape, though I would advise against this. Because a sliced clip is a copy of the master clip, you can now access any shot in the reel from inside any sliced clip.

That's the upside; the downside is scrubbing. It's difficult to scrub in the **Viewer** because even a tiny movement will move the playhead a long way up and down the **Viewer Scrubber Bar**. Unfortunately, FCP does not allow you to zoom into the **Viewer Scrubber Bar**, or change its scale, like you can in the **Timeline**. It is a feature available in a number of other nonlinear editing systems and would be a beneficial addition to FCP.

Edit Points

A note on where edit points occur. The shot change between edits actually takes place between the frames. That is, you see one frame, and the next frame you see is the first frame of a different shot. So when you're marking In and Out points, you should know where the shot change is actually taking place. If you mark the In point for a frame that you're looking at in the **Viewer**, that will be the first frame of the new clip. The edit will take place in the space before that frame. If you mark the frame you're looking at as an Out point, that will be the last frame in the clip, and the edit will take place after that frame.

Let's push on.

1. Double-click again on *Damine.mov* in the **Browser**.

You'll notice it still has In and Out points marked into **Viewer**, those points you marked for the clip that became *StoneBasin*.

2. Hit **Shift-O**, which, if you're not already there, will take you to the Out point you marked for *StoneBasin*.

3. Using the **Mark In/Mark Out** technique, cut out a few more shots from *Damine.mov*.

4. As you mark them, drag each into the **Clips** bin, naming the clip appropriately.

Now you're building up a collection of shots that you can edit together in any order you want. This is the first Slice method in the **Viewer**.

Slice 2

The second Slice method is in the **Timeline**. This is where you really are slicing with a digital razor blade.

1. First open *Damine.mov* from the **Browser** into the **Viewer**.

It will probably have an In and Out point marked. We need to clear those.

2. **Control-click** on the **Scrubber Bar** at the bottom of the **Viewer** to evoke a contextual menu.

3. Select **Clear In and Out**. This will — surprise, surprise — clear the In and Out points (Figure 3.5).

4. Open the empty **Timeline** by double-clicking on *Sequence 1* in the **Browser** and drag *Damine.mov* into it, dropping the clip on **V1**.

When you place a clip in the **Timeline**, the playhead automatically jumps to the end of the clip, ready for you to place another clip in position. In this case, we don't want to do that.

5. Click in the **Timeline** window to make it active (or use **Command-3**), and then press the **Home** key to take you back to the beginning of the **Timeline** (Figure 3.6).

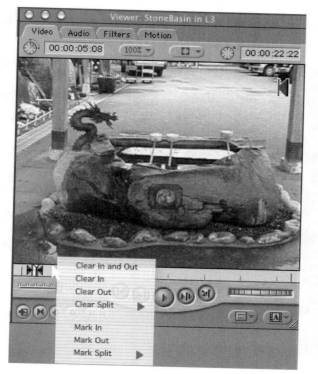

Figure 3.5   Viewer Scrubber Bar Contextual Menu   Figure 3.6   Timeline Window

6. Press the spacebar to play *Damine.mov*. The video plays in
   the Canvas.

Tip

Clearing from the Browser: If you've opened a clip from the **Browser** and want to clear its In and Out points,
you can use the keyboard shortcut **Option-X.** You can use this way to clear In and Out points in the **Timeline**
also. You can't, however, clear the In and Out from a clip that's been opened from the **Timeline.**

7. Again use the spacebar to stop and the **Left** and **Right** arrow
   keys to find the start of the shot of the stone basin. When
   you've found it, press Control-V.

Note

Real Time Vs. Render: Notice the two thin darker gray lines at the top of the **Timeline** window. These indicate
that the clip will play back in real time. The upper line indicates the video, the lower the audio. If either of these
lines were red, it would indicate that the material needed to be rendered before it would play back. Different colors on these lines will have different meanings, which will be explained as we go along.

Figure 3.7   Cutting in the Timeline

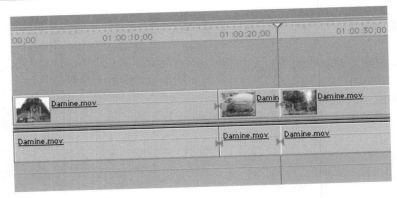

Edit Points Redux

We talked about where the cut takes place when you're editing, that the In point cuts the space before the frame you're looking at, and the Out point cuts after the frame you're looking at. The **Razor Blade** always cuts on the gap in front of the frame you're seeing in the **Canvas**. So to get the last frame of *StoneBasin* in the Slice method, you have to be looking at the first frame of the shot after it. If you do **Control-V** on the last frame of the basin shot, the next shot will have one frame of the stone basin at its head.

This will cut the video and audio on the clip as though you were cutting it with a knife or a razor blade, which is what used to be used to cut film and audio tape, and even videotape when it was first edited. What you are doing is the digital metaphor for the same process. When you make the edit, notice the little red triangular marks that appear. These are the **Through Edit** marks that can be switched on and off in the **General Preferences** panel. They indicate where there is a cut between two shots with contiguous time code.

8. Now that you've made one cut, find the end of the shot of the stone basin. Again use **Control-V** to cut the shot (Figure 3.7).

Let's make a second bin for these clips.

9. Use **Command-B** to create the new bin and name it **New-Clips**.

10. Grab the cut clip from the **Timeline** and drag it into **New-Clips**. Again rename the clip *StoneBasin*.

11. In the **Timeline** window, click on the piece that you've cut from the master clip. This will highlight the edited section.

12. Press **Delete**. This will remove the clip from the timeline, but it will also leave a gap in the timeline. So let's undo that using **Command-Z**.

The undo will make the shot reappear in the hole in the timeline. Instead of simply deleting it, we will do what's called a *ripple delete*.

1. Select the clip, hold down the **Shift** key, and hit **Delete**.

In addition to removing the clip, the ripple delete also pulls up all the other material in *Damine.mov*, shortening the timeline.

2. Use the spacebar and the arrow keys to find some more shots. With **Control-V** cut up the material and drag the shots into the **NewClips** bin.

3. Continue to use ripple delete to remove material as you move it into the bin in the **Browser.**

Working like this, you can quickly cut material into shots. You can use this process to weed out the bad shots, removing the chaff from the wheat, as it were.

Immediately after the stone basin clip, you'll find a shot of a temple. The shot begins looking toward a canopied bell in the foreground with a stand of pines and late afternoon sun shining through them. The shot then pans right from the trees to the temple. The camera is set to auto-iris, and as the shot pans it darkens so that the temple is hardly visible. Immediately afterwards, the shot repeats itself, this time properly exposed.

4. Select the darker, poorer shot, and cut it up with the keyboard shortcuts. Now instead of dragging it into the **New-Clips** bin to be saved, simply ripple delete it to remove it from the sequence.

Slice 3

With the Slice 2 method, you're cutting the pieces you want to keep and moving them into the **Browser.** Let's look at another method that works almost exclusively in the **Timeline.** Here we'll simply cut away the pieces we don't want to use and leave behind in the **Timeline** the shots that contain the good material.

1. Undo your ripple delete of the dark shot.

2. Undo the edit at the end of the shot. Use **Command-Z** as many times as necessary to get back to where the dark shot is still unedited in the sequence.

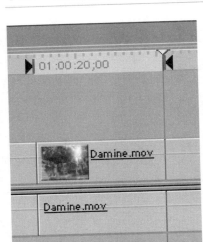

Figure 3.8   In and Out Point
Marked in the
Timeline Window

3. With the playhead parked at the beginning of the shot in the **Timeline**, press the I key to enter an In point in the **Timeline** window.

4. Play forward till you find the end of the shot.

5. Again use the **Left** and **Right** arrow keys to find the last frame of the dark shot, *not* the first frame of the next shot as you did in Slice 2.

6. Press the **O** key to enter an **Out** point in the **Timeline**, which should look like Figure 3.8.

7. Now simply hit **Shift-Delete** to execute a ripple delete to remove that section of the video.

> **Note**
>
> **Important:** It is critical that you have nothing selected in the sequence when you use this technique. Anything that is selected — clip, audio, title, anything — will be ripple deleted instead of the marked In and Out section. The simplest way to avoid this is to press **Command-D** for **Drop** or **Deselect All**. This drops anything that's been selected. A good habit to get into before you execute this technique is to always make the Timeline the active window and press **Command-D**, or if you really like the menus, **Edit>Deselect All**, the opposite of **Command-A**, **Select All**.

This method is a fast and efficient way to cut material quickly. You end up with the shots you want to keep in the **Timeline**. Simply pull them into the bins in which you want to store them and rename. I'd use this method for working on something like a news story, where fast turnaround and quick cutting is necessary, and you're not concerned with storage, organization, or logging your material carefully.

Slicing, whether in the **Viewer** or the **Timeline**, has the advantage of quickly and easily accessing all your material while still cutting it up into shots for editing. It has a couple of disadvantages:

- The problem of not being able to scrub easily in the **Viewer**, as we discussed earlier on page 113

- The problem of transitions

I'll talk about that later in "Comparison" on page 120 after I show you the Dice or Subclip method.

 Note _____

Browser and Timeline Clips: This is a good point to explain a bit about the relationship between the clips in the **Browser** and the clips in Timeline. Quite simply, there is no relationship — no direct, linked relationship any-way. They are two separate and distinct items. They may be copies of each other, but they are quite separate clips that share the same media. So in the first Slice method, when you mark up the master clip with In and Out points, you are marking one clip and making copies of it in the **Clips** bin. When you drag the master clip from the **Browser** and place it in a Timeline, you are placing a copy of the master clip. So when you razor blade and ripple delete the clip in the Timeline, you are not in any way affecting the master clip that remains untouched in your **Browser.**

👉 **Tip** _____

Razor Blade: In addition to the keyboard shortcut **Control-V** for blading the clip in the Timeline, you can also cut it up with the **Blade** tool from the tools. The letter **B** will call up the **Blade** tool (Figure 3.9). As you move along your clip in the Timeline, your cursor will show the **Blade** tool, rather than the **Selector**. The letter **A** is the shortcut that will return you to the **Selection** tool. (Think A for arrow.) Of course, with the cursor in **Blade** mode you cannot select a clip. Trying to select a clip will cut it. So to do ripple deletes, you

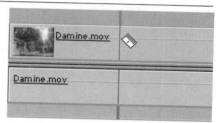

Figure 3.9   Razor Blade

would need to switch back and forth between the **Blade** and the **Selector**. You can do this quickly using **A** and **B**. Or you can leave your cursor in **Blade** mode, and instead of click-ing to select a clip, hold down the **Control** key when the cursor is above the clip you want to remove. Holding down the **Control** key will change the cursor from the **Blade** to the contextual menu. Mousing down will open the menu, and from the menu you can select the function **Ripple Delete**. Neat, isn't it?

Dice

I call it dicing because, as you'll see, we're making clips, which, though the same size as the clips in the Slice method, are more finely honed so only the clip's defined duration remains with each clip.

1. Once again, open *Damine.mov* into the **Viewer** and remove any marked In or Out points with **Option-X**.

2. Create a new bin in the **Browser** and name it **Clips2**.

3. Go back in the **Viewer** to that now-familiar shot toward the beginning of the stone basin. Mark up the In and Out points as you did in the first Slice method.

4. Now instead of just dragging the clip into the **Browser**, hit **Command-U**.

Command-U creates a subclip that automatically appears in the **Browser** with the same name as the clip it was taken from and with the name highlighted. In this case it will be *Damine.mov subclip*.

5. Before we do anything else, let's drag the new subclip into **Clips2**, and again let's rename it *StoneBasin*.

This is the subclip method of cutting up a long clip. Notice the different icon created for subclips, indicating that they are torn out of another clip (Figure 3.10).

Figure 3.10   Subclip in Bin

Comparison

Let's see how the Dice method is different from slicing. Open the newly created subclip called *StoneBasin*. This is the version of *StoneBasin* we just moved into **Clips2**. The others were sliced clips; this one is the diced clip. Unlike a sliced clip with its In and Out marking a small portion of the master clip, in the diced sub-clip the In point and Out point do not appear at all (Figure 3.11).

The subclip is treated as a separate piece of media, though in real-ity it's not. Notice the film sprocket holes on the left side of the frame in Figure 3.11. These holes on the left or right edge of the frame indicate that you're at the limit of the media for that clip. Though the subclip is only a portion of the piece of media on your hard drive called *Damine.mov*, it's treated in FCP as a com-plete, self-contained piece of media. Hence the film sprocket indi-cator. The advantage to working in the subclip method is that it's easy to scrub the clip, running the mouse along the length of the media.

Figure 3.11   Subclip in the Viewer

If you need to access more of the media within that subclip, select **Remove Subclip Limits** from the **Modify** menu (Figure 3.12). When you do this, the clip, if it's in the **Viewer**, will suddenly disappear, and a slug will be loaded in its place. I'm not sure why the application does that. If you again open that clip after the subclip limits are removed, the clip will revert to its whole length, without In or Out points.

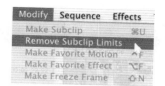

Figure 3.12   Modify>Remove Subclip Limits

You can also remove subclip limits from a shot or a whole bin of shots directly in the **Browser**. Just select the bin and pull down **Remove Subclip Limits** from the **Modify** menu. All the subclips will revert to full-length clips.

 Tip

Keeping Ins and Outs: If you want subclips to retain their In and Out points after the subclip limits are removed, you need to set In and Out points for them. The simplest way is to drag them into a sequence first. Dragging the subclips into a timeline will immediately define In and Out points for the clips. If you then **Remove Subclip Limits**, the clips will behave as sliced clips, their Ins and Outs defined, but the whole lengths of the media available on either side.

The fact that you can't normally exceed the limits of the subclip is also an advantage, while being a problem with the Slice method described earlier. The problem is transitions. These take extra media, extending the shot to create space for themselves. Transitions will take any available media. In the Slice method, that media may include sudden zooms, garbage frames, or bits of another shot. These appear as a sudden flash during a transition, barely noticeable, but disconcerting.

Because subclips can't extend the media beyond their duration, this will never happen with a subclip. The trick to dicing is to make sure that you include in your subclip not just the really good bit of the shot you want to use, but as much extra material as you safely can without including any garbage or spurious frames. This allows the transition room to extend the material.

Figure 3.13   DV Start/Stop Detection Menu

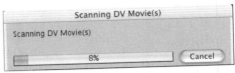

Figure 3.14   Scanning DV Movie(s)

DV Start/Stop Detection

This tool was first made available by Apple in iMovie. It works only on DV material and uses DV's shot marking system. It works slightly differently in Final Cut Pro, which uses the start/stop information to create markers on your video. They can be used to either slice or dice the master clip. Here's how it works.

1. Bring your long clip of DV material, either batch captured or with **Capture Now**, into FCP.

2. Select the clip or clips.

3. From the **Tools** menu, select **DV Start/Stop Detection** (Figure 3.13).

You will immediately see the FCP scanning monitor (Figure 3.14) scan multiple clips at once. It can handle even whole bins. It produces clips with markers at each camera start/stop.

Note

DV & Clock: DV Start/Stop Detection only works if you've set the clock in your camera. What's being detected is the time difference between the end of one clip and the beginning of the next. No clock, no time difference.

These markers can actually be turned into subclip segments. They appear in the **Browser** as a clip with markers (Figure 3.15).

You'll see that there are now markers for each shot change. You'll also notice that the In point for each segment is defined, but that neither duration nor Out point are. If you double-click on the clip itself, it opens in the **Viewer** with all its segments (Figure 3.16).

Match Framing

It's sometimes important to find the master clip material from which either a sliced clip, or more importantly a diced subclip, is extracted. In the Slice method, you have the master clip to hand in every clip you make, but in the subclip, the original material is probably hidden in your **Browser**. Fortunately, Final Cut provides a simple, efficient method to find your place in the original material. If you open the subclip in the **Viewer**, all you have to do is press **Shift-F,** which matchframes you back to the original material. In other words, Final Cut immediately loads into the **Viewer** the original master clip parked at exactly the same frame that you were looking at in the subclip. It can be an extremely useful tool.

Miyajima3	00 :04 :32 ;22	Not Set	Not Set
Segment 1	00 :00 :00 ;00	00 :00 :02 ;29	Not Set
Segment 2	00 :00 :00 ;00	00 :00 :27 ;22	Not Set
Segment 3	00 :00 :00 ;00	00 :00 :36 ;06	Not Set
Segment 4	00 :00 :00 ;00	00 :00 :48 ;19	Not Set
Segment 5	00 :00 :00 ;00	00 :01 :00 ;24	Not Set
Segment 6	00 :00 :00 ;00	00 :01 :13 ;21	Not Set
Segment 7	00 :00 :00 ;00	00 :01 :26 ;15	Not Set
Segment 8	00 :00 :00 ;00	00 :01 :49 ;05	Not Set
Segment 9	00 :00 :00 ;00	00 :01 :56 ;02	Not Set
Segment 10	00 :00 :00 ;00	00 :02 :05 ;21	Not Set

Figure 3.15   Segmented Clip in Browser

Tip

Shortcuts: You can easily move between segments with keyboard shortcuts.

Shift-M (or **Shift-Down** arrow) takes you to the next marker.

Option-M (or **Shift-Up** arrow) takes you to the previous marker.

Command-` or the **Delete** button: the **Marker** dialog box deletes the marker you're positioned on.

If you double-click on one of the segment markers in the **Browser,** the segment will open in the **Viewer** as if it were a subclip. You only see the limits of the media as the segment defines them. You can either drag it into a **Timeline,** or you can drag the segment back into the **Browser** or into a bin, rename it, and treat it just like any other subclip.

Figure 3.16   Master Clips with Segments in Viewer

Tip

Subclip Conversion: Another way to turn all the segments from a **DV Start/Stop** clip into subclips is to drag a marquee around markers in the **Browser**. Then press **Command-U**. Or you can select the markers you want and drag them into a bin. Either hitting **Command-U** or dragging the clips into a bin will copy each of the segments and turn them into subclips.

In addition to making markers in segments, FCP3 has introduced the ability to make each segment of a marked-up clip not only into a subclip, but also into a separate clip of its own. Simply place the playhead anywhere between two markers, and press the keyboard shortcut **Control-A.** This is called **Mark to Markers** and

Figure 3.17   Mark to Markers

will immediately mark and In and Out point on the nearest markers on either side of the playhead (Figure 3.17).

You can also do this by selecting **Mark to Markers** from the **Mark** menu. (Though note that as of this writing the menu selection is sometimes dimmed when working in the **Viewer**, while the keyboard shortcut still functions.) **Mark to Markers** will slice your clip, marking the In and Out points and leaving the entire length of the material intact. You can now drag the marked shot into a bin to be stored and renamed. I'll show you another use for the **Control-A** technique on page 291 in Lesson 7 when we look at working with music.

Power Dicing

The ability of Final Cut to make subclips from markers is not confined to **DV Start/Stop**. Any master clip or any clip segmented with markers can be made into subclips.

1. Open the master clip into the **Viewer** and press the spacebar.

2. As you play the clip, tap the **M** key.

Each time you hit **M**, a marker will be added to the clip. Each marker can become the In point for a new subclip.

3. As with **DV Start/Stop Detect**, you can now simply use **Command-U** or drag to a bin to turn the segments into subclips.

You don't have to add markers on the fly. You can add them with more precision by scrubbing or using the arrow keys to find a frame before marking. You can also go through the long clip before you turn them into subclips and fine tune the marker positions. You can position the marker later in time using **Shift-`**.

It's not quite so simple to move a marker earlier in time.

1. With the playhead on a marker, press **M to** call up a **Marker** dialog window.

2. Change the start time. You can also change the duration, delete the marker, or add comments and on-screen text.

Once you've set the markers as you like, you can turn the master clip into precisely defined subclips.

Markers are very useful for a variety of tasks, and we'll look at them more closely in Lesson 6, "Using Markers" on page 256.

🖎 *Tip*

Adding Out Points: Adding markers only adds In points to your clip. If you really want to get slick, you can add Out points as well by using FCP's **Extend Marker** feature. After you've set the markers, go forward in time and hit **Option-`** to extend the marker to that frame. This will be taken as the clip's Out point. If you're really quick and practiced, you can do this on the fly while a clip is playing with your left thumb and finger poised over **Option-`** and a right finger poised over the **M** key.

Range Clipping

Another technique for slicing or dicing is to use the **Range** tool on the **Timeline**. Some people prefer this method because it offers a visual display of the cut point.

1. Let's try this by dragging the master clip *Damine.mov* into an empty **Timeline**.

2. Next select the **Range** tool from the tools. It's under the second icon from the top. You can also call it up by hitting **GGG** (the letter **G** three times) (Figure 3.18).

3. Position the playhead in the **Timeline** where you want the clip selection to begin.

4. With the **Range** tool, stroke a section of the clip (Figure 3.19).

Unfortunately the **Range** tool, unlike the **Razor Blade**, does not respond to snapping, but the crosshairs let you position the **Range** selector very precisely. As you stroke the clip to make the selection, the **Canvas** will give you a two-up display that shows you the start and end frames as well as the timecode (Figure 3.20).

5. Now simply grab the selection from the **Timeline** and drag it to the **Viewer**, where it will load as a sliced clip.

6. As always, **Command-U** will turn it into a subclip.

Figure 3.18   Range Tool

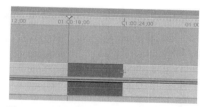

Figure 3.19   Range Tool in the Timeline

Figure 3.20   Range Selection Two-Up Display in the Canvas

Tip

Renaming Clips: As you make sub-clips from a master shot, you'll probably want to rename the shots immediately. What usually happens, though, is that as soon as you change the name of the subclip, it leaps off somewhere as the **Browser** order is changed. To avoid this, before you go naming the clips, try clicking on any blank column header — **Label**, perhaps — or a column in which everything is the same, like **Frame Size**. Then when you rename the clips, they won't change position in the **Browser** order.

You can also drag it directly from the **Timeline** into the **Browser**. The In and Out points will remain with the clip, as well as the rest of the media.

Organizing the Clips

Once you've got your material diced up, you should spend some time getting it put away so that you can find it again. There are no firm rules about this, and I find each project tends to dictate its own organizational structure. Usually I begin with one bin that holds all the master shots. These are usually pretty big chunks of video: 10, 20, 30 minutes, usually not smaller. From the master shots, clips are separated out into bins. Keeping the master shots has the advantage that you can go back to the material in bulk to look through it again. As the project nears completion, I like to do this to see if I overlooked or discarded anything, which can be useful in light of the way the material gets cut together.

The separate bins can be organized in a variety of ways. Narrative projects tend to have material broken down in scene bins, with sub-bins for different types of shots or characters, depending on how complex the scene. Documentary projects tend to break the material down into subject matter: a bin for all the forest shots, another for logging scenes, another for road work, another for weather, another for all the interviews, another for sound, another for narration tracks, another for music, another for graphics. As I said, there are no hard and fast rules on how material is organized. It's a bit like the Eskimos. If your subject is snow, you may have 20 different bins for different types of snow, but if your project is weather in general, you may have only a single generic snow bin.

The real trick is to break down your material into enough bins so that your material is organized, but not so many bins that it becomes difficult to find material. As you move clips into bins, add notes — lots of them. The more information you include on the clips, the easier it will be to find them.

Cutting up your shots and organizing them into bins is critical to working efficiently, particularly for long-form work. The longer the project, the more tapes you have, the more sequences, the more complex everything becomes. Having your material well organized is crucial. Fortunately FCP provides ways to help you.

Principally you have bins, and bins within bins. But at the most visible level you have color-coded and user-definable labels, as we saw in the **Browser** on page 31. The **Browser** also gives you:

- **Comment** fields
- A **Label** field
- A **Description** field
- **Log Notes**
- A **Good** check mark

Do not overlook or hurry through the note-taking and entering process. All editors have their own ways of organizing material, loading information into the computer, and keeping it consistent. However you do it, it opens up to you one of computer-based editing's great boons, the computer's ability to search through huge amounts of data almost instantly. But you have to enter the information first. You can enter it either directly in the **Browser** fields, or by **Control**-clicking the clip and selecting **Item Properties**. The information can be entered in the tabbed **Logging Info** panel (Figure 3.21).

What is entered here also appears in the **Browser** columns and will be searchable with FCP's search engine. You can access a

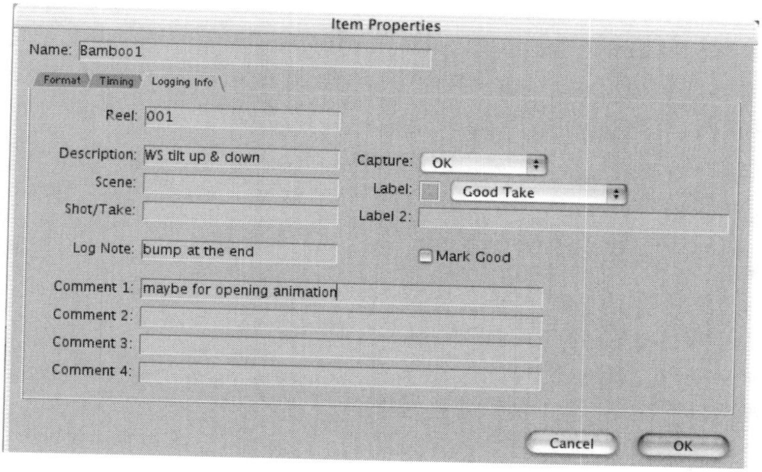

Figure 3.21 Logging Info Panel

Clips					
Name	Goo	Log Note	Description	Comment 1	Comment 2
Bamboo1		bump at the end	WS tilt up & down	maybe for open	
Bamboo2			CS pan right & back		
Ceremony1	✓		MS priest bowing & standing	push to scroll	
Ceremony2	✓		MS attendants bow	pan to priest pull to wide	
Ceremony3		wobbly	CA attendants bowing		
Ceremony4			pull from altar	priest reading from scroll	
Ceremony5			priest bowing and kneeling	double pull	
Ceremony6		dark	MS priest with drum bowing	can't find chopsticks	
Ceremony7		dark	CS priest drum & chant		
Ceremony8			WS attendants	push to attendant in corner	
Ceremony9			Wide drum & chant	push to priest in corner	sound bed
Dance1			CS feet facing R		sound bed
Dance2	✓		WS dance troupe from beside drummer	dance end	
Dance3			MS pan right across troupe	end on musicians	
Food1			CS food trays	pan R	
Food2		looking at camera	MS man at grill	push to tight skewers	
Food3			CS ladling in tray	pan L to kettle tilt to chef	3 shots
Food4		3 and 4	WS ladling in tray		
Food5	✓	watch bumps	Girl buys biscuit	moves around girl	
Food6		5 and 6	biscuit vendor couple	pan R woman to man	
Food7			CU corn		
Food8		7 and 8	corn pan R to corn		
Stairs1			WS stairs to temple		
Stairs2			Closer stairs to temple		
StoneBasin			CS stone basin		
Temple			WS temple grounds	Pan R to temple and back to bell	
Village1	✓		LS village	tea bushes in foreground	
Village2			LS village	radio mast	
Village3			LS looking down on village	push & pull to houses	

Figure 3.22   Browser Logging Info

clip's **Item Properties** directly from the **Viewer** with the keyboard shortcut **Command-9**. I find the simplest way to enter information for clips is in the **Browser** as I make and rename subclips (Figure 3.22).

Another excellent tool for entering information is FCP's **Marker** screen. With the playhead sitting on an existing marker, tap **M**, or when creating a marker, tap **M** twice to call up the **Edit Marker** screen where you can enter descriptive information and comments (Figure 3.23).

The **Marker** screens will actually appear over the media on the computer screen, at least while the clip isn't playing and the playhead is on the marker (Figure 3.24).

If the marker is extended, the text will appear over all the frames the marker covers. If you add the comments to the markers before you make the subclips, the information will be carried over into the subclips themselves.

Figure 3.23   Edit Marker Screen

New to FCP3 in the **Marker** dialog window is the ability to add chapter markers and compression markers. These are markers that are usually applied to sequences in the **Timeline** window. These chapter and compression markers can be exported for use with DVD creation.

All these tools are a great help to editors, but nothing helps an editor in long form more than a good visual and aural memory. Simply being able to remember material over perhaps hundreds of reels is a real gift, but even without this talent, looking closely at all your material, making good notes, and having a decent search engine will go a long way toward making your life a lot easier.

Figure 3.24   Marker Display in Viewer

Note

Search Engine: This is the **Browser's** search engine, so unfortunately FCP cannot at this time search through marker screen information. It would be very useful if it could, but as of this writing, it has not been implemented. If you use the search feature in a specific sequence, you will get a more limited search engine, but one that does look for text in the marker screen information (Figure 3.25).

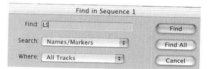

Figure 3.25   Sequence Search Window

Final Cut has an excellent search tool, which is why adding the notes is so important (Figure 3.26). The first popup in the **Find** window lets you search:

- The open project
- All open projects
- The *Effects* folder

It searches anything tabbed into the **Browser**.

The second popup selects **All Media** or a choice of **Used** or **Unused Media,** while the third popup lets you replace or add to existing results. The two popups at the bottom define parameters. The left one sets where it's going to look (Figure 3.27).

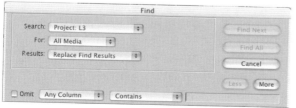

Figure 3.26   Find Dialog

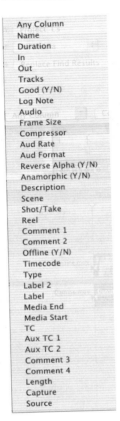

Figure 3.27 **Search Parameters**

| Starts With |
| Contains |
| Equals |
| Ends With |
| Less Than |
| Greater Than |

Figure 3.28 **Search Options**

⤳ Tip

Using Find to Keep Track: Because FCP doesn't keep track of shots that are taken from the **Browser** and put in a sequence, the **Find** window is one way to do this. By selecting the **Unused** popup, you can find the material. You can then use the check mark in the **Good** column to marked the unused clips. Unfortunately, **Find** only searches media, not subclips, so if any part of a piece of media is used, even one subclip, then all the subclips based on the same media are considered used.

Unless you have pretty good idea where the information is — for instance, if you're looking for a specific type of file — just leave it on the default **Any Column**. The right popup lets you limit the search parameters to speed up the process by limiting the number of results (Figure 3.28).

If you press the **Find All button** rather than the default **Find Next**, the requested clips appear in a new **Browser** window (Figure 3.29).

Note the two buttons at the bottom, which let you:

- Show a selected item in the regular **Browser** bins
- Remove selected items from project

This is not the powerful **Make Offline** tool we saw earlier on page 42, which lets you delete the media; this simply deletes the clip in the **Browser** window.

An important point to understand about this **Finder** is that all the items it locates are directly related to the items in the **Browser**. Unlike FCP's usual behavior where clips in sequences and bins can be copies of each other, here the found clips are directly linked to the clips in the **Browser**. Highlight a clip here and it's highlighted in the **Browser**. Delete a clip here and it's deleted from the **Browser**.

For some reason that escapes me, the **Find Results** window cannot be changed to Icon view from the **View** menu, but can be changed to icon view using the **Control** key and the contextual menu in the **Name** column.

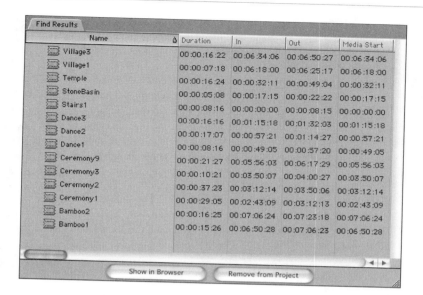

Figure 3.29   Finder Results

Look Before You Cut

However you work your video into clips or subclips, what you're really doing is looking through your material. What you should watch for is relationships, shots that can easily be cut together. Getting familiar with the material is an important part of the editing process, learning what you have to work with and looking for cutting points. I think this is one reason why many editors still like to use the batch capture method. It allows them another opportunity, the first opportunity to look at the available material.

While looking through the material in the **Timeline**, some editors even like to roughly cut up the shots into sequences as they sort through the pictures. As they come to groups of shots that work together, some editors put them together in sequences. This is easy to do in Final Cut Pro. Simply use **Command-N**, which creates a new sequence.

Spend a little time going over *Damine.mov*. Slice it up and drag the clips into the bins, or dice it up into subclips and drag them into bins. It won't take that long, and you'll find you work faster and faster as you get familiar with the tools and using the keyboard. You'll be able to slice and dice these shots fairly quickly. It's a short reel, less than eight minutes long.

Tip

Other Searches: The search engine isn't only for finding shots. You can search for anything in FCP. You might want to find a filter or a transition. You can search for those as well.

Tip

Sequence Handling: Sequences require precise settings to be compatible with the material placed in them. Rather than creating a new sequence, it might be simpler for these lessons to duplicate an existing sequence, which duplicates its settings as well.

1. Select the sequence that appeared in the **Browser** when you opened *L3*.

2. Then go to the **Edit** menu and select **Duplicate,** or use the keyboard shortcut **Option-D.** This duplicates everything currently in that sequence and automatically names it *Sequence 1 Copy.*

3. Rename this sequence something appropriate.

4. Open it, press **Command-A** to select everything that may be in the **Timeline,** and press the **Delete** key.

Everything's gone, and you now have a brand new, pristine, empty **Timeline,** which you're sure has the right settings for your work.

Tip

Pulling Windows: To separate the timelines just grab the tab and tear one timeline away from the other. You can always stick them back together again by pushing one tab back next to the other. Any tabbed window call be pulled apart like this. All the elements of the Viewer can be in separate windows as can the contents of the Browser. Bins can be opened separately and tabbed together into clusters. It can be a very useful tool.

You can have multiple sequences open at the same time. Timelines normally tab together into one **Timeline** window, but you can pull the timelines apart so that you have two sequences open on the screen at the same time. You can simply pull shots from one sequence into another. By doing this, you're actually copying the shot from one sequence into the new sequence.

While you edit, you just put together the shots you want to work with — edit them, rearrange them, shorten and lengthen them how you like. You can just park your edited sequence to be used later, either as an edited group of shots or just as a holding bin for a group of shots, but unlike a simple bin, here the shots are laid out in the specific order you have arranged.

One way some editors like to work is to build storyboards in bins. Working in Large or Medium Icon mode, you can:

- Trim and set the clips
- Set the Poster frame
- Arrange the layout order of the shots in the **Timeline.**

It's a fast, easy way to move shot order around, to try different arrangements and sequences. Though you can't play the clips back as a sequence, you can make a quick arrangement of shots. Then simply marquee through the shots and drag them into the **Timeline** (Figure 3.30).

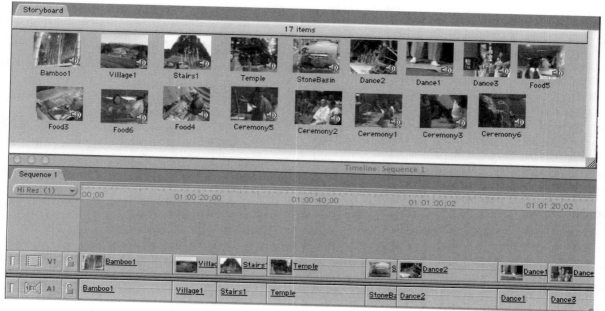

Figure 3.30   Storyboarded Bin and Shots in the Timeline

The shots will appear in the sequence in the order they are in the bin. Notice the shots in the **Timeline** in Figure 3.30 follow the bin order as they are laid out, left to right, top to bottom. Be careful with the row heights: clips that are placed higher up in the bin will appear earlier.

Making Selects

As I wrote in the introduction, an editor can only make a film or video if the material has first been shot and been shot correctly. Some video simply cannot be edited well. When they're shooting a project, the director and cameraperson are trying to get the necessary material to make an editable sequence. One way this is done is by shooting a variety of shots that can be used in different combinations effectively. Let's look at the material in *Damine.mov* more closely for different ways the material can be cut. Also look at the variety of shots and shot combinations the cameraperson has given the editor. This is the process of making selects, choosing the pieces you want to work. It's the first culling out of your material, a process that might be repeated a number of times and revisited again before the project is completed.

The first shots you come to are the two shots of the stairs leading up to the temple at Damine. The shots are quite similar, not so similar in angle, size and composition to jump if you cut them together, but close enough not to be a very pleasant edit. If I could avoid it, I would only use one shot or the other, unless I absolutely, positively had to have both shots to make up for time. In which case I would just grin and bear it and wince through the edit, but use them both anyway.

The next shot is *StoneBasin*, which you've probably seen enough times now. I'd keep it in a bin. I may not use it, but it's a nice, tranquil shot and it might fit in somewhere.

As I mentioned earlier, we cut out the badly exposed shot. Don't even bother saving it. The shot that follows, beginning at 30:22, is the repeat of the pan to the temple. It shows how a good, professional cameraperson shoots this shot. The pan goes from left to right, from the sun shining through the trees to the front of the temple, and then the shot pans back from right to left, from the temple to the trees. It's shot that way so the editor has a choice, a decision that can be affected by many factors. You may choose one because the previous shot pans in the opposite direction and might look clumsy together. Or you want to continue a move in the same direction and perhaps dissolve to it. Or it might be dictated by the script. If the line says something like, "The sun was shining through the trees onto the temple," you would use the first part of the shot, the pan from the trees to the temple. On the other hand, if the script reads, "The temple stood on the hill top under the late afternoon sunlight shining through the trees," you might use the second half of the shot. Two other shots are hidden that can be used equally well — the static shot of the sun through the trees and the static shot of the temple. All the choices are available to the editor only because the cameraperson had the foresight to create them. Good shooters shoot material that's editable in a variety of ways.

☞ Tip _____

Check for Mistakes: Watch out for the little flip up at the end of some shots. Even under a dissolve or other transition, it can appear as something odd and distracting to the viewer. Learn to really look at video as it plays so you can see even momentary mistakes, flashes of the wrong frame, or a frame of black. Lay a couple of clips in the timeline and use the > key to nudge the second clip one frame down the timeline. Play that section of the timeline around the edit. Did you see the flash frame of black? It's easy to miss, but once you see it, you'll see it every time, and the more times you see it, the more annoying it will get.

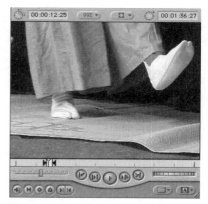

Figure 3.31   Normal

The next three shots are of a dance troupe with a small group of musicians. The first of three is a close-up of a pair of feet with *tabi*, Japanese socks with split toes. The movement of the feet is predominantly from left facing right. This may be important because in the following shot the line of dancers is clearly facing from right to left. In this situation, a wonderfully useful video effect often saves an editor. In Final Cut Pro it's called **Flop**. Go to the close-up of the feet, go to the **Effects** menu, and select **Video Filters>Perspective>Flop**. You will immediately see what how effective this is (Figures 3.31 and 3.32).

🖋 Note _____

Warning: Be careful with the Flop effect. Make sure you check the background. Watch out for any graphics, or other telltale signs that a shot has been flopped. If you look closely in the tabi shot there actually is a Japanese calligraphic character painted on the mat. If your audience will be Japanese you might not get away with this trick, but a Western audience would most probably not notice.

Figure 3.32   Flopped

The second shot of the three should be used as the musical bed for the other shots, first because it's an elegantly composed shot, second because the musicians are clearly visible in the foreground, and third because it's a nice, longish piece of music. The music is repetitive enough that you could easily loop it to play a couple of times, if necessary. It might be useful also to lay in a section of the music under earlier shots, at a low level, to lead into the dance troupe, and perhaps again at a reduced level over the shots following it, to continue the aural continuity of the scene.

The dance troupe is followed by a series of shots of food stalls. The third of the eight is interesting because it can be used in a variety of ways. The close-up of the steaming cooking tray at the start can be used to cut with the wide shot that comes later. Or you could use:

- The small pullout from the close-up to the medium-close shot

- The move from the steam tray to the large pot

- The move from the pot to the cook with the ladle

- Any of these elements as a static shot without the move.

How you use the elements in the shot will be dictated by the rhythm and pace you set for yourself. If you want a vigorous, high-energy sequence, you'll use a lot of the moves, cut together quickly. If you want a slower, more deliberate feel to the scene, you might use just the static parts of the shot cut slowly. We'll look at this and other editing problems in the next lesson.

The religious portion of the ceremony follows immediately afterwards on the reel. The ceremony itself presents some interesting, common problems in editing, those of cutting on movement and of condensing time. We shall look at these issues in Lesson 7. In the scene there are a number of camera flashes. Many editors like to use flashbulb pops as cutting points. If they're conveniently timed, they can make an interesting edit. Be careful though: sometimes they work, sometimes they don't.

Finish looking through the material. Once you've cut up the ceremonial part into its shots, all that's left is a few shots of the village itself and of the surrounding bamboo.

As you look through this material and cut it up, you can see that the quality of the material shot is critical to your ability to edit it properly. The key to good editing is timing, and that timing starts in the camera. In this material, you'll notice how short the movements are. Whether zooming or panning, the camera movement itself will last no more than a few seconds. Shots are generally not on the screen more than 5–10 seconds. For faster paced editing — in commercials, for instance — shots often last a second or even less. You'll also notice little random wandering, no slow panning around movements. The camera movements are deliberate and precise: the pan goes from object A to object B and stops; the zoom starts on the steam tray and reveals the man with the ladle and stops.

There is a tendency for cameramen, particularly novices, to use moves to make static material more interesting. Pans and tilts and zooms enliven what might otherwise be dull or static material. The difficulty for the editor is that this often means having to cope with great many movements that may or may not work together. If you have some shots that zoom in, do you put them together so that the viewer seems to be going every closer inward, or do you follow a zoom in with a zoom out (what many editors call *tromboning*)? Do you follow a pan to the right with another pan to the right or with a pan that goes back to the left? Tromboning is generally to be avoided, as is the swinging-door effect of panning right and then panning left, but a move in one direction followed by a move in the same direction can look equally awkward. If there is something that carries the viewer's eye, such as if the camera is following someone walking down the street, then repeated pans in the same direction work effectively, but over static objects this is a problem.

The best solution in most cases is not to always use the movement, however enticing, but to complement the pans, tilts, and zooms the cameraman so thoughtfully provided with some static shots as well. A series of static shots is often better than an uncertain movement, a mushy pan or zoom, an unclear, or imprecise movement. If the pan or zoom is too big, it will inevitably take too long or be too fast, a crash move, leaving the editor with options that are only bad or worse.

👉 *Tip*

No Edits in Moves: An edit during a movement is almost always ugly. It jars an audience to come into a movement in progress, and it is even more jarring to leave a movement before it finishes. Usually the editor will use the end of the movement rather than the beginning, so that the movement comes to rest before the shot changes. If you have to cut into a movement in progress, the most common device is to use a short dissolve, perhaps 16 frames or less, to smooth out that lurching feeling you get when cutting into the movement. This applies to anything in motion, even someone speaking. It always seems to work best to cut away from the action at some moment, however brief, when the action is at rest. When cutting away from someone speaking, place the cut on a frame when the lips are closed rather than when the mouth is open. (This doesn't apply to screams, of course.)

A video needs to be shot with the final goal always in mind. What do you want to create? What do you want to convey to the audience? How much depth do you want to go into: short or long, fast or slow, information or impression? The outcome determines every step in the video-making process, every minute detail:

- Where you place the camera
- What you point it at
- How you light the subject
- What happens in front of the camera, of course

Finally, all the pieces are strung together to make a coherent, meaningful whole that conveys the message or tells the story that ultimately moves the audience to tears, to laughter, to think, to act, to buy — whatever your final goal.

Media Manager

At some stage in the editing process you may want to remove all the excess material from your hard drives and just keep the core of material that your project needs. You may do this housecleaning more than once in the course of creating a longer project. You may do it fairly early once you've gleaned out the good material, and you may do it toward the end of the project as you're finalizing it. Or you may want to do it at the very end of the project after everything is edited and reduced to one sequence and its media for archiving purposes. In other editing systems, this pro-

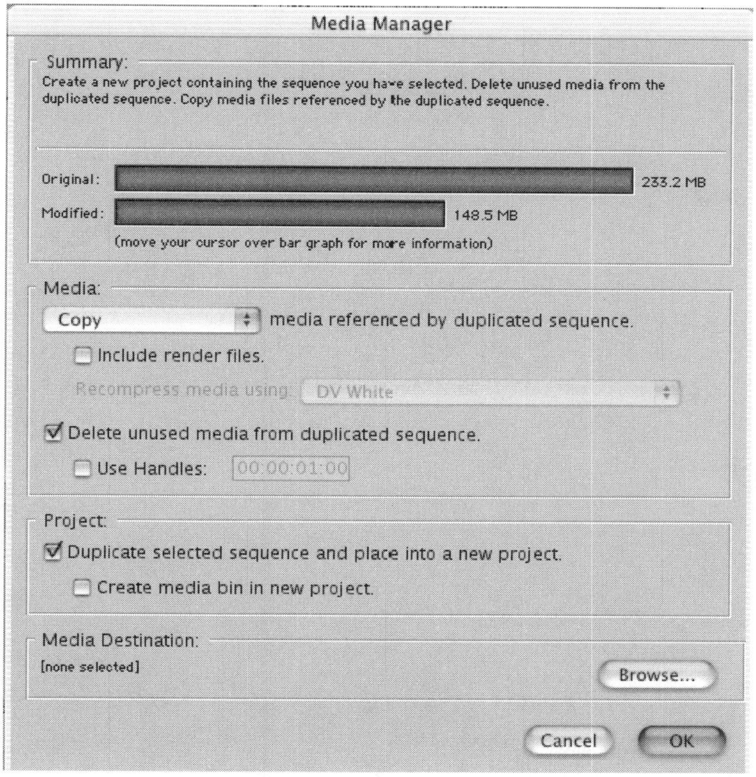

Media Manager

Summary:
Create a new project containing the sequence you have selected. Delete unused media from the duplicated sequence. Copy media files referenced by the duplicated sequence.

Original: 233.2 MB
Modified: 148.5 MB
(move your cursor over bar graph for more information)

Media:
[Copy   ▼] media referenced by duplicated sequence.
☐ Include render files.
Recompress media using [DV White   ▼]

☑ Delete unused media from duplicated sequence.
☐ Use Handles: [00:00:01:00]

Project:
☑ Duplicate selected sequence and place into a new project.
☐ Create media bin in new project.

Media Destination:
[none selected]   (Browse...)

(Cancel)   (OK)

Figure 3.33   Media Manager

cess is called consolidating. You do it in Final Cut Pro with the **Media Manager** (Figure 3.33).

You can select **Media Manager** from the **File** menu. You can apply **Media Manager** to a single sequence or multiple sequences, or multiple clips or bins. Whatever you selected, **Media Manager** will only include those items in the consolidation.

The panel is self-explanatory. It clearly lists your options and what the system will do. The summary information at the top of the window explains what your options are doing. Below that the bar graphs show the amount of media involved, how long it is, and how much media your media management will produce.

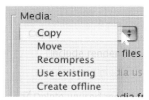

Figure 3.34   Media Manager Popup

The media popup offers a number of options (Figure 3.34). The default copies the media to a new location picked with the **Browse** button. With the **Copy** process, the media is copied and the unused deleted or not, as requested, and a new project is created. The new project opens immediately into FCP. If clips in a sequence have the same name, which often happens, the names are incremented with a suffix to distinguish them from each other. The names of the clips in the copied folder remain the same as the original files, which can lead to confusion because separate folders will hold clips with the same name but containing different media.

The **Move** option actually moves the media to the new location. When moving to a different drive or partition, the media will have to copy over, but after the operation is completed, the original media will disappear from the original location. If you use the **Move** option and other clips are associated with the media, a dialog box comes up (Figure 3.36).

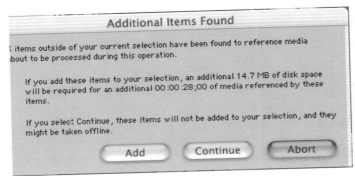

Figure 3.35   Moving Dialog

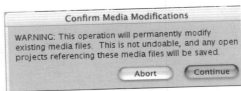

Figure 3.36   Warning Dialog

Selecting **Add** will maintain the link to clips in other projects. Choosing **Continue** will break the link. Because this is undoable, choosing either **Add** or **Continue** will bring up a further warning (Figure 3.36).

The media that's moved is transferred to the designated place and put in a folder named after the project that's being moved. This folder, in turn, is inside another folder called *Media*. Though the filing system seems convoluted, the process is efficient and works remarkably well. Unlike the **Copy** option, a new project is not created; the media is just moved to a new location specified with the **Browse** button.

The **Use Existing** option is really the opposite of the **Move** option. While **Move** transfers the material but does nothing to the project, **Use Existing** creates a new project with whatever you included in the **Media Manager**. If you have **Delete Unused Media** selected, it will immediately delete the unneeded portions from your hard drive and replace them with only the media required for your new project. This is fatal and final. I would recommend using this option only if you are pressed for drive space. If you have the space available, use **Copy** or **Move**.

The **Create Offline** option simply makes a new project with sequences or clips as requested in **Media Manager,** but it leaves all the clips marked **Offline,** ready for recapturing.

Media Manager defaults to no handles and not moving render files. I would recommend making some handles; one second is usually good. Probably dumping the render files is a good idea, unless the project is render intensive. Then it might be worthwhile preserving them as well to save time later.

 Tip

Getting Offline to the Client: Because **OfflineRT** is only visible on your computer monitor and does not get fed to an NTSC monitor via FireWire — it's in Photo-JPEG after all, not DV — you need to know how to get your offline material to tape to be seen by a client for approval.

There are a couple of ways around this. One is to simply drop your OfflineRT sequence into a DV sequence. You can either leave the OfflineRT sequence as a small box in the window, or you can scale it up to fit the DV screen. The latter may make the image too soft and pixilated to be watchable. Or you could do some compromise between the two: scale the material partially to make it bigger without getting it uglier than it already is. Whichever way you handle the offline material in the DV sequence, the whole timeline will have to be rendered out into the DV codec to play back to video. That can be a long, time-consuming and hard drive–consuming experience.

The second way is to get a video card or scan converter that will output your computer screen. Again, either play the video full screen or use some compromise setting of screen size and pixelization. The audio show be fed out of the computer's headphone jack to the recording deck. Neither solution is ideal, but those are the only available options at the moment.

Summary

In this lesson we've covered slicing and dicing clips, consolidating with the **Media Manager,** and organizing our material so we can work efficiently. In the next lesson we'll look at editing sequences.

OfflineRT

FCP3 has introduced the ability to capture DV material at low resolution using Photo-JPEG at a reduced frame size. There are a couple of different strategies to use this feature.

If you computer is fast enough, a G4/500 or a G4/633 PowerBook, you can capture directly to this format. If your computer isn't fast enough — an older PowerBook or a G3-based iBook, for instance — you can use a faster computer to capture the material and then transfer it to the slower machine for portable editing.

Or you can use **Media Manager**:

1. Capture your material in DV.

2. From the **Media** popup, choose **Recompress**.

3. From the **Recompress** codec popup, choose **OfflineRT NTSC (Photo-JPEG)** (Figure 3.37).

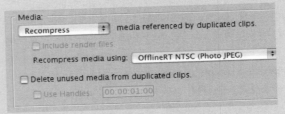

You probably want to leave off **Delete Unused Media from Duplicated Clips** because you'll want as much material as possible for your edit. If you're short of drive space, you can capture a couple of reels of DV, recompress them to **Offline**, then capture a couple more reels in DV, and so on.

Figure 3.37 Recompress to OfflineRT

After you've finished your edit in **OfflineRT**, you'll want to recapture your final sequence in DV quality.

1. Again, use **Media Manager** to do the recapture.

2. Now select **Create Offline** from the media popup and choose the format you want to convert your sequences to — **DV NTSC Superwhite**, for instance.

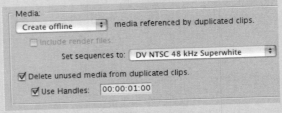

3. Make sure you check **Delete Unused Media** and add handles if you wish (Figure 3.38).

4. Then batch capture all the material needed for your project.

Figure 3.38 Create Offline

Lesson 4

Editing Basics: Building Your Sequence

Now that you've got your material into Final Cut Pro and sliced and/or diced it up, we're ready to begin putting it all together.

Loading the Lesson

As in the previous lesson, start by loading the CD into your CD drive. When you begin any lesson that needs material from the CD, you should first drag the needed folders onto the media drive of your computer. The sound and video clips included there will play much better and more smoothly from your computer's high-speed media drive than from any CD drive. For this lesson you'll also need the folders called *Media1* (if you haven't dragged it over already) and *Lesson 4*, which is inside the *Projects* folder on the CD.

1. Drag *Lesson04* onto your internal system drive. Again, probably the best place for it is in the *Shared* folder in the *Users* folder.

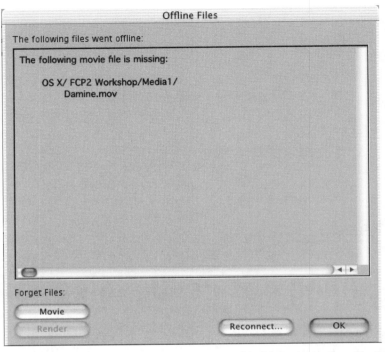

Figure 4.1 Offline Files Dialog Box

Figure 4.2 Reconnect Options Dialog Box

You have to have both folders because this lesson's project file is in the *Lesson 4* folder, while the media, which will again be *Damine.mov*, is in the *Media1* folder.

2. Before opening anything, eject the CD from your computer.

3. Now open the *Lesson 4* folder on your hard drive and double-click the project file, *L4*, to launch the application.

When the project finishes loading, you'll be greeted with the dialog box in Figure 4.1.

4. Do *not* press **Enter** or click **OK**. Instead click on the **Reconnect** button.

Do not click the **Movie** button underneath **Forget Files** either, because the application will do exactly that: forget that it needs the media. After you click **Reconnect**, you will get the **Reconnect Options** dialog box in Figure 4.2.

The computer will now search through your hard drives looking for *Damine.mov*. When the file is found, you'll get a dialog box that looks similar to the one in Figure 4.3.

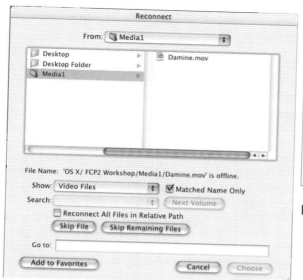

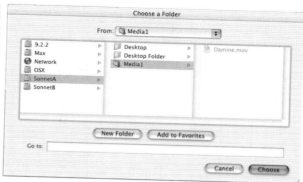

Figure 4.4   Scratch Disk Navigation Menu

Figure 4.3   Reconnect Selection Box

5. If this is the correct file on your media drive, click the **Select** button.

Final Cut will now reconnect all the material for the project and you're ready to go.

Setting up the Project

The first step you should take after your project has reconnected is to save the project with a new name inside the *Lesson 4* folder. Use **Save Project As** from the **File** menu. If something goes wrong with your project, or if you accidentally delete an element, you can open the original project and drag that element into your working project.

Also, whenever you start a new project or open a project you haven't worked on in a while, assign the scratch disk. Immediately go to the **Final Cut Pro** menu, select **Preferences (Option-Q)** and click on the **Scratch Disk**s tab. Click on the **Set** button and navigate to your media hard drive that holds the *Media1* folder. Click on the *Media1* folder to highlight it and then click on the **Choose** button shown in Figure 4.4.

Also make sure that in the **Scratch Disk** panel of your **Preferences**, your **Autosave Vault** is set to the *Shared* folder as well.

Inside the **Browser** of your copy of *L4*, you'll see a couple of sequences:

- *Sequence 1*
- *Food Sequence*

Sequence 1 is empty. We'll look at *Food Sequence* in a moment. In the **Browser** there is also the master clip, *Damine.mov*, together with a bin called **Clips**. Open the **Clips** bin and you'll see the shots from *Damine.mov* diced into subclips. Because of the nature of the material — distinctly different shots — I felt that dicing was a better method in this case to avoid the transition problem we discussed on page 120 in Lesson 3.

Though subclips normally appear without In points and Out points set, I've marked Ins and Outs at the beginning and end of each subclip. The advantage this gives you is that you can order the subclips in reel order based on their timecode In point, rather than their alphabetical order. So if you look at **Clips** in List view (**View>Browser Items>as List**) and click on the column header **In**. The clips will arrange themselves in TC order.

You can also do this by clicking on the **Media Start** column and use this as the basis for the sort order.

Working with the Clips

I'd like to focus on one particular section of the video in this lesson: the food material. Take a quick look at *Food Sequence*. This is where we're going. To begin, let's look at where we're coming from, the material we have to work with.

1. Open the empty *Sequence 1* and double-click on the clip in the **Clips** bin called *Food1*, which will bring it into the **Viewer**.

The shot is 6:04 long, six seconds and four frames.

2. Play the shot, let it pan from left to right across the trays of food, let the pan end, give it a beat, and then stop.

3. Enter an Out point.

This is probably around 1:36:18, making the shot about four seconds in length.

Try it a few times till you get the pacing of the movement down. You might find that the more times you try it, the more you're shaving off the shot. Perhaps you'll feel the front needs to be shortened as well. Instead of beginning right at the start of the shot, enter an In point just before the camera pans right. When you have it the way you want it, you're ready to move it into the **Timeline**.

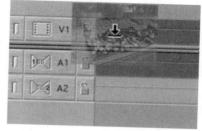

Figure 4.5   Dragging into the Timeline

There are essentially three ways to get material from the **Viewer** to the **Timeline**:

- Simply drag it there. Grab the image from the **Viewer** and pull it directly into the **Timeline**, dropping it onto **V1** as in Figure 4.5.

Figure 4.6   Edit Buttons

- The second way is to press the little red button, the middle button, in the group of three at the bottom left of the **Canvas** (Figure 4.6), or use its keyboard shortcut, **F10**.

- The third method is unique to Final Cut Pro. Drag the clip from the **Viewer** to the **Canvas**, and the visual dialog box in Figure 4.7 appears immediately.

Note

Dropped Frames: One of the most common causes of dropped frames, especially for new users of FCP, is that their viewing window is not fit to the video. If you look at your DV video in a small frame while the material is set to full size, you're expecting the computer to display only portion of the video while playing it back. If this doesn't produce dropped frames on playback, it will at the very least show as stuttering video on your computer monitor. You can always tell if the image is too large for the viewing window when you see scroll bars on the sides, as in Figure 4.8. To correct this, simply select **Fit to Window** from the **Viewer Size** popup.

Figure 4.7   Canvas Edit Overlay (CEO)

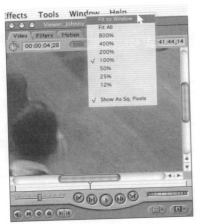

Figure 4.8   Fit to Window

Figure 4.9   In Point Mark in the Timeline

The Canvas Edit Overlay
Overwrite

Let's look at the **Canvas Edit Overlay (CEO)**(Figure 4.7). It offers a number of different editing options. The most commonly used is the **Overwrite** command.

1. Drag the clip from the **Viewer** until the box marked **Overwrite** highlights.

2. Then drop the clip.

It will overwrite whatever is in the timeline beginning at the point at which the playhead is parked.

> 👉 *Tip*
> **Target Tracks:** When you drag a clip onto the **CEO**, you'll notice the target tracks at the top of the display. Your clip will be placed on these tracks. The indicators serve as a handy last warning before you execute the edit.

This is a three-point edit. In a three-point edit you're defining three elements required to execute the edit function:

- Where you want the clip to start
- Where you want the clip to end
- Where you want to place the clip

The three points are most commonly defined by:

- Marking In and Out points in the **Viewer,** the equivalent of marking In and Out points in a linear system's play deck
- Using the playhead as the marker for the In point in the Timeline, the record deck in a linear system.

> 📌 *Note*
> **Different In Point:** You can also define the In point in the **Timeline** to be a different point from the playhead. Go to the **Canvas** or the **Timeline** window and press the **I** key to mark an In point (Figure 4.9). This will be the In point for the next edit, and when you drag the clip from **Viewer** to **Canvas**, or hit **F10** or the red **Overwrite** button, the clip will drop at the marked In point and not at the playhead's current position.

Why Three-Point Editing?

The origin of three-point editing goes back to linear videotape editing. To perform a clean edit into the tape, you had to instruct the machines through an edit controller on the point where edits were to be performed. You marked on the record deck, using the timecode on the tape, the point at which you wanted the recording to beginning. You then marked on the play deck the point from which you wanted the material to begin copying. The third point could be marked on either the record deck or the play deck. You could mark either the duration or Out point on the record deck where you wanted the edit to finish, or you could mark the point on the play deck at the end of the material you wanted to record. This is closest to the general working practice in Final Cut Pro. In the reality of editing videotape, many editors simply used a two-point editing system. Entering In points on both the record and play decks, beginning the edit, letting the tapes run at least as long as was needed, perhaps a bit longer, and then aborting the edit. You can even simulate two-point editing in FCP. Mark an In point in the **Viewer** and an In point in the **Timeline**. Do an overwrite or insert edit to put the clip in the **Timeline** at the marked In point. Then play the **Timeline** till you get to the point at which you want to place the next clip. Mark a new In point in the **Timeline** and go and find the next shot. When you've found it, again only mark its In before executing the edit. This is quick and easy two-point editing analogous to linear videotape production.

So that we can look at the functionality offered in the **CEO**, let's quickly drag a few shots into the **Timeline** to see how they work.

1. If you haven't already done it, drag *Food1* from the **Viewer** and drop it on **Overwrite**.

2. Then select clips *Food2* and *Food3* in the **Browser** and drag them directly to the **Overwrite** box in the **CEO**.

The clips will appear in the **Timeline** following *Food1* in their bin order. Note that every time you place a clip in the **Timeline**, the playhead automatically leaps to end of the clip, ready for the next edit event, and the **Canvas** displays the last frame of the sequence. Also notice that in the **Timeline**, *Food2* and *Food3* will appear with **Through Edit** markings if you have that switched on in *Preferences*. This happens because the shots have contiguous timecode, as will all the shots taken sequentially from the *Damine.mov* master shot.

 Note _____

Overwrite Constraint: Note that F10 does not overwrite directly from the **Browser**. F10 only works when overwriting from the **Viewer**. If the **Viewer** is closed, F10 will simply input a slug, a long section of black with a stereo audio track.

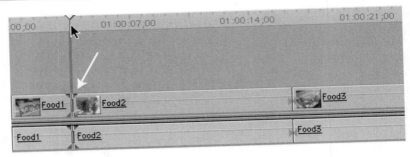

Figure 4.10   Snap Markings

Insert

If **Overwrite** is the most commonly used of the **CEO** features, then the next most used must be **Insert**. This is where an NLE system shows its power.

1. Move the playhead to the edit between *Food1* and *Food2*.

As you move the playhead onto the edit point, it should snap strongly to the join and display on the tracks the marks in Figure 4.10. If you don't see the snap marks, **Snapping** is turned off.

2. Press the **N** key. Try it several times, toggling the **Snapping** function on and off.

The Magic Frame

If the playhead moves to the end of the last clip in a sequence, the **Canvas** displays the last frame of the clip with a blue bar down the right side. This is the Magic Frame, because the playhead is actually sitting on the next frame of video — the blank, empty frame — but the display shows the previous frame. Try it.

1. Place a clip in an empty sequence and use the **Up** and **Down** arrow keys to move back and forth between the beginning and the end of the clip. You see the first and last frames of the clip.

2. Now, leaving a gap in the Timeline, place another clip in the sequence.

This time when you use the **Up** and **Down** keys to toggle, at the beginning you see the first frame of video, but at the end you see the first frame of black, the empty space. This is important to remember that the playhead is always sitting at the start of the video frame, despite what the Magic Frame shows you.

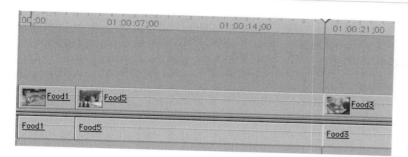

Figure 4.11   Accidental
Overwrite

Figure 4.12   The Insert Edit

The **N** key may get to be one of your most often-used keys in Final Cut Pro. You'll find as you work with the application that you'll be constantly changing from one mode to the other.

Now with snapping on, you should have the playhead parked between the clips.

3. Grab *Food5* directly from the **Browser** and drag into across to the **Canvas**, calling up the **CEO**.

4. Drop it on **Overwrite** to see what happens.

Food5 wipes out all of *Food2* and some of *Food3*, as shown in Figure 4.11.

5. Quickly undo that with **Command-Z**.

6. This time, instead of dragging *Food5* onto **Overwrite**, drag it onto **Insert**.

Immediately the **Timeline** rearranges itself. *Food5* drops into the **Timeline**, appears between *Food1* and *Food2*, and pushes everything further down in the **Timeline**, as shown in Figure 4.12.

Insert will move everything down the track regardless of a clip's position. So if you insert into the middle of the clip, the clip will be cut, and everything on all the tracks will be pushed out of the

Figure 4.13 Track Locks

way. This applies to all tracks, including music or narration, which you may not want to cut.

Track locks are useful in these circumstances. For instance, to prevent an insert from slicing into a music track, lock the track or tracks. All the other tracks will move, but the locked tracks will remain stationary. Just click on the track locks (Figure 4.13) at the head of each track. (Remember to lock or unlock both tracks of a stereo pair.)

Tip

Keyboard Shortcuts: As usual in FCP, there are keyboard shortcuts for locking and unlocking tracks. To lock a video track, press **F4** and the track number. To lock an audio track, press **F5** and the track number. If you want to lock all the video tracks, use **Shift-F4**. For all the audio tracks, **Shift-F5**. These key commands are toggles: unlocked tracks will lock, and locked tracks will unlock.

Sometimes it's handy to lock all the video or audio tracks except one. Use **Option**-click on the lock, and that track will remain unlocked while all the other tracks of that type, video or audio, will lock. Do **Option**-click on the track again to unlock everything.

Figure 4.14 Overwrite Arrow

Figure 4.15 Insert Arrow

7. Before we go any further, let's undo the insert edit we just did using **Command-Z**, bringing the **Timeline** back to just three clips, *Food1*, *Food2*, and *Food3*.

You can also use **Control** and the contextual menu to do a ripple delete, or ripple delete with **Shift-Delete**.

Alternative Overwrite and Insert

Overwrite and **Insert** are the primary functions in the **CEO**, but let's look at another way to do them.

Drag *Food5* directly from the **Browser** to the **Timeline**. As you drag it onto the edit point between *Food1* and *Food2*, a little arrow appears, indicating how the edit will be performed. If the arrow is pointing downward as in Figure 4.14, the edit will overwrite. If the little arrow is pointing to the right as in Figure 4.15, you will be doing an insert, which will push the material out of the way.

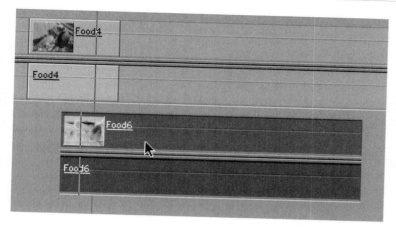

Figure 4.16   One Clip Trying to
Replace Another

You'll notice also as you work in the application that in addition to the arrow indicators, the clip colors change. In **Overwrite**, the track color changes to the highlighted brown color. In **Insert**, the track simply has an outline box.

Replace

We'll skip **Overwrite with Transition** and **Insert with Transition** for the next lesson and look at:

- **Replace**

- **Fit to Fill**

- **Superimpose**

These functions have specific uses and are a little tricky to understand, particularly as they are implemented in Final Cut.

Replace is remarkably sophisticated in the way it works. It will replace a clip in the **Timeline** with another clip either from the **Viewer** or dragged from the **Browser** to the **CEO**. The trick to understanding how **Replace** works is to understand that it works precisely from the point at which the playhead is positioned. Take a look at the clips in Figure 4.16.

The clip in the **Timeline**, *Food4*, has the playhead parked near the end of the shot. I want to replace it with the clip *Food6*. In the **Viewer** *Food6* is near the beginning of the shot. The current position of the playhead in *Food6* is indicated. I won't be able to replace *Food4* with *Food6* even though the new clip is much longer than the clip it's replacing. Why? Because FCP calculates the **Replace** edit from the position of the playhead. There just aren't enough frames in front of the current position of the playhead in *Food6* to replace all the frames in front of the current position of the playhead in *Food4*.

Let's see what happens when we try to do this in our sequence.

1. In the **Timeline**, place the playhead somewhere toward the middle of the *Food2* clip.

2. Double-click *Food5* in the **Browser** to bring it into the **Viewer**.

3. Make sure the playhead in the **Viewer** is at the beginning of the clip.

4. Drag the clip from the **Viewer** onto the **Canvas** and drop it on the **Replace** box.

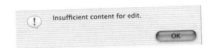

You get is the unpleasant and highly uninformative dialog box in Figure 4.17.

Figure 4.17   Insufficient Content Message

You know you have enough material to do the edit. *Food5* is quite a bit longer than *Food2*. What FCP is trying to do is match the frame in the middle of *Food2* with the point where the playhead is parked in the **Viewer**. Because you're in the middle of the clip in the sequence and there isn't sufficient media in front of the playhead, you can't perform the edit. In Figure 4.18 the playhead is 5:04 into the clip *Food2*.

If you want to replace *Food2* with *Food5*, *Food5* in the Viewer has to be at least 5:04 from the beginning of the clip as in Figure 4.19, otherwise the **Replace** can't happen.

Remember, to move to a specific point in the clip you can simply type in the timecode number on the keypad of your keyboard and press the **Enter** key.

5. Go to the start of the clip, type *+504*, and press **Enter**.

Figure 4.18   Food2 and its Position in the Timeline

That will take you five seconds and four frames forward from where you are.

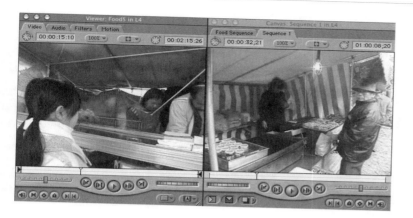

Figure 4.19   Food5 in the Viewer
and the Canvas with
Food2

6. Now drag *Food5* from the **Viewer** to the **Canvas** and drop it
    on the **Replace** box.

The frame containing the playhead in the **Viewer** will replace
exactly the frame that's sitting in the **Canvas**. *Food2* will extend
back toward the beginning of the clip from its current point at
and forward for the length of the clip it is replacing. It will only
replace the current clip; it won't extend backwards into *Food1*,
nor will it cut off any of *Food3*. Your **Timeline** should now look
like Figure 4.20. Notice also that the **Through Edit** marks have
disappeared because the timecode is no longer contiguous
between the shots.

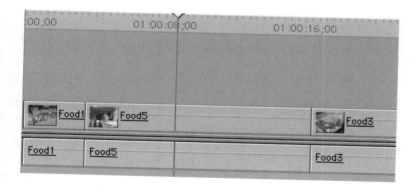

Figure 4.20   Sequence 1

Figure 4.21   Ins and Outs in the Timeline

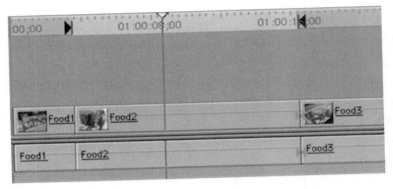

Avoiding the Math: If you don't want to hassle with working out the time difference to get the clips to line up, simply take both clips back to their In points and do **Replace** from there. Or you can use **Overwrite** after first defining the limits of the shot you want to replace. That's easy to do in FCP. With the playhead parked over the shot, press the **X** key. This sets In and Out points on the timeline that are exactly the length of the clip, as in Figure 4.21. If you now do an overwrite edit, it will effectively replace the shot in the **Timeline**.

Fit to Fill

Fit to Fill functions similarly to **Replace** except that it's never hampered by lack of media. **Fit to Fill** simply adjusts the speed of the clip to match the area it needs to occupy. This sounds like a fantastic tool, but in practical terms, it raises serious problems.

1.   Open the clip *Food7* in the **Viewer**.

You can see by the duration in the upper left corner of the **Viewer** that *Food7* is quite a bit shorter than *Food5*.

2.   With the playhead parked over the middle of *Food5* in the **Timeline**, drag the clip from the **Viewer** and drop it on the **Fit to Fill** box.

The clip will immediately drop into the **Timeline**, and unless it is exactly the same size as the clip it's replacing, a red line will appear at the top of the **Timeline**. The red line indicates that the section of the **Timeline** needs to be rendered. This section needs to be rendered because of the speed change to *Food7*, which is now in slow motion to accommodate the **Fit to Fill** edit. The clip

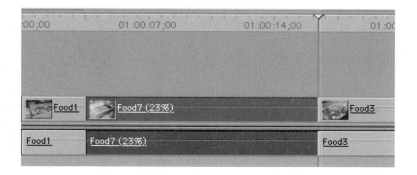

Figure 4.22   Slow Motion Clip in
the Timeline

in the timeline also shows the speed change, in this case, 23% of
real speed — pretty slow (Figure 4.22).

But that's not quite true. Let's check the speed.

3. Select the clip in the **Timeline** and hit **Command-J**, which
    calls up the **Speed** dialog box (Figure 4.23).

In this case the speed is 23.26%. Let's render this out to see what
it looks like.

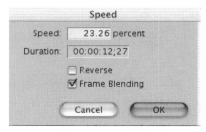

Figure 4.23   Speed Dialog Box

4. Close the dialog box, select the clip in the **Timeline**, and press
    Command-R for render.

You will quickly get the blue progress bar in Figure 4.24, showing
you how long it will take to render. Notice in this version of FCP,
for the first time you also get estimated time remaining information. Will there be time for a bathroom break? Maybe we could
fit lunch in.

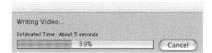

Figure 4.24   Render Progress
Bar

Fortunately Photo-JPEG renders quite quickly, especially on a fast
computer. When you play back the render, you'll probably notice
that the sound is also slomoed in addition to the picture. This
may be an interesting effect on some occasions, but it certainly
calls attention to itself and can be distracting for the audience.

Modify>Speed (**Command-J**) is where all clip speed changes are
made. It is unfortunately not possible to ramp speed up or down
so that it accelerates and decelerates.

Problems with Speed Changes

The real problem with speed changes is that it is difficult to create smooth motion, particularly at odd speeds such as 23.26%. This may not be noticeable using the small Photo-JPEG clips we're working with, but at full-size DV or other interlaced video, you can get some nasty stuttering effects, particularly if the clips are speeded up. In slow motion we get some unpleasant-looking artifacts because it becomes difficult for the application to make sensible intermediate frames. The program needs to extrapolate and create frames that don't exist and blend together at the correct frame rate of 29.97fps. It's better if you want to do slow or fast motion to use simple multiples: 50%, 150%, 25%, or 200%. These are much easier to calculate and generally produce better results. **Fit to Fill** calculates an absolute number and, as you can see, usually a bizarre one.

Interlaced video by its very nature does not handle speed changes well. Frame blending can help, but it will slow down render time. The default is to have **Frame Blending** turned on. With **Frame Blending** off, FCP merely duplicates or drops frames as necessary to make up the right speed, which can appear as juddering video. With **Frame Blending** on, FCP tries to create intermediary frames based on fields. However, if you speed up your video, **Frame Blending** can produce strange results — even with slow motion speeds greater than 50%. Extremely slow motion, under 20%, will also produce rather jerky output. All in all, you have a fairly small window for making decent slow motion without more sophisticated software than FCP can offer.

Rather than using **Fit to Fill**, if you do want to slow down or speed up a shot to fit a gap in your sequence, I recommend the following procedure:

1. Place the clip on the track above the gap you want to fill.

2. Use **Command-J** to change the speed, lengthening or shortening the clip as necessary, using a common increment such as 150%, 200%, 50%, or 25% so that it covers the gap.

3. Then trim the clip to fit the hole.

I think this will make the smoothest **Fit to Fill**, especially for interlaced video.

Tip

Changing to Slomo: When a speed change is done in a sequence, a ripple edit is performed, i.e., the contents of the **Timeline** shift, based on the new length of the clip. This is usually good, but sometimes you just don't want that to happen. If you're speeding up the material, the easiest way is to go to the head of the clip in the **Timeline** and double-click to open it into the **Viewer**. Use **Shift-F** to match back to the clip in the **Browser**. Mark an In point and use **Cmd-J** to call up the speed change dialog. Change the speed to say 200% and then **Overwrite** back into the **Timeline**, cutting away what's left of the clip that you don't need. If you're slowing down the material, it's slightly different. Here with the playhead in the **Timeline** at the start of the clip, double-click to bring it into the **Viewer**. Again use **Shift-F** to match back and then mark an In point. Execute the speed change, say to 50%, and now drag the clip to **Replace**. The slomo will be the duration of the clip it's replacing without rippling the sequence.

Superimpose

Superimpose doesn't work quite as I would like. I would have thought that it would work like **Overwrite** onto the track above. It works a bit like that, except it uses the **Replace** mindset. The clip you're superimposing has to be the duration of the clip you're placing it above. Simply positioning the playhead where you want the superimposition is not sufficient. So the easiest way I find to work with **Superimpose** is to define the In point in the **Timeline**, or simply drag the clip into the space above the clip you want to superimpose it on.

Let's ripple delete the middle shot of the three in the Timeline so that we're left with only *Food1* and *Food3*.

1. Place the playhead somewhere over the middle of the *Food3*.
2. Drag *Food5* from the **Browser** to the **Canvas** and drop it on the **Superimpose** box.
3. When the **Insufficient Content** dialog box appears, click **OK**.
4. Go to the **Timeline** and press **I** to mark an In point.
5. Go to the **Browser** and drag *Food5* to the **Superimpose** box.

The clip appears in the **Timeline** above the target track beginning at the marked In point as in Figure 4.25. Notice where the audio track has gone — not onto **A2**, which is empty — onto **A3**, the

 Note

Superimpose: There is often some misunderstanding about the term *superimpose*. In FCP it is used to mean simply placing a clip on the track above the currently targeted track. It does not mean what many people expect in the sense that the superimposed image will appear partially transparent and the underlying image will still be visible beneath it.

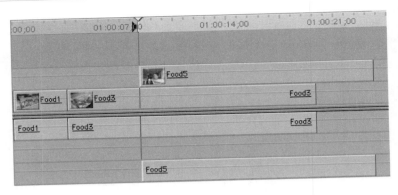

Figure 4.25 Superimposed Clip

track below the target track. Also notice that the In point marked in the **Timeline** remains. Normally when you perform an edit to a targeted track using a marked In point in the **Timeline**, the In point disappears after the edit is performed.

Note _____
Superimpose Effect: If you do a **Superimpose** edit onto a **Timeline** that already has a track above the target track, **Superimpose** will push the other tracks out of the way to make room for itself, as in Figure 4.26. It will not cut off a clip, like **Overwrite** or **Insert**.

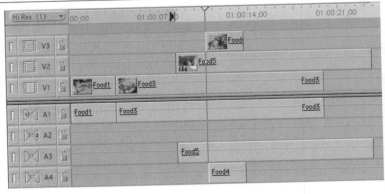

Figure 4.26 Superimposing after a Superimposition

Figure 4.27 All the Edit Buttons

Tip _____
Finding Buttons: If you like using the buttons at the bottom of the Canvas, you are not limited to the three normally visible. You can also have **Superimpose**, **Fit to Fill**, and the transition edits. Mouse down on the **Replace** button, and the others will appear as in Figure 4.27.

Let's Start Editing

Now that we've gone through the principal means of going from **Viewer** to **Canvas**, let's edit in the **Timeline** itself, trimming and adjusting the clips. We'll edit together a quickly paced, dynamic sequence of shots.

I like to begin by looking at the material I'm going to use for the sequence. The simplest way to do this is to lay everything out in shot order in the sequence.

1. Use **Command-A** in the **Timeline** and then **Delete** to remove everything you have there.

2. Set the **Browser** to In point list order by clicking on the **In** column.

3. Select the clips *Food1* through *Food8*, drag them onto the **Canvas**, and drop them on **Overwrite**.

4. Click on the **Timeline** window and press the **Home** key.

You're ready to start viewing. We're looking for movement and shots that can be cut together. Once I've looked at the clips in reel order, I then start looking at the clips individually, cutting them down to size and rearranging them.

Making a Sequence

Rather than working on the clips in the **Timeline**, let's start afresh with the first clip.

1. Again, delete everything in the **Timeline**.

2. Double-click on *Food1* in the **Browser** to open it into the **Viewer.**

3. Scrub through to the point where the camera starts moving from left to right.

4. Find the beginning of the movement and mark the In point.

5. Now find the end of the movement and mark the Out point. We can leave the shots a little loose at this stage.

6. After you've marked the In and Out points, drag the clip to **Overwrite** or press **F10**.

I'm not sure which part of the second shot, *Food2*, I'll use at this stage, but I'll probably use something.

1. Take *Food2* from just before the zoom starts and let it run almost to the end, leaving the hands turning the skewers.

2. Again **Overwrite** to the **Timeline**.

Food3 is a little more complex. I want to use more than one part of the shot.

1. Start by marking the In at the beginning of the shot.

2. Mark the Out just before the small pull back.

3. **Overwrite**.

Because the shot was loaded from the **Browser**, it is not the shot that I just placed in the **Timeline**. By putting the shot in the **Timeline**, I made a copy of the shot that's currently loaded in the **Viewer**. So now I can simply set new Ins and Outs without affecting what I've already done to the shot in the sequence.

1. Set a new In point just before the pan left begins.

2. Let the shot carry over to the steaming kettle, until about the 2:00:00 mark.

3. Add that to the **Timeline**.

4. Take a third section from that clip, from just before the camera tilts up until shortly before the shot ends.

Food4 is a very short shot, but it might fit nicely before the close-up of the steaming tray.

1. Position the **Timeline** playhead between *Food2* and *Food3* in sequence.

2. Drag the clip to **Insert** or use the shortcut **F9**.

Let's look at *Food5*. It's the most human part of the material, the little girl at the food stall. My thought is to use it as bookends: the little girl at the beginning of the sequence and at the end.

1. Make the first part of the shot one clip, basically until after she hands the vendor her money.

2. Make sure the playhead is at the start of the **Timeline**, then drag to **Insert**.

3. Make the second part of *Food5* begin shortly before the vendor reaches for the biscuit and let it go till just before the end.

4. Move the playhead to the end of the **Timeline**.

5. Drag the second half of *Food5* from the **Viewer** to **Overwrite**, or use **F10**.

We want *Food6* before the last shot.

1. Open up *Food6* in the **Viewer** and play it.

2. Start it near the beginning.

3. End it after the move with the biscuits, around 2:32:28.

4. In the **Timeline** the playhead is probably at the end of the material. Use the **Up** arrow to move backwards one edit.

5. Now drag the clip from **Viewer** to **Insert**, or use **F9**.

After looking at *Food7* again, I decided to drop it from the scene altogether. I want a short piece of *Food8* before the last shot.

1. Take the piece of the movement of the pan right of the steaming corn to the tray of roasted corn.

2. Insert it so it's before the last shot, as in the previous steps.

Editing the Sequence

The total duration of this little sequence should be roughly about 42 seconds, depending on how tightly you cut the shots. Looking through it, it's obvious it needs to be tightened up as well as have the order rearranged.

Swap Edit

Let's begin by pulling *Food8* from the end of the sequence and placing it as the second shot. This is called a *swap edit*.

1. Grab the shot and start to pull it along the timeline.

2. After you've started the movement, hold down the **Option** key.

 Tip

Timecode Location: To go to a specific timecode point in either the **Canvas**, the **Viewer**, or the **Timeline**, simply tap out the number on your keypad (in this case, **23228**) and press **Enter**. The playhead will immediately move to that point.

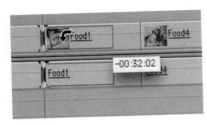

Figure 4.28 Swap Edit Option Drag Arrow

It has to be after you've started to move the clip while you're already in mouse-down mode. As you move, a downward hooked arrow appears on the clip (Figure 4.28).

3. When you get to the edit point between the first and second shot in the sequence, drop the clip.

If you look at the **Timeline**, you'll see that you've done an insert edit as well a ripple delete. You've removed the clip from one point on the timeline, placed it somewhere else in the timeline, and pushed everything out of the way to make room for it. This is a great hidden tool. I use it often. Also notice in Figure 4.28 the **32:02**. This shows how far in the sequence you've moved the clip: 32 seconds and two frames from its original position.

Once you've done this, you'll discover something unfortunate. Now we have two shots one after the other that pan from left to right. Sometimes it works —not very often. In this instance I think it looks dumb. Let's put *Food4* and the first *Food3* clip right after *Food8*. However, if you select both clips with a marquee drag and then drag them along the **Timeline**, you'll get the downward **Overwrite** arrow as in Figure 4.29. So don't do that.

1. If you hold down the **Option** key while dragging the two clips as you did earlier, you'll get the **Insert** edit arrow in Figure 4.30.

Unlike moving a single clip however, your **Option**-drag insert edit will not ripple delete as it did earlier. It will leave a hole in the sequence.

2. Hold down the **Control** key and click on the empty space.

3. Then select **Close Gap** as in Figure 4.31.

Figure 4.29 Overwrite Arrow when Dragging (Left)

Figure 4.30 Insert Arrow when Dragging (Right)

Figure 4.31 Close Gap Contextual Menu (Bottom Right)

Tip _____

Gaps and Syncing: FCP defines a gap as a space in the Timeline that extends across all tracks. So if you have a music track on **A3** and **A4**, for instance, FCP will not see the space between the shots on the video tracks as a gap. This is where the ability to lock tracks really helps. If you lock those music tracks, you can then close the gap. Or use **Option**-lock to lock all other tracks, and again you can close the gap.

Besides the contextual menu, there are two other ways to close a gap in the track:

• With the playhead over the gap, hit **Control-G**

• Click on it to select the gap and then hit the **Delete** key.

Be careful, though, with closing gaps like this. It can throw shots out of sync with elements on other tracks like music or narration tracks.

_____

There is another way to do this operation rather than **Option**-dragging the group of clips.

1. Select the clips.

2. Cut them with **Shift-X** instead of **Command-X**.

Shift-X performs a ripple delete instead of a simple lift edit that leaves a gap in the track. This not only cuts the clips out of the timeline, but also closes the gap the missing clips created.

3. Now go to wherever you want to place the clips and use **Shift-V**, which will paste the clips as an insert edit. **Command-V** would also paste, but as an overwrite edit.

Let's look through the sequence again. It's getting better, but there are still a few edits I don't like and quite a few shots that need trimming. We'll get to trimming in a moment, but let's rearrange a few more shots.

In the first shot, I like the way the camera moves around the girl at the beginning, and I like the way she hands over her money with her fingers splayed out. I don't care for the hesitation in the middle.

1. Double-click on the first shot in the sequence to bring it into the **Viewer**.

2. Scrub or play the shot until you find the point just after the camera finishes moving around the girl, about 2:12:09.

3. Press the **F** key.

This is the **Match Frame** key. It immediately moves the playhead in the **Timeline** to the frame that corresponds to the one on the **Viewer**, and displays the matching frame in the **Canvas**. It also makes the **Canvas** the active window so you can immediately use **Control-V** to slice the clip in the sequence. There are now two halves to the first shot in the sequence.

4. Open the second half in the **Viewer**. Find the point just before the vendor reaches his hand out for the money, about 2:13:19.

5. Repeat the process: Hit **F** and **Control-V**. You have now isolated the section you want to cut out.

6. Ripple delete it either by **Control**-clicking to call up the contextual menu or by selecting it and hitting **Shift-Delete**.

☞**Tip** _____
Moving the Playhead: Shift-Left or Right arrow will move the playhead forward or backward in one-second increments.

The F key is a very useful tool as a means of finding your place in the **Timeline**.

In the previous lesson, I showed you a simpler technique that would work well here. Undo all these steps that cut a section out of _Food5_, and we'll do the edit entire in the **Timeline** window.

1. Go to the head of the sequence and start to play it, stopping again just after the first camera move around the girl.

2. Press **I** to enter an In point in the **Timeline**, around 1:18.

3. Play until just before the vendor reaches for the money. Scrub the playhead if it's easier; use the **J, K,** and **L** keys, or the **Left** and **Right** arrow keys.

4. With the playhead at about 3:00, press **O** to enter an Out point in the **Timeline**.

5. Now do a ripple delete.

6. Press **Shift-Delete** to remove that short section of the shot.

Obviously the sequence now has a jump cut. So let's take the third shot in the sequence, the shot of the corn, _Food8_, and do an insert edit. Drag with **Option** to drop _Food8_ between the two halves of _Food5_ at the beginning of the sequence. The beginning of the **Timeline** should look like Figure 4.32.

As you go through the sequence, you'll see another jump cut between two parts of _Food3_. The camera pans right from the cooking tray to the steaming kettle and then in a separate shot

Figure 4.32 Food Sequence Beginning

tilts up from the kettle to the cook. I would remove the first of these shots, taking out the pan. I've seen that cooking tray already, but the kettle and the chef are new.

The arrangement is almost right, but there is a problem with the very last shot that I don't care for. Just after the vendor puts the biscuit in the bag, the camera jiggles. I'd like to remove this. So let's do this in the **Timeline**.

1. Scrub or play the **Timeline** to the frame when the biscuit just disappears into the bag behind the counter.

2. Use **Control-V** to split the clip.

Right after this the camera is jostled.

3. Move further down to where the vendor is about to reach forward with the bag, as his hands separate. This is about midway through *Food5*, the last shot in the sequence.

4. **Control-V** and ripple delete the middle portion.

Now we have the same problem we had in the first shot.

This time we're going to move *Food3* from its earlier position. This is the shot of the tilt from kettle to cook.

Jump Cuts

The sequence as we've laid it out so far has the most obvious form of jump cut, which is any abrupt edit that jars the viewer. This is generally considered a *faux pas*. The most common cause is placing side-by-side shots, such as the two halves of *Food5*, that are very similar, but not the same. You get this disconcerting little jump, as if you blacked out for a fraction of a second. It suddenly pulls the viewers out from the content of the video as they say to themselves, or perhaps even out loud, "What was that?" You can also get a jump cut if you put together two very different shots, such as the shot of a long street with the small figure of a person in the distance, cutting to a tight closeup. It's disorienting because the viewer has no reference that the close-up belongs to the person seen in the far distance in the previous shot. These are jump cuts. The general rule is to avoid them if you can. Or use them so often that it becomes your style. Then it's art.

5. Drag with **Option** and drop it between the two halves of
    Food5 that you just split.

If you look through the sequence, you'll see that the shots are in
the order we want, but we still need to tighten it up, trimming the
shots to make them faster paced.

Tip

Figure 4.33   Scaling Slider
              and Tabbed
              Slider

Timeline Scaling: You can change the scale of the Timeline to zoom in and
out with the tabbed slider at the bottom of the window. Pulling either end
of the tab will change the scale of the Timeline window. At the bottom left
is a little slider that will adjust the scale (Figure 4.33).

My personal favorite is to use the keyboard shortcuts **Command-=** (think
Command-+) to zoom in and **Command--** (that's **Command minus**) to
zoom out. What's nice about using the keyboard shortcuts is that it leaves the playhead centered in the Timeline
as you zoom in and out. Just be careful a clip isn't selected in the Timeline because the scaling will then take
place around that rather than around the playhead. Sometimes when you're in the **Viewer** or the **Canvas** window, you may want to scale the Timeline window. The easy way to do this without switching the active window
is to use **Option-+** or **Option--** to scale the Timeline window in and out. Using **Command-+** or **Command--**
would just scale the active window.

Figure 4.34   The Tools

The Trim Tools

The trim tools — **Roll** and **Ripple**, **Slip** and **Slide** — are among
the tools shown in Figure 4.34. The trim tools themselves are
clustered in the fourth and fifth buttons.

The first two trim tools, **Ripple** and **Roll**, change the duration of
clips, while the second two, **Slip** and **Slide**, leave the clip duration
intact.

A **Ripple** edit moves an edit point up and down the timeline by
pushing or pulling all the material on the track, shortening or
lengthening the whole sequence. In a ripple edit, only one clip
changes duration, getting longer or shorter. Everything else that
comes after it in the track adjusts to accommodate it.

A **Roll** edit moves an edit point up and down the timeline
between two adjacent shots. Only those two shots have their
durations changed. While one gets longer, the adjacent shot gets
shorter to accommodate it. The overall length of the track
remains unchanged.

A **Slip** edit changes the In and Out points of a single clip. The duration of the clip remains the same, and all the clips around it remain the same. Only the In and Out of the slipped clip change. If more frames are added on the front, the same amount are cut off the end, and vice versa, if some are added to the end, an equal amount are taken off the beginning.

A **Slide** edit moves a clip forward or backward along the timeline. The clip itself, its duration and In and Out points remain unchanged. Only its position on the timeline, earlier or later, shortens and lengthens the adjacent shots as it slides up and down the track.

The Ripple Tool

We're first going to work with the **Ripple** tool. Press the fourth button and extend the popout to select the tool as in Figure 4.35. You can also call it up by pressing **RR**; that's the **R** key twice.

Let's use it on some of the shots we want to work on. Start with the edit between shots *Food4* and *Food3*. Take the tool and place it near the edit. Notice it changes direction as you move it across the edit as in Figures 4.36 and 4.37.

When the tool is on the right side it will ripple the second shot; when it's on the left side it will ripple the first shot.

In this case, we want to ripple the second shot. The edit almost works, but it can perhaps be a little improved by tightening up. The hesitation at the beginning of *Food3* looks awkward. You can ripple right in the timeline. As you grab the clip, you will get a small two-up display in the **Canvas** as in Figure 4.38.

Figure 4.35 The Ripple Tool

Figure 4.36 Ripple Tool Right

Figure 4.37 Ripple Tool Left

Figure 4.38 Canvas Trim
Window

Notice the small triangle indicators between the two little windows, pointing away from each other. This is the indicator that the two-up display is in **Ripple** (or **Roll** or **Slide**) mode. You'll see a different indicator in a moment.

If you're going to be doing a lot of trimming, you can call up a separate **Trim Edit** window where you can work with the **Ripple** tool.

1. You open the **Trim Edit** window by moving the playhead to an edit point and using the menu **Sequence>Trim Edit** or the keyboard shortcut **Command-7**.

2. Place the **Ripple** tool on the **Trim Edit** window timeline at the edit point as in Figures 4.39.

3. Pull the edit point to the right. You'll notice that not only does the **Trim Edit** window display change, but also that the clip in the **Timeline** window is shortening, pulling up all the material behind it.

Figure 4.39 Trim Edit Window

You can also use the little plus and minus buttons at the bottom of the window to make incremental edits on either side of the **Trim Edit** window. You might also want to trim a little off the end of *Food4*. This is the place to do it, to fine tune your edit point.

The spacebar serves an interesting function in the **Trim Edit** window. It acts in play-around loop mode. It will play around the edit point again and again so you can view it repeatedly. Fine tune the edit as much as you can. It will never be a perfect match, but it can be made to look pretty good. Similarly fine tune the edit between *Food6* and the second appearance of *Food5*. Trim it so that as the vendor reaches for the biscuit in *Food6* around 2:29:24 it comes close to matching the girl reaching for a biscuit in *Food5* around 2:19:20.

There's a lot of useful timecode information at the top of the **Trim Edit** window (Figure 4.40):

- The center number under the track indicator is the current time in the sequence.

- The number to the far left is the duration of the outgoing shot, *Food6* in this case.

- The timecode between these is the Out point of the outgoing shot.

- On the far right of the window, the number is the current In point of the incoming shot, *Food5*.

- Finally, the number displayed between the In point and track indicator is the duration of the incoming shot.

A word of caution about rippling. If you're working with material that's cut to narration or music, rippling will easily upset the timing of the sequence, as it's pulling and pushing the entire track and its sync sound. So what's working for you at this moment in the edit, may be ruining something else further down the timeline. In these cases, the **Roll** tool may work better for you.

Tip
Working in Trim Edit: A really neat trick is to work with the J, K, and L keys in the **Trim Edit** window. Using either the **Ripple** tool or the **Roll** tool, which we'll see in a moment, the playback functions work perfectly as well as the I and O keys, allowing you to playback and input In and Out points on the fly. You switch to rippling either side of the edit point by clicking in either the left or right window. If you want to roll the edit point, click between the two windows. Once you get used to it, the **Trim Edit** window is an excellent way to work.

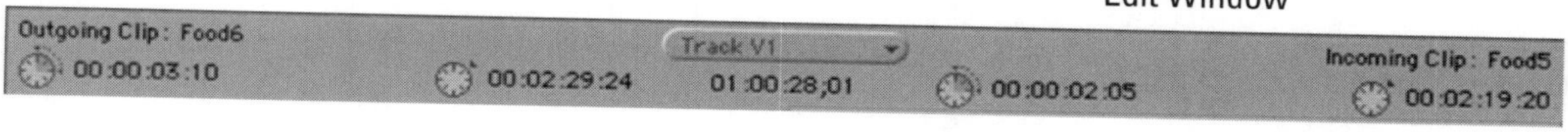

Figure 4.40   Timecode Displays in the Trim Edit Window

Outgoing Clip: Food6		Track V1			Incoming Clip: Food5
00:00:03:10	00:02:29:24	01:00:28,01	00:00:02:05		00:02:19:20

The Roll Tool

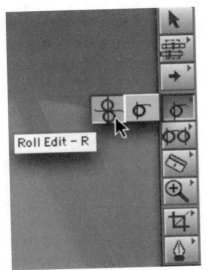

Figure 4.41   The Roll Tool

Figure 4.42   The Roll Tool in the
Timeline

The **Roll** tool is also under the fourth button in the tools as in Figures 4.41. In can be evoked with the **R** key. It works similarly to **Ripple**, also either in the **Trim Edit** window or in the timeline as in Figures 4.42.

The **Roll** tool acts on both shots, extending one shot while shortening the other. While the **Ripple** tool changes the enter length of the sequence by moving everything up and down the line, the **Roll** tool only affects the two adjacent shots. Generally I find the **Ripple** tool more practical than the **Roll** tool, but it's easy to switch back and forth between the two in the **Trim Edit** window. Notice in Figure 4.39 there is a bar across the top of the **Canvas** side. It's colored green in the application and indicates that you're in **Ripple** mode on the right clip. If you click on the space between the two windows, the bar will appear on both clips and you will now be in **Roll** mode. Clicking on the **Viewer** side will of course put you back in **Ripple** on the left clip.

You can toggle between the **Ripple** and **Roll** tools in the **Trim Edit** window with the **U** key. This can be very handy but is slightly deceptive because the cursor doesn't change, just the marking on the clip. Sometimes you want to change just one side of a cut; other times you want to change both sides. The **U** key cycles between **Ripple Left, Ripple Right,** and the **Roll tool.**

Using **Roll** and **Ripple,** tighten up some of the shots in the sequence. I rippled the zoom into the skewers in *Food2* until all you see are the hands turning over the sticks on the grill.

👉 **Tip**

Ripple and Roll Shortcuts: You can also use the **Ripple** and **Roll** tools incrementally with keyboard shortcuts in the Timeline. Select the edit point by moving the playhead over it and pressing the **V** key. Now, by using the **U** key, you can toggle through **Ripple Right, Ripple Left,** and **Roll.** Whichever edit you have selected, you can now move incremental with the less-than bracket < and the greater-than bracket >. (Actually, it's the comma and period, but most people think of it as < and >.) Each tap will move the edit one frame left or right in the direction the bracket is pointed. **Shift-<** and **Shift->** will move the edit whatever duration you have set for **Multi-Frame Trimming** in your **General Preferences.** This also works if you select a clip in the Timeline and chose either the **Slip** or **Slide** tools.

The Slip Tool

Let's look at **Slip** and **Slide** next. These work in the **Timeline** and the **Viewer** and do pretty much what their names imply. **Slip** is one of my favorite tools, though I'm not very keen on the display in Final Cut Pro. Select the **Slip** tool from the fifth button in the tools as in Figures 4.43. Call up the **Slip** tool with the **S** key.

Grab one of the clips in the sequence with the **Slip** tool and start moving it from side to side as in Figure 4.44. What you're doing is slipping the media for the clip up and down its length. The overall duration of the clip remains unchanged but the section of media for that duration is adjusted. The **Canvas** shows you a two-up display as in Figure 4.45.

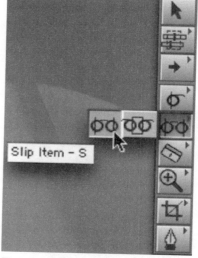

This is showing you the first and the last frames of the video. It will help you from slipping the clip too far into some unwanted material. If you're working in the Slice mode we discussed in the last lesson, you can see if you're slipping into the next shot. Also notice the small triangle indicators on the outer edges of the little frames. This indicates that the two-up display is in **Slip** mode.

It is also possible to slip in the **Viewer**, which can be especially beneficial when you're adjusting a clip before you bring it into the **Timeline**.

Figure 4.43   The Slip Tool

1. To slip in the **Viewer**, double-click the clip to load it into the **Viewer**.

2. Hold down the **Shift** key as you grab either the In point or the Out point and drag. This way you will drag both points together and maintain a constant duration (Figure 4.46).

This is **Slipping**, and what you see in the display is the start frame in the **Viewer** and the end frame in the **Canvas**. It doesn't matter which end you grab to pull, the display is always the same, start in the **Viewer**, end in the **Canvas**.

Figure 4.44   The Slip Tool in the Timeline (Above)

Figure 4.45   The Canvas Slip Display (Right)

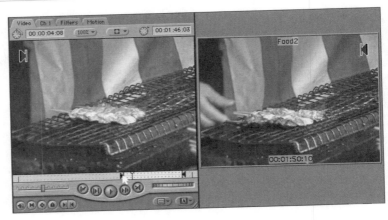

Figure 4.46 Slipping in the Viewer with the Canvas Display

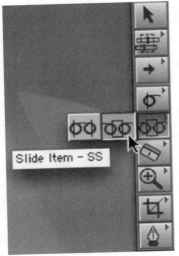

Figure 4.47 The Slide Tool

The Slide Tool

Let's look at the last trimming tool, the **Slide** tool, also in the fifth tools button (Figure 4.47). The **Slide** tool can be brought out with **SS** (S twice).

It also works only in the **Timeline** similarly to the **Slip** tool. The **Slide** tool doesn't change anything in the clip you're working on; it simply grabs the clip and pulls it forward or backward along the **Timeline**, wiping out material on one side, extending the material on the other side as in Figure 4.48.

Notice that you're not only moving the clip, you're also affecting the two adjacent clips, which is why they're highlighted with boxes in Figure 4.48.

The **Canvas** display (Figure 4.49) is similar to the **Slip** tool. You don't see the clip you're moving at all. What's displayed are the two adjacent shots:

- On the left, the end of the shot before the one you're moving

- On the right, the beginning of the shot after the one you're moving

Figure 4.48 The Slide Tool in the Timeline

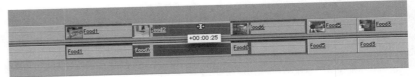

How Long is Long Enough?

A static shot, either close-up or medium shot, needs to be on the screen a much shorter time than a long shot in which the audience is following a movement. A shot that has been seen before, a repeat, can be on the screen quite briefly for the audience to get the information. Though there is no hard and fast rule, generally shots without dialog remain on the screen no more than six to eight seconds on television with its small screen. In feature films shots can be held for quite a bit longer because the viewer's eye simply has a lot more traveling to do to take in the full scope of the image. This is probably why movies seem much slower on the television screen than they do in the theater. While a close-up can be on the screen quite briefly, a long shot will often contain a great deal of information and needs to be held longer so that your viewer has time for his or her eye to rove around it. A moving shot, such as a pan, you can often hold longer because the audience is basically looking at two shots, one at the beginning and the other at the end. If the movement is well shot, a fairly brisk move, no more than about five seconds, you can also cut it quite tightly. All you need to show is a brief glimpse of the static shot, the movement, and then cut out as soon as the camera settles at the end of the move.

You are limited in how far you can slide a clip by the amount of media available in the adjacent shots. Notice in Figure 4.49 the right frame shows the telltale sprocket holes marking the end of the media. I have slipped the clip I'm moving as far to the left as I can, as early in time as I am able with the **Slide** tool. If you need to move the clip more, you'll have to use some other technique, perhaps dragging along the timeline to **Insert** or to **Overwrite**, perhaps placing it on the track above and sliding it along, but we're getting a bit ahead of ourselves.

Look at your finished sequence. It should look something like *Food Sequence* in the **Browser.** I still wouldn't be very happy with the piece, principally because the audio is so abrupt and choppy,

Figure 4.49   The Slide Tool
Canvas Display

marking each cut. Work would need to be done to smooth out the sound, perhaps extend sound from a single clip, or add some constant underlying sound from somewhere else. But that's for another lesson.

Summary

You've learned how to use the **Canvas** editing tools:

- Overwrite
- Insert
- Fit to Fill
- Replace
- Superimpose

You've learned how to use the various **Sequence** editing tools:

- **Roll** and **Ripple**
- **Slip** and **Slide**

When you want to smooth out cuts or to change between scenes, you might want to use transitions. That's what we're going to look at in the next lesson: lots and lots of transitions, how they work, and how to use them.

Lesson 5

Adding Transitions

Transitions can add life to a sequence, ease a difficult edit into something smoother, or give you a way to mark a change of time or place. The traditional grammar of film that audiences still accept is that dissolves denote small changes, while a fade to black followed by a fade from black mark a greater passage of time. With the introduction of digital effects, any imaginable movement or contortion of the image to replace one with another quickly became possible — and were quickly applied everywhere, seemingly randomly, to every possible edit. They can be hideously inappropriate, garish, and ugly. But to each his own taste. Transitions can be used effectively, or they can look terribly hackneyed. Final Cut Pro gives you the option to do either or anything in between. Let's look at the transitions FCP has to offer. There are quite a few of them, as well as some odd omissions.

Loading the Lesson

Let's begin by loading the material you need on the hard drive of your computer.

1. If you don't already have it on your media drive, drag the *Media1* folder from the CD to it. Again, this contains the media for the project.

2. You should also drag the folder called *Transitions* from the CD onto your media drive. This contains samples of each of the 76 transitions available in FCP3, including the new **FXScript DVE's**.

3. Also drag onto your system drive from the CD *Projects* folder the folder called *Lesson 5*. Put it in the *Shared* folder inside *Users*.

4. Eject the CD and open the *Lesson 5* folder on your hard drive.

5. Double-click the project file, *L5*, to launch FCP3.

6. Once again go through the reconnect process as in the previous "Loading the Lesson" on page 143 in Lesson 4.

Setting up the Project

1. Again, the first step you should take after your project has reconnected is to use **Save Project As** from the **File** menu and save the project with a new name inside the *Lesson 5* folder on your internal hard drive.

This ensures that if something goes wrong with your project or, or you accidentally delete an element, you can easily open the original project and drag that element into your working project. You should also make sure to assign the scratch disk.

2. Go to **Final Cut Pro>Preferences (Option-Q)**.

3. Click on the **Scratch Disks** tab.

4. Click on the **Set** button and navigate to the hard drive that holds the *Media1* folder.

5. Click on the *Media1* folder to highlight it and then click on button marked **Choose** as in Figure 5.1.

6. Also in the **Scratch Disks** panel, make sure your *Autosave Vault* is set to the *Shared* folder.

Remember to do this each time you move between projects.

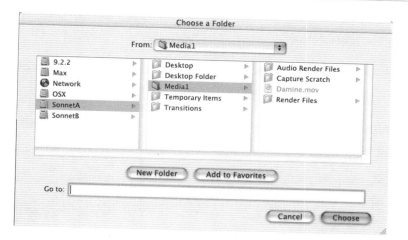

Figure 5.1   Scratch Disk Navigation Menu

Inside your copy of the project *L5* you'll find in the **Browser**:

- An empty sequence called *Sequence 1*
- The master clip *Damine.mov*
- A still image called *Gradient.pct*, which we'll use later
- The bin called **Clips**
- The bin called **Transitions**

Last time we worked with the food clips. This time we'll be working with a different section of the master clip. When you open the **Clips** bin, you'll see most of the shots from *Damine.mov* diced into subclips so that each clip is self-contained, as in the previous lesson.

Applying Transitions

Next let's look at the transitions themselves. In the **Browser**, usually behind the **Project** window, is a tab called **Effects**. If you open it, you see a window with a group of folders — sorry, bins — as in Figure 5.2. You'll notice more than transitions in this window. For the moment, we're going to concentrate on the **Video Transitions** bin.

This window does not maintain strict interface standards: for some reason, the **Name** column does not force alphanumeric ordering. The order is created internally in FCP, and the first bin is **Favorites**. You can park your special transitions and effects here. It's probably empty now.

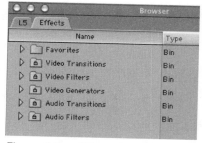

Figure 5.2   Effects Window

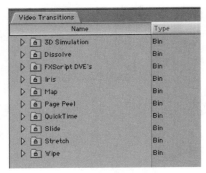

Figure 5.3   Video Transitions
Window

Double-click on **Video Transitions** to open the bin. It should look like Figure 5.3. The **Video Transitions** window shows yet more bins, and these bins contain a total of 76 video transitions. I'd be very surprised if any one has actually ever used them all in earnest on real projects, not just playing with them to try them out. The **Transitions** bin in your **Browser** contains previews of each of the transitions available in FCP3. We're going to try them out in this lesson, but first let's see how the **Favorites** bin works.

Note

If your **Video Transitions** bin is missing the **FXScript DVE's** bin, you will need to go back to your install CD and load it. Quit the application first. Load the install CD and run the FCP installer or upgrade. When you get to the **Software Selection** window, check the **FXScript DVE's from CGM** box and click the **Continue** button (Figure 5.4). This will load the FXScript DVE's into the appropriate folder of your system.

Favorite Transitions

Twirl open **Dissolves**, which holds seven different types of dissolves. Who would have thought there were so many ways to do a dissolve?

1. Grab the most commonly used transition in video or film, the **Cross Dissolve**, and drag and drop the transition over to the **Favorites** bin.

Figure 5.4   Installing FXScript
DVE's

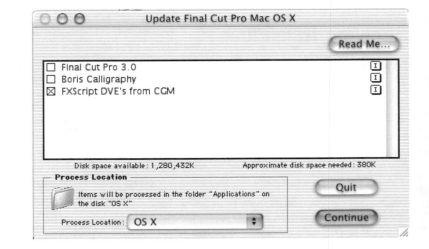

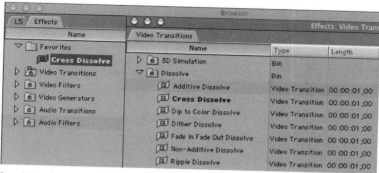

Figure 5.5   Favorites Bin

2. Twirl open **Favorites** as in Figure 5.5.

You may notice that the transition in the **Favorites** bin is a dupli-cate. The usual behavior when moving items from one bin to another is that the item is relocated. But when moving an element to **Favorites**, a copy is created. You can put any transitions, video or audio; any effect; or even a generator into **Favorites**. Though multiple types of items can be placed into this bin, only the appropriate items will appear in the **Effects** menu below **Video Transitions** in **Favorites**, as in Figure 5.6. You can rename the transition or effect anything you want, so perhaps you'd like to keep handy an eight-frame dissolve. Just copy **Cross Dissolve** in **Favorites**. Change its name to something like **8Frames**, and then change its duration to your favorite length.

Notice in Figure 5.6 that below the **Favorites** menu item that's selected is the default effect, in this case, **Cross Dissolve**. It's sim-ple to set the default transition. You can either set it with the menus or by the selecting the transition in the **Video Transitions** bin, and choosing **Set Default** from the **Effects** menu.

You can also do this directly to a transition with the contextual menu.

1. In **Video Transitions**, select the transition you want to desig-nate as default.

2. Hold down the **Control** key.

3. In the menu select **Set Default Transition** as in Figure 5.7.

> **Note**
>
> **Real-time Transitions:** Whenever a transition's name appears in bold in either the **Video Transitions** folder or in a menu, that indicates that the transition can be played back in real-time. These transitions only appear like this if your system is capable of real-time preview.

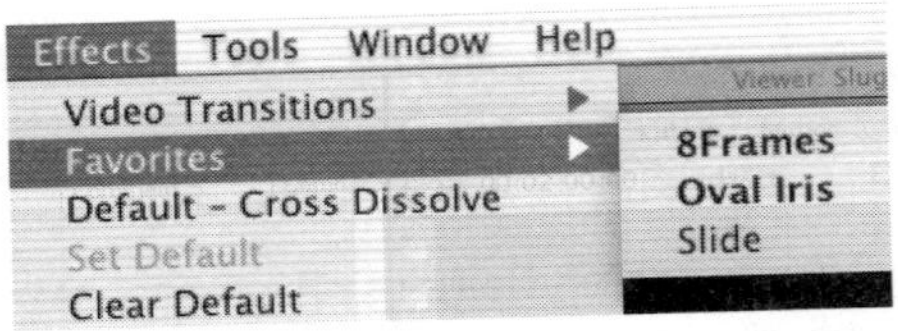

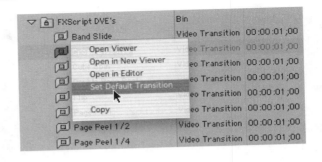

Figure 5.6   Video Transition Favorites Menu

Figure 5.7   Set Default Transition

👉 Tip

Saving Favorites: Remember that **Favorites** are saved as part of your preferences. If you trash your **Prefer-ences** file, your **Favorites** go with it. There is a simple solution to this. Drag the **Favorites** bin from the **Effects** panel and place it in your **Browser**. This is a copy of the **Favorites** bin in **Effects**, and will remain with the project, even if the prefs are trashed. I simply use the **Browser** bin as my **Favorites** bin, and move it from project to project whenever I like, as well as backing it up on a Zip disk.

After the default transition is set, it will appear underlined in the bin.

In Figure 5.7 you'll see that all the transitions are set with a duration of one second. This is the default duration for all transitions in Final Cut Pro. You can set any duration you want in the **Transitions** bin, and that will be the default duration for that transition.

So what's all this about default transitions? In the last lesson we skipped two items in the **Canvas Edit Overlay**:

- **Insert with Transition**

- **Overwrite with Transition**

The default transition sets the transition that will appear in your sequence when you select **Insert with Transition** (**Shift-F9**) or **Overwrite with Transition** (**Shift-F10.**)

Checking the Media

1. Let's begin by opening up *Sequence 1*.

2. Next select the three clips at the bottom of the **Clips** bin called *Village* and drag them directly to the sequence.

Remember these are all subclips, and so each shot you just placed in the timeline contains the full extent of the media for that clip on the hard drive. Or at least Final Cut Pro thinks so.

Let's try putting a transition onto the sequence we've laid out, the three *Village* shots.

3. Grab the **Cross Dissolve** transition from either the **Dissolve** bin or from **Favorites** and drag it onto the edit point between *Village1* and *Village2*.

You see that this isn't possible because you get the transition drag icon with a small **X** as in Figure 5.8. Why is this happening? The answer is simple. There isn't enough media in either clip to perform the transition. The shots must overlap; frames from both shots must appear on the screen simultaneously. For a one-second transition, both shots have to have one second of media that overlaps with the other shot (Figure 5.9).

The pale shot on the left has to overlap the dark shot on the right by half the length of the transition, and vice versa. If that media does not exist, you can't do the transition. FCP always assumes as a default that the transition takes place centered around the marked edit point, not that it ends at the edit point. Therefore, to

Tip

Quick Transition: The quickest way to add a transition to an edit is to go to the edit point, park the playhead over it, and hit **Command-T**. This will add the default transition with the default duration.

Figure 5.8   Transition Error

Figure 5.9   Overlapping Video

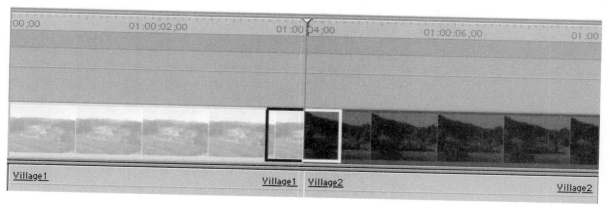

execute the default one-second transition, you need at least half a second, 15 frames, of available media after the Out point on the outgoing shot, and 15 frames in front of the In point of the incoming shot. In this case there is nothing, hence the **X**. Unless you think of it ahead of time, which many times you don't, you'll have to deal with it when you're fine tuning your edit. Often you'd rather not deal with transitions while you're laying out your sequence, leaving them until you've laid out the shot order.

If you know you have extra media in the original clip, you can always go back to extend the media. If this option is available, it's easy to do in FCP. Select **Remove Subclip Limits** from the **Modify** menu (Figure 5.10).

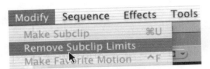

Figure 5.10 Remove Subclip Limits from the Modify Menu

However, in this case, extending the media will extend it into another shot, producing a flash frame during the transition, something to be avoided. To be able to put in transitions, we'll have to trim the Out point on *Village1* and the In point of *Village2*. Let's do that in the **Trim Edit** window.

1. Navigate to the edit point between *Village1* and *Village2* using the **Up** or **Down** arrow keys.

2. Hit **Command-7** to call up the **Trim Edit** window, which appears in **Roll** mode.

3. Click in the left hand window to bring up the **Ripple** tool (or use the U key to cycle through the window's tools).

4. With the left window active, type in *–15* for 15 frames and enter it.

We know this is the navigation shortcut for going backward half a second. Because we're in the **Ripple** tool, we're not only going back one-half second on *Village1*, we're rippling it backwards one-half second.

5. Next click on the right window (or use U to get to the **Ripple Right** tool activating the right window) and type in *+15* and **Enter** (or **Return**).

Figure 5.11   Rippled Trim Edit
Window

We've now rippled *Village2's* In point by half a second, half a second off the end of the first shot, half a second off the beginning of the second. Figure 5.11 shows the **Trim Edit** window after the two shots have been rippled.

Over these three shots, if I ripple the Ins and Outs on both edits in the **Timeline**, taking 15 frames off the end and the beginning of each shot, I reduce the overall duration by two seconds. This will substantially change the timing of my sequence. If you plan to use transitions between shots, it's best to allow for the extra material within the shot before you lay it in the timeline.

6. Once you've rippled the two edits, go the edit point in the sequence between *Village1* and *Village2*.

7. From the menus, select **Effects>Video Transitions> Dissolve>Cross Dissolve** (Figure 5.12). Notice that **Cross Dissolve** is bold, indicating that this computer is capable of some real-time transitions, at least real-time preview of transitions.

Tip

Trim Edit Shortcut: In the **Trim Edit** window, you could also use the little –5 and +5 buttons to shift the In and Out points. When you're rippling left, click three times on the –5 button (**Shift-[**). When you're rippling right, click three times on the +5 button (**Shift-]**) if you prefer not to type in the numbers. If you don't see the number 5 on the little buttons, it's because you have changed your **Multi-Frame Trim Size** in the **General** preferences.

Figure 5.12 Effects>Video Transitions>Dissolve > Cross Dissolve

Note

Insufficient Overlap: If you only have video available for the transition overlap on one side of the edit, you can drag a transition from the **Effects** bin and place it on that side. If you try to execute the transition from the menu or with **Command-T**, it will always execute the default centered on transition edit. If one of the shots does not have enough material to do a centered on edit transitions, what will happen is that you'll get a one frame-transition. Personally I'd prefer if FCP threw up the usual insufficient content error message rather than doing the one-frame transition. Just be careful, because it may seem that a transition has been entered into your sequence when there really isn't anything there of value.

This adds a cross dissolve transition to the edit point. You can also go to the **Transitions** bin, either from the **Dissolves** bin or from **Favorites**, and drag and drop the transition onto the edit point. The transition does not need to be dragged only to the center line. It can also be dragged to the out clip so that the transition ends at the edit point, or to the in clip so the transition begins at the start of the clip. This can only be done, of course, if there is sufficient material for this type of transition.

If you double-click on the transition itself in the **Timeline**, it will open into the **Viewer**. This is the **Transition Editor**, which we'll look at in detail in a moment. Here you can see how the video overlaps and why extra material — handles — are needed on either end of the transition to create the effect (Figure 5.13).

Once it's in the **Timeline**, the transition displays in one of three ways, depending on how it was placed. Figure 5.14 shows the center position; the other two appear as in Figures 5.15 and 5.16.

Notice the sloping line indicators showing the type of alignment in each case, and also note that the two latter transitions can only be half-second dissolves. When the sequence was rippled by 15 frames on each side of the edit point, only enough media was made available for a center-aligned transition. If the transition is to end on the edit point, the incoming shot has to be extended a whole second underneath the outgoing shot to accommodate it.

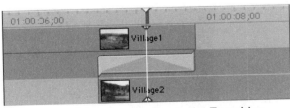

Figure 5.13 Clips Overlapping in the Transition Editor

Figure 5.14 Center on Edit Transition

Figure 5.15   End on Edit Transition

Figure 5.16   Start on Edit Transition

Similarly, if you wanted to start the transition on the edit point, the outgoing shot has to extend one second into the incoming shot, one second beyond the start of the edit point. If we made these changes, then we could also easily change the type of transition alignment with a control contextual menu on the transition in the **Timeline** (Figure 5.17).

Using the Canvas Edit Overlay

Let's back up a bit to see a better way to do this.

1. Delete everything in the **Timeline**.

2. Open up *Village1* from the **Browser** into the **Viewer**.

Because this will be the first shot in the timeline, I won't need to shorten the front of the clip.

3. Hit the **End** key or the **Down** arrow to take you to the end of the shot.

4. Type *−1.* (minus one period) and enter. This will move the playhead back one second.

5. Press **O** to enter the Out point and drag to the **CEO Overwrite** box, or hit **F10** to overwrite it into the **Timeline**.

6. Open *Village2* in the **Viewer** from the **Browser**. This clip we should shorten front and end.

Figure 5.17   Transition Contextual Menu

7. Go to the beginning of the clip and type *+1.* and enter an In point.

8. Then go to the end of the clip and enter an Out point one second before the end (type *−1.* and press **O**).

9. Drag *Village2* from the **Viewer** to **Overwrite with Transition** as in Figure 5.18 — not to **Overwrite**. Or enter **Shift-F10**.

The clip immediately drops into the **Timeline** after the first clip. The default transition has been added at the beginning of the clip, as well as a default audio crossfade. Adding the audio crossfade is a bonus that enhances the edit and helps to smooth the transition.

Contextual Menu Transition

A third method can be used to add the default transition.

1. **Control**-click on an edit point as in Figure 5.18.

2. Select **Add Transition**.

This procedure will evoke the default transition type and default duration, if sufficient media is available in the clips. If not, FCP will make a transition of whatever length is available. If no media is available, no transition will be created. If media is available only on one shot, the transition will be created offset on one side or the other. The contextual menu transition will also add the audio crossfade.

Rendering

Now we need to discuss rendering. In adding your transition to your sequence, you may have encountered the need for rendering for the first time. After you've entered a transition, you'll see that the narrow bar at the top of the **Timeline** has changed color from the normal mid-gray. It will have changed to red or green, depending on your system capabilities. If you are working with a system with no real-time capabilities, then a bright red line will appear over the transition, indicating that a portion of the sequence needs to be rendered (Figure 5.20).

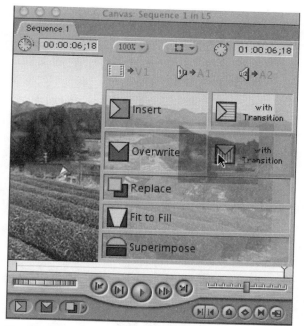

Figure 5.18   Overwrite with Transition

Figure 5.19   Transition Context Menu

Figure 5.20   Render Bar

I've circled the red bar because the grayscale image doesn't show it clearly. If your system were capable of real-time transitions, this bar would appear green. Real-time transitions will be highlighted in bold in your bins and in the menu. All other transitions will need to be rendered out.

Rendering means that the application has to create media for which none exists. Most of the two shots are on your hard drive, but not for the 30 frames that make up this one-second cross dissolve, during which one shot is changing into the other. The material of one shot mixed together with another is not on your hard drive. All you've done is give the computer instructions to create that media. If you try to play across that part of the timeline with a non–real-time system, the **Canvas** will momentarily display the message in Figure 5.21.

If you have a real-time capabilities, Final Cut can play through the timeline without prior rendering. It processes the transition on the fly in real time as it plays.

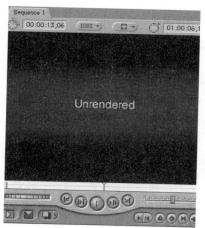

Figure 5.21   Unrendered Warning

Real-time Preview

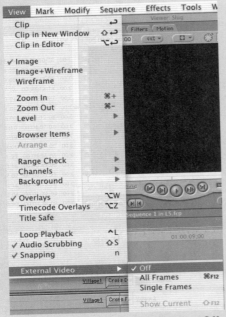

Figure 5.22   View>External Video>Off

Using FCP's real-time capabilities, real-time preview is only available on the desktop and only available when using DV material or OfflineRT material. (Some Motion-JPEG boards will do this as well through their hardware support.) FCP's real time can only be seen in the **Canvas** and only when the external viewing is switched off. It will not send a real-time DV signal out the FireWire cable. So you have a choice: either monitor through FireWire but not in real time, or monitor on your desktop screen. There is a third choice: to use a video card such as the ATI Radeon card that will output your video through an S-video cable.

So if you think you have real-time capabilities and you're still seeing a red line in your sequence, it's probably because you have **External Viewing** turn on. You can switch it off from the **View** menu, right down at the bottom the selection **External Video** (Figure 5.22). Fortunately there is a keyboard shortcut that will quickly toggle this on and off: **Command-F12.**

Remember, this is real-time preview only. As soon as you revert to viewing your video externally or you want to output your material to tape, all those items that were in real time on your desktop a moment ago now have to be rendered out.

Aside from the real-time effects, there are also the so-called **Proxy Effects**. These effects have a yellow rather than red or green render bar. A **Proxy Effect** is one that plays in real time but only as an approximation of the full effect; some of its controls and features will not be included in real time. There are many ways to render out these various effects. Unfortunately, Apple has made this process far more complex than is necessary. The various render commands are shown in Table 5.1.

Table 5.1   **Render Commands**

Render All	Option-R	Render Real Time Effects	Control-R
Render Selection	Command-R	Render Proxy Effects	Command-Option-R
Render In to Out	Command-R (yes, the same shortcut)	Mixdown Audio	Command-Option-R (yes, it's the same)
Render nonRT Effects	Command-R (one more time)		

FCP3 has introduced a new tool that allows you to see quickly material needing to be rendered before rendering. This is the **QuickView** window, called up from the **Tools** menu (Figure 5.23). The window allows you to play through a section of video by building a cache file in RAM. The more RAM you have available, the more the application will able to store.

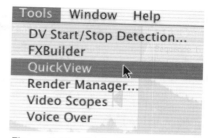

Figure 5.23   Tools>QuickView

There's only one button on the window, a **Play** button (Figure 5.24). Click to play; click to stop. Of course, you can also use the spacebar. No J, K, and L keys however. There is only one direction and one speed, forward and looping. The **QuickView** window is like the Energizer bunny: it just keeps playing and playing, trying to cache as much as it can with any available RAM, until you press the spacebar to stop it. With the window set to **Auto** (in the **View** popup menu at the upper right), it will keep doing RAM previews of whatever is in the active window. Switch to the **Timeline**, and it will start previewing around the position of the playhead. Switch to the **Viewer**, and it will start playing that. The little popup also allows you to designate a screen to preview: **Canvas, Viewer,** or **None** (Figure 5.25). I don't know why there is a **None** option, to be honest.

Figure 5.24   QuickView Window

The popup in the upper left **Resolution** does just that: sets the resolution of playback to **Full, Half,** or **Quarter** (Figure 5.26). The lower the resolution, the more you'll be able to preview, but the poorer the quality. The default duration for **QuickView** is two seconds, which is ideal for checking one-second transitions. To increase the amount of time previewed, use the **Range** slider at the bottom of the window. It goes up to 10 seconds. If you do increase the range to its maximum and you don't have enough RAM to hold 10 seconds of video as well as do the processing, **QuickView** will never be able to get the preview up to speed. It will always be dumping cached frames to pick up new ones. So either reduce the range or reduce the resolution.

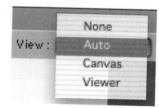

Figure 5.25   View Popup

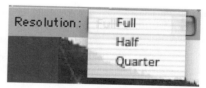

Figure 5.26   Resolution Popup

Render Settings

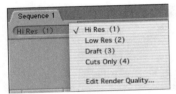

Figure 5.27 **Render Settings Menu**

Rendering is still a key component of most work in FCP, so let's look at the options available. The **Render Settings** button in the upper left corner of the **Timeline** window opens a contextual menu, as in Figure 5.27. The settings are:

- **Hi Res**
- **Low Res**
- **Draft**
- **Cuts Only**

Each of these can be changed to whatever you find most comfortable to work with. Inevitably, you balance between speed and quality. For simple transitions on a fast computer with spare drive space, it may be just as easy to work always at **Hi Res.** If you're going to be doing a lot of effects work, and you really only need to get rough previews of what you doing, one of the other settings might be suitable. You can change them by selecting **Edit Render Quality** in the contextual menu to bring up the tabbed window shown in Figure 5.28. It allows you to change the settings for each of the preset resolutions.

The **Hi Res** window is your final output quality, full frame rate, and full resolution. I'd advise against changing this from its maximum settings.

Look at the checkboxes. **Draft Render** lets you speed up the render process by rendering transitions (or effects) at the lowest

Figure 5.28 Hi Res Render
Quality Editor

quality. It won't look as good, but the process will be faster. Be sure to switch off **Draft Render** before you record to tape.

For most purposes, **Field Rendering** should be turned on for final output for any interlaced video. Separate fields that combine to create a single frame is what gives video its sharp temporal resolution. You're really dividing up a second into 60 slices, rather than 30 slices if fields are switched off, or the 24 slices of film. Each frame of video with moving objects looks sharper and crisper. Again, you can switch this off to speed up the render process.

Turning on **Motion Blur** will only affect clips that have motion applied to them — scaling, rotation, position, which we shall look at in Lesson 9, "Motion Window" on page 364. Switching it off will speed up rendering, but also produces unsmooth movements. If no motion has been applied to the clip, **Motion Blur** will have no effect.

The **Include Filters** checkbox is pretty obvious. Again, you can switch these off. Having to render filters in long clips can be time consuming. Being able to switch off **Filter Rendering** means clips will appear without the filter and play straight through, even though a filter has been applied. You just won't see it. With **Include Filters** unchecked, you not only won't see filters during playback, you also won't see them when the playhead is stopped. The **Canvas** will not update to show the filter effects.

Enabling **Frame Blending**, as we saw in Lesson 4's "Problems with Speed Changes" on page 158, will improve the appearance of speed changes, but will have a substantial impact on render times. **Frame Blending** takes quite a bit longer to calculate than simply dropping or adding frames. Switching it off will, of course, speed up the process.

Play Base Layer Only does exactly what it says. You can apply multiple layers to a sequence — effects and transitions, to your heart's content — making it necessary for everything to be rendered, turning the bar in the whole **Timeline** bright red. However, with this box checked, everything will play back smoothly. It will just play back without any effects, transitions, or motion appearing in the **Canvas**. Unlike the **Include Filter** checkbox, here the frame in the **Canvas** will update to show your filters and transitions correctly rendered out, as soon as you stop playing.

Figure 5.29   Low Res Render Quality Editor

The **High Quality Playback (Slower)** option is an interesting tool. Normally the DV display in the **Canvas** is low quality, not best. This allows for smoother playback and less chance of dropped frames. With this option checked, the **Canvas** display will be at highest quality, which can be useful for compositing, but it greatly increases the probability of getting dropped frames during playback, or getting slowdown playback. This checkbox only affects DV, not any Motion-JPEG system.

The two popups allow you to control the frame rate of the playback and image resolution. Reducing the levels from 100% will speed up rendering as well.

Though you should probably leave **Hi Res** untouched, the **Low Res** window (Figure 5.29), on the other hand, gives you the opportunity for some flexibility. **Low Res** defaults to using full frame rate but half resolution. This is a good setting for quick checking of your work if you have a fast computer. The full frame rate playback means you need to render out each of the 30 frames in the transition.

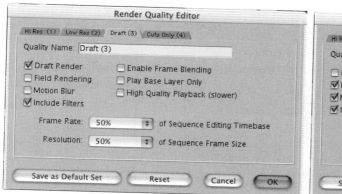

Figure 5.30   Draft Render Quality Editor

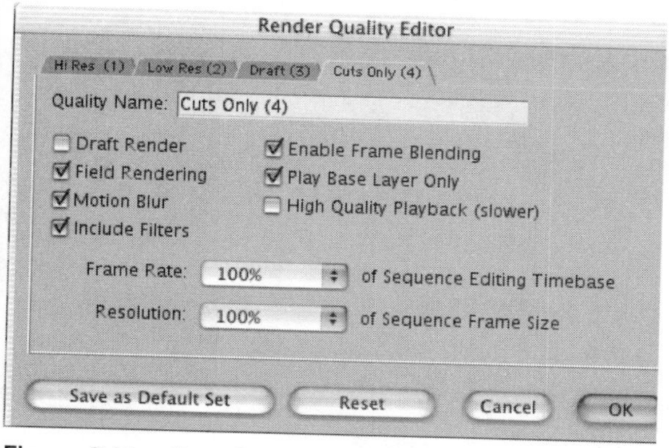

Figure 5.31   Cuts Only Render Editor

Draft, however, (Figure 5.30) works well for older machines because it halves the number of frames needed to play back.

Cuts Only setting (Figure 5.31) looks impressive, full resolution, full frame rate, very much like the **Hi Res** setting. The trick is in the checkbox marked **Play Base Layer Only.**

This is an excellent way to work if you're dealing only with a few transitions and titles. It allows you to edit quickly, without breaking up the work flow with pauses for rendering. When your session is complete, or it's time for a break, simply switch to **Hi Res** and let the computer do its thing.

There are two simple ways to render material in Final Cut Pro:

- Select the element or elements you want to render and press **Command-R** or

- Press **Option-R** and FCP will render everything it has to render, starting at the beginning of the sequence, using the render setting you have selected.

If nothing is selected, **Command-R** will work as **Option-R.** While rendering, FCP will display the window we saw in the last lesson when we did **Fit to Fill.**

✎ Note

Change Render Settings: Changing render settings of sequences that have material already rendered will mark the sections that need rendering as unrendered. This happens because FCP saves different render settings separately from each other. So if you render material at **High Res** and then change to **Draft**, all your transitions will appear with a red bar. However, when you change back to **High Res**, the bars disappear because FCP knows that it already holds rendered media at the higher resolution.

Render Manager

The **Render Manager** is in the menus under **Tools>Render Manager**. This feature lets you selectively delete unwanted or old render files from your hard drive. What's nice about the **Render Manager** is that you can delete files not only from the project you're working on at the moment, but also from any other projects on any of your hard drives. (Figure 5.32).

It's simple to delete files. Check in the **Remove** column the items you wanted deleted and press **OK** or the **Enter** key. It's good practice to go through the **Render Manager** periodically to weed out old render files. You might find some lingering items you'd long forgotten. It's probably a good idea to check through the **Render Manager** about every month or so.

Figure 5.32 Render Manager Window

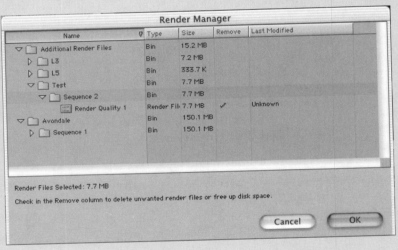

Tip

Entering Ins & Outs: You can also enter In and Out points in the Timeline, then FCP will on **Command-R** only render what needs to be rendered in the marked portion of the sequence between the In and Out points.

The render bar shows your render progress while it's writing the media to your hard drive. You can stop the render process at any time with the **Cancel** button or by pressing **Command-.** (period). If you interrupt the render part way through, none of what you've already rendered will be lost. When you resume rendering, FCP will continue where it left off. This switching on and off during renders can lead to disk fragmentation however, so avoid it when possible.

Figure 5.33   Lengthening Transition in the Timeline

Figure 5.34   Two-Up Display in Canvas

Controlling Transitions

Once you've played back your transition a few times in **Quick-View,** you may discover that it doesn't look quite the way you'd want it to. You may want to shorten or lengthen it or shift the actual edit point. Assuming you have material available for this, it is easiest to do in the **Timeline** itself. To change the duration of the transition, simply grab one end of it and pull, as in Figure 5.33. It's a good idea to switch **Snapping** off before you do this, because it's easy to snap the transition down to nothing. As you pull the transition, a little window displays the amount of change as well as the new duration of the transition. If you have an audio crossfade as well as a transition, that will also change with your action. While you're dragging the transition end, you'll get the two-up display in the **Canvas** that shows you the frames at the edit point (Figure 5.34). Notice the tell-tale film sprocket holes on the right edge of the frame. While extending the transition, I reached the limits of media available to one shot. When you're extending a transition, however, you can force it to extend beyond the media. The transition simply becomes offset and jumps rather than changing smoothly from one shot to the other.

You can also change the edit point in the center of the transition. Simply move the **Selector** to the center of the edit, and it will immediately change to the **Roll** tool, allowing you to move the edit point, together with the transition along the **Timeline,** left and right as desired (Figure 5.35). You can also ripple either shot, but to do that you have to call up the **Ripple** tool (**RR**) and then pull either shot left or right, shortening or lengthening the sequence while not affecting the transition (Figure 5.36). Again, the two-up display in the **Canvas** will show you the frames you're working on.

Figure 5.35 Rolling the Transition Edit Point

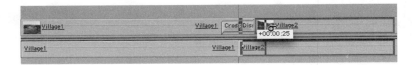

Figure 5.36 Rippling the Transition Edit Point

Transition Editor

Final Cut gives you another way to control the transition and fine tune it. This is done in the **Transition Editor** (Figure 5.37, bottom), which we saw briefly earlier.

Double-click on the transition itself in the **Timeline** window to evoke the **Transition Edit** window. It opens in the **Viewer**. The **Viewer** displays the transition as a separate track between the two video tracks on which the clips sit. This is a conventional display in systems such as Premiere and Media100.

The **Transition Edit** window allows you to control the transition. At the top is a small group of buttons (Figure 5.38) that let you position where the transition will occur. The transition will be placed in the default centered position between the two clips, shown by the middle button in Figure 5.38. Using the left button moves the transition so that it begins at the edit point. The right button in moves the transition so that it ends at the edit point.

Figure 5.38 Transition Buttons

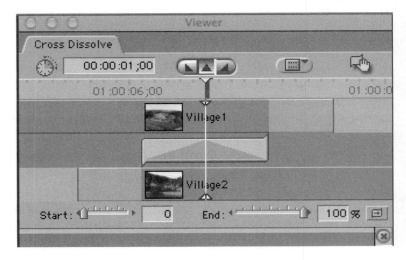

Figure 5.37 The Transition Edit Window

The primary purpose of the **Transition Edit** window is to access the controls some transitions offer you. Here you can also fine tune the effect, to shorten or lengthen it as needed. As in the **Timeline**, you can do this by dragging either end of the transition. The **Canvas** displays the end and start frames for the two shots.

By grabbing the center of the transition, you evoke the **Roll** tool, which allows you to drag the transition forward and backward along the clips, provided there is available media.

You can also ripple edit either the end of either outgoing or incoming clip by pulling it (Figure 5.39). You don't have to call up the **Ripple** tool. Simply by moving the cursor into position, it will change to the appropriate tool. Different shades of blue indicate the limits of the media. As with all ripple edits, you are changing the duration of the tracks involved and may be pulling the alignment of clips on different tracks out of kilter.

Notice in the **Transition Edit** window the two sliders, one for Start and the other for End, each with percentage boxes adjacent. The transition starts at zero percent completed and ends at 100 percent completion. You can adjust these sliders so that the **Cross Dissolve** will pop in at more than zero to start or suddenly finish before the transition reaches completion. In **Cross Dissolve** this produces a rather ugly effect. There is also a small arrow button to the right of the End slider. This will swap the effect for you.

Tip

Alignment Shortcuts: You can switch between the three transition alignment types with keyboard shortcuts. **Option-1** sets to begin at the edit point, **Option-2** to center on the edit point, and **Option-3** to end on the edit point.

Note

Navigating the Transition Editor: The **Grab Handle** in the upper right corner lets you pull a transition from the **Transition Editor** onto an edit point in the **Timeline**. This is useful if you've opened the editor directly from the **Transitions** bin. This is the only way you can grab it drag the transition. There is also a popup for recent clips in the **Transition Editor**, though why it's here I'm not sure.

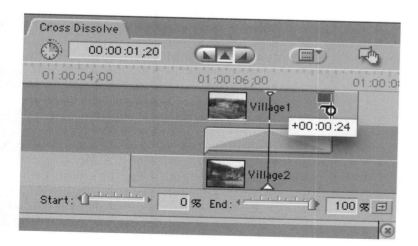

Figure 5.39   Rippling Clip in Transition Editor

Transitions between Sequences

Because FCP allows you to place sequences within sequences, it sometimes becomes necessary to create transitions between them. This presents some problems, which have been exacerbated in the latest version of the application. FCP treats each sequence as a complete piece of media. So as we've seen, if you have used the media to its limits, you can't create a transition. In earlier versions of FCP, the problem could be solved by opening the sequence and extending in the material inside it. No more. Now if you extend the contents of a sequence, all versions of the sequence will become longer, rippling the sequences that hold them.

As we shall see in a later lesson, because multilayer Photoshop files become sequences of their own when they're imported into FCP, they present the same problem. Though each layer in a PS sequence can be any length you want, when the PS sequence is laid into another sequence, the final sequence assumes that the limit of the media is the limit of the nested sequence. It will not go burrowing into the nest to extend the media for each layer to make room for the transition.

So if you want to create a transition between sequences, you have to open the edit point into the Trim Edit window, as we did earlier, and ripple the outgoing sequence and the incoming sequence to allow room for the transition.

Below that is a small circle with a red cross in it. This is the **Parameters Reset** button. Neither of these has value in **Cross Dissolve** but will be important later for more complex transitions, as we shall see in a moment. Also note that the **Reset** button does not reset the sliders, nor the arrow, only the other parameters.

Using Transitions

Now that we know how to add and trim transitions, let's look at the transitions themselves. To change the transition:

- Drag the new transition from transitions folder in the **Effects** window and drop it on the existing transition in the timeline or

- Select the transition in the timeline by clicking on it and then select a new choice from the **Effects>Video Transitions** menu.

I'd like to go through the many transitions because they offer a number of surprises and hidden capabilities. The introduction of the **FXScript DVE's** means that there is now a good deal of redundancy in transitions. You will now find this throughout the application: as new elements are put in, others become obsolete but are retained simply to maintain compatibility with old projects. Personally I would have preferred if loading redundant, legacy transitions and effects were a choice for the user, rather than cluttering the interface with more and more duplication. Rather than detailing every transition as I did in the first edition, I'll skip redundant transitions and point you to the one mostly likely to be useful. There are a lot of transitions in FCP3. Many are fairly ugly and probably would best be avoided; others, including some of the newly introduced ones, are quite good. Let's begin with the first group of transitions, **3D Simulation**.

3D Simulation

Cross Zoom

The **Cross Zoom** transition pushes into the image until the midpoint of the transition is reached and then pulls back out of the second shot (Figure 5.40).

The **Center** point is a function you will see in various places in Final Cut Pro. It allows you to position an image by clicking on the crosshairs and then clicking in the **Canvas** to pinpoint where in the **Canvas** the cross zoom will push into and pull out from.

The amount of **Zoom** controls how far into the image the zoom with push in, while **Blur** controls how much softening is applied to the image as it goes into it. Because this is a purely digital effect, by zooming into the image you're increasing the pixel size, until it looks very blocky. Using **Blur** mitigates this. The default of 10 is a good number to work with.

Setting up **QuickView** to the side and keeping it loading frames while you try different settings really does makes it easy to experiment with effects, to quickly get them just the way you want them.

Figure 5.40 Cross Zoom Control Panel

Cube Spin

Cube Spin will roll your clips around as if they were stuck to either the outside or to the inside of a cube. Popups let you switch between spinning the cube: left, right, up, and down. This is one of many transitions that allow you to add a colored border to the image (Figure 5.41).

Unless you want to have the colored border, the **Cube Spin** you really want to use is in the **FXScript DVE's**, which has more

Figure 5.41 Cube Spin

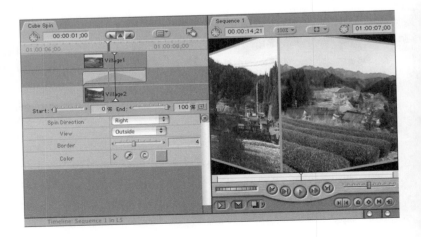

controls, including highlights, and produces a cleaner effect, though it doesn't have the colored border.

Spin 3D

Spin 3D turns the image away from you so that it's on edge and disappears.

As Figure 5.42 shows, **Angle of Axis** lets you control the direction for the plane to spin back. The default action is to make the outgoing shot spin away so it disappears. The little toggle arrow will let you switch it, so that rather than having the outgoing shot spin away, the incoming shot spins in to fill the screen.

The antialiasing on the 3D effects doesn't seem very good. You don't get nice clean edges, but you see nasty looking stair-stepping on the edges of the image. This is clearly visible in Figure 5.42. This is a common problem with a number of 3D-type transitions.

Spinback 3D

This is similar to **Spin 3D**, except that the image turns away to nothing and then turns back to reveal the second shot. It would be nice if the spin movement could continue as if one image was on the back of another, but it doesn't. I don't find it an attractive transition because of this. There is an **FXScript DVE** version of this called **Flip** that does follow through so that the second image is on the back of the first. It looks far superior.

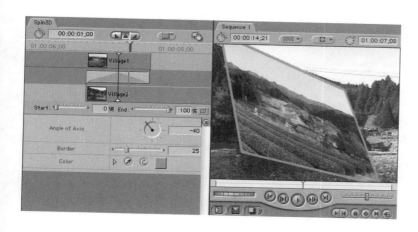

Figure 5.42   Spin 3D

Swing

Swing acts like a door that's hinged on one side. The controls allow you to make the door swing inward or outward. This is a legacy transition. We'll look at the controls in the more fully featured **FXScript DVE's Swing** transition on page 220.

Zoom

Skip right over **Zoom and** go to **FXScript DVE's Zoom/Rotate** transition, which we'll look at shortly on page 221.

Dissolve

Additive Dissolve

Unlike the standard cross dissolve that fades out one image while the other fades in, the **Additive Dissolve** combines the luminance values of the two images so that it brightens sharply toward the midpoint of the transition. Figure 5.43 shows FCP's standard **Cross Dissolve** on the left, and on the right the same transition done as an **Additive Dissolve**. Be careful with this transition. It is easy to exceed acceptable, NTSC-legal luminance values using it, albeit only momentarily.

Cross Dissolve

The only reason I might prefer to use FCP's own legacy **Cross Dissolve** rather than the **FXScript DVE's Cross Dissolve** is that FCP's **Cross Dissolve** will play back in real time on real-time capable systems, while **FXScript DVE's** will not.

Figure 5.43 Cross Dissolve and Additive Dissolve

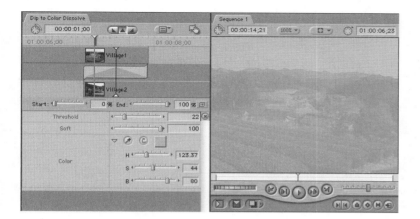

Figure 5.44   Dip to Color Dissolve

Dip to Color Dissolve

This is a handy way to do a quick fade to black and back again. Or you can do a fade to white or green or red or pink or mauve or chartreuse (Figure 5.44).

Threshold determines when the color will appear in the transition. The earlier the threshold, as in Figure 5.44, the faster the dip to the color will be, and the slower going back from the color to the second shot. The higher the threshold, the slower the fade out and the faster the fade back in.

Dither Dissolve

This dissolve gives creates a flickering, speckled look to the transition, as if ants were racing madly all over the screen (Figure 5.45).

Figure 5.45   Dither Dissolve

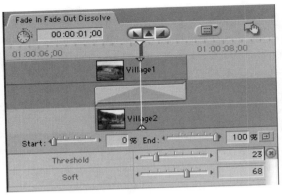

Figure 5.46   Fade In Fade Out Dissolve

Fade In Fade Out Dissolve

I confess to not fully understanding the purpose of the **Fade In Fade Out Dissolve**. By the way, it should really be called the **Fade Out Fade In Dissolve** because that's what it's doing. In most instances, it does basically the same transition as **Dip to Color**, except that it dips to transparency. So if the clips are on an upper track, in the middle of the transition, the video on the underlying track will be visible. Normally though you just see a fade to black and a fade up from black. The default one-second transition means that you get a half-second fade out, which is pretty brisk for most purposes, so you might want to lengthen it to two seconds to get a full one second out and one second in. You could also change the default duration in the **Effects** tab of the **Browser**, as we saw earlier.

FIFO has the added benefit of having the **Threshold** and **Softness** sliders (Figure 5.46). **Threshold** sets where the center of the fade point is. Move the slider to the left, and the fade out will happen sooner and sit there longer before a smooth fade up. Move the slider to the right, and the outgoing shot will behave normally, but the incoming shot will fade up more quickly. **Softness** sets how long the screen stays empty. At the default 100, the screen is empty for one frame. Increasing the amount will increase the duration of the pause, as well as increasing the corresponding speed of the fade out and the fade in. If used unwisely, as in the settings in Figure 5.46, the two sliders will fight against each other, producing unpleasant results.

Non-Additive Dissolve

There may be some difference between this and a **Cross Dissolve**, but it's too subtle for my eyes, especially if seen only in a second or two.

Ripple Dissolve

If **Non-Additive** doesn't seem to have much value, **Ripple Dissolve** adds something different to a dissolve, though a horribly

Figure 5.47   Ripple Dissolve

overused one. As its name says, it gives you a pond ripple effect (Figure 5.47).

The controls let you adjust the shape and force of the ripple to some degree. **Acceleration** is a bit fierce for my taste, and it's difficult to get the transition to do a slow ripple. Even at low values, it moves quickly.

The toggle arrow has an interesting effect: the default movement is outwards, like the pond ripple. Click the toggle arrow to reverse the movement so that the ripple moves inwards like water going down a drain hole.

FXScript DVE's

Next are the **FXScript DVE's**, all new to Final Cut Pro 3. Created by Klaus Eiperle of Eiperle CGM tv, these are a great addition to the application, not only for their transitions, but for their special effects, as we shall see. The transitions are created using FCP's built-in **FXBuilder**, a wonderful tool to bring out the programmer in you. Many of these transitions are classics and serve to replace the existing transitions. Klaus also has a new collection of special effects, **FXScript DVE's Volume II**, which are available through his website http://www.cgm-online.com. All the **FXScript DVE's** add a **Cropping** tool. This is very important because many digitizing cards produce black borders around the image. This is in the blanking area outside the television mask and not seen by the viewer, but it's recorded on every clip, though it's never seen unless the clip is moved, such as in a DVE transition. As soon as the image moves so that its edges become visible, then the few lines of black on the edge of the frame can be seen. For this reason, the Eiperle filters give you the option of cropping off these

Figure 5.48   Left: FXScript DVE's Band Slide Showing Black Edge of Video Frame Without Cropping
Right: Transition Without Black Edge After Cropping

edges. In Figure 5.48, on the left you see the black edge of the clip as it slides across the screen. On the right, with the transition's cropping applied, the clip passes with the black edge removed.

Band Slide

Band Slide is a classic DVE transition (Figure 5.49). It's very similar to the standard FCP filter with one addition. You can set the bands to slide horizontally or vertically, from two up to 30 bands to make very narrow slices of your clips.

Of course, you have the controls at the bottom to crop the edges of the frame if necessary.

Cross Dissolve

The **FXScript DVE's Cross Dissolve** ramps up a little more slowly than the standard **Cross Dissolve**. Note the checkbox for **Ease**

Figure 5.49   FXScript DVE's Band Slide

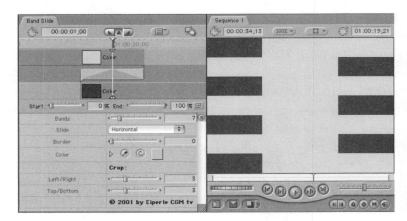

In/Out in Figure 5.50. Without it, the transition is very much the same as the regular **Cross Dissolve**. It's really just a question of taste; some might prefer the smoothness of this dissolve over the slightly more punchy effect you get with FCP's traditional dissolve.

Cube Spin

This brings something really special to FCP's transitions and effects, the ability to add and control highlights on 3D effects (Figure 5.51).

The **Spin Direction** popup lets you set the direction of the motion: **Right, Left, Up,** or **Down.** The **View** popup switches between the default outside of the cube and the option of images being on the inside of the cube.

The **Jump** slider lets you set how far away you want to cube to pull so that the action is more clearly visible. Set to zero, there is no pull back. So as the cube spins, some of the image is cut off. The default 5 a good place to start, while 10 makes the image quite small in the screen.

Again, there is a **Border** control that lets you set an edge color. The default is bright yellow, which is better than the conventional black.

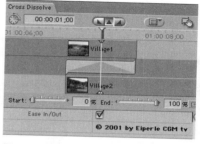

Figure 5.50   FXScript DVE's Cross Dissolve Controls

Figure 5.51   FXScript DVE's Cube Spin

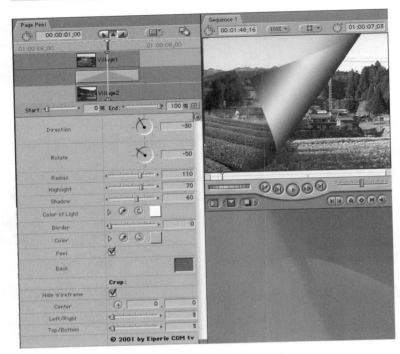

Figure 5.52   FXScript DVE's Page Peel

Figure 5.53   The Well

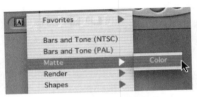

Figure 5.54   Generators Button

Below that are the controls for **Highlight**. The first slider lets you set the amount of the highlight, how shiny it will seem. Below that you can set the color of the highlight, and **Width** controls how broad a band the highlight produces.

Finally there are the **Crop** tools, which should always be applied if your material has black edge banding.

Page Peels

There are a number of these **Page Peels,** and though **Double Page Peel** is the first, let's look at them together, starting with the base **FXScript DVE's** transition **Page Peel** (Figure 5.52).

Page Peel is often overused, but sometimes it really is the right effect, especially for wedding videos. This is also the first time we meet FCP's **Well** (Figure 5.53).

The **Well** lets you use another image as part of an effect. In this case, the **Well** lets you map another image onto the back of the **Page Peel**. The default is to place the same image, flopped, on the back of the page, but you can use any image in your project.

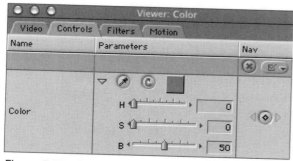

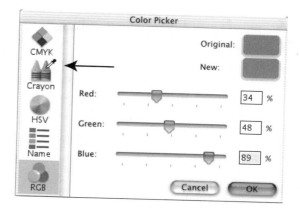

Figure 5.55 Color Matte Controls Tab (Above)

Figure 5.56 Eyedropper in the Color Selector (Right)

To put a color on the back, as in Figure 5.52, use the **Video Generator** in the **Viewer** to create a color matte.

1. Open any clip into the **Viewer**. The **A** with the **Filmstrip** icon in the lower left corner evokes the **Generators** (Figure 5.54).

2. Select **Matte>Color**.

3. Choose a color from the **Control** tab (Figure 5.55) and drag it into the **Browser**.

4. Reopen the **Page Peel** transition from the **Timeline**, and pull the **Color Matte** from the **Browser**. Drop it into the **Well**, making it part of the transition.

Note

Static Well: Unfortunately the **Well** won't track an image or change if a video clip is used. The **Well** simply uses the In point of the video clip as its map. In the case of **Page Peel**, there is no movement on the backside of the page. Sorry.

Tip

Selecting Color: Whenever you need to select a color from anywhere on your desktop, simply click on the color swatch to open the **Color Selector**. If you hold down the **Option** key, you will get an **Eyedropper** that will let you select a color from anywhere on the computer desktop (Figure 5.56).

Note

Color Picker: The Color Picker that's called up by clicking on the swatch offers a number of different color samplers, none of them very suitable for video. The RGB picker works in percentages, unlike the Photoshop standard of 0–255 colors. CMYK is only suitable for print. HSV is not video friendly because it doesn't the follow vectorscope standard layout for hue. I haven't used crayons myself since sometime in early childhood, though I understand their nostalgia value. To keep colors NTSC safe, use the RGB picker and don't let the slider for any color exceed 85%. This may produce color on the computer screen that looks quite muddy, but in video they'll be vivid without being oversaturated.

Page Peel has a number of controls to affect its parameters:

1. **Direction** sets the angle at which the pages turns back. The default −30 pulls it toward the upper left corner.

2. **Rotate** controls how much the peel pivots as it turns under. With **Rotate** you can make it seem as though the page will peel in one direction, and then swing it around so that it turns back into another.

3. **Radius** sets the arc of the page peel. A small number will make it peel very tightly, while a high number will make the turn of the page quite loose.

4. **Highlight**, as in other **FXScript DVE's**, puts a gleam of light on the back of the turning page, which is controlled by the **Color of Light**. There is no control of the width.

5. **Shadow** controls a shadow area created by the page peel. It also acts to darken the back of the image, emphasizing the highlight and the underlying shadow. It's an attractive, subtle, soft shadow.

6. **Border** and the second **Color** swatch set a colored edge to the page, while **Back**, as we've seen, allows you to place a color or image on the back of the turning page.

7. The **Peel** checkbox is defaulted on. With it unchecked, the page doesn't only peel back, it also curls under as it goes. The smaller the **Radius** value, the tighter the curl becomes.

8. Leave **Hide Wireframe** checked on. Without it, a gray box is added to the frame during the transition.

9. Again, you have the **Crop** tools to trim the black edges of the image.

Figure 5.57   Double Page Peel
Controls

10. The **Arrow** checkbox at the top toggles between peeling the page off, the default, and peeling the page on, an unusual variation.

Now that you've seen the controls in **Page Peel**, the **FXScript DVE**'s other page peels are just variations.

Double Page Peel

The controls in **Double Page Peel** should be familiar to you now. In the **Double Page Peel**, one is peeled off while the other is peeled on (Figure 5.57). There is **Direction** and **Radius**, of course, but no **Rotation** control. **Distance** controls the gap between the two images; you probably want to keep it low. **Highlight**, **Shadow**, **Border**, and **Color** are as in the standard **Page Peel**. This transition actually defaults to curl, with **Peel** unchecked, unlike the standard **Page Peel**. **Back of Scene 1** is the image on the backside of the outgoing shot, while **Back of Scene 2** is the image on the back of the incoming shot. Again you have the **Crop** controls, but apparently no **Hide Wireframe** is necessary here.

Page Peel 1/2

Page Peel 1/2 splits the outgoing page in half, either horizontally, the default, or vertically, selected in the first popup (Figure 5.58). The second popup, **Direction**, changes the page from either the default (the two halves ripping in opposite directions) to the two halves ripping and peeling back, but in the same direction. The rest of the controls are the standard **Page Peel** controls.

Page Peel 1/4

In **Page Peel 1/4** the outgoing splits apart in the middle — either in a rhombus shape (the default) or a rectangular shape (Figure 5.59). By flipping the arrow toggle, the incoming shot will peel over the other image, closing on the center point.

Flip

This is the **FXScript DVE's** version of **Spinback 3D.** Here not only does the image turn away, but the incoming image then swings back into view on the back of the outgoing image. With the added highlight, this is a very slick effect (Figure 5.60). The little jump back that the transition uses as the default helps the illusion of a card flipping over seem all the more realistic.

Figure 5.58 Page Peel 1/2

Figure 5.59   Page Peel 1/4

Though the **Direction** control clock would seem to give you full angle control, it only works in 90° increments: right, left, up, or down. You can, however, type in an angle value in the box and enter any direction you want.

Slide

Slide actually defaults to being a **Push** (Figure 5.61), one of my favorite transitions. One image pushes the other image out of the frame and replaces it. With the first popup set to **Both**, the incoming image slides onto the screen pushing the outgoing image off the screen. Set to **Out**, the incoming shot slides off the screen,

Figure 5.60   Flip

Figure 5.61   Slide

revealing the next shot behind it. Set to **In**, the incoming shot slides in over the top of the outgoing shot.

Again, the **Direction** clock only works in 90° increments, but the value box will allow you to enter any number. The **Fade** controller is interesting. If the transition is set to **In** or **Out**, the image fades off as the transition finishes, which speeds the effect up slightly but makes for an interesting variation. With the popup set to **Both**, **Fade** has no effect.

Softwipe

Softwipe looks deceptively simple, but under its simplicity of control is disguised a huge amount of power. The power is in the **Method** popup under **Pattern**, coupled with the **Pattern Well** (Figure 5.62).

Let's first look at the default controls, which activate the soft-edged color bar that wipes one image off, replacing it with another. The **Softness** control at the top regulates how blurry the edges of the transition are where one image replaces another. The **Width** slider at the bottom sets the width of the color bar. Set **Width** to zero, and you get a soft-edge directional wipe with no color overlay. The **Direction** clock sets the angle at which the wipe moves. It's fully controllable, anywhere in the 360° circumference.

Figure 5.62   Softwipe Controls

With the popup set to **Direction**, the **Center** point crosshairs have no effect, but if you switch the popup to **Radial**, you now get a soft-edged radial wipe. Now the **Center** point crosshairs controls where the radial generates. Click the **Crosshairs** button and then click in the **Canvas** where you want the wipe to originate (Figure 5.63).

Pattern is what makes **Softwipe** a crucial tool in Final Cut. In the project **Browser** is an image called *Gradient.pct*. If you open it up and take a look at it in the **Viewer**, you'll see that it's a complex, grayscale checkerboard pattern. This is the basis of patterning in **Softwipe** or any gradient wipe. The image will be wiped on or off, based on the grayscale values of pattern image. The darkest parts of the pattern image will be where the incoming image will appear first, and the lightest parts will be where the image will appear last. In the gradient pattern we have, some of the outside boxes will appear first, while as the transition approaches midpoint as in Figure 5.64, the lower left to upper right diagonal of the image will still be from the outgoing shot. There is no end to the huge variety of patterns you can get to manipulate this control. If you don't like a pattern, simply replace it another.

Figure 5.63   Softwipe Radial

Figure 5.64 Softwipe Pattern

Figure 5.65 Softwipe Pattern in Both Wells

To really see the power of transition effects, you should look at what Michael Feerer has created with his Video Spices. Check them out at http://www.pixelan.com. They add an important tool to Final Cut's transitions. His patterns can be used not only inside his own transitions, but inside **Softwipe** as well.

The **Temporary Pattern Well** allows you to place a pattern or other image on the screen that's actually visible as the transition takes place. This will replace the **Color Width** if it's active. Setting the same gradient pattern in the **Wipe Pattern Well** and the **Temporary Pattern Well** creates an interesting effect (Figure 5.65).

There is a folder of *Softwipe Patterns* on the FCP3 installation CD that gives you 65 grayscale images. Copy these onto your computer to make them available to use with this transition. They are inside the *Extras* folder, inside *FXScript DVE's by CGM*. There is also a *Tutorial* folder that's a useful resource for some of the CGM effects.

Softwipe is probably my favorite and most used transition, after a simple **Cross Dissolve**. I like it because it is so infinitely variable, and you can always find some way to make it look just a little different and just right for the effect. A trick I've used in the past is to use a grayscale frame of either the outgoing shot or the incoming shot as the image for the **Pattern Well**. It makes the transition like a slightly sharp-edged dissolve because the elements of the shot itself are affecting how the transition happens.

Split Slide

This simple little transition goes one step better than FCP's legacy **Split Slide**, which only divided the image in two, horizontally or vertically. In **FXScript DVE's Split Slide**, the default is to split two ways from the middle (Figure 5.66). Set in 2-axis method, the **Split** will open up in four pieces from the center. The popup for vertical or horizontal control has no effect, but the **Center** crosshairs do, allowing you to position the split wherever you want in the **Canvas**. In the more conventional 1-axis method, you can set the split to be either vertical or horizontal. If set to vertical, the x value of the **Center** point has effect; if set to horizontal, only the y value has any effect.

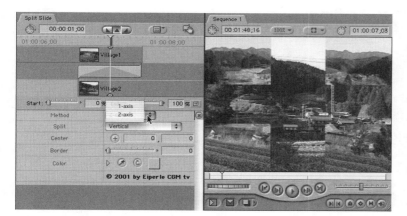

Figure 5.66   Split Slide

Stretch

This is another classic DVE transition with a couple of interesting enhancements (Figure 5.67). The first popup lets you choice between stretch the default **Both,** or stretching **In,** which stretches the incoming shot over the top of the outgoing shot. Set to **Out,** the outgoing shot is squeezed off the screen. The default **End** position is to the **Edge** of the frame, controlled in the second popup. Or you can set it to **Center,** in which case squeezing takes place around the center line of the frame. With **End** set to **Center** and **Method** set to **Both,** the outgoing shot will squeeze to nothing on the center line of the frame, and then incoming shot will stretch out from there. The **Direction** dial itself only works in 90° increments again. Here entering a value in the box will not change the real direction, which will only happen at right angles.

Figure 5.67   FXScript DVE's Stretch

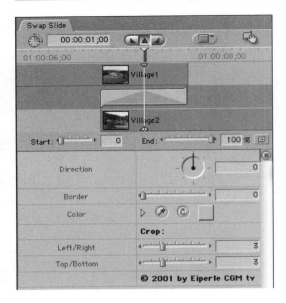

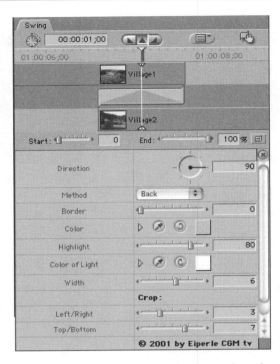

Figure 5.68   FXScript DVE's Swap Slide Controls (Above)

Figure 5.69   FXScript DVE's Swing Controls (Right)

The **Stretch** slider has an interesting effect. Set at high number, the image seems to start very broad, as though it were much broader than the frame. It seems to squeeze down to the frame size as it comes into position. This gives the effect of the movement being a slight arc, as though the image were being bent into place.

Swap Slide

Swap is similar to the **Push** except that it moves only halfway before the second image starts to replace it, like you're cutting a deck of cards in one hand. Again, you can set the **Direction** of the swap to any angle you want by using the **Value** box, though the **Direction** dial is confined to 90° sections (Figure 5.68).

Swing

The barn door swings either away from you (**Back** in the **Method** popup) or toward you (**Front** in the popup). You can add a **Border** and, of course, a colored **Highlight**. You can make the image swing in any direction, but keeping it to 90° is probably a good idea (Figure 5.69).

Zoom/Rotate

This is the last **FXScript DVE's**. It makes a very good transition, and when used as an effect, as we'll see later, it provides FCP with a better way to control large format images. More on that in "Roll/Scroll (Title)" on page 459 in Lesson 11. **Zoom/Rotate** does exactly what it says: the image zooms away into the distance. The default is a straight zoom back without rotation. Where the image disappears to is set with the **Endpoint** crosshairs. Click the crosshairs, and then click in the **Canvas**.

Z axis Rotation allows you to spin the image one full revolution either clockwise or counterclockwise, but only one revolution. Leave **Hide Wireframe** checked on (Figure 5.70).

Iris

Cross Iris

The **Iris** group of transitions are very old effects that go back to the early days of film. They are often used to point up particular parts of the frame. Two features they all have in common are the ability to center the iris on any part of the frame and to feather the edges of the iris. In FCP you can either have a feathered edge as in Figure 5.71 or you can have a border — unfortunately, not both.

All of the **Iris** transitions are real-time — sort of. They will all appear with a yellow bar on top of them, indicating that playback will be an approximation only. Anything that you alter in the controls, such as **Feather** or **Border** will not be visible in real-time

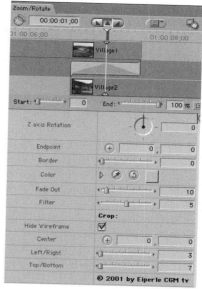

Figure 5.70   FXScript DVE's Zoom/Rotate

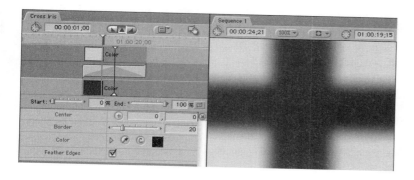

Figure 5.71   Cross Iris

Figure 5.72   Diamond Iris

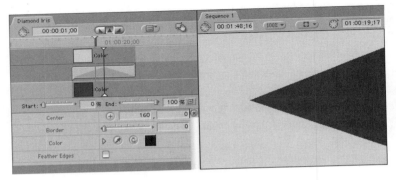

playback, only when the playhead is parked over a frame or in **QuickView**, of course.

Cross Iris is a typical iris that opens up the image from the center point in a cross shape. The toggle switches between opening the cross up and closing the cross down from the edges. Setting the center point in one of the corners will create a transition that opens out or closes like a wedge from the opposite corner.

Diamond Iris

This transition creates a standard diamond shape that opens or closes. Setting the center point off to one edge will create a wedge shaped wipe that slices in from one side (Figure 5.72).

I would have liked some way to control the shape of the diamond vertically and horizontally, so that it was either a flat, wide diamond or a tall, narrow diamond.

Oval Iris

This is actually a circle iris with controls. The default with an **Aspect** setting of 1 makes a circle. Changing the aspect will create an oval. An **Aspect** of 0.5, the lowest setting, will make a horizontal oval as in Figure 5.73, while a high **Aspect** number will orient that oval vertically.

Again, setting the center point off to one edge will make an iris that appears as an arc sweeping across the screen.

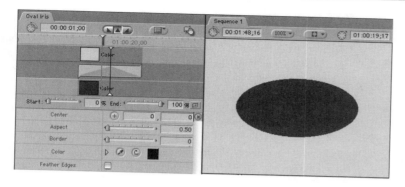

Figure 5.73 Oval Iris

Point Iris

This is the same as the **Cross Iris** with the opposite orientation (Figure 5.74). The **Cross Iris** is the English Cross of St. George and the **Point Iris** is the Scottish Cross of St. Andrew.

Offsetting the center point to one edge will create a wedge-shaped iris that will slice across the screen. It can be very effective when you want a dynamic transition.

Figure 5.74 Point Iris

Rectangle Iris

In addition to generating a rectangular-shaped iris, this transition lets you round the corners using the **Corner Radius**, creating an old-fashioned TV look (Figure 5.75).

You can feather or border the edges, as well as control the center. It would be nice if the shape of rectangle could be controlled, perhaps so that you could make a square.

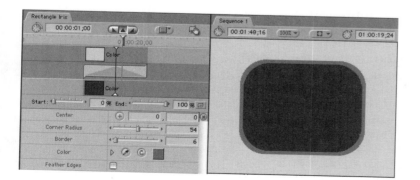

Figure 5.75 Rectangle Iris

Figure 5.76   Star Iris

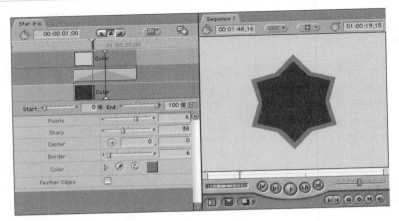

Star Iris

The final iris in the bin is the **Star Iris,** which does exactly what its name says: creates the ever-popular star-shaped iris. The controls include the number of points and the sharpness of the effects. Adjusting the sharpness as shown in Figure 5.76 will allow you to create some unusual shapes, freeing you from the ubiquitous default star.

Map

There are two effects in the **Map** transition bin:

- **Channel Map**
- **Luminance Map**

They work similarly and produce interesting and unusual transition effects.

Channel Map

Channel Map allows you to select any channel alpha, red, green, and blue from the channels of either **Source 1,** the outgoing shot, or **Source 2,** the incoming shot.

Leaving the default settings produces no real effect. Each channel is mapped to its own channel, resulting in a cross dissolve. Each of the four channels can also be inverted using a small checkbox.

Changing the channels around produces interesting effects (Figure 5.77). For most video clips, the alpha channel will be the full size of the image. Replacing it with another channel will have little discernible effect. Replacing **Red** with **Source 1 Blue** produces a soft blue-green tint during the transition. I would like some softening controls to allow the channels to blur slightly. This would create interesting effects.

Inverting all the channels creates a negative appearance during the transition. Making each of the RGB channels from a single source as in Figure 5.78 will make the image dip to grayscale during the transition.

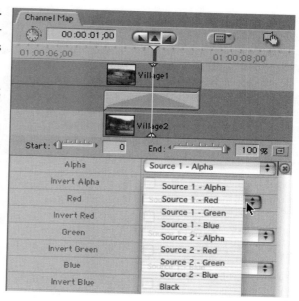

Figure 5.77   Channel Map Controls

Luminance Map

Luma Map has only one control, which lets you set a color that the transition will map to. So using a blue map color will make the image go predominantly blue during the effect. Luma map is a handy way to make an interesting effect. Using a near white, say 85% saturation, on a very short transition will create something like a film flash frame effect.

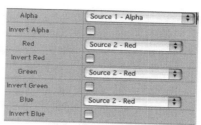

Figure 5.78   Grayscale setting of Channel Map

Page Peel

We've done enough page peeling by now. For all the variations, go back to page 210 and use **FXScript DVE's** page peel of your choice.

QuickTime

I guess Final Cut had to include the QuickTime transitions, though many somewhat duplicate FCP's own transitions, and

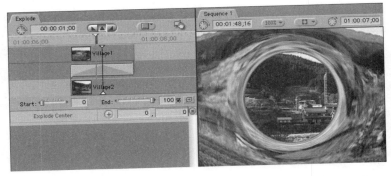

Figure 5.80 Explode

some don't have much benefit. The first, **Alpha Compositor**, seems to have little value, and its inclusion puzzles me. A **Chroma Key** transition is also pretty useless. **Crossfade** is the basic **Cross Dissolve**.

Explode

This effect squeezes the image out of a circle to create an expanding hole (Figure 5.80). The arrow toggle will make the incoming shot collapse in around the center, which is a bizarre effect, espe-

What's a Channel?

Digital images like video are made by combining primary colors, often red, green, and blue. These are the channels R, G, and B. A fourth channel, the alpha channel, defines the image's transparency. It is usually represented as a grayscale image. You can see channels for a digital image most clearly in Photoshop's **Channels** panel (Figure 5.79).

Figure 5.79 Photoshop Channels Panel

Each of the color channels displays the amount of its primary color. The redder portions in an image will appear paler in the red channel, while the blue portions will be the paler in the blue channel, and similarly for the green channel. Different colors will use different proportions of the three primary colors. Wherever you have all the channels with full luminance, you get pure white.

In the alpha channel, the luminance value represents transparent. White is fully opaque, while black is fully transparent; the shades of gray in between will make more or less of the image visible.

cially in a slow transition where the images appears to be oozing onto the screen from the edges.

Gradient Wipe

As we have seen with **FXScript DVE's Softwipe** on page 216, gradient wipes are some of the best weapons in the transition arsenal. **Gradient Wipe** functions just like **Softwipe** using its **Pattern** method, and **Softwipe** gives you more flexibility in one control panel.

Implode

This function is the reverse of **Explode,** except instead of opening into a hole it collapses into points (Figure 5.81). The toggle arrow will make the incoming shot open out from the points in the center.

Iris

QuickTime **Iris** provides many of FCP's **Iris** effects as well as a host of others, including the ever popular heart iris seen in many wedding videos (Figure 5.82). QuickTime also allows the ability to tile the effects (Figure 5.83). The irises can be tiled both horizontally and vertically up to nine iterations in each direction. This function allows a variety of interesting and unusual transitions. The **Soft Edges** switch doesn't make a soft-edged iris as you might expect, but it does improve the antialiasing on the pattern edges.

Random Effect and **Random Iris** at the bottom of the **Iris** popup produce a truly ugly effect, randomly switching through iris affects every frame of the transition.

Matrix Wipe

This produces a staggering number of block-based transitions that ripple across the screen (Figure 5.84). The effects range from a classic horizontal matrix effect to complex effects like **Quad Spiral Vertical** and **Horizontal Waterfall.**

Implode
00:00:01;00
01:00:06;00
01:00:08;00
Village1
Village2
Start:
0
End:
100 %
Implode Center
0
0
Sequence 1
00:01:48;16
100%
01:00:07;04

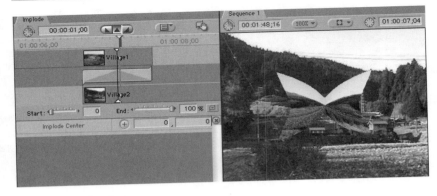

Figure 5.81 Implode

Rectangle
Diamond
Triangle
Triangle right
Triangle upside down
Triangle left
Arrowhead
Arrowhead right
Arrowhead upside down
Arrowhead left
Pentagon
Pentagon upside down
Hexagon
Hexagon side
Circle
Oval
Oval side
Cat eye
Cat eye side
Round rect
Round rect side
4 point star
5 point star
6 point star
Heart
Keyhole
Random Effect
Random Iris

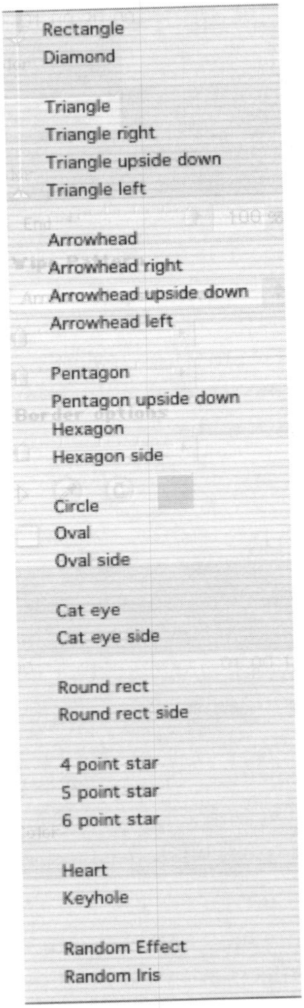

Figure 5.82 QuickTime Iris

Iris
00:00:01;00
01:00:20;00
Color
Color
Start:
0 %
End:
100 %
Wipe Pattern
Wipe Type
5 point star
Horizontal repeat
4
Vertical repeat
4
Border options
Border width
4
Border color
Soft edges
Sequence 1
00:01:48;16
100%
01:00:19;16

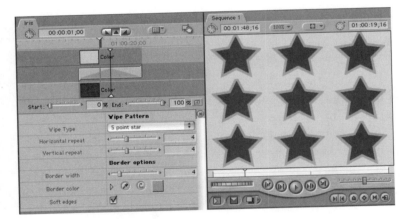

Figure 5.83 QuickTime Iris Control

Push

The **FXScript DVE's Slide** (see page 215) works just as well with more options.

Radial

Radial offers a staggering variety of wipe patterns (Figure 5.85). The default settings, **Rotating Top**, will generate a radial clock wipe that can be used to create the old Academy film leader, beginning at 8 and ending with the 2-pop before going to black. This transition also offers horizontal and vertical repeats as well as colored borders. The toggle arrow will reverse the movement. For instance, **Rotating Top** goes counterclockwise, rather than the traditional clockwise.

Slide

Use **FXScript DVE's Slide.**

Wipe

The QuickTime **Wipe** transition offers a popup with a whole slew of wipe effects (Figure 5.86). These wipes must provide everything you could want, plus multiple iterations horizontally and vertically. You might be hesitant to use these wipes because none of them offer real-time capabilities, which does appear in some of FCP's own built-in wipes, as we shall see shortly.

Zoom

The QuickTime **Zoom** has a few interesting variations that set apart from the **Zoom** transitions in FCP (Figure 5.87).

Zooming B Over A is the standard zoom effect. Increasing the **Distance** slider will reduce the size at which the zooming image starts. It doesn't, however, really start from infinity as the **FXScript DVE's Zoom** does.

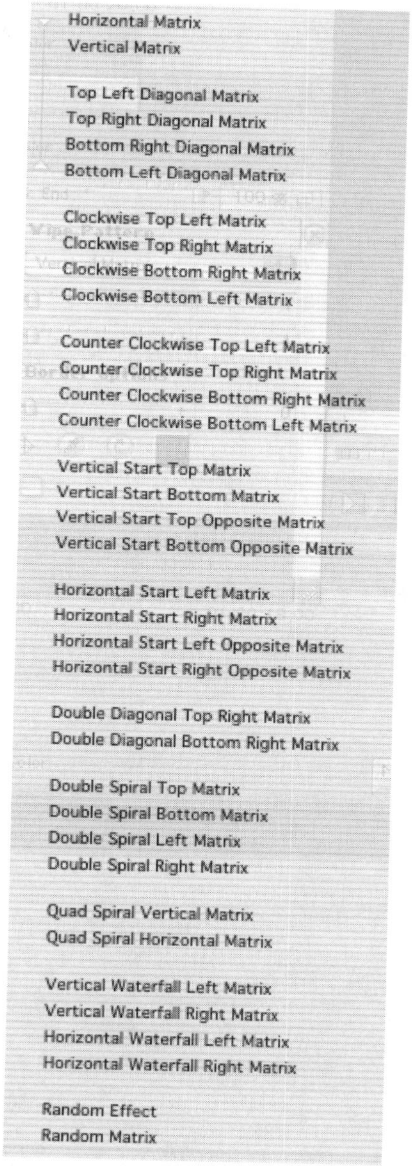

Horizontal Matrix
Vertical Matrix

Top Left Diagonal Matrix
Top Right Diagonal Matrix
Bottom Right Diagonal Matrix
Bottom Left Diagonal Matrix

Clockwise Top Left Matrix
Clockwise Top Right Matrix
Clockwise Bottom Right Matrix
Clockwise Bottom Left Matrix

Counter Clockwise Top Left Matrix
Counter Clockwise Top Right Matrix
Counter Clockwise Bottom Right Matrix
Counter Clockwise Bottom Left Matrix

Vertical Start Top Matrix
Vertical Start Bottom Matrix
Vertical Start Top Opposite Matrix
Vertical Start Bottom Opposite Matrix

Horizontal Start Left Matrix
Horizontal Start Right Matrix
Horizontal Start Left Opposite Matrix
Horizontal Start Right Opposite Matrix

Double Diagonal Top Right Matrix
Double Diagonal Bottom Right Matrix

Double Spiral Top Matrix
Double Spiral Bottom Matrix
Double Spiral Left Matrix
Double Spiral Right Matrix

Quad Spiral Vertical Matrix
Quad Spiral Horizontal Matrix

Vertical Waterfall Left Matrix
Vertical Waterfall Right Matrix
Horizontal Waterfall Left Matrix
Horizontal Waterfall Right Matrix

Random Effect
Random Matrix

Figure 5.84   Matrix Wipe

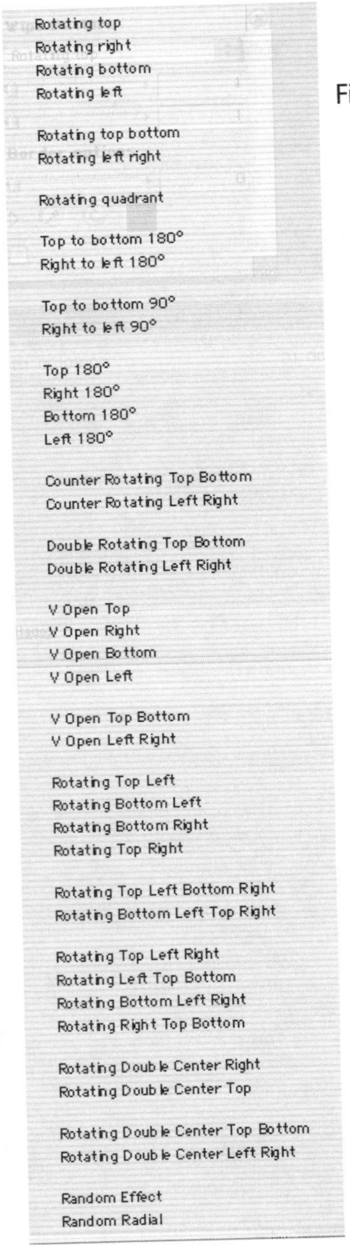

Rotating top
Rotating right
Rotating bottom
Rotating left
Rotating top bottom
Rotating left right
Rotating quadrant
Top to bottom 180°
Right to left 180°
Top to bottom 90°
Right to left 90°
Top 180°
Right 180°
Bottom 180°
Left 180°
Counter Rotating Top Bottom
Counter Rotating Left Right
Double Rotating Top Bottom
Double Rotating Left Right
V Open Top
V Open Right
V Open Bottom
V Open Left
V Open Top Bottom
V Open Left Right
Rotating Top Left
Rotating Bottom Left
Rotating Bottom Right
Rotating Top Right
Rotating Top Left Bottom Right
Rotating Bottom Left Top Right
Rotating Top Left Right
Rotating Left Top Bottom
Rotating Bottom Left Right
Rotating Right Top Bottom
Rotating Double Center Right
Rotating Double Center Top
Rotating Double Center Top Bottom
Rotating Double Center Left Right
Random Effect
Random Radial

Figure 5.85 Radial Wipes

Slide horizontal
Slide vertical
Top left
Top right
Bottom right
Bottom left
Four corner
Four box
Barn vertical
Barn horizontal
Top center
Right center
Bottom center
Left center
Diagonal left down
Diagonal right down
Vertical bow tie
Horizontal bow tie
Diagonal left out
Diagonal right out
Diagonal cross
Diagonal box
Filled V
Filled V right
Filled V bottom
Filled V left
Hollow V
Hollow V right
Hollow V bottom
Hollow V left
Vertical zig zag
Horizontal zig zag
Vertical barn zig zag
Horizontal barn zig zag
Random Effect
Random Wipe

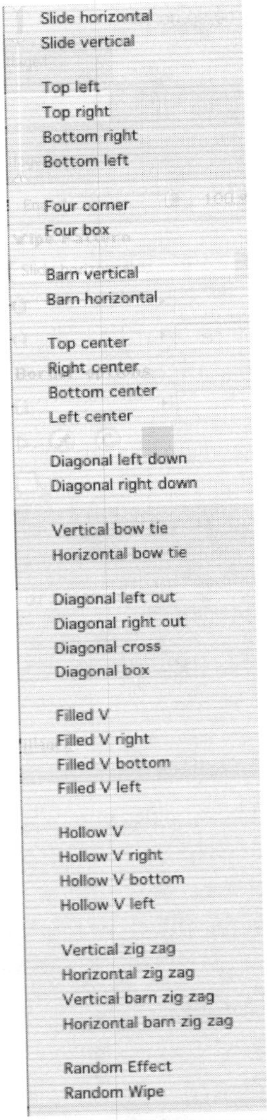

Figure 5.86 QuickTime Wipes

Figure 5.87 QuickTime Zoom

Zoom
00:00:01;00
01:00:06;00
01:00:08;00
Village1
Village2
Start:
Zooming B over A
Zooming B over zooming A
Zooming A
Zoom Type
X
Y
Distance
Sequence 1
00:01:48;16
01:00:07;13

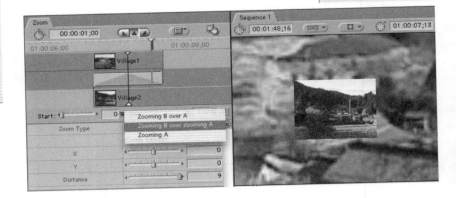

Zooming B over Zooming A digitally zooms into the outgoing shot creating unpleasant artifacting, similar to FCP's **Cross Zoom.**

The third option, **Zooming A,** makes the blockiness of the image even more pronounced as the image zooms digitally before the second shot appears. Unless you have a specific need for one of these effects, they're probably best left unused.

Slide

The **Slide** bin has eight slide effects, each with the ability to let you add borders.

Band Slide

Use **FXScript DVE's Band Slide** (see page 208) rather than this one. FXScript gives you edge cropping as well a more choices in the number of bands.

Box Slide

Box Slide also lets you set from two to 10 box shapes, and have the box shape slide in from any edge (Figure 5.88).

The default is to have the new image slide onto the screen in sections. The arrow toggle switch lets you send the box sections of the outgoing shot sliding off the screen.

Center Split Slide

FXScript DVE's Split Slide (see page 218) has exactly the same functionality as this transition.

Multi-Spin Slide

Multi-Spin, however, offers a host of possibilities, if not the most attractive of effects. It has a complex control panel (Figure 5.89). The clock dials allow you to set the spin direction and number of revolutions. **Spin 1** sets the overall spin direction, while **Spin 2** sets the direction of each panel. Zero spin with one row and one

Figure 5.88   Box Slide

column will just give you a zoom back, so if you want to have the image just tumble away without slicing up into boxes, set **Row** and **Column** to **1** and dial up the spin number, which will allow a much faster spin cycle than **FXScript DVE's Zoom/Rotate** (see page 221).

Push Slide

There isn't anything here that you haven't seen before. If you missed it, it's in **FXScript DVE's Slide** on page 215.

Spin Slide

Spin Slide is a simpler variant of **Multi-Spin Slide**. In **Multi-Spin**, all the rows and columns converge on the center point. In **Spin Slide**, all the rows and columns spin straight back from their cut point (Figure 5.90).

Figure 5.89   Multi-Spin Slide

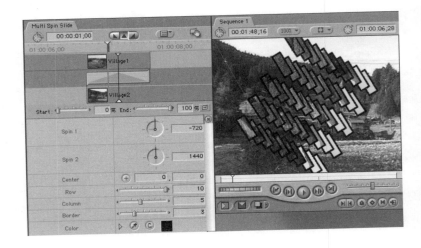

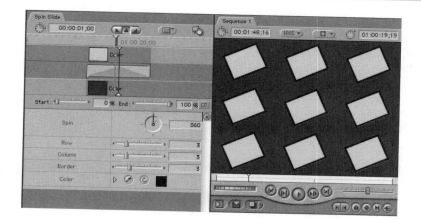

Figure 5.90 Spin Slide

Split Slide

This transition simply splits in half either vertically or horizontally. Use **FXScript DVE's Split Slide** with **1-axis** instead (see page 218).

Swap Slide

Use **FXScript DVE's Swap Slide** on page 220 instead.

Stretch

All of the **Stretch** transitions are built into the single **FXScript DVE's Stretch** (see page 219). They are all the variations that the Klaus Eiperle transition provides by changing the popups in his control panel.

Wipe

Many of the 14 wipes are similar to other effects in the package, particularly the **Slide** effects. In **Wipes**, instead of the images actually moving, portions of the image simply get wiped away, hence the name. The difference between a **Wipe** and an **Iris** is subtle. **Irises** always have a center point, albeit one that can move around, while **Wipes** usually don't have a center. Other than that, the effect of wiping or irising on or off the image is the same.

Figure 5.91   Band Wipe

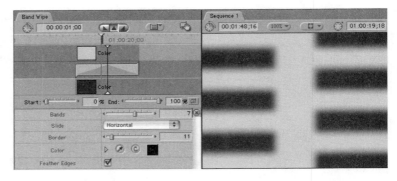

And, like the **Iris** transitions, some of these can playback in real time without resorting to **QuickView**.

Band Wipe

If you've seen a **Band Slide**, you've seen a **Band Wipe**. In the slide, the image actually moves into place; in the wipe, it doesn't (Figure 5.91).

The toggle arrow swaps which image appears in the top row. Again, you can specify from two to 10 rows. Unlike **Band Slide**, though, **Band Wipe** not only has borders, it also allows feathered rows.

Center Wipe

Center Wipe is one of five real-time wipe transitions available in Final Cut. It opens up from the middle of the image at the specified angle (Figure 5.92).

Figure 5.92   Center Wipe

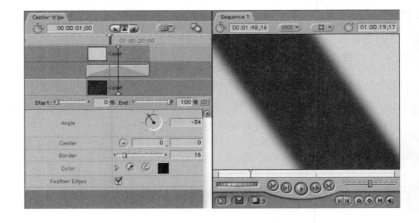

You can set the angle of the wipe as well as the center point. This is one of the few wipes with a center-point control. The toggle arrow switches between splitting the image open and closing in the second shot from the edges.

Checker Wipe

This has to be one of my least favorite transitions (Figure 5.93). It breaks the image up into little boxes, up to 16 columns of them, but only 12 rows. The incoming image is wiped on in these little boxes over the outgoing shot. Adding the **Zigzag** checkbox makes an even uglier back and forth movement.

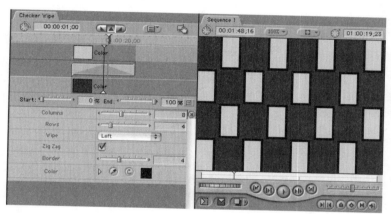

Figure 5.93   Checker Wipe (Left)

Figure 5.94   Checkerboard

Checkerboard

Unlike **Checker** that creates little boxes all over the screen, **Checkerboard** starts creating them in one of the four corners of the frame and ripples them across the screen (Figure 5.94).

At the midpoint, the screen is full of little boxes, which then start disappearing off the screen, starting from their original corner.

Clock Wipe

This is a real-time transition and much the same as the Quick-Time **Radial** wipe, except it has more individual controls, such as **Border** and **Feathering**, but without the huge number of variations built into **Radial**.

Figure 5.96   Jaws Wipe

Edge Wipe

This is also a real-time effect and does exactly what its name says. It wipes the image in from any side you want. An **Angle** dial lets you pick the point from which the wipe moves. **FXScript DVE's Softwipe** on page 216 will do almost the same effect, but not in real-time preview.

Gradient Wipes

Of all the **Gradient Wipes** in FCP, **FXScript DVE's Softwipe** on page 216 has the most options and possibilities. This one is really now a legacy transition.

Inset Wipe

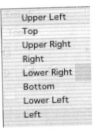

Figure 5.95   Inset Wipe Popup

This is also a real-time wipe also and will open up the image from any one of eight positions set with a popup (Figure 5.95). The default wipes the new image on, while the toggle switches to wiping the old image off.

Jaws Wipe

Every transitions package has to have one seriously gross effect. Final Cut has kept them to a minimum, but here's one (Figure 5.96). At least the designers have a sense of humor about it, with controls like the number of teeth (up to 10) and their sharpness. The default is to have the jaws open, which strikes me as odd. The toggle switch, however, will change it to the shark's teeth biting down.

Random Edge Wipe

I'm not a big fan of **Jaws,** but I really do like **Random Edge** wipe (Figure 5.97). Instead of a simple feathered edge that blurs the shape, **Random Edge** uses a dithered effect that makes a nice change from soft wipes. The width of the dithering can be set with a slider. Set to zero, the wipe is just a straight line. Set at 100 as in Figure 5.97, the band of dithering can be quite broad. You can set the wipe angle with a dial.

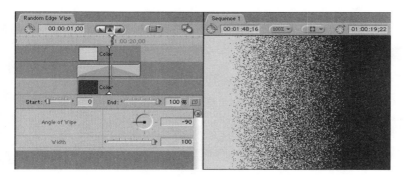

Figure 5.97   Random Edge Wipe

V Wipe

The **V Wipe** is a real-time wipe that slices in from one of the four sides of the screen (Figure 5.98). The black band in the image is called its **Width** in the controls rather than its **Border**. The toggle makes the **V** go backward, opening wide into the image rather than point first.

Venetian Blind Wipe

This is a classic, though the default doesn't set it to the classic mode (Figure 5.99). The default is **Vertical Blinds** rather than the true **Horizontal Venetian Blinds**. A dial lets you set the blinds to any angle, up to 10 blinds.

Figure 5.98   V Wipe

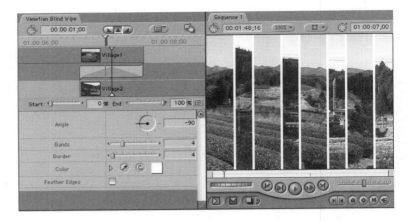

Figure 5.99   Venetian Blinds

Wrap Wipe

The **Wrap Wipe** moves bands across the screen starting from one of the corners (Figure 5.100). Each band wipes from the same direction, defaulting from left to right. Up to 10 bands can be moved horizontally or vertically.

Zigzag Wipe

This is exactly the same is **Wrap** only instead of the bands going in the same direction, they go back and forth across the screen.

Conclusion

Whew! That's a lot of transitions, but there are more third-party transitions, such as Pixelan's and the package made by Joe Maller,

Figure 5.100 Wrap Wipe

which can be found at http://www.joemaller.com, as well as others, such as Klaus Eiperle's second collection, demos of which are on the book's CD. If you have a programming bent, you can also make your own digital transitions with Final Cut Pro's **FXBuilder**. It lets you script your own transitions and special effects.

That's it for transitions. Everybody has their favorites, I'm sure. mine are fairly simple: **Cross Dissolves, FXScript Softwipe**, and **Slide**. Many I've never used. Many should probably never be used, and most you'll probably never see. Next we go on to advanced editing techniques and editing for different forms of program.

Lesson 6

Advanced Editing: Using Sound

Film and video are primarily visual media. Oddly enough, though, the moment an edit occurs is often driven as much by the sound as by the picture. So let's take a look at editing sound in Final Cut Pro. How sound is used, where it comes in, and how long it lasts are key to good editing. With few exceptions, sound almost never cuts with the picture. Sometimes the sound comes first and then the picture; sometimes the picture leads the sound. The principal reason video and audio are so often cut separately is that we see and hear quite differently. We see in cuts. I look from one person to another, from one object to another, from the keyboard to the monitor. Though my head turns or my eyes travel across the room, I really only see the objects I'm interested in looking at. We hear, on the other hand, in fades. I walk into a room, the door closes behind me, and the sound of the other room fades away. As a car approaches, the sound gets louder. Screams, gunshots, and doors slamming being exceptions, our aural perception is based on smooth transitions from one to another. Sounds, especially background sounds, generally need to overlap to smooth out the jarring abruptness of the hard cut. As

241

we shall see, dialog poses a special, interesting problem for the editor when it comes to overlapping sound.

Loading the Lesson

This is going to sound familiar, but it's worth repeating. Begin by loading the material you need on the media hard drive of your computer.

1. If you don't already have it on your drive, drag the *Media1* folder from the CD to your media drive.

2. Open the *Projects* folder on the CD and drag the *Lesson 6* folder into the *Shared* folder on your system hard drive.

3. Eject the CD, open the *Lesson 6* folder, and double-click the project file *L6to* launch the application.

4. Once again, choose the **Reconnect** option to relink the media files when the **Offline Files** dialog appears.

5. Again, the first step you should take after your project has reconnected is to save it.

6. Choose **Save Project As** from the **File** menu and save the project with a new name inside the *Lesson 6* folder.

Next make sure the scratch disk is properly assigned.

7. Go to **Final Cut Pro>Preferences** and click on the **Scratch Disks** tab.

8. Click on the **Set** button and navigate to the hard drive that holds the *Media1* folder.

9. Click on the *Media1* folder to highlight it and then click on **Choose** button.

10. Set your *Autosave Vault* to the *Shared* folder on your system hard drive.

Setting up the Project

You'll find in the project's **Browser** an empty sequence called *Sequence 1* and a number of other sequences that we'll look at during this lesson. There is also the master clip *Damine.mov* and the folder called **Clips**, which contains the subclips pulled from the master.

Viewing Your Material

In this lesson we're going to look at the religious ceremony at the heart of the Dengaku festival itself. Let's look at the subclips we'll be working with, *Ceremony1* through *Ceremony9*, in the **Clips** bin.

1. Start as usual by opening the blank *Sequence 1* and dragging the nine clips to the beginning of the **Timeline**. Or drag them to **Overwrite** in the **Canvas Edit Overlay**, making sure the playhead is parked at the beginning of the sequence.

2. Click on the **Timeline** window to make it active, or press **Command-3**.

3. Press the **Home** key to take you back to the beginning.

Because the **Timeline** doesn't scroll while the sequence plays, some people like to view material with all of it visible in the **Timeline**.

4. To show all the material, select **View>Level>Fit to Window** from the menus, or hit **Shift-Z** (Figure 6.1).

5. We're ready to go. Hit the spacebar to look at your rushes.

Tip

Thumbnails: Before you get going, you may want to turn the thumbnails off. Use **Command-zero** to access **Sequence Settings**. In the Timeline Options panel, change the **Thumbnail Display** to **Name**. Personally, I prefer working with thumbnails on in the Timeline.

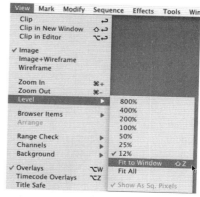

Figure 6.1   View>Level>Fit to Window

The Split Edit

A common method of editing is to first lay down the shots in scene order entirely as straight cuts. After you've laid the material out as cuts, you can begin applying transitions, as you did in the last chapter. But audio and video so seldom cut in parallel in a finished video, you will have to offset video and audio. We need to see how this is done.

Viewing Rushes

Old habits die hard. I can't get over using the British term for overnight film processing, *rushes*, rather than the American term, *dailies*. Whatever you call them — rushes, dailies, tape, cassettes, reels — this is the raw material editors work with. Watching this material for the first time, whether it's in a darkened screening room, on a tape deck in a room crowded with humming electronic equipment, in the viewfinder of your camcorder, or even on the **Viewer** in Final Cut Pro — that first moment has a magic of its own. It's a moment not to missed. Use it. Use it to grasp those first impressions, to find those visceral moments that affect you. As you watch, think about the relationships between pictures, between moments in time. Think about and watch for those moments that repeat themselves in various forms. This first viewing is crucial to editing.

When audio and video have separate In and Out points that aren't at the same time, the edit is called a split edit, J-edit, or L-edit. Whatever you call it, the effect is the same. There are many ways to create a split edit.

In the Timeline

Many instructors tell you to perform these edits in the **Viewer**, but I think the **Viewer** is the least flexible place to create them. Let's set up a split edit inside the **Timeline**. It's a much more logical place to perform this type of work and very effective. Personally, I prefer using the **Trim Edit** window, and we'll look at it on page 250.

In making split edits, particularly in the **Timeline**, you will be frequently linking and unlinking clips, switching off the link between synced video and audio. You can do this with the little switch in the upper right corner of the **Timeline** window (Figure 6.2).

Figure 6.2   Left: Snapping and Linking On Right: Snapping and Linking Off

You might want to switch **Linking** off if you want to move a lot of sync sound clips, splitting the audio and the video. But I don't think it's ever a good idea to switch off **Linking**. I think it should be maintained at all times and only toggled on and off for individual clips when needed. You might get away with leaving it off most of the time, but one day it will leap up and bite you hard. So for the purposes of these lessons, let's just leave **Linking** on.

The Cutaway

Any editor will tell you that cutaways are the most useful shots. You can never have too many, and you never seem to have enough. No editor will ever complain that you have shot too many cutaways. A cutaway shot shows a subsidiary action or reaction that you can use to bridge an edit. It's usually used to contract time, as we'll see a bit later. It's the shot of the onlookers watching. It's that overly used shot of a person's hands. The shot of the interviewer nodding in response to an answer is called in England a *noddie*. The noddie allows you to bridge a portion of the interviewee's answer where the person has stumbled over the words or has digressed into something pointless. A wide shot that shows the whole scene can often be used as a cutaway. Make note of these useful shots as you're watching your material.

In *Sequence 1* you should have laid out the shots *Ceremony1* through *Ceremony9*. If so, let's first delete the contents of *Sequence1* so we can use it for our edit. Let's look at the second shot, *Ceremony2*. Rather than opening it into the **Viewer,** just bring it straight into the **Timeline** play through it there. This shot starts out as a cutaway and then later pans across to the principal priest. You may notice that the priest's chanting begins before the camera reaches him. This will create a small problem for us that we'll quickly fix. The finished split edit can be seen in the **Browser** inside the *Split Edit Sequence*.

Let's first cut out the pan to the priest reading.

1. Working in the **Timeline,** find the point just before the camera pans from right to left.

2. Use **Control-V** to cut the shot.

3. Play forward till you find the point where the camera settles on the priest reading from the scroll.

4. Again use **Control-V** and the **Ripple Delete** (keyboard shortcut: **Shift-Delete**) to remove the section of the shot that contains the pan.

5. Play across the edit you've created.

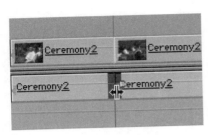

Figure 6.3 **Selecting Audio Edit**

Figure 6.4 **Dragging the Audio Roll Tool**

✎ Note _____

Toggling Linking: Option-clicking the audio (or video) edit point will only toggle off **Linking**, if **Linking** is turned on. If **Linking** is off, Option-clicking the edit point will toggle it on.

Split Edit Process

You'll see at once that the sound of the priest when he begins chanting has been cut off. This sounds quite ugly, but it's not a problem. It can be easily repaired with a split edit.

1. Hold down the **Option** key and click on the edit point as in Figure 6.3-to select only the audio portion of the edit.

2. If you have used **View>Level>Fit to Window**, it would probably be a good idea to zoom into the edit point a bit. Remember **Command-+** and **Command- -** will zoom in and zoom out from your selection or from the playhead.

It may be helpful if you turn on the audio waveform display in the **Timeline**. You can do this with the keyboard shortcut **Command-Option-W.**

3. Once the audio edit has been selected, hit **R** to call up the **Roll** tool.

4. Holding down the **Option** key, drag the audio edit point toward the head of the **Timeline**, well past where the chanting will begin (Figure 6.4). If **Snapping** is turned on, it may be helpful to toggle it off with the **N** key.

Notice a small box appears that gives you a time duration change for the edit you are making. We know the chanting is just a second or so before the start of the edit, so drag back well past that. You're overshooting the point at which you want to make the edit. I find this makes it easier to find a good cut point than simply trying to edge it into place. The **Timeline** audio waveform display will make it easy to see where the chanting begins, though often the clip name at the head of the track gets in the way. I wish there was a preference that allowed you to toggle clip names on and off as needed.

5. Scrub the **Timeline** or play that portion of the **Timeline** around the voice entrance back and forth a few times.

6. Use the arrow keys to precisely find the point where the audio starts. Once you've found the spot, leave the playhead parked there.

7. Again use the **Option**-Roll edit on the audio edit point and pull it back to the voice in point. Now it would be helpful if you toggled **Snapping** on with the **N** key. The roll edit will snap right to the playhead as in Figure 6.5.

Now the sound should play smoothly, coming in while the acolytes are bowing and then continuing after the cut to the priest.

 Tip _____

Cueing with Markers: We could have added a marker to the clip where the chanting begins before we ripple deleted the pan from the shot. This would have meant that we could use that as a visual cue to snap the roll edit to. Often, though, you've made the visual edit first and are then coming back to making the split edit later, which is where the **Trim Edit** window shows its benefits.

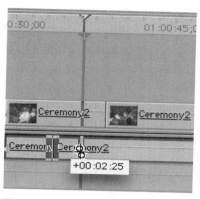

Figure 6.5   Dragging Audio Roll Edit to the Playhead

In this case the edit works quite smoothly because you're cutting within the same scene with basically the same audio ambience. However, this type of edit between scenes can create a jarring sound track. I often prefer to use a variation of this technique.

Alternative Method

Instead of simply doing the roll edit on the same inline audio track, I first move the audio down to an empty track so that the sound of the two shots overlap. This is easy to do.

1. Before beginning the split edit, **Option**-click on the audio portion of the track. This selects it independently from the video portion — temporarily unlinks it.

2. Now drag the audio track down to an empty audio track. Do not hold down the **Option** key, or you'll create a duplicate audio track rather than moving the audio track. As you drag it downwards, hold down the **Shift** key to constrain the movement to the vertical axis (Figure 6.6).

If there is no track in the space below the current track, a new audio track will be created. If you don't hold down the **Shift** key, the sound can easily slip out of sync with the picture. If that happens, you'll see time indicators in the **Timeline** tracks (Figure 6.7) showing you how far out of sync the clips have slipped.

Figure 6.6   Dragging Audio to New Track

Figure 6.7   Out of Sync Audio

The time slippage shows in a red box. The plus number means that the audio is three frames behind the picture. A minus number indicates that the audio is ahead of the video.

👉 *Tip*

Syncing: If the audio does slip out of sync, the easiest way to get it back in sync is to **Control**-click on the red box and choice **Move to Sync** from the popup menu (Figure 6.8).

You could also nudge the clip back into sync. **Option**-click on the audio to select the audio portion of the clip. If you just click on the audio, you'll select both video and audio even though they are out of sync. With only the audio selected, use the < or > keys to slide the clip forward or backwards.

As it moves, the time displays will update and finally disappear when the clip is back in sync. Every hit of the < or > keys nudges the clip one frame. Holding down the **Shift** will nudge the clip the trim amount you selected in your **Multi-Frame Trim Size** in the **General** preferences.

You can also select the audio portion of the clip (or whichever portion has free track space around it) and type plus or minus the value in the red box as in Figure 6.9. Then press the **Enter** key to move the clip.

Figure 6.8   Move to Sync

Figure 6.9   Typing in Numeric
Value to Move Audio

With the audio now on a separate track, you can now use the basic arrow tool, the **Selector,** to drag the audio edit point.

3. Hold down the **Option** key before you grab the end of the audio and drag the sound under the audio of the previous shot as in Figure 6.10.

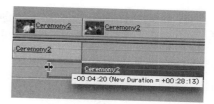

Figure 6.10 Option-Dragging Audio Edit to Overlap Sound

Extend Edit

Final Cut's **Extend Edit** is another nice way to perform a roll edit. It's a simple way to move an edit point, even one with a transition.

1. Choose an edit and click on it to select it.

2. Find your new edit point in the **Timeline** (or in the **Canvas**) and hit **E** or select **Sequence>Extend Edit**.

If the selection is dimmed or you hear a system warning, it's because you don't have enough media to perform the **Extend Edit**. What's nice about **Extend Edit** is that, like **Roll**, you can do it to sync picture and sound or to audio and video separately.

Removing Jiggle

Now that you've done the split edit, you may still have a little jiggle on the end of the first *Ceremony2* clip. A moment after the camera pans down the group of bowing men, just after it settles, it moves up and down a bit before beginning the pan that you've cut out. The simplest way to remove this bobble is to ripple the video.

Figure 6.11 Rippling Video

1. Select the **Ripple** tool (**RR**) and place the cursor slightly to the left of the edit point, as shown in Figure 6.11.

As soon as you let go of the mouse, something bad happens, I'm afraid. I think Final Cut's behavior is unfortunate in this technique. It actually breaks the sync link on the second shot (Figure 6.12). This does not occur when the audio tracks are inline. But there is a way around this problem.

Figure 6.12 SyncLinkBrokenAfter Ripple Edit

2. With the **Ripple** tool, click in the video portion to the left of the edit as before.

3. **Command**-click in the empty space right next to the audio on **A2** to select the space on the empty side of the edit (Figure 6.13).

Figure 6.13 Selecting Empty Side of Audio Edit Point

Figure 6.14 Rippling Split Edit with Empty Space

Now if you do the ripple edit, the empty space will be rippled as well, pulling the sync-linked audio with it (Figure 6.14).

Editing in the **Timeline** is a quick and easy way to work. Many people like it because it keeps you flowing through your material without taking you away from the sequence of shots. There are two other methods of doing split edits:

- One in the **Trim Edit** window

- The other in the **Viewer**

In the Trim Edit Window

This is where I prefer to do split edits. It's simple to use, efficient, and gives you good control over the material.

So that you won't have to go back and make up the edit again, I've prepared the sequence *Pan Edit Sequence*. Before we open it, though, let's duplicate it.

1. Select *Pan Edit Sequence* in the Browser and from the menus select **Edit>Duplicate** or use the keyboard shortcut **Option-D**.

2. Open up the duplicate you just created and look at the two halves of *Ceremony2* that are in the **Timeline**.

The pan has been cut out, but the audio of the chanting is still clipped, so you're ready to do the split edit.

3. **Option**-double-click on the audio track on the edit point between the two parts of *Ceremony2*.

We have to **Option**-double-click because we want to open the audio separately without affecting the video edit point. You can also **Option**-click on the audio edit point to highlight the edit and then hit **Command-7**. Either way will open the **Trim Edit** window as shown in Figure 6.15. It would be really nice if actual waveform displays of the audio showed up here rather than simply the large speaker icons.

If you drop the sound track to **A2** so that the audio will overlap as you did earlier, then **Option**-double-clicking on the end of the audio track will call up the **Trim Edit** window with black on the left and the speaker icon in the right window.

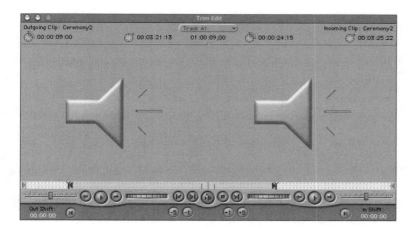

Figure 6.15   Audio Trim Edit Window

In either case, if you open the **Trim Edit** window with the standard **Selector** (**Arrow**) tool, the window defaults to working in **Roll** tool mode, which is what we want.

I like several using the **Trim** window because:

- You can listen to the audio track by scrubbing it.

- You can use the **J, K**, and **L** keys to rock and roll the playhead.

- You can use the **I** or **O** keys to set In or Out points.

When you use these features, the **Timeline** will immediately update the track position, sliding the audio of the second half of the shot under the first.

4. Use the play keys or scrub the track in the right window to find the In point for the start of the priest's chanting.

5. Press **I**.

It's a simple and efficient way to work.

These tools are key to creating interesting and effective audio tracks in Final Cut. Learn them and get comfortable using them.

Tip

Moving Slowly in the Trim Window: Unfortunately, the arrow keys will not move the playhead slowly in the **Trim Edit** window. You can though click and hold down the **Next Frame** or the **Previous Frame** buttons to move slowly forward and backward. You can also move forward slowly by holding down the **K** and **L** keys together. To move backwards slowly, hold down the **K** and **J** keys together. To go forward one frame, hold down the **K** key and tap **L**. Backwards one frame, tap **J**. Remember the spacebar here works to preview the edit point, which is very useful. And use the **U** key to toggle between the **Roll** tool and **Ripple First Shot** and **Ripple Second Shot**.

In the Viewer

Figure 6.16   Audio Panel

You can work in the **Viewer** similarly to the way you work in the **Trim Edit** window, but in the **Viewer** you have even greater control because you can actually see the audio waveform displayed. You can edit with precision.

1. Start by undoing the audio trim you just did in the duplicate of the *Pan Edit Sequence*. You should be back to the two halves of *Ceremony2*.

2. This time, **Option**-double-click on the audio portion of the second half of the shot. This will open the **Audio** panel in the **Viewer** (Figure 6.16).

3. Scrub through the audio to find the beginning of the chanting, and position the playhead at the start of the sound.

4. Use **Command-+** to zoom in around the playhead to see the waveform in real detail.

5. Before you enter a new In point, switch to the **Roll** tool (**R**) and then enter **I** for in.

This will do the same as the **Trim Edit** window, the **Timeline** will update with the new edit point.

In the Viewer 2

Figure 6.17   Split Edit in Viewer

There is another way to create a split edit in the **Viewer**, which is often shown to new users. I find it has little practical value. If you need it, here's how to do it.

1. Open *Ceremony1* into the Viewer from the **Browser**.

2. Play the clip until you find the point where you want the video to begin. In this case, we'll choose 02:47:21.

3. Instead of hitting **I** to enter the In point, hit **Control-I**.

This marks an In point for the video, leaving the audio at the original length. Note the markings in the **Viewer Scrubber Bar** and on screen in Figure 6.17-that indicate the split edit.

You can also make a split Out point using **Control-O**, which we'll be doing shortly.

Viewer To Timeline

The simplest way to work with the split edit in the **Viewer** is to drag and drop to the **Timeline**.

1. If you have the *Pan Edit Sequence* open, move the playhead to the end of the last shot. Drag the clip from the **Viewer** to the audio portion of the **Timeline**, as in Figure 6.18.

If there is no spare track there, FCP will create one for you. This is a bit of a clumsy way to do it. A more precise way would be to mark a split edit in the **Timeline**.

2. Undo the drag and drop if you have performed it.

3. With the playhead at the end of the sequence, press **Control-I** to mark an In point in the **Timeline** (Figure 6.19).

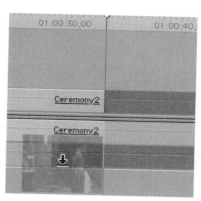

Figure 6.18   Dragging Split Edit to the Timeline

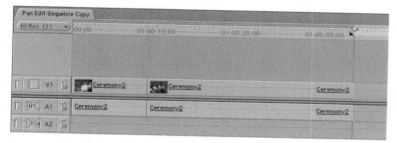

Figure 6.19   Split Edit Marked in Timeline

This will determine the video track that the picture will go to. If you want to cut the audio of *Ceremony2* on **A1**, drag to the **CEO** to **Overwrite**, or use **F10**. The edit will be performed as in Figure 6.20.

To place the audio of *Ceremony1* onto a lower track so that it overlaps the audio on **A1**, we need to change the targeted audio track.

4. Click the **1** position on **A2** (Figure 6.21). Then **Overwrite**. The edit will look like Figure 6.22.

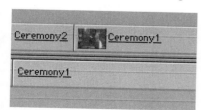

Figure 6.20   Split Edit Performed

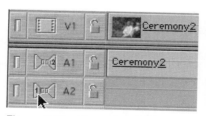

Figure 6.21   Targeting Audio Track Position

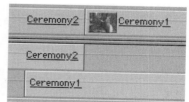

Figure 6.22   Overlapping Split Edit Performed

This technique of creating the split edit in the **Viewer** works best if you have the foresight to figure ahead of time where you want sound and video to come in and how you want them to overlap.

Backtiming

The crucial decision on editing audio, whether in the **Viewer**, the **Timeline**, or the **Trim Edit** window, is what leads and what follows. Will the audio come in first before the picture, as in the edits we did in *Ceremony2*? Or will the audio follow after the video starts, so that the audio of the first shot carries into the second? With one obvious exception, audio generally leads video, coming in before the picture appears. The obvious exception is music, which generally trails into the second shot and dies away as the next scene begins. We'll get to controlling audio levels on page 265, but first let's talk about how to control the video and lay it over picture so that the audio comes in first, a technique called backtiming. In the days of videotape editing, this meant some careful calculation on the part of the editor and the edit controller, but in nonlinear digital editing, this process is simplified.

Creating the Bed

To explain this concept, let's built a new sequence. My finished sequence *Drum Sequence* is in the **Browser**. You may want to look at it first. Or you may want to do the exercise and watch it later or not at all. But you should start by duplicating *Sequence 1* (**Option-D**). Open the new sequence and delete anything that's in the **Timeline**. To begin the sequence, let's look at the shot *Ceremony7*. It's about 20 seconds long and shows a medium-close shot of a priest chanting and banging a drum. Obviously this shot is too long to play as it is. On the other hand, I do want to see the priest in a closeup at some point. Because this shot contains the music, I want to use it as the basis for the scene. This will be the key shot in the scene. It's often useful to establish the key shot first, and then build the rest of the scene around it. Using

Figure 6.23   Marking Split In Point

Figure 6.24   Marked Split In and Out Points

this shot allows me to create a continuous event, with a couple of added bonuses:

- I don't have to cut the music, though in this case its repetitive nature would make cutting fairly simple.

- When I come to the priest banging the drum, he will be in sync.

1. Double-click on *Ceremony7* in the **Browser** to open it in the **Viewer.**

2. Play the clip from the beginning.

3. It starts with the priest chanting and then there is a response from the others. Around 05:29:18 the priest chants again. This is the point at which we want to come to him.

4. At 05:29:18 in the **Viewer Scrubber Bar,** hold down the **Control** key, and from the contextual menu, select **Mark Split>Video In** (Figure 6.23).
   Or use the keyboard shortcut **Control-I.**

This will create a split edit as we saw earlier.

5. Now play the clip until the priest finishes his chant, about 05:33:26.

6. Again use the **Control** key in the **Viewer Scrubber Bar**, but this time from the contextual menu select **Mark Split>Video Out** (or **Control-O**).

The clip in **Viewer** should look something like Figure 6.24.

7. Drag *Ceremony7* to the **Canvas Edit Overlay**, to either **Insert** or **Overwrite**, so that it drops into the **Timeline** at the beginning of the sequence.

Filling in the Blanks

What we need to do next is fill in the blanks, the area at the beginning of the shot and at the end. To do this we'll use some of the other shots from the event. I used the close shot as the bed for the scene because audio/video synchronization is more critical in the closer view than in the long shot such as in *Ceremony9*. This shot starts wide and at the end pushes into a priest sitting in the corner. It would be a classic way to begin the scene, with a wide, establishing shot. The trick here is to use the sound of the bed with the picture of this shot, the problem being to match sync the two. FCP gives you some tools to do this. Markers are the most important.

Using Markers

We looked at markers before as tools for logging and making subclips in "Organizing the Clips" on page 126 in Lesson 3. Now we'll work with them as editing tools. As we've seen before, these visual references points can be placed:

- On clips in the **Viewer**
- On a selected clip in the **Timeline**
- On the **Timeline** itself

To sync up the sound in the bed with the picture of another shot, we're going to place markers on both shots. First let's put a marker in *Ceremony7*.

1. **Option**-double-click on the sound track to open it in the **Viewer**.

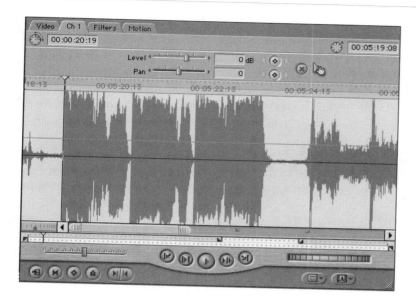

Figure 6.25 Audio Waveform

The first major burst of sound on the track, led by a clearly defined spike, is the sound of the drum (Figure 6.25).

2. Scrub the track till you've found the very beginning of the sound. Hit the **M** key to add a marker.

Now we want to match this frame with another shot.

3. Open *Ceremony9* in the **Viewer** and play the video till the priest strikes the drum.

It's quite hard in the small Viewer screen to see precisely when that moment is, but again the audio track gives us a much better clue.

☞ *Tip*

Waveform Cache: Sometimes the computer will have trouble displaying the waveform, particularly of subclips. It's helpful if you can open the master clip and go to the Audio tab to allow FCP to build up a waveform cache of the display. Once it's cached the master clip's waveform, it's much easier for it to load the subclip's waveform. It helps if you shorten the **Scaling** tab at the bottom of the **Viewer** (Figure 6.26). If you minimize the **Scaling** tab, you should see the waveform of the audio. It might help also to expand the scale of the Viewer window.

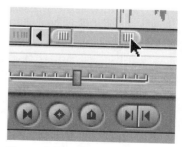

Figure 6.26 Scaling Tab

4. Click on the **Ch 1 Audio** tab in the **Viewer** and scrub the track till you find the drum sound and match it up with the spike on in the audio waveform.

Because the waveform gives a visual representation of the sound, it can be much easier to edit the sound in the **Audio** tab then it is by simply listening to it.

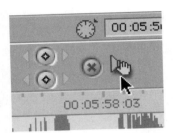

Figure 6.27   Audio Grab Handle

5. Once you've found the sound, put a marker on the clip with the **M** key. Grab the clip with the **Loudspeaker** grab handle at the top of the **Viewer** (Figure 6.27) and pull the clip into the **Timeline**.

Lining Up the Clips

1. Drag the clip onto the empty space above **V1**. As you do this, new tracks will be created for you, a new video track, **V2**, and a new audio track, **A3**.

Make sure the arrow indicator is pointing downward as you drag the clip. This will perform an overwrite edit, which is what you want to do, overwrite onto **V2** and **A3**. If you only drag the clip so that it is in the top third of a track, the arrow will be pointed to the right. This will slice everything on all unlocked tracks and push it down the timeline. This can be very useful, but in this case that would be a bad thing.

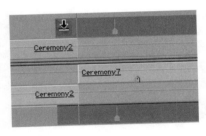

Figure 6.28   Aligning Markers in the Timeline

2. With **Snapping** toggled on (**N** key), slide *Ceremony9* along the **Timeline** until the markers line up as in Figure 6.28. You'll probably find that by coincidence, the beginning of the two shots line up.

✏ Tip

Deleting a Marker: You can delete a marker you're sitting with **Command-`**. Or you can hit the **M** key to call the dialog box and click the **Delete** button. Remember you can move to go to the next marker with **Shift-M** (or **Shift-Down** arrow) and **Option-M** (or **Shift-Up** arrow) to go to the previous marker. You can use the menus delete all the markers in a clip with **Mark>Markers>Delete All** (Figure 6.29). You can also use the keyboard shortcut **Control-`**. You can extend the duration of a marker with the keyboard shortcut **Option-`**.

It may be easier if you zoom into the timeline with either the scaling tab at the bottom of the Timeline window or with the **Zoom** tool (Figure 6.30), the **Z** key (**Z** for zoom). You hold down the **Option** key while you click in the **Timeline** to zoom out.

Remember, you can also use **Command-+** to zoom in and **Command- -** to zoom out.

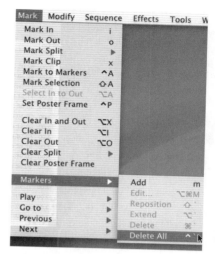

Figure 6.29   Mark>Markers> Delete All

👉 *Tip* _____

Zoom a Marquee: You can also use the **Zoom** tool to drag a marquee along a section of the **Timeline** (on a screen if you're in the **Viewer** or **Canvas**) to zoom into just that portion of the Timeline.

Once you've got the clips lined up, play through the area.

Notice that even though the clips are overlapped, Final Cut will simply play across the overlap as if it were a straight cut edit, switching from *Ceremony2* to *Ceremony9* on the upper track. Playing like this you should hear both sound tracks.

3. If the clips sound slightly out of sync, the drums not banging together, simply slide *Ceremony9* up or down the **Timeline** until the sounds match up.

4. As you line up the sounds, it may be helpful to toggle one of the sound tracks off so you can tell exactly which of the tracks you're hearing. To toggle off and on a track, click on the green button light on the left edge of the **Timeline** (Figure 6.31). The length of track will dim as you toggle the sound off.

Once you've got the first strike of the drum lined up, you'll notice that the rhythm is not very consistent and wanders fairly quickly.

Figure 6.30   Zoom Tool in the Timeline

👉 *Tip* _____

Invisibility: You can also switch off the visibility of an individual clip or audio track. To switch off just the audio portion, **Option**-click the audio to select it separately from the video. From the menus choose **Modify>Clip Visibility** (**Control-B**) (Figure 6.32). You can also use the Clip contextual menu to **Control**-click on the audio and choose **Clip Visibility** (Figure 6.33). New to FCP3 is the ability to solo items. If you wish to see only one video track or hear only one audio track, you can **Option**-click it to select it and choose **Sequence>Solo Item(s)** (Figure 6.34) or use the keyboard shortcut **Control-S**. This new function is not available in the contextual menus.

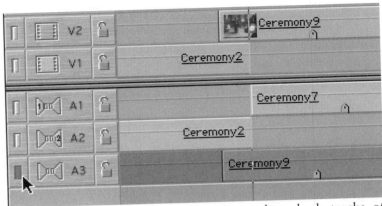

Figure 6.31   Toggling Sound
                      Track Off

5. Because you probably don't want to hear both tracks of audio, toggle off the sound for *Ceremony9*. Don't delete the track for *Ceremony9*; you may still want to hear it while you're working on the scene. But once the scene has been edited, you can safely delete the audio on **A3** from the **Time-line**.

6. When you do want to do that, **Option**-click on the audio for *Ceremony9* to select it separately from the video, and then simply delete it.

Because of the small size of the picture, you can easily get away with two drum hits, but I would suggest cutting away from the wide shot of the priest just before the third drum strike to mask the creeping loss of synchronization.

7. Use the **Blade** tool (**B**) to cut *Ceremony9* just before the third strike of the drum. Your timeline should look something like Figure 6.36.

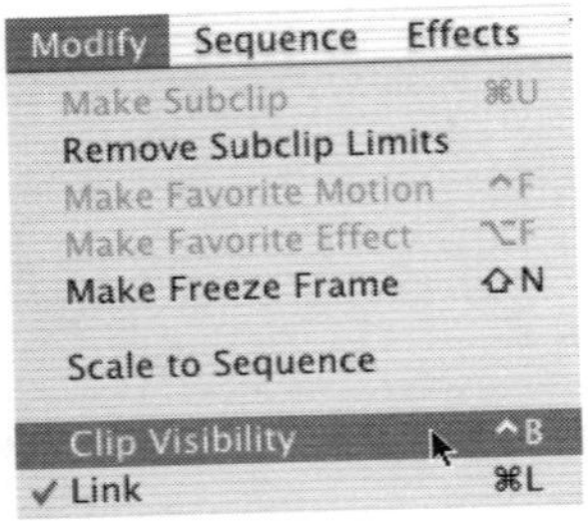

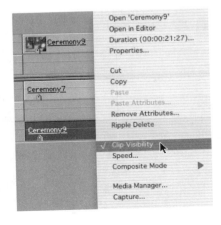

Figure 6.32   Modify>Clip Visibility

Figure 6.33   Contextual Menu>Clip Visibility

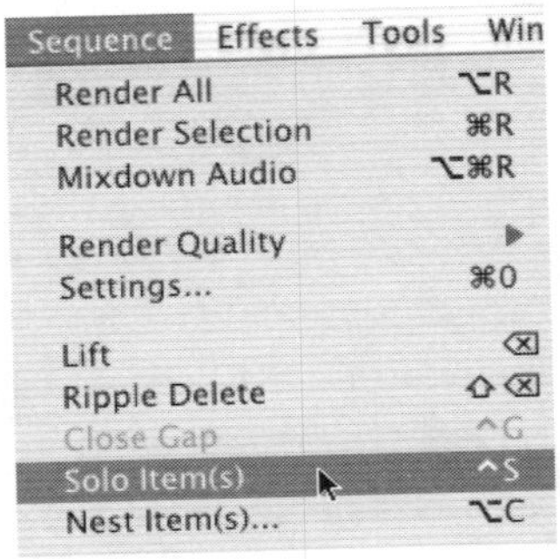

Figure 6.34   Sequence>Solo Item(s)

Waveform in the Timeline

It might also be beneficial to turn on the waveform display in Timeline window (Figure 6.35).

Figure 6.35   Waveform in Timeline

1. Do this by going to the **Sequence Settings** (Command-Zero).

2. Click on the **Timeline Options** tab

3. In the **Timeline Options** window, check the box marked **Show Audio Waveform**.

Because displaying the **Audio Waveform** in the **Timeline** takes a good deal of computer processing power, prereading the audio and then displaying it, the redraw ability and video playback capabilities of the computer are markedly slowed down. So it's a good idea to toggle the waveform display on and off as needed. Fortunately there is a simple keyboard shortcut to do this, **Command-Option-W**.

Second Edit

Rather than deleting the remainder of the shot, let's open the second part of *Ceremony9* in the **Viewer** from the **Timeline** and look at it. We could use the long section of drumming again later, as well as the zoom into the kneeling priest at the end of the shot. We'll use that next, but we'll cut out the zoom itself.

1. Go down to about 06:12:18 and mark a new In point.

Figure 6.36   Timeline with Bladed Clip on V2

Figure 6.37   Timeline After
Second Edit

2. Now pull the shot up against the first part of *Ceremony9* as in Figure 6.37.

3. Lock **V1**.

4. After cutting the clip with the **Blade**, you could also use the **Ripple** tool to pull up the beginning of the shot in the **Timeline**, watching the two-up display until you find where you want the second shot to start.

In this case, the **Ripple** technique will work, but in other circumstances, where you're not working at the head of a sequence, you can get in trouble because you'll be rippling the shot on **V1** as well, pulling it out of the sync with the material edited onto **V2**.

5. Play the scene a couple of times.

I think you'll see that the shot of the kneeling priest probably needs to be shortened. The nature of editing is that it creates patterns of rhythm. In this case, because of the music, the patterns are quite strong. We have also created a visual pattern. By cutting the long shot of priest before the third beat of the drum, we have determined to some extent the visual rhythm we'll follow for this short scene. If you play the sequence, you'll find a natural edit point after the call of the priest with the drum to the response of the gathered men. We need to find a shot for this.

Third Edit

At the beginning of the *Ceremony8* is the response of the acolytes, so this is what we'll use next. We want to place this shot onto **V2** cutting into the second portion of *Ceremony9*.

1. Park the **Timeline** playhead at the point you'll make the edit.

2. Now target the correct tracks, V2 and A3, either with the Target button on the left edge of the tracks (Figure 6.38) or with the keyboard shortcuts.

The keyboard shortcuts to target the video track are **F6** followed by the track number, in this case **2**. To target a particular channel of your audio, use **F7** for Channel 1 and **F8** for Channel 2. To set and audio track for that channel, follow the **F** key with the track number. So to target **Channel 1** to A3, press **F7** and **3**. We use **F7** because the audio on these clips is Channel 1.

3. Open up *Ceremony8* from the **Browser** into the **Viewer**.

4. When the tracks are targeted, cut *Ceremony9* as shown in Figure 6.39 in one of these ways:

   • Pull *Ceremony8* to **Overwrite** in the **CEO**.

   • Click on the red **Overwrite** button at the bottom of the **Canvas**.

   • Press **F10**.

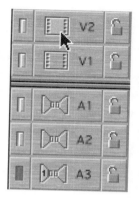

Figure 6.38   Track Target Buttons

👉 *Tip*

Foresight: If we had thought about it ahead of time, we could have added the Out point to the **Timeline**. Then when we did the **Overwrite**, not only would the shot have dropped in at the right spot, but it would have been cut off at the right spot. I tend to do the edit and then adjust it, rather than line it up perfectly and then perform the edit.

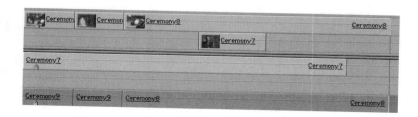

Figure 6.39   Timeline after Third Edit

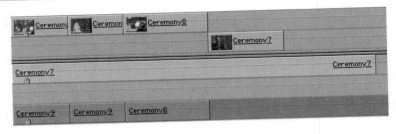

Figure 6.40   Timeline after Fourth
Edit

Fourth Edit

Obviously we have much more of *Ceremony8* than we need. Let's cut that down further. The logical place to make the cut is to let the shot extend until it reaches the video on **V1** or the base shot *Ceremony7* (Figure 6.40).

Fifth Edit

After the priest's call in *Ceremony7*, the acolytes make another response to end the scene.

1. Open up *Ceremony8* from the **Browser** again.

Notice that toward the end of the shot the camera pushes into a closer shot of the men in the corner. We'll use this portion of the shot next.

2. Mark an In point after the zoom, about 05:48:18.

3. Drag the shot onto V2, butting it to the end of the shot on V1 (Figure 6.41).

Be careful you don't drag the shot onto V1 or it will cut your primary audio track, unless you've locked the audio track already.

Sixth Edit

I probably wouldn't want to end the scene with this shot, but rather with the long shot of the priest again. Because we set the

Figure 6.41   Timeline after Fifth
Edit

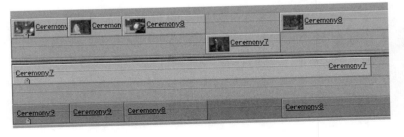

rhythm early on of two drum strikes then a shot change, we'll do the same again. We'll make the cut just before the third drum strike so we see the drum being struck in *Ceremony9*, the wider shot. Again the problem is syncing the drum hits. To do this, we'll again set markers in the audio of the base shot *Ceremony7* and in the **Browser** clip *Ceremony9*.

1. Open the audio from the **Timeline** for *Ceremony7* and set the marker for the drum strike as in Figure 6.42.

2. Open *Ceremony9* from the **Browser** and play the clip till the response section.

3. Set a marker on the first drum strike.

4. After you've set the marker, then back up a few frames and set the In point (Figure 6.43).

You really want to cut to the shot before the strike so that you see it happen, rather than cutting on the strike, when all you would see in the shot is the hand coming away from the drum.

5. After you've set the In point, pull *Ceremony9* from the **Viewer** into the **Timeline** and drop it onto the area above **V2** to create yet another video track as in Figure 6.44.

6. Fiddle the tracks, sliding *Ceremony9* up and down the **Timeline**, till drum strikes match up.

This time, however, we're not going to mute the audio for *Ceremony9* as we did for the audio on **A3**; we're going to mix the two tracks using the level controls.

Controlling Audio Levels

You can adjust audio levels in two primary areas:

*   Viewer

*   Timeline

We'll look at adjusting levels in the **Viewer** first.

In the Viewer

1. Open the audio *Ceremony7* into the Viewer.

Figure 6.42   Setting Marker in the Audio Clip

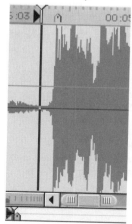

Figure 6.43   Setting Marker in the Audio Clip with a New In Point

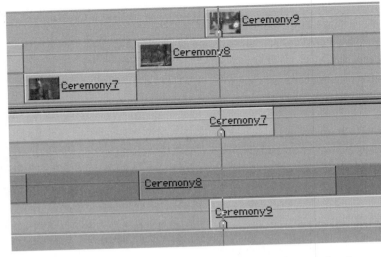

Figure 6.44 Timeline after Sixth Edit

Notice the mauve line in the center of the audio track. As you move the cursor over the line, it changes to a line-moving tool (Figure 6.45).

At the top of the Figure 6.45 you'll notice the **Level** slider and the **Indicator** window. It's currently at 0, which is the level at which the audio was digitized or captured.

2. With the line-moving cursor, grab the audio level line and push it up or pull it down.

This moves the level for the overall audio level of the whole clip. As you move the line up or down, both the **Level** slider and the **Decibel Indicator** window at the top move. A small window appears in the waveform as well that shows the amount in decibels (dB) that you're changing the audio level (Figure 6.46). The computer sometimes has difficulty redrawing the screen.

You often don't want to move the whole level of the audio, just a portion. To do this, you need to put keyframes on the **Audio Level** line, which allow you to bend the line, ramping the audio level value up or down.

3. To add a keyframe, hold down the **Option** key as the cursor approaches the **Level** line. The cursor then changes into the **Pen** tool (Figure 6.47).

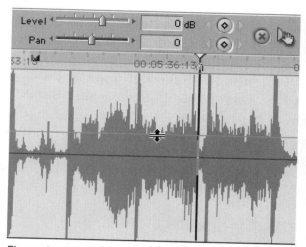
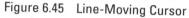

Figure 6.45   Line-Moving Cursor

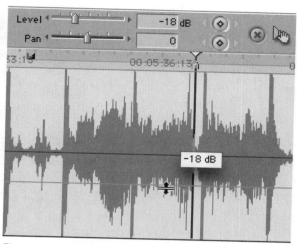

Figure 6.46   Decibel Level
Change Indicators

You can also select the **Pen** from the tools or call it up with the **P** key.

4. Go further along the timeline and add another keyframe with the **Pen** tool.

5. Then pull the level line down so that the audio fades out over time (Figure 6.48).

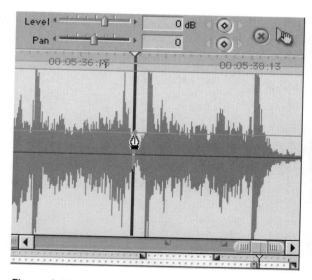

Figure 6.47   Pen Tool in the Viewer

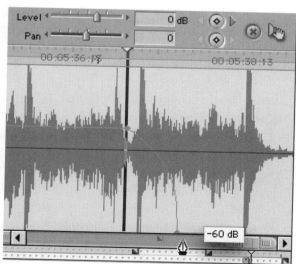

Figure 6.48   Audio Fade Out

Pan and Spread

In addition to the mauve **Level** line in the **Viewer**, there is also a purple **Pan** line. This allows you to move the audio from one side of the stereo speakers to the other. In the **Mono Mix** used in these clips, audio with only one channel, only a single **Audio** tab appears in the **Viewer**. The audio for *Damine.mov* defaults to a **Pan** value of zero, centered between the two speakers of a stereo system (Figure 6.49).

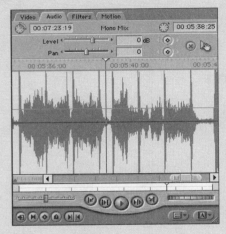

Figure 6.49   Default Pan Value

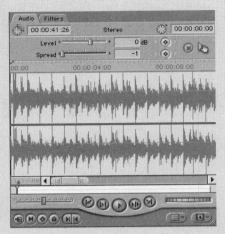

Figure 6.50   Stereo Pair Audio Panel

Using the **Pan** line, you can shift the sound to come from either the left side or the right side. Moving the **Pan** slider to the left to −1 will move all the sound to the left speaker, and moving the **Pan** slider all the way to the right to 1 will move the sound to the right speaker. Like **Levels**, **Pan** values can be keyframed. The classic example is the racing car that approaches from the left with all sound coming from the left speaker, roars by and disappears to the right, while the sounds sweeps past to the right speaker.

When you have a multitrack recording with separate **Channel 1** and **Channel 2** sound, the **Viewer** appears with separate tabs, one for each channel. **Levels** and **Pan** values can then be set separately for each track.

In a stereo clip, on the other hand, both audio tracks appear in one panel (Figure 6.50). When there is a stereo pair of audio, the purple lines display **Spread** instead of **Pan** and is defaulted down to −1 so that the two tracks are centered between the speakers. Spreading the audio will move the stereo sound farther and farther apart.

A multitrack recording can be changed into a stereo pair from the **Modify** menu by selecting **Stereo Pair**. This will toggle the audio between being a stereo pair with both audio tracks changing level in unison and being two separate channels of audio whose **Levels** and **Pan** values can be controlled separately.

You can also add keyframes with the little diamond button next to **Levels** slider. Click the little button, which will turn green while adding a keyframe to the level line. Go to a different point in time. Then pull the **Levels** slider up or down to change the sound volume, and another keyframe will be added.

There are several ways to delete an audio keyframe:

- Grab it and pull it down out of the audio timeline

- Hold down the **Option** key when you're over the keyframe. The cursor will change into the **Pen Delete** tool (Figure 6.51).

- Use the contextual menu, clicking on the keyframe and selecting Clear.

- If the playhead is sitting on a keyframe, you can also remove it by simply clicking the little green keyframe diamond next to the **Levels** slider. This will turn the keyframe button gray and remove the keyframe in the **Level** line.

To delete all the keyframes in the audio, click the **Reset** button, the button with the red X next to the **Grabber** at the top of the panel (Figure 6.52).

To move the keyframe, grab it and slide it left and right along the line.

In the Timeline

It's often easier to control audio levels in the **Timeline** itself. The controls work in exactly the same fashion as in the **Viewer**. The first step to take is to activate the **Level** lines, which normally remain hidden — a good thing, so that you don't accidentally grab the **Level** line and change the setting when you're grabbing a clip.

To turn on the **Level** lines:

- Click on the **Clip Overlays** button on the lower left corner of the **Timeline** (Figure 6.53) or

- Use the keyboard shortcut **Option-W**.

 Tip

No Switching Necessary: If there already is a keyframe on the level line, then you don't need to switch to the **Pen** tool with the **Option** key. The cursor will automatically change to a crosshairs as you move over the audio node. If you are working with the **Pen** tool and you want to switch to the straight-level line-moving tool, hold down the **Command** key.

Tip

Fixing Soft Audio: Sometimes audio is just too low to be as forceful as you'd like, even after you crank it up with FCP's level controls. A neat little trick is to double up the audio tracks. Just put another copy of the same sound on the track below and push that audio level up as well. Double your pleasure. It's saved me more than once in a pinch.

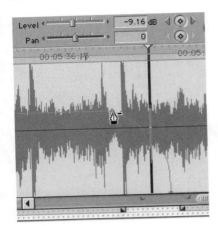

Figure 6.51 Pen Delete Tool

Figure 6.52 Reset Button

Figure 6.53 Clip Overlay Button

 Tip

Nesting: If you nest your audio into a new sequence, you can push it up quite a bit. We'll talk about nesting in "Nesting" on page 334 in Lesson 8.

As when editing in the **Viewer**, you can shift the red **Level** line up and down. Adding the **Option** key lets you add a keyframe. By adding another keyframe farther down the line, you can pull down the level in a curve that fades the sound out (Figure 6.54).

You can also select a single track, multiple tracks forward and backward, a single track forward and backward, or a whole track of audio and adjust their levels globally.

Select the items or the track with the **Track** tool (**T**) (Figure 6.55). Once you have your track or clips selected, go to **Modify>Levels** (**Command-Option-L**).

This command calls up a dialog box that allows you to adjust the audio levels of the clips (Figure 6.56). The slider or the value box will change the gain setting for all the clips selected.

Tip

Changing Levels: A new way to change levels for clips has been introduced in FCP3. You can copy an audio clip by selecting it and pressing **Command-C**. Now select by marqueeing or **Command**-clicking the clips you want, and then use the **Paste Attributes** function from the **Edit** menu or pressing **Option-V**. Then check the attributes you want to paste to the other clips' **Levels** or **Pan** values (Figure 6.57). We shall look at pasting attributes more closely in Lessons 9, 11, and 12.

Changing Levels in Keyframes: You can also change the relative or absolute levels of a group of audio keyframes. Use the **Range** tool to select the area that includes the audio keyframes. If you then apply the **Levels** tool, it will raise or lower the relative or absolute values of the keyframes in the selected area.

Figure 6.54 Fade Out in the Timeline

Figure 6.55 Track Tool

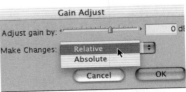

Figure 6.56 Audio Controls

The **Relative** and **Absolute** popup sets how the gain is affected. **Absolute** will make the level you set affect the whole of all the clips, eliminating any fades. Using the **Relative** setting will change the value of the levels relative to each other. This global levels control not only works on audio, but also works on other levels, such as opacity.

1. On *Ceremony7*, set the first level keyframe just after the drum strike.

2. Place the second keyframe at the end of the fade out shortly before the next drum strike.

3. Fade up the sound on *Ceremony9* as shown in Figure 6.58 so that the drum strike is inaudible and the next drum strike you hear is the sound on *Ceremony9*.

You have now created a crossfade between the tracks on A1 and A4.

Level Markers

New to FCP is the ability of the application to analyze the audio levels of a clip or a sequence and place markers indicating where the sound exceeds acceptable levels. You can then simply pull down the levels, or keyframe the area around the overloaded audio and pull it down that way. It's very simple to do. Start by selecting the clip you want analyzed, either in the **Browser** or in the **Timeline**. Or select an entire sequence, or have an open **Timeline** window active. Then choose from the **Tools** menu **Mark Audio Peaks** (Figure 6.59). The application will quickly look through the clip or sequence and place a marker wherever it detects an audio peak.

It's probably not a good idea to select multiple clips in a sequence and run the analysis because markers will be placed on each of the clips in the **Timeline**. This may show you where the audio is overloaded on individual clips, but it will not tell you if the cumulative effect of multiple tracks of audio will exceed peak levels. With sequence markers, the analysis is done quite quickly, and with waveforms displayed in the **Timeline**, it's pretty easy to see where the peaks are occurring, especially if you zoom into a section of the **Timeline** more closely, as in Figure 6.60.

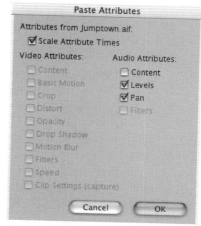

Figure 6.57 Pasting Audio Attributes

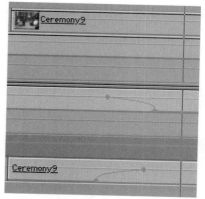

Figure 6.58 Crossfading Audio Tracks

Figure 6.59 Tools>Mark Audio

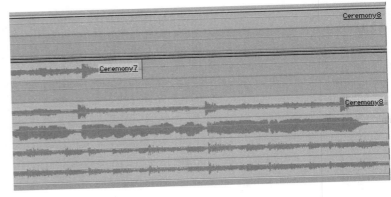

Figure 6.60 Audio Marks in the Timeline

Notice also that if there are extended portions of peak audio, FCP will place extended markers in the **Timeline**. It may be an idea to bring down the overall levels on some of these clips to make the audio levels acceptable. Simple lower the levels with the tools we've seen, and run the analysis again.

You can clear audio peak markers either with the standard marker clearing tools (**Control- tilde**) or individual markers. To specifically delete audio peak markers choose from the **Tools** menu, **Clear Peak Marks**.

Voice Over

Final Cut Pro 3 has another new feature called **Voice Over** that allows you to record audio tracks directly to your hard drive while playing back your **Timeline**. **Voice Over** is most valuable for making *scratch tracks*, test narrations used to try out pacing and content with picture. It could be used for final recording, though you'd probably want to isolate the computer and other extraneous sounds from the recording artist. Many people actually prefer to record narrations prior to beginning final editing, so the picture and sound can be controlled more tightly. Others feel that recording to the picture allows for a more spontaneous delivery from the narrator. However you use it, **Voice Over** is an important new addition to the application.

Voice Over is part of the new **Tool Bench**, and is called up from the **Tools** menu (Figure 6.61). This brings up the window in Figure 6.62.

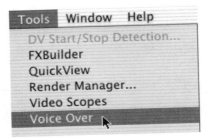

Figure 6.61 Tools>Voice Over

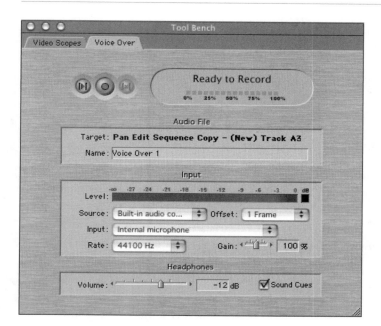

Figure 6.62   Voice Over Tool

It's probably best to work with **Voice Over** in the **Three-Up** arrangement. This places the **Viewer** on the left, the **Canvas** in the center, and the **Voice Over** panel itself on the right. I always prefer working with a longer **Timeline**, and so I use a variation of this. If you load the book's CD you can select the layout from the **Window** menu, **Window>Arrange>Restore Layout (Shift-Option-U)** and navigate to the CD itself. Open the folder *Window Layouts* and select *Voice Over*.

The first steps you'll have to take are to configure your recording setup for your **Source, Input,** and **Sampling Rate**.

✎ *Note*

More RAM for VO: Because **Voice Over** works in RAM, storing the sound before recording it to disk, you may need to put more RAM into your computer over and above the minimum requirements asked for by FCP3 because the audio is buffered in RAM as it's recorded. 48kHz audio consumes 6MB per minute. So a half-hour track would take 180MB. All of these recordings are stored in your *Capture Scratch* folder with the project name.

✎ *Tip*

iMic: The iMic from Griffin Technologies is a handy little device that's very useful for working with **Voice Over**. It's a small analog-to-digital converter that allows you to connect a microphone to your computer through its USB port. The iMic allows you to digitize audio at 16-bit, 48kHz, the standard for most DV work. The internal mic input on the Mac digitizes at 44.1, the CD audio standard, which may mean you are mixing sampling rates within your sequence.

Source defines where the sound is coming from: the computer mic input, a USB device, a camcorder, or an installed digitizing card.

Input controls the type of signal being received, whether it's line level, balanced audio in, digital audio, or whatever your source device is capable of handling.

Offset adjusts for the delay taken by the analog to digital conversion. USB devices typically take one frame. DV cameras can be three frames or more.

Let's look at some of the controls in this panel. The large red button, the middle of the three in the top portion of the window, is the **Record** button. It will also stop the recording, as will the **Escape** key. The button to its left is the **Preview/Review** button and will play the selected area of your sequence. The button to the right is the **Discard** button. Immediately after a recording or after aborting a recording, pressing the **Discard** button will delete the file from your hard drive, which is why you get the warning dialog in Figure 6.63.

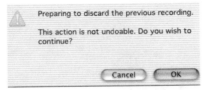

Figure 6.63   Discard Warning Dialog

The **Gain** slider, next to the **Input** popup, allows you to control the recording level based on the horizontal LCD display meter. This is fine for scratch tracks, but for finished work, it would probably be better to have a hardware mixer before the input for good mic level control.

Note _____

Playback Levels: Don't be fooled by FCP's vertical audio meters. These display the playback levels, and do not show the recording level.

The **Headphones** volume does just what it says. If there is nothing jacked into the headphone output of your computer, the sound will come out of the computer speaker itself. To avoid recording it or the **Sound Cues**, pull the **Volume** slider down to the minimum level.

FCP gives the recording artist elaborate **Sound Cues**, which are turned on with the little checkbox. Together with the aural sound cues in the headphones, there is visual cuing as well, which appears in the window to the right of the **Record** button. As the recording starts, a countdown begins, with cue tones as the display, that starts pale yellow (Figure 6.64) becomes darker and more orange until when recording begins. Then the display changes to red (Figure 6.65). There is a cue tone at 15 seconds from the end of the recording as well as beeps counting down the last five seconds to the end of the recording (Figure 6.66). Recording actually begins during countdown and continues two seconds after the end of the recording during **Finishing**. Though this doesn't appear in the **Timeline** after the recording, you can simply drag out the front and end of the clip if the voice started early or overran the end.

I think the best way to work with **Voice Over** in the **Timeline** is to define an In and Out point as in Figure 6.67. If no points are defined, recording will begin at the point at which the playhead is parked and go until the end of the sequence, or until you run out of available memory, whichever comes first. You can also simply define an In point and go from there, or define an Out and go from the playhead until the Out is reached. Because the **Timeline** doesn't scroll as the sequence plays, it might be helpful to reduce the sequence to fit the **Timeline** window. **Shift-Z** will do this with a keystroke.

Recording is always done to a targeted track that has free space. If there is no free space within the defined area of the recording, **Voice Over** will *always* create a new track. So if you record multiple takes, they will record onto the next lower track or onto a new track. The **Audio File** window will give you the track information. If there is no free space, a new track will be created, as in Figure 6.68. You can name the recording in the **Audio File** window, and each take will be numbered incrementally.

Figure 6.64   Starting

Figure 6.65   Recording

Figure 6.66   Finishing

Figure 6.67   Timeline Marked for Voice Over

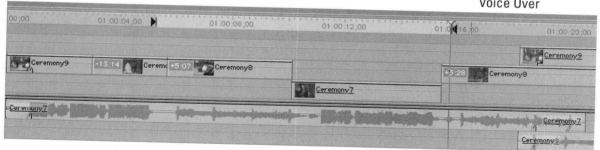

After a discarded take, **Voice Over** will record to the previously assigned track with the previously assigned name. After a few takes, you may want to discard a previous take and reassign the targeted track so that **Voice Over** will work with the empty tracks you vacated as in Figure 6.69, which shows an aborted recording on a higher track.

Figure 6.68   Audio File Window

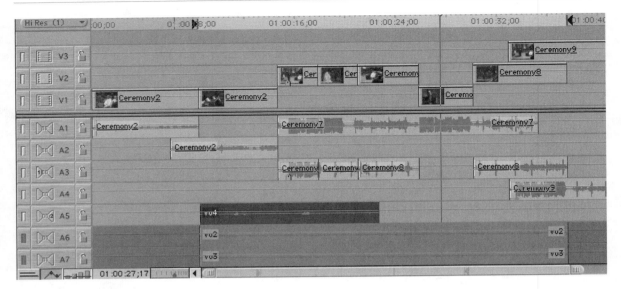

Figure 6.69 Timeline after
Recording Takes

The next recording will take place on a new **A6** between *vo4* and *vo2*. Or I could simply discard *vo4*, and the next recording will be on the blank **A5** again, using the recording name *vo4*. Also, you should switch off previous takes as you go so that the talent doesn't hear the previous recording in the headphones while recording.

After a recording session with **Voice Over**, it would not be a bad idea to go into your hard drive and root out old tracks that aren't needed and may be filling up your drive. It's probably simplest to do this from the application. Those takes you recorded that you no longer want can be deleted from your sequence, but they aren't automatically deleted from your hard drive. You can't make something offline from inside a sequence, but you can drag the unneeded takes into a bin in your **Browser** and from there make them offline, deleting them from the drive. Also remember, the recordings are only a part of your sequence and will not appear in your **Browser** at all, unless you put them there.

I confess **Voice Over** would not have been on the top of my priority list to put into this version of the software, but that said, I think Apple has done an outstanding job in implementing it.

Summary

In this lesson we looked at working with sound in Final Cut. Performing split edits, overlapping sound, cutting with sound, overlapping and crossfading-tracks, as well as FCP's new **Voice Over** tool. Sound is often overlooked, seeming insignificant or of minor importance, but it is crucial to making a sequence appear professionally edited.

In the next lesson we'll look at the different forms of editing — documentary, music, action, and dialog — and how to work in them using Final Cut Pro 3.

Tip

No Timecode in Voice Over: There is no timecode or other identifying information other than the assigned name with any **Voice Over** recording, if you need to reconstruct your project at a later date. It may be an idea to keep this recording preserved on tape if you want to use it again.

Lesson 7
<u>Lesson 7</u>

Advanced Editing: The Moment

The French film director Jean-Luc Godard called cinema "truth 24 times a second." For the film editor, the moment of the truth is choosing which 24 instances in a second to change the image from one to another. In the case of a video editor, that moment of truth comes every 29.97th of a second. An edit is that precise, that fraction of a moment in time, which may not seem that important, but a moment that has a fundamental effect on the way the viewer perceives the scene. We're going to spend this lesson looking at the moment, how to find it, and how to use it. You have by now learned the fundamentals of how to use this application. Now we need to hone those skills. The moment of the edit is nowhere more clear than in the classic question of where to cut on an action. We'll look at that later in this lesson.

The moment of the edit is dictated by rhythm, sometimes by an internal rhythm the visuals present, sometimes by a musical track, more often than not by the rhythm of language. All language, dialog or narration, has a rhythm, a cadence or pattern, dictated by the words and based on grammar. Grammar marks language with punctuation: commas are short pauses; semicolons are slightly longer pauses; periods (full stops, as they're called in England) are the end of an idea. The new sentence begins a new idea, a new thought, and it is natural that as the new thought begins, a new image is introduced to illustrate that idea. The shot comes, not on the end of the sentence, not in the pause, but on the beginning of the new thought. This is the natural place to cut, and it's this rhythm of language that drives the rhythm of film and video. We'll look at this more closely in this lesson.

Loading the Lesson

Let's begin by loading our material. This is going to sound familiar, but it's worth repeating. Begin by loading the material you need onto the media hard drive of your computer.

1. If you don't already have it on your drive, drag the *Media1* folder from the CD to your media drive.

2. This time also drag the folder *Media2* to your media drive.

3. Open the *Projects* folder on the CD, drag the *Lesson 7* folder onto your system hard drive, and place it inside your *Shared* folder.

4. Eject the CD, open the folder on your system drive, and double-click the project file *L7* to launch the application.

5. Once again choose the **Reconnect** option to relink the media files when the **Offline Files** dialog appears.

Again, the first step you should take after your project has reconnected is to save it.

6. Use **Save Project As** from the **File** menu and save the project with a new name inside the *Lesson7* folder.

Next make sure the scratch disk is properly assigned.

7. Go to **Final Cut Pro>Preferences** and click on the **Scratch Disks** tab.

8. Click on the **Set** button and navigate to the hard drive that holds the *Media1* folder.

9. Click on the *Media1* folder to highlight it and then click on the **Choose** button.

10. Make sure that *Autosave Vault* is also set to your *Shared* folder.

Setting up the Project

Inside the project, you'll find these sequences in the **Browser**:

- An empty sequence called *Sequence 1*
- *Action Cut Sequence*
- *Chopsticks*

We'll look at *Action Cut* and *Chopsticks* later in the lesson. Other items include:

- The master clip called *Damine.mov*
- The folder called *Clips*, which contains the subclips pulled from *Damine.mov*, as well as another folder called *Heartwood*

Editing Forms

One of the first points to consider in any production is the form in which it will be delivered. This should not be happening when you are in postproduction, but rather when you are writing, and congruent to that, when you are planning production, when you are shooting, and then finally when you are editing. If your end product is a film to be seen on a large screen, it's shot in a certain way and edited in a certain way. Shots can be held longer because there is so much to see and so much space for the eye to cover and travel around. The same movie seen on the small screen of a television set will appear to be cut too slowly, because you take in the whole image without your eye moving, so you take it in more quickly. Of course, you also see less detail.

If your project is intended for delivery on television, it should be shot for television's limitations of luma and chroma values. If it's shot for delivery on a computer screen, you aren't bound by those limits, but perhaps by greater limits dictated by compression. If you're going to squeeze your video down for web delivery, you need to shoot it with as few moves as possible, use few transitions (which don't compress well), and shoot plainer, less busy backgrounds. Delivery should be the first consideration in a production, not the last, and every step of the process, from scripting through final editing, should bear the delivery mechanism in mind.

Film and video production, not unlike book production, is a team effort, starting with an idea and expanding outward. It grows, getting fuller and more detailed, but all refers back to the original idea. What determines how the production is edited is that original idea. It goes from the script to govern:

- What and how the video is shot
- Where the emphasis is placed
- What is looked at in the scene and from what angle
- What elements are created for juxtaposition

The elements are the shots, called clips when they are collected in Final Cut Pro's **Browser**. Often a scene will be shot from a number of different camera angles all the way through to give the editor the greatest variety of selection material.

But a director who knows in his mind how the shots will be cut together will probably be more effective than one who shoots lots of cover material without a clear idea of how it will come together. Without having an idea how the material will be put together, it's difficult for the director to judge the pacing within each shot. If the action is slow within the shot, then the shots will have to be cut together slowly. If the action is fast paced, it will force the editing to be fast. In dialog films, the order of shots often goes all the way back to the writer. His choice of words, the sequence of imparting information within the dialog, will be the first steps in determining the order of shots. Eventually we arrive at the editor, who has a selection of material and an order of shots to some degree determined by the content, be it dialog, narration, or intellectual logic.

Each of the many common editing forms requires a different approach to the material. The forms I'd like to look are:

- Documentary
- Music
- Action
- Dialog

Obviously these will all overlap to some extent or other. Each has its own variations, and techniques that apply to one will get used in others, but these four offer the principal challenges an editor might face. Though narrative film, the Hollywood and independent feature film, is the most visible film and video production, it makes up only a very small portion of production in America and around the world. Final Cut Pro is being used on a vast range of projects. On any single weekend day in June, probably more wedding videos are produced in America than all the feature films made in Hollywood in a year, and some of those wedding videos are longer than feature films. Or maybe they just seem that way.

There are many different ways to work, perhaps as many different ways as there are editors. Probably the longer the project, the more variations in work flow. How you organize your material is critical in long-form production. Many people like to work in organized bins; some prefer to work with multiple sequences with very few bins. Those coming from the Media100 editing software often work like this: one or two bins for the major material, then sequences with the shots gathered together by scene or subject matter. The final scene is then made up by selecting shots for multiple open **Timelines** and moving them to the final sequence. This way of working is best with very large computer monitors.

Others prefer to work with multiple bins, all of them open at once, all in Icon view. A second computer monitor is almost a prerequisite for working like this. Others prefer to work with toggled open bins set in list view with the **Comments** and **Log Notes** columns pulled over next to the **Name** column. Others like to use the **Find** tool, leaving found multiple lists open at the same time. As you become more experienced, you'll find yourself working with some methods more than others. You'll probably also find that on different projects, you work in different ways. Some material lends itself to working with multiple sequences; other material might not. Some workflows are faster than others. Laying out clips in bins that you trim in the **Viewer** and then rearrange as a storyboard might sound good, but cutting up and rearranging material entirely in a **Timeline** is probably a lot quicker for small amounts of material.

Documentary

Documentary is a loosely used term for factual film or video production. Generally these are productions that usually present facts and have a narration, either a disembodied voice or one made up from those appearing in the video. Documentaries are the type of shows you might see on the Discovery Channel or National Geographic. Documentary, news, reportage, informational, and even instructional are all variations of the same type of video, much like the type of material we're dealing with in this lesson. Some documentaries are tightly scripted to start, shot to a prewritten narration, and edited from that, with few changes along the way. Others are wholly made up in the editing room, usually when they have mediocre shots. Good, experienced camerapersons, whether they realize it or not, are actually scripting the story as they shoot it. Certainly every good news cameraperson is shooting with the correspondent's voice reading the lines in his head. Chances are if it isn't shot for any particular purpose, it will probably not find any use at all.

Documentary can be a factual, accurate representation of events, or it can be an imaginative, poetical, loose interpretation of reality. Either way, documentary can start fully scripted, wholly unscripted, or something in between. One feature that both forms have in common is the tendency to shoot vastly more material than necessary, sometimes with shooting ratios as high as 25:1, even 100:1.

Documentary scripts aren't written so much as found, or so says my friend Loren Miller, and there's much truth to that. The mass of material in a documentary is often best sorted out on paper before the picture is attacked. The paper edit is crucial, and the paper edit is the mining for the script that's in the material, Michelangelo finding the statue that's in the stone. The paper edit can be done from transcripts, from log notes, on an Excel spreadsheet, or on 3×5 cards. The idea is always the same: move the information around, find the links, find what flows together, find the conflicts, the drama, and visual strength in the material and put it together into a coherent plan that can be taken into the cutting room.

Music and Narration

I have been asked if it is better to cut the music or the narration in a sequence. Personally I don't think you should be having to make a choice between cutting on the music or cutting on the narration. If you're having to make that choice, then there is probably something more fundamentally wrong with the sequence. There should either be music which you're cutting to or there should be narration. I very much dislike productions that lather music under everything. You should bring the music up for a purpose, and while it's up full, you should be cutting to the music. Then when you bring in the narration, you should fade out the music under the narration, but just keeping it there as a bed I think is almost always wrong (unless it's integral to the scene that's being narrated).

If you're having to chose between cutting to one or the other, the music or the narration, then either the music doesn't belong there: it's the wrong music, or it's the wrong narration. Even in a sequence where music is a key element — a video about dance, for instance — you are cutting to the rhythm of the music while the music is up, and then to the narration when it's up, even if the music continues underneath. Often with this kind of production, it's better to make the narration quite sparse, and punctuated more frequently than you normally would with sections of music. So you get a phrase or a sentence or two at most, then go back to the music and dance briefly, before returning to another short piece of narration. What should be avoided in almost every instance is the tendency to have a blanket of narration lying on top of a blanket of music.

The unscripted documentary benefits greatly from the advent of nonlinear editing systems, because not only does it give the editor very powerful search tools, but it also allows quickly trying many combinations of images. Organizing your material is crucial to working efficiently in the documentary form. Well-organized bins with many notes throughout are very beneficial. After working through various shot orders, the frames themselves seem to impose a continuity by being adjacent to each other. Certain shots will seem to want to go together, as will others. Then groups of images coalesce into clusters, and the clusters form logical strings, until the whole is built out of the parts and a structure has imposed itself on the material.

Documentary generally uses a narration track to carry the information, whether it's a disembodied voice of God speaking truths, or an ever-present narrator who wanders through the scene, or even if it's pieced together from interviews. The narration becomes the bed for the video.

What many editors like to do is build a bed of the primary audio track and its synchronous video. So if the video starts with a short piece of music, lay down the music on a lower audio track, leaving the primary tracks open for the video. Then the narration comes in. Lay down the narration on a separate track. Then a piece of an interview comes in, so lay in the sound bites in their entirety with the sync picture, jump cuts and all. The picture can always be covered later. Then perhaps more narration, and then another musical break. You can go on and on building the entire sound track like this if you wish so it looks something like Figure 7.1. This is where FCP3's new **Voice Over** feature comes in handy, for recording the kind of scratch recording, a rough narration, to lay down as the basis for the bed.

At this stage, the laid-out video might have a distinctly blocky look to it, but as the material is worked, more and more overlapping of sound and picture will begin to appear.

Some people like to work in a very linear fashion, tightly editing the material as they go. It's quite natural to build a sequence this way, this is the natural way a story progresses, linearly. On the other hand, I think the benefit of laying out the bed is that you get to see what the whole structure is like, where emphasis needs to be placed, where more graphical explanation is needed perhaps, where there are parts that may need to be cut because they're taking too much time, or a minor point is being dwelt on too long.

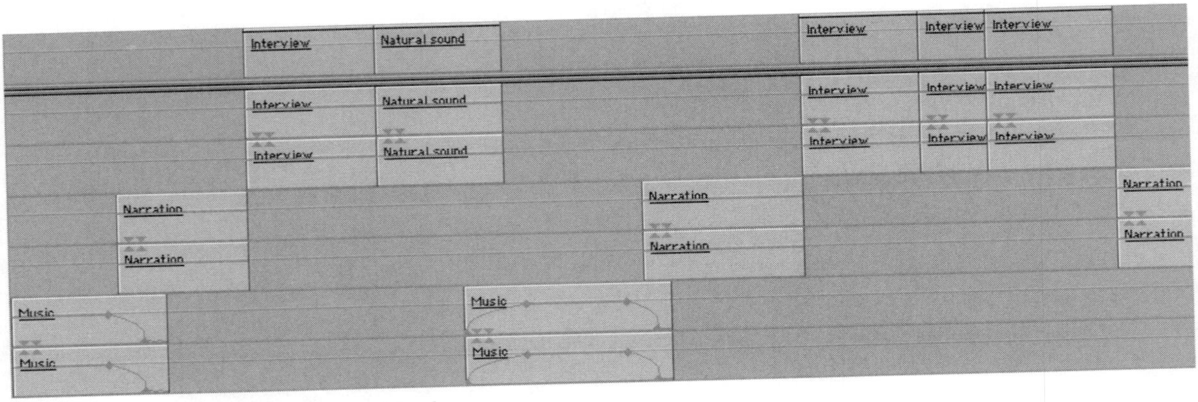

Figure 7.1   Documentary Sound Bed

Without the whole, it's hard to get that sense of how the material is paced and stands up as a structure.

Once the bed is laid out, the sound track flowing smoothly, the content making sense, progressing sensibly from point to point to conclusion like a well-crafted essay, then the pictures are put in to fill the gaps in the track. Having laid down your bed, you're ready to put in the B Roll material. The pacing of the editing is now dictated by language, the rhythm and cadence of speech, which can vary greatly from speaker to speaker, from language to language.

Speech has a flow. It has natural breaks, such as the punctuation marked in this sentence, that determine the rhythm of the spoken words. This natural flow will determine, by and large, where edits take place. It is much more natural for edits to occur on the breaks in the speech, on the point when the next phrase starts, than in the middle of a phrase. Cutting in the middle of a phrase would be analogous to cutting off the beat of a piece of music, as opposed to the more natural and expected form of cutting on the beat of the music.

In practice, of course, an hour-long documentary is usually not laid out as a single bed, but rather broken into sequences that are edited separately and then brought together into a final sequence. Opens are often built separately, often by entirely separate companies that specialize in motion graphics, 3D, and compositing using tools such as After Effects. Even while staying in-house, specialist sequences can be laid down separately.

Editing documentaries is not often about continuity of action, but rather about continuity of ideas, putting together images that separately have one meaning, but together have a different meaning and present a new idea. This is the concept of montage. The term is used for a variety of different techniques, but the original form established by Russian filmmakers in the 1920s was based on this idea.

In this powerful concept you can put together two shots that have no direct relationship with each other and thereby create in the audience's mind a quite different idea, separate from the meaning of its parts. This juxtaposition of unrelated images to make the audience draw a continuity of ideas is often done with a sequence of usually quick, impressionistic shots, often with motion. The

What is a B Roll?

You may have noticed that one of the FCP default **Labels** is called **B Roll**. In the old days that were not so long ago, a television anchorman or reporter would lay down a commentary track or do an entire on-camera narration, originally as film and later as videotape. Called the A Roll, it would be loaded on a machine, either telecine or VTR. Then shots illustrating the narration would be cut together and loaded on a second machine. This would be the B Roll. Both would be fed into a control room and gang-synced together so that the director could either cut back and forth or use effects to switch between the two. B Roll became the generic term for any cover video, regardless of how it was assembled into the production.

term has come to mean a collection of shots used to contract or expand time, either simply by being cut together, or using some complex compositing effects to overlay multiple, changing images on the screen.

Montage can be used to create the sense of location or process — for instance, shots of various aspects of car production build up to create an impression of the process. A variety of shots of the Damine festival produce an effect that gives the flavor of the town and the event. The common trick to make montage effective is fast pacing, using speed to quickly build block on block, shot on shot, to construct the whole. Because of time limitations, montage is often used in commercials. It's a quick and concise way to convey a variety of impressions that make up a single whole. It would be a good exercise to take the material in the **Clips** bin and edit together a fast montage to give the flavor of the festival. Use one or two shots from each group, each shot no more than a few seconds, and see what you can do.

The juxtaposition of shots with very different audio may preclude the use of natural sound because of the harshness of the edit. It often becomes necessary to use unnatural sound or music or to use a split edit to reinforce the point of the intellectual edit. By splitting the sound, the edit happens twice, multiplying its effect. When intercutting material to create tension, what's commonly done is not to cut the sound with the picture, but to keep a constant sound or music to which the editing and the action paces itself.

Note

Misused Montage: Montage in its weakest form is used as a quick way to convey information. The travel sequence is the most clichéd: character leaves, plane takes off, plane lands, character walks out of terminal and gets in a cab, cab pulls up at curb, character walks into a building. This is superficial montage to convey minimal information.

The most commonly seen form of montage is a program opening, like the opening to last year's Super Bowl. We see small boys playing football on a lawn, then NFL stars repeating their motions in a stadium while the narration talks about a uniquely American

---

Foreign Language Versions

French and Spanish are often spoken very quickly, yet seem to take many more words to say the same thing as English, so despite the rapid speech, the editing often seems contrapuntal because it is paced so slowly. Re-editing for different languages can be a frustrating experience. Extending material to fit a sentence or shot may not always be best. Because of the rapid speech, new material might have to be introduced. So more shots are used to match the cadence while maintaining the coverage of a single scene. If the material was originally shot for English, finding extra clips to fit foreign language versions can be an exercise in futility.

sport, the spectacle, the fun, the camaraderie in play and performance, and the celebration as fans, as participants, both as children and as professionals, as Americans. It is deeply complex, emotional, full of evocative ideas and concepts, and brought together through images, music, and special effects. It creates a powerful, persuasive impact. Even something as simple as two shots, football player and lightning. The shots have no direct relationship, but together form a continuity of ideas. Music videos are often montages, metaphors repeated often enough to become cliché, such as the suitcase in the Country & Western video. One good thing about cliché is that the repetition can be honed ever finer. A shot of a guy flirting with a girl, shot of another girl's hand picking up the suitcase tells the whole tale of any number of C&W songs.

Montage isn't confined to documentary or music videos and is occasionally seen in feature films such as the climatic baptism scene in *The Godfather*. Here, with Bach's music and the Roman Catholic liturgy as a background, Michael Corleone literally becomes a godfather while eliminating his principal enemies, the two intercut and built up together into a classic piece of cinema editing.

Documentary, I'd like to think, is about truth, but truth can be a malleable commodity. Look at the clip called *Ceremony6*. There is a moment in this shot when the priest fumbles around in his robes for his *hachi* (chopsticks). *Hachi* are used because this is, after all, a rice festival. What better way to strike the drum and call up the spirits? It takes him a long time to find them, quite a bit longer than in *Ceremony6*, but I spared you the full time. The editor could be cruel and leave every excruciating frame of this, or even make it worse and slow it down, or cut it up and use other shots in between to repeat the action. Perhaps it would be amusing, but it's probably not true to the spirit of the occasion or of the ceremony. You could use a cutaway, such as the beginning of *Ceremony2*, so that the priest reaches for his chopsticks, a brief cutaway follows, and then we return to the priest just as he's striking the drum. Actually I'd put the first drum strike across the edit back to the priest, so the sound begins on the cutaway. Open the sequence in your project called *Chopsticks* and see what I mean. Which is truth?

Music

Music videos are the staple of MTV, VH1, and CMT. Every popular music recording artist has a video made to accompany their music. It's an essential ingredient in artist and record promotion. The key point to remember about editing music videos is that it's about the music. Everything is dictated by the rhythm, the tone, and texture of the music — whether you're working on a project that will be created entirely from computer-generated animation or from a multi-camera shoot of a performance — where the edit point comes on each shot is driven by the beat of the music. Finding the beat is the first step you'll have to take. The simplest way is to mark it up. You probably have an excellent piece of music to try this out on; if not, use the music that comes with your FCP3 Tutorial CD.

1. Open your project and import the music track named *Jumptown.aiff*. It's normally located here: *NTSC TUTORIAL/ Dance Shots/Jumptown.aiff*.

2. Once the file is imported, open it into the **Viewer** and play it.

3. Once you've got the rhythm, start again. As it plays, tap out the beat on the **M** key. You'll quickly fill it up with little green markers (Figure 7.2).

You'll probably notice how not all the markers line up exactly with the spikes in the beat. The visual display of the waveform is really helpful here.

4. Step through the markers (**Shift-M** takes you to the next marker; **Option-M** takes you to the previous marker), repositioning them as you go.

5. If the marker is late (after the beat), just add a new marker on the beat. Then go to the incorrectly positioned marker and delete it (**Command-`**).

6. If the marker is early (before the spike in the waveform), reposition the marker with **Shift-`**, which will pull the marker up to the playhead.

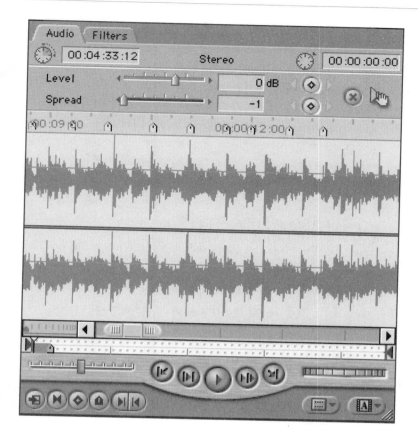

Figure 7.2   Music Markers

Once you get into the groove of it, you can very quickly clean up your markers till they're exactly placed.

Now that you've marked up, you're ready to start laying in picture, but first lock those music tracks with the handy little locks on left end of the **Timeline** (Figure 7.3).

That music track shouldn't be going anywhere, and you don't want to accidentally overwrite it when you put in some video.

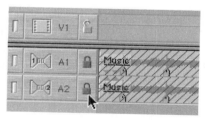

Figure 7.3   Track Locks

FCP3 has created a great new way to work with markers for music videos. We saw in an earlier lesson FCP3's **Mark to Markers**. These can also be used very effectively with music. Rather than placing the markers on the audio track itself, you can tap out the markers in the **Timeline**.

1. Place *Jumptown.aiff* in the **Timeline.**

2. Lock the audio tracks so that nothing can move them or **Overwrite** them.

3. With the playhead at the start of the sequence, begin playing the track, tapping **M** to the beat as the music plays.

4. After you've placed the markers in the **Timeline**, move the playhead to a point anywhere between the first pair of markers, and select from the **Mark** menu **Mark to Markers.** Or press the keyboard shortcut **Control-A.**

Now all you have to do is find the shot to place between those markers and the In and Out points you've created.

5. Open a clip from the **Browser** into the **Viewer** by double-clicking on it.

6. Find where you want the clip to begin, and mark an In point.

7. Press **F10** to **Overwrite.** The shot will be inserted into the **Timeline** in the marked position.

8. Move the playhead between the next pair of markers, and hit **Control-A.**

By repeating the process a couple of times, your **Timeline** will soon look like Figure 7.4. It's a very efficient way for quickly roughing out your shots for a music video.

If you to want to use any natural or sync sound with your music video, you might want to add a couple of tracks and move the music down, leaving the primary tracks, *A1* and *A2*, free for the video.

Figure 7.4   Mark to Markers in the Timeline

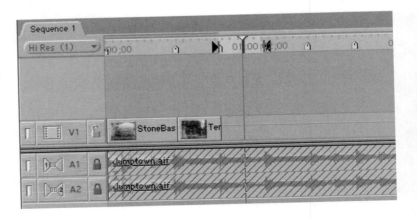

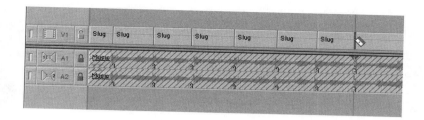

Figure 7.5   Bladed Slug

It's no coincidence that many editors are musicians at heart and often play musical instruments. Editing is so much about rhythm and cadence, both of which are usually dictated by sound. Edit on the beat: either the cut on the beat or the event in the shot on the beat. When you cut on the beat, the edit appears on the moment of the beat, on the spike in the waveform. If you are cutting a drummer pounding the skins, if you cut on the beat, you are cutting on the moment he is striking the drum. The strike on the drumhead explodes the edit into the next shot. However, to see the drummer beat the drum, you really need to cut off the beat so that the edit occurs in the gaps between strikes. This way the action is placed on the moment of the beat, on the spike in the waveform.

For most music you can cut either on the beat or off the beat. I'd guess most music is cut on the beat, as in the slug tip. This works pretty well and will always produce acceptable results. Placing the cut on the beat works especially well for stills or other images without much action. However, if there is strong action in the shot, it's often better to cut off the beat.

Take the obvious example of a shot of a drummer striking his drum. If you're cutting on the beat, you're cutting to or away from the drum on the very frame on which it's struck. Here you might want to set up a rhythm that has you cutting off the beat and placing the action on the beat:

- The fist strikes the table.
- The door slams.
- The drum is pounded.
- The guitar chord is struck.
- The couple kisses.

All of these moments need to be seen. The impact event should happen on the beat; the edit, hidden between the beats. No video will have just one or the other, which would make it horribly monotonous, but a mixture of the two, changing back and forth through the rhythm of the music and of the images.

> 👉 **Tip**
>
> **Sequence Chorus:** Music is about repetition, passages, and choruses that often repeat. Using FCP you can create a sequence that repeats for each chorus. You may not want each chorus to be exactly the same, but have small variations, though the structure and rhythm and many of the shots may repeat. The simplest way to do this is to duplicate copies of the first chorus sequence, as many as you need, and make the variations in them. The various chorus sequences can then simply be dropped into the final sequence as needed.

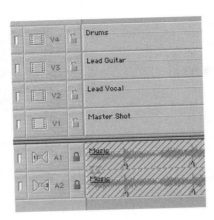

Figure 7.6   Multi-camera Track Layout

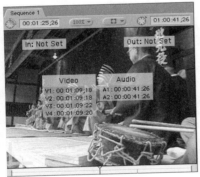

Figure 7.7   Timecode Overlay

Multi-camera performance recordings are edited somewhat differently. There are many ways to work, but I think the easiest is to lay all the shots in sync with each other out on the **Timeline** (Figure 7.6).

One of the trickiest parts of working with multi-camera material is to sync up the video. Ideally, the material is shot with cameras that can slave-timecode to each other. One camera becomes the master camera, and all the other cameras run timecode that is jam-synced to the master, so that the timecode on each camera is identical. This means that at any single moment in a performance, you can see what each camera is doing.

FCP3 provides a handy new way to slip each camera into sync and to make sure they are in sync. It will display the TC for each of the shots stacked up in the **Timeline** (Figure 7.7). This can be called up from the **View** menu, **Timecode Overlays (Option-Z)**.

Notice in the graphic that a couple of the tracks are slightly out of sync by a few frames. It's easy enough to nudge them back into sync. Simply select the clip and tap the left or right bracket (< or >) to move the clip along the **Timeline**.

Often it isn't possible to shoot the material with cameras with synced timecode. Then it becomes necessary to sync the clips manually. Sometimes the waveforms of the various clips can be used to help do this; sometimes it's just a matter of fiddling with the clips. It really helps, however, to shoot it properly in the first place. As the shoot begins, all cameras should point to a common place and record a syncable event like a clapperboard strike, or a handclap, or a camera flash — anything that all the cameras can see at the same time. Once the clapperboard is taped, the cameras shouldn't stop rolling until the performance is over or their tape runs out.

There is new technique to aid multitrack, multi-camera editing that allows you to see one or more tracks in the **Canvas** at a time. It's calling *soloing*. Select the clip you want to see, even if it's on V1 underneath layers of other video, and choose **Solo Item(s)** from the **Sequence** menu, or use the keyboard shortcut **Control-S**. This will toggle off the visibility of all but the selected tracks. Use this to see the what material is available at any one time and use the **Blade** tool or **Control-V** to slice away the layers you don't need to see. Upper most tracks are visible, so wherever you cut away the upper tracks, the layers beneath become visible.

When working with multiple tracks like this, it's generally best to get most of your editing done before you begin to put in transitions or do effects that require rendering. Switching track visibility off and on will delete your render files, so edit before you affect. Or work with your **Render Settings** set to **Cuts Only** so that you don't have to deal with render files and losing them, while still being able to play through video with transitions and effects applied to them.

To maintain sync across all the cameras — which probably don't have matched timecode, unless they were all slaved to a single generator during recording — the easiest way to do this is use **Auxiliary Timecode**. In the **Browser**, **Control**-click in the column header and from the menu select **Show Aux TC 1** (Figure 7.8). In the **Browser** you can type in (or copy and paste) matching TC for each of the clips as in Figure 7.9.

Note

No Warning for Solos: You may remember in the **General Preferences** there was a checkbox for a warning if visibility changes will delete rendered files. Be warned that the warning does not apply to soloing. It only applies to switching off visibility of whole tracks. Switching off visibility of tracks using soloing **will** delete your render files and will do so without warning. Consider this your one-time-only warning.

Tip

Multi-camera: For multi-camera editing, some people like to work with wide tracks with the **Timeline** switched to filmstrip mode. This way you can actually see the pictures in the sequence to help while you're razor blading the shots.

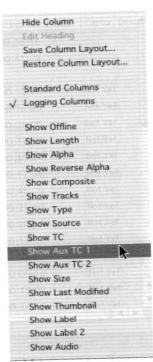

Figure 7.8   Menu Showing
             Auxiliary Timecode
             Item in Browser

Note

Free Music: If you are looking for some music to try out these techniques, Apple has provide a huge quantity of royalty free music of all styles available from its website and found in your iDisk, in ***Software>Extras.*** There are 350 titles in 35 categories — each in six lengths.

You can also change the **Auxiliary Timecode** for a clip that's been opened into the **Viewer** from either the **Browser** or the **Timeline**. With the clip in the **Viewer**, choose **Timecode** from the **Modify** menu. This will bring up the dialog box in Figure 7.10. Notice in this box that you can change not only the **Auxiliary Timecode**, but also the **Source Timecode**. Use this with great care. This is one of the few functions within FCP that will actually affect the media on your hard drive. If you change the **Source Timecode** in this window, you will permanently change the timecode of your source media on your hard drive.

Note

Aux TC: As of this writing, the ability to change to **Auxiliary Timecode** and bring that into the **Timeline** and then change to **Aux TC** in the **Viewer** has been broken in FCP3. Also, **Aux TC** does not display in **Timecode Overlay**. I hope by the time you read this that this feature will have been fixed in a maintenance release of the software. However, if you change the **Auxiliary Timecode** in the **Viewer**, it does stick.

Now when the clips are laid out in the **Timeline** and opened in the **Viewer** you can switch to **Aux TC** by control clicking in the current time window in the upper right of the **Viewer** and select **Aux 1** (Figure 7.11).

You can help this further by changing the **Timeline** start time to match the timecode of the clips, so everything, each clip and the **Timeline** itself are all running to matching timecode references. You can change the **Timeline** start time in **Sequence** settings (**Command-Zero**) under the **Timeline** tab, dial a new **Starting Timecode** number (Figure 7.12).

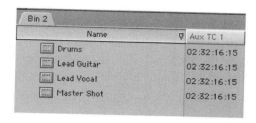

Figure 7.9   Aux TC in the Browser

Figure 7.10   Modify>Timecode

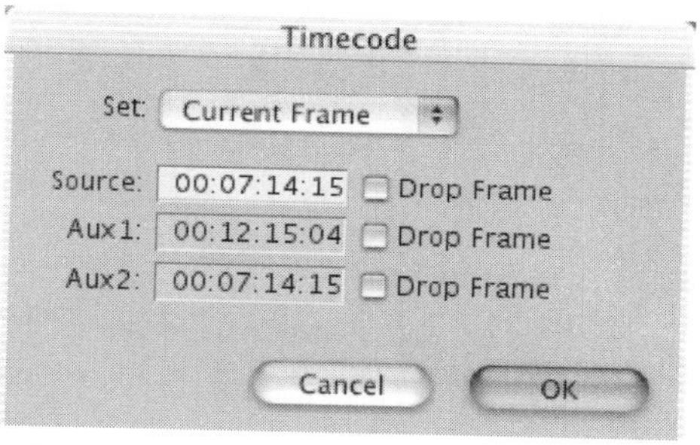

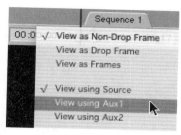

Figure 7.11   Switching to Aux TC in the Viewer

Figure 7.12   Setting Starting Timecode for Timeline

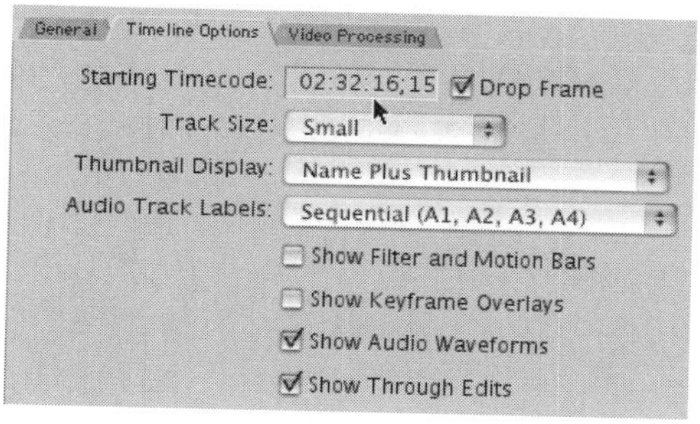

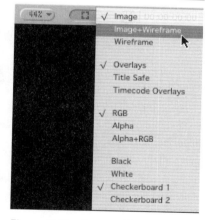

Tip _____

From Charles (Chawla) Roberts, a fellow Guide on the 2-pop Final Cut Pro website http://www.2-pop.com. For multi-camera work, lay four shots in sync in the sequence as before. Scale each clip back to quarter size so each fits into a different quadrant of the Canvas. We'll look at scaling and reposition clips in greater detail in "Scaling Text Files" on page 385 and "Repositioning the Clip" on page 394 in Lesson 9. The simplest way is to change the **Image Layers** popup in the **Canvas** to **Image+Wireframe** (Figure 7.13). You can then drag a corner of the selected clip to resize it, and grab the image itself to reposition it. Export the sequence as a QuickTime movie. You can now reimport and have a single clip that plays all your camera shots gang-synced together. Keep that shot open in a separate **Viewer**, and you can quickly find any shot for any moment by matching auxiliary timecodes.

Figure 7.13   Image+Wireframe

Audio Delay

If you are working in DV, be careful of how you work, whether with a video monitor or the computer monitor. The latter shows you what your computer is doing, the former what's being fed out of your computer through some device that converts the digital signal to an analog display. The problem is that there is a delay in the signal getting through the FireWire and being converted. The audio needs to come from the video monitor as well. Connect your speakers to your video monitor. Don't feed them directly from the computer.

So either:

- Work entirely on the computer monitor and set your audio output to internal. Everything is on the computer screen.

- Or switch off **Mirror on Desktop** so you don't see any video display in the **Canvas** during playback, and work entirely on the video monitor with your speakers connected to the analog monitor.

I would suggest the latter. If you mix the two, you'll be marking the music at the wrong spot and making edits on the wrong point. When you get it looking right and then output it, you'll find that the recording is off. The cuts aren't coming at the right point.

Action

By action I don't mean only the movies of Arnold Schwarzenegger or Sylvester Stallone. Action might any feature or short narrative film. All forms of video might use elements and techniques of action, where what occurs in one shot continues smoothly into the next. While documentary is often based on noncontinuous shots and juxtaposes apparently unrelated images, action films are based, within each scene, almost exclusively on continuity, a smoothness that makes the film appear almost seamless. The director has to shoot the scene so that the elements match as precisely as possible, that movements repeat as exactly as possible, that the appearance of people and things (and the content of objects like beer glasses) change as little as possible from shot to shot. Editing action is often about finding that precise moment to match two events together as closely as possible, as we did, for instance, in Lesson 4.

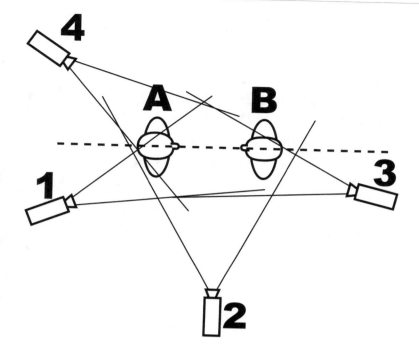

Figure 7.14   The Line

The Line

The first lesson they teach budding directors in film schools is the Rule of the Line, sometimes called the 180° rule. It's a simple rule, and because it's simple, it always works. The rule is basically that through every scene the director stages there runs a line, an axis, which his camera cannot cross. If a couple are speaking to each other — let's say the man on the left and the woman on the right — then the Line runs through their heads (Figure 7.14).

The director must keep his camera on the one side of his chosen line. He can move the camera anywhere he wants within that 180 degree arc. As long as he does, the man (A) will always remain on the left side of the screen and the woman (B) on the right. As long as the scene is shot from any position in that 180 degree arc, such as camera positions 1, 2, or 3, A will always be looking from the left side of the screen toward the right, and B will always be looking from the right side of the screen toward the left. As soon as the camera crosses the Line, such as in position 4, the relationship between the two will suddenly change. A will now be looking from right to left, B from left to right. The audience will become disoriented, thinking that one has turned his or her back on the other.

The same principles apply to objects or people in motion. If a direction of movement is established, such as left to right, movement must continue in that direction, or the audience will think that the objects or people have turned around and are going back where they came from.

To get over the problem of getting to the other side of the line, directors use simple tricks like tracking around the subject, which visually defines for the audience that the line is being crossed. Or for objects in motion, the common trick is simply to place the camera directly on the line so the car, for instance, is either going directly away from you or coming straight at you. After that shot, the director can then place the camera on either side of the line, because again the audience has received a visual clue that the line is being violated.

To achieve this continuity of action and avoid a lot of jump cuts, the director should vary the shot by changing the size and/or the angle of the shot. As we saw, a small change will create a jump cut. Shots should change a full size greater, close shot to medium shot to long shot, not closeup to close shot, nor medium shot to medium long shot. The angle change should be 40° or more to make it effective.

These are the most basic rules of action direction, but they do work and work effectively, but like most rules not only are they often broken, but they're really made to be broken. If you do break them, though, you should know why, and break them on purpose to good effect.

These ground rules, of course, carry over to editing, so that the directions established on the stage or location are maintained in the cutting room.

The basis of this type of editing is cutting on action. An action can be any movement:

- The moment when someone walks in the door

- When someone sits in the chair

- When the hero pulls the heroine into his arms

It's the moment the editor uses to draw the audience into the action or back them out of it.

There are three possible places to cut an action:

- Just before the action takes place

- During the action

- After the action is completed

Each of these has a different contextual meaning for the audience. Inside your copy of the *L7* project is a sequence called *Action Cut Sequence*. In this sequence, four separate edits are shown:

- In the first, the cut to the closer shot of the priest takes place before the priest rises. Placing the cut before the action occurs emphasizes the action.

- In the next edit, the cut occurs after the action is completed. This emphasizes not the action but the object or person you're cutting to. Cutting before the action begins or after the action is completed makes the edit more pointed, more apparent to the audience.

- The third edit shows the cut during the movement itself. Cutting during the movement has the tendency to conceal the edit. The is probably the preferred edit is many circumstances.

- The fourth edit cuts away before the action takes place, but unlike the others, it moves from a close shot to wider shot.

Sometimes it is important to mark the event before it occurs. Sometimes it is necessary not to disrupt the action but to let it complete before we move on. Sometimes it's best to make the action flow as smoothly as possible, to conceal the edit within the movement. In the first three edits in *Action Cut Sequence,* the edit goes from a medium shot to a closer shot. If the cut is going the other way as in the fourth edit (close shot to wider shot) it generally works better to place the edit before the action takes place rather than during the action. None of these rules are by any means hard and fast. Every situation will vary; every cut will be different and require a different decision. These are the decisions you have to make, and you have to make them somewhere in one of those 29.97ths of a second.

Dialog

Dialog is the other key ingredient in feature and short-form narrative film and video. Action editing and dialog together form the main techniques used in narrative film. As so often in editing, sound is the principal driving force behind the timing of edits, probably none more so than in dialog sequences. This does not mean the edits come with the sound; they may in fact come against the sound, and most often do. You almost never slavishly cut with the person speaking; you often cut ahead or more commonly behind the person speaking. It's often unnatural to cut on the gap; either you cut after the response begins, as if you're an observer reacting, or you cut while the first person is still speaking, anticipating the response.

Because editing dialog is such a unique, yet common, problem, let's look at a short, simple scene and see how to put it together. There is no right way to edit any scene of dialog; no two editors will pick exactly the same frames, or perhaps even the same takes, or the same pacing, to assemble a scene.

In your **Browser** is a bin called **Heartwood**, inside of which is the clip *Hearwtood.mov*. This is a master clip made up from the slightly edited rushes of a movie called *Heartwood*, an independent production, directed by Lanny Cotler and produced by Steve Cotler, starring Hilary Swank, Eddie Mills, and the late Jason Robards. This is a short scene between Sylvia (Hilary Swank) and Frank (Eddie Mills) in which he's trying to persuade her to run away with him. The scene was shot, as is common in film production, with a single camera. Editing the scene shot with multiple cameras is somewhat easier, as in a multi-camera musical performance, but the techniques and the end result is very similar.

This scene opens as the couple come out from an old trailer. The camera tracks slightly with them to their marks, and then becomes the master wide shot for the scene. The wide shot is followed by singles of Frank and Sylvia, closeups of each of the actors' performances. There are a couple of flubs at the beginning, but the singles are only one take of many. By giving you only one real take, I've simplified your editing choices considerably. In reality, you could choose lines from any one of a number of takes, as long as you maintained the integrity of the performance.

1. Look through the material. It's only a little over four minutes long.

2. Next cut the shot up into usable bits: top and tail the master shot, cut off the slate and the director's action, and the runout, the bit where the director calls cut and the camera stops.

3. Do the same for the single of Frank and the single of Sylvia.

4. Make each of them subclips to limit the media you bring into the **Viewer.** In the **Heartwood** bin I have already made up the subclips for you, *Frank, Sylvia,* and *Master,* which is the wide, two-shot of the argument.

Once the three subclips are ready, you can begin editing. In the bin is a blank sequence called *Edit Sequence,* ready for you to use. In this scene, let's begin with the wide shot because that's the only cover until the actors reach their marks.

5. Drag the subclip *Master* and lay it in the **Timeline** in the space above **V1,** creating a new video track, **V2,** with the audio on a lower audio track. Leave it stretched out for the whole length of the scene.

6. Play the master shot until the first line of dialog, "Look, we can make it."

7. With the **Razor Blade,** cut the master shot. The timing can be trimmed and adjusted later, but just leave it there for the moment.

8. Switch off the video and audio for the master shot and target **V1** and its audio track (Figure 7.15).

9. Next open up Frank's and Sylvia's subclips into separate viewers. **Control**-click on one of the clips and select **Open in New Viewer.**

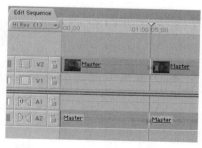

Figure 7.15   Master Shot Hidden in Timeline

Though you can't gang-sync the two **Viewers** in FCP — both windows playing at the same time — it's nice to have them open at the same time (Figure 7.16).

10. Cut the dialog up in the subclips line by line and overwrite into the targeted tracks each line of dialog, back and forth between the couple, into the **Timeline**.

Sometimes it's easier to find the edit point in the **Audio** tab of the **Viewer**, such as when Frank says, "I'll do anything for you." (Figure 7.17).

Once you've worked through the lines you'll have the basic structure of the scene in close-ups, cut in its most boring, conventional manner. The audience sees who's speaking, each in turn. By leaving the master shot on **V2**, but invisible, you can cut the scene in closeups (Figure 7.18).

At any point when you want to pull back to the master shot — for instance, where Sylvia shoves Frank — turn on the visibility for **V2** and razor blade the section you want. Unfortunately, Sylvia's shove doesn't come in the same place in the dialog in the master shot as it does in the closeups. You might need to slide the

Figure 7.16 Two Viewers, Canvas, and Timeline

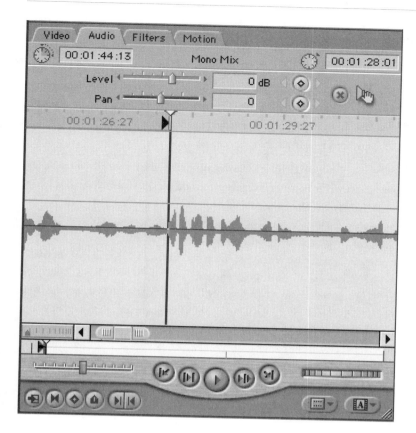

Figure 7.17 In Point Marked in the Audio Tab

master clip up the timeline a bit. Generally good, professional actors will keep the pacing of a scene and the timing of each take remarkably consistent so that shots can match easily. Because Frank's performance varies a bit, you'll probably need to cut off some of the closeup so the lines don't repeat in the wide shot, but if you pull it up and then delete the audio on the close-up track, **A1**, it'll match pretty closely. I'd probably want to fix the audio later, replace the line, or take Sylvia's "No" from somewhere else so it isn't stepped on. Delete what you don't need, then make **V2** invisible again as you work on the dialog closeups on **V1**. Lock

Figure 7.18 Closeups Laid in Timeline

V2 and **A2** when you need to pull up the closeups. You might want to return to the wide shot for the end after Sylvia turns away (Figure 7.19).

Despite the inconsistent dialog, the performances here are paced carefully. There is nothing worse than trying to cut together a scene in which the actors rush the performance for the takes on which they are off camera.

After you've cut through the dialog like this, you'll immediately see how arid it is, the beginning rushed as the lines trade back and forth quickly, the middle section slower where they're longer pieces of dialog. Where you adjust the shots is up to you and the director, and the weight you want to give the scene. The basic question is usually, whose scene is it? Though *Heartwood* is really Frank's movie, a coming of age story complicated by timber and environmental issues, the scene is more Sylvia's, I think, and Hilary Swank gives a lovely performance. If you accept the premise that it is Sylvia's scene, you should cut it so it weighs more heavily in her favor; if it's Frank's scene, it'll weigh more on his performance and on his reaction to what she says.

I find it best to leave the sound pretty much untouched, except to tweak it for any extraneous dialog. I work primarily by **Option**-clicking the video edits and either using the **Roll** tool in the **Time-line** or **E** to **Extend Edit** to alter the cut point while leaving the sound track as the bed.

At the end of the first closeup of Sylvia, I let her remain on screen over the beginning of Frank's line, "I'll do anything." Letting the dialog start first motivates the cut as if you are a bystander following it. You hear the voice, and then you turn to see Frank. Because Frank's line is short, I again waited for Sylvia's responding question "Anything?" before turning to her.

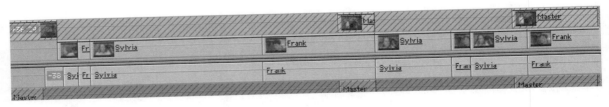

Figure 7.19   Razor Bladed Sections and Locked Master Shot on V2

Figure 7.20   Option-Shift Drag to V3

One problem is the type of lengthy speech like Sylvia's where you might want to drop in a cutaway of Frank to see his reaction to her words. I like to do this by **Option-Shift**-dragging a copy of the adjacent video clip onto **V3** (Figure 7.20).

Option-dragging will make a copy of the video portion of the clip, the **Shift** will constrain the movement to the vertical as you move it. Why to **V3**? So you can keep **V2** open to stretch out the master shot to any point that you might need it. Then with the **Option** key stretch out the clip on **V3** to meet roughly the point at which I want the cutaway to appear. You can now cut the clip on **V3** to provide the cutaway reaction shot of Frank during Sylvia's speech. Again you might need to nudge the reaction shot up or down the timeline so it comes in exactly as you want it.

I also added a couple of other cutaways, one of Sylvia when Frank says. "This is what people do," and another of Frank when Sylvia says, "I'm not going to run away all half-cocked." Perhaps I got carried away with the cutaways, but I think it gives the audience a chance to see the other person and their response without losing the intimacy of the scene by backing out to the wide shot.

In the **Browser** there is a sequence called *Heartwood Sequence*, which is my version of the scene. There are endless possible variations. In the film the scene was played largely in the master shot with one closeup of Sylvia and one of Frank. The movie edit is in *Movie Sequence*. It was probably right for the movie, but for this little exercise, I went for the intensity of the closeups rather than standoffish look of the wider shot.

You might not have the opportunity to edit material shot by an excellent director and cameraperson, with an Academy Award winning actor and outstanding performances. If the direction, camerawork, and acting isn't there, it's much harder to edit the scenes. There is only so much you can do, and sometimes no amounting of stitching will be able to make a silk purse out of a sow's ear.

Summary

Modern editing is based on the idea of seamlessness; the narrative film especially stresses the hidden edit, both in action and in dialog. The editor in these types of film is often looking for the most natural place to cut. Editing is the decision of the moment, the one frame that precisely defines the moment of change from one image to another, the moment the great Walter Murch calls the blink of an eye. This is the moment the viewer blinks, the moment he has enough of one image and is ready for the next. In a carefully edited sequence, that moment is predicated by the edits that came before it and by the sound that links them together.

Think of how you watch a conversation. You generally look at the speaker, perhaps occasionally glancing at the listener. When the listener interjects, you hear the voice and then turn to the source of the sound. This rule generally applies to most edits. The audio precedes the video; you hear the sound and then see the source of the sound. Sometimes this is overt, such as the famous Hitchcock transition from a woman's mouth opening to scream, hearing a train whistle, and then seeing the rushing train. More usually, the transition is considerably more subtle. In narrative film the editor often works on the assumption that the viewer grasps the situation and anticipates the response. One person speaks, and while they're talking, you cut to the other, to see the reaction and anticipate the response before it begins. The second person responds, and during the response, after the subject and verb establishes the sense, you cut back to the first person to await another response. Murch contends that you blink as you change your point of view, and this blink is the edit. You hear the door open; you turn to see who is entering the room. When we turn our heads, we often blink. When we're looking at the door to see who has entered, the door is already open. It is unnatural to see the door before it begins to open, though it's often used to create anticipation and suspense.

Sometimes you hold longer on the listener, especially when they're being told some piece of news that you already know. When your wife is telling a story that you've heard many times, usually you don't watch her retelling the tale. You watch her audience to see the reactions. This is especially true when someone is being told terrible news like a death in the family. If you know the news, you watch the reaction, but if you don't know the news, if it is being revealed to you for the first time, you usually watch the messenger.

How long you hold an image on the screen is dictated by how long you want the viewer to look at it. Sometimes this is very brief. You look left and right to cross a street, and you see the two images of the street for only the briefest of moments, probably less a second each. Often you hold on an image much longer to give the viewer a chance to look around, to study the image. The more complex the image the longer it needs to be on the screen. The word STOP in white letters in a black ground can on seen in a few frames; an Ansel Adams photograph of Yosemite's Half Dome needs to be lingered over.

There are many film and video forms, and the lines between them are sometimes blurred, sometimes to the detriment of the content and of the medium. Sometimes though the blurring of documentary and narrative film, music, and dialog, which is basis of the American musical, can give a richness and texture to a film that would be missed if the story were simply told conventionally.

We've only looked at some of the most common editing forms, but there are others that have conventions of their own, corporate videos, informational, weddings, special interest videos, and on and on. In the next lesson, we'll get back to working more closely with FCP as we look at titles and how to create them and what you can do with them using Final Cut Pro.

Lesson 8

Adding Titles

Any industry that radically changes how it works within 10 years can be said to have undergone a revolution. This revolution happened in desktop publishing about 20 years ago and has happened to video production over the last 10. This revolution means that where once an industry worked by compartmentalization, it now works in free form. Now producers are editors, directors are cameramen, soundmen are making graphics. For those who have come from a more structured, traditional workplace, this new open-work model can be intimidating. Many of my clients are producers who now find that they are in a position to essentially do an entire production themselves, from script to screen. Yet they reach a point where they feel intimidated by finishing a project, fine tuning it, and creating the graphics, the simple animations, and the opening montages. They are happy to make the big decisions but reluctant to do the final polish. They would rather leave the finishing — with its esoteric details of luminance ranges, color saturation, black level, pixel aspect ratios, interlace flicker, antialiasing and others — to someone else. Regardless of whether you do it yourself or have someone else do it for you, in the new era of video production you should have a working knowledge of some of these details yourself, especially if you're working in Final Cut Pro.

Every program is enhanced with graphics, whether they are a simple opening title and closing credits or elaborate motion graphics sequences illuminating some obscure point that can best be expressed in animation. This could be simply a map with a path snaking across it or a full-scale 3D animation explaining the details of an airline crash. Obviously, the latter is beyond the scope of both this book and of Final Cut Pro alone. But many simpler graphics can be easily created within FCP. That said, I think all experienced users of this application will agree that the character generator/titler included with the first version of Final Cut Pro was not as good as it could have been. With every full new version of the software, additional capabilities have added to the titler, functions such as built-in scripts for standard animations, scrolls (vertical movement), crawls (horizontal movement), and a typewriter effect, which is pretty neat. In version 2 Boris Script was added as an effect, and now Boris Calligraphy has been added as one of the **Generators**, providing more options for titling motion and 3D animation.

In this lesson, we will look at typical titling problems and how to deal with them. As always, we begin by loading the project.

Loading the Lesson

This should be familiar to you by now. Let's begin by loading the material you need onto your media drive.

1. If you don't already have it there, drag over the *Media1* folder from the CD.

2. Also drag *Lesson 8* from inside the *Projects* folder on the CD into your *Shared* folder.

3. Open the *Lesson 8* folder on your hard drive. It should contain a folder called *Circles* and the project file *L8*. Double-click the project file to launch the application.

4. Reconnect the media file and reassign the scratch disk if needed.

5. After you've reconnected the media, you should use **Save Project As** and give the new project a new name in the *Lesson 8* folder on your system drive.

6. If you did not load Boris Calligraphy when you first installed FCP, now would be a good time to do so. Put in your install CD and run the installer. Make sure the **Boris Calligraphy** checkbox is marked, and press **Install**. The software will be put into your *Plugins* folder in *Library>Application Support>Final Cut Pro System Support*.

Setting up the Project

Inside the project in the **Browser** you'll find eight sequences, which we shall look at in the course of this lesson. One of the sequences, *Sequence 1*, is empty, ready for you to use. There is also the master clip, *Damine.mov*, and the **Clips** bin.

1. Begin by opening *Sequence 1*.

2. Drag a clip, let's say *Dance2*, from the **Clips** bin and drop it onto **Overwrite** in the CEO (**Canvas Edit Overlay**).

Text Generator

Now let's look at the **Titler**, which FCP calls a **Text Generator**.

1. To get to it, click the small **A** in the lower right corner of the **Viewer**.

2. Go into the popup menu, drop down to **Text**, slide across and pick **Text** again, as in Figure 8.1.

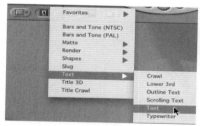

Figure 8.1   Text Generator

You'll notice the new version of Final Cut Pro, in addition to **Text**, **Lower Third**, **Outline Text**, and the basic animations **Scroll**, **Crawl**, and **Typewriter**, has added the Boris title tools **Title 3D** and **Title Crawl**. We'll look at the Boris tools a bit later in the lesson, but let's start by looking at the way FCP's basic **Text** tool works.

Text

This is for very basic text graphics indeed, simple on-screen words. Select **Text** from the **Generator** popup, which immediately loads a generic text generator into the **Viewer** (Figure 8.2).

Notice that this generator has:

- A default duration of 10 seconds.

- A default length of two minutes.

☞Tip

Launching Text Generator: The default, basic text generator can be opened into the **Viewer** with the keyboard shortcut **Control-X**. It's handy if you need to create a lot of basic titles quickly.

You can designate any duration for a text file up to four hours. However, once the text file has been placed in a sequence, its duration can no longer be extended beyond the designated duration. So if I accept the default length and I place the text file in a sequence, I can no longer make the duration go beyond two minutes. I don't know why it's limited this way. In the **Browser** you can designate any duration for a text file up to four hours. However, once the text file has been placed in a sequence, its duration can no longer be extended beyond the designated duration. If you know you're going to need to make a very long text file, you can simply drag it into the **Browser** and dial in a very long duration to start with and then place it in the sequence. You can always make it shorter, but not longer. It's a good way to create a video bug, that little graphic that's always in the bottom right of your TV screen — or your warning that a tape is only a check copy and not for distribution.

The first point to realize about this text generator is that at the moment it only exists in the **Viewer**. Usually the next step I take is to put it somewhere useful, either into the **Browser** or the **Timeline**. If you park the playhead anywhere over the shot that's in the **Timeline** and then drag the generic text generator from the **Viewer** to the **CEO** to **Superimpose**, the text will appear above the shot, with the same duration as the shot (Figure 8.3).

You can also simply drag and drop the generator into the **Timeline** onto an empty track or the space above the tracks. Either way, you'll immediately see that the render line above the generator in the **Timeline** changes color. If your system has real-time capabilities, the line will be green. If not, it will be red, telling you that section of the sequence needs to be rendered.

Whether you drag the generic text generator to the **Timeline** or the **Browser**, remember that you are creating a copy of that generator. Be careful not to do anything to the generator in the **Viewer**. I've seen countless people do this. They lay the generator

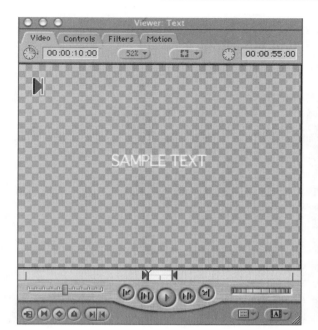

Figure 8.2   Generic Sample Text in Viewer

Figure 8.3   Supered Text in the Timeline

in the **Timeline**, work in the **Viewer**, and then wonder why the text in the sequence still says "Sample Text."

First, you should open the new generator you created in the **Timeline**. Open it by double-clicking on the **Text Generator** in the **Timeline** window. The **Viewer** screen will look exactly the same, of course, except now you'll be working on the generator in the **Timeline**, which is what you want. The label area at the top of the **Viewer** will tell you where the text came from. Figure 8.4 shows the label for text generated in the **Viewer**. Figure 8.5 shows the label for text that's been opened from a sequence.

The other telltale sign that indicates whether a title or a clip has been opened from the **Browser** (or generated in the **Viewer**) or has been opened from a sequence is in the **Scrubber Bar** at the bottom of the **Viewer**. In Figure 8.6 the clip has been opened from the **Browser**. The **Scrubber Bar** is plain. In Figure 8.7 the clip have been opened from the **Timeline**. The **Scrubber Bar** shows a double row of dots, like film sprocket holes.

Figure 8.4   Viewer:Text

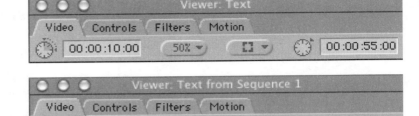

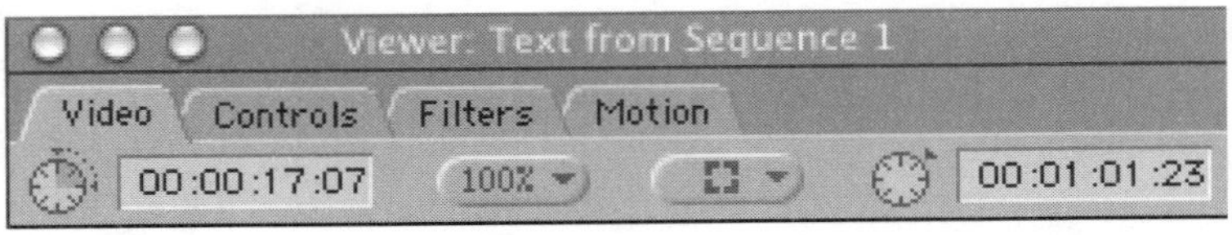

Figure 8.5   Viewer:Text from
Sequence 1

☛ *Tip*

Dropping Bread Crumbs and Viewing Nothing: I always leave the playhead in the **Timeline** parked over the middle of the clip with the text supered on it. That way whatever I do in the **Text** controls appears a moment later supered on the clip in the **Canvas**. If you place a clip in the **Timeline** over nothing, the blackness you see in the **Canvas** behind the clip is the emptiness of space. You can make it any color, including checkerboard under the **View** menu, but this is only for viewing purposes. If you want an actual color layer, use the **Generators** to make a color matte. Make it any color you want and place it on the layer below all other material. For instance, if you're scaling down video clips and moving them about the screen, you may want to place an interesting color behind them. Or make something in Photoshop with a fancy design or gradient.

Now we're ready to start making that graphic.

1.   After you've opened the generator from the **Timeline** into the **Viewer,** click on the **Controls** tab at the top. You might also want to stretch down the **Viewer** to see all the controls (Figure 8.8).

Figure 8.6   Plain Scrubber Bar
on Clip Opened from
Browser

Figure 8.7   Dotted Scrubber Bar
on Clip Opened from
Timeline

These are the default settings. At the top is the text input window in which you type whatever you want to appear on the screen.

2. Click on **SAMPLE TEXT** and type in *Dance*, then do a return, and type *Title*.

3. Click out of the window, or tab to the **Size** box. The default is 36 point, which is small even for these clips.

4. Type in a size of *72* and press **Enter**, which loads the size setting.

Above the **Size** slider is the **Font** popup, in which you can pick whatever TrueType fonts you have loaded in your system. If you have fonts on your computer that are not showing up here, then they are most probably PostScript fonts. Unfortunately FCP's **Text** tool does not work with PostScript, only TrueType fonts. Boris Calligraphy — that is, **Title 3D** and **Title Crawl** — will work with both True-Type and PostScript.

An important point to note: the **Font** popup and all the settings in the text block will change all the letters for everything in the text block. You cannot control individual letters, or words, or lines of text. This applies to all of Final Cut Pro's text generators except for Boris. Both **Title 3D** and **Title Crawl** have full text control as we shall see. The one unintentional benefit of FCP's limitations is that it may minimize users going wild with tons of fonts and sizes and colors.

The **Style** popup (Figure 8.9) lets you set text styles such as bold and italic.

Below **Style** is the **Alignment** popup (Figure 8.10), what's usually called **Justification**.

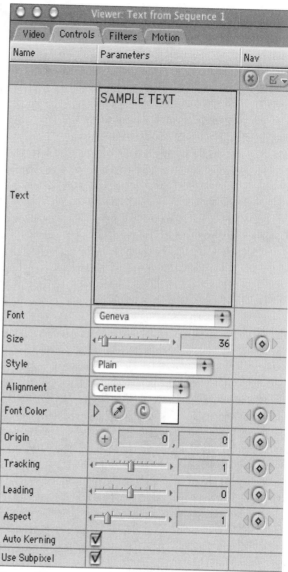

Figure 8.8   Text Control Window

Note _____

No Word Wrapping: FCP's titler is limited in many ways, and word wrapping is one of them. You have to put in the line breaks where appropriate, or your text is liable to run off the screen.

Figure 8.9   **Style Popup**

Figure 8.10   **Alignment Popup**

A word of caution: though the default setting is **Center,** the words in the text window are left justified. Ignore that. The popup rules; the text window just doesn't display intelligently.

The left and right alignment is not to the screen but to the origin point, the way it works in Illustrator and Photoshop. So if you want left alignment on the left side of the screen, you have to move the origin point about −300 or a little less to keep it in the **Safe Title Area,** depending on your format. This only applies in the **Text** tool. Other tools such as **Scrolling Text,** as we shall see, align to the screen as you might expect, with left as the left edge of the **STA,** and right as the right edge of **STA.**

Fonts and Size

Figure 8.11   **Serif Fonts**

Not all fonts are equally good for video. You can't just pick something you fancy and hope it will work for you. One of the main problems with video is its interlacing. Because video is made up of thin lines of information — the odd lines making up one field and the even lines the other field — each line is essentially switching on and off 30 times a second. If you happen to place a thin horizontal line on your video that falls on one of those lines but not the adjacent line, that thin, horizontal line will be switching on and off at a very rapid rate, appearing to flicker. The problem with text is that a lot of fonts have thin horizontal lines called serifs, the little footer that some letters sit on (Figure 8.11).

Unless you're going to make text of a fairly large size, it's generally best to avoid serif fonts. You're better off using a sans-serif font for most video work. You should probably avoid small fonts as well. Video resolution is not very high, the print equivalent of 72dpi. You can read this book in 10 point comfortably, but a 10-point line of text on television would be an illegible smear. I generally never use font sizes below 24, and prefer to use something larger if possible.

Safe Title Area and Safe Action Area

Televisions have a mask on the edge that cuts off some of the displayed picture area. What you see in the **Viewer** and the **Canvas** is not what you get — far from WYSIWYG — and can vary substantially from television to television. That is why the **Canvas** and **Viewer** are thoughtfully marked with a **Safe Action Area** and a smaller area still that is defined as the **Safe Title Area** (Figure 8.12)

These are turned on with the **View** popup at the top of the **Viewer** and **Canvas**. Make sure that both **Overlay** and **Title Safe** are checked to see the **Safe Action and Safe Title areas**. What's within the **SAA** will appear on

Figure 8.12   Safe Action and Safe Title Areas

every television set. Because television tubes used to be curved, and many still are, a smaller area was defined as the **Safe Title Area** in which text could appear without distortion if viewed at an angle. Titles should remain, if possible, within the **Safe Title Area**. This is not important for graphics destined only for web or computer display, but for anything that might be shown on a television within the course of its life, it would be best to maintain them. That said, more often you're seeing titles that are well outside the **STA** and lying partially outside even the **SAA**. Also note that FCP uses an **SAA** and **STA** that are smaller than most other editing systems, which usually only reduce the area 10–20%. The *Extras* folder on your CD contains a 720x486 NTSC CCIR601 format image called *SafeTitle.pct* that shows a more conventionally scribed **Safe Title** and **Safe Action Area**. It's in PICT format with an alpha channel so it will lay over video in FCP. The *Extras* folder also contains a 720x486 PICT file that has been scribed with a grid. I find this helpful to lay over an image. I use it as a guide in the **Canvas** to line up graphic and video elements in a composition.

Font Color (Figure 8.13) is self-explanatory. It includes a color picker and a color swatch as well as a twirly triangle that opens up the **HSB** sliders and **Value** boxes seen in Figure 8.13.

The small icon between the **Eyedropper** and the **Color Swatch** changes the direction in which the color moves if it's animated. We'll get to animation later on page 322.

Figure 8.13   Font Color

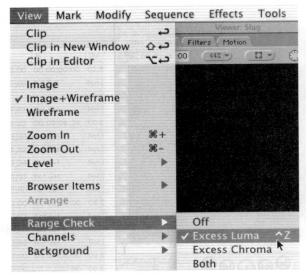

Figure 8.14   View>Range Check>Excess Luma

Figure 8.15   Range Check in the Canvas

Note

Controlling Chroma & Luma: FCP has a new tool for checked luminance and chrominance levels. From the **View** menu, select **Range Check**, and from the submenu, choose **Excess Luma (Control-Z)** (Figure 8.14). You will see the **Canvas** display with diagonal lines called zebra that mark the areas of excessive luminance and a yellow triangle with a warning exclamation mark (Figure 8.15). In the case of our title, that is the whole title. We'll look at the **Range Check** tool again in the lesson on color correction.

The default color for the titles is white — pure, unblemished, high–luminance value white. In fact, it's whiter than white, at least as far as NTSC video goes. This white exceeds the standards set for maximum luminance in NTSC. The slug that FCP generates is blacker than black. Analog NTSC, which is what we watch on television sets, stipulates that black level be at 7.5IRE rather than zero luminance. It's important that you try to keep your luminance and chrominance values within the correct range. Oversaturated colors or video levels that are too high will bloom and smear on a television set. Set the HSB value so that brightness is no more than 92%. This may look pale gray on the computer screen, but as far as NTSC video is concerned, this is white, and it will look white on a television screen.

This is often a problem with using artwork which hasn't been specifically designed for video. Interlacing, limitation in chroma and luminance range, moire patterns, compression, all sorts of issues affect images used in video. Unless the artist makes the necessary adjustments while creating the work, it often looks unsatisfactory when incorporated into a video production.

Set the origin with a **Crosshair** button or with *x,y* values (see Figure 8.8). You can use the crosshairs by clicking on the button

Figure 8.16   Flipped Letters with Tracking Value of −25

Figure 8.17   Leading at −100

Figure 8.18   Left: Aspect with a Value of.4
Right: Aspect with a Value of 0.3

Figure 8.19   Left with Auto Kerning
Right without Auto Kerning

and then clicking wherever in the **Canvas** you want the center point for the origin of the text to be. The value windows are more precise, of course. The first window is the horizontal, or x value; the second window is the vertical, or y value. The default is the center of the screen. This is centered on the baseline of the first line of text, in this case somewhere right under the **n** in **Dance**.

Tracking is the spacing distance between letters, the higher the tracking value, the farther apart the letters will get. Small increases in tracking will have a large impact on letter separation, and animated subtlety makes a pleasing enhancement to a title. As you move tracking down below zero, the letters will scrunch together, and if you go low enough into negative values, the letters will actually flip over, as shown in Figure 8.16.

Leading (pronounced ledding, as in little bits of lead spacing used in hot metal typesetting) is the spacing between lines. The default is zero. A setting of −100 moves the text up so that it's all on one

Note

Tracking: The Auto Kerning check-box near the bottom of the controls as to be checked on or **Tracking** will not function.

line like in Figure 8.17. A value of 100 moves the text down a whole line.

Aspect adjusts the vertical shape of the text. Low numbers stretch text, and higher numbers squeeze the text (Figure 8.18).

Be careful with the **Aspect** control. Very little movement from the default of 1 will cause ugly antialiasing (stair-stepped edges) to appear around the text.

Auto Kerning adjusts the letter spacing based on the letters' shape rather than absolute values (Figure 8.19). Personally I think **Auto Kerning** is too tight for most video, where any blooming will run the letters into each other, particularly serif fonts at smaller font sizes.

Check the **Use Subpixel** box for better quality.

Tip

Flickering Text: Interlace flickering caused by serifs and other fine lines can be alleviated somewhat by smearing the image across the interlace lines. It is easiest to do this with text created in Photoshop, where you can simply applying a one-pixel vertical motion blur. You don't have to soften the whole image like this. If there are particular portions that appear to flicker, you can select them with a marquee or lasso, slightly feathered, and then apply the vertical motion blur to just that portion of the image.

Or in FCP you can duplicate the **Text Generator** in the sequence and stack one on top of the other. Apply a slight **Blur** or **Antialias** filter to the bottom copy. Only the slightly blurred edge that sticks out from underneath the unblurred copy will be visible, smearing the edge. You can also darken the lower copy to give the text a slightly harder edge.

Basic Animation

You can animate all of the items with little diamond buttons shown in Figure 8.8: **Color, Font Size, Origin, Tracking, Leading,** and **Aspect.**

Because this is the first lesson we've talked about animation, we'll need to run through some of the basic concepts. The basis of digital animation is the concept of keyframes. When you change the properties of an image — in text, for instance — you define how it looks. When you apply a keyframe, you define how it looks at a

Subtitles

Subtitling is a laborious, time-consuming business. The first problem is always the translation, especially making it match brisk dialog or narration. The best advice I can offer is to keep it simple and easy to read. The important thing is not to translate the text literally but to convey the sense. The text needs to follow the spoken words closely, which is why subtitles often need to be shortened and condensed.

Technically, the easiest way to generate subtitles in FCP is to make a couple of templates in your **Favorites** bin or in the **Browser** and keep bringing those into the sequence. Because text is so small for video, you should always use a sans serif font. I prefer good old Helvetica. The size should be about 28. I prefer to use yellow with a saturation of about 85% for the text color, with a slight, black drop shadow. Yellow shows against a white or pale shirt better than white with a drop shadow, I think. The text should sit on the edge of the **Safe Title Area.** Set the text at the bottom of the screen with the origin point of a 720 image with a *y* value of about 160. Try to keep to one line of text. Only go to a second line if you have to, but never go to three lines; it encroaches too much into the picture area. For two lines of text, set the *y* axis a little higher. A value of about 135 should do it.

Another trick is to use a black color matte behind the text. Keep it to just the size of the text and reduce the **Opacity** down to 10% or 20%, creating a translucent shadow area behind the text, making it more legible and reducing flickering in the text.

The **Superimpose** function can be useful in subtitling because it creates text clips that are exactly the length of a particular clip.

particular moment in time, a specific frame of video. If you then go to another moment in time, say 10 seconds farther into your video and change that color value, you will then create another keyframe, which will define how it will look at that point in time, 10 seconds later. The computer will figure out what each of the intermediate frames should look like over those 10 seconds.

1. In your **Browser** open the sequence *ColorAnimation.*
2. Double-click on the *Text* clip on **V2** to open it in the **Viewer.**

Animating Size

Though **Size** can be animated, I would advise against it. For text to animate size, it also has to animate the auto kerning to match, which can produce odd behavior. To scale text properly, make the text at the largest font size you can fit on the screen and then use **Scale** in the **Motion** tab to create the animation. Open the sequence in the **Browser** called *Size Test* and take a look at the difference. To see the animation, you may have to render it out. The major gotcha in FCP is that **Size** in **Text** is not really point size, though it defaults to a common point size 36. The problem is obvious if you look at 36-point text created in FCP in either a 320 sequence or a 720 sequence. It looks the same, when clearly it shouldn't be. FCP makes the size relative to the frame dimensions. So to scale text beyond the dimensions of the sequence, you are forced to scale the size. Because of that you'll get ugly behavior such as produced in *Size Test*. Fortunately there is a savior for this problem, and his name is Boris (see page 340).

When working on animations, I like to use a desktop arrangement which was available in previous versions of FCP, but which was removed in v3. The arrangement is called **Compositing** and is available on the CD that accompanies this book. Simply insert the CD, and from the **Window>Arrange** menu, go to **Restore Layout**. When the navigation box opens, find the CD in your computer, and open the folder called **Window Layouts**. From that folder chose the layout called **Compositing**. If you prefer, you can bring all three layouts in the folder into your own computer. Place them in *User>Library>Preferences>Final Cut Pro User Data>Window Layouts*. You can access them at any time you want without loading the CD.

3. Change the screen layout to **Compositing** arrangement.

4. Click on the **Controls** tab and take a look at the **Font Color** property (Figure 8.20).

Notice the highlighted diamond with the darker triangle next to it. The diamond means there is a keyframe for that property.

5. Click the triangle to move to the next keyframe.

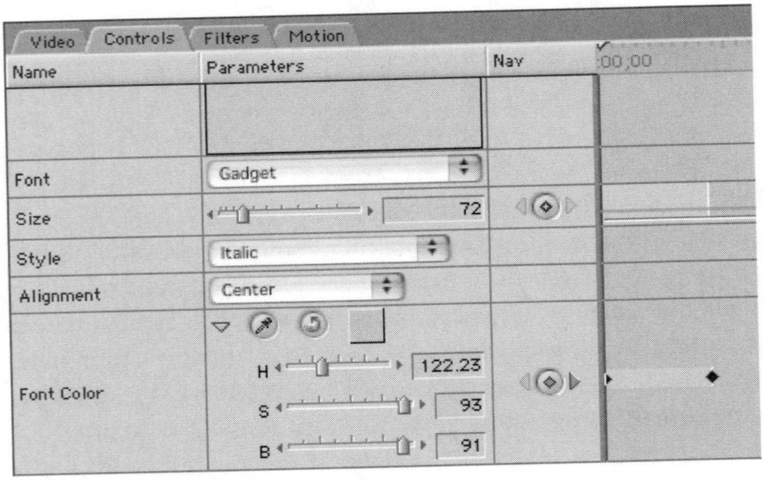

Figure 8.20   Animated Color Property

The right portion of Figure 8.20 shows the timeline with the clip you're working on marked out. You can navigate along the sequence in this window as far as the limits of the media of your clip, beyond the length of the clip's duration.

Usually, though, you only work in the area your clip is visible. The timeline portion of the window indicates with the two little diamonds that there are two keyframes on this clip, one at the beginning and the other at the end.

6. Go to the end keyframe. You'll see that the color is almost the same green.

7. Scrub in the timeline. You'll see that the color of the title changes through the whole spectrum over the course of the 10 seconds of the clip.

The little toggle next to the color swatch sets the direction around the color wheel that the animation moves. If you change that toggle to the opposite setting over the course of the clip, the green will hardly change at all.

Animation in Final Cut is as simple as that. Let's do a small animation.

1. Open up *Sequence 1*, which should have *Dance2* and a *Text* clip in it on **V2**.

Let's animate the **Tracking**.

2. Open the *Text* clip in **Viewer** and go to the **Controls** tab. Make sure you're at the beginning of the clip in the timeline.

3. Either grab the **Tracking** slider and pull it down to –2 or dial in –2 in the value box. The text should look scrunched together as in Figure 8.21.

Figure 8.21 Text at –2 Tracking

4. Now click on the empty diamond keyframe button (Figure 8.22).

You have just created a keyframe. The little button will go green.

5. Scroll down to the timeline to the last frame of the clip and change the tracking value to 18.

Figure 8.22 Keyframe Button

A new keyframe is immediately created and the green line that shows the property value in the timeline slopes upward, indicating that the value increases over time (Figure 8.23).

Figure 8.23 Keyframes in the Viewer Timeline

Note _____

Navigating with Keyframes: Be careful with using the **Down** arrow key to go to the end of a clip. When FCP takes you to the next edit, it takes you to first frame of the next clip. So to get to the last frame of the clip, you need to use the **Down** arrow and then the **Left** arrow to take you back one frame. Where you want to go is not the next edit, but rather to the Out point, the last frame of the clip. So rather than using the **Down** arrow, use the keyboard shortcut **Shift-O** to go to the Out point.

6. Scrub the timeline to see the effect of the animation in the **Canvas**.

7. If you have a system with real-time capabilities, you're done. If not, you'll have to render out the animation to see it, or use **QuickView** from the **Tools** menu. Depending on your RAM availability, you might need to reduce the resolution in **QuickView** to see the whole 10 seconds of the animation.

That's it. You've created your first Final Cut Pro motion graphics animation. We'll talk about animation in much greater detail in the next lesson.

Lower Thirds

A lower third is the graphic you often see near the bottom of the screen identifying a speaker or location. They're simple to create in Final Cut, though they are fairly limited. If you want to create something more exciting or stylish, you'll probably find it easier to do in Photoshop or in **Title**

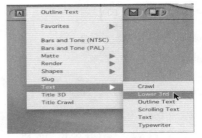

Figure 8.24   Text Generator and Lower Third Menu

3D, which we'll look at later on page 340. Because **Lower Third** is so limited, it's easy to use.

Click on the **Generators** button, and in the menu drop down to **Lower Third** (Figure 8.24).

Figure 8.25 shows the simple lower third Final Cut generates. It's set down in the lower left corner of the **Safe Title Area** for you.

You can create the graphic in the **Viewer** before you move it to the **Timeline**, but remember once you've moved it to the **Timeline**, what's there is now a copy. I always find there is less chance of a mistake if I move the graphic to the **Timeline** first and then open it from there. Also, once it's in the **Timeline**, you can put the playhead over it and quickly see what you're doing in the **Canvas**. Open the **Controls** tab in the **Viewer** (Figure 8.26), and you'll see that the **Controls** are quite different for lower thirds. You have

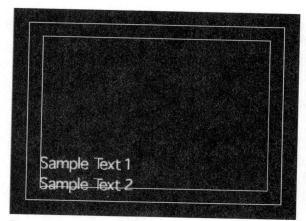

Figure 8.25   Lower Third

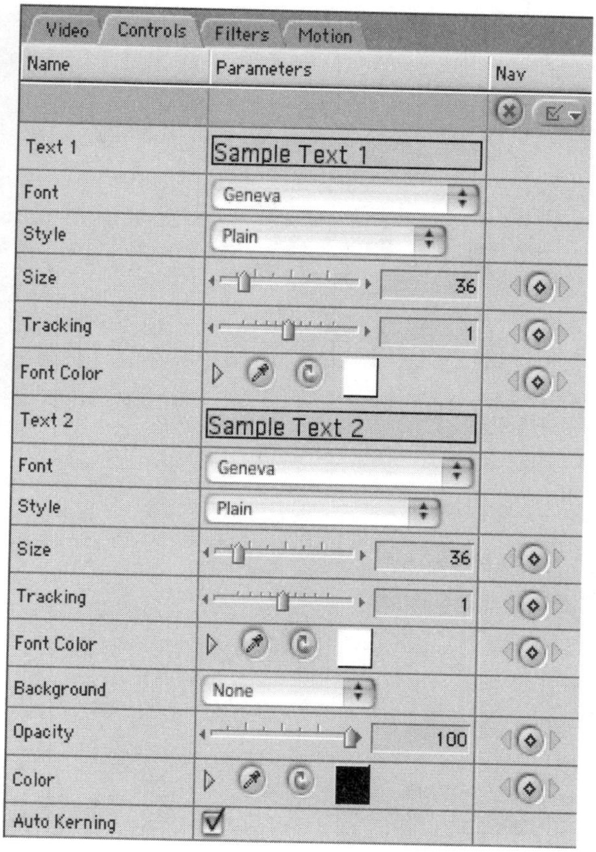

Figure 8.26   Lower Third Controls

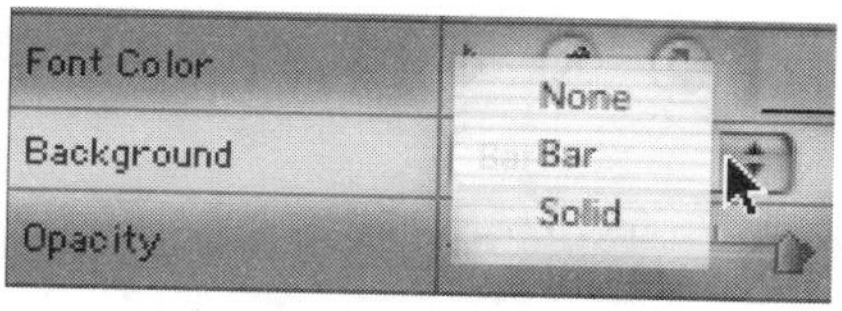

Figure 8.27   Lower Third Backgrounds

some new parameters, and you are missing a property as well. There is, for instance, no alignment popup.

You have two lines of text, for which you set any font, size, or color. You can make a line as long as you want — of course, if you make it too long, it will run off the screen. Unlike the regular text window, each text box here can only hold one line of text. At the bottom of the controls, you have the ability to create a background for the text (Figure 8.27) and to adjust the opacity of the background.

Bar appears as a line between the text blocks. Despite having an opacity of 100%, it will still show some of the underlying video through it. **Solid** is a block of color that appears behind the two text blocks. You can apply one or the other, but not both. You could always add another lower third beneath it, with no text, just the background, as shown in Figure 8.28.

Scrolling Text

FCP's **Scrolling Text** is called up the same way as the other text elements in the **Text Generator** menu (Figure 8.29). It looks startling at first because it opens in the **Viewer** with a blank screen, checkerboard, or black. Don't panic. Drag it to the **Timeline** or **Browser** and then double-click the new version to open it back into the **Viewer**. Go straight to the **Controls** tab (Figure 8.30), which looks pretty familiar, especially the top few items.

The control called **Spacing** is actually **Tracking**. I have no idea why it's called **Spacing** here. It does not mean vertical spacing. For that you use **Leading**. I'm not sure either why **Leading** is represented as a percentage rather than value, as in other Generators.

Indent only works with left- or right-justified text. With left justified (or aligned) the text indents about 10%, about the safe title area. To move the text block farther to the right use the **Indent** slider (Figure 8.31).

Gap Width lets you set the spacing between vertical columns of text. This space is often called the gutter. It defaults to 5%, which is rather small. **Gap Width** only works with center alignment. You activate it by typing an asterisk in your text where you want the column to separate, as in "Producer*Paul Temme" (Figure 8.32). You can't make your font size too large because the text will quickly run off the screen. Entering returns to make two lines will not honor the gutter, unfortunately, so you'll get a rather odd layout.

Fade Size is an interesting control. It allows the scroll to fade in as it comes in off the bottom of the screen and fade out as it disappears off the top (Figure 8.33).

Direction is set in a popup and can be the conventional upward movement, or it can be changed to downward. How fast the scroll moves is determined by the length of the scroll in the sequence. The longer the scroll, the slower the movement. This is one of the places where **QuickView** is a godsend. It's the easiest way to check your scroll speed to see if it's right. Simply set the

Figure 8.28 Lower Third with Bar and Background

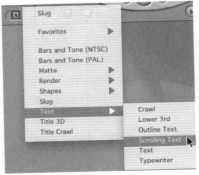

Figure 8.29 Generators>Text> Scrolling Text

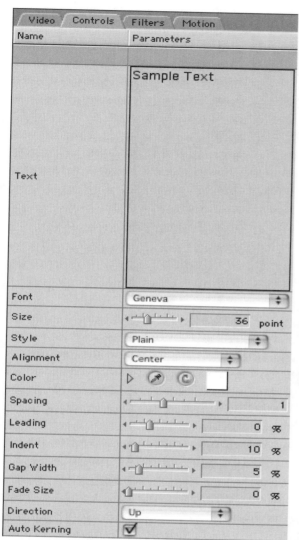

Figure 8.30   Scrolling Text Controls

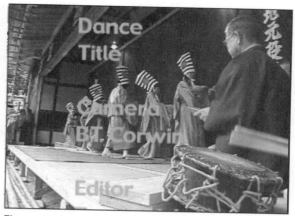

Figure 8.31   Indent Set to 25%

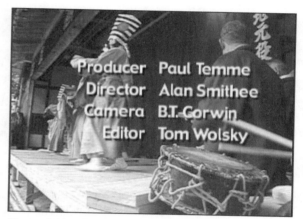

Figure 8.32   Gap Width Default 5%

Figure 8.33   Fade Set to 25%

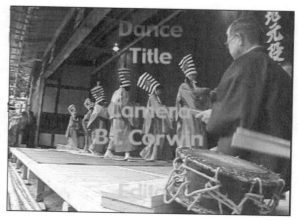

playhead in your sequence somewhere in the scroll and activate **QuickView**. The two-second default should be enough to tell you if your scroll is moved at the speed you want. If it's too slow make the scroll shorter, if it's too fast make the scroll longer. Change the duration either by typing in a new duration in the **Viewer**, or by dragging the end of scroll in the **Timeline**.

Crawl Text

Crawl is the horizontal version of a scroll. The controls are a little different, but they should be pretty familiar by now (Figure 8.34).

Spacing again is tracking. The **Location** slider defaults to **85**, which is the bottom of the **Safe Title Area**. Reducing the number will move the crawl higher up in the screen. A value of about **20**, depending on the font and size, puts it at the top of the **Safe Title Area**.

Typewriter

Let's look at **Typewriter** next. This is a neat addition to FCP introduced in version 2. It looks especially good if you use a typewriter monospace font such as Courier.

The controls give you a small degree of flexibility (Figure 8.35).

Alignment defaults to **Left** so that the typing begins on the left edge of the **Safe Title Area** and works its way across. Be careful with the line layout, because it's easy to type right off the screen. Because the text doesn't wrap, you have to put in a return wherever you need a line break.

Location sets the vertical height of the typing. The default is 50, the center line of the screen. A setting of about 20 moves the text block to the top of the **Safe Title Area**, which is probably where you should start if you have more than a few of lines to type on.

Indent sets how far in from the edge the text is set if it is either left or right aligned.

Center alignment has an odd effect. The typing happens in the center of the screen, and the line of text spreads out from the center. It's unusual and may be worth playing with.

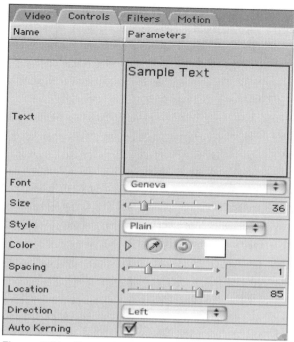

Figure 8.34 Crawl Controls

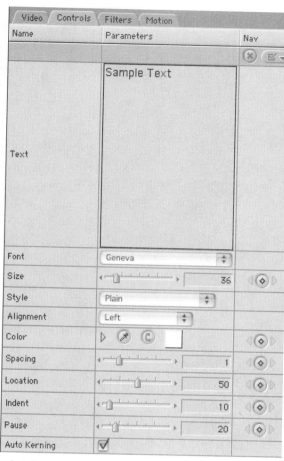

Figure 8.35 Typewriter Controls

The default **Pause** value of 20 produces the action of a brisk typist, depending on how much text there is to type. The way it works is that the higher the **Pause** value, the longer the text is held on the screen before the end of the clip. So the three variables are:

- The length of the clip

- How long the text holds after the typing is completed (that's the **Pause** value)

- How much you have to type

If you have a lot to type, set the **Pause** value fairly low. If you set the **Pause** value very high — for instance, 100 — no typing will occur; the text will just be there and spend 100% of the time paused on the screen.

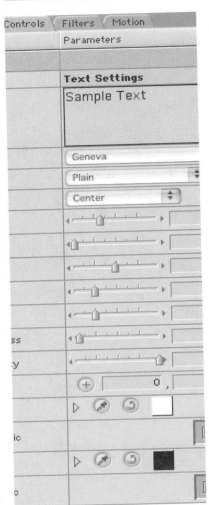

Figure 8.36 Default Outline Text Controls

Mattias Sandström has created a typewriter plugin of his own using FXScript. It's in the *Extras* folder of the CD, part of the plugin package called *TMTSfree*. His typewriter is also a generator and works well. It has the advantage of being able to vary the typing speed so the letters don't just appear as a steady stream but at variable rates.

Outline Text

I saved **Outline Text** for last because it's the most complex of FCP's Text Generators, with the greatest number of controls. Figure 8.36 shows only part of the controls. They're so long they won't fit vertically on most computer screens without scrolling the controls box. We'll examine the rest of them later.

Because **Outline** is meant to be a big bold text, perhaps with video in it, the default font size is 64. It defaults to white text with a broad black outline.

In the **Outline Text** controls, **Tracking** returns instead of spacing, and **Aspect** returns as well. This is useful if you want an image to fill the letters. It lets you make the lettering taller or shorter. Again, be careful of antialiasing if you pull it around too much.

Line Width is more conventionally called *stroke*. It's the edging around the letter. You can make it disappear to nothing, or you can make quite large, up to 200 (Figure 8.37). You can, as we shall see in Lesson 12, "Adding Video" on page 531, insert video into the outline itself to make some really quite bizarre visual effects.

The **Softness** setting is for the stroke. It defaults to 5. I wouldn't put it any lower; the edges would start to look quite blocky. If you push the values up near 100 with a very large stroke, you get a kind of wispy background (Figure 8.38).

The **Text Opacity** control is self-explanatory, though I'm not quite sure why it's here. Note that this controls the opacity for all the text as well as the stroke. You cannot, unfortunately, use this tool to create an outline with a transparent interior. I'll show you the way to do this using FCP's **Filters** and **Compositing** tools in Lesson 12, "Empty Outline Text" on page 536.

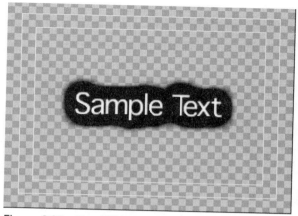

Figure 8.37   Line Width Value of 200

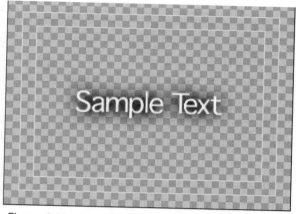

Figure 8.38   Line Width 200 and softness at 75

Center is what's called **Origin** in the standard **Text** tool, 0,0 being the middle of the screen.

👉 *Tip*

Seeing the Border: Because Outline Text starts out as white with a black border, when you put the Timeline playhead over the title on **V1**, you probably won't see the border being black on black. The easiest way to make it visible is to change the background of the **Canvas** to checkerboard with the popup at the top of the window (Figure 8.39).

Now we come to **Text Graphic** and **Line Graphic**. These allow you to insert still images into the outline using the **Well**. We saw the **Well** on page 210 in Lesson 5 on transitions, and it works the same way here: simply drag the image or clip from the **Browser** and drop it in. It would be nice if the sequence played the video inside the **Outline Text**; it doesn't, unfortunately, neither in the text nor in the **Line Width**. It only displays the In point of the video. Don't despair, though. It's possible, even simple, using FCP, to have video moving inside your text. We'll look at that also in Lesson 12 on compositing.

Let's look at the rest of **Outline Text**'s text control panel (Figure 8.40).

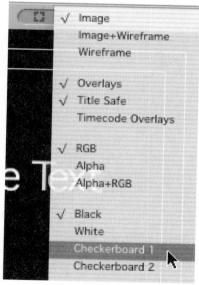

Figure 8.39   Background Popup

Background Settings		
Horizontal Size		0
Vertical Size		0
Horizontal Offset		0
Vertical Offset		0
Back Soft		0
Back Opacity		50
Back Color		
Back Graphic		
Crop		
Auto Kerning		

Figure 8.40 Background Settings Panel

The default is for the background to be off. You turn it on by increasing the horizontal and vertical size. The horizontal size acts in relationship to the amount of text you have — the less text, the less effect the horizontal value has; the more text, the farther the background extends (Figure 8.41).

Horizontal and **Vertical Offsets** set the screen position relative to the text, so it's not strictly an origin point. If the text is set high in the screen, so will the background. On the other hand, with the text high in the screen and the **Vertical Offset** set to negative numbers, the background will be pulled down in the screen (Figure 8.42).

If you're older, you probably remember the Brylcreem ads: "a little dab'll do ya." Well, a little dab of **Softness** will do ya. Small amounts of **Softness** will have a big impact on the blurring of the background. You'll probably need to make the background size quite large so that the softening doesn't dissipate the image too much. **Softness** and **Opacity** add great tools to background and can be used for other elements besides **Outline Text**. The problem is that the background seems to be tied to the text. That's easy to overcome. In the **Text** window, use a bunch of spaces, even blocks of spaces with returns to make shapes that the background will work behind.

Nesting

In the project **Browser** is another sequence called *Title and Background*, which is made up of a number of FCP titling tools. The output appears in Figure 8.43, but if you open it in FCP, you'll see it in color. I'll show you how it was built up.

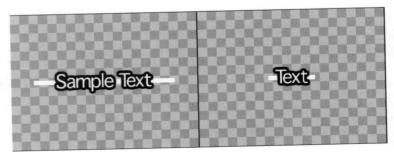

Figure 8.41 Both with Background Set With Horizontal Size 150 Vertical Size 20

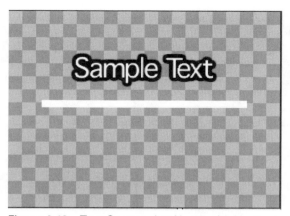

Figure 8.42 Text Centered at Y –50 with Vertical Offset Set to –100

Figure 8.43 Title and Background

If you open the sequence *Title and Background*, you'll see that it is made up of two layers. On **V1** is the video clip *Dance2*, and on **V2** is a text block called *Title Composite* and another called *Title Composite Japan*. These are nests. Nesting is an important concept to understand in Final Cut. Because you can have sequences within sequences in FCP, you can also group layers together into nests to form a sequence of their own. You'll notice in the **Browser** there are sequences called *Title Composite* and *Title Composite Japan*. These are the elements that appear on **V2** in *Title and Background*. Let's build these nests together.

Text

1. Start by duplicating *Title and Background* in the **Browser**. Select the sequence and use **Edit>Duplicate** (**Option-D**).

2. Open the duplicate *Title and Background copy* by double-clicking on it, or simply select it and hit **Enter** or **Return.**

3. Use **Command-A** to select everything in the **Timeline** and then delete to the empty the sequence.

4. Next drag the clip *Dance2* into the beginning of the **Timeline** on **V1**.

5. In the **Viewer**, from the **Text Generator** popup select **Outline Text.**

6. Drag the **Sample Text** block onto **V2** of your sequence.

7. Double-click it to bring it back into the **Viewer** and go to the **Controls** tab.

8. First change the text to *DAMINE*, the name of the village where this video was shot.

9. You can, of course, use whatever text, color, or settings you want, but this is how I built this image:

Font	Arial
Style	Bold
Point Size	98
Tracking	4
Line Width	23
Color	muted red: R 79%, G 27%, B 35%

Because the letters looked too jammed together, I set the **Tracking** to 4.

That's it. You have the basic text block. Now let's set the background white glow.

☞ Tip

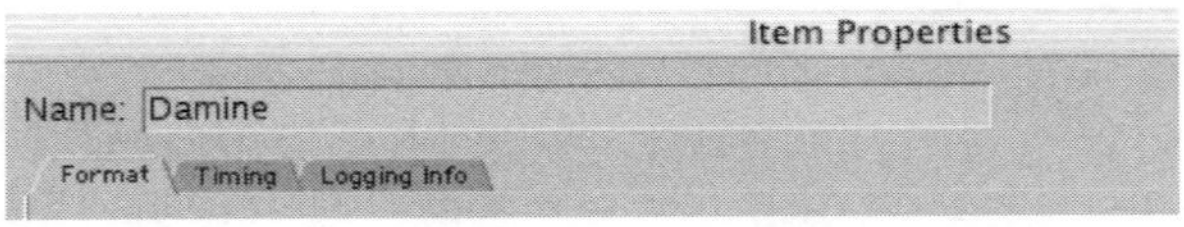

Figure 8.44 Changing Name in Item Properties

Renaming: It's helpful to rename the **Outline Text** before we create a new one. **Control**-click on the **Outline Text** on the top track and select **Properties** from the menu. In the **Item Properties** dialog you might want to change the name to something like **DAMINE** (Figure 8.44).

Background

1. Set the **Duration** for the clip to the length you want.

I left it at the default 10 seconds.

2. Next pull the **Text** block upward, holding down the **Shift** key to constrain movement to the vertical and drop it on the empty space above.

This will create a new track and leave **V2** empty for the background.

3. In the **Viewer** create a new **Outline Text** block.

4. Drag it to **V2** and open the clip from the **Timeline** back into the **Viewer**.

This is going to be the background white glow.

5. In the text block, hit the spacebar 13 or 14 times; that is, type in 13 or 14 empty spaces. Use the default font size, which is fine.

We've now made "text" for the background to work with.

6. Scroll to the **Background** controls and set the following:

Horizontal	200
Vertical	200
Back Soft	50 (blurs the background considerably)
Opacity	100

Your **Canvas** should like something like Figure 8.45.

7. Placing the cursor on the **Filmstrip** icon at the head of **V2**, hold down the **Control** key, and from the contextual menu, select **Add Track** (Figure 8.46).

8. Do this three times so that you have three empty tracks between the two layers with the **Outline Text** blocks.

9. In the **Viewer** from the **Generators** button, select **Matte>Color,** as we did to make the color backing for the **Page Peel** transition in Lesson 5. Again this will fill the screen with midtone gray.

10. Drag it to **Timeline** and place it on the empty **V3** you created.

11. Double click the **Color** in the sequence to open it back into the **Viewer.**

12. Go to the **Controls** tab and set the color to the same dark rose as the DAMINE title. Use the color picker if the title is visible in the **Canvas.** It should be if the playhead is sitting over the clips.

Figure 8.45 Text and Background with Two Layers

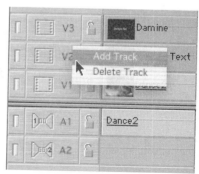

Figure 8.46 Adding Tracks

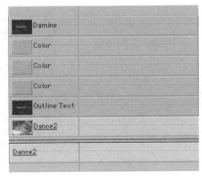

Figure 8.47   Crop and Opacity Settings in Motion Tab

13. After setting the color, go to the **Motion** tab and twirl open the **Crop** controls (Figure 8.47). I used these settings:

Top Crop	64
Bottom Crop	32
Opacity	75

We'll look at the other controls in the **Motion** tab in detail in the next lesson.

14. Open another **Color Matte,** and place it in the sequence above the red bar you just created. Or you can **Option-Shift-**drag to duplicate the **Color** and place it on the track above.

15. Make the color of this matte green (R 8%, G 38%, B 7%), and in the **Motion** tab set:

Top Crop	64
Bottom Crop	38

16. One more color matte to make. Generate the matte and bring it to the sequence below the top **Outline Text** block.

17. Set the same green color and these **Crop** values:

Top Crop	70
Bottom Crop	32

Your sequence should have six layers in it (Figure 8.48):

- The video clip on **V1**
- **Outline Text** block on **V2**
- Three color mattes on the layers above
- At the top, another **Outline Text** block, the one that holds the actual text DAMINE.

Figure 8.48   Timeline After Making Text and Matte Layers

Putting It All Together

1. Make a marquee selection in the **Timeline** window, or **Shift-**click all the layers, *except* the video layer on **V1**. Leave that unselected.

2. From the **Sequence** menu, select **Nest Item(s)** (Figure 8.49) or use the keyboard shortcut **Option-C**.

This will bring up a dialog box that lets you name the new sequence you're creating.

3. Call it *Title Composite 2*, to distinguish it from the sequence in your **Browser** already called *Title Composite* (Figure 8.50).

This nest appears in the **Timeline** as a block called *Title Composite 2*. It will also appear in your **Browser** as a sequence. That block of text in your sequence can be moved around wherever you like and used again and again.

Drop Shadow

You thought I forgot the drop shadow on DAMINE. Here is the beauty of nested sequences.

1. Double-click the nest. It opens as a whole separate sequence in a new tab in the **Timeline** window.

2. Double-click on the **Outline Text** block at the top to open it in the **Viewer.**

3. Go to the **Motion** tab, and check the box for **Drop Shadow.** Enter these settings:

Angle	135
Offset	4
Shadow color	Green: R 24%, G 55%, B 21%
Softness	15
Opacity	80

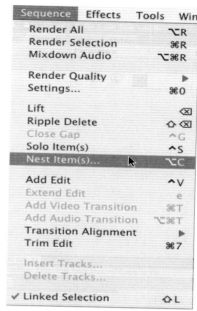

Figure 8.49 Sequence>Nest Item(s)

Figure 8.50 Nesting Dialog

The drop shadow is done. This change will now appear in every iteration of that sequence wherever it appears anywhere in my project.

Here's what else makes this beautiful: suppose I've built this complex text block, and I want to change the actual text, but nothing else.

1. Duplicate *Title Composite 2* in your **Browser**.
2. Change the name of the duplicate to *Title Composite Japan 2*.
3. Open the duplicate in the **Timeline**.
4. Double-click on the top outline text block to open it into the **Viewer**, and replace the word *DAMINE* with the word *JAPAN*.

Nothing else changes, just the text block and its drop shadow. Easy, isn't it?

If you want to apply an effect to a nest or reposition the block — lower in the frame for instance — you can do this without adjusting each layer individually.

Title 3D

Title 3D is a wonderful new addition to Final Cut Pro. It really supersedes FCP's titlers in many ways, giving the user great control and flexibility with text. It is a hugely feature-packed tool, an application within itself really. I'm going to show you some of its principal tools, but for a thorough look at its capabilities, there is an excellent PDF on the Final Cut CD that details its operation.

Title 3D and **Title Crawl** are Boris Calligraphy and should be installed when you install FCP3. Because they are built into FCP's **Generators**, they are really now an integral part of the application.

Call up **Title 3D** from the **Generators** (Figure 8.51) and it will launch a separate titling window that is part of the Boris interface (Figure 8.52). This is the first of five tabbed windows that allow you access to **Title 3D**'s powerful and complex tools. In fact, **Title 3D** has so many controls that there seem to be controls for the controls.

Figure 8.51 Generators>Title 3D

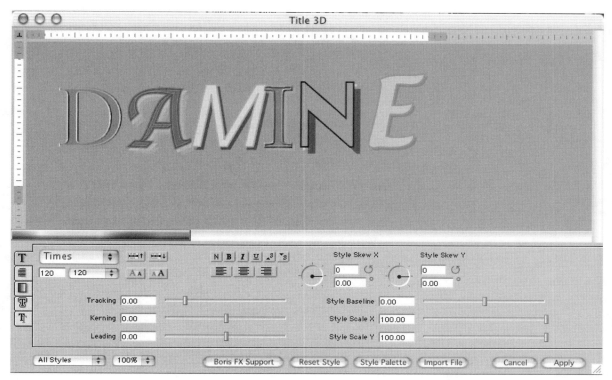

Figure 8.52   Title 3D Interface

The first tabbed window is obviously the text window.

Unlike the FCP text box, it is truly WYSIWYG. Most importantly, each control can be applied to each letter or group of letters separately. So now, with little trouble, you can make a garish combination of colors and fonts, such as I have done in the sequence *Calligraphy*.

Before you do anything in this window, you may want to click on the second tab and change the default **No Wrap** to **Wrap** (Figure 8.53). I don't know why it defaults to **No Wrap**. You can leave the wrap default at 512. It doesn't seem to matter what the dimensions of your frame size are nor what font point size is. They are arbitrary numbers that scale to the dimensions of the image. 512 will give you word wrapping that will fit inside a standard 720 video image's Safe Title Area.

Figure 8.53 Word Wrapping

The **Top-down Text** and **Right-to-left Reading** checkboxes at the bottom of the window are great if you want vertical text or if you're doing Hebrew or Arabic text.

After you've set **Word Wrapping**, go back to the text window to enter your text. The main window allows you to enter and select text, which you can then adjust with the controls at the bottom part of the window.

The text window works very much like most text applications such as Word. At the top of the **Text** window is a ruler that allows you to set tabs for precise positioning of text elements (Figure 8.54). Use the **Tab** key to navigate from one tab indent to the next. After you've set a tab, you can double-click on it to toggle from left justified, to right justified, to center justified. This tool is especially useful when making long scrolls like movie credits that often use columns and indents for different sections.

The white area seen in the ruler is the active text part of the screen, while the gray area is beyond the word wrapping.

Let's look quickly at some of the phenomenal text control in Calligraphy. In the bottom portion of the screen, the first popup obviously sets the font. The two buttons to the right will move you up and down through your font list. Below the **Font** popup is a **Point Size Value** box. The two buttons to the right will

Figure 8.54 Title 3D Text Window Ruler

incrementally raise and lower your point. To the right of the font controls are six buttons that let you set:

- Normal
- Bold
- Italic
- Underline
- Superscript
- Subscript

Below that, three **Paragraph** buttons let you set justification:

- Left
- Center
- Right

The **Tracking** slider adjusts the letter spacing globally.

Kerning-adjusts the spacing between individual pairs or groups of letters without affecting the overall spacing. It allows you to control individual letter spacing. It's important for many fonts, especially when you are writing words like AVE, where you need to slide the A and V closer together than fonts normally place them.

Leading controls the line gap between all the lines in the window.

The **Style** controls (Figure 8.55) allow you a truly astonishing degree of control over text and begin to show why this text tool is called **Title 3D**. Individual letters or groups of letters can be skew left and right on the baseline with **Style Skew X**. They can be swung like doors with **Style Skew Y** as in Figure 8.56. The value boxes in these controls let you set the degrees of skew (the lower

Figure 8.55   Style Controls

Figure 8.56   Style Skew Y 45 degrees

Tip

Text Control Shortcuts: If the Kerning, Tracking, or Leading value box is active, you can make the values go up or down by holding down the **Option** key and tapping the Up and **Down** arrow keys to raise and lower the values.

Bitmap or Vector

How is this enormous flexibility of text possible? When we scaled text created with the FCP titler, the image quickly became jagged around the edges, yet here we're separately scaling individual letters, twisting and skewing them, and yet you'll see no apparent antialiasing or stair-stepping on the edges of the letters. This is possible because Calligraphy works with vector graphics, while FCP text creates bit-mapped graphics.

When a bitmapped graphic is created, the color and position of each pixel in the image is defined. If you then scale that image, you have to scale the pixels, trying to create pixels where none previously existed. When a vector graphic is created, no pixels are actually defined. Only the shape, based on lines and curves, is defined. So if you scale a vector graphic, you're simply redefining the shape; no actual pixels need be created until the image is displayed on the screen.

Figure 8.57 shows what happens when a bitmapped text file (Apple Chancery 76 point) is scaled 300% and when a vector-based text file is scaled the same amount. The scaling for the vector graphic has to be done within Title 3D and not using the **Scale** slider in the **Motion** tab.

Figure 8.57 Left: Bitmapped
Right: Vector

box) and numbers of rotations (the upper box), which can be used with the animation controls.

Style Baseline will allow you to raise and lower letters separately, while **Style Scale X** and **Style Scale Y** will let you scale individual characters on the x and/or y axis independently from each other.

The **All Styles** popup at the bottom lets you change to **Basic Style**. You see basic limits in the text window. It does speed up preview, which can get quite slow with long text windows.

The **Percentage** popup lets you change the display size of the text window, a useful feature if you have a lot of text and want to quickly move around in it.

Boris FX Support will connect you to Boris's online web support system.

The **Reset Style** button will reset all the parameters for the words in the text window. It will not, however, reset wrapping, tabs, justification, or margins.

The **Style Palette** is a great tool (Figure 8.58). It allows you to create your own text style and to name and save it. This way you can replicate styles from file to file and even project to project simply and efficiently. You can download many **Style** presets from the Boris FX website http://www.borisfx.com.

The **Import File** button allows you to bring into the **Text** window a previously created plain text file or RTF (Rich Text Format) file. All the justification and styles applied there will be honored in **Title 3D**.

Cancel and **Apply** are self-explanatory.

This is only the first couple of tabs in **Title 3D**.

The third tabbed panel, **Text Color**, lets you set the text fill and opacity (Figure 8.59). Notice the little checkbox in the upper left corner that let's you turn off the fill, so that you only have the text outline if you want. The **Text Fill** popup lets you choose to fill the text with a color or with a gradient. If you choose **Color** the **Style Color** swatch allows access to the system color picker that we saw earlier. If you choose **Gradient** you will get access to an incredibly powerful gradient editor (Figure 8.60), which allows multiple color points as well as transparency. To add color points, click below the gradient bar display.

The fourth tabbed window lets you set the width and opacity for the **Text Edge**, and not just a single edge, but up five separate edges for each letter (Figure 8.61). Each edge can be **Plain, Bevel** or **Glow**, and can be **Center, Inside,** or **Outside**. The slider on the right controls the softening blur for each edge. The variations possible with five edges are nearing infinite. More than anyone could need.

The fifth panel sets the five separate **Drop Shadows**. These can be either a standard **Drop**; a **Cast** shadow, which slopes away from the text; or a **Solid** shadow with sides (Figure 8.62). **Drop** and

Figure 8.58   Style Palette

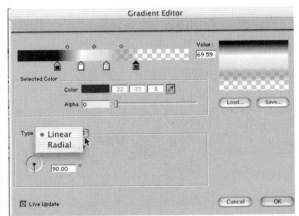

Figure 8.59   Text Color

Figure 8.60   Gradient Editor

Figure 8.61   Text Edge

Figure 8.62   Drop Shadow

Cast shadows don't have **Highlight** or **Shade** color, but they have a **Softness** control that appears when the shadow popup is changed. Each shadow also has controls for color, distance, opacity, and angle.

Unfortunately, while you're working in **Title 3D**, you cannot see the text composited on top of the image, but once you've created your text, drag it to the **Timeline** or **Superimpose** it over a clip that's already there.

If you need to change or adjust the text, double-click the **Title 3D** file in the **Timeline** to open it into the **Viewer**. Then click on the **Control** tab to open all the controls for **Title 3D** (Figure 8.63).

To access the text window to change the letters or styles or any of the other controls, click on the **Title 3D** logo at the top of the controls panel. Notice that all of the items that have the little diamond keyframe button on the right. Each of these parameters is keyframable, though there are some that you probably don't want to animate.

Note _____

Interlace Flickering: If you're doing text animation on interlaced video, check the 1:2:1 **Deflicker** box to reduce interlace flickering.

The **Geometry** section controls the text overall, changing:

- Position
- Distance
- Scale
- Tumble
- Spin
- Rotate

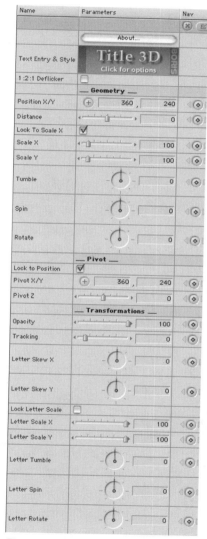

Figure 8.63   Title 3D Controls

While **Position** places the text in the screen, **Distance** makes the text appear nearer or farther away. If you want to make the text seem as if it's coming from the distance to the camera, animate the **Distance** parameter, not the **Scale**. The movement of **Scale** will get slower and slower as it gets bigger. This does not happen when animating **Distance**. Unfortunately, the smallest distance is 5, moving the slider to the right, which may not be enough to make the text disappear into infinity. Nor can the largest scale value 800 make the text seem to fly from the horizon toward the camera and past it. To do that, you'll need to use a combination of primarily animating **Distance** and adding a bit of **Scale** animation to make the text start from zero. This is the **Scale** value you want to adjust to get clean, large fonts, not the **Scale** in the **Motion** tab.

Tumble, Spin, and **Rotate** will turn the entire text block around on the *x*, *y*, and *z* axes, respectively.

Pivot controls the point around which the text **Tumbles, Spins,** and **Rotates**. If the **Lock to Position** box is checked, the controls have no effect. With the box checked, the text will **Rotate** around the selected **Pivot** point, which can be set with numeric values or with the crosshairs button. Neither **Tumble** nor **Spin** controls function with the **X/Y** controls, but their movement is affected when the **Z** slider is activated.

Transformation affects all the letters in the text block, but it affects them individually. In Figure 8.64 the image on the left has its **Geometry** tumbled –45 ° and spun 70°, while the image on the right has its **Transformation** tumbled –45 and spun 50. Notice that on the right each letter is moving, while on the left they are moving together. Also notice that on the right the **Tumble** factor appears quite limited when **Spin** is applied. You'll get more

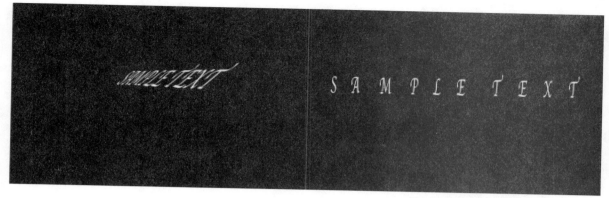

Figure 8.64   Geometry vs. Transformation

displacement of the text using **Letter Skew** rather than **Letter Tumble** if **Spin** is added.

It's probably not a good idea to use **Letter Scale** because this can cause strange kerning behavior, as shown in Figure 8.65.

Title Crawl

Title Crawl is accessed from the bottom of the **Generators** popup and shares many of the same controls as **Title 3D**. The text window that's evoked when **Title Crawl** is called up functions identically in both Calligraphy title tools. The real difference is seen in the **Controls** tab of the **Viewer** (Figure 8.66). Here there are far fewer keyframable options, no **Geometry**, no **Transformation**.

Figure 8.65   Letter Scaling

The **Animation** popup lets you set:

- **None**, the default

- **Roll** (Scroll)

- **Crawl**

Mask Start and End, Blend Start and End are the same as FCP's **Fade Size** tool, only with more control. Here you can fade the start and end separately as well as controlling the amount of fade, here called blend. The **Reverse Direction** checkbox does just that, makes a roll reverse from the default bottom-to-top direction to top-to-bottom, and reverses direction of the standard right-to-left crawl to left-to-right.

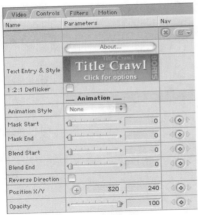

Figure 8.66 Title Crawl Controls

To do a **Crawl**, make sure **Word Wrap** is switched off.

The speed of the **Roll** or **Crawl** is determined by the amount of text in the text window and the duration of the text block in the **Timeline**, the longer the block the slower the motion. Again this is where **QuickView** is especially useful: to determine whether the text speed is appropriate, a couple of seconds will be enough to give you an idea if the scroll is moving too fast or too slow.

Photoshop Titles

Because the titler was so weak in earlier versions of Final Cut, many people, myself included, took to using Photoshop as the FCP titler. What a great titler it is, infinitely malleable, with many additional elements, like banners and bars and gradients, which are more difficult to construct in FCP than in this great graphics application. Anything you can imagine is possible. I use it often, particularly for lower thirds, but also for working with still images that need to be incorporated into a project.

What you should first know about working in PS is that you should only use RGB color space — no CMYK, no grayscale, no indexed color. They don't translate to video.

One problem with using PS is the issue of square versus non-square pixels. Because PS is a computer program, it works in square pixels exclusively, while most video uses the CCIR601 or rectangular pixel. This presents a minor problem. The important point is to understand how FCP handles still image files. It handles different sized images in different ways. Single layer files are treated one way, multilayer Photoshop files or PS files with transparency are treated another way.

1. If you're working in the DV format using CCIR601 pixels at 720×480, create your PS files at 720×534.
   If you're working in standard CCIR601 format, 720×486, then create your PS files at 720×540.

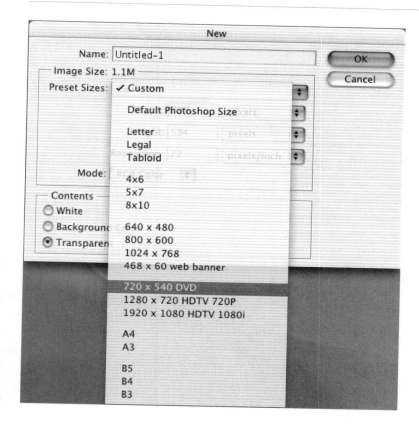

Figure 8.67   Photoshop Preset Popup

2. After you've made your graphic, go to **Image Size** and, making sure **Constrain Proportions** is deselected and **Bicubic** is selected, change the height of the image to 480 or 486, as appropriate.

This squashes the image down, distorting it, changing it to a file that FCP recognizes as using CCIR601 rectangular pixels.

3. Save your file. I save out a separate PS file that has been converted to CCIR601 format and keep the original so I can correct the typos I usually make.

When you bring a PS file that's 720×480 into FCP, the editing software assumes it's been prepared for use in a DV sequence. When placed in a DV sequence, the image will work perfectly and be treated as a nonsquare pixel image.

There are templates for these formats as well as for the 16:9 format in the *Extras* folder of the book's CD.

Tip

Preset Sizes: If you're working with Photoshop 7, there's a neat new feature that allows you to select preset custom sizes when you make a new file. Use the **Preset Sizes** popup and select **720x540 DVD** (Figure 8.67).

You're not always making a graphic that needs to fit in the video format. Sometimes you're making a graphic that is much larger, one you want to move around on to make it seem as if you're panning across the image or zooming in or out of the image. To do this, you need to make the image much greater than your video format, perhaps 2,000×2,000 pixels or more.

If you are working with a Photoshop layer image, you still should squeeze the image down to nonsquare pixels before you bring it into FCP. To do this, rather than using pixel values, use percentages and reduce the height of the image to 90% or, if you want to be anally precise about it, 89.886%. Again, you should not resize these images if they are single layer images without Photoshop transparency. FCP understands these are square pixel images brought into a CCIR601 world and will handle them appropriately. If they are PS layered files with transparency, FCP treats these as separate sequences and does not adjust for CCIR601 pixels. The rules of the road are probably unnecessarily complex, but the bottom line is if it's a single-layer file, let FCP do the resizing; if it's a PS file, squeeze it before you import it.

Open the sequence in your **Browser** called *CircleTest*. This is a DV format sequence, not the multimedia size we have been working with so far. The sequence contains eight short animations. You can render it out if you wish or just scrub through the **Timeline**. There are markers placed in the sequence at the beginning of each shot that illustrate various images in a DV sequence and how FCP interprets them. Make sure the **Size** popup at the top of the **Canvas** has **Show as Square Pixels** checked; that is, it's switched on.

- **Marker 1**, the first animation, shows what happens to a circle in a Photoshop file that's made in the DV size of 720×480. The image immediately appears distorted and egg-shaped. As it rotates, you see that the circle is not a true circle because the correct pixel aspect ratio has not been allowed for when the image was created.

- **Marker 2** shows a single layer PS file that's 720×534. FCP interprets this correctly as a square pixel image intended for use in a DV sequence. As the circle rotates, it holds its shape.

Widescreen

If you're working in widescreen format, shooting and editing using the 16:9 anamorphic aspect ratio, making graphics requires different pixel sizes. The Photoshop file should be created at 960x534 if you're working in DV, or 960x540 if you're working in standard definition CCIR601 that uses an image height of 486 Pixels.

- **Marker 3** is also 720×534. But this is a Photoshop multi-layer file, so no account is taken by the application of its square pixel origins. The circle is distorted, and as the image rotates, it's clear that the shape is not correct.

- **Marker 4** shows the same PS layered file, only this time it was squeezed to 720×480 prior to being imported into the application. The circle remains a circle throughout the animation.

- **Marker 5** presents a different situation. Here we have a circle inside a 1,000×1,000 still image. The dimensions have no relation to DV or to CCIR601 pixels. Yet as the circle turns, it remains true. This is because it is a single-layer PICT file that Final Cut interprets correctly as a square pixel image that has been brought into a nonsquare pixel world.

- **Marker 6** shows what happens when you take the same 1,000×1,000 image and squeeze it fit the DV aspect ratio. The circle looks squeezed, and as it rotates, it's clear the image is not behaving circularly.

- **Marker 7** displays what happens when you bring in a 1,000×1,000 image that's created as a Photoshop file. It doesn't look right, and as the circle turns, the image shows its noncircular behavior.

- **Marker 8** is the final image. It shows how a 1,000×1,000 multilayered image is treated when it has been squeezed vertically 89.9% in PS before being imported. The circle remains a circle throughout its rotation.

The easiest way to work with Photoshop files that you want to lay over video is to create your PS files over transparency, PS's checkerboard background. This transparency will be honored when you import the file into FCP. It's important to understand that PS files come into Final Cut as separate sequences. This means that when you bring a PS file with multiple layers, all its layers remain intact as separate layers in a FCP sequence. There each layer can be animated and affected separately, just as we recently saw with nested sequences.

Figure 8.68   Select>Save Selection

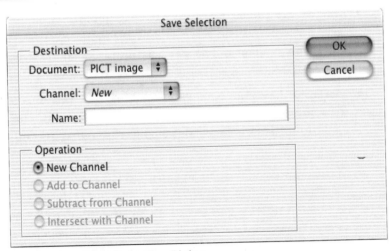

Figure 8.69   Save Selection Dialog

The only time Photoshop files do not import as a sequence is when they are made up of a single background layer or are saved as flattened images or in some other file format, such as PICT or TIFF. Then they import as an image file with a different icon, as can be seen in the **Browser** inside the bin called *Circles*.

PS to PICT

Because it's simpler to work with a single-layer file, I often convert my PS files to PICT images, preserving the transparency information in an alpha channel, a simple procedure and easy enough to create a PS Action for. I retain the PS file to make changes after the following procedure.

1. Collapse the PS layers so that they merge over transparency.

2. **Command**-click the layer to select the contents of the layer.

3. Go to the menu bar to **Select>Save Selection** (Figure 8.68) to bring up the **Save Selection** dialog box.

4. Save it as a new channel, as shown in Figure 8.69.

If you look in your **Channels** tab, usually behind the **Layers** window, you'll see that you now have four channels, the three color channels — **Red**, **Green**, and **Blue** — and a channel called an **Alpha** channel (Figure 8.70).

This is a grayscale representation of opacity. Whatever is white in the alpha channel will be opaque on the screen; whatever is black in the alpha channel will be transparent. Various shades of gray in between will define greater or lesser amounts of opacity.

Because video is interlaced and often produces flicker in text, I like to apply a slight amount of blur to mitigate this.

You have to select the whole layer — not just the content — or the blur won't have any effect.

1. Use **Command-A** to select the entire layer.

2. Then from the **Filters** menu select **Motion Blur** (Figure 8.71).

This opens up the **Motion Blur** dialog box (Figure 8.72).

3. Set the blur to vertical and the amount to one pixel.

This produces an ever-so-slight vertical smearing, just enough usually to offset the jittering created by interlaced fields.

4. Put a black layer behind the content layer.

I do this because PS collapses an image to a white background, producing white fringing around the alpha edges of the content. It premultiplies the image with white, mixing the antialiasing on the edges of the text with white. This doesn't look very good over video. Adding the black layer will force PS to premultiply and mix the antialiasing with black, which looks better on video.

5. To save this file, you have to use **Save As**, which brings up the **Save** dialog in Figure 8.73.

6. From the **Format** popup, select **PICT File**. Make sure the **Alpha Channel** checkbox is checked.

7. Click the **Save** button to call up one more dialog box (Figure 8.74).

8. Set the **Resolution** to 32-bit.

It's eight bits per color channel, plus another eight bits for the alpha channel. Do not compress the image. Compression will lose the alpha channel.

That's it — you've made your PS file into a single layer PICT file with transparency.

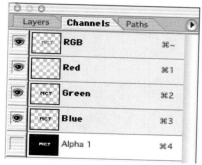

Figure 8.70   Channels Palette

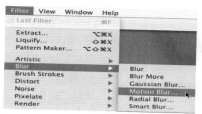

Figure 8.71   Motion Blur Menu

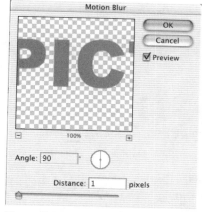

Figure 8.72   Motion Blur Dialog

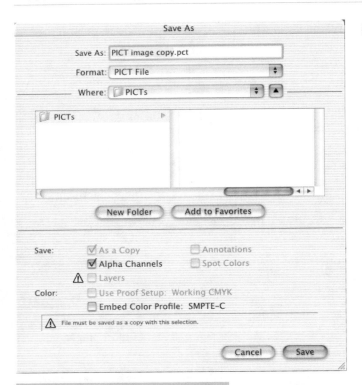

Figure 8.73 Save Dialog Box

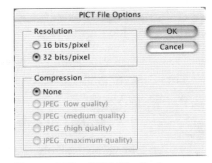

Figure 8.74 PICT File Options

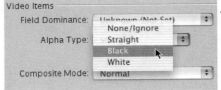

Figure 8.75 Alpha Type Popup

Tip

Alpha Changes: For premultiplied images, you can change the alpha type within FCP to accommodate the premultiplied color, either white or black. Do this in the clips' **Item Properties**, with the **Alpha Type** popup in the **Video Items** portion of the dialog box (Figure 8.75).

Tip

Bringing in the Layers: If you do bring your PS sequence into Final Cut as layers, and you decide you'd rather work with it as a single-layer file, use this easy trick: Open the PS sequence, select all the layers, and go to the **Modify>Make Freeze Frame (Shift-N)**. That will make a still image of all the layers. You can then drag that still into the **Browser**, rename it, move it wherever you want, and use it again and again. What's nice about this technique is that it preserves the transparency of the Photoshop file; all the layers will be merged, but the transparency will remain intact. If you want to preserve the layers as individual images, just select all the layers in the PS sequence and drag them to the **Browser**. They will appear as individual images with their PS layer names.

When you import an oversized Photoshop file and place it inside a sequence, FCP will immediately scale the image. If the still is

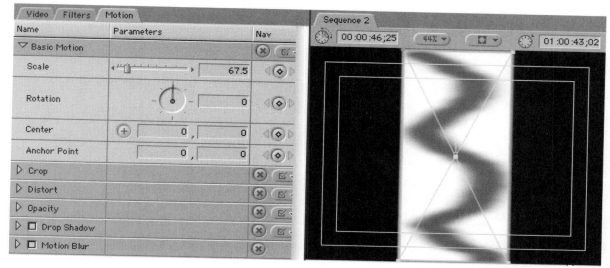

Figure 8.76   Large Image in Canvas
Showing Scale in Viewer

smaller than the image resolution, say a 500×200 image in a 720×480 DV sequence, the application will simply place it in the center of the screen with blackness around it. If the image is, say, 400 pixels wide but 800 pixels tall, FCP will scale it down to fit inside the window, as in Figure 8.76. If you do want to use the image at its full size, so that you can move across it, for instance, the first step you'll have to do is to return it to its full size.

1. Select the image in the **Timeline** and hit the **Enter** or **Return** key. Or **Option-double click** on it to open it into the **Viewer**.

2. Click on the **Motion** tab in the **Viewer.**

3. Set the **Scale** value back to 100.

Resolution

For people who come from a print background, the important point to note is that video doesn't have a changeable resolution. It's not like print where you can jam more and more pixels into an inch of space and make your print cleaner, clearer, and crisper. Pixels in video occupy a fixed space and have a fixed size, the equivalent of 72dpi in the print world, which happens to be the Macintosh screen resolution. Dots per inch are a printing concern. Forget about resolution. Think in terms of size: the more

✎ Note

Out of Memory Message: Be careful that any Photoshop file you import into FCP3 has no empty layers, or adjustment layers, or layers with effects applied that have not been rasterized. Trying to import a file like this can cause an **Out of Memory** error message when you try to bring the file into FCP3.

Pulling Photoshop Effects

Figure 8.77 Merge Down

One problem many users encounter with Photoshop images is with effects applied in PS, such as drop shadows to text layers or any of the hundreds of image effects the application can do. None of the effects seem to appear when the file is imported into FCP. In fact, in OS X, if you have an adjustment layer applied in the file, you will get an **Out of Memory** error message if you try to import the Photoshop document. The problem is the effects are not applied to the image, but remain with PS so they can be changed at any time without having to recreate the layer. It's like nondestructive editing in Final Cut Pro. There is a way around this, however. Just merge the layer with the effect into an empty PS layer. Make a new blank layer beneath each layer you want to rasterize, then from the **Wing** menu of **Layers** palette choose **Merge Down** (Figure 8.77). This fixes the effect with the image onto the empty layer. Of course, now the layer effects are no longer editable

Another method, if you only have a few layers that you don't mind merging together, is to use **Merge Visible**. Create a blank layer at the bottom of the layer stack and then use **Command-Option-Shift-E**. Unlike the normal **Merge Visible** from the Photoshop Layer menu, this keyboard command will not collapse the layers into a single layer but will copy the content of all the visible layers and merge them into the single blank layer. With this method you still have the editable layers in the PS document. If you switch off the visibility for the upper layers in PS, when the file is imported into FCP, the merge layer will be visible, and the other layers will be present as well, only with their track visibility switched off as they were in Photoshop.

This is something you should do at the very end: merge the layers as needed, and squish the file to its CCIR601 format, while still keeping an original PS file copy in its original format with the original images, text layers, and effects, separated and still editable.

pixels, the bigger the picture. Do not think that you can make an image 720×480 at a high resolution like 300dpi or 600dpi and be able to move it around in FCP. Certainly you'll be able to scale it up, but it will look soft, and if you scale it far enough — to 300%, for instance — the image will start to show pixelization. FCP is good at hiding the defects by blurring and softening, but the results are not really as good as they should be. FCP is a video application and only deals with pixel numbers, not with dpi.

Scanners, on the other hand, are designed for the print world where dpi is an issue. Because scanners generate lots and lots of pixels, this is very handy for the person working in video. This means that you can scan an image at, let's say, 300 or 600dpi, even a quite small image, and your scanner will produce thousands and thousands of pixels, which will translate into video as a very large image. You now have an image that's very much larger than your video format of 720×486 pixels. If your scanner can generate an image that's 2,880 pixels across, it's making an image four times greater than your CCIR601 video frame. You can now move that very large image around on the screen, and make it seem as if a camera is panning across the image. Or you can scale back the image, and it will look as if the camera is zooming back from a point in the image. Or reverse the process and make it look as if the camera is zooming into the image. We'll look at these in Lesson 9, "Pan and Scan" on page 382. Also check out the *ScanGuideII.pdf* in the Extras folder on the CD — a handy scan/scaling guide.

Working with a single-layer file within FCP has one advantage: it's simpler. One of the issues that arise with PS sequences in Final Cut is the problem of doing transitions between them, as we saw in Lesson 5.

 Tip

Transitions with Still Images: If you want to put together a group of still images with transitions between them, you can simplify the process in a couple of ways. When you import the files, make sure you leave enough room in your **Still/Freeze Duration** preference to accommodate the transitions. Sequentially number the stills you want to import and place them into a separate folder on your hard drive. Next import all your stills as a single folder using **Import>Folder** so that they come in as a bin. Set a default transition that you want to use for the effect. If it's something unusual like a special page peel, put it in **Favorites** before you make it the default. Then drag the bin from the **Browser** straight to the **Canvas Edit Overlay** and drop on **Overwrite** (or **Insert**) with Transition. All the stills will miraculously dump out of the bin and appear in the Timeline with the page peel between them. The technique works beautifully with flattened PS files or other image formats.

It's a little quirky when used with a regular PS file that comes in as a sequence. The first transition will come as a start-on-edit transition and be the correct duration. The others will be end-on-edit transitions and half the duration because they can't overlap the material between sequences by extending them. So if you want a one-second transition, set your default effect to two seconds. Then all the stills will come in as one-second end-on-edit transitions, except for the first one. It will be start-on-edit and the full two seconds, but that's easier to fix than fixing every transition between every still image.

Figure 8.78 Overlay Button

Very often you'll want to fade in the graphic and fade it out again. Take another look at the sequence called *Title and Background*.

1. Click on the **Overlay** button (**Option-W**), the middle of the three buttons in the lower left corner on the **Timeline** window (Figure 8.78).

The files now have lines in them near the top. This is the opacity value of the clips. With the lines all the way to the top, their values are 100%. You'll notice that the line ramps down at the

Importing Image Sequences

Figure 8.79 Image Sequence Import Dialog

At some time you might want to import an entire folder of still images as a sequence, one frame for each picture. There are a couple of simple ways to do this. Start off by making sure that the stills are properly numbered sequentially, such as PICT001, PICT002, PICT003, and so on. One way to bring this material into FCP is to use the QuickTime Player. With the player open, select from its **File** menu **Select Open Image Sequence**. Navigate to the folder and select the first image in the list. When you hit **Open**, you'll get the dialog box in Figure 8.79, which allows you to set the frame rate for the still images. The sequence will open as a QuickTime movie. Now simply export from the QT Player to whatever file format you're working in setting the compressor, frame size and frame rate.

The second way is simply to import the image sequence directly into FCP. Before you import the correctly sequentially numbered still images, go to your FCP Preferences and set the **Still/Freeze Duration** to one frame, or whatever frame rate you want to use. Two frames for every still is common in animation. Now import the whole folder containing the still images. This will bring the folder in as a bin. Create a new sequence. Open the bin of one or two frame still images, select all, copy, and paste into the new sequence, or just drag the bin into **Overwrite** or **Insert** in the **CEO**. You can now use that sequence as a nest that acts like any other clip in FCP.

The important advantage of doing this within the QT player is that once the sequence is exported, it's a clip like any other and no longer needs to go through the render process in FCP each time you make a change.

beginning and end of each of the graphics clips in the lesson sequence. This will fade in and fade out the **Opacity** from 0 to a 100 and back again. This works exactly like the control for audio levels.

2. Grab the level line and pull it down. The overall level will change.

3. Use the **Pen** tool (**P**) to make opacity keyframes on the level line and to pull down the opacity as needed.

Also, the global-level **Changing Box** tool, **Sequence>Levels** (**Command-Option-L**), will also affect the levels of multiple video or title clips. We saw this feature in Lesson 6, "Controlling Audio Levels" on page 265. Unlike audio keyframes, though, you can also smooth the opacity keyframes to ease into the fade.

☞ Tip

Fading Graphics: Another way I like to do a fade in or a fade out from a graphic is to lay a **Cross Dissolve** just before the edit point. If you place it too close to the edit, it will drop in as a one-frame dissolve, but if you place it slightly away from the edit, it will drop in as dissolve to the edit point, as in Figure 8.80. This only works if there aren't two graphics inline with each other, butted up one to the other.

Figure 8.80   Cross Dissolve to Fade Out Graphic

Summary

In this lesson we've gone through FCP's title tools, Boris Calligraphy, and the task of bringing Photoshop title files into Final Cut. But that isn't all there is to titling. There are still some issues with graphics images in Final Cut, particularly images in motion, that we'll look at in the next lesson on creating animation in FCP.

Lesson 9

Animating Images

Final Cut Pro has considerable capabilities for animating images, allowing you to enhance your productions and creating exciting, interesting and artistic scenes. We touched briefly on keyframing in the last lesson, but in this lesson we will concentrate on FCP's motion capabilities.

Loading the Lesson

One more time, begin by loading the material you need onto your media drive.

1. If you don't already have it there, drag over to your media hard drive the *Media1* folder from the CD.

2. For this lesson, also drag the folder *Media3* onto your media drive.

3. Also bring into the *Shared* folder of your system drive the folder *Lesson 9* from inside the *Projects* folder.

4. Eject the CD and open the *Lesson 9* folder on your hard drive.

5. For this lesson you need to have Boris Calligraphy loaded on your computer. If you haven't already done so, install it from your FCP3 CD.

6. When you have all the software installed on your computer, double-click your copy of the project file, *L9*, to launch the application.

7. Reconnect the media, and reassign the scratch disk if needed.

8. Finally, use **Save Project As** to save it with a new name, keeping the original as a backup.

Motion Window

Let's first take a look at how to create motion in Final Cut.

Figure 9.1 Compositing View

1. Open *Sequence 1*.

2. Drag a clip — let's say *Village1* — from the **Clips** bin and drop it onto **Overwrite** or **Insert** in the **Canvas Edit Overlay** (**CEO**).

Let's also set the window arrangement for compositing.

3. Because this arrangement is no longer available with FCP, we'll have to use **Restore Layout**. Choose **Window>Arrange>Restore Layout** (**Option-Shift-U**).

4. Insert the book's CD. If you have already copied the *Window Layouts* folder to your hard drive you can skip this step.

5. In the navigation dialog, go to either the *Window Layouts* folder on the CD or in your computer and choose **Compositing**. If you have *Sequence 1* open, your monitor looks something like Figure 9.1.

6. Use the popup menu at the top of the **Canvas** to select **Image+Wireframe** (Figure 9.2), the one with the square icon to the right of screen size percentage popup.

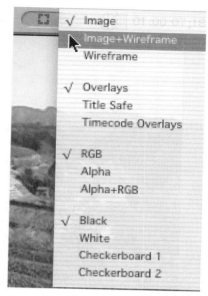

Figure 9.2   Canvas Popup Menu

Select the clip in the **Timeline**, and the image in the **Canvas** will appear with a wireframe indicator. The large cross through it defines the corners and boundaries (Figure 9.3).

7. Double-click on the clip in the **Timeline** to open it in the **Viewer**, and open the **Motion** tab at the top.

If you're in Compositing view, you should see FCP's motion controls and a timeline in an area called the **Keyframe Graph** (Figure 9.4).

Here all the motion elements are laid out for you with a time ruler for keyframing. Everything is keyframable except, unfortunately, **Motion Blur**. Once you start twirling open the little triangles, which the FCP manual calls disclosure triangles, you might need to stretch down the window.

Figure 9.3   Image+Wireframe
Clip in Canvas

Once a keyframe has been set for a parameter, if you move to another point on the timeline and change the parameter values, a new keyframe will be set. The speed of the change is determined by the time between the keyframes, the farther apart in time the keyframes, the slower the motion.

Figure 9.4 Motion Control Window

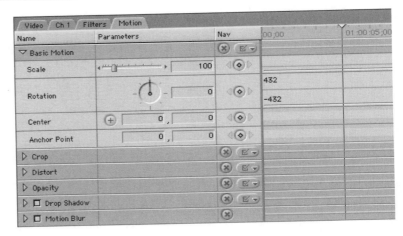

You can adjust the green line in the **Keyframe Graph Ruler** either:

- With the **Line Grabber,** as in audio levels or
- By grabbing and moving a keyframe

Keyframing in the Canvas

Figure 9.5 Keyframe Button

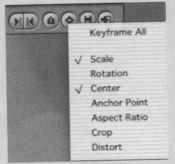

Figure 9.6 Keyframe Contextual Menu in Canvas

If you are going to do complex motion paths, it might be simpler to set a global keyframe, rather than keyframing individual parameters. It's easy to do. Click the **Keyframe** button at the bottom of the **Canvas** or of the **Viewer**, or press **Control-K** (Figure 9.5).

This sets an initial keyframe for most of the properties in the **Motion** tab. It will not set keyframes for **Opacity** nor for **Drop Shadow**. Because these need keyframing less often, they remain independent and have to be entered separately. When you **Control**-click the **Keyframe** button in the **Canvas**, it calls up a contextual menu, which allows you to set or clear a keyframe for a specific parameter or parameters (Figure 9.6).

If you are on a keyframe, this process can also be used to remove keyframes from specific parameters. The keyframed parameters appear with a check mark. Unchecking the parameter will remove the keyframe for the parameter.

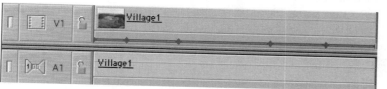

Figure 9.7 Moving Keyframes in the Graph

Figure 9.8 Timeline with Keyframes

If you grab a keyframe, you can either:

- Move its value up or down or
- Shift it along the **Keyframe Graph Ruler.**

A display will show you the value change or the time change. As you move the keyframe, it tends to be sticky to change either its time position or its value, not both. If you hold down the **Shift** key while moving a keyframe, you switch off the stickiness and can move it easily in time and value, with both displayed simultaneously, as shown in Figure 9.7.

The first number in the display, **+00:00:11**, indicates that the keyframe has moved ahead eleven frames, while the second number, 65, shows the new value for the keyframe.

A keyframe can be added or, if one is already there, removed by holding down the **Option** key. You can also select the **Pen** tool and use that.

Keyframes can also be seen in the **Timeline** (Figure 9.8). You can call the keyframe line with the button in the extreme lower left corner of the **Timeline** window (Figure 9.9).

Keyframes can be moved in the timeline. Just grab one and pull it along. Values can't be changed, but their time position can be.

Tip

I'm Moving! I often find when I'm working on animations that I'm moving back and forth between the **Viewer** and the **Canvas**. Well, there's a keyboard shortcut for this: the letter **Q**. It toggles back and forth between the two windows.

Figure 9.9 Filters and Motion Bar Button

Tip

Reset: Notice that each of the control panels — **Basic Motion, Crop, Distort, Opacity, Drop Shadow,** and **Motion Blur** — has a button with a red **X** on it (Figure 9.10). This allows you to reset the values for that parameter. Note the little popup next to it: this controls which keyframes display on the Timeline's blue line, the **Motion Bar.**

Figure 9.10 Reset Button

Tip

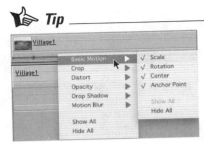

Figure 9.11 Parameter Control Contextual Menu in the Timeline

Moving Keyframes: What's neat is the way you can move keyframes in the **Motion Bar** in the **Timeline** window. If you grab the blue line of the **Motion Bar** between keyframes and pull up or down the **Timeline**, all the keyframes will move together, maintaining the same relative position. You can only do this in the **Timeline**. In previous versions of the application, you could pull them right off the clip and pull them back on again. In v3 you seem to be restricted to sliding the keyframes until one of them hits the end of the clip, either the start or the beginning. Whether the addition of this limitation was intentional (a feature) or not (a bug), I don't know.

If you **Control**-click on the blue **Motion Bar** in the **Timeline**, you'll call up a contextual menu that allows you to select which parameter's keyframes are displayed (Figure 9.11).

Scale

The first keyframable property in the **Motion** window is **Scale**, a simple slider and value box that lets you set a size. Unfortunately, the scale of the **Scale** slider is quite limiting. Because FCP deals exclusively in bitmapped images, stills, video, and text files made up of pixels, it's generally not a good idea to scale upwards, not much above 110% to 120%. Even scaling motion graphics within FCP can make the image quite soft, though if it's done quickly, it can be effective. The slider ranges from zero to 1,000%, while most of the useful part of scale is jammed into about one-tenth of the slider's travel. I would have preferred if FCP used a system seen in other applications, in which the slider controlled the most useful portion of the parameters, while the value boxes let you create values outside that range.

Tip

Controlling Sliders: Because there is so little travel in the slider's useful range, I usually use it holding down the **Command** key, which gives smaller increments of movement. The **Command** key works like this in many drag movements in FCP, such as dragging clips to lengthen and shorten them in the **Timeline**.

If you hold down the **Shift** key, you'll get increments up to two decimal places. Unfortunately, if you do both, you'll get the two decimal places, but then the change will be confined to going up or down a whole number at a time. These controls work on any sliders in FCP.

Fortunately, you can also scale the image in the **Canvas**. With the **Canvas** set to **Image+Wireframe**, grab one of the corners and drag. The image will, by default, scale proportionately. If you want the image to be distorted, hold down the **Shift** key while you drag (Figure 9.12).

Most graphic programs work exactly the opposite, so be careful that you don't hold **Shift** down out of habit to constrain proportions, because it will have quite the opposite effect.

If you hold down the **Command** key while you drag an image's corner to scale it, you add the **Rotation** tool so you can scale and rotate at the same time.

One common use for scaling is in animating large format images and text. As much as possible, try to avoid scaling up:

- Instead, create your stills at large size and scale down, or

- Create your text using fonts at very large point sizes so you're again scaling downward.

We'll look at how to work with large size images and text after we've looked at the other controls in the **Motion** panel.

Rotation

Rotation is controlled with the clock dial or with values (Figure 9.13).

There is a limit on how far you can take rotation, no more than 24 rotations seems possible. To get there, you can either:

- Keep dialing in more and more turns of the screw or

- Type in a value

Each notch of the "hour" hand is one revolution. It would be nice if separate value boxes for revolutions and degrees had been included. At the moment, you either have to:

- Twist the dial around and around lots of times or

- Calculate, such as 22 revolutions times 360° equals 7,920°

By the way, 24 revolutions are 8,640°.

Figure 9.12   Image Scaling Distorted

Tip

On Keyframe: When the playhead is on a keyframe, different indicators in the **Image+Wireframe** turn green. A green cross through the wireframe indicates a Scale keyframe.

Figure 9.13   Rotation Controls

Figure 9.14   Rotation Tool

Like **Scale**, **Rotation** can be created in the **Canvas**. As you move the cursor near one of the edges of the image, it changes into a rotation tool (Figure 9.14). You can now grab the image and swing it around the anchor point, which we'll see in a minute. For the moment, rotation is happening around the middle of the image. It's a little easier if you grab near the corner of the image, but don't get too close or you'll grab the **Scale** point.

☞ **Tip**

Rotation Tips:

Tip 1: Holding down the **Shift** key will constrain the dial to 45° increments, while holding down the Command key will give you a little finer control over the movement of the dial.

Tip 2: The clip bounding box in the **Canvas** turns green if the playhead is sitting on a rotational keyframe, though it's impossible to see this when the clip is selected because the blue edge highlight obscures it.

Tip 3: The upper left corner dot is round, while all the rest are square. If you're rotating an image a lot in **Wireframe**, or if it's small and scaled down, this can be useful to indicate which way is up.

Figure 9.15   Size Popup

Center

Center is position: where the image is on the screen. Unlike some other applications that count position from the upper left corner of the image, FCP counts the default center position, 0,0, and counts outwards from there, minus x to the left, plus x to the right, minus y upwards, plus y downwards. The crosshairs allow you to position an image with a click in the **Canvas**.

Straight Motion

Let's set up a simple motion for a clip.

1. Place the clip *Village2* at the beginning of an empty sequence.

2. Make sure the **Canvas** is in **Image+Wireframe** and that the playhead is back at the start of the sequence.

We're now going to move the clip off the screen.

3. If you need to position an image outside of the **Canvas**, first reduce the size of the display in the **Canvas** with the **Size** popup (Figure 9.15), then stretch open the **Canvas**.

4. Grab the image and move it off the screen (Figure 9.16).

   Or use the **Center** crosshairs to click on a point out in the grayboard.

5. Once the clip is positioned off the screen, use **Control-K** to set a keyframe.

6. Go forward five seconds in time.

7. Drag the clip across the screen to the other side, creating a line with a string of dots on it.

You have now created a straight linear motion of the image across the screen (Figure 9.17).

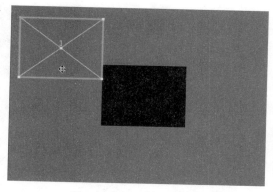

Figure 9.16   Moving Image Off the Screen

 Tip

Navigation Tips

Tip 1: In the **Canvas**, the center point turns green when the playhead is on the keyframe. It's only visible when the clip is selected. When the clip isn't selected, there is no indicator.

Tip 2: If you are moving a clip or multiple clips off the screen, it's handy to use **Fit All** (Figure 9.15). This will adjust the **Canvas** to include all the clips off the screen.

Tip 3: The spacing of the little dots along the motion path indicates the speed of the motion, so if the dots are all bunched together the motion is slow, whereas if they're more separated from each other the motion is quite fast. Other applications use the dots of indicate frame points, but this is not so in FCP.

Curved Motion

There are two ways to create a curved path:

- Pull out the path from the linear motion.

- Create a curved path by using Bezier handles.

In the first method, when you place the cursor on the line, it changes from the regular **Selection** into the **Pen** tool. You can then drag out the line so it's a curve (Figure 9.18). This creates a new keyframe in your timeline.

Notice also the two bars sticking out from the dot on the curve. The bars have two handles each, represented by little dots, one slightly darker than the other. These bars are the Bezier handles.

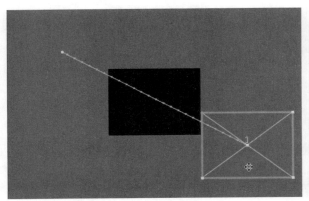

Figure 9.17   Linear Motion Path

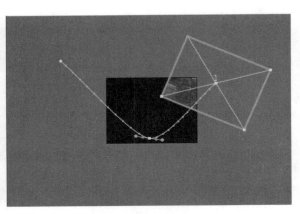

Figure 9.18   Curved Motion Path

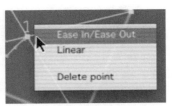

Figure 9.19   Ease In/Ease Out
Menu

The second method doesn't create an intermediate keyframe. There are normally no handles to adjust the arc on either the start point or the end point of the motion. You can quickly add these by **Control**-clicking on the point and from the contextual menu selecting **Ease In/Ease Out** (Figure 9.19).

When you select **Ease In/Ease Out**, the handles appear. These can be used to pull the line into an arc. Unfortunately, the handles are quite small, and minor adjustments can have a major impact on the motion path. The outer handles allow you to adjust the arc of the curve. Each side of arc can be adjusted separately to make complex movements.

Tip

Zoom: To zoom into a portion of the **Canvas**, select the **Zoom** tool, **Z**, and lasso a rectangular area (like drawing a marquee) around a section of the screen. **Zoom** will fill the **Canvas** with that section. **Option-Zoom** will take you back out.

Changing Speed

Normally objects don't arrive at speed instantly, nor do they stop instantly. So if your image is starting or stopping on the screen you probably want it to accelerate or decelerate, rather than jerking into motion. In graphics animation this is called *easing*: you ease into a motion and you ease out of a motion. This is what the darker set of handles, the **Acceleration Handles**, do. They control the speed at which the image moves through the keyframe, the rate of deceleration as it approaches the keyframe and then acceleration as it leaves the keyframe. If you want the motion to smoothly pass through the point without changing speed, make sure those handles are not moved, or **Control**-click on the keyframe and choose **Linear.** If you pull the handles apart, the motion will be faster. If you push the handles inward toward the keyframe point, the motion will slow down. The image will decelerate as it comes to the keyframe, and then accelerate away. I have created a simple motion path that shows this.

1. Open *Curved Path Sequence.*

2. Render out the motion path.

You'll clearly see the deceleration and acceleration as the image passes through the intermediate keyframe. Notice that the image moves much quicker in the first part of the movement and then slower in the second portion. This happens because the first portion of the movement is shorter both in time and distance.

👉 *Tip*

Adjusting Bezier Handles: If you want to make the curves or the motion even more complex, you can adjust each end of the Bezier handles independently. Hold down the **Command** key and grab a handle and it will move separately from the other (Figure 9.20).

Figure 9.20   Separate Bezier Control Handles

The ease handles in the **Canvas** only control Center point or Position keyframes. Ease controls for other keyframes such as **Scale** have to be applied in the **Motion** controls timeline. If you **Control**-click on the keyframe in the **Keyframe Graph Ruler,** the contextual menu appears that allows you to change the keyframe to **Smooth** (Figure 9.21).

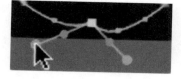

Figure 9.21   Contextual Menu Change to Smooth

Changing to **Smooth** will make the ease handles appear in the **Keyframe Graph Ruler** for **Scale and Rotation.** If the ease handles are hard to control in the **Canvas,** they are even more difficult to manipulate here, quite impractical in my opinion, unless you expand the **Viewer** to take up most of your monitor. You can get finer control by opening up the graph area. If you grab the bar that separates the parameters, you can pull it down, which increases the area for the graph (Figure 9.22). It doesn't help much with ease control, but for finer control of the whole motion it is helpful.

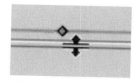

Figure 9.22   Expanding Graph Area

Scale's and **Rotation's** graphical displays in the **Motion** tab have Bezier handles to control speed. However, for some reason, Bezier handles are only provided in the **Canvas** for both center and anchor point animation. I think this makes precise control much more difficult, especially for pan and scan, as we shall see later on page 382. A wide, moveable graph, such as in the one in **Scale**, would be very useful.

New to FCP3 is the ability to move the entire motion path you've created. You can move the whole path as a single entity to whatever position on the screen you want. This can be very useful, if, for instance, you've made a horizontal movement — say, left to right across the screen — that slides a clip through the upper portion of the screen. Later you decide it would be better for it to slide across the lower portion of the screen. Rather than resetting all the motion path keyframes, simply move the entire path. To do this, make sure the **Canvas** is in **Image+Wireframe** mode. Hold down **Command-Shift**, and when the cursor is over the clip, it will change to the **Hand** tool (Figure 9.23). Simply grab the clip and move it. The whole motion path will move as a single group.

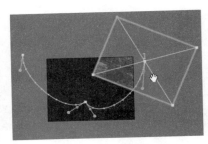

Figure 9.23   Hand Tool to Move a Motion Path

Anchor Point

The anchor point is the pivot point around which the image swings. It's also the point around which scaling takes place. For some reason that escapes me, the anchor point does not have crosshairs for positioning it. Fortunately there is a way to move it in the **Canvas** (Figure 9.24).

Figure 9.24   Anchor Point Moved with Distort Tool

1. Select the **Distort** tool (keyboard **D** for distort) and grab the center point of the clip. Drag it to where you want to position the anchor point. Note that holding the **Shift** key does *not* constrain the movement direction as in many other applications. You have to either do it by eyeball or use the value boxes in the **Motion** tab.

Anchor Point and Text Block

The anchor point for text created in FCP is the center of the screen, which in default settings is the center of the first line of text. This is the origin point of the text. This is important to note if you want to create text in FCP and then rotate it. If you have multiple lines of text, the anchor point being in the center of the first line will cause the text to rotate around that point. If you actually want to make the whole block of text rotate around the center of the screen, you'll have to move the origin point of the text higher up on the *y* axis, into negative numbers. That way the text starts higher up the screen, while the anchor point remains at the center. Take a look at *Rotate Sequence*. In the first clip, the rotation is around the first line, while in the second, the text file is moved higher in the frame and rotates around the **Anchor Point** correctly.

We'll look at the **Distort** tool on page 377. The point you're moving with this tool is actually the anchor point.

2.   Apply a rotation to the image.

Notice that it doesn't swing around the center of the image but around this new point. If you pull it out to the upper right corner, that's where the image will pivot. Take a look at *Anchor Point Sequence*. Two images swing through the frame with opposing anchor points.

Notice that on the second clip *Village2* I have animated the center as well as repositioning the anchor point. It makes movement slightly different, more tumbling than simply rotating. Be careful with animating multiple parameters: once the anchor point's been moved, as it can lead to unexpected results.

Because images not only rotate around the anchor point but also scale around it, this becomes an important issue when moving large-scale images, as we shall see.

☞Tip

Anchor Point Keyframe: If the clip is deselected, the anchor point keyframe is not indicated in the **Canvas**. If the clip is selected, however, the track number will turn green to show that the playhead is over an Anchor Point keyframe.

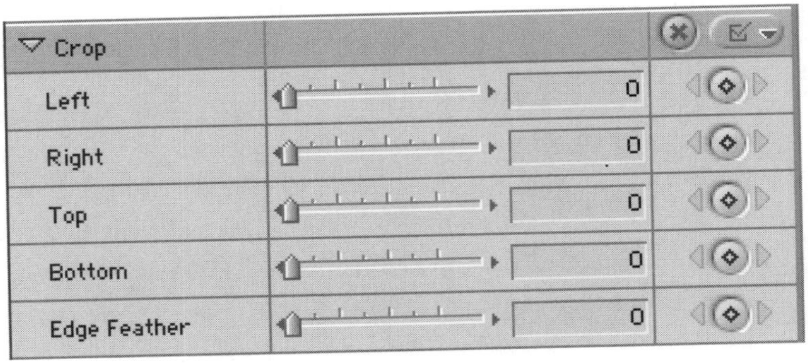

▽ Crop		⊗	☑ ▾
Left	◁─┈┈┈┈┈─▷	0	◁◈▷
Right	◁─┈┈┈┈┈─▷	0	◁◈▷
Top	◁─┈┈┈┈┈─▷	0	◁◈▷
Bottom	◁─┈┈┈┈┈─▷	0	◁◈▷
Edge Feather	◁─┈┈┈┈┈─▷	0	◁◈▷

Figure 9.25   Crop Controls

Crop

Crop allows you to cut the image from the sides. This can be done with the controls hidden under the twirly triangle (Figure 9.25).

If you have specific values, or if you want to reduce the image by precise amounts — such as equally from all sides — then this is place to do it. You can also, however, use the **Crop** tool in the **Canvas**, which may be easier to work with. The **Crop** tool is in the tools and can be called up with the letter **C**, just as in Photoshop (Figure 9.26).

The **Crop** tool in Final Cut doesn't work very much like Photoshop's. You can't simply drag a marquee across the image to define the section you want to keep.

1.   You have to select the image, and with the **Crop** tool you grab the corner of the image.

As the tool gets near the edge, it changes into the **Crop** icon, indicating the cursor is acting in **Crop**.

2.   Grab the edge and pull in the image to crop (Figure 9.27). Or you can grab the corner and pull in two sides at once.

Figure 9.26   Crop Tool

Notice at the bottom of the **Crop** control panel the slider for **Edge Feather**. This softens the edges of the image and can be very attractive, particularly when there are multiple images on the screen (Figure 9.28). Also notice the number **2** in the figure. The number appears in the wireframe, indicating which layer has been selected. The selected clip is on **V2**.

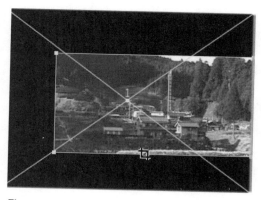

Figure 9.27 Cropping the Image in the Canvas

Figure 9.28 Two Clips in Canvas Cropped and Feathered to 80

Distort

This tool allows you to squeeze or expand the image, either maintaining its shape or pulling it apart. Be careful though, remember these are pixels you're dealing with, and making pixels bigger will make them blocky and ugly looking. What's remarkable is how much you can distort the image and still get away with it. As with other tools there are two or more places to do everything. We already saw one way to distort the image by grabbing a corner with the **Selector** (the standard arrow tool) and dragging the image around holding down the **Shift** key. This distort alters the aspect ratio of the image but maintains its rectangular shape. This can also be done with the slider at the bottom of the **Distort** control panel (Figure 9.29).

Moving the **Aspect Ratio** slider to the left, into negative numbers, will squeeze the image vertically so it mashes down into a narrow

Tip

On the Fly: If you're working with the **Distort** tool and want to change the overall scale of the image, with the mouse released, hold down the **Option** key. When you grab the image and pull, it will scale proportionately. Similarly, if you're moving the image and hold down the **Shift** key, you'll have changed to rotation. Be careful, though: the image may move in unpredictable ways, so nudge it gently.

▽ Distort				
Upper Left	-160	,	-120	
Upper Right	160	,	-120	
Lower Right	160	,	120	
Lower Left	-160	,	120	
Aspect Ratio			0	

Figure 9.29 Distort Control Panel

slit; while pulling the slider to the right into large positive numbers will squeeze it horizontally, so it's a tall, thin image. The slider ranges from –1,000 to 1,000. The image can't be squeezed until it's gone, but it does come close.

The distortion corner points in the control panel are determined by the size of the image you're working in. The numbers you see in Figure 9.29 represent the corner points for the 320×240 Photo-JPEG material in the CD projects. You can dial in values into the corner point boxes, which will move the corner points to any position you want.

Or you can use the **Distort** tool from the tools. Select it or call it up with the **D** key (Figure 9.30).

Figure 9.30 Distort Tool

The **Distort** tool lets you grab a corner in the **Canvas** and pull it around and really mess the image up (Figure 9.31).

👉 *Tip*
_____

Proportional Distortion: If you use the **Distort** tool and grab one corner while holding down the **Shift** key, you will distort the image proportionately. Dragging the upper left corner in, for instance, will make the upper left corner move inward the same amount. It's a easy way to create perspective. It's also an easy way to bend the image inside out so half of it is flipped over on itself.

_____

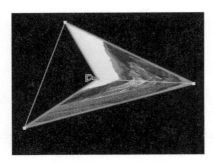

Figure 9.31 Distorted Image in the Canvas

Anything becomes possible with these kinds of tools. Now that images are digital, they can be twisted and distorted, shaped and sized, and blended any way you can imagine. I hope you see the potential for creating almost any transition you can imagine.

I've made a simple one using **Distort, Scale,** and center animation. Look at *Transition Sequence*. That's only the beginning. A few pulls on **Distort** tool, a little scaling, and the image shoots off. If you apply motion or any other effects to a clip, the whole clip has to be rendered out, even if for the greater part of its duration, all the values remain at default.

The simplest way to get around this problem is to cut the clip — **Control-V** or **Blade** — and separate the normal section from the twisted section. You can see what I did in *Transition Sequence*.

Just be careful you don't move elements around so that the two parts get dislocated from each other.

There is another way to crop and distort an image that affords a great deal of control and combines the two tools into a single interface. That is to use the **FXScript DVE's Distort** filter, which we shall look at on page 456 in Lesson 11. These tools give you the ability to make a greater variety of transitions and far more interesting and varied ones than any of the 61 provided by FCP. You can add many other tools — blurring, rippling, solarizing, and a host of others — to the mix of video effects. These will give you an almost limitless supply of arrows for your bow.

There are still a few more elements to look at in the **Motion** panel. **Opacity** is next.

 Tip

Easy Flop: In Lesson 3 we needed to flop a shot. It was facing right to left, and we wanted it left to right. The easy way to do this using the **Distort** controls is to swap all the values in the **Distort** settings from left to right. So in these Photo-JPEG files we're using, upper left is –160, –120 and upper right is 160, –120; lower right is 160, 120 and lower left is –160, 120. Set upper left to 160,–120 and upper right to –160, 120. Set lower right to –160, 120 and lower left to 160,120. This sounds more difficult than using Flop, but the advantage is that some real-time boards can use the Distort tool to make this effect instantly, while they can't using the Flop filter. An example is the RTMac, which can do real-time motion effects, but not real-time filters.

Opacity

This effect is pretty obvious. The transparency of the image decreases from a 100% opaque to zero opacity. It's a useful way to do simple fades, as we saw in the timeline with titles in the previous lesson on page 360. Whatever is adjusted in the **Timeline** with the **Pen** tool will also appear reproduced here. Using the **Pen** tool, you can fade video in and out the same way you can audio.

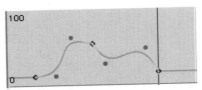

Figure 9.32 Beziered Keyframes in Keyframe Graph

☞ Tip _____

Linear to Bezier: By **Control**-clicking the keyframe in the **Motion** tab **Keyframe Graph,** you change the keyframe back and forth between a corner (linear) keyframe and a smooth (Bezier) keyframe. This is easier to do if you pull open the **Keyframe Graph** with bar that separates the parameters. When the keyframe's in Bezier mode, a blue handle appears that allows you to adjust the curve of the fade. Bezier handles can be attached to any keyframe and can either change the shape for both sides of the curve, or by pressing the **Command** key, the handles can be pulled independently, adjusting the curve on either side of the keyframe separately (Figure 9.32). Be careful with the Bezier handles: there is a bug in this version of the application that makes them tend to shoot off toward infinity, and they become hard to pull back.

A nice new addition to FCP3 is that opacity changes only need to be rendered if they fall below 100%. In previous versions of the application, if you added an opacity keyframe and then reduced the opacity of the clip, the entire clip would need to be rendered out, included those portions that had no modifications and were fully opaque.

Drop Shadow

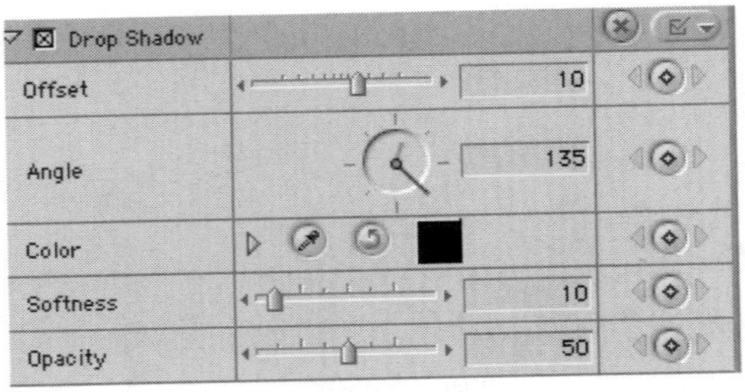

Drop Shadow is one of my favorites. It gives titles and moving images some depth and separation. FCP's **Drop Shadow** is pretty basic, but it works fine. The control panel has all the expected features of offset, angle of offset, shadow color, softness, and opacity (Figure 9.33). Note that **Drop Shadow** has to be activated with the little checkbox in the upper left corner of the control panel.

Figure 9.33 Drop Shadow Control

What might seem puzzling about the **Offset** slider is that it goes into to negative numbers. Surely you think this will just change the direction of the shadow. Doesn't the angle do that already? Yes, it does, but when you animate them they behave differently.

Open *Shadow Sequence* in your **Browser** and play through the first two shots either by rendering them out if you have to or by using **Option-P** or by using **QuickView** on sections of the sequence. In the first shot, animating Offset, the shadow slides underneath clip as if the light were passing across it, while in the second shot, animating Angle, the light seems to be circling the clip — different effects for different applications.

The **Angle** control lets you spin multiple times around the dial. I'm not sure if you'd want to use that a lot, but it's there. Its rotation travel is from 720 to –720, or four full circuits of the object by its shadow.

Softness lets you control the amount of blurring on the edges of the shadow. Though the slider goes up to 100, I'm quite disappointed in how little effect it has. In other applications, high values will makes the shadows very dissipated, as if on an overcast day. Shadow softness in FCP really reaches no more than about 10% into the shadow area, so you're forced to rely on **Opacity** to soften the shadow area, which is not the same look. It lacks the subtlety of other compositing applications.

Look at the third clip in *Shadow Sequence*. It uses the shadow to help create the illusion of three dimensionality in 2D space. By hardening the shadow and reducing the offset, while increasing the opacity of the shadow as the clip becomes smaller, you can create the impression that the clip is getting closer to the grayscale background. It would work even better if FCP produced a greater range of softness.

The default drop shadow settings work well for stills and other large images, but not so well for text. If you're using this drop shadow with the basic text tool, you should bring down the offset value and push up the opacity value. For thin objects like text, the first is too high and the second too low.

Motion Blur

Motion Blur is also activated with a checkbox in the upper left of its control panel. Figure 9.34 shows FCP's **Motion Blur** at a setting of 1,000 with four samples and with 32 samples. This was created by applying **Motion Blur** to a fast, horizontally moving

Figure 9.34 Motion Blur Set to 1,000 with Four Samples on the Left and 32 Samples on the Right

clip. It gives the clip the appearance of great speed because of the added blur. Sampling goes down to 1, which produces no **Motion Blur** at all. The stepping that occurs in the lower sampling rates is ugly and best avoided. The low sample settings can be used, though, to produce interesting effects in images that contain fast moving objects. You will see a ghosting effect as the object moves through the screen.

Use **Motion Blur** if you're trying to make it look as though your animations are moving very quickly, but be warned that **Motion Blur** adds considerable time to all renders. It's a very long and slow calculation for each frame. If you are going to apply it, always add it last just before you're finally going to render out your sequence.

Pan and Scan

Pan and scan is the slang term for doing motion on large-size images such as stills. I have set up a sequence that illustrates some of the problems. If you open *Pan Sequence*, you'll see that it contains four copies of a still image. It's a PICT file called *Pic*, but it could as easily be a Photoshop file, Targa file, or TIFF. I try to work with PICT files for single-layer images because they're simpler to deal with in FCP. *Pic* is a very large image, much larger than our **Canvas**. It's 1,494×1,033.

In an earlier lesson, I said you should forget about image resolution as far as video is concerned, and think only in numbers of pixels. In the print world for which scanners are designed, resolution is critically important. If you're scanning images such as this one to use in FCP, you can scan it at a high resolution, like 300 or 600dpi. Ideally you'd want to calculate the area you're going to zoom into based on an image that's 720 pixels across at 72dpi.

There's a useful chart for scan sizes in the *Extras* folder of the CD called *ScanGuideII.pdf*, from Loren Miller, the creator of the KeyGuide that accompanies this book. Often times it's simpler just to scan more than you need, and adjust it in Photoshop, or even leave it to Final Cut. By scanning at high resolutions, the scanner will make lots of pixels. FCP will translate this into a very large image, not a small image at high resolution as a print system would do.

In *Pan Sequence*, I've panned and scanned *Pic* using four different methods. Look at them one at a time. On real-time systems, these movements will not need rendering to playback on the computer screen.

1. In the first, the image starts out center in the screen and zooms into a point in the bottom right corner of the image.

A couple of problems are apparent:

- The image jerks into motion; acceleration is not smooth.

- The zoom-in seems to get slower and slower as it progresses.

This latter is a difficult problem and pretty much impossible to deal with when using the **Motion** controls in FCP. It is totally unnatural and the bane of trying to create motion that looks like a camera moving over an image and zooming as it goes.

2. To try to solve the jerking problem, I applied smoothing to the **Scale** parameter in the second copy of *Pic*.

As you can see, the rate of movement is linear and far faster than the scaling so that the image shoots off the **Canvas** and slowly comes back into frame. This obviously isn't going to work.

3. For the third clip, I applied **Ease In/Ease Out** to the center point animation.

Better, but it still doesn't work. The smoothing rate of scale and the **Ease In/Ease Out** rate of center point animation are different. You could go in and tweak the two to make them match. It's difficult with the tiny little Bezier handles in the **Canvas**. You can zoom in on the **Canvas** to make it easier.

4. The fourth version of *Pic* compromises smoothing the scaling with keeping the center point animation linear.

Scaling takes place around the anchor point, so if you scale to zoom and pan off to one corner at the same time, the image is moving farther and farther away from the point on which the scale is changing. To try and get around this problem and the problem of the mismatched animations, a third animation is added, the anchor point. Like the center point animation, this is also kept linear.

You can use the **Distort** tool to pull out the anchor point to match position at the movement's end. Because scaling happens around the anchor point, by moving it with the center point animation, you keep the scaling happening around the center point, which prevents the image from shooting off the screen. The downside is that neither the anchor point nor the center point have smooth motion applied. I would advise against applying FCP's **Ease In/Ease Out** to either. Because **Ease In/Ease Out** and **Smooth** use different acceleration rates — we saw this on the third *Pic* clip — in trying to ease the anchor point, the Bezier curve pulls the movement in the opposite direction to start and then overshoots at the end.

The bottom line is, if you confine yourself to simple linear movements or small amounts of scaling, FCP's **Motion** panel will work for you. If you need to do anything like large map movements, you'll need to use the updated **FXScript DVE's Roll/Scroll** (**Title**), which we'll look at on page 459 in Lesson 11 on Special Effects.

The other problem with scaling, as we saw, is the speed of the scale, which doesn't work very well in FCP. If you're doing a large movement from wide to close, the image seems to move much faster at the start and slower and slower as you zoom in. This happens because **Scale** is a logarithmic value, while position and other keyframable elements are simple arithmetic. **Scale** is a movement in 3D space, but it's using a two-dimensional movement. True compositing applications perform exponential scaling, where the scaling remains a constant speed because it accelerates or decelerates as the image changes size. Unfortunately, FCP cannot do exponential scaling easily. There should be a way to select between the current scaling behavior and exponential scaling. It can be simulated with considerable difficulty in FCP using the Bezier controls to adjust the speed. It's fiddly, and on images that are much larger in size than the screen, such as *Pic*, I have never been able to make it look good.

Scaling Text Files

The problems of pan and scale apply equally to animating text files, such as titles created in FCP. As with graphics files, you don't want to scale images up because the text becomes pixelated if you do (Figure 9.35).

So use a larger size and scale down, you say. That works up to a point. But what if the point size is larger than the screen and you scale down? Figure 9.36 shows what happens.

The text is cut off. So how do you solve this? The simplest way is to use **Title 3D**. This allows you to set the point size to whatever you want and to scale the text larger than the screen (so you can fly through it) and down to infinitely small so that it disappears into the horizon. To do this, you animate **Title 3D's Scale** and **Distance** settings. Do not animate the scale in the **Motion** panel.

Split Screen

This is a common request for all sorts of purposes, for showing parallel action such as in two sides of a phone conversation, or to show a wide shot and a closeup in the same screen. It's easy to do if the video was actually shot for a split screen. For a phone conversation, for instance, it should be shot so that one person in the phone conversation is on the left side of the frame, leaving the right side empty, and the other person is shot on the right side of the screen, leaving the left empty.

Take a look at *Split Screen Sequence* in your **Browser**. Don't bother rendering it out; they're just still frames. In the first clip, Nathan was shot on the left of the screen and Victoria on the right. I just had to crop the picture of Victoria from one side, and it fit without problem. This is the easiest way to do it. It helps a lot if your actors don't emote too much and move about the screen.

Figure 9.35   Text at 48 Scaled to 300

Figure 9.36   Text at 200 Scaled to 50

In the second clip, the two were shot centered in the screen, here you have to move one clip to the left — Nathan, in this case — and the other to the right. Then because Victoria was on top, **Crop** was applied to her picture.

Some people like to add a bar that separates the two images as in Figure 9.37. That's easy to do. Use the **Generators** to create a color matte (Figure 9.38) and place it on the top track, as in *Split Screen Sequence*. Crop the matte left and right so that only a narrow stripe is visible over the join of the two frames

Other modifications, like blurred edges, use filters. We'll look at those in Lesson 11.

Figure 9.37   Split Screen with Bar

Chasing Stills

A common request is to create a slide show of still images moving at a regular speed, sliding across the screen one after the other. This is fairly easy to do, especially with a few simple tricks to help automate the process.

In the *Stills* folder are four freeze frames, *Still 1* through *Still 4*.

1. Duplicate *Sequence 1* and drag one of these stills onto the **Timeline**.

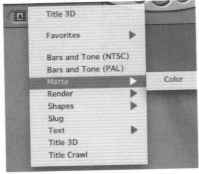

Figure 9.38   Generators>Matte>
Color

Each of the stills has a duration of five seconds. It's important that this duration is the same for each image so that they can process steadily across the screen. The duration of the clip will in large part determine the speed of the motion. So let's animate the motion of image across the screen. This should be fairly simple for you by now.

2. Reduce the **Canvas** size to 50%.

3. Turn on **Image+Wireframe**.

4. Move the image off the right side of the screen, holding down the **Shift** key to constrain it to a horizontal path.

5. Make sure you're at the beginning of the sequence and create a starting **Center** keyframe for the clip.

6. Its starting **Center** point position should be *x* 320, *y* 0.

7. Move two seconds into the timeline and animate the still so that over two seconds it slides into the center of the screen.

8. The **Center** point position now should be, of course, *x* 0, *y* 0. By creating a starting point at the beginning and then changing the position later in time, you're adding a new **Center** keyframe.

9. Go forward another second in time. You're now three seconds into the timeline. Add another **Center** keyframe.

You have to do this because the keyframe will not be added automatically when none of the image's parameters change.

Here's the trick to creating this type of continuous motion: the next keyframe you place is not actually on the clip itself, but on the frame after the clip, what will be the first frame that the next image appears.

10. To go to the frame past the clip, you want to use the **Down** arrow key, which will take you to the next edit point.

11. Change the **Center** point value to *x* –320, *y* 0.

You should still see a tiny fraction of the image on the left edge of the frame and the blue bar on the right indicating you're at the end of the sequence. You see the small bit of video on the left edge because you're looking at the Magic Frame, the frame before the edit point, while the keyframe you made is one frame later.

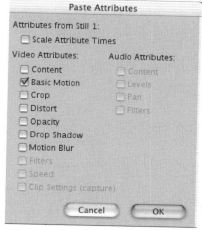

Figure 9.39 Paste Attributes

12. Render the motion and try it out.

13. Select the clip in the **Timeline** and copy it.

14. Position the playhead in the **Timeline** at the 3:00 point, which is where the *Still 1* starts to move off the screen and where we want *Still 2* to start to move on.

15. Drag *Still 2* into the space above **V1** to create **V2**.

16. Drop the image on the track at the playhead.

17. Select the clip on **V2** and go to the **Edit** menu and choose **Paste Attributes** (**Option-V**). This brings up the dialog box in Figure 9.39.

18. Check the box for **Basic Motion**.

19. Make sure the box for **Content** is unchecked. **Scale Attribute Times** is checked by default. Uncheck this box so that you do not **Scale Attribute Times**.

20. You do not want to scale the attributes to the duration of the clip because you are in fact putting in keyframes longer than the clip.

If the durations of the clips are the same, and they have identical keyframes, they will move across the screen at the same speed, chasing on another. Now you just have to line up the third image to the end of the second so that it too chases the other across the screen.

1. Move the playhead to the third keyframe in *Still 2*.

2. Target **V1**, and drag *Still 3* to **Overwrite**.

3. Click the new clip to highlight it, and **Option-V** to call **Paste Attributes**.

4. Apply the **Basic Motion** that should still be saved in the system scrapbook, and switch off **Scale Attribute Times**.

5. Repeat back and forth between **V1** and **V2** for however many times you want.

The completed sequence is in the **Browser** called *Chase Sequence*. I also added, as in the Split Screen technique, a color matte bar that separates the images. I laid it on **V3**, and after the motion was created, I copied and pasted as many times as needed on **V3** to separate the images and mask the unsightly black edges you might see in stills taken from video frames.

Once you've set up the motion the way you want, you can save it as a **Favorite**. Select the clip, and choose **Make Favorite Motion** from the **Modify** menu, or use **Option-F**.

Once you've made the motion a **Favorite**, you can replicate it for any clip by selecting it from the **Effects>Motion Favorites** menu while the clip is in the **Viewer**. When applied, the motion favorite adjusts to fit the duration of the clip it's applied to from In to Out point.

Brady Bunch Open

This is one of the classic opens on American television. It's easy to reproduce in Final Cut Pro using the techniques we've learned here.

Play the clip in your **Browser** called *BB.mov*. This is the sequence, with the faces silhouetted to protect the innocent. The timing is based on the original sequence. If you know the tune, sing along. In building this sequence, we'll use still images rather than movie clips to conserve storage space on the hard drive.

1. Open the *Brady Bunch Sequence*.
2. You'll probably have to render it out to play it at real speed, but it shouldn't take very long with these Photo-JPEG 320-size images.

We're going to replicate this sequence. Look through it closely to get an idea of where we're going.

3. Duplicate the one in your **Browser** and delete the contents of the dupe.

You could simply make a new sequence, but be careful that your **Sequence Presets** match these in every parameter.

4. It might be easier to work with the two sequences open, or you might want to lay *BB.mov* on **V1** in your **Timeline** and lock the track. That way, it could act as a guide.

Sliding White Bar

The first step we have to take is to create the white bar that slides across the screen. Easy enough.

1. Make a color matte. In **Controls**, change the color from the default gray to full white.
2. Crop the top and bottom with the **Crop** tool in the **Canvas**. In the **Crop** controls, the **Top** value is 48.75 and the **Bottom** value is 47.92, creating a narrow bar.
3. Lay the bar on **V3**, leaving a video track free below it.

Figure 9.40   Headshot and White Bar

I'm assuming that you've placed *BB.mov* on **V1** as a guide and have locked that track.

4. Slide the bar off the screen to the left so that you start in black.

5. Keyframe the white bar either with the **Keyframe** button at the bottom of the **Canvas**, or with a **Center** (position) keyframe.

We're going to animate only its position value.

6. Using *BB.mov* as a guide, slide the bar across the screen to its end position, which is when about half the bar is off the screen on the right side. Hold down the **Shift** key as you slide it to constraint the movement to horizontal.

7. Use **Opacity** controls to fade it out. It fades out very quickly, over three or four frames.

Fixing the Headshot

1. Open the bin in your **Browser** called **Graphics**.

It's probably best to just leave it open. In the **Graphics** bin are the headshots of this sequence and the image for the pan and scan sequence we dealt with earlier. These are mostly PICT files and a few titles made with **Title 3D**. We'll get to those later on page 397.

2. Drag *HeadshotPink.pct* to **V2** to the point where the bar stops and begins fading out (Figure 9.40).

Obviously at this point the headshot will fill the frame with the white bar over it. What we have to do is scale down and reposition the headshot.

3. Grab one corner of the headshot in **Canvas** and pull it in.

4. Grab the image and slide it to the right so it's positioned under the bar (Figure 9.41). I scaled it down to 63.76% and positioned it to *x* 75, *y* –1.

Next we have to crop the image.

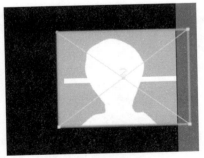

Figure 9.41   Scaled and
Positioned Headshot

5. Select the **Crop** tool from the tools (keyboard shortcut **C** for crop). With the **Crop** tool, pull in the left and right edges a little bit.

6. Then crop the top and bottom till the headshot is a narrow slit hidden underneath the bar. The settings used in the sequence are:

Left	6.38
Right	11.28
Top	50
Bottom	48.57

7. Set a keyframe in the **Canvas** or on the **Motion** panel of the **Viewer.**

8. Set the keyframes for **Crop Top** and **Bottom.**

Those are the only parameters that will animate on this image.

9. Go forward about 14 frames in the timeline. With the **Timeline** or **Canvas** active, press **Command-D** to make sure no clips are selected, and type *+14*.

If you don't drop any select clips, you'll actually move them 14 frames in the **Timeline** rather than moving the playhead 14 frames. This only happens in the **Timeline**, not in the **Canvas** or in the **Viewer.**

10. Pull open the top and bottom crop lines to the full height of the image.

You've made the first part of the animation: the bar slides across the screen, stops, and fades out, and the headshot wipes open to reveal the picture. Don't worry about the lengths of the clips yet. We'll fix that later.

Middle Headshots

Now we're ready to bring in the next set of headshots.

1. Go down to Marker 1 in the timeline.

Shift-M takes you to the next marker; **Option-M** takes you to the previous marker. Three headshots appear on the left.

2. From the **Graphics** bin, drag in the image *HeadshotGreen.pct* and place it on **V3**, the track above the pink headshot.

3. Again, first we have to scale and position it so that it's in the lower left corner of the screen. The settings I used are:

Scale	29.59
Center	x –107, y 76
Crop Right	3.85

4. Then we need to fade in the image, either in the **Timeline** with the **Pen** tool (**P**), or in the **Motion** panel of the **Viewer** with the **Opacity** slider.

This again is a fairly quick fade in, about 14 frames.

5. Select the clip in the **Timeline**.

6. Now **Option-Shift**-drag from **V3** to **V4** to make a copy of the clip on the track above.

7. Repeat to place a third copy on **V5**.

At this stage, all three copies of *HeadshotGreen.pct* are on top of each other.

8. Select the clip on **V4** and in the **Canvas** drag it upward, holding down the **Shift** key to constrain direction, and position the image about the center line of the screen.

9. Repeat for the clip on **V5**, dragging it up vertically to the top third of the screen. I used these **Center** position settings for the three layers:

V5	x –107, y –78
V4	x–107, y –1
V3	x –107, y 76

At Marker 2, where the fade-ups on the green headshots end, the screen should look like Figure 9.42.

Extending

So far so good. Next you should extend the image files in the timeline all the way down to Marker 3.

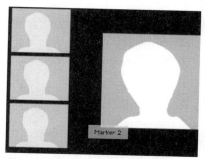

Figure 9.42 Four Headshots on Screen, Marker 2

1. Drag them out to Marker 3 with the **Selector** tool (**A**). **Command**-click on the edits at the end of each clip in the **Timeline**. Once all the edits are selected, move the playhead to Marker 3. Hit **E** to do an **Extend** edit. Voilà. All the clips will be extended to Marker 3.

At Marker 3, all four shots end, and we cut to black, but not for long. Next we have to bring in a new white bar from the right side.

2. Copy the white line from the beginning and paste it at the next marker on **V3**.

The line will appear with all its motion and opacity just like the first time you made it. The only problem is that it's moving in the wrong direction.

3. Open the copied clip at Marker 4 into the **Viewer**.

4. Go to the **Motion** tab and move the playhead to the bar's first keyframe.

5. Holding down the **Shift** key, slide the clip in the **Canvas**, which should still be in **Image+Wireframe** mode, across the screen to the other side.

This is the bar's new start position.

6. Go to the point where the fade-out begins, which should also be the bar's second **Center** keyframe.

7. Slide the bar to the left to its end position, mirrored from the first time you did it.

8. Select the clip *HeadshotPink.pct* that's on **V2** and copy it.

9. From the **Graphics** bin, drag *HeadshotBlue.pct* onto **V2** in the **Timeline**, placing it at the point where the bar begins its fade-out.

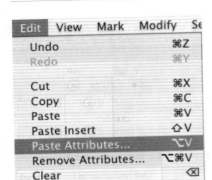

Figure 9.43   Edit>Paste
             Attributes

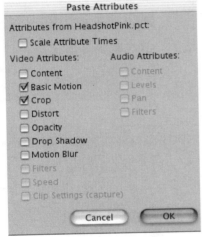

Figure 9.44   Paste Attributes

10. With *HeadshotBlue.pct* selected in the **Timeline**, go to the **Edit** menu and choose **Paste Attributes** (**Option-V**) (Figure 9.43). This brings up the dialog box in Figure 9.44.

11. Select **Basic Motion** and **Crop** from the dialog box. Because we've lengthened *HeadshotPink.pct*, make sure that the checkbox at the top of the window for **Scale Attribute Times** is deselected. The default is for the box to be checked.

This duplicates the position and animation of the earlier shot. Now all we have to do is reposition the clip to the left side of the screen.

Repositioning the Clip

1. Holding down the **Shift** key, slide the image in the **Canvas** to the left so that it's underneath the white bar.

2. Jump down to Marker 5 and bring in the clip *HeadshotRed.pct* from the **Graphics** bin and place it on V3.

3. Copy the green headshot that's earlier on **V3**.

4. Select the new red headshot and again use **Paste Attributes** (**Option-V**).

5. Apply **Basic Motion**, **Crop**, and **Opacity**. Again with **Scale Attribute Times** deselected.

Now reposition its center so that it's on the opposite side of the screen.

6. Again, **Option-Shift**-drag the copies of the clip from **V3** to **V4** and **V5**.

7. Holding down the **Shift** key to constrain movement, reposition the clips so they appear one above the other on the right side of the screen. The **Center** values I used these three shots are:

V5	x 109, y –78
V4	x 109, y –1
V3	x 109, y 76

8. Again, extend the green headshots and the blue headshot all the way down to Marker 7.

Again the screen cuts to black.

New Headshots

9. Go down to Marker 8 and bring in the clip called *Head-PinkSmall.pct* and place it on **V2**.

10. The image is the right size for the start of this section, but it's in the wrong place.

11. In the **Canvas**, drag it straight up to the top of the frame so that the top edge of the image is at the top edge of the screen. My setting for the **Center** was y –61.

12. Go to Marker 9 and set a keyframe for **Crop Bottom**.

That's the only part we have to animate at the moment. It's often easier to work backwards in animation, to start with the end position on the screen and then animate the wipe on.

13. Now go back to Marker 8 and with the **Crop** tool (**C**), grab the bottom crop line and pull it upward off the screen.

This is why it's easier to make the end position first, because the two crop lines are now right next to each other, and they're much harder to separate. That's your Start keyframe position. It will give you a quick wipe on of the picture.

Marker 10 is where the next image comes in.

1. Place *HeadBlueSmall.pct* on **V**

2. Reposition to the bottom center of the screen. My **Center** value was y 6.

3. Go to Marker 11 to set a **Crop Top** keyframe.

4. Go back to Marker 10, and this time take the top crop line and drag it down to hide the image.

At Marker 11 both pictures should now be on the screen as shown in Figure 9.45. We're ready now to bring in the rest of the headshots.

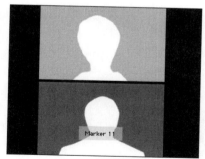

Figure 9.45 Two Headshots on Screen, Marker 11

Final Headshots

At Marker 12 we'll first have to place a keyframe on both the pink and blue head shots. Both images need to scale down slightly and have the left and right sides cropped so the images fit into their final position.

1. With the playhead at Marker 12, select both headshots and click on the **Keyframe** button in the **Canvas** to set a global motion keyframe for the two headshots.

2. Change the scale of the **Timeline** window so that you can see most of the **Timeline**.

3. Position the playhead at Marker 13 to place the next head-shots. **Shift**-select the three green headshots from near the beginning of the sequence.

4. Hold down the **Option** key and grab them, dragging them along the timeline and up one track to the playhead at Marker 13. Release the **Option** key before you let go of the clips to perform an **Overwrite** edit.

The three duplicate green headshots should be on **V4**, **V5**, and **V6**, leaving **V2** and **V3** for the pink and blue headshots. Next do the same for the red headshots in the timeline.

5. Select the red headshots, hold the **Option** key, and drag to **V7**, **V8**, and **V9**. Again, make sure you release the **Option** key before you let go to execute an overwrite.

If you don't, the edit will be an insert that will push the green headshots along the timeline.

Between Marker 12 and Marker 14 where the green and red headshots reach full opacity, the pink and blue headshots scale, crop, and slightly reposition to their final locations.

For the pink headshot my values at Marker 14 are:

Scale	63.81
Center	*x* 1, *y* –78
Crop Left	2.83
Crop Right	5.23
Crop Top	4.29
Crop Bottom	4.29

For the blue headshot my values at Marker 14 are:

Scale	69.62
Center	*x* 0, *y* 70
Crop Left	8.23
Crop Right	11.16
Crop Top	12.89
Crop Bottom	0

When you've positioned the clips about the screen, you should end up with the **Canvas** looking like Figure 9.46.

One more step needs to be taken before we put in the titles: extend the headshots down to the end of the sequence. Move the playhead all the way down to Marker 24, then **Command**-click on the edits at the ends of all the headshots: pink, blue, the three greens, and the three reds. Now do an **Extend** edit to stretch them out to the playhead.

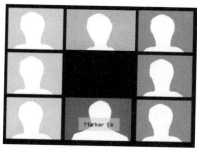

Figure 9.46   Eight Headshots on Screen, Marker 14

Titles

We're finished with almost all the headshots. Next we have to get the titles on the screen. I've prebuilt them for you using **Title 3D**. They are made with the Textile font, which the closest in the basic Apple font collection to the original title style.

1. Lay the first title, *Main Title* in the **Graphics** bin, at Marker 15 on the topmost track, **V10**.

You'll see that it's at its full size. In fact, there is a small scaling of the title in the open. The parameter we're going to animate is not the **Scale** value in the **Motion** panel, but the **Distance** value inside the text controls.

2. Double click *Main Title* from **V10** of the **Timeline** to open it into the **Viewer**. Go to the **Controls tab** and set a keyframe for **Distance**.

3. Go to Marker 16 and now reduce the **Distance** value. I set it to –0.87. This will move the title closer, making it larger.

4. Next go down to Marker 17 and with the **Razor Blade (B)**, cut the title and throw away the rest of it.

At Marker 18, the next title, *Starring Title*, appears.

5. Drop *Starring Title* onto the same track as the main title.

6. Cut this title off at Marker 19.

7. At Marker 20 introduce *Mom Title*. Because it overlaps with the final headshot we're going to bring in, it needs to be placed on a higher track, **V11**.

8. At Marker 21 set an **Opacity** keyframe for *Mom Title*. The frame before Marker 22 set the **Opacity** down to zero. This will fade it out quickly.

9. **Razor Blade** *Mom Title* at Marker 22.

Final Polishing

We're on the home straight, just a few more steps to take. At Marker 21, while *Mom Title* is fading out, one more headshot is fading in.

1. Drag one more copy of the green headshot into the center of the screen. Place it on **V10** underneath **Mom Title**.

2. The final green headshot needs to be positioned, scaled, and cropped top and bottom to fit the center square in the screen. The values I used are:

Scale	34.18
Center	$x -2, y -2$
Crop Top	6.11
Crop Bottom	6.11

3. Set an **Opacity** keyframe for the green headshot at Marker 21 and set the value to zero. Ramp up the **Opacity** to 100 at Marker 22.

At Marker 22 the last title, *Alice Title*, just cuts in. Place it on **V11**.

4. Cut off both *Alice Title* and the center headshot at Marker 24.

Fade to Black

The last step we want to do is to fade to black. We could keyframe and ramp down the opacity on each of 10 layers now on the screen, but there's an easier way.

1. Make a short slug and place it on the topmost video track at Marker 23.
2. Set its **Opacity** down to zero and keyframe it.
3. At Marker 24 bring its opacity up to 100% so black fills the screen.

Congratulations. You've made the Brady Bunch open. The original open was made with a good deal more precision than I invested in it, but if you want, you can precisely align and shape the images using exact values in the **Motion** tab.

Picture in Picture

By the time you've done this lesson, it must be pretty obvious how to do a PIP, a Picture in Picture.

One note of caution about PIPs: many digitized video formats such as DV and Motion-JPEG leave a few lines of black on the edges of the frame as we saw when doing transitions. This is actually the rough edge of the CCD, where the pixels end. It's normally hidden in the overscan area of your television set and never seen. However, as soon as you start scaling down images and moving them about the screen, the black line becomes apparent. The easiest way to do this is to take the **Crop** tool and just slightly crop the image before you do your PIP so as not to get the black lines, which give the video an amateur look. You might also want to add a border to the PIP to set it off, but that's for Lesson 11 when we look at "Video Filters" on page 496, but next we'll look at FCP's new **Color Correction** tools as well as its keying capabilities.

Lesson 10

Color Correction

Unlike **Transitions** that go between clips, **Filters** are applied to single clips, or parts of clips. FCP offers a great variety of excellent effects, including **Color Correction**, which is a new collection of filters available in Final Cut Pro 3. We'll look at the other filters in the next lesson, but this lesson is primarily for image control, color, and luminance and how you can manipulate them. Because keying uses many of the same controls as the **Color Correction** filters, we'll also look at that here as well.

Good exposure and color begins in the shooting. It's actually easier and always better to do it right to start rather than trying to fix it in post. That means lighting the scene well, correctly exposing it, setting your white balance correctly and not leaving the camera's auto white balance to guess , recording camera color bars, and finally shooting a chip chart that shows a full gradation of pure white to pure black without any color cast (Figure 10.1).

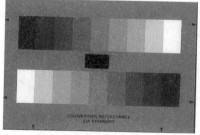

Figure 10.1   EIA Chip Chart

In Hollywood there is a job called colorist, one that is part art and part science. It requires great skill, talent, training, and experience to do well. Whole books have been written on color theory, and books could be written on the art of the colorist and on color correction. Because I am not nor do I aspire to be a colorist, you will be getting only a rudimentary look at the tools FCP offers and possibilities of color correction using them. Anyone you says they can explain it to you in an chapter or a few QuickTime movies is either deluding themselves or trying to pull one over on you. I'll show you the tools, but if you really want to become accomplished, you'll need to practice often and train your eyes to see color correctly in all its subtleties.

Loading the Lesson

As always, let's begin by loading the material you need onto your media drive.

1. If you don't already have it there, drag over the *Media1* folder from the CD.

2. Also drag onto your system drive the folder *Lesson 10*.

3. Eject the CD, open the *Lesson 10* folder on your hard drive and double-click the project file, *L10*, to launch the application.

4. After you've reconnected the media, be sure to set the **Scratch Disk Preferences** to the *Media1* folder, as well as setting the *AutoSave Vault* location to the *Shared* folder.

5. Finally, use **Save Project As** and give the project a new name.

Inside your project copy, you'll find in the **Browser**, the **Clips** bin, *Damine.mov*, and other files that we'll look at in this lesson. Let's start by opening *Sequence 1* and loading a clip into it. Let's work with *Stairs2*.

Applying Video Filters

It really couldn't be simpler to apply an effect in Final Cut Pro.

1. Select the clip in the **Timeline** and from the menu bar select **Effects>Video Filters** (Figure 10.2).

2. Pick a submenu and pick an effect.

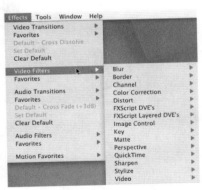

Figure 10.2   Effects>Video Filters

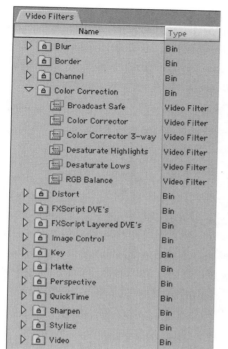

Figure 10.3   Video Effects Bin

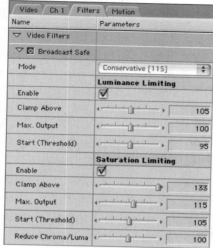

Figure 10.4   Selected Effect in Filters Panel

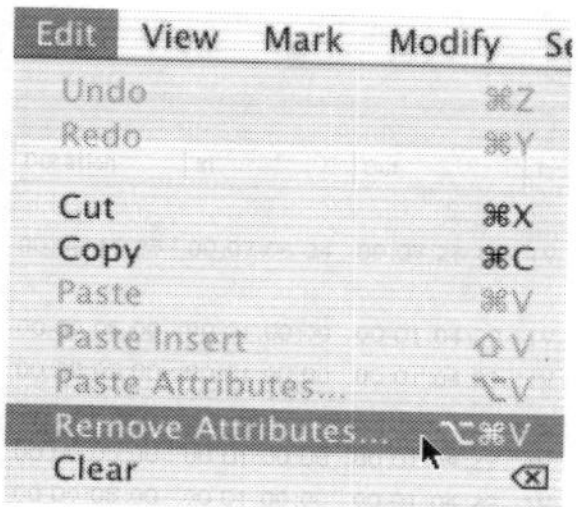

Figure 10.5   Edit>Remove Attributes

It is immediately applied with its default settings to the clip. If you prefer, you can drag the effect from the **Video Filter** bin inside the **Effects** panel of the **Browser** (Figure 10.3).

It's just as easy to remove an effect. Simply open the clip into the **Viewer**, go to the **Filters** tab, select the effect by clicking on its name, and press the **Delete** key (Figure 10.4).

You can also select a clip or a number of clips in the **Timeline**, and from the **Edit** menu chose **Remove Attributes**, or use the keyboard shortcut **Command-Option-V** (Figure 10.5). Make sure the **Filters** box is checked in the **Remove Attributes** dialog box (Figure 10.6), and the filter or multiple filters will all be removed. It could be simpler only if this could be done from the clip's contextual menu right in the **Timeline**.

Notice also the little checkbox next to the effect's name in the **Filters** tab of the **Viewer**. The checkbox allows you to switch off an effect, while leaving it and all its settings loaded in the clip.

Figure 10.6   Remove Attributes Dialog Box

Almost all effects still need to be rendered, even when working in DV. The only one that doesn't is **Color Corrector 3-way**. Some systems allow other filters to be real-time as well, but using the Mac's internal capabilities, **CC 3-way** is only real-time with DV material, and it's real-time preview to the computer monitor only.

This is certainly not the filter you want to use when you're working only on your computer monitor. If you're producing work for output on a television set, it is essential that you view your color correction work on a properly set-up production monitor, not the computer monitor, so while you're actually doing color correction, real-time preview of **CC 3-way** is fairly pointless. Once it's done, however, you can switch to real-time preview and leave the rendering until your work is finished and you're ready to output. Unless you have a system that outputs in real time, any filters you apply will have to be rendered out, so the faster your computer, the better off you'll be. Some effects, especially with extreme settings, render quite slowly.

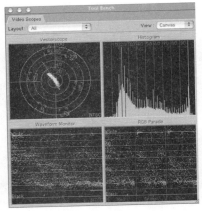

Figure 10.7 Video Scopes

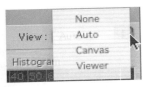

Figure 10.8 View Popup

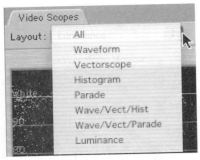

Figure 10.9 Layout Popup

Video Scopes

Before we get into using the new **Color Correction** filters in FCP3, let's first take a look at the video scopes that come with it. These are in the **Tool Bench**. When you open the **Tool Bench** (**Option-5**), it defaults to showing a four-up display of the FCP scopes, **Vectorscope**, **Histogram**, **RGB Parade**, and **Waveform Monitor** (Figure 10.7).

The **View** popup in the upper right allows you to set which screen you're looking at (Figure 10.8). It defaults to **Canvas**, but I usually prefer to set it to **Auto**, which allows it to scope whichever is the active window, **Viewer** or **Canvas**. I'm not quite sure why there is a **None** setting.

The **Layout** popup on the right lets you see a variety of scope combinations (Figure 10.9). **Luminance** at the bottom of the popup gives you a combination of **Waveform Monitor** and **Parade**. Because of the size of the **Tool Bench**, it's probably easiest to use one scope at a time.

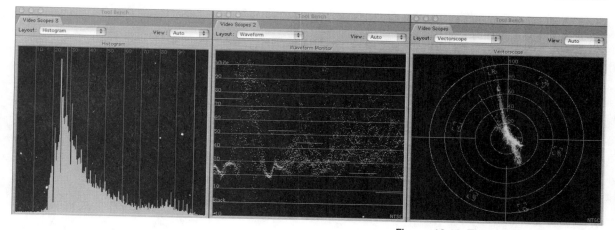

Figure 10.10 Three Video Scopes
Open at the Same Time

As you look through the scopes, open up your own material of the clips in *L10* and see how the various scopes respond to the different images.

Histogram

Let's look at the scopes in more detail, starting with **Histogram** (Figure 10.11). If you're familiar at all with Photoshop's **Levels** control, the **Histogram** will not to be strange to you. The left edge of the **Histogram** is pure black, and the right side is pure white. What's displayed in the graph is the amount of luminance in each area. Figure 10.11 shows a fairly typical histogram graph. Not too much in the darkest areas nor too much in the brightest areas, most of the image is in the central area of the graph, the midrange of luminance values. If there is too much in the dark end with little in the middle and none on the right, then the image is probably underexposed and needs correcting. Vice versa, if there is a lot in the highlight side of the **Histogram** and little in the middle or dark end, the image is probably overexposed and should be adjusted. High contrast images, such as night scenes, often have a pronounced U-shaped graph, a lot in the dark area, very little in the midtone area, and building to a spike in the highlight side (Figure 10.12).

Notice that as you move the cursor over the **Histogram**, it displays the luminance value for that spike in the upper right corner. Also notice the lower right corner of the graph that has

Tip

Viewing Scopes: Actually you can have multiple scopes open at the same time, assuming you have screen space for them all. If you go to **Tools>Video Scopes** repeatedly, you can open a second and a third or even fourth scope, which will all look at the same frame of video (Figure 10.10).

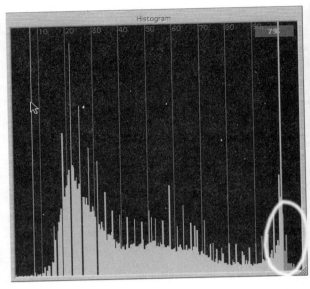

Figure 10.11 Histogram

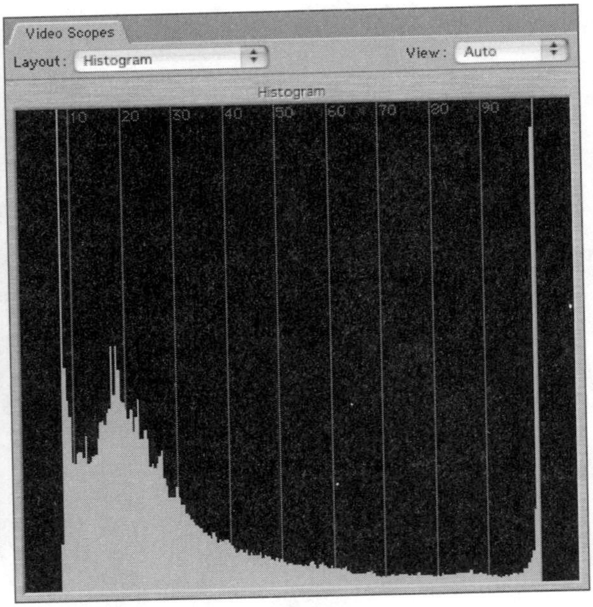

Figure 10.12 High Contrast Histogram

Figure 10.13 Histogram
Contextual Menu

been circled. This indicates that a portion of the image exceeds a luminance value of 100, beyond what is considered broadcast safe. There is a quick and easy-to-use filter, **Broadcast Safe**, that will fix this problem.

The **Histogram** is most useful for adjusting the gamma of an image. *Gamma* is the slope of a picture's luminance from dark to light. Ideally it's a steady rise, but sometimes adjusting it, forcing the image's luminance levels one way or the other, will improve the picture. Increasing the pitch of the slope, so that it reaches highlight levels more quickly, gives the image more contrast, while decreasing the pitch so that the darkest portion of the image is not so black will reduce the contrast. How the gamma distributes light and dark in an image is displayed in the **Histogram**.

As so often in FCP, the **Control** key will call up a contextual menu that will allow you to adjust the **Histogram** display (Figure 10.13). You can set the display from the default white to the traditional green. **Include Black** should be left on. It's important to see if there is pure black in the image. The **High, Medium, Low,** and **Off** setting controls the intensity of the scale markings.

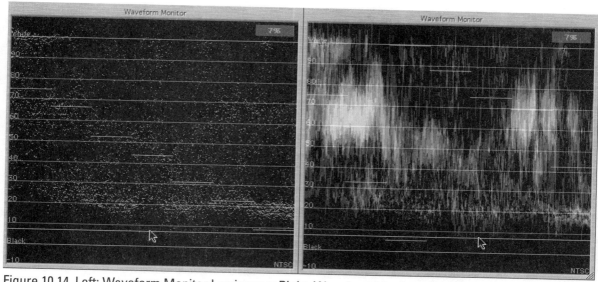

Figure 10.14 Left: Waveform Monitor Luminance; Right: Waveform Monitor with Saturation

Waveform Monitor

The **Waveform Monitor** is probably the most useful scope for setting levels and calibrating your equipment. It can be displayed either only as luminance values or can include saturation information, showing how much chrominance there is in an image (Figure 10.14). This is selectable by **Control**-clicking in the window and choosing it from the contextual menu (Figure 10.15).

The waveform in Figure 10.14 is again pretty average, perhaps a little higher than it should be in some areas, but this can easily be controlled. You do not want your video to look like Figure 10.16, in which it is clearly crushed into the blacks, with not enough in the midrange. The **Histogram** on the right indicates that there is very little of the image values in the acceptable range. If you look closely, you can see the spike at the left edge of the **Histogram**. Figure 10.17 shows the opposite. The video levels are too high. There is again not enough in the midrange and almost no dark areas.

The diagonal of steps are the targets used to calibrate color bars, starting on the left with white at 75, then yellow, cyan, green, magenta, red, and blue at 9. The waveform displays the image as you see it on the screen from left to right.

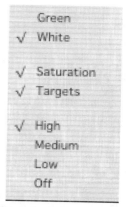

Figure 10.15 Waveform Monitor Contextual Menu

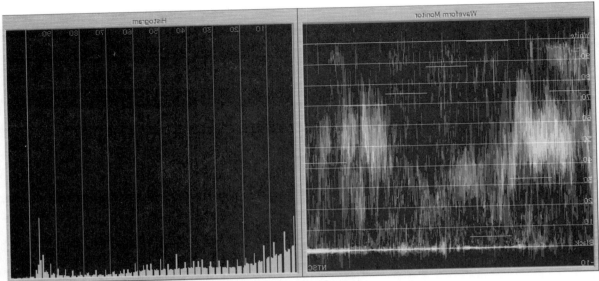

Figure 10.16 Waveform and Histogram of Underexposed Image

Vectorscope

The **Vectorscope** is used to display color information about an image (Figure 10.18). The targets that appear on the scope are points that color bars should hit when they are generating correct amounts of chrominance. Starting from just left of upper center

Figure 10.17 Waveform and Histogram of Overexposed Image

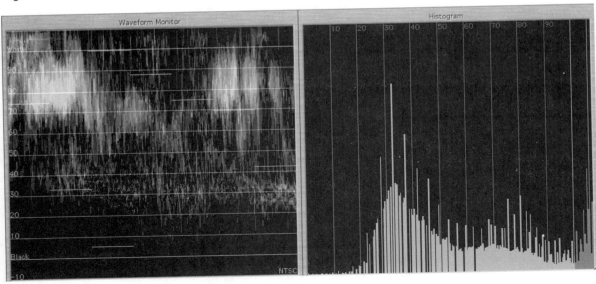

Figure 10.18 Vectorscope

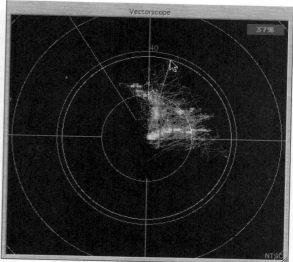

Figure 10.19 Vectorscope Magnified Showing Strong Color Cast

and going clockwise, the target points are the basic color wheel red, magenta, blue, cyan, green, and yellow.

Notice the diagonal line sticking out from the center point about halfway between yellow and red. This is the flesh tone line. Any image of a human, especially a close-up, will have a mass of color along the fleshtone line. Regardless of race, human skin falls into a very narrow spectrum of color centered along this line. If your scope shows a considerable shift off the fleshtone line as in Figure 10.19, it's because your video has a serious color cast.

You can then use FCP's filters to shift the image into the correct part of the spectrum. Because the **Vectorscope** tends to use only a fairly small part of its range for most video images, the contextual menu allows you to magnify the central portion of the image as in Figure 10.19.

RGB Parade

The final scope **RGB Parade** also is used to measure color values, but it is similar in display to the **Waveform Monitor** in that it shows again, bottom to top, the amounts of the primary colors, red, green, and blue in each luminance value (Figure 10.20). The **Parade** is most useful for comparing shots, to see how much of a

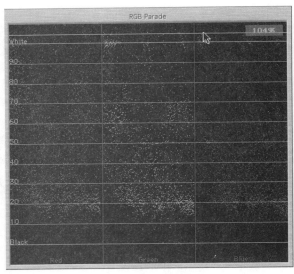

Figure 10.20 Average RGB Parade

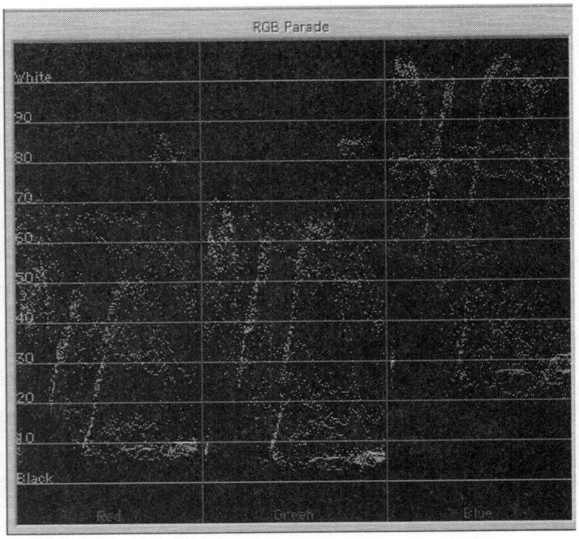

Figure 10.21 RGB Parade with More Blue

particular color is in it when you're trying to match them as closely as possible.

Figure 10.20 shows a fairly typical parade, even distributions of the primary colors, a little less in the blues. Figure 10.21 shows a parade with a heavier concentration of blue, which may be typical against a blue sky. Figure 10.22 shows a parade that is predominantly red.

Black is Black

There is no mark on the FCP graticule to indicate North American NTSC black, which should be at 7.5. The DV format in prosumer cameras uses Japanese NTSC black set to zero. Higher end DV and DVCAM cameras can usually be set to record black at either zero or raised to 7.5. Most analog cameras such as BetacamSP are always set to 7.5. Zero black is the digital standard, however, and that is what is used within FCP. Be aware though that if you intend your material for broadcast, or to be seen on a North American television, for that matter, the black level should be set to 7.5. If you don't do it, the broadcaster in all probability will, either by raising the level to bring it to black, or by crushing the signal, so that nothing falls below 7.5. American television sets are designed to receive black at 7.5IRE.

The same is true of chrominance values. Many camcorders record quite high levels of chroma. Televisions sets are designed to receive NTSC levels of saturation, which are not very high, and have features built into them to enhance the chroma values. This is why it is critical that levels be controlled carefully. This is especially true for graphics than show large areas of a single color, which can easily become over-chromaed and bleed into other colors when displayed on a television set.

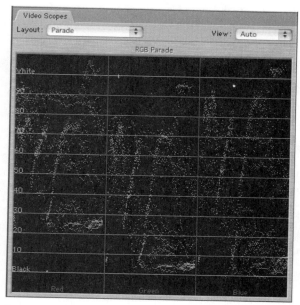

Figure 10.22 RGB Parade with More Red

Figure 10.23 View>Range Check>Excess Luma

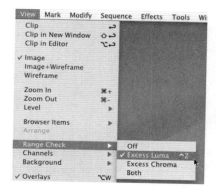

Range Check

Range Check is not a traditional video scope, but rather an FCP display that will show if your image exceeds legal luminance and chrominance values. **Range Check** can be turned on and off from the **View** menu by choosing **Range Check** and then picking an option in the submenu (Figure 10.23). The most commonly used check **Excess Luma** can be toggled on and off with the keyboard shortcut **Control-Z**.

When it's turned on, you will see *zebra* in either the **Viewer** or the **Canvas** (they can be turned on and off independently). Zebra are the diagonal lines you see running through the image in Figure 10.24.

Users of professional cameras will be familiar with this feature because it appears in their camera viewfinders. The presence of zebra tells the cameraperson which parts of the image are reaching peak values. In cameras zebra is normally set by a technician to whatever the cameraperson prefers. Many like to have it set to 77–80IRE, a point just above the value of the white bar on the left edge of the color bar chart. Obviously, with the value set so low, most images will show some zebra. A Caucasian face will usually show some zebra, usually in the highlights on a cheek.

White shirts will certainly be a mass of diagonal lines. In FCP zebra appears at a somewhat higher level, usually not before 90%. In Figure 10.24 you'll see the warning sign with the exclamation sign indicating that the frame exceeds 100, higher than it should be. If you saw this in color, you would see that the mass of diagonal lines in the upper left quadrant of the image were almost all green, indicating that the luma values were between 90 and 100. If you looked closely at the figure, you can see that small portions of the line would be in red. The red areas exceed 100 units and should be reduced.

> ### 🐿 *Note* _____
> ***Range Check*** should be turned off when not in use. At the moment, it seems to disturb a number of functions within FCP, most notably the ability to export video correctly. It also has an adverse effect on some **Color Correction** functions. That said, it's a useful tool for quickly checking through your material.

Sometimes when **Range Check** is active, you will also see a different symbol, the one in Figure 10.25. The check mark with the upward pointing arrow is on a green field and indicates that the video level is between 90 and 100. There is also still a great deal of zebra present in the image. When the luminance values fall below 90, you'll see just the check mark as in Figure 10.26 and all traces of zebra will have disappeared. Taking video levels down below 90 is probably a bit excessive, especially if there is a lot of white sky as in *Stairs2*. If, however, the shot is a close-up of a face against a neutral color background, levels even of 90 might be too high.

Figure 10.24 Range Check in the Canvas

Figure 10.25 Range Check Between 90 and 100

Figure 10.26 Range Check Below 90

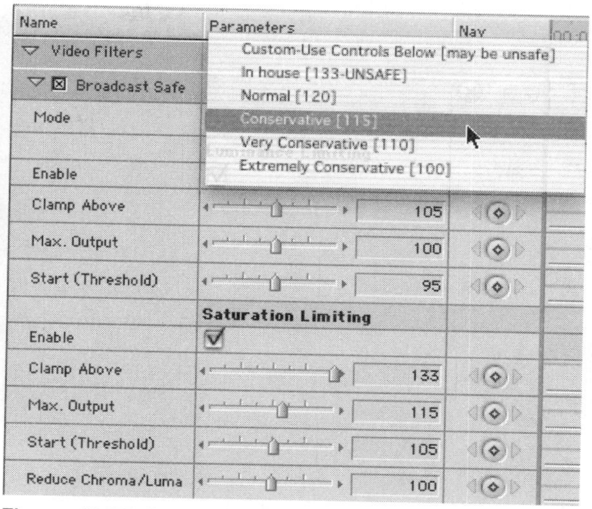

Figure 10.27 Broadcast Safe Default Settings

Color Correction

Broadcast Safe

Now you know how to tell if your video is not what it should be, what do you do about it? FCP3 has given you a number of excellent tools to not only fix problems, but also to enhance your images, and even alter them in surprising ways.

There are six filters in the **Color Correction** submenu, starting with **Broadcast Safe,** the simplest tool to use for images such as *Stairs2* that are perhaps a touch hotter than they should be. Simply select the clip in the **Timeline,** the **Canvas,** or the **Viewer,** and from the **Effects** menu choose **Video Filters>Color Correction>Broadcast Safe.** The **Canvas** will immediately change to look like Figure 10.25, indicating that the highest values have been reduced to between 90 and 100.

Broadcast Safe isn't just a magic bullet; you do have quite a bit of control on the filter to set it to whatever parameters you want (Figure 10.27). The default is be **Conservative,** allowing a maximum value of 115 at which point the video signal will be clipped off. These are not the settings you see displayed in the sliders. Changing the popup value unfortunately does not change the

Figure 10.28 Top of the Viewer
Window with Color
Correction

slider values, so you have only a guess what the actually filter is doing. None of the standard settings show an appreciable difference, and personally I think the default setting works very well.

Notice that as the default you limit both the luminance values and the chrominance values. If you want to keep the luminance in an acceptable range but do something outrageous with the color, you can uncheck the **Saturation Limiting** checkbox. You also have to make sure **Custom — Use Controls Below** is selected from the popup.

The **Threshold** slider controls the point at which the luminance starts to roll off. With the default of 95, there is smooth ramp down to 105. You could, if you wanted, pull the **Threshold** lower, which would change the slope of the gamma. Instead of being a straight ramp with a fairly sharp curve between 95 and 105, it would be a more gradual curve, tapering to the clip point.

Color Corrector

Unlike most filters, **Color Corrector**, as well as **Color Corrector 3-way** and **Chroma Keyer** in the **Key** submenu, have two panels in the **Viewer** (Figure 10.28). One marked **Filter** has sliders and numerical controls to adjust the values, and a useful button at the top that lets you switch to the **Visual** display (Figure 10.29). The second panel with the name of the filter has the visual interface that you are most likely to use (Figure 10.30, page 416).

I'm not entirely sure why there needs to be a separate panel for the filter itself, when the visual panel has all the controls necessary in a graphical interface that's much more appealing to the user. A couple of key features are on the **Filter** panel only. One is the little button with the red X to reset the entire filter. The other items that seem to be missing from the **Visual** panel are **Edge Control**, **Thin/Spread**, and **Softening**. We'll look at those later on page 423 when we see secondary color correction. Why these could not have been incorporated into the **Visual** panel, especially the **Reset** button, I don't understand. There are, however, **Reset** buttons that allow you to reset individual parameters. They're the small white radio buttons, for instance, the one to the bottom right of the **Hue** color wheel.

Let's take a look at the visual controls for **Color Corrector**. At the top is a grouping of useful buttons (Figure 10.31). The **Numeric** button takes you to the **Filter** panel. There is a **Keyframe** button linked to the **Keyframe Graph** on the right. This timeline will only cover the area of the clip and not extend beyond it as other filter windows do. There is also the little checkbox that allows you to toggle the filter on and off. The **Eye** icon simply tells you that you're in the **Visual** panel, if you didn't realize that already. Below the **Keyframe Graph** are the basic timeline controls and timecode reference.

There is the **Grab Handle**, which lets you pull the effect onto a clip, similar to the **Grab Handle** in the audio panel. On either side of the **Grab Handle** are some very useful buttons. The first to the right of **Grabber**, with the number **1** on it, allows you to copy your **Color Corrector** settings to the next clip in the **Timeline**. With this button you can very quickly copy the settings to a whole series of clips. Click the button and you'll have copied the settings to the next clip. Press the **Down** arrow and you'll go to the next edit point, also changing the contents of the **Viewer** and the **Visual** panel.

Though it may not be immediately apparent, you're in the **Color Corrector** panel for the next clip in the **Timeline**. Press the button again and the **Down** arrow, and the button and the **Down** arrow, and with a few keystrokes you can scoot along the **Timeline** and copy the settings to every clip.

 Note _____

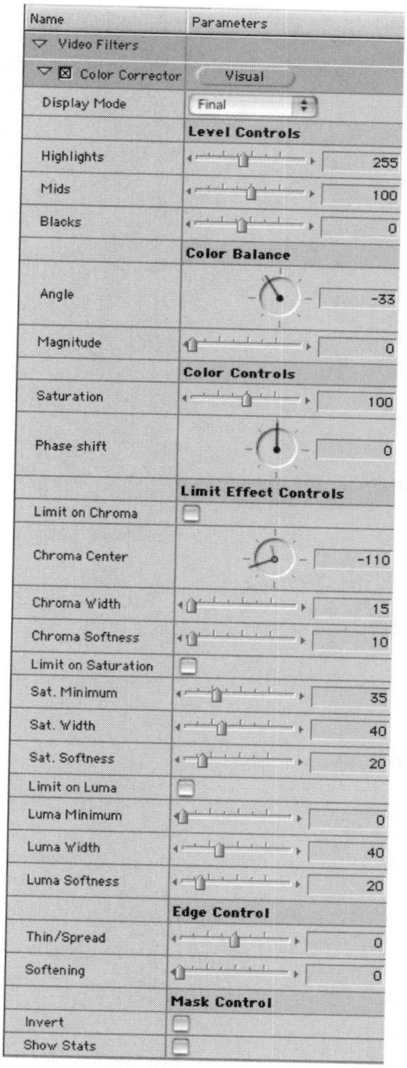

Smart Buttons: The **Color Corrector Copy** buttons are intelligent. That is, you can't keep clicking repeatedly on the **Copy** button and find you've applied **CC** a dozen times. It copies to the next clip or second clip only once.

The second button to the right of the **Grabber**, marked with the number **2**, can be even more useful. This copies the settings not to the next clip in the **Timeline**, but to the second clip down the

Figure 10.29 Color Correction Filter Panel

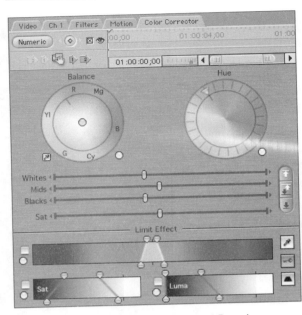

Figure 10.30 Color Correction Visual Panel

Figure 10.31 Top of the Color Corrector Visual Panel

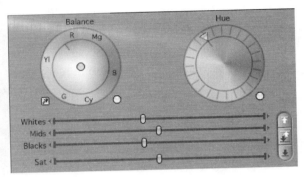

Figure 10.32 Main Color Corrector Controls

Timeline. For instance, if you have a two-camera interview that basically switches back and forth between the two cameras and you want to color balance one camera to the other, you need to color correct every other shot in the **Timeline**. Clicking the **2** button will copy the settings to the next shot for that camera. You can quickly copy the settings to every other shot in the **Timeline**. Copying it to multiple copies is not quite as straight forward as click, **Down** arrow, click, **Down** arrow. If you click on **2** and **Down** arrow, you get to the next edit point that has no **CC** applied, so you get to the **Filter** tab. Another **Down** arrow takes you unfortunately to the **Filter** tab of the clip with CC applied, but not to the **Visual** panel. So you have to click, **Down** arrow, **Down** arrow, switch to **Visual** panel, click on **2**, and repeat the process.

The two buttons marked with a **1** and **2** to the left of the **Grab Handle** act similarly. They let you copy the **Color Corrector** settings to the clip you're working on from either the shot before, the **1** button, or from the shot before last in the **Timeline**, the **2** button.

Let's take a look at the central control panel in **Color Corrector,** which has two color wheels, four sliders, and a few buttons (Figure 10.32).

The left wheel controls the white balance of the image, while the right changes the hue, just like the hue knob on a television set. Below are four self-explanatory sliders. The first controls the white levels; the second, the midtones; and the third, the black level. The controls are needed to adjust the levels that we looked at earlier in the **Histogram** and the **Waveform Monitor.** Below is the fourth slider to adjust the **Saturation** or amount of chroma in the image. The three buttons stacked together on the right are auto setting buttons. These are the best place to start with any

Pluge

It's always important to set up your production monitor properly when doing video work. It's critical when you're doing color correction, which is one reason FCP provides standard NTSC color bars in the **Generators.** This is where it is so important to have hardware scopes, so you can calibrate your monitor and your video after it leaves your computer.

First, set the pluge (pronounced plooj, not plug), which stands for Picture Line Up Generator. Pluge is the array of black squares on the bottom of the color bars. They help you calibrate your monitor to the correct NTSC black level specification of 7.5IRE. In the black swatch along the bottom, there are a set of three slightly different values of black. The bar farthest to right of the three should be slightly lighter than the others, set to 11.5 units. The two black areas to the left should be indistinguishable.

1. Turn up the brightness on your monitor until you can tell them apart. The bar in the middle should be correct NTSC black, while the one to the left is set to zero black.

2. Turn the brightness back down just until you can't see the separation between the zero block and the 7.5. That's the point you're shooting for.

3. Next set the white level to 75, using the white bar on the left side of the color bars. The bright white square in the bottom portion of the screen should reach 100. You may have to retweak the black settings.

4. Next set the color. Adjust the chroma so the bars shoot out to the targets on the vectorscope.

5. Finally, set the phase dial so that the bars fall onto the right color targets on the vectorscope. If one or more of the bars is outside the tolerance range by a good way, it might be time for a new monitor or at least to get it serviced by a technician.

image. From the top the buttons are **Auto White**, **Auto Contrast** and **Auto Black**.

Open the sequence called *Color*. The first clip is a still image called *Color1*, which is probably a bit darker than it should be. If you look at the **Histogram** (Figure 10.33), you'll see that the mass of the picture information is down toward the dark end of the scale. (Ignore the spike of black on the left. That's the blanking on the edge of the video frame that we saw in the lesson on transitions.)

To correct the image, apply the simple **Color Corrector** filter, open the visual panel, and click the **Auto Contrast** button, the middle of the three-button stack. This will shift the contrast up the scale a bit (Figure 10.34). There is less of a hill at the dark end of the range and a bit of a plateau in the brighter areas. But still more work needs to be done on it.

The blacks aren't bad, but we want to raise the mids and the whites. Start with the mids, and then do the same for the whites Push up the sliders until you get just a touch of red zebra on the roof of the van, and then back it off a bit. Remember, as with almost all FCP sliders, if you hold down the **Command** key you'll "gear down" the drag, giving you finer control.

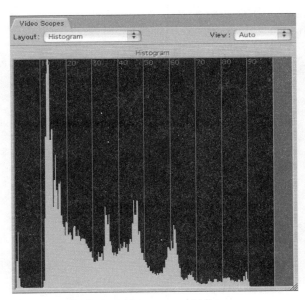

Figure 10.33 Color1 Uncorrected Histogram

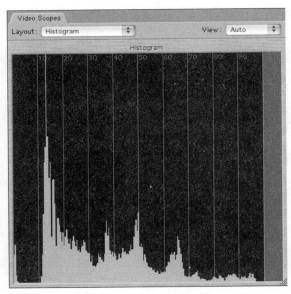

Figure 10.34 Color1 Auto Contrast Histogram

Color2 in the *Color* sequence shows the image improved. This is the basic process for color correction. It should always being with setting the luminance values first before adjusting the color.

Color3 is an image that's overexposed rather than underexposed. Use it to try your hand at reversing the process.

Color Corrector obviously is for color as well as luminance and contrast. Take a look at *Color4* in the sequence. Something's certainly gone wrong here. It looks like the white balance hasn't been set correctly. **CC** is the easiest tool to fix this.

First start with the **Auto Contrast** button, and then set your luminance levels with the **Histogram**. It's not going to take much work. The exposure is correct; just the color is wrong.

Take a look at the **Vectorscope** (Figure 10.35), though you don't need it to tell you what's wrong. It's too blue. The mass of the color information is shifted toward the blue side of the monitor.

What we're going to do is pick white in the picture and use that to set the correct color balance. There are a couple of tricks to this. First, take the **Saturation** slider and crank it way to the right, terribly oversaturating the image. What this simply does is to emphasize any color cast in the image, making it easier to pick

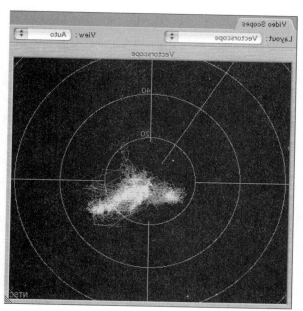

Figure 10.35 Vectorscope of Blue Cast Image

out what's wrong. The second trick is to find the right bit of white. The temptation is to use something that's very bright, but the problem is that what's very bright often is quite washed out and has almost no color information in it. Look for something that's white but not at full luminance or something that's neutral gray. Here's how you do it with **Color Corrector.**

1. Just to the bottom left of the **Balance** wheel is a tiny **Eyedropper.** Use this to pick something in the scene that should be white or gray. In this image there isn't really anything that's very oversaturated, so I'd pick something off the white of the roof of the van.

This will immediately pull the color back toward a truer representation of the image. You'll also notice that the button in the center of the **Balance** wheel has shifted toward the red direction. When I pulled the white, it gave the image a slightly more magenta tinge than I would have liked. Again, this was apparent because the **Saturation** was turned up. You'll want to fine tune the color more toward the yellow-red direction of the **Balance** wheel.

2. Before you do that, slide the **Saturation** slider back down to normal, and you'll see the image is close to coming good.

3. Finally, push the **Balance** button in the center of the **Balance** wheel a little farther to yellow-red. I also swung the **Hue** wheel a bit around to yellow.

There's a little gotcha here. All the color wheels are by default "geared down." So you have to move the button a lot to get any effect. In the color wheels, like **Balance,** you use the **Command** key to "gear up." This is the only place in FCP that this occurs. It's done this way because colorists prefer the fine control of a geared down track ball.

Color5 shows the corrected image as I did it. It's acceptable, I think, and certainly better than the original.

For greater control of the color of the image, we'll need FCP's next effect, **Color Corrector 3-way,** which is where we'll look at the bottom part of the **Color Corrector** controls called **Limit Effect,** more usually called secondary color correction.

Tip

Color Balance: If you want to color balance two cameras or two shots that have a slightly different color cast, open one shot into the **Viewer** and go its **Visual** control panel while the playhead in the **Timeline** is parked over the shot to be color corrected. Now select the shot you want to match it to and open it into a new **Viewer** (Shift-Enter). You can now use the **White Balance Eyedropper** to pick white out of the second shot in the new **Viewer**. You're now balancing the white of one shot to the white of the other. It's a good first step in color matching.

Color Corrector 3-way

Take a look at the visual panel controls (Figure 10.36). Instead of one color balance wheel, there are three wheels, for blacks, mids and whites, each with its own eyedropper. The sliders beneath the color wheels control the luminance for blacks, mids, and whites. The Auto control buttons are clustered horizontally in the middle. Below that is a long **Saturation** slider.

Take a look at *Color6* in the *Color* sequence. This was the same shot as *Color4* and *Color5*. I used the same procedure as I did for *Color5*:

1. Set the **Auto Contrast.**

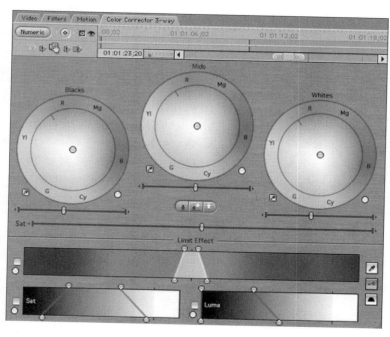

Figure 10.36 Color Corrector 3-way Controls

2. Crank up the **Saturation**.

3. With the **White Eyedropper**, pick the white from the roof of the van.

4. Turned down the **Saturation**.

5. Adjust each of the color wheels starting with **White**, moving it toward yellow-red.

6. Do the same for the **Mids** wheel and for the **Blacks** wheel.

With this kind of color control, I can not only bring the color in to acceptable levels, but I can also make it match — or come pretty close to matching — the color and look of another shot. Compare *Color6*, which started out blue, with *Color2*. They're not identical, and I'm sure an expert colorist could make them match better with these tools, but it's not too bad, I think.

When it comes to matching shots, FCP has given this version of the application some handy new shortcuts for switching between clips (Table 10.1). They all work around the **Control** key and are used to switch to specific places in the **Timeline**. What's neat is that they only switch to that point while the keys are held down. When released, the playhead leaps back to its previous position in the **Timeline**, so you can flick back and forth between two shots. I find the first two the most useful because they let you toggle back and forth between exactly the frames you want to look at, which often isn't the beginning or the ends of shots.

Color Persistence

Video works on the basis of persistence of vision, the retina holding onto one image as the next is displayed, creating the impression of smooth motion. Persistence of vision also effects color perception. If you stare at a face against a pale blue ground, and then turn away, you will see for a moment a negative of the face burned into your vision. Because your retina retains color information like this, most colorists carry color neutral charts they can look at while they're working. Sheets of pure white, or pure midtone gray, that have no color values or tints are used to "reset" their retinas. A few moments of looking at a color free image can help you achieve a consistent balance in your color control.

In addition, your eyes tire. It's important to change the luminance and focal distance of what you're looking at. Do this regularly while you're working. Take eye breaks often. Stare out the window at something far away. Close your eyes and look at the back of your eyelids for a while. It's important to maintaining your vision and color perception.

Table 10.1 Shortcuts for Switching between Clips

Control-Left arrow	In point marked in the Timeline
Control-Right arrow	Out point marked in the Timeline
Control-Up arrow	Out point of the shot before
Control-Shift-Up arrow	Out point two shots before
Control-Down arrow	In point of the next shot
Control-Shift-Down arrow	In point of the shot after next

Take a look at shots *Color7* and *Color8* in the *Color* sequence. This is a typical exposure/color problem. The close-up has pretty good exposure for the face, but the sky seems washed out. The medium shot shows a blue sky, but the face is shadowed. Because of video's limited color and luminance range, exposure is often a compromise, especially on documentaries, where there is often no time or budget to fully light a scene.

You could try to correct one shot to match the other, but it's probably best to adjust both, and this is where secondary color correction, **Limit Effect**, becomes really useful (Figure 10.37).

The controls show a **Color Range** slider at the top and below that, a **Sat** (saturation) control on the left and a **Luma** (luminance) control on the right. Each has a round radio button that allows you to reset the parameter and a square checkbox that lets you toggle the parameter on and off.

On the right are three important buttons. At the top is the critical **Eyedropper**. Below that, in the middle, is a three-way toggle switch with a **Key** icon. Its default position is colored gray, which shows the final output of the image. Click it and it will change to

Figure 10.37 Limit Effect

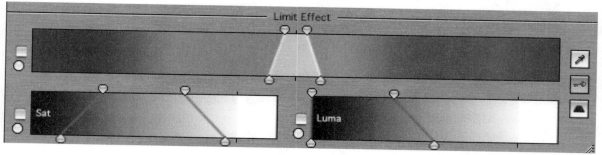

white, which will show you a black and white representation of what you're keying. Click it again and the button goes blue, which shows you the original source material. The bottom button with the keystone icon will invert the key, which can be very useful.

Let's see how these work in practice on *Color7*.

1. Start by running **Auto Contrast**. Make it a habit.

2. Next use the **Limit Effect Eyedropper** to pick some of the pale sky. Immediately all three controls in secondary color correction will become active.

3. Click the key button to toggle to see the grayscale image of the matte (Figure 10.38).

What's white is selected, and what's black is not.

Figure 10.38 Grayscale Matte Display

Obviously more work needs to be done. In each of the **Limit Effect** controls, there are handles that can be adjusted. Pulling the buttons on the top of the sliders will increase or decrease the range of the effect, while pulling on the buttons at the bottom of the slider will control the tolerance, how widely the control will be applied to adjacent colors.

Next we want to widen the **Color Range** and increase the tolerance controls.

4. Because the sky area is pretty low in chroma, we'll want to pull down the **Saturation** control and widen it. The **Luma** controls will have little effect.

At this stage you should have a fairly significant portion of the image selected (Figure 10.39, facing page). You'll also notice a bit of chunkiness in the sky, on the right side particularly.

5. To mitigate this, switch to the **Filter** tab, scroll down to the bottom to **Edge Control**, and push up the **Softening** slider, which will blur the matte (Figure 10.40).

6. Now that you've made the selection, go to the **Visual** panel, and in **Limit Effect**, switch the key button to show the output.

Tip

Limit Effect: If you hold down the **Shift** key you can click on multiple points and the **Limit Effect** controls will extend the range of values, color, saturation, or luminance as needed. Also, if you hold down the **Shift** key and stroke a line through the area you want to sample, the tool will use the range of values along the line to set up the **Limit Effect** controls.

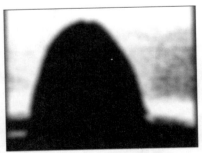

Figure 10.40 Softened Matte

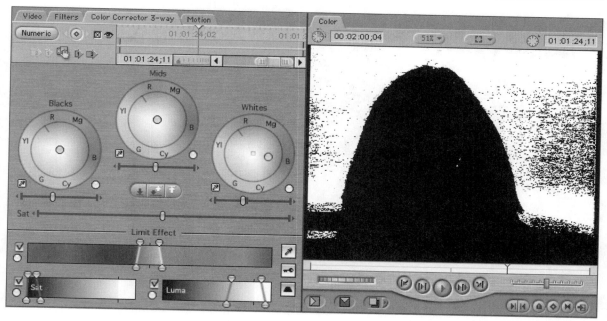

Figure 10.39 Controls and Matte Display

7. Finally, use the **Whites** color wheel to skew the selected area of the image strongly toward blue.

8. *Color9* will give you some idea of what can be done with these controls.

Tip

Correcting Multiple Clips: It's can often helpful to apply a filter like **CC 3-way** to a clip more than once. Using the **Limit Effect** controls, you can apply a color effect to a portion of the image, then selecting a slightly different chroma or luma value again, apply the same effect. This multiple iteration use of **CC 3-way** can give you great control over you work. This is where the **Numeric** display becomes really useful, because you can precisely copy the chroma and luma values from one filter to another, without trying to eyeball it.

Let's now do some work on *Color8*. The technique is almost exactly the same here.

1. We start by color picking the sky with the **Limit Effect Eye-dropper.**

2. Open up the **Color Range** controls, and widen the **Saturation** control and the **Luma** control.

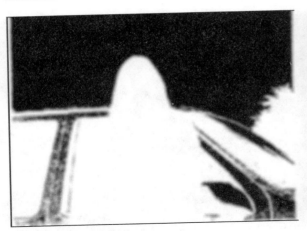

Figure 10.41 Matte Display

Figure 10.42 Matte Display

It doesn't matter if you pick up a great deal of the van. In effect, the more that's picked up, the better.

3. When you've got as much of the sky as you can, click the **Keystone** icon to invert the matte.

We're inverting the matte because we want to adjust the exposure on the woman's face. The problem is that if we simply turn up the exposure, the sky will wash out and lose its blue color. By inverting the selection, we can now work easily on the face and body and not affect the sky at all.

4. Once again, go to the **Filters** tab and turn up the **Softening** control so the matte isn't too harsh (Figure 10.41).

5. Finally, adjust the **Mids** slider to push up the values in the midrange of tonal values, brightening her face.

Color10 is my shot at the problem. This and *Color9* look pretty similar in tone and in sky color.

But color correction doesn't have to be used only for correction; it can also be used for useful purposes like costume changes. Take a look at *Color11* and *Color12*. The young woman's penchant for lime-green jackets can be attenuated by putting her in a more conservative tan color. This was done by using the **Color Corrector's Limit Effect** controls. I picked the jacket color with the **Eyedropper** and adjusted the **Color Range**, **Sat**, and **Luma** controls until I got most of the jacket area and even its reflection in the van's window. You can see in Figure 10.42 that some of the tree leaves were also picked up the matte. To cut out that portion of the image, I'd use a **f4-Point Garbage Matte**, but that's for the next lesson (page 453) on the rest of FCP's special effect filters.

Color correction is amazing in FCP, and you can easily spend hours endlessly tweaking color and luminance values long into the night.

 Tip _____

Removing Color: It's easy to make an image black and white or tinted using the **Color Corrector** or **CC 3-way**. Simply apply the filter and, as always, first run **Auto Contrast** and adjust the luminance levels using **Histogram** and **Waveform Monitor** as guides. Then drag the **Saturation** slider down to nothing. Pure black and white. To tint the image, apply **CC** or **CC 3-way** again. If you're using **CC**, push the **Balance** wheel toward the color you want to tint the image. If you're using **CC 3-way**, start by shifting the **Mids** in the direction in which you want to color the image. **CC 3-way** allows you to do interesting enhancements by tinting the **blacks** and **whites** to different parts of the spectrum. There are simpler ways to do this, using FCP's **Sepia** filter, for instance, which we'll see in the next lesson on page 473, but **CC** does give exceptional control.

Desaturate Highlights and Desaturate Lows

There are a few other filters in **Color Correction**. The next two are **Desaturate Highlights** and **Desaturate Lows**. I'm not sure why there are actually two of them. They both have the same controls, except one is toggled on and the other toggled off (Figure 10.43).

This filter is a quick way to attenuate chroma values in either the whites or the blacks of an image, with adjustable roll off. Notice the **Show Stats** checkbox at the bottom of the filter controls. If you have it checked on, and have both desaturated highlights and lows activated, you'll get a displace in the **Canvas** like Figure 10.44. This shows you roughly where the chroma roll-off begins for the lows and highs.

RGB Balance

The last filter in **Color Correction** is **RGB Balance**. This is a relatively simple tool that adjusts color values and works very well with the **Parade** when you're trying to adjust the color balance in shots from the same scene (Figure 10.45). Using **RGB Balance**, you can easily match colors from a two-camera shoot, though

Name	Parameters
▽ Video Filters	
▽ ☒ Desaturate Highlights	
	Highlight Desaturation
Enable	☑
Begin At	70
Softness	15
Amount of Desaturation	100
	Lows Desaturation
Enable	☐
Begin At	15
Softness	15
Amount of Desaturation	100
Show Stats	☐

Figure 10.43 Desaturate Highlights Controls

Figure 10.44 Shows Stats Display

most people would probably use **CC 3-way** for the full-featured luminance and chroma controls.

Keying

Keying is used to create mattes that cut out areas of the image. The three most common types are:

- Chromakeying
- Luminance keying
- Difference keying

Figure 10.45 RGB Balance Controls, Canvas, and Parade

FCP has tools to do these, but they really weren't very good in earlier versions of the application, but that has changed with the introduction of secondary color correction and a new **Chroma Keyer.**

The key to keying is to shoot it well. Poorly shot material just will not key properly. For chromakeying, the background blue or green screen must be evenly lit and correctly exposed so that the color is as pure as possible. Video, of course, and DV even more so, have many limitations of color depth and saturation that make good keying difficult. Because of the way the format works, DV actually keys green easier than it does blue.

In your copy of the *L10* project is a bin called **Keying,** which holds the elements we'll work with. Open the *Keying* sequence. This has a couple of still images to work with. On **V1** in the sequence is a still of the Stanford University clarion tower called *Background.pct*, while on **V2** is the image to chromakey called *Blue.pct*. The sequence is in the NTSC 640×480 format.

Chroma Keyer

If the material is properly shot and lit, there is really no trick to chromakeying in FCP. Ignore the legacy tools **Blue and Green Screen** and **Color Key.** I think these are here for when you're working on old projects that have these filters applied. If you do work on an old project with these tools, I'd suggest removing them and simply using the new **Chroma Keyer,** which has tools you should now be familiar with.

1. Apply **Chroma Keyer** to *Blue.pct* on **V2.**
2. Open the **Visual** panel into the **Viewer,** and you'll see the **Limit Effect** controls (Figure 10.46).
3. Click on the **Eyedropper,** click in the blue screen behind the flowers in the **Canvas,** and you're practically done.

Almost instantly the bulk of the blue has disappeared.

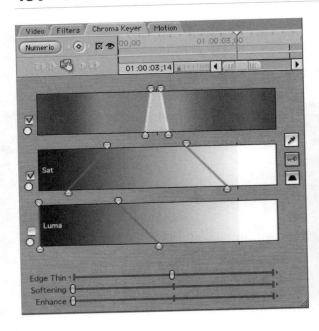

Figure 10.46 Chroma Keyer Controls

Figure 10.47 Matte Display

4. Check the matte by clicking on the **Matte/Key** icon. You'll see most of the background has been keyed out as in Figure 10.47.

5. Widen the **Color Range** slightly and reduce the **Luma** controls a bit, and you'll have a pretty good key (Figure 10.48).

If you look closely, though, you'll see a rather unnatural color fringe around the edges of the flower. This is fairly easy to get rid of.

6. Push up the **Edge Thin** control a bit.

7. At the very end of the **Softening** control is a tiny little triangle. Give it a few clicks. This will move **Softening** incrementally.

8. Try adding a little **Enhance**, but not too much, or the edges will start to turn yellow.

Matte Choker

Again, if the material is properly shot and lit there is really no trick to chromakeying in FCP. Adding another tool in the mix here may be helpful. For some reason I've never understood, the

Figure 10.48 Nearly Keyed Blue
Screen

Matte Choker isn't in the **Key** package, but in the **Matte** package, which we'll see in the next lesson on page 473. It's mostly commonly used as a keying tool, however, and adding it to the key will improve the image.

The controls are basically the same as the **Edge Thin** and **Softening** controls in the **Chroma Keyer** (Figure 10.49), but adding a second line of choking to the key's edges will make it easier to get a tight, sharp line between the edges and the background.

The **Edge** controls are not the greatest in the world, but all in all, the **Chroma Keyer** is a vast improvement over the earlier tools, which were a bit of an embarrassment. If you'll be doing a great deal of keying work, you might want to look at specialized, dedicated keying software such as Primate or Ultimatte for truly astonishing keying control. Or as an add-on package, Boris RED includes an outstanding keyer that works as a plugin within FCP.

Spill Suppressor-Blue and Spill Suppressor-Green

The **Spill Suppressors** are used if there a blue cast on the edges of the image (Figure 10.50). This often happens when you get

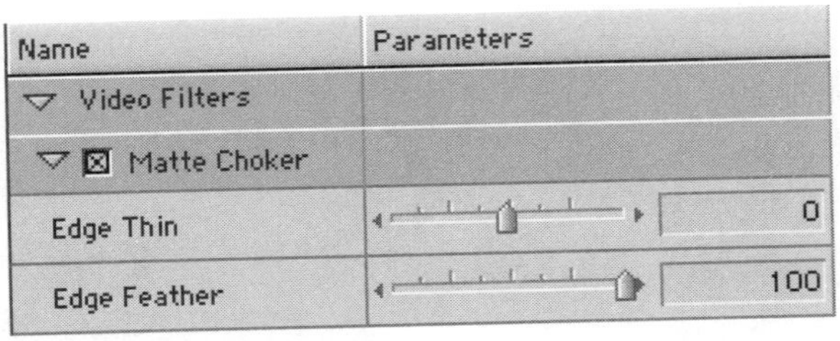

Figure 10.49 Matte Choker

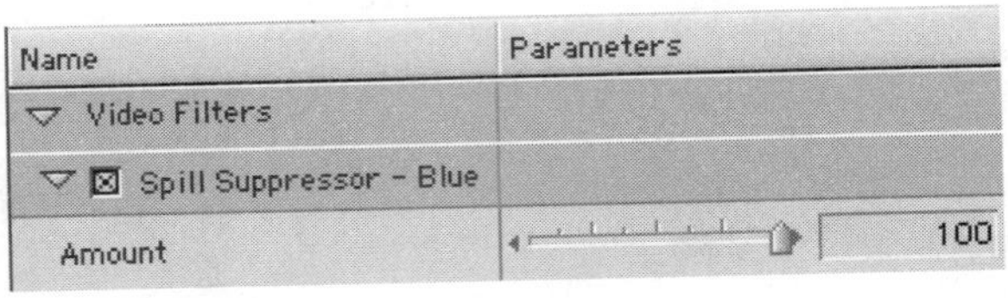

Figure 10.50 Spill Suppressor Control

reflected light for the blue screen wall falling on the edges of a curved object, like a person's shoulders. The **Spill Suppressor** takes the blue in the image and replaces it with black, like a shadow area. This is fine on the object you want to leave, but if the background color has not been keyed out sufficiently, it can leave a dark edging on the screen.

Lower the **Suppressor** slider substantially. Usually only a small amount will be sufficient to do the work.

Difference Matte

This filter works differently than the chromakeying tools. It calculates the differences between two images and keys out what's constant. If you can shoot a scene with exactly the same setup, once with the object you want to key around and once without, you can then use the **Difference Matte** to remove the background, leaving only the object, what's different between the two shots.

1. From the **Keying** bin place the image *Difference.pct* into the *Keying* sequence.

This is the image of the orchids with the Stanford picture behind it.

2. Apply the **Difference Matte** filter to it.

The image in the **Canvas** will simply disappear. In the **Filters** tab of the **Viewer**, you see a popup that lets you set the **Canvas** display (Figure 10.51). The four-up display shows the **Source**, **Difference Layer**, **Matte**, and **Final**, basically what the **Key** button toggles through in the **Color Corrector**.

3. To activate the matte, drop the still image *Background.pct* into the **Difference Layer Well**.

Figure 10.51 Difference Matte Controls and Canvas Four Screen Display

Immediately most of the image will disappear, including much of the flowers and vase.

4. To bring them back, reduce the **Threshold** slider.

With a little care, you will be left with the vase of orchids and nothing behind it, ready to have a piece of video dropped onto **V1**.

Luma Key

This keys out luminance values, either lighter, darker, or dissimilar (Figure 10.52). Again, there is a four-up display showing the various mattes and layers.

Luma keying almost never works properly because almost inevitably some darker or lighter area of the image will key out.

1. Drag the image *Luma.pct* from the **Keying** bin into the **Timeline** of the *Key* sequence, dropping it on **V2**.

2. Drag *Background.pct* onto **V1** to set something to view it against.

3. Apply **Luma Key**.

4. Change the **Key Mode** popup to **Key Out Darker**.

Figure 10.52 Luma Key Controls and Four Screen Display

Again, much of the image will disappear, including quite a bit of the vase. You'll have to drag down the **Threshold** value pretty low. Even at –100, you'll still be cutting out bits of the vase while leaving an unsightly black ring around the edges.

One interesting use of this filter is to copy the key to the RGB channel to create a silhouette.

Summary

FCP3 has brought to the table an astonishing array of world-class color correction tools. With practice and experience you can do pretty much anything you can imagine with color correction, not only correcting chroma and luma values, but using it to modify and enhance images, adding a warm glow to an image, turning it blue and cold, heightening to contrast for a sinister effect, or reduced it to a more natural look, enriching chroma to vibrant, eye-searing levels, or muting to a pale tonal values of the true image. By controlling portions of the image, adjusting them separately, you can change the whole look and feel of a video production.

Lesson 11

Adding Special Effects Filters

In this lesson we're going to look at and work with Final Cut's filters to create some special effects. FCP offers a great variety of excellent effects, some new to FCP3. In addition, other programmers are creating effects using FCP's FXBuilder, such as the collection of filters written by Klaus Eiperle, who wrote the new filters for FCP3. A demo version of his next collection of filters **CGM DV Vol. 2+** is included in the *Extras* folder of the CD. These filters are well worth investing in and provide many useful tools such as **TimeWarp**, which gradually changes the speed of clips. There is also a collection of free filters from Mattias Sandström called TMTS Free.

FCP also has the ability to use third-party plugin effects based on the Adobe After Effects plugin architecture. There are various packages, such as those from Boris Effects, RED, Continuum, and FX, that give the application fantastic capabilities. With OS X, only those AE plugins written specifically for or upgraded to work with the new operating system can be used in OS X. Earlier plugins, such as Final Effects, will only work in OS9. For this lesson, we'll confine ourselves to the FCP built-in effects package, including the new groups of **FXScript DVE's**. If you have not

435

already done so, you should install the new **FXScript DVE's** that came with FCP3. Just run the installer and check the box for **FXScript DVE's from CGM.**

Inside *Extras* folder on the book's CD, there is a folder called *CGM DVE Vol.1.1*, which contains updates for some of the current CGM filters. You should copy these plugins into the folder containing the CGM DVE's, replacing the current ones. The CGM filters normally install into the folder *Library/Application Support/Final Cut Pro Support/Plugins/FXScript DVEs by CGM.*

Loading the Lesson

One more time, let's begin by loading the material you need onto your media drive.

1. If you don't already have it there, drag over the *Media1* folder from the CD.

2. Also drag onto your system drive the folder *Lesson 11.*

3. Eject the CD, open the *Lesson 11* folder on your hard drive and double-click the project file, *L11*, to launch the application.

4. After you've reconnected the media, what's the very first step we take, boys and girls? Yes, that's right, we set the **Scratch Disk Preferences** to the *Media1* folder, as well as setting the *AutoSave Vault* location to the *Shared* folder.

5. And the next step? Yes, we use **Save Project As** and give the project a new name.

Inside your project copy, you'll find the usual suspects in the **Browser, Clips** bin, *Damine.mov,* and other files. Two of the sequences are called *Effects Builder* and *Effects Builder 2.* These demonstrate some of the filters we'll see in this lesson. You can copy and save the settings of these effects in your **Favorites** bin and use them with your own media.

As we go through the lesson, I'll show you how the effects in these two sequences were made. Let's begin by opening up the empty *Sequence 1* and dragging one of the clips from the **Clips** bin into it. Why don't we start with *Dance2?*

Renamed Slugs in a Favorites Sequence

Favorites are a great way to save effects, because you can not only save them as their default settings, but you can also save them as an effects pack, a number of effects that work together to produce a result. It's simple to do.

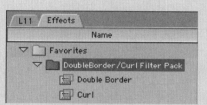

Figure 11.1   Modify>Make Favorite Effect

1. Apply the effects and adjust them as you as you want them.

2. Then with the **Filters** tab of the **Viewer** open, but without any of the effects selected in the **Viewer**, go to the **Modify** menu and chose **Make Favorite Effect** (Figure 11.1).

3. The effects will appear as a folder in the **Favorites** bin, where you can rename it anything you want (Figure 11.2).

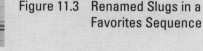

Figure 11.2   Filter Pack in Favorites Bin

This sounds great, but it has a serious downside, which is that **Favorites** are part of the application's preferences. So if you have to trash your prefs file, your favorites are gone with it.

1. Another way to do this is to create a *Favorites* sequence, a new sequence with a slug in it.

2. Cut the slug up into short sections, and apply the filter stack to a portion of the slug.

3. You can rename the slugs appropriately in its **Item Properties (Command-9)** as in Figure 11.3.

4. Just keep the *Favorites* sequence and move it from project to project, and keeping a separate project with these kinds of elements in a project backup folder.

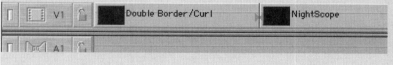

Figure 11.3   Renamed Slugs in a Favorites Sequence

You may have thought there were a lot of transitions. There are even more filters — 104 of them, in fact — some of which we've already seen in the previous lesson. There are still quite a few to look at. One of the reasons there are so many filters, I believe, is that many still remain solely to support legacy projects created on older versions of the application. This is an admirable thought, but I think it leads to a great deal of confusion. Personally I would prefer if only the current versions of filters were normally installed, while legacy filters were a separate installation if needed, much as the **Boris Calligraphy** or the **FXScript DVE's** are installed. Because there is now so much redundancy, I will only look closely at those filters that I think are still useful. At the end of the lesson on page 503 is a table of all the normally included 104 filters that will tell you which filters have more useful current versions. Let's begin by looking at the first folder of effects.

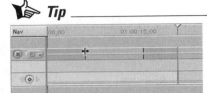

Figure 11.4 Selecting Effect's Range in the Keyframe Graph

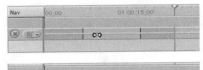

Figure 11.5 Slipping the Effect's Range in the Keyframe Graph

> ⇨ *Tip*
>
> **Partially Filtered:** You can actually add a filter to only a section of the length of a clip, which can be useful if you want to ramp up an effect, while most of the length of the shot remains unchanged. To avoid having to render out the entire shot, you can apply the filter by selecting a section of the clip you want to affect with the **Range Selection** tool (**GGG**). Stroke along the clip, or group of clips, or sections of the Timeline to select those that you want to affect. Choose the filter from the **Effects** menu, and you'll immediately see that only the portion of the Timeline picked with **Range Selection** will change render color to red, green, or yellow, as appropriate. You can also limit the range of the effect in the **Viewer** using the **Keyframe Graph**. There are two thin black lines that normally default to the ends of the clip, but you can grab them and pull them to limit the section of the clip that the filter will affect (Figure 11.4). If you grab the horizontal bar, the **Filter Start/End Bar**, between the two black lines you'll get the **Slip** tool cursor (Figure 11.5), which will allow you to slip the affected area forward and back along the **Keyframe Graph**.

Blur

The longer I do effects work, the more surprised I am at how many ways there are to blur something. FCP only has four of them, however.

Gaussian Blur

Gaussian (pronounced gousian), named after the 19th century German mathematician, Karl Friedrich Gauss, produces a smooth blurring of the image. This blur does more, though, than softening the picture. It allows you to blur channels separately through a popup (Figure 11.6).

Figure 11.6 Gaussian Blur Controls

Selecting different channels can produce some interesting and unusual effects. If you want to blur the **Red** and **Green** channels, just apply the effect twice, once selecting red and the other time green.

Try blurring one color channel to 20, and apply the effect again. In the second effect, blur the **Luminance** the same amount. The order in which the effects are applied always makes a difference. Don't assume that because you apply **Luminance Gaussian** and **Blue Gaussian** you get the same effect by applying them the other way around. FCP processes the filters from the top down as they're stacked in the **Filters** tab. If you blur **Luminance** first, the color values smear, and you'll get less impact than if you blur the color value first.

Try it on *Dance2*. It doesn't reproduce well in grayscale, but I've set it up in the first clip of the sequence called *Effects Builder*. A word of caution: be careful with blurring the **Luminance** value of an image. It can produce nasty blotchiness.

It's simple to change the stack order in the **Filters** tab and consequently, the order in which the filters are processed. Just grab one and pull it up or down in the stack to the position you want and the order will change.

In **Gaussian Blur,** the slider goes up to 100, which will make a video clip blurry and soft-looking. The real power of the blur is seen when you apply it to text. Even large text with **Gaussian** at 100 will be dissipated to a mere wisp. It's a nice way to bring text in and out, a variation from a simple fade-up. I've set it up on the second clip with a text file in *Effects Builder* at Marker 2. I used **Opacity** to simply finish off the effect so that it disappears completely.

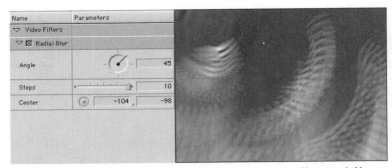

Figure 11.7 Radial Blur Settings and Result

Gaussian is not, however, a camera blur, so the effect is different from that of a camera going out of focus, which produces circles of confusion around highlights. If a camera goes far enough out of focus, it will actually resolve itself to sharp-edged polygons based on the lens' aperture. **Gaussian Blur** is a smooth blurring of all values selected in the popup.

Radial Blur

This is an okay effect, especially when animated. The controls are limited, however, and it isn't as well done as it could be (Figure 11.7).

The dial at zero produces no blurring effect. It only goes up to 90°. Beyond that, it's just repeating itself. **Radial** uses the same step system we saw in **Motion Blur**, and it's not very good. **Radial** does not produce the smooth, circular blur of Photoshop's **Radial Blur**. It does have a **Center** point control so that you can set where in the image the **Radial** spins. Try animating this so that it moves around the screen.

Wind Blur

Wind looks similar to **Radial**, except that it's unidirectional. It's also stepped, unfortunately. The dial in **Wind** lets you select anywhere in the 360° compass for a direction. An interesting effect is to use **Wind** doubled — once to the left, once to the right — and to animate it to make a streaky blur text coming into focus and then going back out. It's an interesting animated effect on titles.

Look at the third clip in *Effects Builder* at Marker 3. I applied Wind twice, once to the left at 270° and once to the right at 90°.

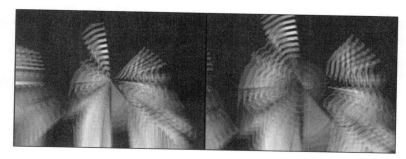

Figure 11.8 Left: Zoom Out
Amount 50
Right: Zoom In
Amount 50

The smearing appears to come from both sides and join in the middle.

Zoom Blur

Zoom is the other half of Photoshop's **Radial** effects filter. FCP's **Radial** is the **Spin** half of the PS **Radial** effect; **Zoom** is the other half. Also a stepped effect, here it's actually quite effective, though you really do have to max out the step values while punching up the amount to make it look decent (Figure 11.8).

Most of these stepped filters, like **Zoom** and **Wind**, often need a little help from **Blur** to reduce the hard edges. **Blur** gives a smooth smearing of the image.

Favorites

Favorites has great value here, perhaps more so than in Transitions. After you've applied all your effects and their settings in the order you want them, use **Command-A** in the **Filters** panel of the **Viewer** to select all the effects. Then hit **Option-F** to **Make Favorites**. All the effects will go into the **Favorites** bin. Because **Favorites** doesn't honor alphanumeric ordering, the effects will remain in stack order with the settings you created. I like to hold groups of effects in a separate bin inside **Favorites**. **Favorites** also remembers animation settings, so if you include keyframed effects changes, these get stored as well. Also note that in OS X, your Preferences, and therefore your Favorites are part of one user's folder and are not available to other users of FCP, even though the project is in the *Shared* folder and available to all users. This is another reason why I like to keep effects attached to a slug or other placeholder in a sequence and keep a sequence with settings in the order I like. I can easily move the effects sequence from project to project. A little oddness: you can't keep a sequence inside **Favorites**, but you can make a new bin inside **Favorites** and keep a sequence inside that bin.

Border

There are two **Borders**:

- Basic
- Bevel

It's important to note that these **Borders** both cut into the image. They do not extend the borders around the bounding box of the image. They're a nice touch to Picture-in-Picture effects (PIPs) and can be used to mask those nasty black edges we talked about in the previous lesson. If you really do need the maximum size of your frame, you could nest the image in a sequence with a slightly larger frame size and then apply the **Border** in the final sequence, using the extra size as room for either a **Basic** or **Bevel** filter.

Basic

As basic as it gets: it just adds a colored border. The controls give you a color picker and the **Border Amount**. The default value of 5 is very thin. You'll probably want to push it up a bit. Oddly, there is no opacity control or fade control for the border; you can't do a feathered inner edge.

Bevel

Strangely, **Bevel** does have an **Opacity** controller. I would have thought it would be the other way around — **Basic** had opacity, while **Bevel** didn't. If you max out the bevel width, you'll fill your image with a pyramid-like effect (Figure 11.9), which might make an interesting reveal for someone.

The color picker is called **Light Color**, like the color of a gel a lighting director might put over a light that's falling across the beveled edges. You can of course also set the angle the light is falling from.

Figure 11.9 Bevel Border with a Width of 87

Channel

The six **Channel** effects allow you an amazing degree of control of color and compositing. We'll look more closely at compositing in Lesson 12 on page 509, but here the **Channel** effects allow you to combine clips and apply color effects to them combined with compositing modes.

Arithmetic

This is a basic **Channel** effect. It composites a color, which can be animated, to any one of the color channels **R**, **G**, or **B**, or all three combined, using one of the compositing modes on a popup (Figure 11.10).

FCP calls them **Operators**, but they are really compositing modes. In the *Arithmetic* sequence in your **Browser**, I have laid out a short clip of *Dance3* 12 times. Each clip has a different **Operator** mode applied to its RGB value using the default color, gray. Look through these to get a basic idea of how the **Operators** work. Most of the **Operators** such as **Add**, **Subtract**, **Darken**, and **Lighten** are commonly known, but there are a couple of unusual **Operators**, **Ceiling** and **Floor**, that produce interesting results. Remember these are only compositing with the color you select, not with the anything else.

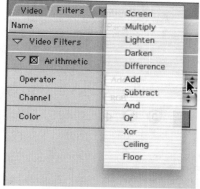

Figure 11.10 Arithmetic Channels Popup

Channel Blur

I confess I can't tell you what this effect gives you that multiple copies of **Gaussian Blur** don't already, except the ability to blur more than one channel at a time (Figure 11.11). In fact, as you can see from the popup, **Gaussian** can blur more elements than the **Channel Blur** sliders.

Channel Offset

If **Channel Blur** is pointless, **Channel Offset** and **Color Offset** are cool. You can easily take them to great extremes, and strange effects will happen, especially if you use the **Repeat Edges** popup. The fourth clip in the *Effects Builder* sequence shows you **Channel Offset** as applied in Figure 11.12.

The fifth clip in *Effects Builder* uses much smaller offsets for each channel, but animates them rapidly. An After Effects-type **Wiggler** would be really useful here, but it can be done by hand, though

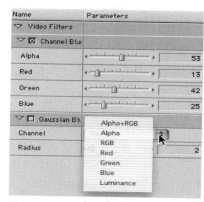

Figure 11.11 Channel Blur Together with Gaussian Blur

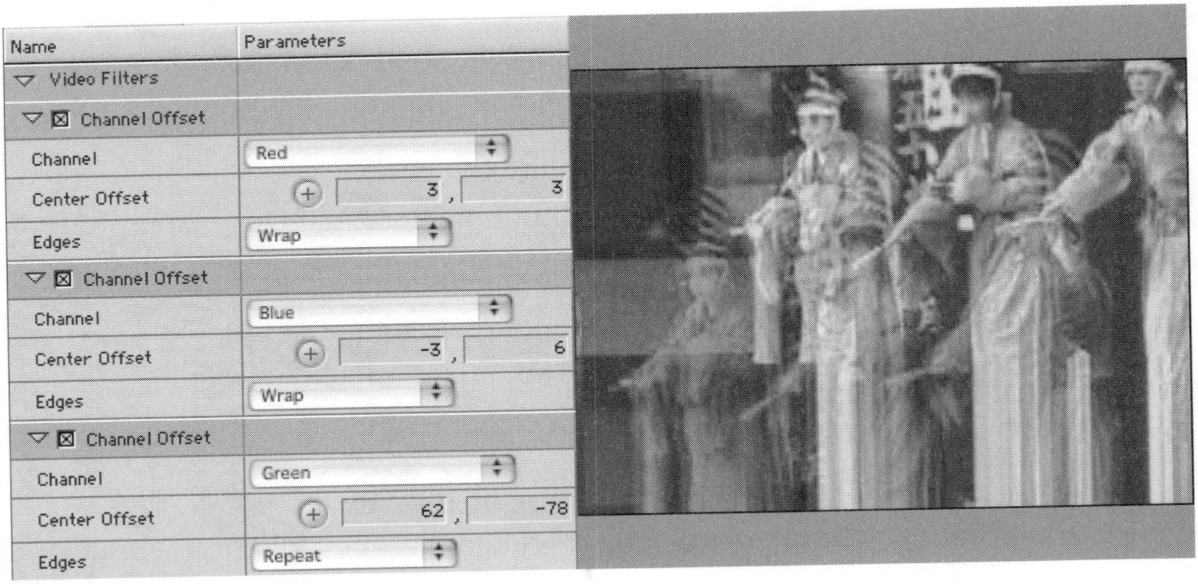

Name	Parameters
▽ Video Filters	
▽ ☒ Channel Offset	
Channel	Red
Center Offset	⊕ 3 , 3
Edges	Wrap
▽ ☒ Channel Offset	
Channel	Blue
Center Offset	⊕ -3 , 6
Edges	Wrap
▽ ☒ Channel Offset	
Channel	Green
Center Offset	⊕ 62 , -78
Edges	Repeat

Figure 11.12 Channel Offset Three Times with Channel with Large Offset and Repeat

laboriously. You just have to **Copy** and **Paste Attributes** using **Scale To Time**. Or you could cut up the clip in six-second long sections and paste attributes into each. Then the speed of the wiggling offset would not change.

Color Offset

The **Color Offset** controls allow you to offset the hue of each of the RGB channels (Figure 11.13). The default **Overflow** popup is set to **Invert** the color of the image. This happens when all sliders are pushed to their full value of 256. In **Invert** mode, dragging the sliders back down to zeros on all sliders will bring the clip back to its normal state. With the popup set to **Wrap**, the sliders act as a color wheel. Either end of the slider will produce normal color, while the center produces the greatest deviation. With a little bit of animation here you'll feel as if you're right back in the 60s, psychedelic city, man.

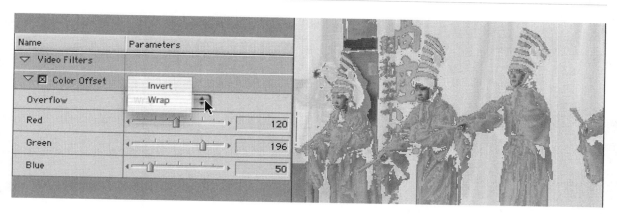

Figure 11.13 Color Offset Controls
Using Wrap

Compound Arithmetic

This is another potentially great effect gone bad because the **Well** doesn't function properly (Figure 11.14). It's unfortunate that video clips dropped into the **Well** don't produce motion but simply stick on the first frame of the clip. This happens regardless of the icon keyframe set in the **Browser** and regardless of the clip's In point. The correct frame appears in the **Well**, but the wrong frame appears in the **Canvas**.

This seems to be a bug that has persisted since FCP2. Other **Wells** will accept the In point, but for some reason, **Compound Arithmetic** does not seem to do so. It always wants to take the first frame of the media. The only way this can be overcome is to create a subclip with a new start point. This will force a new first frame and load that frame into the **Well**. **CA** lets you blend the still frame, image, or text file using one of the 12 **Operators** we saw in Arithmetic.

Without an image in the **Well**, the **Operator** popup produces little effect. It does not change by compositing with the layer below, simply with itself. If an image is in the **Well**, the **Operator** will apply to the image. Try it with text such as that on the sixth clip in *Effects Builder*.

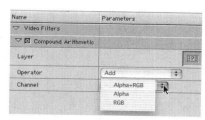

Figure 11.14 Compound
Arithmetic Controls

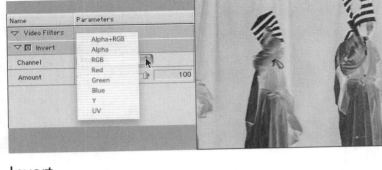

Figure 11.15 Invert Controls

Invert

Invert is the last of the **Channel** effects. You can not only invert the color of the image, but you can invert selectively choosing from a popup (Figure 11.15).

Notice that you can change the Y value separately from UV as well as each of the color channels and the alpha channel. Inverting the alpha channel 100% does nothing. You would think it would affect the opacity of the image, but it has no effect at all. Inverting the alpha channel of a text file produced in FCP produces a jagged-edged text over black. Inverting the alpha of Photoshop file is cleaner (Figure 11.15).

Figure 11.16 Photoshop File Over Clip with Invert Alpha Effect Applied

By inverting the alpha of the text block, you allow the underlying image to show through. The black you see is not transparent, however. We'll look at showing letters through text over transparency in a later lesson on compositing (see page 528).

If you combine **Invert** with the **Desaturate** filter, which we'll see on page 472, you can produce the look of a black-and-white negative photograph.

Color Correction

We have already looked at the **Color Correction** filters in the previous lesson.

Distort

The **Distort** effects have some real gems in them, some of which can be used in subtle ways.

Bumpmap

Bumpmapping and displacement are common tools in compositing and special effects. Neither this effect, nor the **Displace** filter, which we'll see in a moment, should be used unless you're working on an old project. They have both been superseded by **FXScript DVE's Displace** filter, which adds a versatile new tool to FCP's filters. All of these effects are most useful for creating motion in images, and are often used to create movement on background layers for motion graphics.

Bumpmap will displace an image based on the values of a grayscale image. The image is dropped in the **Well**, and the amount of displacement is set with a slider (Figure 11.17).

Ignore the **Luma Scale** slider for the moment. The real controls are the **Outset** slider and the **Direction** dial. The **Bumpmap** controls work like **Drop Shadow** controls: **Setting**, **Angle**, and **Amount**. The distortion is created by shifting the portions of the video image based on the grayscale of the image in the **Well**. The closer to white the **Well** image, the more the shifting will occur. The darker part of the image will shift less. The grossest distortion will be in areas of pure white, with no distortion at all in areas of black. In Figure 11.17 the image in the **Well** is a gradient from white in the lower right corner to black in the upper left.

Figure 11.17 Bumpmap Controls With
Result on the Right

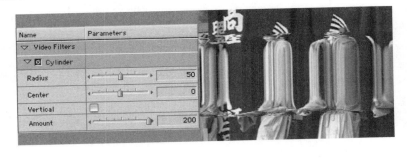

Figure 11.18 Cylinder Effect and Resulting Image

The resulting image shows the bottom right area of the picture heavily distorted, while the upper left has no displacement at all.

The image is shifted up toward the center of the screen, with maximum **Outset**. If the little **Repeat Edge** checkbox hadn't been clicked, the lower right corner would be black; the repeat extends the frame to the edges like a smear of colors.

The values **Outset** and **Direction** can be animated. Unfortunately, the map that's bumping can't; it's always a still frame.

Luma Scale adds to the mix the visibility of the grayscale luminance map in the **Well**. The white portions will show in the video; the black portions will be transparent and unseen.

Cylinder

Cylinder isn't really cylindrical. It doesn't actually wrap the image around a cylinder, which would be quite neat and useful for generating DVE transitions (Figure 11.18). The only sense that the distortion is cylindrical is that it's more smeared in the center of the distortion and more shifted at the edges.

The controls let you adjust the **Amount** with a slider and the **Radius**, which sets the amount of separation between the curved parts of the image. Setting either value to zero will produce no distortion. The **Center** control will shift the effect along the axis, in the case of the default position, the shift will be along the *y* axis. By clicking the vertical checkbox, the cylinder will be vertical and the **Center** control will affect the *x* axis.

Figure 11.19 Displace Controls with Resulting Image

Displace

When comparing Figure 11.19 to Figure 11.17, you can see that it's difficult to tell the difference between **Displace** and **Bumpmap**. They function in exactly the same fashion except that the controls are built into two sliders, **Horizontal** and **Vertical**, as opposed to the **Direction** dial and the **Outset** amount. The only difference is that **Displace** lets you push the slider up to 200 in either direction, while **Bumpmap** has an offset of only 100. If the values in Figure 11.19 had been set to −100 and 100, the image distortions would have been the same. Neither should be used, but rather the superior **FXScript DVE's Displace** filter.

Fisheye

Fisheye is a neat effect. It bulges the image outward, or if the **Amount** slider is pushed into negative numbers, the image sucks into a point, as shown in Figure 11.20.

Radius controls how wide the fisheye effect is, while **Amount** obviously controls the bulge or suck value. **Center** positions the bulge and is animatable. Look at the seventh clip in *Effects Builder.* Animating the Center point makes the bulge look as if it were a magnifying glass moving across the screen. If you animate the Center far enough out beyond the edge of the image, the

11.20 Fisheye Controls with Resulting Image

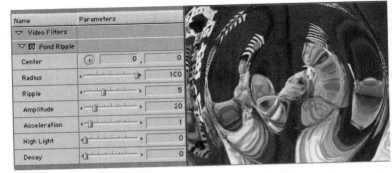

Figure 11.21 Default Pond Ripple
Effect with Controls

Fisheye will have no effect. Reducing either the **Radius** or the **Amount** to zero or moving the Center way off the screen somewhere will eliminate the effect. Animating the **Amount** value up and down will give the image a pulsating look, like a heart throbbing. Try setting the keyframe to a musical beat, low **Amount** on the offbeat, a large value on the beat. Use the waveform of the music, either in the **Viewer** or in the **Timeline** (**Command-Option-W**).

Pond Ripple

As you see from Figure 11.21, **Pond Ripple** is a neat effect, with a nice amount of control. It's similar to the **Ripple Dissolve**, but here the ripple will continue for the duration of the clip. Look at the clip at Marker 8 in *Effects Builder*. It shows the **Pond Ripple** starting from nothing, rising, and then dying away. The ramp of the ripple is created by raising the **Radius** over time. This works well to start the ripple movement. The ripple doesn't fade out as nicely, however. Because the ripple is not a true generator, ramping down the ripple only makes it retreat back to its origin point if you reduce the **Radius** value. It reduces in strength if you lower the **Amplitude** down to zero. Animating the **Amplitude** is the more pleasing effect, I think. It would be nice if the ripple were a true generator so that it stopped producing wave action and the waves simply dissipated as they spread away from the center point. That would look better, more natural than the current behavior.

Most of the controls will quickly push the rippling up to very exaggerated levels. The **Radius** slider controls how far out the ripples go. Less than a 100 won't make it across from corner to cor-

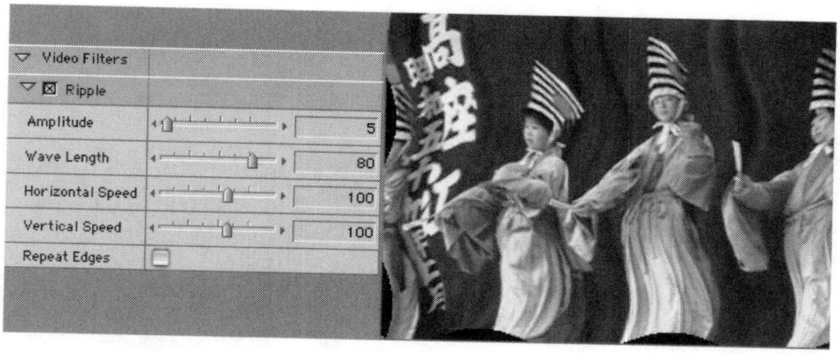

Figure 11.22 Ripple Controls with Affected Image

ner, regardless of the size of the format you're working in. If you push the **Ripple** number much above five, there quickly won't be any troughs between the ripples. **Amplitude** broadens the distorted part of the image, and again will quickly fill in the troughs. **Acceleration** is in the Ferrari league. Give it any amount above the default value and the ripples will fly across the screen. **High Light** adds a gray banding around the distortion rings. Unfortunately, the high lighting appears on both sides of the wave rather than on one side, as if it were coming from a light source. This can pretty well kill the effect. **Decay**, on the other hand has remarkably little effect, only reducing the **Amplitude** even slightly when set to its full level.

Ripple

Ripple creates a waviness across the screen (Figure 11.22). The wave is controlled primarily with **Amplitude** and **Wave Length**, which is frequency. At the top end of **Wave Length**, the ripples are smooth, gentle curve, while at the low end, around **1**, the image looks as if it had electricity shot through it. At that setting, **Ripple** creates terrible interlace flicker in video and is almost painful to watch.

There is both horizontal and vertical rippling, controlled with the speed sliders. These are positive and negative speeds, forward and backward. Positive horizontal motion is left to right; negative, right to left. For vertical motion, positive is downward; negative is upward. If you set speeds of zero, you'll get waves that don't move. The default settings of 100 will give you pretty leisurely movement in the wave. For real speed, you'll need to push the sliders close to maximum.

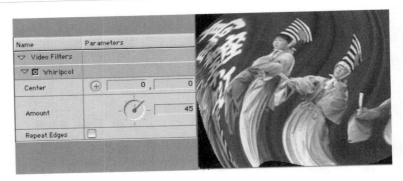

Figure 11.23 Whirlpool with Affected Image

Wave

This filter is half of **Ripple**. The wave motion is only in one direction, either horizontal or vertical, and is set with a checkbox. The default **Wave Length** of 100 is a slow, lazy wave, almost like a giant flag. The default **Amplitude** of 10, down near the left edge of the slider, is pretty big, especially if you bring the **Wave Length** slider down.

Whirlpool

Whirlpool is the last of the **Distort** filters. Unlike **Wave** or **Ripple**, it has no motion of its own, just a shape (Figure 11.23).

It's not difficult to create a real **Whirlpool** effect. Animate the **Amount** dial, which can go through two full revolutions in one direction. 720° is the limit. It will also go into negative numbers, down to –720°. Positive values give the whirlpool a clockwise spin, while negative values give a counterclockwise spin. I've animated the **Whirlpool** effect on the clip in *Effects Builder* at Marker 9.

FXScript DVE's

The **FXScript DVE's** and the **FXScript Layered DVE's** were written by Klaus Eiperle and sold as a separate plugin package until Apple included them in FCP3. Klaus has a new collection of effects, **Volume II**; a demo version with small QuickTime clips is included in the *Extras* folder of the CD.

4-Point Garbage Matte

A garbage matte allows you to roughly cut out a section of the image by selected points on the screen that define the four corners of the picture. It works similarly to the **Distort** tool, except that instead of twisting the image, you cut it. There is a legacy FCP **Four-point Garbage Matte** as well, but this one has superior capabilities. FCP also has an **Eight-point Garbage Matte**, which we'll look at shortly.

The controls in **4-point Garbage Matte** allow you to set four points on the image, beginning with **Point 1** in the upper left corner, **Point 2** in the upper right, **Point 3** in the lower right, and finally **Point 4** in the lower left (Figure 11.24).

To make a diagonal, for instance, you would think I could simply move **Point 3** over to where **Point 4** is, cutting the screen from the upper right to lower left, as in Figure 11.25. FCP's **Four-point Garbage Matte** would do it like that, but because of the greater control available in **FXScript's** version, it's a little more complex. This matte lets you soften the edges of the image with the **Smooth Edge** controls.

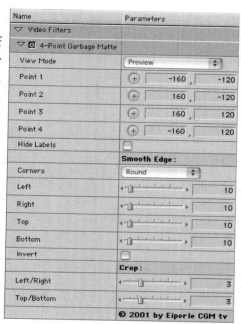

Figure 11.24 FXScript DVE's 4-point Garbage Matte Controls

Unfortunately, the controls only go down to 1 and not to zero. So even if you set the values down to the minimum and reduce the **Crop** settings to zero as well, you would still see a bit piece of the underlying image on the edges of the frame. For most video applications, this will not be a problem, because it will be well outside the television set's masking. If you need the whole frame, as in Figure 11.25, then you have to extend the edges further out. Unlike FCP's version of **Four-point Garbage Matte**, this version allows you to move the corner points out beyond the edges of the image into the grayboard. So to see the whole of the image, move **Point 1** off beyond the upper left corner, **Point 2** beyond the upper right corner, and **Point 4** beyond the lower left corner.

Figure 11.25 4-Point Garbage Matte used for a Diagonal

In Lesson 9, I talked about the problem of feathering the center line of a split screen. Here's the tool to do it. It's simple to do with this version of the **4-point Garbage Matte**. Set the points as in Figure 11.25, **Point 2** near the top middle of the **Canvas**, and **Point 3** near the bottom middle of the **Canvas**. Again I extended

Figure 11.26 Soft Edge Split Screen using FXScript DVE's 4-point Garbage Matte

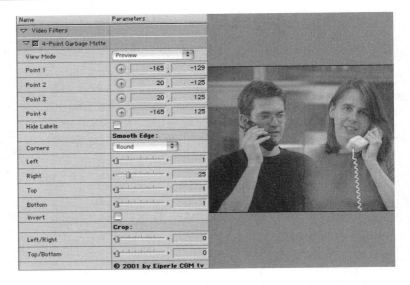

the points out into the grayboard so as not to show the underlying image around the edges.

Take a look at Marker 10 in the *Effects Builder* sequence. It will show you the clips laid out on two layers with the filter applied to the top layer. The layer on **V1** is shifted a little to the right to fit better underneath the image on **V2**.

Brightness and Contrast

There are a number of different ways to control brightness and contrast in FCP, most made obsolete by the introduction of FCP's new, powerful **Color Correction** tools. Usually when you want to adjust the brightness and contrast of an image, you usually adjust the mid gamma, shifting the histogram up or down as we saw in the previous lesson. This simply cannot be done properly with these controls but only with **Color Corrector 3-way**.

In addition to this **Brightness and Contrast** filter in **FXScript DVE's**, there is FCP's own **Brightness and Contrast (Bezier)**, another **Brightness and Contrast** filter in the QuickTime group of filters, as well as the brightness and contrast tools available in **Color Corrector 3-way**, which would be my first choice for image control. One feature the **FXScript DVE's Brightness and Contrast** offers is the unique ability to make a simple and quick split screen

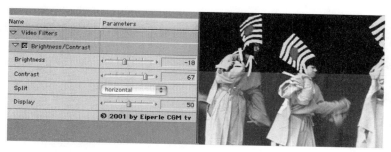

Figure 11.27 FXScript DVE's Brightness and Contrast with Split Screen

showing the image before and after the brightness and contrast is applied (Figure 11.27).

The **Split** popup allows you to choice either a vertical or horizontal split. The **Display** slider lets you set where the split will occur. At 100 there will be no split at all. It's an interesting feature, though probably of limited application.

Color Balance

This filter is similar to FCP's legacy **Color Balance**, providing RGB control for highlights, midtones, and shadow areas separately (Figure 11.28). This filter also has the additional benefit of the same split-screen capability as **FXScript DVE's Brightness and Contrast**. I would suggest, though, that you will have superior control using **Color Corrector 3-way**. If you want to create the split-screen effect, do it with two layers and use the **Crop** tool to create the split.

Displace

FXScript DVE's Displace filter brings a unique capability to FCP. For the first time, clips can interact with each other based on a moving image placed in a well (Figure 11.29). This is unique to this filter. By putting a clip in the **Map Movie** well, the movement of the luminance value will displace the image that the filter is applied to. Take a look at Marker 11 in the *Effects Builder* sequence. *Dance3* is being displaced by the movement in the clip *Ceremony5*. Because the clip in the **Map Movie** does not have particularly high contrast values, I had to use extreme settings,

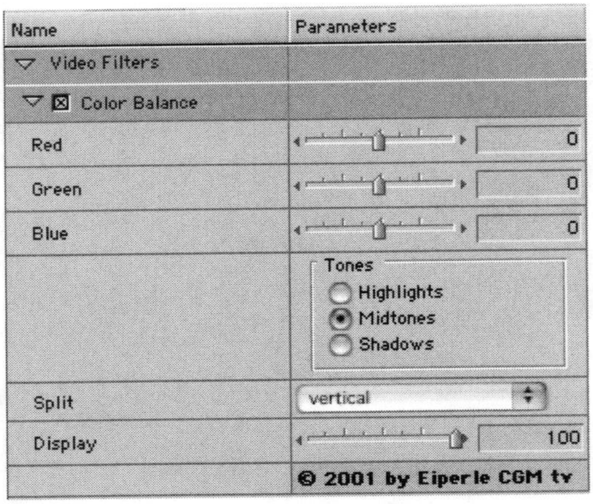

Name	Parameters
▽ Video Filters	
▽ ☒ Color Balance	
Red	◄———⊡———► 0
Green	◄———⊡———► 0
Blue	◄———⊡———► 0
	Tones
	○ Highlights
	● Midtones
	○ Shadows
Split	vertical ⬍
Display	◄————⊡—— 100
	© 2001 by Eiperle CGM tv

Figure 11.28 FXScript DVE's Color Balance Controls

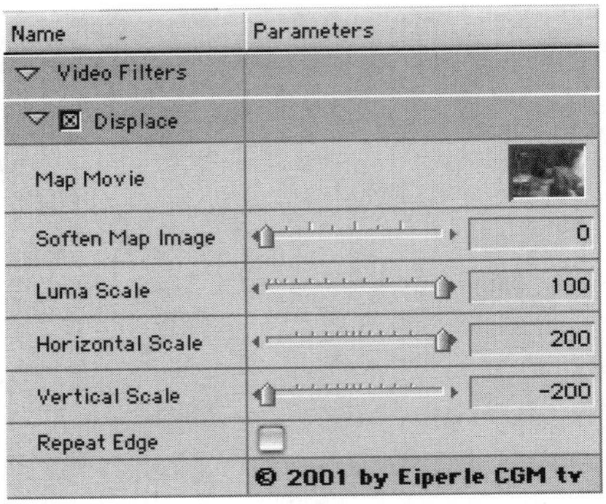

Name	Parameters
▽ Video Filters	
▽ ☒ Displace	
Map Movie	
Soften Map Image	⊡————► 0
Luma Scale	◄————⊡ 100
Horizontal Scale	◄————⊡ 200
Vertical Scale	⊡————► -200
Repeat Edge	☐
	© 2001 by Eiperle CGM tv

Figure 11.29 FXScript DVE's Displace Controls

but you can clearly see *Ceremony5* displacing the image in the **Timeline**.

Luma Scale will increase or decrease the contrast range of the clip in the **Map Movie** well, similar to sliding the **Histogram** up and down, as we were doing in the previous lesson on color correction.

Horizontal Scale and **Vertical Scale** control how much the image is displaced by the **Map Movie**, which doesn't have to be a movie of course. You can put a still in **Map Movie**.

Distort

While this filter's controls might look very similar to the **4-point Garbage Matte**, here the points will not cut the image. Like the FCP tool, they will actually distort the shape of the image (Figure 11.31). Unlike using the **Distort** tool, this **Distort** filter allows you to softened the edges of the image.

Switching on **Use Translucence** at the top of the panel will switch off the **Smooth Edges** option. It gives you full width of the image without any softening. The ability to soften the edges of the distorted image inside one control panel is quite useful. If you need to do that, this is the superior tool to use.

The **Hide Labels** checkbox lets you make the little number boxes that you see in Figure 11.30 disappear. The labels do not appear

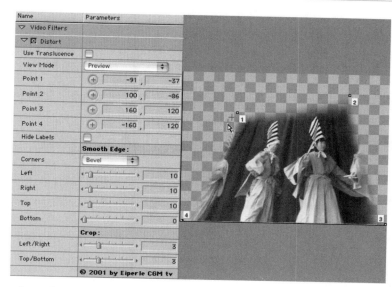

Figure 11.30 FXScript DVE's Distort

when the points are out in the grayboard, only when they are in the viewable portion of the screen.

Tip

Distort Preview: If you want to see how the image will look while you're trying to distort it, click one of the points' crosshairs in the **Control** panel and then mouse down in the **Canvas**, which will update as soon as it can. If you hold the mouse down and drag the point around the screen, the image will be pulled around on the screen as quickly as your computer can manage it. The faster your computer, the sooner this will happen. It's handy for positioning the distort points accurately. This mouse-down technique will work with any pointer crosshairs in the application: the **Distort** tool itself, **4-point** and **8-point Garbage Mattes**, and others.

Double Border

Double Border gives you an interesting capability, to use the border to crop the image. In the default settings seen in Figure 11.31, the **Scale Border** slider is actually cutting into the image, reducing its size. If you check the **Scale Scene** box, the slider won't crop the image, but will actually scale it, reducing it in size from full size at 100 to nothing when the slider is pulled down to zero. Unlike the scaling problems we saw on page 385 in Lesson 9, "Animating Images," this effect scales back smoothly without accelerating as it shrinks back.

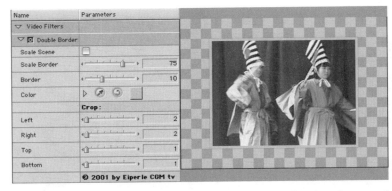

Figure 11.31 Double Border
Default Settings

The **Border** slider increases the width of the color band around the image. Even at its highest value of 30, it doesn't make a very deep border. It's about the same as a setting of 70 for **Basic Border**.

Replicate

Replicate is cool filter (Figure 11.32). The default output produces only four images on the screen, but if you push the sliders, you can get 16 horizontal and 16 vertical. That's 256 very small images on the screen. It's a nice effect when it steps back every few seconds: 4, 9, 16, 25, 36, and so on.

If animated, it steps through the replication in whole numbers. Look at the first clip in *Effects Builder 2*. It shows the animation of **Replicate** applied to a clip. As in all the **FXScript DVE's** filters, the image is by default cropped left and right. This is unnecessary for these Photo-JPEG pictures; so I've removed the cropping.

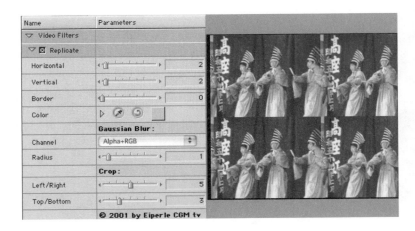

Figure 11.32 Replicate Controls
and Default Output

Notice also that this filter allows you to blur the image within it. The default is a **Radius** of 1, but if you don't want any blurring, you can set it down to zero. In *Effects Builder 2*, **Gaussian Blur** has been removed.

There is also a FCP legacy version of **Replicate**, but this one has the additional feature of being able to add borders to the images with a slider.

Roll/Scroll (Title)

Though it can be used to move a clip across the screen, either horizontally or vertically, it's designed primarily to quickly animate long Photoshop files scrolling or crawling title. Because of Photoshop's great capabilities to make complex images, it's a wonderful tool for titling.

The filter works by creating a scroll (or crawl) similar to what you might do by animating the **Center** point in the **Motion** tab, but much more simply and with less possibility of error. The controls require you to set the project dimensions (Figure 11.33). You first have to set the project resolution from the popup near the bottom. Your choices are:

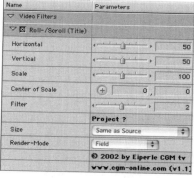

Figure 11.33 Roll-Scroll (Title) Default Controls

- Same as

- 320×240

- 720×480 (DV-NTSC)

- 720×576 (DV-PAL)

- 1,280×720 (High Definition 720p)

- 1,920×1,080 (High Definition 1080i)

- 2,048×1536 (Film)

1. Using **Roll-/Scroll (Title)** begins by creating a vertically long PS file for a scroll, such as the file *Scroll.psd* in the **Browser**, or a horizontally long PS file for a crawl.

2. Import the Photoshop file and place it in the sequence.

3. Apply the effect to the PS file, which is probably a sequence of its own.

4. Select the image in the sequence, and hit **Enter** or **Option-double-click** on it to bring it into the **Viewer.**

5. You will probably have to go to the **Motion** tab to reset the **Scale** value back to 100 so the image isn't shrunk down.

6. Go to the **Filter** tab, and with the playhead at the beginning of the clip, set either a **Horizontal** keyframe for a crawl or a **Vertical** keyframe for a scroll, and set the value down to zero.

7. Go to the end of the clip (**Shift-O**) to go to the Out point, and set the slider of the keyframed value up to 100.

That completes the effect. For a scroll, it slides the contents of the PS file up the screen. By reversing the keyframes, you could make the scroll slide down the screen, if you wanted to. You could also add keyframes part way through to stop the scroll.

Take a look at the sequence *Roll/Scroll (Title) Sequence,* which uses the Photoshop file *Scroll.psd.* This is a DV-format sequence and will only display properly on an NTSC monitor. The display in the **Canvas** may look strangely aligned. Only the NTSC monitor should be used as an alignment guide to control this effect.

Pan and Scan

As I said in Lesson 9, **Roll-/Scroll (Title)** can also be used to animate across large-format images. Take a look at the sequence called *Pan and Scan.* This uses the same image file called *Pic* that we used in Lesson 9. Over the 15-second duration of the clip, the camera zooms into the lower left corner of the image, pauses, moves up to the upper right corner of the image, pauses again, and then pulls back out. Take a look at the "flight plan" in Figure 11.34. This shows the keyframing that was done to create the motion. The key to this effect is the **Center of Scale** value. Because we want to zoom not around the anchor point but around the direction in which we're going, we need to set the **Center of Scale** point.

Using this keyframing scheme as a guide, let's create the animation.

1. Start by duplicating the *Pan and Scan* sequence, deleting the *Pic* image that's in it and placing a fresh copy of *Pic* in the **Timeline,**

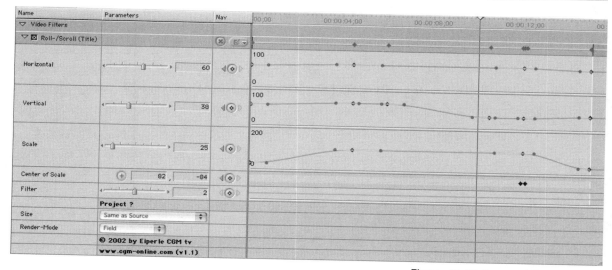

Figure 11.34 Pan and Scan Keyframing

2. Because FCP's trying to be helpful, it will scale the image to fit into the **Canvas**, so the next step will be go into the **Motion** tab and reset the **Motion** values. Just hit the little red **X** button.

The image will now fill the screen, and you will be zoomed right into it.

3. Next set some keyframes for **Horizontal**, **Vertical**, and **Scale**. You don't need to set a keyframe for **Center of Scale** at this point.

4. Set the **Scale** value down to about 25, so that the image fits into the **Canvas** and you can see the whole picture.

5. Next use the **Center of Scale** crosshairs and click in the lower right quadrant of the image, approximately where the center of screen will be when you zoom into the image.

The picture will immediately leap off to the side, showing black at the top and left. This is because the **Scale** value we set is happening around the **Center of Scale** point that you just moved to the lower right of the screen.

6. To reset the image back to the center of the screen, use the **Horizontal** and **Vertical** sliders, which sets our start position. We're ready to take off.

7. Go forward in time to 4:15, and change the **Scale** value to 100%, which will zoom you into the center of the image.

8. Use the **Horizontal** and **Vertical** sliders to reposition the image into the lower right quadrant. We've now created the push in. New keyframes have automatically been created for **Scale, Horizontal,** and **Vertical**.

9. Go to 6:00 and set a keyframe for the **Vertical** value.

We'll only move vertically in the next portion of the animation. You set the keyframe because you want the image to remain still between 4:15 and 6:00.

10. Go forward to 10:15 and, using the **Vertical** slider, move the image so it's high in the frame, in the upper right quadrant, showing the sky. A new **Vertical** keyframe is created.

11. Next, move to 12:00 where we need to set a lot of keyframes because we're now going to change all the values. Set keyframes for **Horizontal, Vertical, Scale,** and **Center of Scale**.

Why do we set a keyframe for **Center of Scale**? Because at the moment, keyframing is happening around the lower right quadrant of the **Canvas**, which is where we zoomed into. Now we want to zoom out of the upper right quadrant, so we need to change the **Center of Scale** to that area, which is what we do next.

12. Move forward one frame in time (**Right** arrow) and, using the **Center of Scale** crosshairs, set a point in the upper right of the **Canvas**.

13. Go to the end of the clip, using **Shift-O** to get to the Out point (not the **Down** arrow, which takes us one frame past the end of the clip), change the **Scale** value back down to 100, and reposition the **Horizontal** and **Vertical** sliders so the image is again centered, back where it started.

14. One last step: **Control**-click on each of the keyframes in the **Keyframe Graph** and from the contextual menu chose **Smooth** to add easing to the motion. Do this for all the keyframes except the two **Center of Scale** keyframes.

That's it. Your motion should be similar to that in the original *Pan and Scan* sequence. We now finally have the true power of

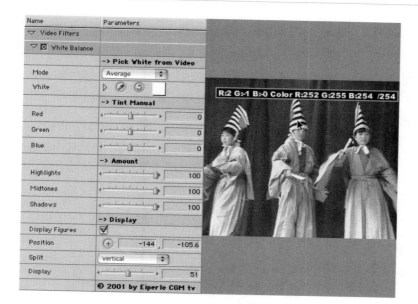

Figure 11.35 White Balance
Controls

the Pan and Scan technique available to us in FCP, an essential tool for most documentary filmmakers.

White Balance

After using the complexity of the **Color Correction** tools in the previous lesson, the simplicity of **FXScript DVE's White Balance** might be a welcome relief. You just use the **Eyedropper** to pick the nearest element to white or pale gray that you can (Figure 11.35). As in the previous lesson, don't try to pick an overexposed area. It will be white, but it will also have no color information. Normally you would use the **Average** mode, but you can also select **Add** from the **Mode** popup. This will not subtract any color elements, only add them, and can produce images with greater chroma saturation.

The **Display** shows two sets of RGB values. The second set shows the RGB values of color you picked, while the first set shows you the difference the filter has shifted the values to produce what it sees as a correctly white balanced image. The RGB display does not appear, of course, in your rendered output. On the other hand, there is also the popup that lets you select a vertical or horizontal split, to get a before-and-after display of your white balancing. This split is not only for your guidance; it will actually render out into your video.

Widescreen

FCP has its own **Widescreen** filter under the **Matte** menu. **FXScript DVE's Widescreen** works exactly the same with the addition of one feature. The filter allows you to take a standard 4:3 video and crop it to one of seven standard cinema shapes (Figure 11.36).

This is a crop, not an overlay, so the area outside the image is empty. If you want to color it something other than the black emptiness of space, place a color matte underneath it.

This version of **Widescreen** also has an **Amount** slider at the top of the controls, which basically allows you to override the presets and create any widescreen crop you would like. It also allows you to animate the **Widescreen** filter. With the slider at 0, you get the full effect of the selected popup. Setting the slider to the maximum value of 300 will give you the full-screen version. So it can start full 4:3 and then cut down to the widescreen shape. You could also ramp up the border or the feather value as you do. As with some transitions we saw earlier, you can have either a colored border or a feathered edge, not both.

The **Offset** slider allows you to move the image up and down without altering the position. Negative numbers drag the image downward; positive numbers move the image upward, opposite of the way the y axis functions in the **Text** tool, for instance.

Figure 11.36 Widescreen Controls

Be wary of the **Offset** slider though. It can make the image look quite blurry and produce unfortunate interlacing problems. Try to move the **Offset** value in even pixel amounts so that you don't reverse the fields of interlaced video.

Making a Sequence Widescreen

If you want to make a whole sequence **Widescreen,** — which is probably the point, rather than applying it to individual clips — nest the whole sequence, and apply the filter to the nest.

1. Select all the clips in a sequence, **Command-A.**

2. Use **Sequence>Nest Item(s)** or **Option-C.**

3. Name the nest something useful.

4. Select the nested sequence in the **Timeline** and apply the **Widescreen** filter.

5. To access the settings for the filter, simply select the nest in the **Timeline** and hit the **Enter** key to open it into the **Viewer.** You can now go to the **Filters** tab to change the settings.

If you need to use **Offset,** you may not want to do it here because it will offset all the clips in the nest. Better would be to open the nest, use the **Motion** tab of any shots you want to offset, and move them up or down in the frame as necessary.

There are other ways to create the widescreen effect. You can use **FXScript DVE's 4-Point Garbage Matte.** Simply create the shape you want for the masked area, and then use the **Invert** button.

Or for a simple widescreen without the border, you could also use the **Crop** tool.

Or you could make a mask in Photoshop, a black area at top and bottom with transparency in the middle. Personally I like this way best, particularly for projects like commercials, because it lets me create interesting effects with the mask edges, graphic elements that overlap the widescreen line, different color masks, text, logos, etc.

FXScript Layered DVE's

The **FXScript Layered DVE's** are a collection of filters based on ten of the **FXScript** transitions we saw earlier, specifically:

- **Band Slide**
- **Page Peel**
- **Page Peel** 1/2
- **Page Peel** 1/4
- **Slide**
- **Split Slide**
- **Stretch**
- **Swing**
- **Zoom/Rotate**

Usually the filters work exactly the same as the transitions, except that they work on a single clip and that they are keyframable, allowing the effect to stop and hold or go back and forth any number of times. The controls for these filters are the same as the controls provided in their transition counterparts.

Band Slide

Band Slide lets you split the screen horizontally or vertically, from two to up to 10 bands, not as many as the 30 available in the transition. An **Amount** slider controls how far into the effect you want to set it at any moment in the **Timeline**.

Figure 11.37 Page Peeled Corner

Page Peel, Page Peel 1/2, and Page Peel 1/4

The **Page Peel** effects have the same controls as the transitions they share names with. **Page Peel** can be used effectively to dog-ear an image to place a chapter marker behind a corner for instance as in Figure 11.37.

The **Amount** slider is set very low, as is the **Radius** value. This makes a very tight peel that shows the back very quickly. It wouldn't work well for most transitions, where you'd use a much higher **Radius** to make the image peel back more slowly. The number is simply created with the basic **Text** tool, with a **Color Matte** behind it.

Slide

This effect can be used to create the type of *Chasing Stills* sequence we did in Lesson 9, "Animating Images."

In the *Stills* folder are the four freeze frames called *Still 1* through *Still 4*, if you want to try **Slide** for yourself. I've built the effect in the sequence called *Chase*. Again, each of the stills has a duration of five seconds. It's important that this duration is the same for each image so that they can move steadily across the screen. The duration of the clip will in large part determine the speed of the motion. So let's animate the motion of image across the screen.

1. Drag one of the stills onto the **Timeline**, return the playhead to the beginning of the sequence, and apply the **Slide** filter to the still.

2. Double-click on it to bring it to the **Viewer** and go to the **Filters** tab.

3. Set the **Direction** dial to 90° and set a keyframe by clicking on the diamond keyframe button.

4. Set the **Amount** slider to 100 and set a keyframe for that as well.

The image should now be off the right edge of the screen.

5. Move two seconds into the timeline (type **+2.** and press **Enter**).

6. Set the **Amount** slider down to zero.

7. Also set another keyframe for the **Direction** dial.

The image should now be in the center of the screen. We set the **Direction** keyframe because we want to lock its movement during the next two seconds of the effect.

8. Go forward another second into the **Timeline** and add another **Amount** keyframe.

9. Turn the **Direction** dial around to 270°. While the image is still, we want to reverse the direction of the **Amount** slider.

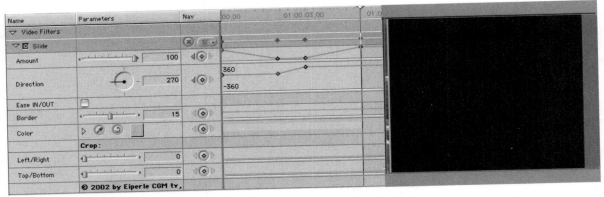

Figure 11.38 Slide Effect with Magic
Frame in the Canvas

10. Go to the edit point with the **Down** arrow, and set the **Amount** slider back up to 100.

Remember, as in Lesson 9, you're setting the final keyframe beyond the end of the clip, on the first frame of what would be the next clip. So what you see in the **Canvas** will the Magic Frame, the last frame of the clip, though the keyframe you've set is actually on the frame after it. That's why you still see a small portion of the image in the frame, as in Figure 11.38.

The motion should now show the still sliding onto the screen from the right, pausing for a second in the center, and then sliding off camera left.

The next step is to apply the same motion path to the second still.

11. Select the clip in the **Timeline** and copy it.

12. Position the playhead in the **Timeline** at the 3:00 point, which is where the *Still 1* starts to move off the screen and where we want *Still 2* to start to move on.

13. Drag *Still 2* into the space above **V1** to create **V2**.

14. Drop the image on the track at the playhead.

15. Select the image on **V2**, and from the **Edit** menu, choose **Paste Attributes** (**Option-V**).

16. From the **Paste Attributes** dialog box choose **Filters** and make sure that **Scale Attribute Times** is unchecked.

Now you just have to line up the third and fourth images so that they too chase the first two across the screen. **Slide** provides another way to create image motion in Final Cut.

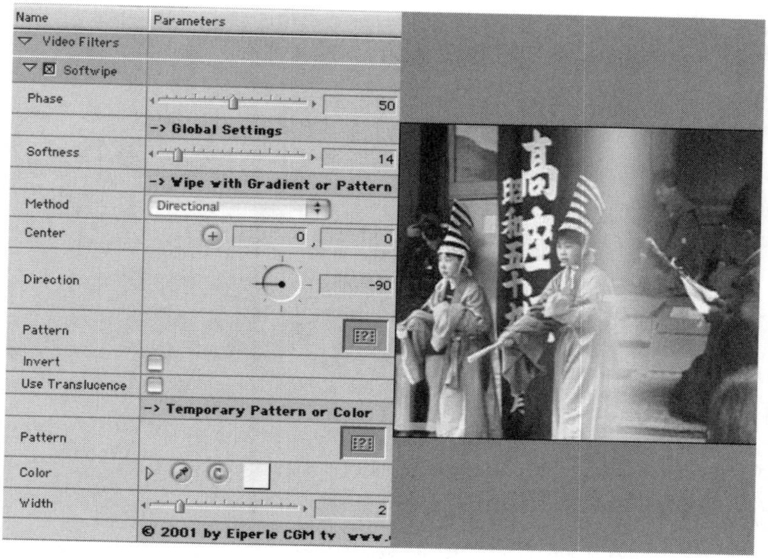
Name
Parameters
Video Filters
Softwipe
Phase
50
-> Global Settings
Softness
14
-> Wipe with Gradient or Pattern
Method
Directional
Center
0
0
Direction
-90
Pattern
Invert
Use Translucence
-> Temporary Pattern or Color
Pattern
Color
Width
2
© 2001 by Eiperle CGM tv www.

Figure 11.39 Softwipe and Output Used for Split Screen

Softwipe

Softwipe can be used to create a great array of interesting effects. It's a simple way to do a fancy split screen as in Figure 11.39.

The **Phase** slider is used to control how far the wipe moves through the screen. If you think of it as a transition, it's how far into the transition the effect holds. The **Softness** control the blurriness of the bar, while the **Width** slider at the bottom controls how wide the color bar is. Put it to zero, and you get softness with no colored bar.

Figure 11.40 Softwipe Radial Positioned in Upper Right Corner

The **Method** popup lets you set **Directional**, **Pattern**, or **Radial**. **Radial's** position can be fixed with the **Center** crosshairs as in Figure 11.40.

The ability to enter patterns into the **Wells** gives the filter its great power. The images can be sized and animated on the luminance value of images; usually grayscale patterns are used. FCP comes with a collection of 65 grayscale images that can be used as patterns, though for this filter, simpler ones like shapes are probably more useful.

The **Temporary Pattern Well** allows you to make the pattern itself visible while using the filter. So you could add a complex shape of the colored band that makes the mask in the image and replaces the color band, fading in the pattern between the two images.

Figure 11.41 Stretch Controls

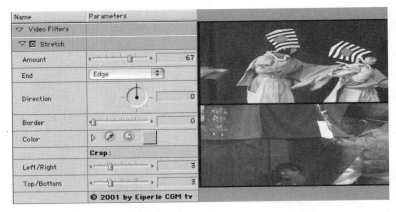

You can create something interesting by using a still of a third image or the same image as the one in the background to create a kind of echo effect.

The **Well** is not recursive, however. Once the file is dropped in, it's locked until it's replaced. Even if I put a text file in there and update it by changing the words or size, those would not be reflected in the **Well**. You could, however, drag the text file out of the well into the **Browser,** make the change you want to it, and then drop it back into the **Well**.

Split Slide

This effect is simply an animatable version of the transition of the same name.

Stretch

Stretch could be quite useful. It allows you to squeeze images so that they fit into the screen. You can do this with the **Distort** tool, but **Stretch** gives you more precision. In Figure 11.41 I have applied **Stretch** twice, once to *Dance3*, which is placed on track **V2**, using the controls seen in the figure. I also applied it to *Ceremony5*, which is on **V1**, and has the same values applied to it, only in the opposite direction.

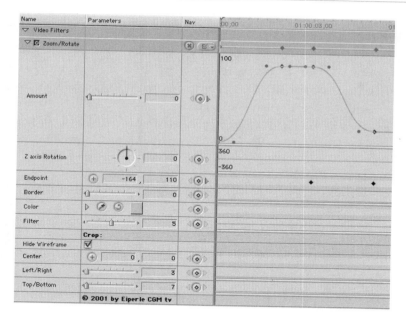

Figure 11.42 Controls for
Zoom/Rotate
Sequence

Swing

Swing is an animatable version of the transition. There isn't much more to say about it. Like the other **FXScript Layered DVE's**, it has the same controls as the transition with the addition of the keyframable **Amount** slider that lets you control the effect.

Zoom/Rotate

This is a really helpful effect. You may remember in we saw how FCP had trouble smoothly scaling large objects, that the motion would either speed up or slow down, depending on the direction you were scaling. **Zoom/Rotate** allows you to create smooth motion in and out. Take a look at the sequence *Effects Builder 2*. At Marker 2 there is a shot that demonstrates **Zoom/Rotate's** capabilities. Here a large object, larger than the sequence size, zooms back into the lower left corner of the image, holds, and then zooms back out again to the upper right, all with smooth, fairly steady motion in both directions (Figure 11.42).

Image Control

The **Image Control** group of filters is now largely made up of a legacy collection of filters, remnants left behind to be used on older projects. For all practical purposes, when working on a new project, for most of what you might want to do, you will be better served using the **Color Correction** filters that we looked at in the previous lesson. There are eight filters in the **Image Control** menu:

- Brightness and Contrast
- Color Balance
- Desaturate
- Gamma Correction
- Levels
- Proc Amp
- Sepia
- Tint

Of these, only **Desaturate** and **Sepia** serve much purpose, and only that of speed, for quick and dirty work. **Brightness and Contrast** and **Color Balance** should certainly either be done with **Color Correction**, or with **FXScript DVE's Brightness and Contrast**, if you want its special split-screen feature. **Gamma Correction** and **Levels** can be controlled far better with **Color Correction**, and the **Proc Amp** controls are too restricted to be very useful. **Tint** was pretty useless in the first package because **Sepia** did whatever **Tint** could do any way.

Desaturate

This is still the quickest, easiest way to remove color. The default **Amount** of 100 is a fully desaturated image, pure black and white. I find it makes a somewhat flat-looking black and white. **Desaturate** does not only *de-*, it will also *over-*. **Desaturate** can go into negative values, which overchromas the image. It won't take much of a push into the negative numbers to get excessively colorful, especially if the scene already has a lot of color, particularly reds. To do anything other than desaturate quickly, you should really use FCP's **Color Correction** filters.

Sepia

The default setting generates a rich brown color, without being too orange (Figure 11.43). Bringing down the **Amount** slider to around 60, blending in the underlying color, makes an interesting look.

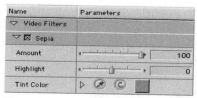

Figure 11.43 Sepia Controls

Though the filter is called **Sepia**, the color picker allows you to tint the image any color you'd like. **Sepia** also has a **Highlight** slider, which increases the brightness in the highlight areas, punching them through the tint color. Pulling the **Highlight** slider into negative numbers will deepen the shadow areas.

Sepia should really only be used for a fast-and-easy tint of the image. For finer and more subtle control, use one of the color correction tools we saw in the previous chapter. The simple **Color Corrector** would be easiest.

Matte

Like the keying tools we looked at in the previous lesson, the purpose of the **Matte** tools is to remove or isolate part of the image without benefit of a keyed screen. The tools are powerful, though somewhat limiting and frustrating to work with. An important use of mattes, particularly garbage mattes, is as the preliminary step in keying. The matte removes the excess area, leaving you less to have to deal with and key out.

The lack of a true Bezier pen tool to draw mattes accurately, however, makes the matte tools difficult to work with. Let's start with the most complex of the collection, the **Eight-point Garbage Matte**.

Eight-Point Garbage Matte

This filter works similarly to **FXScript DVE's 4-Point Garbage Matte** except that it allows you to crudely draw shapes on the screen with up to eight separate points. Each point is animatable

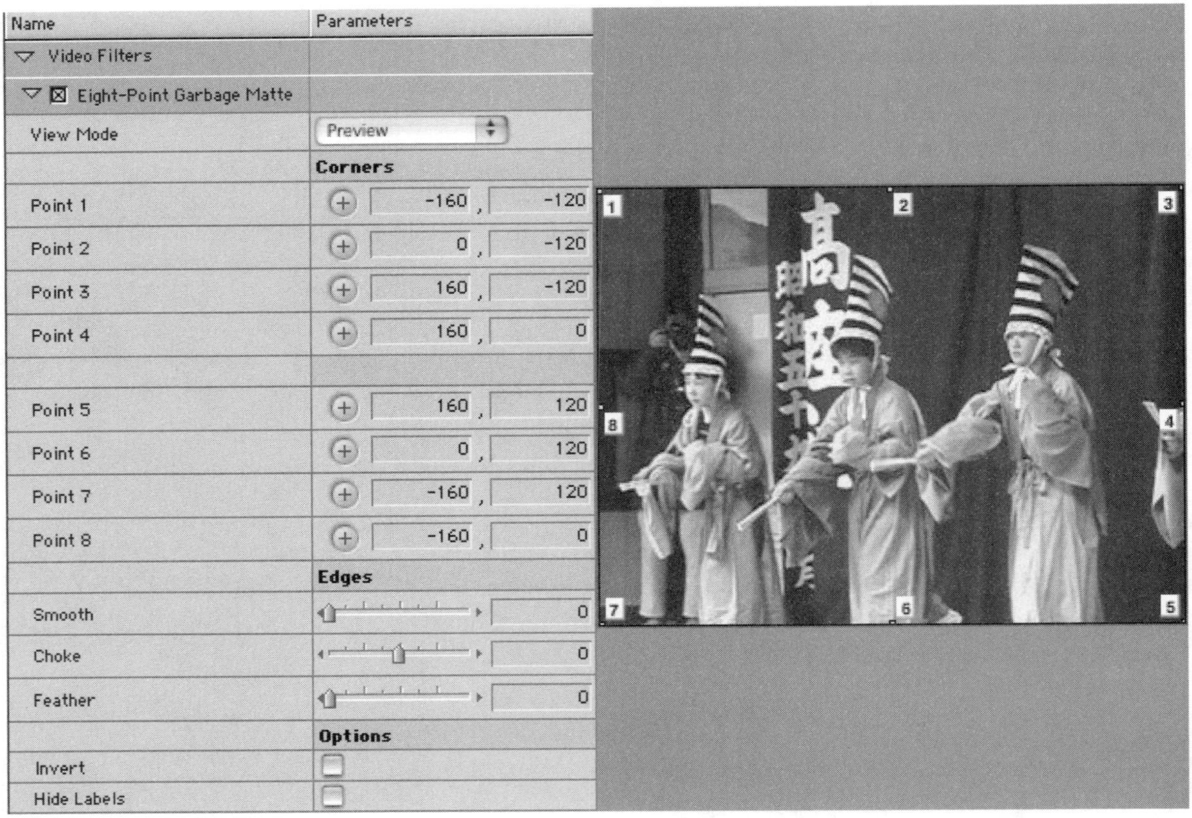

Name	Parameters	
▽ Video Filters		
▽ ☒ Eight-Point Garbage Matte		
View Mode	Preview ⬍	
	Corners	
Point 1	⊕ -160 ,	-120
Point 2	⊕ 0 ,	-120
Point 3	⊕ 160 ,	-120
Point 4	⊕ 160 ,	0
Point 5	⊕ 160 ,	120
Point 6	⊕ 0 ,	120
Point 7	⊕ -160 ,	120
Point 8	⊕ -160 ,	0
	Edges	
Smooth	◁———▷	0
Choke	◁———▷	0
Feather	◁———▷	0
	Options	
Invert	☐	
Hide Labels	☐	

Figure 11.44 Eight-Point Garbage
Matte Controls and
Canvas Display

so the matte can change shape over time. Look at the controls in Figure 11.44.

As you can see from the controls, there are eight points which can be placed anywhere on the screen using the **Crosshairs** button. Click in the crosshairs for **Point 1** and click in the **Canvas** and the point will be placed there. It's as simple and as difficult as that.

❧ Note

Labels: These are only visible when the **Canvas** or **Viewer** is not in Image+Wireframe mode. When you're in Image+Wireframe, labels are automatically hidden.

Point 1 is in the upper left corner of the image, **Point 2** in the upper middle, **Point 3** in the upper right, **Point 4** in the middle right, **Point 5** in the lower right, **Point 6** in the lower middle, **Point 7** in the lower left, and finally **Point 8** in the middle left. Basically the points go around the screen starting in the upper left corner. It's best to try to keep the points in those relative positions. Because lines connect the points to each other — **1** to **2** to **3**

to 4 and so on — it's important to avoid having the lines cross each other. Bizarre shapes can be created with your image if the lines cross, though it can be used to good effect as an interesting transition (Figure 11.45).

Though you have those nice markers on the **Canvas** displaying where the points are located, unfortunately you can't actually grab one of the markers and pull it about the screen. You have to work either from the crosshairs to the **Canvas** or with numerical values. If you're trying to matte a small part of the image, the point markers sometimes get in the way, which is why they can be toggled on and off with a checkbox at the bottom of the **Control** window.

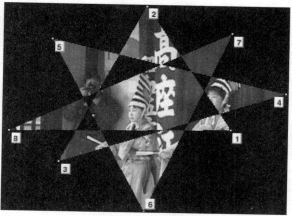

Figure 11.45 Crossed Lines in Eight-Point Garbage Matte

The three **View Modes** can be selected from a popup at the top of the controller.

- **Final** is the output as seen on the screen along with the underlying layers, but without any point markers. The **Hide Labels** checkbox has no effect.

- **Preview** is the same as **Final**, only with the points indicated and with the point numbers. The number display can be toggled with the checkbox.

- **Wireframe** shows you the matte outline but only on the layer on which you're working, without cutting away the rest of the image to reveal the underlying layer.

Below the points are some important tools. The first is **Smooth**. This rounds out the corners in your matte. You can combine it with **Feather** to create soft-edged mattes with interesting organic shapes (Figure 11.46).

Without **Smooth** applied, **Choke** is a subtle adjustment of the matte shape. Moving **Choke** into negative numbers will slightly reduce the matte, while pushing the value up will increase the size of the matte. The more smoothing that's applied, the more powerful **Choke** becomes. With maximum smoothness, **Choke** can double the size of the matte. If pushed down to −100, it will make the matte disappear.

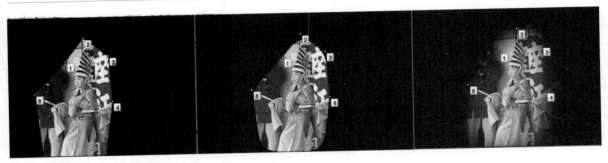

Figure 11.46 Matte without Smooth, with
Smooth, and Feather at 50

Note _____

Matte Boundaries: Though you can extend the points out into the grayboard, the matte doesn't actually extend out there. If only it would. The matte is still bound by the edges of frame. So if you hope that extending the points out from the screen so that **Feather** will not affect one edge of the image, give up. **Feather** will unfortunately occur around the frame edges.

Finally, an important but often overlooked checkbox is **Invert.** This feature allows you to create a matte around an object that you want to remove, and then rather than keeping the area you defined, by checking the **Invert** box, you'll cut it out.

The real beauty of the garbage mattes is that they allow you to create complex shapes with soft edges, allowing you to layer multiple images together in interesting and shifting patterns.

The **Eight-Point Garbage Matte** can be used for some simple wipes as well for complex animations, though it is a bit fiddly. A couple in your **Browser** will show you what I mean. The first is a simple animated X on an image. It's the third group in _Effects Builder_ 2 at Marker 3. On top of a shot is a PS file _Cross.psd_ made up of two layers. The top layer is the slash from upper left to lower right, and the bottom layer is the slash from upper right to lower left. If you put _Cross.psd_ into its **Timeline** window, you'll see that an **Eight-Point Garbage Matte** has been applied to each layer, first to the top and then to the bottom. None of the points are in the start positions, but on the top layer, animating **Points 5** and **6** produced the slash of red paint across the screen. A few frames later, the bottom layer animation begins where **Points 6** and **7** are primarily animated.

I could have done the red X with a simpler matte, but then I couldn't have done the next animation. It's also a PS file with two layers, a base layer and an overlay. Open the sequence called _RouteMap_ in its **Timeline** window. This sequence is actually a multilayer Photoshop file. The bottom layer is the map and the top layer (animated with an **Eight-Point Garbage Matte**) is the

Figure 11.47 Extract Controls and Three-Up Display

route Little Red Riding Hood has to take to get to Grandma's house. It's simple, but tricky to get the line to move smoothly around the corner.

 Tip

Fudging the Bounding Box: I did a little trick with these layers and with the next demonstration as well. Because the contents of a Photoshop layer are defined by a bounding box, when the file is brought into FCP that bounding box remains with it. When a garbage matte is applied to one of the layers, the point markers of the matte appear on the bounding box rather then on the edges of the frame. But that is not where the points actually are. If you click on a point crosshair, the point will show in the **Canvas** but not at the point marker. I get around this problem by expanding the bounding box in Photoshop so that it stretches all the way to the edges of the frame. To do that on each layer, I place a tiny dot of paint in diagonally opposite corners of the frame. Because I know I'm going to matte the image, the dot will never be seen, but if you open *Cross.psd* in Photoshop and look carefully at the upper left corner and the bottom right corner of each layer, you'll see the tiny paint dot. When the file is imported into FCP, the bounding box extends to the edge of the frame, and FCP's garbage matte points behave normally and can be more easily controlled.

Extract

Sandwiched in between the two garbage matte filters is **Extract**, and what a beauty it is. It's a little unpredictable to work with, but with luck it will create interesting combinations of matte shapes, especially when used with a garbage to define a core area (Figure 11.47).

Extract gives you deceptively simple controls with a three-up display in the **Canvas**:

- **Source**
- **Matte**
- **Final**

Figure 11.48 Extract Applied to RGB Channel

The bottom right corner is empty. A popup lets you select if you want the extraction applied to RGB or to the alpha channel of the image. Applying it to RGB will make a high-contrast black-and-white image (Figure 11.48). By adjusting **Threshold, Tolerance,** and **Softness,** you can vary the image substantially.

Extract works like a luminance keyer and probably should be in the key package. It gets really interesting when you apply it to the alpha channel instead of the RGB value. Then you cut through to an underlying layer with a great amount of control. It's useful for pulling an alpha channel from an image that doesn't have one.

Look at the TIFF file in the **Browser** called *TIFF.tif*. Apply the **Extract** filter to it with **Copy Result to Alpha Channel,** and you'll see that with hardly a tweak of the sliders, the white will disappear from around the word.

Tip

NightScope: If you apply **Color Corrector** to a clip, taking down the black level a bit, then use the **Extract** filter, followed by **Color Corrector** again with a green tint and the white level brought down considerably, as well as the mids choked down, you can create quite a credible NightScope look for your image. Look at the fourth clip in *Effects Builder 2.* It needs a little fiddling, depending on the image, but it's fun, especially if you can add a little blurred glow to it with a composite mode, which we'll talk about on page 543 in Lesson 12.

Four-Point Garbage Matte

The **Four-Point Garbage Matte** has really been superseded by the **FXScript DVE** version of the filter, so this should really be considered only a legacy filter for old projects that still need to be worked on.

Image Mask

This filter is a simple compositing tool based on FCP's **Well.** It has nowhere near the sophistication and capabilities of **FXScript Layered DVE's Softwipe,** which should be used in its place for most

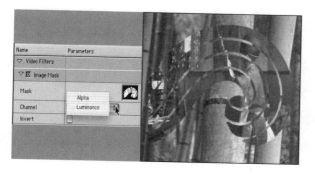

Figure 11.49 Image Mask Controls

Figure 11.50 Mask Feather Control

effects. For a simple effect as using static text or a logo as a mask, it is very easy to use. In Figure 11.49 I have applied the filter to *Ceremony1*, which in on layer **V2**. *Bamboo2* is on layer **V1**. The Photoshop file *Logo.psd* has been dropped into the **Well**. *Logo.psd* acts as the mask shape that cuts the image revealing *Bamboo2* on the layer below.

Mask Feather

This feature is specifically designed to feather the edges of masks, to soften any sharpness or jaggedness (Figure 11.50). By raising the values high, it can also be used to blow out the mask so that it smears the image. Unfortunately, the lowest value is two; so it's difficult to start from no feathering to a very feathered image. The filter cannot be used to feather the edges of an image or of its crop. It will only feather masks.

Mask Shape

Mask Shape has to be one of the most useful filters because of its ability to shape the image. Let's first look at how the controls work, and then I'll show you a practical application (Figure 11.51).

In Lesson 5 on transitions, I decried the lack of a square wipe. Using this filter, you can make your own. Set the **Horizontal** and **Vertical** sliders down to zero and keyframe it. Ramp up the slider values over time, and your have your square wipe. Because of the limitations of FCP transition architecture in starting, holding, and finishing a transition, effects like **Mask Shape** have an extra importance. With these effects, you can bring in a wipe, hold on a

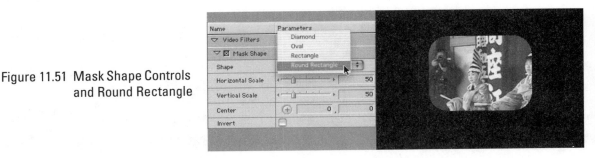

Figure 11.51 Mask Shape Controls and Round Rectangle

particular point, and then finish the wipe at a different rate. The other popups, such as **Round Rectangle**, allow you to create interesting wipe patterns and ones that vary over time. Marker 5 in *Effects Builder 2* shows the **Diamond** wipe changing shape as it comes in.

Another interesting use for **Mask Shape** is to create borders using color mattes. It's simple to do. Look at the sixth clip stack in *Effects Builder 2*. On **V1** is the dance clip with **Mask Shape>Round Rectangle** applied. On **V2** is a color matte in a stylish pale yellow. The color also has **Round Rectangle** applied to it twice. The first time it's applied inverted. This leaves the matte with the picture showing through and fills the rest of the screen with the color. Applying the shape again, only slightly larger and not inverted, will cut the color outside in the **Round Rectangle**. I also used **Mask Feather** at its lowest setting to soften the aliasing.

Hiding ID with Mask Shape

There seems to be an increasing need to hide the identity of a person, license plate, house number, or some other part of a video image. **Mask Shape** is a useful tool for making this happen. Let's go through this step by step.

1. Bring two copies of *Dance3* into a sequence.

2. Stack them one on top of the other on **V1** and **V2**.

The clip on **V1** will be the rest of the shot, while the clip on **V2** will be just the portion that's altered. We're going to mask out the face of the first boy in the line.

3. Apply the filter **Mask Shape Oval** to the clip on **V2**.

4. You won't see anything change in the **Canvas** because both the clips on **V1** and **V2** are the same.

5. To see what you're doing, switch off visibility on **V1** with the green button at the end of the track.

Another trick is to temporarily place the **Desaturate** filter on the clip below, which will show you which piece is on the upper layer.

6. Using the sliders, adjust the shape and size of the oval until it's about the right dimensions.

7. Use the **Center** crosshairs to position the shape on the boy's face.

8. Don't make it too tight or it'll be difficult to work with and also perhaps not mask the face well enough.

You should now see Figure 11.52.

Once you have that right, set a keyframe for **Center**. You could also set keyframes for the shape dimensions, but in this case it's not necessary as the size doesn't change appreciably as it might if the boy walked up to the camera. Next we need to animate the oval.

Figure 11.52 Clip with Mask Shape Oval Applied

9. To do this step through the sequence, and every few frames, use the **Center** crosshairs to readjust the position of the oval. For this kind of thing, you usually put the crosshairs right on the subject's nose.

Once you've set all the keyframes, use **Option-P** to play through the unrendered clip to check your tracking. So far so good. It's a bit laborious, but nobody said animation was quick and easy.

10. Add a small amount of feathering to the mask with **Mask Feather.**

11. For the final piece of the puzzle, apply a filter to schmutz up the image on **V2**.

Gaussian Blur is a very common solution. Or use **Diffuse** from the **Stylize** group of filters.

The seventh clip stack in *Effects Builder 2* shows the completed effect using **Diffuse**.

You could do something similar using **Mask Shape** to create a color matte like a blue dot that positions over the face. Then rather than animating Center in the filter, simply animate the

Tip

Circle: To make a circle, set **Oval's** Horizontal to **75** and **Vertical** to **100**, or some other proportions of 4:3.

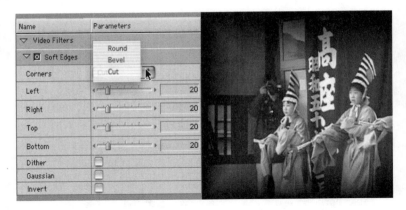

Figure 11.53 Soft Edges Controls with Image Set to Bevel at 20

position of the dot in the **Canvas** by setting keyframes, grabbing it, and moving it about.

Soft Edges

Soft Edges is a lovely filter. It creates very diffused edges to the sides of images (Figure 11.53).

The **Corners** popup sets the way the diffusion acts in corners:

- **Round** is smooth curve.

- **Bevel** leaves the corners square looking, less rounded by the softening.

- **Cut** chops off the corners diagonally. If you push up the blur values with **Cut**, you will create a diamond-shaped pattern.

The **Dither** and **Gaussian** checkboxes make subtle variations in the way the image blurs.

Soft Edges only acts on the bounding box of the image. It will not blur the crop lines of a cropped image.

Widescreen

We have already looked at the **FXScript DVE's Widescreen** filter, which does the same work as this one, with more controls.

Perspective

Basic 3D

Basic it is, but it does the job and can be used effectively for customized effects and transitions from tumbles to spins to bow ties. The controls for *x,y,z* axes are self-explanatory (Figure 11.54).

Notice the **Center** and **Scale** controls. Set these functions here and not in the **Motion** window. If you scale or reposition in **Motion**, the 3D will be cut off by the bounding box as in Figure 11.55.

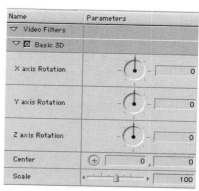

Figure 11.54 Basic 3D Controls

 Tip
_____

Constraining Dials: Holding down the **Shift** key will constrain the dials to 45° increments.

_____

Star Wars Scroll

Let's do something useful with this. Let's create the classic *Star Wars* scrolling title, the one where the scroll seems to disappear toward the horizon. It's tricky, but it can be done. I've made a separate project in your *Lesson11* folder called *StarWars Scroll*. The project is made up of a couple of sequences and a text block, though the text block doesn't need to be outside of a sequence.

The text block, *Scrolling Text*, was made with the FCP **Scrolling Text** tool. I could have made it with **Title Crawl** and its roll animation for additional fine tuning. I placed *Scrolling Text* inside a sequence called *Tall Text*. Note that this sequence is 320 pixels across — though it could be 720 pixels — and it's 800 pixels tall. It's important to create this sequence that will be nested in the final sequence so that the image can be tilted without being cut off by the bounding box.

Figure 11.55 3D Scaled in Motion Tab and Scaled in 3D Controls

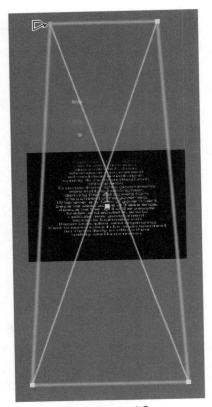

Figure 11.56 Distorted Corners
for 3D Perspective

Tall Text has been placed inside a 320 x 240 sequence called *3D*. If you open *3D* and **Option**-double-click the nested sequence *Tall Text* inside it, you'll open it in the **Viewer**. If you look at the **Filters** tab you'll see I set the **Basic 3D** filter to *x* –65, which tilts the image backwards away from us. Because of the tilt, the text does not now appear immediately. In fact I lopped off six seconds from the beginning of the *Tall Text* so that it would start scrolling close to the beginning of the sequence.

I also added **FXScript DVE's 4-Point Garbage Matte**. This cuts off the top of the screen. I smoothed the top edge, which allows the *Tall Text* to fade out and disappear as it nears the top. I did this with the garbage matte rather than the **Fade** feature in the FCP scrolling because I only wanted it to fade out at the top, not both top and bottom.

If this is not enough sloping away perspective for you, you can also help it along by using the **Distort** tools on the two upper corners of the image as in Figure 11.56.

Be warned, all of this is going to be a pretty slow render even on a fast computer.

Bow Tie

At the beginning of this section I mentioned a bow tie, and some of you probably scratched your heads a bit. Go back to the **Browser** and take a look at the stack at Marker 8 in *Effects Builder 2*. That's a bow tie, most commonly used in two-ways (interviews from a remote site). Both clips are tilted backwards on the *y* axis, one 45° and the other –45°. The center points are shifted 70 and –70 to move the images left and right, and both are scaled down to 60 to fit the screen. You can add all sorts of graphical embellishments like borders and bars and logos across the bottom. There is a tendency to make bow ties too busy, which is probably not a good idea.

Curl

Curl is quite unnecessary now. The **FXScript Layered DVE's Page Peels** provide a huge number of possibilities, far more than are offered in this filter. To make the image curl rather than peel using

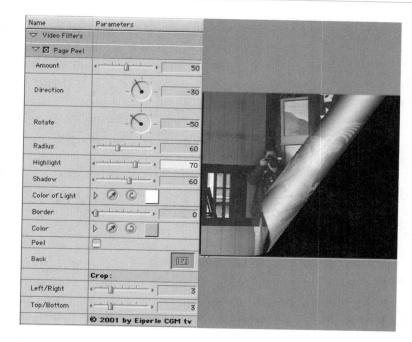

Figure 11.57 FXScript Layered DVE's Page Peel Used to Curl

Page Peel, simply uncheck the **Peel** checkbox, and tighten up the **Radius** as in Figure 11.57.

Flop

We've already seen **Flop** on page 135 in Lesson 3. It simply turns the image around, either horizontally, vertically, or both at the same time (Figure 11.58). It's so simple, but such a useful filter. It might save you if you cross "The Line" (see page 299). I've often seen it used to change the direction of action, so instead of someone running along a street from right to left, they go from left to right.

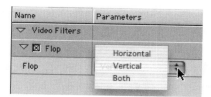

Figure 11.58 Flop Controls

Mirror

Mirror can be used for some interesting effects. The default is to mirror the right side of the screen into the left side (Figure 11.59).

Changing the **Reflection Angle** to 180 will mirror the left side in the right, and anything in between will tilt the angle of the mirroring. Because the **Reflection Angle** will go from 360° to –360°, you can do some interesting spins of the mirror.

Figure 11.59 Mirror Controls and Image

Rotate

Rotate is one of the few effects that can't be animated. It has only a single popup that sets rotation in 90° increments: 90° clockwise, 90° counterclockwise, and 180° (Figure 11.60).

The 180° popup has exactly the same effect as **Flop** set to both vertical and horizontal. The 90° rotations distort the image, as can be seen in Figure 11.58, which keeps the image size constant despite changing its aspect.

QuickTime

QuickTime offers a selection of effects, some of which duplicate FCP filters. The notable absence from the QT list is **Film Noise**, which would be quite useful for those wanting to give their video a film look. You can add it in the QuickTime Player but not in FCP.

Alpha Gain

This is a strange filter. It's another one of those complex effects where the default settings make no change to the image when first applied. When you move the sliders, you'll be able to see the

> **Note**
>
> **Film Look:** When you download the upgrade to v3.0.2 from Apple, you will also get a free film look plugin from Klaus Eiperle that works very nicely indeed. It does add a little film scratches however, even at its lowest settings, when you may not want any.

Figure 11.60 Rotation Controls with Image

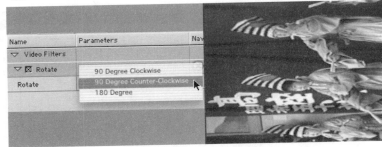

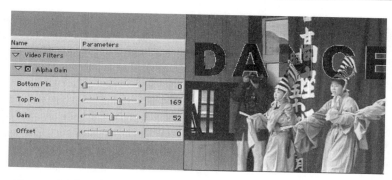

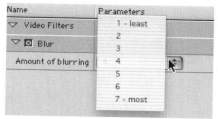

Figure 11.61 Alpha Gain Controls with Image

effect, which adjusts the luminance values of the image's alpha channel (Figure 11.61).

Bottom Pin and **Top Pin** peg luminance values, with no change being **Bottom** 0 and **Top** 255. Reducing **Top** makes the more opaque parts of the image become transparent, while raising **Bottom** will make more transparent portions become opaque, bringing up the black of the alpha, darkening the image below.

Gain increases the level of the alpha. The default is 1; zero is complete transparency. Raising it higher will have very little effect.

Increasing **Offset** will make the image darker, while going into negative numbers will have little effect.

This effect may be especially useful if you have a reversed alpha, with black opaque and white transparent. **Alpha Gain** will allow you to fix it.

Blur

Blur does pretty much what you'd expect it do, though it has neither FCP's **Gaussian Blur**'s simple controls nor the range (Figure 11.62).

Figure 11.62 Blur Controls

Brightness and Contrast

QuickTime's **Brightness and Contrast** should not be used. For luminance control use the simple **Color Corrector** or **Color Corrector 3-way**.

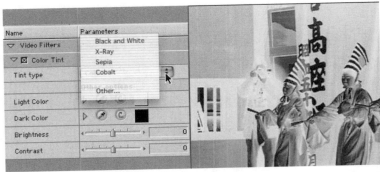

Figure 11.63 Color Style Controls
with Image Output

Color Style

This combines **Solarize** and **Posterize** into one interface (Figure 11.63). I think FCP's **Solarize** and **Posterize** effects, which we'll see on page 496, are much better. They have better and subtler control.

we'll see on page 496

☞Tip

Updating Color: With the filter applied but switched off in the checkbox, you can use the **Eye-droppers** to pick color from the original image in the **Canvas**. Hold down the mouse and drag it around the **Canvas** with the **Eyedropper**, and the color swatch will update as it picks through the colors.

Color Tint

Color Tint has one feature that is difficult to duplicate with any other tools. It allows you to create an X-ray negative effect (Figure 11.64). It also has a subtle sepia tint, much less garish and orange than FCP's **Sepia**.

Color Tint also has **Other,** a wonderful tool. It allows you to set extremely different colors for light and dark. You can have a warm light color and a cold dark, a very nice duotone effect.

The **Brightness** and **Contrast** controls really help with the duotone, letting you put in rich color while keeping the luminance from looking too washed out. Take a look at Marker 9 in *Effects Builder 2*. It shows you the type of duotone effect **Color Tint** can create.

Figure 11.64 Color Tint Controls
with X-ray Image

ColorSync

You'll only use this filter if you're working for a specific computer display. It allows you to use Apple's **ColorSync** to adjust your source material to a specific monitor configuration.

Edge Detection

Edge is an interesting effect, especially when composited with itself (Figure 11.65).

The **Colorize** checkbox will return the color to the image but with the edges still highlighted. The default setting of **Thinnest** produces the best results, I think, especially when overlaid on another image using a composite mode (Figure 11.66). We'll look at the wonderful world of compositing modes next in Lesson 12 on page 509.

Figure 11.65 Edge Detection with Screen Mode Composite

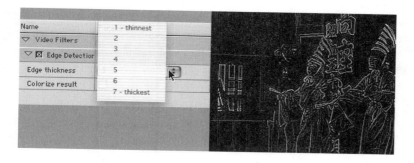

Figure 11.66 Edge Detection with Screen Mode Composite

Emboss

Emboss is **Edge Detection** with highlights and shadows added to the edge lines (Figure 11.67). This works well when composited with itself so that color can be reintroduced.

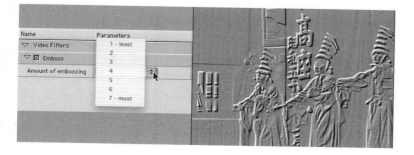

Figure 11.67 Emboss Control with Default Least Image Output

General Convolution

General Convolution is another filter for messing up the image. The default settings show no effect on the image — **Cell 5** is set to a value of one and the other cells are set to zero. (With **Cell 5** set to zero, the image is black.) Increasing the value of a slider will brighten an image, while decreasing it will make the image darker and more embossed-looking (Figure 11.68).

Multiple copies of **GC** applied to a clip will produce even more bizarre effects. Pushing the sliders so some are lower and others are higher will make the image fight itself, producing an ever-more stylized look.

Unfortunately, I don't know how the filter works except by trial and error.

General Convolution doesn't only have to be used to distort an image; it can also have practical applications. Mattias Sandström of Sweden devised this elegantly simple method to give a film look to video. It's a simple way to remove the effects of interlacing without adversely affecting the resolution. It also softens the image slightly. Use the following cell values in Table 11.1 to create the effect.

Table 11.1 Sandström's General Convolution Recipe for a Film Look

Cell 1	0
Cell 2	.25
Cell 3	0
Cell 4	0
Cell 5	.5
Cell 6	0
Cell 7	0
Cell 8	.25
Cell 9	0

HSL Balance

These **Hue**, **Saturation**, and **Lightness** (brightness) controls should only be used for projects already created using them. Otherwise stick to FCP3's **Color Corrector** tools.

Lens Flare

Lens Flare is another one of those filters that opens up to default settings that produce no result. You look at a long list of controls, start moving the sliders around, and only after the fourth or fifth slider does anything actually start to happen (Figure 11.69).

The key control is the second **Size** slider under **Spot Info**. The first **Size** slider controls intensity. The **Spot Info Size** slider adjusts the size of the flare, except for **Star Burst**, which also needs to have

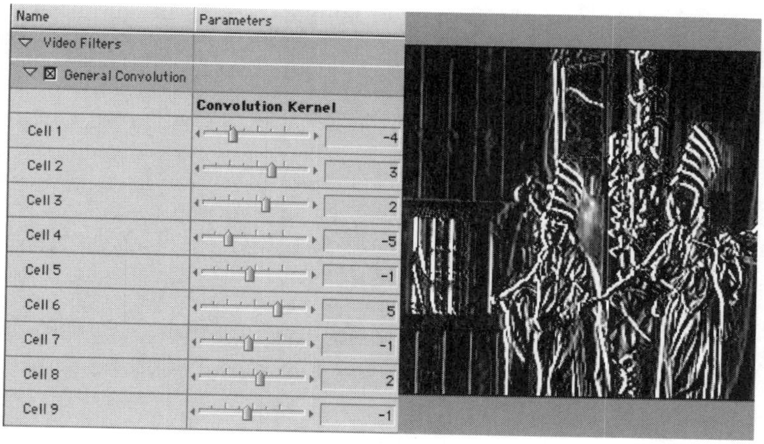

Figure 11.68 General Convolution Controls with Image Output Using Filter Twice

the **Solid** slider pushed up. With the other flare types, **Solid** should be kept at zero.

Lens Flare's resemblance to a real lens flare is only very tangential. It can create swatches of colored flares that radiated from the center. Positioning is almost impossible. The **Well** only works if you actually put a lens flare in it and then use the crosshairs to position it. But then, of course, the flare won't rotate properly as

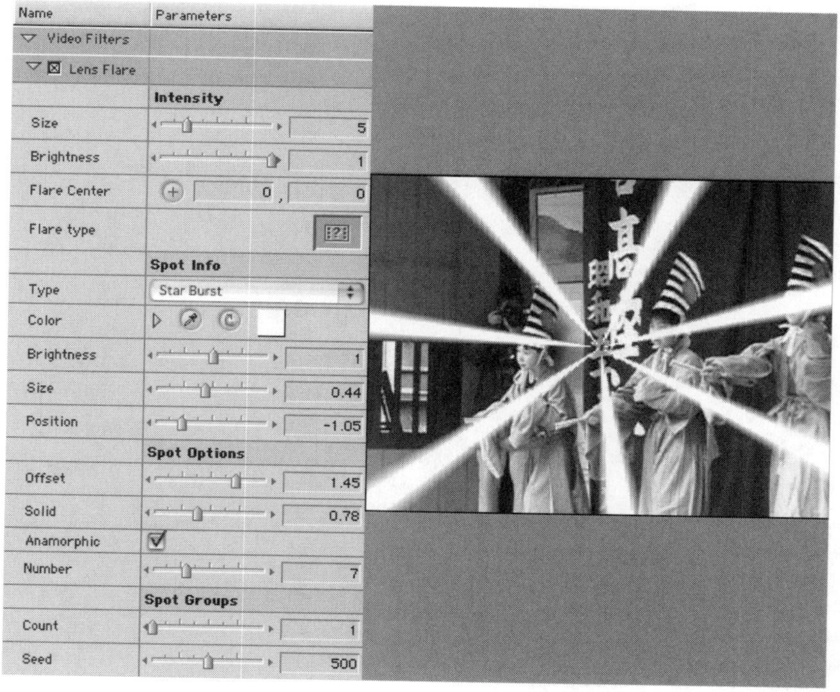

Figure 11.69 Lens Flare Controls and Output

a true lens flare would, so it's not animatable. All in all, rather a waste of time, and the flare that it is able to produce with **Star Burst**, for instance, is truly ugly (Figure 11.69). If you want to do a decent lens flare, get the Knoll Light Factory, now part of Pinnacle Systems.

RGB Balance

This works exactly the same as the FCP **Color Balance**, only without the highlights, midtones, and shadows controls. If you want to work with a cruder tool with less control, use this one. Otherwise, stick to FCP's **Color Corrector** tools.

Sharpen

Skip right over QuickTime's **Sharpen** and head straight to FCP's. Again, the built-in version has finer, more subtle control that the QuickTime version, which simply offers a seven-step popup for different levels of sharpening.

Sharpen

The two effects under **Sharpen** are **Sharpen** and **Unsharp Mask**. Be careful with both of them, particularly with compressed video. Most cameras shoot with a certain amount of edge enhancement, Sony's are particularly notorious for it, adding a dark line of edging to enhance separation. This can look quite ugly when it is sharpened.

Sharpen

Sharpening will nicely bring out all the compression pixelization around the edges of objects. In Figure 11.70, the little dots you see around edges are caused by this. Even at a lower value can emphasize unsightly pixelization. Small amounts of **Sharpen** in less compressed images can help to enhance an image that looks a little soft.

The **Luminosity** checkbox may as well stay off. It doesn't add much to the effect, unlike in the next filter.

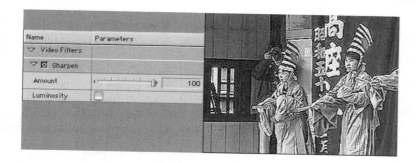

Figure 11.70 Sharpen at Default Settings with Image Output

Unsharp Mask

Unsharp Mask is really a sharpening tool and doesn't unsharpen. At its default settings, most video images will bloom horribly, blowing out the luminance values (Figure 11.71).

With just a little touch of **UM**, settings around 60 with **Radius** down to 8 or so will crisp up an image, brightening the highlights. Pushing the **Radius** up around 25 with the **Threshold** up to 100 works quite well also. At low levels, the **Luminosity** checkbox has little effect. At the higher levels, when **UM** can be used for special effects, the checkbox bleaches out even more of the color.

Stylize

This is mostly a collection of special effects, except for the first one, which produce neat visual results.

Antialias

Antialias has a default setting of one, which is probably right for what it does best: slightly blurring an image to soften sharp outlines, such as those that occur around text. It does soften the

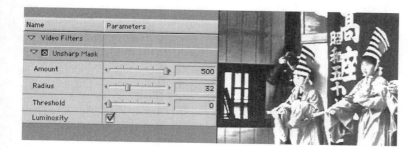

Figure 11.71 Unsharp Mask at Default Settings with Image Output

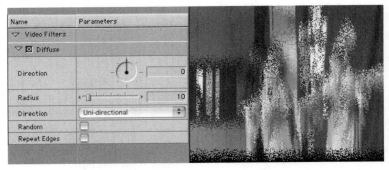

Figure 11.72 Diffuse Controls and Image Output

whole image, but it can be useful for toning down the jaggedness around effects like **Page Peel**.

Diffuse

Diffuse is dithering, making the image speckled with pixels. The effect works well, though, and animates nicely (Figure 11.72). Even small amounts of **Diffuse** will smear the screen heavily.

Emboss

I don't care for the way FCP's **Emboss** works. The default setting doesn't look bad, though I'd prefer any direction other than the default zero (Figure 11.73). By reducing the **Amount** slider, you'll bring color back into the image.

Find Edges

This effect gives a nice, stylized look (Figure 11.74). Try it with the **Invert** checkbox on, which puts a hard black outline on the edges. Both ways have their uses and can work well.

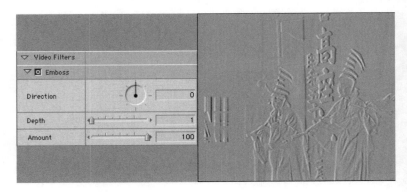

Figure 11.73 Emboss Controls with Image Output

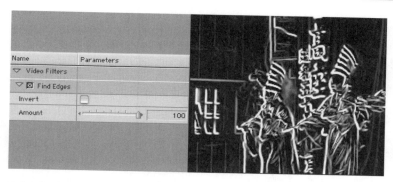

Figure 11.74 Find Edges Controls
with Default Output

I think this filter is much more useful than QT's **Edge Detection**, which really only works usefully set at thinnest and composited with another image. **Find Edges**, on the other hand, creates interesting effects with good control.

Posterize

Final Cut's **Posterize** is unusual because you can set separate values for each RGB channel (Figure 11.75).

The default setting of 8 for each channel produces a result on many images; you'll probably need to use low numbers to generate good posterization. I prefer the QuickTime **Color Style** effect. Though it doesn't have channel control, its slider range is much more useful for making little adjustments.

Replicate

We have already looked at a better **Replicate** filter in the **FXScript DVE's** menu that does exactly what this one does, only better.

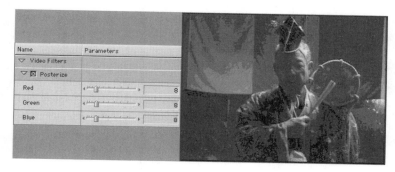

Figure 11.75 Posterize Control with
Image Output Set to 2

Solarize

I like **Solarize**, especially when it's inverted, as shown in Figure 11.76. The default is to not inverted, but what's nice is that even with it inverted, if you set the amount down to zero, the image looks unaffected. Only as you increase the value does the inversion take place.

Figure 11.76 Solarize Controls with Image Inverted

Video

Video is the last group of effects in Final Cut Pro, and contains some of its really most useful and most often used filters.

Blink

Blink does exactly what it says, switches to black at a set rate (Figure 11.77). You can enhance the effect, though, by keyframing the values, so that the rate is not constant. Just give it some crazy numbers and let it flash erratically. A randomizing control would have been a nice feature for this effect.

De-interlace

This has got to be the most used filter in FCP, if for no other reason than that it's used to remove video interlacing when making still images. If you don't remove the interlacing on an image with movement, you get a still that looks like Figure 11.78.

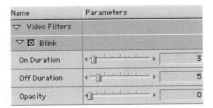

Figure 11.77 Blink Controls

If you place that image back into a video stream, it will flicker horribly as the interlacing switches on and off. The way around the problem is to apply the **De-interlace** filter before you export the frame. In that case, the frame will look like Figure 11.79. This frame will now play back smoothly when edited into video.

The **De-interlace** filter has only a single control, a popup that lets you select a field. Choose whichever looks better.

The other important use for the **De-interlace** filter is to help make video look more like film. The high temporal resolution of NTSC video, giving 60 discrete fields every second, is one of the reasons that makes video look like video, while film, which has a lower frame rate and no interlacing, produces a more blurred motion, a softer look which we associate with film. Removing interlacing is the first step toward trying to recreate that ever-popular film look.

Film Look

This recipe was created by Shawn Bockoven, the manager of Kids Merced Educational Television, who shared it with fellow FCP users on the 2-pop forums.

1. Lay two copies of a clip, one on top of the other.
2. Apply the **De-interlace** filter to the lower clip.
3. Select the dominant field — **Upper** or **Lower** — from the popup.
4. Reduce **Opacity** on the upper clip to about 30%.

This frame blending of the fields will slightly soften the image and simulate the temporal resolution of film. Hiroshi Kumatani has a variation of this method.

Figure 11.78 Interlaced Still Frame

Figure 11.79 De-interlaced Still Frame

1. Apply **De-interlace** to both clips, with upper dominance on the top clip and the lower dominance on the bottom.

2. Reduce **Opacity** on the upper clip by 50%.

3. You can also composite a little noise on the clip, but we'll look at that in Lesson 12 in "Noise" on page 513.

If you want a dirty and scratched film look, use the Film plugin that comes with the 3.0.2 upgrade, or export the clips and apply the QuickTime **Film Noise** filter. We'll look at this filter a little more closely in the lesson on exporting, Lesson 13 on page 549.

Flicker

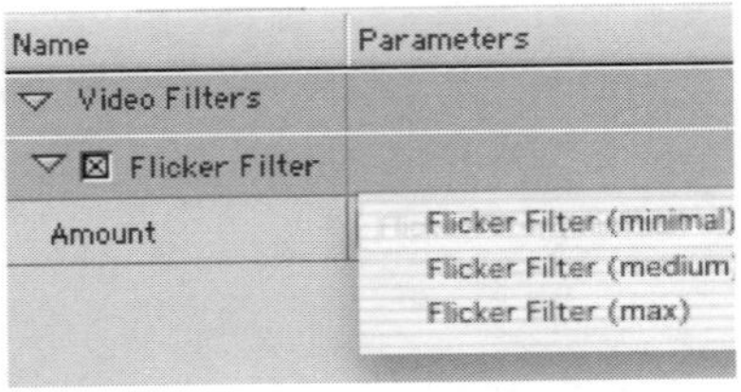

This is not a filter that creates a flickering image like an old silent movie. This filter, new to FCP3, helps remove flicker from an image. It is another of the few FCP filters that cannot be animated. It simply lets you set one of three amounts of flicker removal (Figure 11.80). **Flicker** is used to overcome that horrible shimmering effect you get when there are thin, horizontal lines across the screen, such as serifs in text, thin lines of newsprint on the screen, stripes in a shirt, Venetian blinds in the distance, and a host of other possible causes. These are all caused by interlace flicker, and **Flicker**, which probably should be called **De-Flicker**, helps to remove it. It's particular useful for minimizing flickering that can occur during scrolling titles as serifed fonts run up the screen.

Figure 11.80 Flicker Controls

Image Stabilizer

Some wags prefer to call it the Image Destabilizer. It doesn't work very well. Figure 11.81 shows the filter's controls as well as the image output.

Figure 11.81 Image Stabilizer Controls with Image Output

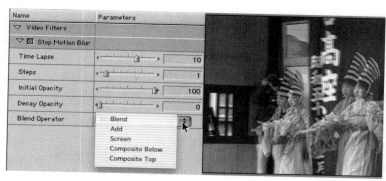

Figure 11.82 Stop Motion Blur Controls with Default Image Output

You can see from the figure how far the stabilizer has moved the image to try to compensate for the motion. The squares on the screen define the area the stabilizer is trying to lock onto. The smaller square defines the area to synchronize to, while the outer square defines how far the filter should look to find the portion of the image it's looking for. The filter will help a little for an image that is fairly stable and doesn't have motion in it, people moving, camera movements like pans and tilts and zoom. The filter is trying to lock a portion of the image and have the picture move to hold that stable. This won't work of course if there is something moving across the screen. Other applications can do this much better; FCP's is pretty much a failure, and you're probably better off leaving it alone than spending a lot of time trying to make it work. It also renders slowly.

Stop Motion Blur

This sounds like something practical, but it's really a special-effect filter (Figure 11.82).

The default setting uses the composite type **Blend**. Try using **Composite Top** or **Composite Below**. I prefer **Composite Top**. To use this, you'll need to turn down the **Initial Opacity** slider.

With **Time Lapse** set to zero, the filter has no effect. The slider defines which frames ahead (positive numbers) or which frames past (negative numbers) are combined with the current frame. Taking **Time Lapse** into low negative numbers will create an echo trail effect. Don't add too many **Steps** to the filter or it will quickly turn into a really bad Futurist painting, especially if there is a good deal of motion in the image or the frame itself is moving.

Name	Parameters	
▽ Video Filters		
▽ ☒ Strobe		
Strobe Duration	◄ ▯───┴───┴ ► │	5

Figure 11.83 Strobe Control

Strobe

Strobe creates a stuttering motion effect. It has one control that lets you set how many frames the image will be still for small amounts (Figure 11.83). The default setting makes it look as if your video has a frame rate of six frames per second. If you go much above 10, the motion is too stuttery.

Timecode Print

This tool creates a timecode display of your sequence and burns it into your video output. It's quite sophisticated (Figure 11.84). The **Mode** type defaults to **Generator**, which will begin counting timecode from the beginning of the clip, which is not in itself very useful. You'll most likely want to generate timecode not for a single shot, but for the whole sequence. To do this, simply select everything in the **Timeline** and nest it (**Option-C**). Apply **Timecode Print** to the nest, and it will write TC onto the screen for each frame. Get set to render out your entire sequence, which could take up a good deal of drive space.

✎ Note

Gaps: Be sure that any gaps in your sequence are filled with slugs. If they aren't, FCP will not print timecode for the gaps, though it will continue to generate numbers correctly. The gaps will simply be missing the timecode display when you output your material.

You have quite a bit of control in design and placement of the TC window as well as its functionality. A couple of important controls are obscured in Figure 11.84. The **Offset** slider allows you to adjust a specified number of frames difference from the real display, from –216,000 to +216,000 frames, which at NTSC video frame rate is plus or minus about two hours, depending if you're counting in drop fame or not.

Figure 11.84 Timecode Print Controls with Default Output

☞ Tip _____

Specific TC Start: Sometimes you might want to use a **Generator** but start at a specific timecode number. The simple way to do this is to use nesting and the **Reader**. You'll avoid having to calculate how many frames in a specific number of minutes, seconds, and frames. Set the start time for your sequence in the **Timeline Options Preference** to the time you want the **Generator** to begin. Then select all the clips in the sequence and hit **Option-C** to nest the clips. To the newly created nest, apply the **Timecode Print** filter. **Option**-double-click the nest to open it into the **Viewer** like any other clip, and change the default mode from **Generator** to **Reader**. The timecode will now start from the assigned time inside the nested sequence.

The other obscured but interesting function is the **Mode** popup, which lets you switch from the default sequence time to **Reader** mode. **Reader** will output the TC for each clip and display it in the window burn.

1. Apply the filter to a clip and set it up the way you want, with **Mode** selected as **Reader.**

2. Copy the clip and then select all the other clips in the sequence.

3. Use **Paste Attributes** to apply the filter to all the other clips.

Presto, all the timecode will be read out.

The other controls are self-explanatory, except for **Opacity**. This is not the opacity of the timecode numbers themselves, only of the background color. Rather than a solid black, perhaps turn the transparency down to about 50, and how about using yellow numbering instead of white? Or maybe a blue background with orange numbers?

I have been asked more than once to make a countdown clock that appears on screen. You can do this using **Timecode Print.**

1. Place a **Slug** in an empty sequence and apply the **Timecode Print** filter to it. (If you need it to run longer than two minutes, simply apply a bunch of slugs to a timeline, nest all the slugs into a sequence, and apply **Timecode Print** to the nest.)

By default the clock will start counting forward from zero.

2. Trim the slug by cropping it with the **Crop** tool. Bring in the sides, top and bottom, so that only the minutes and seconds are visible. This is your _Countdown_ sequence.

Name	Parameters
▽ Video Filters	
▽ ☒ View Finder	
Mode	REC
Custom Text	MONO
Font	Times
Size	20
Color	▷ 🌀 Ⓒ
Location	⊕ -102.4 , -67.2
Lamp Color	▷ 🌀 Ⓒ
Blink	6

Figure 11.85 View Finder Controls with Default Image Output

3. Place the *Countdown* sequence in your final sequence on top of your video.

4. Select the nested *Countdown* sequence and from the **Modify** menu select **Speed** (**Command-J**).

5. In the **Speed** dialog box, check the box for **Reverse** and uncheck the box for **Frame Blending**.

That's it. You'll have a little black box with time starting at whatever length your slug is, and counting down to zero. If you want to get rid of the black around the numbers, apply the compositing mode **Screen**. But we're getting ahead of ourselves. That's for the next lesson.

View Finder

The very last of Final Cut's filters, **View Finder,** is a nice touch, and it's not just any old view finder. Look at the controls (Figure 11.85).

I wish more cameras had view finders like this one: full **Safe Title** and **Safe Action Area,** center crosshairs, programmable message, variable blink rate — even size, style, and color of font can be set in this view finder. You can change what text appears in the view finder from a popup, or you can enter whatever text you want by selecting **Custom.**

👉**Tip**

TMTS Free: You might also want to take a look at the *TMTS Free* filters from Mattias Sandström. These contain an FXScript file for a countdown clock that will actually work as a **Generator.** Simply drag the *TMTS Free* folder into your *Plugins* folder to have access to the **Too Much Too Soon** filters.

Summary

This brings us to the end of another long chapter on the many, many capabilities of Final Cut Pro. Table 11.2 summarizes the filters for you. By now you should have a fairly good idea of what you can do with this application and should be well on your way to creating exciting, interesting and original video productions.

We need to explore one more aspect of FCP before we're ready to put our creations out on tape, the web, or some other delivery format, and that is compositing, the topic of our next lesson.

Table 11.2   Special Effects Filters

Filter	Description	Page
Blur		page 438
Gaussian Blur	Overall image blur or separate channels	page 439
Radial Blur	Spinning blur	page 440
Wind Effect	Directional blur	page 440
Zoom Blur	Streaks inward	page 441
Border		page 442
Basic	Colored edge around frame	page 442
Bevel	Raised 3D look to the frame edge	page 442
Channel		page 442
Arithmetic	Composites color to individual RGB channels	page 443
Channel Blur	Use Gaussian Blur	page 443
Channel Offset	Offsets RGB channels	page 443
Color Offset	Psychedelic colors	page 444
Compound Arithmetic	Composites still image to RGB or alpha channel	page 445
Invert	Inverts image channels	page 446

Table 11.2 Special Effects Filters (Continued)

Filter	Description	Page
Color Correction		page 401
Broadcast Safe	Keeps video to NTSC safe levels	page 413
Color Corrector	Adjusts chroma and luma values with secondary color correction	page 414
Color Corrector 3-way	Adjust chroma and luma in lows, mids and highs with secondary color correction	page 421
Desaturate Highlights	Reduces chroma in highlight areas	page 427
Desaturate Lows	Reduces chroma in darks	page 427
RGB Balance	Adjusts amounts of red, green & blue	page 427
Distort		page 446
Bumpmap	Use FXScript Displace	page 447
Cylinder	Distorts a portion of the image, doesn't wrap it around the cylinder	page 448
Displace	Use FXScript Displace	page 449
Fisheye	Very wide angle lens effect	page 449
Pond Ripple	Ripples out from a point on the screens	page 450
Ripple	Waves the image like a flag	page 451
Wave	Half of Ripple. One direction only.	page 452
Whirlpool	Spinning distortion. Needs to be animated.	page 452
FXScript DVE's		page 452
4-point Garbage Matte	Draws a four point shape to remove portion of image	page 453
Brightness/Contrast	Image control plus before/after split screen	page 455
Color Balance	Limited color control with split screen	page 455
Displace	Distorts clip based on luma value of moving image	page 455

Table 11.2   Special Effects Filters (Continued)

Filter	Description	Page
Distort	Like the Distort tool with soft edges	page 456
Double Border	Border that can crop the image	page 457
Replicate	Multiple copies of the image with borders	page 458
Roll-/Scroll (Title)	Pa and scan as well as scrolling PS titles that can be paused	page 459
White Balance	Simple to use color corrector	page 463
Widescreen	Creates letterboxing with borders	page 464
FXScript Layered DVE's		page 466
Band Slide	Animatable transitions	page 466
Page Peel	Animatable transitions	page 466
Page Peel 1/2	Animatable transitions	page 466
Page Peel 1/4	Animatable transitions	page 466
Slide	Moving images across the screen	page 467
Softwipe	Any mask shape applied to clip	page 469
Split Slide	Animatable transitions	page 470
Stretch	Distorting image	page 470
Swing	Animatable transitions	page 471
Zoom/Rotate	Smooth zoom in and out of clips	page 471
Image Control		page 472
Brightness & Contrast	Use Color Corrector	page 454
Color Balance	Use Color Corrector 3-way	page 455
Desaturate	Quick color removal	page 455
Gamma Correction	Use Color Corrector 3-way	
Levels	Use Color Corrector 3-way	

Table 11.2   Special Effects Filters (Continued)

Filter	Description	Page
Proc Amp	Use Color Corrector 3-way	
Sepia	Tint with highlight control	page 473
Tint	Use QT's Color Tint	
Key		
Blue and Green Screen	Use Chroma Keyer	
Chroma Keyer	Removes selected color	
Color Key	Use Chroma Keyer	
Difference Matte	Removes what's the same in two images	
Luma Key	Removes portion of image based on luminance value	
Spill Suppressor – Blue	Removes blue edge fringing	
Spill Suppressor – Green	Removes green edge fringing	
Matte		page 473
Eight-Point Garbage Matte	Draws eight-point shape to remove portion of the image	page 473
Extract	Another way to luminance key	page 477
Four-Point Garbage Matte	Use FXScript 4-point Garbage Mask	page 478
Image Mask	Use FXScript Softwipe	page 478
Mask Feather	Softens edges of applied mask	
Mask Shape	Creates regular shaped mask	page 479
Matte Choker	Tightens or expands keyed matte	
Soft Edges	Blurs edges of image alpha	
Widescreen	Use Fxscript Widescreen	page 464

Table 11.2   Special Effects Filters (Continued)

Filter	Description	Page
Perspective		page 483
Basic 3D	Allows moving image in 3D space	
Curl	Use FXScript Page Peel	page 484
Flop	Reverses image aspect	page 485
Mirror	Mirrors the image on itself	page 485
Rotate	Turns the images squeezing it to fit the screen	page 486
QuickTime		page 486
Alpha Gain	Controls luma value of alpha channel	page 486
Blur	Use FCP Blur	page 487
Brightness & Contrast	Use Color Corrector	page 487
Color Style	Solarize & Posterize together	page 488
Color Tint	Better than FCP's Sepia	page 488
Color Sync	To match computer monitor color	page 489
Edge Detection	Selects contrast edges	page 489
Emboss	Adds highlights and shadows to contrast edges	page 489
General Convolution	Complex stylization	page 490
HSL Balance	Use Color Corrector	page 490
Lens Flare	Doesn't work	page 490
RGB Balance	Use FCP's Color Corrector	page 492
Sharpen	Skip it	page 492
Sharpen		page 492
Sharpen	Brings out compression artifacts	page 492
Unsharpen Sharp	Brightens highlight areas	page 493

Table 11.2   Special Effects Filters (Continued)

Filter	Description	Page
Stylize		page 493
Anti-alias	Use to soften text edges	page 493
Diffuse	Dithers the images	page 494
Emboss	Like QT Emboss	page 494
Find Edges	Stylized edge detection	page 494
Posterize	Reduces image to areas of color	page 495
Replicate	Use FXScript Replicate	page 495
Solarize	Color & luma inversion	page 496
Video		page 496
Blink	Rapid switching to black on and off	page 496
De-Interlace	Removes one video field	page 496
Flicker	Removes fine-line flickering	page 498
Image Stabilizer	Doesn't work very well	page 498
Stop Motion Blur	Echo effect	page 499
Strobe	Stutters the video	page 500
Timecode Print	Burns timecode into image	page 500
Viewfinder	Puts camera viewfinder on image	page 502

Lesson 12

Compositing

Compositing is the ability to combine multiple layers of video on a single screen and have them interact with each other. This capability really adds depth to FCP. I confess I love compositing and wish I had opportunity to do more of it. Compositing often allows you to create a montage of images and graphics that can explain some esoteric point more clearly than some piece of wallpaper footage. Good compositing work can raise the perceived quality of a production. Be warned, though, that compositing and graphics animation is not quick and easy to do, which is why it's so often contracted out. All animation requires patience, skill, and hard work. With more and more small production companies having to do projects entirely on their own, it becomes more important for every producer to have a working knowledge of motion graphics. Fortunately, this ability has become accessible through tools such as After Effects and now Final Cut Pro, with its ability to access AE plugins such as Boris RED. Though FCP is not a full-bore compositing application such as After Effects, Commotion, or Combustion, it does have excellent tools to do some simple work.

Loading the Lesson

Let's load the material you need onto your media drive.

1. If you don't already have it, drag over the *Media1* folder from the CD. Also drag the folder *Lesson12* onto your drive and put it in your *Shared* folder.

2. Eject the CD, open the *Lesson12* on your hard drive, and launch the project *L12*.

3. Reconnect the media, reassign the scratch disk to the correct folder as well as the *Autosave Vault*.

4. Duplicate the project file, and we're ready to go.

Inside your copy of the project *L12*, you'll find the **Clips** bin, *Damine.mov*, and a number of sequences.

As in the previous lesson, a couple of sequences contain examples of effects used in the lesson. They're called *Composite Stacks* and *Composite Modes*. Before we get into compositing, we should take a quick look at the **Generators**, because these provide us some useful compositing tools.

Generators

We used the **Generator** popup to create text files, but let's take a moment to have a look at what else is under that little **A**.

Bars and Tone

First is **Bars and Tone**, both NTSC and PAL. It creates two SMPTE-style bar sets with 1,000Hz tone, useful for dropping on the front of pieces that are going to broadcast or for dubbing. The audio default is –12dB. These give engineers standard reference signals for aligning their equipment.

Matte

We've already seen how useful the **Color Matte** generator can be. It defaults to producing midtone gray, but if you go into **Controls**, you get a color swatch that allows you to set and animate the color, as we saw earlier in Lesson 8 on titles, "Basic Animation" on page 322.

Render

The **Render** generators are a great tool and a hidden secret inside FCP's **Generators**. They allow you to create animatable compositing tools that will alter the shapes and textures of video and graphics images. Be aware that the blackness you see in **Render** items and in the **Shapes** we'll look at shortly is not the emptiness you normally see in the **Viewer** or **Canvas** around text or animated images. What you see in the gradients and shapes is actual opaque black without any transparency.

Custom Gradient

Custom Gradient lets you create gradient ramps or radials, either from the default black and white or from two colors (Figure 12.1).

Gradients are easiest to work with. Like with titles, you can pull one into the **Timeline**, double-click on it, and use the controls in the **Viewer** while seeing your work updated in the **Canvas**.

The default is a white-to-black gradient. The crosshairs let you pick where the white point or start color begins, and **Gradient Direction** obviously controls the angle at which the gradient proceeds, the default being pure white on the left and going to pure black on the right. In a **Radial Gradient** only the crosshairs have effect; there is no direction, of course. Generally you should leave **Dither** off, but if you see banding in the gradient, **Dither** will add some noise to the image to break up the banding, which is usually due to the way codecs compress the video. They often are not able to make the fine distinctions in color and tone needed to produce smooth gradients. **Gaussian** makes the gradient tighter looking and seems to have less of a ramp.

Creating gradients allows you to make wonderful, complex layered images using traveling mattes, as we shall see on page 520. By animating the gradients, you can make opacity vary and change over time, revealing and fading out layered images and graphics.

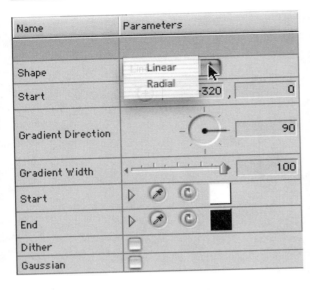

Figure 12.1 Custom Gradient Controls

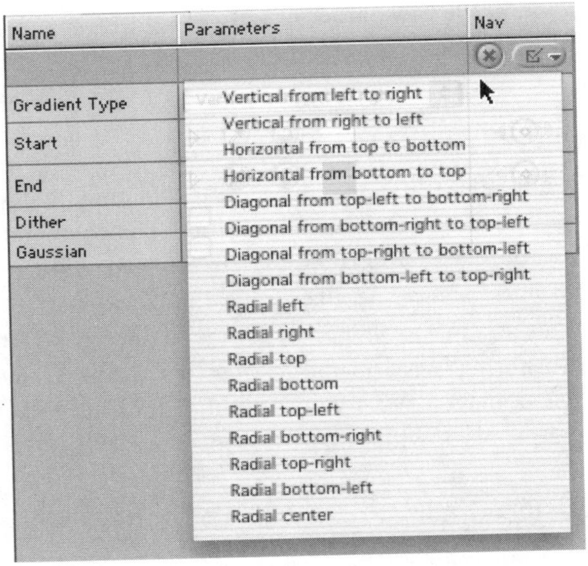

Figure 12.2 Gradient Popup

Gradient

I'm not sure why there is a **Custom Gradient** and a **Gradient**. You have some of the controls in **Gradient**, but no crosshairs or **Gradient Direction**. You do, however, have a popup that generates a long list of standard gradient shapes (Figure 12.2).

Highlight

The **Highlight** render is great for generating quick highlights that race across images or text (Figure 12.3).

Figure 12.3 Highlight and Its Controls

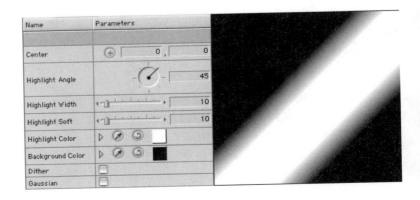

The default sets the highlight to 90. I usually use it at 45 and with a much narrower highlight width than the default 10. You can animate it using the origin point. Set values that place it outside one of the corners, and then about a second later sweep it across to the opposite corner. When you combine it with a compositing mode, it produces effects that give a quick sparkle to your images.

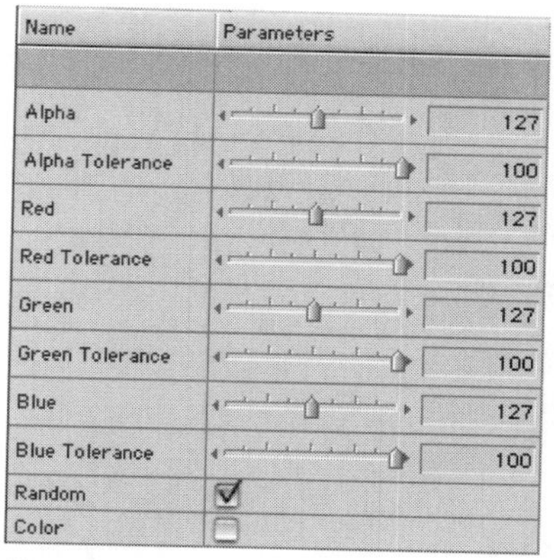

Noise

Using composite modes, this render generator can be used to create film grain–type noise that blends with your video (Figure 12.4). It's perhaps a bit too "noisy" for most film grain, but it helps to enhance the illusion. Small quantities of **Noise** can also be used to break up banding similar to the effect of **Dither,** which we saw in the **Custom Gradient.**

Noise defaults to black and white, but the checkbox at the bottom of the controls can set color noise as well. You can also randomize it, which you probably want, otherwise the noise looks stuck on top of the image. If you want to make a white-noise generator, then crank the sliders around and animate them with lots of keyframes.

Particle Noise

Particle Noise is unique to Final Cut (Figure 12.5). It makes chunks of shapes that scatter about the screen randomly. The controls are self-explanatory. **Density** controls how many shapes appear on the screen, while **Time Lapse** controls how many frames — up to 30 — the generator will hold before creating a new set of shapes. It's a neat little toy, but I've never used it in a

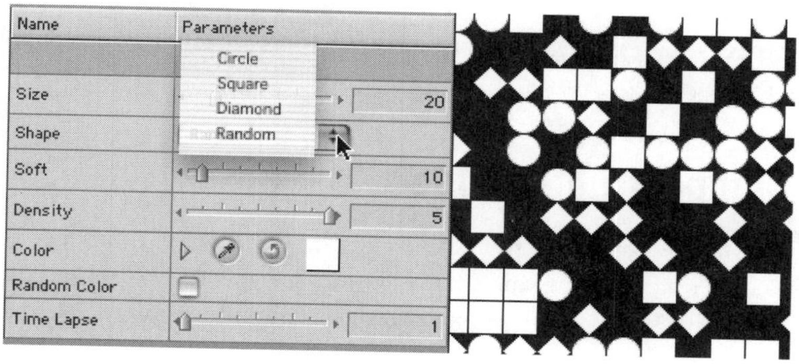

Figure 12.4   Noise Controls

Figure 12.5   Particle Noise and Controls

Figure 12.6 Oval Shape and Controls

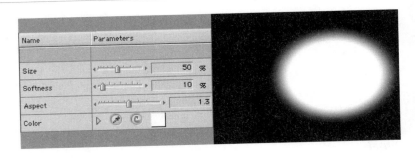

project. Maybe someday I'll need it for a weird animation. There's a clip composited with **Particle Noise** in *Composite Stacks* that we'll look at in the exercise beginning on page 518.

Shapes

New to FCP3 are the **Shapes** generators. Like the **Render** generators, they produce black-and-white customizable shapes:

- Circle
- Oval
- Rectangle
- Square

The controls for the **Shapes** are all pretty much the same. Two of them, **Oval** (Figure 12.6) and **Rectangle**, have controls that allow you to change the **Aspect**, while **Circle** and **Square** do not.

Rectangle starts out with a 1.3 **Aspect**, which coincidentally is the same as standard definition television. All of them can be scaled to 150%, except **Circle**, which can go up to 250%. None of them will go down to a size small enough so they actually disappear. The smallest they can be is 1%. Using **Circle** with very large **Aspect** settings can create interesting shapes, especially when softened.

Compositing Modes

One of the best ways to combine render elements with images is to use compositing modes. If you're familiar with Photoshop, you probably already know that a compositing mode is a way that the values of one image can be combined with the values of another image. Final Cut has 13 compositing modes, including two traveling mattes, which we'll look at on page 520. For the moment, we'll deal only with the first 11:

- **Normal,** the way clips usually appear
- **Add**
- **Subtract**
- **Difference**
- **Multiply**
- **Screen**
- **Overlay**
- **Hard Light**
- **Soft Light**
- **Darken**
- **Lighten**
- **Travel Matte - Alpha**
- **Travel Matte - Luma**

Compositing Exercise

1. Open up the sequence *Composite Modes.*

This sequence contains 11 iterations of two clips, one on top of the other. Each clip on **V2** is composited onto the clip on **V1** using a different compositing mode. A marker on the first frame of each section identifies the compositing mode applied to the clip stack. I put it on the first frame only so it doesn't obscure the image.

No two compositing modes are the same, though the differences are subtle. Some will make the output darker; some will make it lighter, but all in a slightly different manner. It's a wonderful tool for controlling image quality.

The two last **Composite Modes, Travel Matte – Alpha** and **Travel Matte – Luma,** have special uses that we'll look at shortly.

2. To change the compositing mode of a clip, select the clip and from the **Modify** menu choose **Composite Mode**

3. Choose a type (Figure 12.7).

You can also select the clip in the **Timeline** and with the **Control** key bring up the contextual menu and select **Composite Mode** (Figure 12.8). This feature is new to FCP3.

Should you want to change the **Composite Mode** of a clip in the **Browser**, it is slightly more complicated. You have to select the clip and with the **Control** key select **Properties** from the contextual menu. This will evoke the **Item Properties** panel. On the right side of the panel is a popup where you can change the compositing mode (Figure 12.9).

That's it. Note that the clip's contextual menu cannot, for some reason, be called up from inside the **Viewer**, though the **Modify>Composite Mode** menu does function.

Instant Sex

Let's look at some of what you can do with **Composite Modes**.

1. Begin by opening the blank *Sequence 1* and bringing in a clip from the **Clips** bin, *Ceremony8*.

2. Lay another copy of the same clip on **V2**, making identical copies on **V1** and **V2**.

You can also use **Option-Shift**-drag the clip from **V1** to the space above to make a copy of the clip and create **V2**.

3. To the top layer, apply a generous amount of **Gaussian Blur** of about 30.

4. The image looks very out of focus now.

5. Turn down the **Opacity** of the layer to something like 40%.

6. Go to **Composite Mode** and change it to **Add**.

7. I prefer **Add**, but try some of the others, such as **Screen**.

8. Try adjusting the **Blur** amount and the **Opacity** levels to different settings.

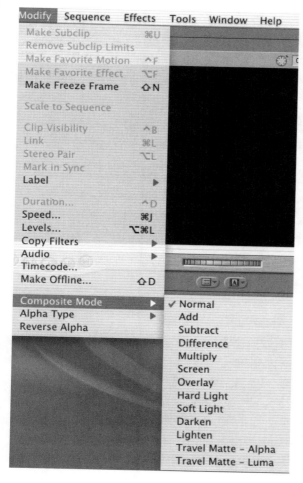

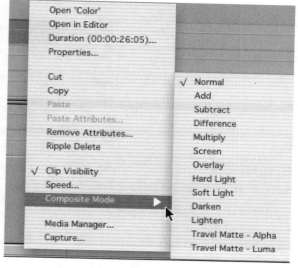

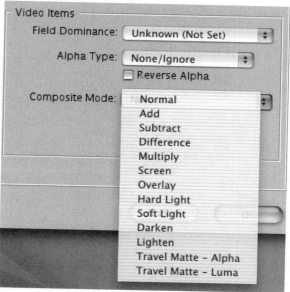

Figure 12.7   Modify>Composite Mode Menu

Figure 12.8   Clip Contextual Menu>Composite Mode

This is the great After Effects artist Trish Meyer's recipe for Instant Sex. Though it was created for After Effects, it adapts readily to Final Cut. The soft, blooming highlights make a wonderful dreamy, romantic effect (Figure 12.10).

Figure 12.10 Left: Original
Right: "Instant
Sex"

Note

NTSC Warning: If you are going to output to NTSC analog, be careful in using **Compositing Modes**, particularly **Add**. It will brighten the image, often beyond the luminance and chrominance values allowable for broadcast transmission. The chroma/luma range in video, even in PAL, is fairly narrow. You should not exceed values of 235 in any RGB channel, particularly in all three when creating white. It's also a very bad idea to exceed 235 in red, which blooms objectionably and smears easily when analog copies are made, particularly VHS copies.

Figure 12.11 Snowy Noise

Noise Exercise

Next let's bring up the noise. We can use **Noise** to add a film-grain effect.

1. Go to the **Generators** popup, and from **Render** select **Noise**.

2. Drag it onto **V3**, above the Instant Sex stack, and stretch it out to the length of the clips below.

3. Change its compositing mode to **Screen**.

4. Remember the piece in the **Timeline** is a copy of the one you created in the **Viewer**, so double-click it to bring it back into the **Viewer**.

5. Go to the **Controls** tab and make sure the **Random** box is checked and the **Color** box unchecked.

In **Color** mode, **Noise** is too strong and generates too many sparkling bits to be useful for our purposes.

Toning It Down

At this stage the **Canvas** should look like a very snowy television picture (Figure 12.11). Now we need to reduce the effect of the **Noise**.

1. First, set the **Alpha** level all the way to zero and pull down the **Alpha Tolerance** to something around 20 or 25, depending on how much graininess you want to introduce.

2. Try also using the **Soft Light** composite mode, but with **Alpha** turned up to perhaps around 120.

Text

Let's not stop there. On top of your video, which should still have strong, glowing highlight areas, as well as a sprinkling of grain, let's add a text element.

1. Use the standard **Text** tool to create the word *JAPAN* in any font you like, fairly large size and a nice, bright color.

I used Textile because it's in the Apple basic font set and used a size of 153 in bright red, the saturation set to 89%. Create whatever text block you like, using any available font.

2. Place your text block on **V4**.

3. **Option-Shift**-drag the *Text* clip to the space above to create a copy on **V5**.

Your stack should look like Figure 12.12.

4. In the controls for the text file on **V5**, change the color to bright yellow.

5. Next, apply a **Gaussian Blur** filter to the text, maybe something in the 20 range.

6. Change the composite mode to **Add** so that it combines with the layers beneath.

The layer blurred out and composited will make it look like a glow over the image (Figure 12.13). But you may not want that top glow layer on the image all the time.

7. Ramp up the **Opacity** quickly over a few frames.

8. Hold **Opacity** for four or five frames.

9. Quickly ramp it down again, so it's just a quick flash of yellow glow.

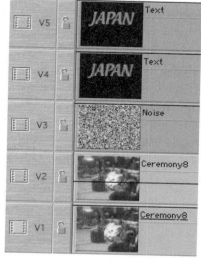

Figure 12.12 Two Video Layers, Noise Layer, and Two Text Layers

Figure 12.13 Composited Layers and Effects

**Figure 12.14 Drop Shadow Glow
Layer Behind**

Finding Markers: Remember you can jump to any sequence marker in the **Timeline** by **Control**-clicking in the **Timeline** ruler and selecting the marker number or name in the popup (Figure 12.15).

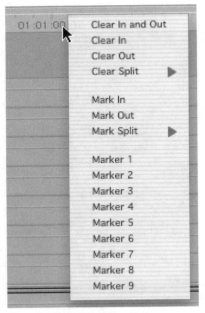

**Figure 12.15 Timeline Ruler
Contextual Menu**

Look at the sequence *Composite Stacks*. I've build the five-layer stack with the quick animation at the beginning of the sequence at Marker 1.

Drop Shadow Exercise

Another variation is to use a composite mode to create a different kind of drop shadow, using this type of glow layer technique only behind the text rather than on top of it (Figure 12.14). Rather than using white in the glow layer, simply keep the same color as the text layer.

1.   Start with two copies of the text stacked on top of each other.

This time, rather than working with the upper text layer, work on the lower text layer.

2.   Scale the lower text layer up in the **Motions** tab of **Viewer** to about 110%.

3.   Add a little **Gaussian Blur** next, something around 10.

4.   At this point the color will be too rich, so change the composite mode to **Multiply** or **Darken**.

The drop shadow glow layer stack is built in the *Composite Stacks* sequence at Marker 2.

Travel Mattes

Technically these are compositing modes as well, though they function in a special way. The two **Travel Mattes** are **Luminance** and **Alpha**. In a travel matte — more commonly a track matte — the layer to which it's applied will take its shape from either the **Luminance** value or the **Alpha** value of the layer directly beneath it. Because it tracks the layer, any animation or change in the layer below will be reflected in the tracking layer. This makes **Travel Matte** an extraordinarily powerful tool.

Split Screen

In its simplest form, **Travel Matte** can be used to create a soft-edge split screen. To do this, create a sandwich of three layers.

1. On the top layer, **V3,** put an image for the left side. I used *Bamboo1.*

2. On the bottom layer, **V1,** put an image on the right side, *Dance3* in this case.

3. In between, on **V2,** place a **Custom Gradient.**

4. To the clip on **V3,** apply **Composite Mode> Travel Matte - Luma.**

5. Adjust to taste the falloff sharpness of the gradient on **V2.**

6. Move the **Gradient Width** slider down to about 30.

7. Move the **Start** *x* point near the middle of the screen, about −10 (Figure 12.16).

8. Animate the gradient's **Start** point to wipe the split screen on or off.

Figure 12.16 Split Screen Using Custom Gradient

Area Highlight

You can also use a **Travel Matte** to highlight an area of the screen. Again start by creating a sandwich of three layers.

1. On **V1** place the image to be highlighted. I used *Dance 3.*

2. On **V2** place the same image and then drag it upward to move it onto **V3.**

3. In between, on **V2,** place an **Oval Shape.**

4. To the clip on **V3,** apply **Composite Mode> Travel Matte - Luma.**

At the moment you're not going to see anything happen because the two layers are identical.

5. To the clip on **V1,** apply **Brightness and Contrast (Bezier)** from the **Image Control** submenu of **Video Filters.** Adjust the **Brightness** value down to about −55.

Figure 12.17 Highlight Area Using
Oval Shape

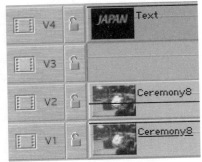

Figure 12.18 Video Tracks in
Timeline

6. The **Oval** should now be clearly visible in the center of the screen.

7. Open the **Oval** controls and set the **Aspect** down to about 0.7, which will make a tall narrow oval.

8. In the **Motion** tab for the **Oval Shape**, move the x point so that it's off toward the left, around –65.

9. You will now have a highlight area of normal exposure, while the rest of the image is darker and obscured. You can of course animate the **Oval** as needed (Figure 12.17).

Highlight Matte

Next we're going to create a **Highlight Matte**. Let's set up a simple animation display. We'll use the two layers of *Ceremony8* that we used earlier. The layer on **V1** is normal; the layer on **V2** as before with **Composite Mode Add**, **Gaussian Blur** about 30, and **Opacity** about 40.

1. Just use the first five seconds of the clips for these layers that are just background to the title.

2. Next add two tracks of video to your sequence above **V2**.

3. Create your text block using a large font with a bright red as we did earlier. Make it the same five-second **Duration** as the other clips.

4. Instead of placing it on **V3**, place it on **V4** as in Figure 12.18.

It's difficult to see in the grayscale figure, but I've targeted **V3**, because that's where I'm going to place the next element.

Select **Highlight** from the **Render Generator** popup and place it on **V3** between the text and the background, which will disappear, of course. Make the **Highlight** five seconds long as well. Simply drag the end so that it snaps to the ends of the other clips.

Let's work on the highlight.

5. Double-click the highlight to bring it into the **Viewer**.

6. Go its **Controls** tab and move the **Highlight Angle** around to 45°.

7. Increase the **Width** and **Softness** a bit, such as 15 of one and 20 of the other.

8. Leave off **Dither** and **Gaussian**; the latter only tightens the sharpness of the fall off.

Your **Canvas** should look something like Figure 12.19.

Animating the Highlight

The next step will be to animate the **Highlight**.

1. Put the playhead at the start of the clip.

2. In the **Highlight** controls, set the **Center X** axis to –400, which should take it off screen left, at least away from the text file on **V4**.

3. Create a **Center** keyframe.

4. Move to the end of the clip (**Shift-O**). Now set the **Center X** point to 400.

Over the five seconds of the clip, the **Highlight** bar will sweep slowly across the screen. Of course, we still don't see the background layer.

5. Next set the **Composite Mode** of the text file on **V4** to **Travel Matte - Luma**.

If you're at the start or end of the clip, everything except the background will suddenly disappear. As you scrub through the sequence, you'll see the text will softly wipe onto the screen and then wipe off again as the **Highlight** layer slides underneath it. The text file's transparency is being directly controlled by the luminance value of the layer beneath it. The matte layer, the **Highlight** in this case, is itself invisible.

To see what's happening to the transparency of the top two layers, switch off the visibility the background layers on **V1** and **V2**. You can check the alpha channel of the **Canvas** or the **Viewer** using the **View** popup to show you the alpha channel of the layer (Figure 12.20).

Figure 12.19 Highlight Under Text

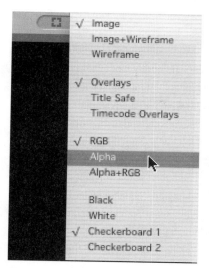

Figure 12.20 View Popup Alpha Channel Select

Figure 12.21 Alpha Channel of Composite Text and Travel Matte Layers

Figure 12.22 Highlight Text with Drop Shadow

What you should see in the **Canvas** when you're about halfway through the clip would be something like Figure 12.21.

If you like, you could nest the text layer and the travel matte layer together into a **Timeline** and use it wherever you want in your project. Simply select both the text file and the animated **Highlight** and hit **Option-C** to nest them into a sequence. The nested sequence is now available for this or any other project.

Try applying a drop shadow to the text layer in the **Motion** tab. It should look Figure 12.22.

Notice that the drop shadow wipes on and off with the text file. The stack at Marker 3 in *Composite Stacks* uses a **Drop Shadow Offset** of 6, with **Softness** at 20 and **Opacity** at 70.

What's nice about this technique is that you can use the animated gradient in so many different ways. It doesn't only have to wipe across the screen. It can open out from the middle, spread across from the edges, or do practically anything you can imagine, while offering great flexibility and control.

Glints

We've seen how we can put a glow on an image and how to use a traveling matte to highlight an image. Next we're going to do something a little more complex, creating a traveling highlight, but one that only goes along the edges of a piece of text, a highlight that glints the edges.

1. We'll begin again with our two base layers, two copies of *Ceremony8*, stacked as before with the top layer blurred, the **Opacity** turned down and composited with **Add** mode.

2. Next we add the text to **V3**.

I made it a little bigger this time, font size 180, nice and fat, right to the edges of the **Safe Title Area** and beyond. Next we'll create a moving highlight area.

3. Use FCP's **Custom Gradient** from the **Generators** popup, Render>Custom Gradient.

4. Set the **Duration** for the **Custom Gradient** to five seconds because that's how long the animation will be, and drag the **Custom Gradient** into the **Timeline** onto V4.

5. Open the **Gradient** from the **Timeline** and the **Control** tab of the **Viewer**; change the **Shape** menu to **Radial**.

6. Set the **Gradient Width** to 35.

7. Make sure both **Dithering** and **Gaussian** are not checked.

Animating the Radial

We'll position the radial gradient in the center of the frame. We want the glint to run along the top edge of the letters.

Figure 12.23 Radial Gradient in the Viewer

1. First let's move the start position of the **Radial Gradient** to *x,y* of 0, −80 as in Figure 12.23.

To animate the gradient, we want it to move from left to right across the screen and then back again staying at the its current height. At the start you want the gradient off one side of the screen.

2. Set the **Start** *x* point to −300, leaving *y* at −80 and keyframe it.

3. Type **+215** to go forward 2:15 (two and one-half seconds), about halfway through the clip.

4. Set the **Start** *x* point way over on the opposite side of the screen, about 300.

5. At the end of the five-second clip, set the *x* value back to its start position of −300.

Over the five seconds of the clip, the radial gradient will sweep across the text and then back again. So far so good.

6. If you scrub the timeline, or play through with **Option-P**, you should see the gradient swing from left to right and back again.

We now have to get rid of the black and just leave the gradient across the text. We could do this by changing the composite mode of the gradient layer to **Screen**. This gets rid of the black and is useful when you want to use these kind of gradient elements on a picture.

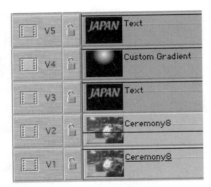

Figure 12.24 Five Layer Video Layers in Sequence

Figure 12.25 Text with Glow Composite

Here, though, the gradient appears not only on the text, but on the background image as well. In this case, we want to confine the gradient to affect only the text portion of the image, so we'll leave the radial gradient layer at normal, not composited.

7. To make the glow appear only on the text, start by copying the text layer on **V3** and placing the copy on **V5**, on top of the gradient.

Your stack should look like Figure 12.24.

8. Open the top text layer into the **Viewer** and use the controls to change its **Color** to white, pale yellow, or whatever glow color you want to use.

This layer will be the glow on top of the text, the radial gradient will be the matte it follows.

9. To the top text layer, apply **Composite Mode>Travel Matte - Luma**.

Immediately the gradient will disappear and the glow will be composited on top of the bottom text layer (Figure 12.25).

Polishing the Glow

That's a nice effect. You could be happy with it and stop there, with the glowing layer animated across the screen with the **Custom Gradient** layer.

What we really want, though, is for the glow not to race across the whole text, but to run just along the top edge of the text. It's not hard to do. We just need to add a few more layers.

1. **Option-Shift**-drag two more copies of the text layer on **V3** up to the top of the stack onto **V6** and **V7**.

These will, of course, completely hide the glow, so what we want to do is create a mask that will hide most of the text except for the very edges.

2. Open up the controls for the topmost layer and set its origin point slightly to one side, away from the side the glow starts from.

3. Also set it slightly lower on the screen if the glow is traveling above the text or slightly higher if the glow is traveling below the text.

I added 3,3 to the text layer's *x,y* values. This will make the text look slightly fatter than it really is, so what we want to do is make a matte that cuts off the bits of text that protrude beyond the correct shape of the text. That's what the layer beneath is for.

4. To the top layer, apply **Composite Mode>Travel Matte-Alpha**.

The **Travel Matte** layer disappears, and you're left with just a glint that travels along the edges of the text (Figure 12.26).

Figure 12.26 Glint on Text

One More Touch

At the moment, the glint brushes across the upper left edge of the letters as it moves back and forth across the screen. If you want to be really crafty and add a little something special, you can shift the glint side as it swings back and forth.

1. For the first pass of the **Radial Gradient**, leave the settings as they are.

2. When the glint reaches the far right side of the screen at 2:15, set a **Center** keyframe on the uppermost offset text layer on **V7**.

3. For the next frame, while the **Radial Gradient** is still off to the right, change that offset text layer's **Center** *x,y* values by −3,−3.

Now when the glint passes back from right to left, the glint will be on the upper right edge of the letters.

Extra Credit Exercise

Next we're going to add a **Drop Shadow**. But we have an apparently moving light, so we'd like to move the drop shadow to appear to be caused by the moving light.

1. Open the bottom text layer on **V3** into the **Viewer**.

2. In the **Motion** tab, turn on the **Drop Shadow**.

3. Change the default settings: make **Offset** 6, leave **Angle** at 135 and the **Color** at black, but change the **Softness** to 20 and the **Opacity** to 70.

Now we're going to animate the drop shadow.

4. At the start of the clip, the **Angle** should be 135. Set an **Angle** keyframe there.

5. Half way through the clip, when the glint is on the right side of the screen, set the **Angle** to 225.

6. At the end of the clip, when the glint is back on the left, set the **Angle** back to 135.

The shadow now swings with the glint as it goes by. The glint stack with the drop shadow animation is at Marker 4 in *Composite Stacks*.

Video In Text

I hope you're getting the hang of this by now and are beginning to understand the huge range of capabilities that these tools make possible. Next let's try an even more complex animation with traveling mattes, the ever-popular video-inside-text effect, the kind of technique that might look familiar from the open of another old television program.

To look at what we're going to do, open the *Composite Stacks* sequence and go to Marker 5. If you click on the clip on **V2** called *Damine Nest* and hit **Command-R**, you will render out the section of sequence defined by the length of the clip. That's what we're going to build.

If you want to make really enormous letters that fill right to the top and bottom edge of the screen, you may need to make them in a stage sequence. The stage sequence is an intermediary sequence, usually larger than your final output that lets you work with a very large text file without cutting it off. The problem usually is that the word will extend beyond the edge of frame, so you need to make a sequence that is as tall as your final is, but a lot wider. For this project, for instance, we'll use a sequence that's 800×240, nearly 500 pixels wider than the normal 4:3 frame, but the same height.

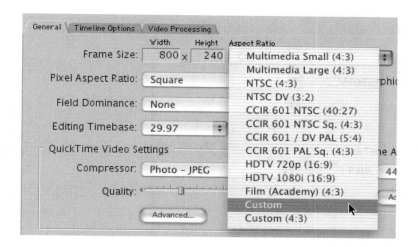

Figure 12.27 Sequence Settings of 800×240 Stage Sequence

1. Start out by duplicating *Sequence 1* (**Option-D**).

2. For the duplicated sequence, which you can call *Stage Sequence*, open **Sequence>Settings** (**Command-Zero**).

3. Change the **Aspect Ratio** popup to **Custom**.

4. Change the **Frame Size Width** to 800, while leaving the height at 240 (Figure 12.27).

Making Text

We need to start with really big blocks of text.

1. From the **Generators** popup, select **Text**.

2. Make the **Duration** of **Text** five seconds.

3. Drag the text into an empty sequence.

4. Open the text from the **Timeline** back into the **Viewer**.

The **Canvas** should still display the text file while you work in the **Controls** tab.

5. Type in the word *DAMINE*, the name of the mountain village in Japan where the clips were shot.

6. Pick a chunky, broad font type.

Don't use a thin, wimpy, serif font. I used Arial Black, but you can use whatever you have at hand.

7. Make the type size large, something in the 120 range.

We're going to not only move images in the text, but we're going to move a different image in each letter of the text.

8. You can make this easier by setting the **Tracking** up a bit to get better separation between letters. Something like 3 or 4 will probably be enough, depending on your font.

Don't worry about the text going outside the **Safe Title Area**. As long as it stays within the confines of the screen and doesn't get cut off, it will be okay.

9. To make the letters bigger, try pulling down the **Aspect** slider a bit.

A very little will move the text a lot. I brought it down to 0.7. Because text starts in the center of the screen, a large text block like this will stretch right off the top of the screen.

10. Set the origin point lower in the frame. Set origin *y* to something like 70 (Figure 12.28).

Figure 12.28 Large Title Block in Canvas

Figure 12.29 Six Layer Stack of Text Blocks

Separating Letters

The text file will be the matte for the video that's inside it. Because we want different video in each letter we need to separate the word into its individual letters.

1. **Option-Shift**-drag the text layer from **V1** onto the layers above again and again, until you have a stack six text layers tall, or one for each letter (Figure 12.29).

Next we want to create a layer for each letter.

After you've created the layer stack, then you need to crop each letter so that only it is visible.

2. If the **Canvas** is not already in **Image+Wireframe** mode, switch to it now.

3. Select the text on **V1** and use **Control-S** to solo it, so none of the other layers are visible.

4. Use the **Crop** tool to pull in the right side of the text layer that's in your sequence (Figure 12.30).

5. Turn on the visibility for the text layer on **V2** and select it.

The number in center of the **Canvas** will tell you which layer is selected.

6. With the **Crop** tool, move the right crop line from the right until you are between the A and the M.

7. Move the left crop line so that it's between the D and the A.

You should now see the A on text layer on **V2** and the D on the text layer on **V1**.

8. Select the text on **V3** and repeat, moving the right crop line to the right until all of the M is visible.

9. Then move its left crop line so that it's between the second and third letters, A and M.

10. Repeat for the other four layers until each layer has one letter visible on it.

Next you need to make space for the video. One more layer has to be added above each layer of text.

11. **Control**-click at the head of the track on **V1** to get a contextual menu that will let you add or delete a track.

The contextual menu will always create a track above the one you've clicked on. After you've done this you should have twice as many tracks as you started out with — in my case, 12 tracks (Figure 12.31).

Adding Video

We're ready now to put in some video. We'll work only with video here.

1. Target **V2**, untarget any audio tracks, and make sure the playhead is at the beginning of the stage sequence.

2. Find a clip in the **Browser** you want to place above the text on **V1**.

I used *Bamboo1* starting at 6:54:19. I chose that point in the shot because there was some movement in the frame.

3. Set the **Duration** to five seconds so that it will be the same length as the text layers.

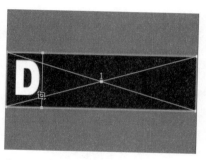

Figure 12.30 Cropped Text Layer

Figure 12.31 Twelve Layers in the Sequence

4. Drag the clip to the **Canvas** to **Overwrite**, slotting the clip into **V2**.

5. Roughly position the clip in the **Canvas** so that it's sitting on the left side of the frame over the letter D.

The next step will be to apply a **Composite Mode**.

6. With the clip on **V2** selected, use the **Control** key to see the contextual menu, and choose **Composite Mode>Travel Matte - Alpha**.

Actually, with white text we could use an alpha matte or a luma matte, and the result would be the same. Remember the image doesn't have to be the whole size of the frame or positioned in the center of the frame. It can be placed anywhere at any size, so long as it covers the letter.

7. Grab a corner of the image and resize it. Hold the **Shift** key and distort image shape, if you want. (Figure 12.32).

Next we need to add some more video to the other layers.

Figure 12.32 Distorted Image Composited over Text

8. Target **V4** and find a clip in the **Browser** for it.

I used *Ceremony7* from right at the beginning of the subclip, giving it a five-second duration so that it was the length of the other layers in the sequence.

9. Place it on **V4** and change its **Composite Mode** to **Travel Matte - Alpha**.

10. Scale the image in the **Canvas** and position it so that it covers the letter A.

The next clip will take its matte from **V5** and fill the letter M. I used the first five seconds of *Temple*.

11. Find a clip to use and bring it onto the empty **V6**.

12. Set the composite mode to **Travel Matte - Alpha**.

13. Scale and position in the **Canvas**.

I used the beginning of *Dance3* for **V8**.

14. Repeat the process for **V8**, and the letter I.

I used *Food3* for **V10**.

15. Repeat the process for **V10** to be matted by the letter N on **V9**.

I used *Ceremony1* for **V12**.

16. Repeat the process for **V12**, the top video layer taking its **Travel Matte - Alpha** from the letter E on **V11**.

Your 12 layers in the sequence should now be made up of six layers of text interspersed with six layers of video scaled and positioned to fit the text layer below it.

Nesting

So far we've created the text in a stage sequence with very large letters, and we've placed moving pictures inside each letter. Next we need to animate the whole composite over another image so that the stage sequence itself moves across another image. The stage sequence we created is a nest of material. The one I've created, which is in your **Browser**, is called *Damine Nest*. This nest is composited over video in the sequence *Composite Stacks*.

Figure 12.33 Damine Nest Composited on Video

1.   Open a copy of *Sequence 1* lay a clip of video in it.

I used the first five seconds of *Village3*.

2.   Next place your stage sequence on **V2** above the video on **V1**.

Sequence 1 is, of course, 320×240, so when you place the much larger stage sequence in it, the stage sequence will extend beyond the sides of the **Canvas** as in Figure 12.33.

Next we'll want to animate the text so that the whole nest slides across the screen from right to left.

1.   **Option**-double-click, or select and press **Enter**, on your stage sequence so that it opens in the **Viewer**.

2.   In the **Motion** tab, set a **Center X** keyframe at the start of the clip of 550, which will push it off the right side of the screen.

3.   At the end of the clip, set a Center position of 550, which will move it off the left side of the screen.

Over the course of the five seconds the text will travel from right to left on top of *Village3*.

Figure 12.34 Resizing the Image

Variation with Fades

At Marker 6 in *Composite Stacks* I've created a variation in which each letter fades in one after the other.

1. Place the background layer *Village3* on **V1** in a new 320×240 sequence, and your stage sequence top of it on **V2**.

For this animation we're going to need the text sequence with the word to fit into the **Canvas**. Rather than rebuild all the text files, with all the all the layers, and all the cropping, we'll simply rescale the stage sequence so that it fits into the 320×240 sequence.

2. Select the stage sequence in the **Timeline** and reduce the view size of the **Canvas** to 50%, which should show you the full width of the stage sequence, as on the left of Figure 12.34.

3. Grab a corner of the image and pull in to reduce the scale. Hold down the **Shift** key so the aspect ratio changes back to 4:3, as on the right of Figure 12.34.

4. Double-click the nested sequence on **V2** to open it up with all its 12 layers.

5. Double-click the video clip on **V2** to bring it into the **Viewer** and go to the **Motion** tab.

6. Set an **Opacity** keyframe of zero at the start of the clip.

7. Go forward half a second, 15 frames, and ramp the **Opacity** up to 100.

8. Now double-click on the video clip on **V4**. You're half a second into the clip. Set an **Opacity** keyframe with a value of zero here.

9. Go forward to the one-second mark. Change the **Opacity** to 100.

10. Double-click on the video clip on **V6**, set its **Opacity** down to zero, and make a keyframe.

11. Bring the **Opacity** up to 100 15 frames later.

12. Do the same for the clips on **V8**, **V10**, and **V12**.

Each letter will now fade onto the screen one after the other, in half second intervals. One last touch will polish it.

Drop Shadow Finale

1. Go back to your final sequence, the one with the rescaled stage sequence and *Village3*.

2. **Option**-double-click on the nested sequence on **V2** to open it in the **Viewer**.

3. In the **Motion** tab, set a **Drop Shadow**.

Now as each letter fades on, its drop shadow will fade on with it. This is easier than doing it for each letter in the nested sequence.

Outline Text

Let's look at a technique for getting video inside outlined text. It's simple to do once you understand the principles behind compositing modes and travel mattes.

1. Start off by creating the **Outline Text** from the **Generator** popup.

2. In the **Controls** tab, type *DAMINE* in the **Text** box. Leave the default black-and-white colors.

3. Again use Arial Black or some other fat font, and set the size up to about 120.

4. Change the **Aspect** to 0.4. This will make the text much taller so you'll see more of the image through it.

5. In **Controls** give the word a large amount of **Line Width** and some **Line Softness**.

I used a **Line Width** of 180 and a **Line Softness** of 50.

6. Lay this Outline Text in *Sequence 1* on **V2**.

7. Put a video clip as a background layer on **V1**.

I used *Village3* again.

8. Before we go further, **Option-Shift**-drag the **Outline Text** from **V2** to **V3** to copy the text.

9. You can now open up the **Outline Text** layer on **V2** and make the **Line Color** anything you want. I went for a bright yellow

10. Put a video clip that you want to appear inside the **Outline Text** on **V4**, above the two layers of **Outline Text.**

I went for *Bamboo2* this time.

11. The final touch is to apply a **Compositing Mode>Travel Matte - Luma** to the video clip on **V4**.

Because a travel matte will always hide the matte layer, the **Outline Text** on **V3**, which provides the matte information for the video clip on **V4**, disappears, leaving you to see the outline color on the layer below. The **Canvas** should look something Figure 12.35. I have prebuilt a sequence for you called *Video in Outline.*

Figure 12.35 Video in Outline Text

Empty Outline Text

Remember in "Outline Text" on page 332 in Lesson 8 I said I'd show you how to make Outline Text that was only an outline and empty where the letters are? You probably can guess how to do this already using **Composite Modes**. The stack of clips that show this technique is in a sequence in your **Browser** called *Empty Outline.*

To make this effect, we'll start as we did for *Video In Outline,* by making **Outline Text** in black and white.

1. Select **Outline Text** from the **Generator** popup.

2. In the **Controls** tab, again type *DAMINE* in the **Text** box.

3. Again use Arial Black at 120.

4. In **Controls** again make **Line Width** 180,-**Line Softness** 50.

5. Lay this Outline Text in a new sequence on **V2**.

6. Put a video clip as a background layer on **V1**.

I used *Village3* again.

7. Again **Option-Shift**-drag the Outline Text from **V2** to **V3** to copy the text.

We haven't finished working with Outline Text on **V2**. To that text block on **V2**, we add a filter from the **Effects** menu.

8. Select **Video Filters>Channel>Invert**. Leave it at its default **Amount** of 100 and the **Channel** at RGB.

This inverts the color of the Outline Text on **V2**; what was black becomes white, and what was white becomes black.

9. Now open the copy on **V3** into the **Viewer**.

10. In the **Controls** tab, leave all the settings untouched, except the **Line Color**. Make that whatever you like.

I chose a bright yellow. Next we want to apply a composite mode to this layer.

11. Use **Composite Mode>Travel Matte - Luma**. Your composite should look like Figure 12.36.

Grunge Edges

Figure 12.36 Empty Outline Text Over Video

Next we'll do something different. We're going to grunge up the edges of a clip.

1. Start out in Photoshop, making a new image that's the same size as your final image — in our material, 320×240.

The technique will work for any image frame size.

2. Make the new image completely black.

3. Take the **Rectangular Marquee** tool and draw a rectangle that's about 20–30 pixels in from the edges of your image.

4. Next fill the selection with white.

5. Now have some fun. Drop the selection and grunge up the edges of the white box.
   Start with PS's **Smudge** tool (**R**), with which you can pull the white into the black and black into white.
   Or you can use one of the PS filters from the **Distort** group, maybe **Ripple** or **Ocean Ripple** set to a small size, but a high magnitude.

Figure 12.37 Grunge.psd

I like to smudge up the edges a bit first and then apply the filter so it doesn't come out too repetitive. Do it by mostly pulling the black into the white because the filter will expand the schmutzing effect. Avoid doing an effect that goes beyond the edges of the frame. It will look cut off when you composite it with the video. You should end up with something that looks like the *Grunge.psd* image in your **Browser** (Figure 12.37).

6. Import your PS file into Final Cut.

7. In a new sequence place your PS file on **V1** and place a video clip on top of it on **V2**.

In the **Browser** is a sequence called *Grunge Comp* that contains *Ceremony2* on **V2** and the Photoshop file *Grunge.psd* on **V1**. To the video clip on I applied **Composite Mode>Travel Matte - Luma**. Because the edges of the video clip looked harsh, I applied a little Gaussian Blur to the PS file, which softened the edges.

Try it without the blur and see how you like it. The video clip and the PS file are nested together in a sequence.

Look at Marker 8 in *Composite Stacks*. Here I've laid a gray color matte on **V1**, while on **V2** I placed the nested sequence *Grunge Comp*. With the **Canvas** in **Image+Wireframe** mode, I scaled and rotated the nested sequence in the **Canvas** (Figure 12.38). As you can see, you can work up millions of variations on the basic idea.

Figure 12.38 Scaled and Rotated Grunge-Edged Clip

Bug

A bug is an insect, a mistake in software coding, and it's also that little icon usually in the lower left corner of your television telling you what station you're watching. There are lots of different ways to make bugs, but I'll show you one using Photoshop and compositing modes. In your **Browser** is a PS file called *Logo.psd*. Double click to open it, and it will open as a sequence with two layers. The bottom layer, which has the visibility switched off, has the bug already made up with the Photoshop effect. The top layer that is visible in the **Canvas** doesn't have the effect applied, and that's the one we're going to work on.

1. Make sure in your **Preferences** that your **External Editor** for still images is set to Photoshop.

2. **Control**-click on the visible layer in the *Logo.psd* sequence, and from the contextual menu choose **Open in Editor** (Figure 12.39).

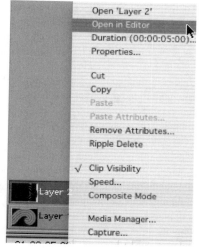

Figure 12.39 Contextual Menu>Open In Editor

3. Once Photoshop has launched, select *Layer 2* and from the little **F** in the bottom left of the **Layers** palette, add a **Layer Style**, choosing **Drop Shadow** (Figure 12.40).

4. Change the **Drop Shadow Angle** to 145 and the **Distance** to 15. Leave the other controls the same (Figure 12.41).

5. Check the **Inner Shadow** check box to add an inner shadow.

6. Also add a **Stroke**. Set the **Size** to 6. I made the color blue.

 Tip

Distinctive Logo: There are any number of different ways to give your logo a distinctive edge by using the power of layer styles. Rather than use the **Inner Shadow** and **Stroke** method, you could also use **Bevel and Emboss**. Change the **Technique** popup to **Chisel Hard**, and push the **Size** slider till the two sides of the bevel meet. This will give you maximum effect. Remember the logo is going to be very reduced in size. Also in bottom part of the **Bevel and Emboss** panel (Figure 12.42), try different types of **Glass Contour** from the little **Arrow** popup.

7. Press **OK**, and you've built the effect.

There is one more step to take before going back to FCP. The effects have to be applied to the layer. The easiest way to do this is to add a layer underneath the effects layer.

8. Add a new layer to your Photoshop composition and in the **Layers** palette drag it below *Layer 2*, which holds the effects.

9. Make sure *Layer 2* is selected. From the **Wing** menu, choose **Merge Down**, or use the keyboard shortcut **Command-E** (Figure 12.43).

10. Save your file and go back to Final Cut Pro.

Layer 2 in the PS sequence *Logo.psd* will have been updated and include your new effects.

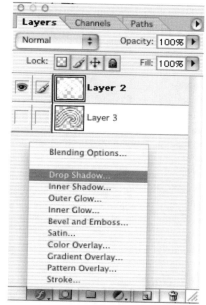

Figure 12.40 Add Layer Style>Drop Shadow

Figure 12.41 Drop Shadow Panel

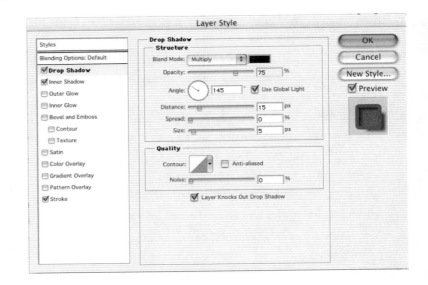

Figure 12.42 Bevel and Emboss
Panel

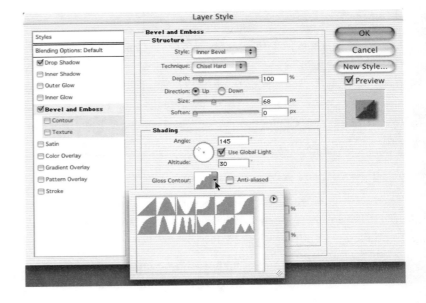

⚲ Note _____

Pixel Shape Reminder: Remember, if you're going to be working in a CCIR601 sequence (such as DV, which has rectangular aspect pixels), which we're not, you'll first need to squeeze the height of the Photoshop file down to 89.9%.

11. Next open a new duplicate *Sequence 1* and drag some video into it. I used *Dance2*.

Now normally you're going to want your bug to run the duration of your sequence, which might be an hour or more. Because you can't drag out still image layers to an unlimited duration once they're in a sequence, you need to set the duration of the bug while it's still in the **Browser**.

12. First open up the sequence *Logo.psd*. Now drag your newly minted effects layer *Layer 2* out into the **Browser**.

This will, of course, be a copy of the *Layer 2* in *Logo.psd*. With *Layer 2* as a single-layer image, before you place the bug into the final sequence, you can change its duration in the **Browser**. Here you can make the duration of the still image anything you want — anything up to four hours anyway, which is the duration limit of any FCP sequence.

13. Set the **Duration** for the bug logo to whatever the duration of the sequence you want to cover. Now you can drag the layer into your final sequence.

14. The first step you should take is to change the logo's composite type.

There are a number of compositing modes that will work for this, but I like to use **Composite Mode>Multiply** (Figure 12.44). This will pretty much make the white of the logo transparent. For a slightly brighter look, try **Soft Light**, and for an even more transparent look, use **Overlay**.

15. At the current size the logo is probably a bit intrusive, especially on a 320×240 image, so you might want to scale it down a bit and reposition it in the corner or your choice.

It'll now be your unobtrusive watermark on the screen. Some like to use effects like displacements or bump maps in addition, but for something this small, I don't really think it's necessary. The simple transparency effect of a composite mode is enough.

Day for Night

Color mattes don't have to be used only for backgrounds or graphical elements as we did in earlier lessons. They can also be

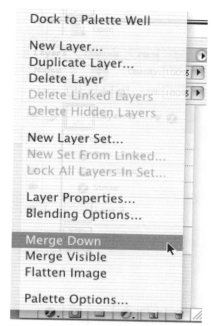

Figure 12.43 Merge Down

Figure 12.44 Logo with Composite Mode> Multiply

used as a color filter. Day for Night is the now seldom-used technique of trying to shoot in daylight and make it look like a moonlit night. Old Westerns almost always used this technique. Basically, you stop down the camera and shoot through a blue or a graduated blue filter. Let's do something similar.

1. Start off by laying the clip you want to affect on **V1** in a new sequence.

I used *Village3* because it presents a typical daylight problem, the bright sky.

2. Darken the image, such as with **Color Corrector.**

I pulled down all the levels — **Whites, Mids, Blacks,** and even **Saturation.** Even with the levels pulled quite far down, the sky remains bright and pale (Figure 12.45). Next we'll use the **Color Matte** to add the blue night filter.

3. Create a deep, dark blue color matte and lay it on **V3.** (You can review color mattes in the Lesson 8 exercise beginning on page 336.)

4. Create a **Custom Gradient** and place it between the two layers on **V2.**

5. Set the **Composite** mode on the **Color Matte** to **Travel Matte - Luma.**

All that's left to do is to make the gradient.

6. Open the controls, leave the default at **Linear** gradient, and change the **Direction** to 180.

Next you need to use the crosshairs to place the start of the gradient. There is a start point, but no end point for the gradient. If you start at the top of the **Canvas,** the blue will carry too far down into the image.

7. Scale down the size of the **Canvas** to something like 50%.

8. Place the start point for the crosshairs somewhere out in the grayboard.

9. Tighten the **Gradient Width** so that it falls off more sharply.

10. Make the end color of the gradient somewhat less than pure black to give the image a cold, blue cast.

Figure 12.45 Darkened Image Bright Sky   Figure 12.46 Day for Night Gradient Filter

The sky should be dark blue, while the center of the image, should still show some light and color (Figure 12.46). The stack is at Marker 9 in *Composite Stacks*.

Jigsaw Puzzle

Let's do one more. This one's somewhat labor intensive, but once you get into a rhythm, you'll work quickly. The effect uses a jigsaw puzzle to piece together an image. There are many variations possible, but here's the basic form. The jigsaw started out as an Illustrator file, but the paths were converted to separate selections in Photoshop, with each piece one of 15 separate layers. I've made it at 720×486 so that it might be more useful and can readily be adapted to DV.

Inside your copy of *L12p*'s **Browser** is the Photoshop sequence *Jigsaw.psd* as well as a 720×486 still image of Stanford University called *Tower.psd*. That's the image we are going to composite into jigsaw, though it could be piece of moving video.

1. Duplicate the 15-layer PS sequence called *Jigsaw.psd* and open the duplicate.
2. Make sure the **Canvas** is set to **Fit to Window** in the **Zoom** popup at the top of the **Canvas**.

It will look almost pure white.

3. Click off the visibility of some of the layers.

You'll see that each of the layers is made up of a piece of a jigsaw puzzle that fitted together form a whole image.

To animate the jigsaw puzzle, we're going to composite a piece of an image, in this case *Tower.psd*, with each of the pieces of the puzzle. We'll to need to add even more tracks to the sequence.

1. Insert above each of tracks a new, empty track until the sequence is 30 layers deep.

2. Target the topmost empty track, **V30**, and place *Tower.psd* on it.

3. Double-click the image *Tower.psd* to open it in the **Viewer**.

Notice the black lines on the left and right edges of the frame. These appear in almost all digital video. Normally these lines are outside the television masking and are never seen, but if you start animating the image, moving it about the screen, the lines will immediately become visible.

4. Make sure the **Viewer** is in **Image+Wireframe** mode.

5. Take the **Crop** tool and in the **Viewer** trim off a bit of the left and right edges.

You're now ready to start the production line.

6. **Option-Shift**-drag tower picture from the top track down into the empty tracks below — **V28**, **V26**, **V24**, **V22**, and so on — until all the tracks are filled, either with a copy of *Tower.psd* or with one of the pieces of the jigsaw puzzle.

7. Go to each of the tower images in the sequence in turn and change its **Composite Mode** to **Travel Matte-Alpha**.

Each layer will now track the alpha information from the PS layer directly beneath it. The top portion of your stack should look like Figure 12.47.

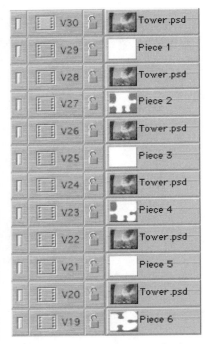

Figure 12.47 Top 12 Layers in the Sequence

Nesting

We're going to animate the jigsaw pieces, so the next step will be to nest each pair of layers.

1. Working from the top of the stack, on **V30** select the tower image and **Command**-select its travel matte on **V29**, *Piece 1*.

2. Press **Option-C** to create nested sequence.

3. Enter a name in the dialog box that appears. I named each pair *Piece 1*, *Piece 2*, *Piece 3*, and so on.

When you've done that, you should be back down to 15 layers, each one a composite nest.

4. To clean up the **Timeline** window, go to the **Sequence** menu and select **Delete Tracks**.

5. In the dialog box, check the **Video** box and **All Empty Tracks**.

Animation

Now we're ready to animate. It's much easier to animate this kind of motion backwards.

1. Go four or five seconds into the timeline and select every layer with **Command-A**.

2. Set a keyframe in the **Canvas**.

3. Go back to the head of sequence and switch off the visibility for all the tracks except one. **Option**-click on one of the green track visibility buttons.

4. Move that layer off into the grayboard somewhere.

5. In the **Canvas**, **Control**-click on the start and end position keyframes and change them to **Ease In/Ease Out**.

6. Grab the Bezier Handle sticking out from the keyframe and pull it out.

7. Give the motion some wild and crazy path.

8. Turn on the visibility for another layer and make a new, different, perhaps even more tortuous route.

9. Make motion paths for each of the layers. All the motion paths seen at once from the start frame might look something like Figure 12.48.

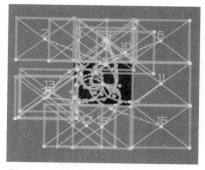

Figure 12.48 Motion Paths in the Canvas

Look at *Jigsaw Final* in the **Browser**. This is the sequence with the all the nested composites animated. I didn't tumble any of the layers by rotating them or by using the **Basic 3D** filter, but you could to increase the complexity of the animation. You can render *Jigsaw Final* if you like, but be warned that it's a long, slow render. It might be easier just to skip through it and look at selected frames.

Drop Shadow

After doing the animation, I like to add a final touch by putting in a drop shadow on each layer.

1. In your own sequence, **Option** double-click the top piece to bring it into the **Viewer**.

2. In the **Motion** tab, apply the **Drop Shadow**.

My settings were:

Shadow	black
Offset	6
Angle	default
Softness	10
Opacity	70

When the jigsaw puzzle movement is complete, we want the drop shadow to disappear.

3. Go to the end of the motion, the end keyframe for Center, and then go back eight frames.

4. Type **–8** and **Enter**.

5. Set a keyframe for the **Drop Shadow** controls **Offset** and **Opacity**.

6. Go back to the end of the motion again and turn the **Offset** and **Opacity** values both down to zero.

7. After you've done the process for the item on the top track, select it in the sequence and copy it.

8. Use **Paste Attributes** (**Option-V**), checking the **Drop Shadow** box for each nested composite on each track below.

9. Leave **Scale Attribute Times** unchecked because you want the keyframing to maintain their current positions. We'd use **Scale Attribute Times** to spread or contract the copied keyframes proportionately over the length of a shot.

Near the middle of the jigsaw motion, your **Canvas** should look like Figure 12.49. Eh voilà! You've built the jigsaw puzzle motion in a full-frame sequence, rather than the 320×240 sequences we've usually used. You can use the *Jigsaw.psd* Photoshop sequence for any full-sized video as well as for DV.

That brings us to the end of this short, but packed lesson on compositing. We're almost ready to export our material from Final Cut and out into the world, which is the subject of our final lesson.

Figure 12.49 Jigsaw Pieces in Motion

Lesson 13

Outputting from Final Cut Pro

Remember I said at the beginning that the hard, technical part of nonlinear editing was at the start, setting up and setting preferences, logging and capturing? The fun part was the editing part in middle, and the easy part was the outputting at the end. We're up to the easy part, the output.

The two basic ways of outputting are:

- Exporting, if you're going to another computer application or CD or DVD or web delivery, or

- Recording to tape, if you're going to traditional broadcast or analog tape delivery

As it's probably the most common requirement for Final Cut Pro users, let's look at outputting to tape first. We see exporting later on page 554.

There are basically three ways to get material from your computer to tape:

- **Record to Tape**
- **Print to Video**
- **Edit to Tape**

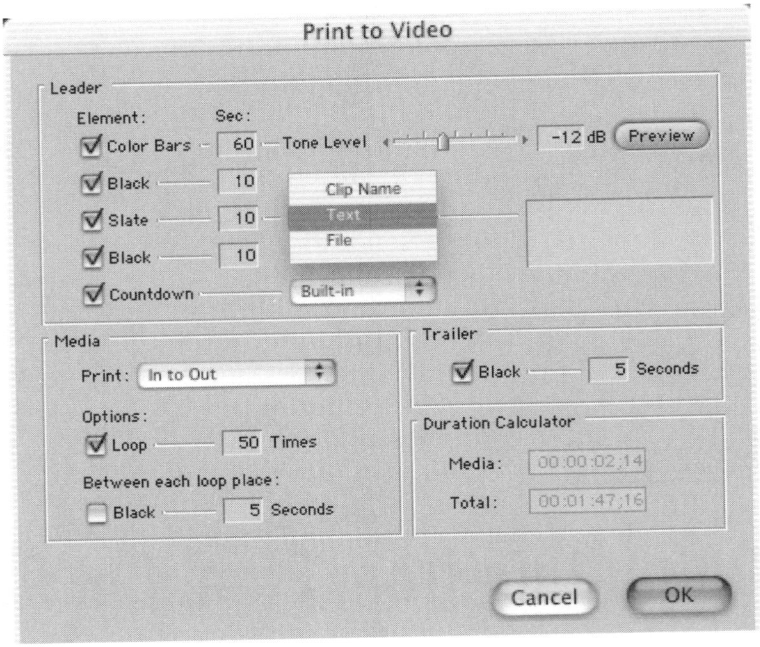

Figure 13.1   Print to Video Dialog

Record to Tape

You can get your edited material back out to tape in several different ways. The simplest one, and probably the most commonly used way, is to record to tape. Put the playhead at the beginning of the timeline, put your deck into record mode, and hit the spacebar. This is a fast, effective, and simple-to-use method.

Using playback from the **Timeline** has some disadvantages; you don't get to put in bars and tone and neat countdowns and slates and black leaders and trailers, unless you physically add them to your sequence. If you want these features, you can use **Print to Video**.

Print to Video

Print to Video and **Edit to Tape** are now both found under the File menu. If you have a sequence selected in the **Browser** or an active **Timeline**, you can call up **Print to Video** from the menu or use **Control-M**. This brings up the dialog box in Figure 13.1.

Tip

Audio Quality: Be sure to set the Audio Quality in **Preferences** to High. It's normally set to **Low**. When you use **Print to Video** and **Edit to Tape**, FCP will automatically switch the audio quality to **High**, but when you're simply recording to tape, it won't.

In this dialog you can set any number of options for program starts and ends. You can add bars and tone and set the tone level, depending on the system you're using. A number of different digital audio standards are used, if you can call anything that has variables as being a standard. Different systems use –12, –14, –16 or –20dB as digital audio standards. Analog uses a variety of other standards around 0dB. Check with your final destination before selecting a tone level.

The **Slate** popup lets you use the:

- **Clip Name**
- **Text**, which you can add in the text window
- **File**, which is any still image, video or audio file

So if you want to record an audio slate, selecting file and navigating to it with the little **Load** button will play the sound during recording.

You can use FCP's built-in countdown, using a form of Academy leader. Or you can use a countdown of your own by selecting **File** in the **Countdown** popup.

When you start **Print to Video**, FCP will write a video, and if necessary, an audio file of any material that needs to be rendered. It will render for every **Print to Video**. After it's finished writing the video and audio files, FCP may prompt you to put your deck into record. Press **OK** and playback will start. It may also be set to **Auto Record**, to automatically put your deck in record mode and set it off after a specified number of seconds. This new function is set in the lower right corner of the **Device Control** in **Audio/Video Settings** (Figure 13.2).

Edit to Tape

Print to Video is an excellent tool, but if you have a professional deck that allows insert and assemble editing to tape, then **Edit to Tape** is the tool for you. It's also called from the **File** menu.

Note

PtV Limits: Though you can loop FCP's **Print to Video** as many times as you want, the sequence had better be fairly short. The duration of any **Print to Video** recording is limited. It can't be longer than four hours, which is probably more than enough for most people.

Tip

Audio Mixdown: One of the hardest tasks for a hard drive to do in digital video is finding, seeking, and playing back multiple tracks of audio simultaneously. Final Cut has a great feature: the ability to mixdown your audio tracks. From the **Sequence** menu, select **Mixdown Audio**, or press **Cmd-Option-R**. That's it. Wait while FCP renders out a single audio file that mixes down all your tracks. Your system will run more easily, and you're less likely to have dropped frames during that crucial playback to tape. I suggest mixing down every time you output to tape, whatever method you use. I also suggest always switching off **Mirror on Desktop** to conserve system resources for outputting.

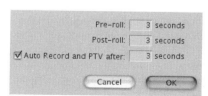

Figure 13.2 Auto Record
Preference

Figure 13.3 Edit to Tape Window

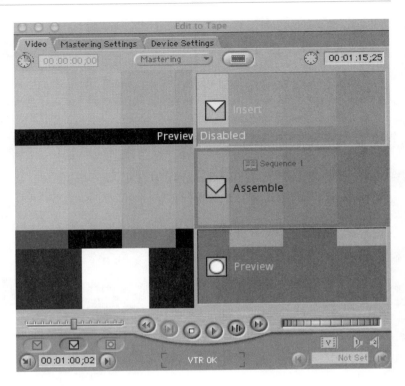

Figure 13.4 Edit Select Buttons and Controller in Edit to Tape Window

Figure 13.5 Insert Selector Buttons in Edit to Tape Window

Edit to Tape uses the same type of window as **Log and Capture**, only with an edit overlay (Figure 13.3). To perform an **Assemble** or **Insert** edit, at least an In point has to be entered. Simply dragging a sequence from the **Browser** into the **Edit to Tape** window will activate the **Edit Overlay**. It offers you the choices of **Assemble**, **Insert**, or **Preview**, assuming your deck is capable of those functions. Most DV camcorders and decks can do an assemble edit. If so, you can select your edit mode here, or with one of the buttons in the lower left corner (Figure 13.4).

The controls will operate your deck with the usual buttons or the **J, K, L** keys. You can assign In and Out points on the deck for assemble or insert edits, either with the usual buttons as in the **Log and Capture** window or with the **I** and **O** keys.

On the lower right side of the **Edit to Tape** window are selector buttons that let you choose the tracks you want to enable for insert editing, any combination of video or two audio tracks (Figure 13.5).

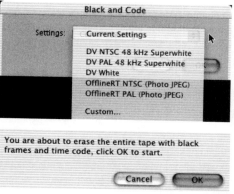

Figure 13.6   Top of the Edit to Tape Window (Above)

Figure 13.7   Black and Code Dialog (Upper Right)

Figure 13.8   Black and Code Warning Dialog (Lower Right)

At the top of the **Edit to Tape** window, in addition to the duration on the left and the current time on the right, are two buttons (Figure 13.6). The one on the left is a popup that lets you select between **Mastering** and **Editing**.

In the **Mastering** panel you have access to **Bars and Tone, Leaders and Trailers,** and **Looping,** just as you do in **Print to Video.** You select them in the **Mastering Settings** tab in the **Edit to Tape** window. In the **Mastering** panel, you can set whether you record whole or part of a sequence by selecting from a popup **Entire Media** or **In to Out.**

With the **Editing** option, you can do an insert edit, assigning both In and Out points on the tape or In and Out points in your sequence in any combination to define a three-point edit. In the **Editing** option, you don't have access to leaders and trailers and the other extras you get with **Mastering.**

The button on the right will black a tape for you. This lays down on your tape a video black signal with continuous timecode. You need this for an **Insert** edit, and you'd certainly want to black at least the first minute of a tape before you did an assemble edit. Clicking the **Black and Code** button brings up dialog where you can select any of your **Sequence Preset** types and use them as the type of Black and Code to be laid down (Figure 13.7).

Or you can simply use the **Current Settings,** or make up a new one with the **Custom** selection. Once you click **OK,** you'll get the warning dialog in Figure 13.8 before you can proceed.

Clicking **OK** will take the tape in the record deck back to the head and begin the process of recording Black and Code to your tape. During the recording you'll see on your computer monitor the video output, poorly displayed as during capture. If you have **Mirror on Desktop During Recording** switched off in your **External Video** preferences, instead of the picture you'll see a large black box the size of your output with the words "**Output of Video in Progress**." You can quit the Black and Code process at any time by hitting the **Escape** key.

When you're ready to begin the edit, drag the sequence into the **Edit Overlay**, and the process will be initiated. As in **Print to Video**, FCP will first render out what's necessary before beginning the **Edit to Tape**. As soon as that is completed, FCP will take control of your deck, queue it to the correct point, pre-roll it, and put it into record mode as frame accurately as your system can manage. Again, during the **Edit to Tape** process, you'll see the video or the **Output of Video in Progress** window. The **Escape** key again will allow you to abort the edit at any time.

If you only want to insert a portion of the timeline into a portion of the tape, you'll have to do an insert edit. If your deck is accurate enough, it's easy to do. What you'll really be doing is a linear, tape-to-tape, three-point edit, only in this case, one of the tape decks (the player deck) is your computer. Set the In and Out points on your record machine, and mark the In point in the timeline to create the three-point edit. Drag the sequence to **Insert** to execute the edit.

> **Note** _____
>
> **Preedit Calibration:** Before doing either an assemble and certainly an insert edit you should calibrate your deck in **Device Control** preferences, making adjustments in **Playback Offset**.

Export

You can access the different formats and ways of exporting from FCP from the **File** menu (Figure 13.9). From here you can export to **Final Cut Pro Movie**, which offers a number of options. You can also export using **Export>Audio to OMF**, an Avid standard audio file format for digital audio applications such as Pro Tools. Other export options include:

- Batch List

- Edit Decision List (EDL)

- QuickTime, which offers a great many options

Figure 13.9   File>Export

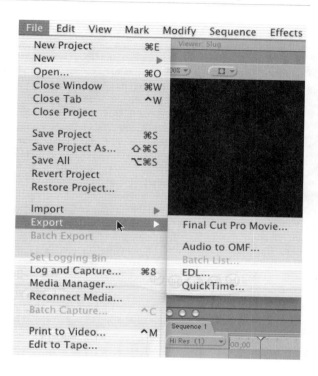

👉 *Tip*

Matching Timecodes: A common request is to lay off to tape a sequence in which the timecode on the tape matches the TC in the timeline. To do this, you need a deck that's at least assemble-edit capable, preferably one that's frame accurately controlled through RS-422. If your deck can address the timecode — that is, allows you to start at whatever TC number you enter — you have an added advantage. I like to start the TC on the deck at 58:00:00 or 59:00:00. This gives me a minute or two with a little fudge factor to begin the tape. That time can be used to lay in bars and tone, slates, countdown, black, whatever you want. Do this with the **Mastering Settings** tab on the back of the **Edit to Tape** window. This allows you access to all the options you had in **Print to Video**. Then at 1:00:00:00 straight up, your program begins. If your timeline begins at the default time of one hour, the TC on your deck will match the TC in the timeline, frame for frame.

If you can't address the TC on your deck, it's still possible to do, though not as neatly. Start by recording a chunk of black at the beginning of your tape. Put a 10-second slug of black at the head of your sequence in the timeline so that your program begins 10 seconds into the timeline. Next, using the **Timeline Options** tab in **Sequence Settings (Command-zero)**, set the **Sequence Start Time** to zero. Mark an In point in the sequence at the beginning of the program, where the 10-second slug ends. Now enter an In point on the tape for the assemble edit at 10:00 exactly. Assemble to that point, and the TC on your tape will match the TC in the timeline. If you want the bars and tone as well, you'll have to add them to the timeline to keep sync with the TC on the tape.

Figure 13.10 Final Cut Pro
              Movie Export
              Dialog

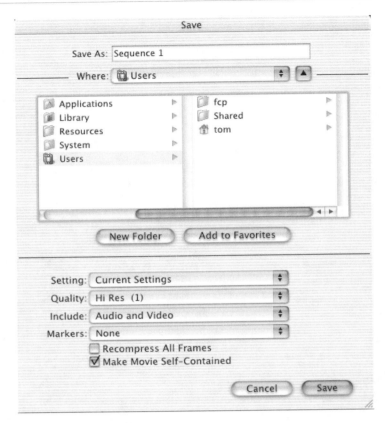

Final Cut Pro Movie

Let's start with Final Cut Pro Movie, the first in the **Export** list. FCP is listed as its creator type, so that if you launch the resulting movie, it will launch FCP. Because Final Cut is a QuickTime-based application, the exported movie will also play using the QuickTime Player.

You can export a sequence as a digital file into a Final Cut Pro movie in several ways:

- From the active **Timeline** window directly from the sequence you're working in

- From an active **Viewer**

- From the **Browser** by exporting a sequence or clip

Click on the item and go to **Export>Final Cut Pro Movie**. Any way will bring up the dialog box in Figure 13.10.

Here you can rename your sequence, if you wish, and you can set standard FCP settings from the **Settings** popup (Figure 13.11).

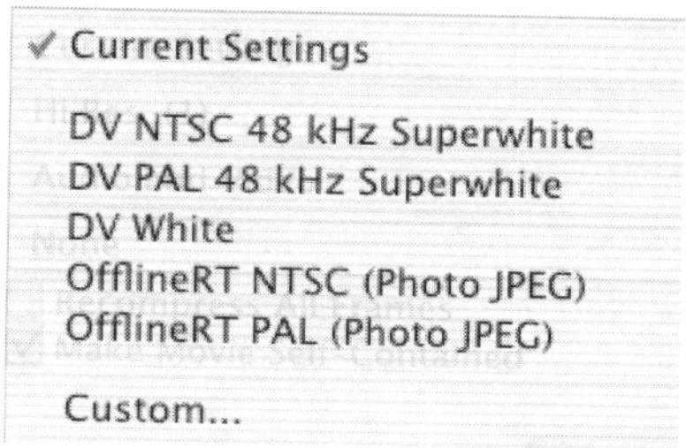

Settings can either be current or selected for anything in your **Sequence Presets Audio/Video Settings** panel. Or you can select **Custom**, which will actually call up the **Sequence Presets** window and let you create a custom preset right there.

The **Quality** popup is the **Render Quality** editor. You can select any of the preset render qualities. Unlike **Sequence Presets** though, you can't access the **Render Quality** editor from here.

The **Audio/Video** popup allows you to export just audio, just video, or both.

The two checkboxes at the bottom of the dialog box are the crucial: **Recompress All Frames** and **Make Movie Self-Contained**. Normally you do not want to recompress the frames; they've probably been compressed already into DV or Motion-JPEG. You want to use the compression that's already there.

You would want to use **Recompress All Frames** only if you have material from different codecs or with different data rates in a single sequence and you want them to use a uniform, fixed codec and data rate. In such cases, you have to use **Make Movie Self-Contained** to create a single video file for your sequence.

But you have another choice. If you uncheck **Make Movie Self-Contained**, FCP will generate a reference movie. This is a relatively small file that points back to the original media source files. It will play the contents of the sequence as you laid them out. The reference movie will play back from the QT player, and it can also be imported into other applications such as After Effects, Commotion, and Cleaner, for compression. The real advantages to making reference movies are the speed in generating the file and the comparatively small file size. If anything in the FCP sequence needs to be rendered, it will still have to be rendered for the reference movie, and the audio files will also be duplicated as a mix-down of your tracks. No other application can call up FCP's effects and motion to do rendering within it. The reference movie is treated just like any other QT clip inside AE or Cleaner. FCP and the importing application do not need to be open at the same time for this to work. You do, of course, need to have access to all

Figure 13.11 Settings Popup

(Settings Popup contents:)

✓ Current Settings

DV NTSC 48 kHz Superwhite
DV PAL 48 kHz Superwhite
DV White
OfflineRT NTSC (Photo JPEG)
OfflineRT PAL (Photo JPEG)

Custom...

the source media included in the sequence, because a reference movie only points to existing media source files on your hard drives. It's not a complete video clip in itself. Be warned: you cannot delete any of the media needed for the reference movie, or it will not play. It will be a broken QuickTime file.

Export to Final Cut Movie is an important tool because it is the only way to export a sequence from FCP without recompressing the video. All other exports, including export to QuickTime, will recompress the frames.

QuickTime

QuickTime is the catch-all for every form of file conversion and still export from FCP. I would have liked if **Still** export were separated, but it's hidden in here as well (Figure 13.12).

Video Export

Final Cut Pro has a number of video export choices for Quick-Time Export. They include:

- FLC, an 8-bit format used for computer animations
- AVI, a PC video format
- DV Stream, DV audio and video encoded on a single track

These are video formats. Some, such as AVI and QuickTime, allow you to use a number of different codecs. DV Stream is used by iMovie, not by FCP. Do not export to DV Stream if you're going to a video-editing application other than iMovie.

In **Quicktime Export**, the **User** popup offers a stack of common Internet or CD settings (Figure 13.13).

To export to DV, use the **Options** button and select the correct video and audio settings (Figure 13.14).

The default compressor is **Video**, but if you click on the **Video** button, you get exactly the same **Settings** dialog box as you get when you press the **Advanced** button in **A/V Settings** for **Sequence Presets** and **Capture Presets**. You can set the compressor, quality, and frame rate just as before. Be sure to set

🦎 **Note** _____

Range Check: Whenever you export from FCP, whether as a Final Cut Pro movie, or as QuickTime, you must make sure that you have **Range Check** switched off. From the **View** menu, select **Range Check>Off**. It is important because **Range Check** will upset the codec and produce a white screen on output, the notorious missing codec symptom. Users are reporting problems on export that appears as a blank white screen on movie or even still frame export. There may be a other bug-like issues involved here, but one certain cause is having **Range Check** active during export.

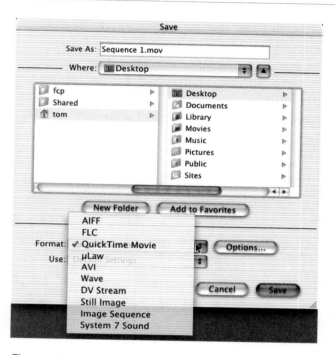

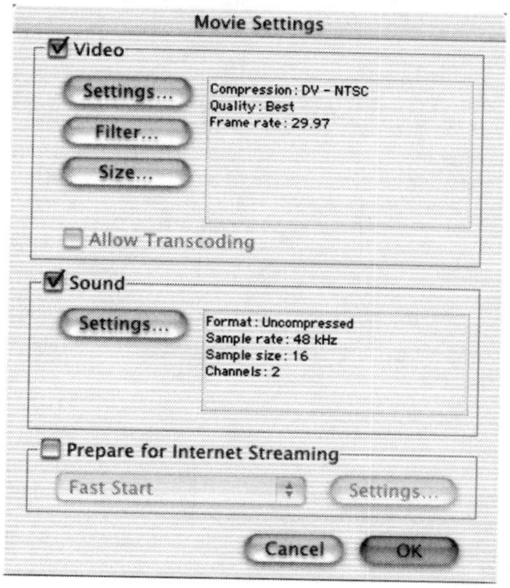

Figure 13.12 QuickTime Export (Above)

Figure 13.13 QuickTime Export User Popup (Upper Right)

Figure 13.14 QuickTime Video and Audio Options (Lower Right)

the **Quality** slider in DV to **Best** for final output. The **Quality** slider will affect the recompression quality. Only use **Low** or **Medium** for a test output or some other intermediary use.

The **Audio** dialog box is also the same as you've seen in **Sequence Presets** and **Capture Presets**.

One setting that's slightly different in the QT export is the **Size**, which offers you either the current frame size or a custom size you can dial in (Figure 13.15).

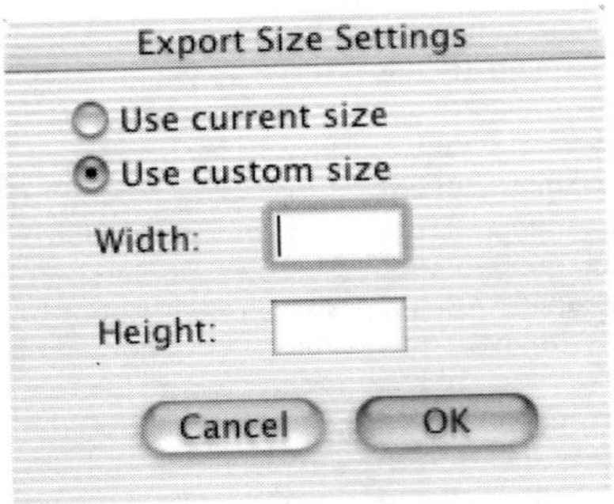

Export Size Settings

○ Use current size
● Use custom size

Width: ☐

Height: ☐

(Cancel) (OK)

Figure 13.15 QuickTime Frame
Size Options

Exporting with QuickTime allows you to use a variety of different codecs for compression, such as, among others:

- Animation

- Cinepak

- DV-NTSC

- Motion-JPEG A

- Photo-JPEG

- Sorenson Video 3

Sorenson Video 3 is an excellent codec for web compression. Photo-JPEG is used for file size reducing and works with FCP's OfflineRT capability. An important codec is Animation, a high data rate, lossless compression codec often used to transfer material between various applications such as After Effects. One advantage that the Animation codec has that others don't is that it can carry alpha channel information with the video. This allows you to create a composition in After Effects, for instance, and bring it into FCP without loss. With an alpha channel, it can be overlaid on other images. When you export with the Animation codec with an alpha channel, make sure that for **Colors** you select **Millions+**. The plus is the alpha channel.

To create good quality web video, you'll need a separate application such as Discreet's Cleaner or Sorenson Squeeze. To create video CDs, you'll need an application, such as Cleaner, that allows compression to the MPEG1 codec. This is a heavily compressed codec, but one which is remarkable in that it can actually play back off the very low output of a CD and still produce a full-screen, full-motion image. To create a DVD, you need another application such as iDVD or DVD Studio Pro. When exporting to iDVD, you should use either a self-contained or a reference Final Cut Pro movie, and iDVD will do the compression to MPEG2 for you. If you're using DVD Studio Pro, one of the options available in the QuickTime **Export** window will be MPEG2, the DVD compression format. Export to MPEG2 and build your DVD project using the MPEG2 assets, which will be separate video and audio, that you export from Final Cut Pro.

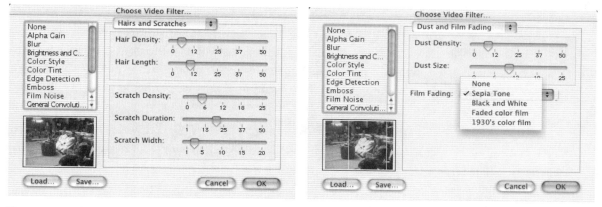

Figure 13.16 Film Noise Hair and Scratches Panel   **Figure 13.17** Dust and Film Fading Panel

Exporting to QuickTime allows you to add filters to your clips or sequences. Most of the QuickTime filters are available directly within FCP, with a notable exception, **Film Noise** (Figure 13.16).

This filter adds an old-time film look to your video, as if it were scratched and dirty. A small QT movie runs in the bottom left corner showing you how much schmutz you've added to the picture. Here you can set amounts of **Hair and Scratches** that appear on your video, from very low to fairly well-destroyed. You can't control the grain, however, but you can add that in FCP before you export. In addition to **Hair and Scratches**, the popup at the top will take you to another panel where you can set the amount of dust on your video as well as tinting the film. The sepia is quite subtle, and the 1930's color film is suitably garish (Figure 13.17).

Image Sequence Export

Two other types of QuickTime export are often used: **Image Sequence** and **Still Image**. Image sequences are useful for rotoscoping and animation work, and provide high quality output without loss. You can set any frame rate, and exporting will create one frame of uncompressed video for every frame you specify. Make sure you first create a folder in which to put your image sequence because this can easily generate a huge number of files (Figure 13.18).

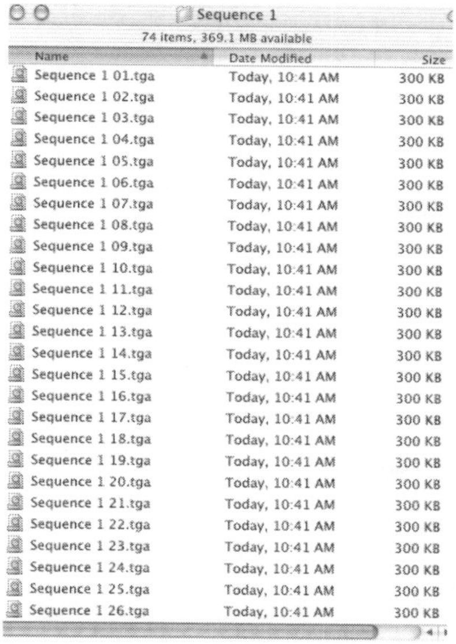

Figure 13.18 Targa Image Sequence in Folder

Still Image Export

Finally, the **Quicktime Export** allows you to export still images. This is how you get frames of video out to your computer for web or print use. Your stills will only be 72dpi, probably not good enough for fine printing. Photoshop plugins such as Genuine Fractals can help improve the image's appearance.

The **Options** button for **Still Image** export uses the same dialog box as **Image Sequence**, together with frame rate. Don't be confused; leave the frame rate blank.

The still you're exporting may very well be in CCIR601 rectangular pixels. This is not a problem if you're going back to a video application, but in print or on a computer display, the stills will look squashed. Photoshop will fix this problem for you. If the still image comes from DV, in PS go to **Image Size**. Switch off the **Constrain Proportions** checkbox, and either upsample the image by changing the size to 720×540 or, for better quality, downsample to 640×480. Either way, you'll end up with a 4:3 image in the correct pixel aspect ratio. If you're working with a 720×486 image, then downsample to 648×486. Check **Resampling** and select **Bicubic** whenever you resize in PS.

If you're going to export stills for web or print work from video, especially video with a lot of motion in it, you'll probably want to de-interlace it. You can do this either in FCP before you export the frame. As we saw in "De-interlace" on page 496 in Lesson 11, you select **Video Filters>Video>De-interlace** from the **Effects** menu. Or you can de-interlace in PS as well. It's in the Filters menu under Video>De-Interlace. I normally do it in Photoshop because I think its **De-interlace** feature works better than FCP's built-in one, which simply drops one of the fields. In the Photoshop **De-Interlace** filter, you have an interpolation option, which works very well (Figure 13.19).

Audio Export

FCP can export to a number of different audio formats including:

- AIFF
- μLaw

- Wave

- System 7

Below the **Format** popup is a Use popup that is contextually sensitive, so if you select **AIFF**, for instance, in the **Use** popup you'll get common audio file settings (Figure 13.20).

Notice that the selection does not include any of the DV sampling rates, although AIFF is the most commonly used format for audio files with Final Cut. Instead of the **Use** popup, use the **Options** button, which is also context sensitive and offers a wider range of options, including 32,000 and 48,000, the DV sampling rates (Figure 13.21).

Export Audio to OMF

OMF stands for Open Media Format, a file format that Avid may have hoped would become the PDF of audio. It hasn't been quite as successful as the Adobe product, but it's widely recognized as an intermediary format for moving audio files between various applications. Exporting to OMF allows you to move your audio tracks as you've laid them out in FCP into a digital audio workstation such as Pro Tools. It works very well, as long as you bear a number of constraints in mind.

Conversion Application Constraints

As with most exports from FCP, it's easy to do and just as easy to get wrong. To export audio to OMF, select the sequence you want to export and go to **File>Export Audio to OMF.**

This brings up a dialog box that offers you a few choices (Figure 13.22). However, your options are limited by the application converting your OMF files and the application massaging your audio. Digidesign offers a free OMF converter called OMF-Tool 2.0.8. This software does not handle crossfades, however, so you should uncheck that box. If you're using Digidesign's Digi-Translator you can export your crossfades.

Another important issue is that neither OMFTool nor DigiTranslator, nor the ProTools mixing software will work in OS X. Once

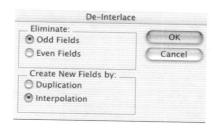

Figure 13.19 Photoshop De-Interlace Options

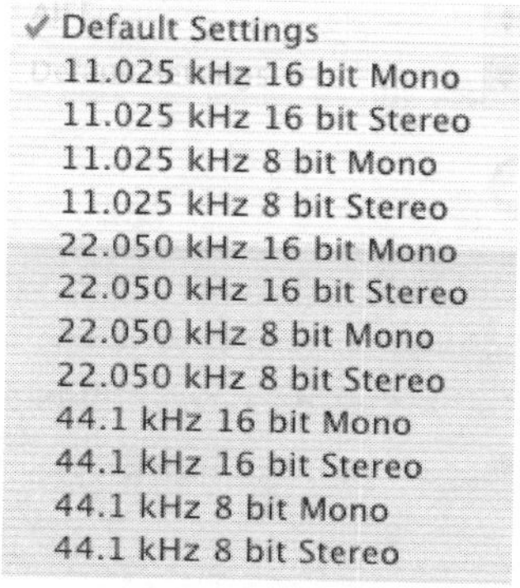

✓ Default Settings
11.025 kHz 16 bit Mono
11.025 kHz 16 bit Stereo
11.025 kHz 8 bit Mono
11.025 kHz 8 bit Stereo
22.050 kHz 16 bit Mono
22.050 kHz 16 bit Stereo
22.050 kHz 8 bit Mono
22.050 kHz 8 bit Stereo
44.1 kHz 16 bit Mono
44.1 kHz 16 bit Stereo
44.1 kHz 8 bit Mono
44.1 kHz 8 bit Stereo

Figure 13.20 AIFF Export Use Popup

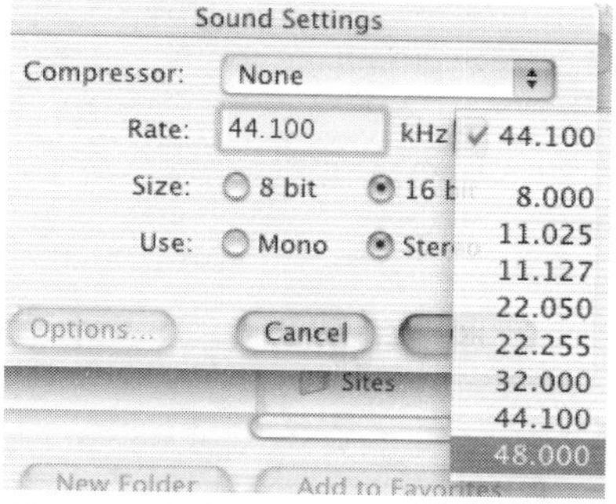

Figure 13.21 AIFF Export Options

you have done your **Export to OMF**, you will have to reboot your computer into OS9 to work with the Digidesign tools, which as of this writing will only work in the older operating system. Nor will they run in Classic mode, that is, using OS9 from within OS X.

Note _____

OMF Considerations: The OMF file does not pass on pans, levels settings, or filters from FCP; all you get are the tracks and media handles. Levels settings and effects are supposed to be added in your audio-mixing software. Also, a small bug in OMFTool 2.0.8 puts an audio pop on the end of each track. The solution is to drop a short audio slug on the end of each track. This doesn't happen with DigiTranslator.

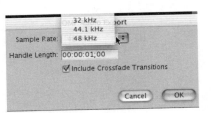

Figure 13.22 Export to OMF Dialog

Sample Rate Limits

There are limitations on the sampling rate you can choose as well. OMFTool will only work with 44.1 and 48; it does not accept 32. DigiTranslator accepts all three. But here are further complications. Digidesign has a free Pro Tools application called ProTools Free. This application will only work with 44.1 as a sampling rate, so that's what you have to choose. Digidesign's other apps will work with whatever sampling rate you pick. If your sampling rates are mixed in FCP, they will all be processed into one sampling rate, whatever you choose in the popup.

Audio Track Limits

Though you can have 99 tracks of audio in FCP, the Digidesign applications have limits on how many they will accept. Pro Tools Free can only handle eight tracks, Pro Tools LE up to 24 and Pro Tools TDM as many as 72.

Bearing in mind these limitations, **Export to OMF** is a powerful feature from those who want to audio sweeten their projects and have the software to take advantage of it. Table 13.1 summarizes these considerations.

Table 13.1   Summary of Digidesign Tool Considerations

	OMFTool*	DigiTranslator	ProTools Free	ProTools LE	ProToolsTDM
Sampling rate	44.1, 48	all	44.1	all	all
# audio tracks			8	24	72

* OMF Tool doesn't handle crossfades, pans, levels settings, or filters.

👉 *Tip* _____

Audio Sync: It's a good idea to add an audio sync pop at the beginning and end of your tracks. Set a one-frame tone two seconds before the first audio and two seconds after the last audio. Just use the **Generators** to go to **Bars and Tone,** make the single frame, and throw away the video bars. This makes an easy sync point when you bring your audio back into FCP for final output.

_____

After you've exported to OMF, you then have to run OMFTools or DigiTranslator to convert your files into a Pro Tools project. A dialog will ask you where you want to save the material. It's probably best to pick a media drive because two folders will be created:

- One with the Pro Tools project

- Another containing the actual audio files for Pro Tools to work with

When you've finished working with your material in ProTools, or whatever audio finishing application you're using, you'll need to export the sound track as an AIFF file and bring it into FCP. If you're working with ProTools Free you'll probably need to resample the audio from 44.1kHz to 48kHz. After importing the AIFF audio track, place it on an empty track in the FCP sequence and carefully line it up with the existing audio. Play the audio and listen for any echoing, which will indicate that the tracks are slightly out of sync. Obviously, all the tracks won't be the same, otherwise there would be no point using ProTools in the first place, but there should be some easy spot on the track where you'll be able to tell if the clips are in sync or not. Do this even if you've placed sync pops at the beginning and end of the tracks, just to check.

Batch List

A Batch List is basically a printout of the contents of a bin. You can only make a batch list when the bin is in List view. Then select **Export>Batch List,** choose either **Tabbed** or **Formatted** output, and you're done (Figure 13.23).

Figure 13.23 Batch List Dialog Box

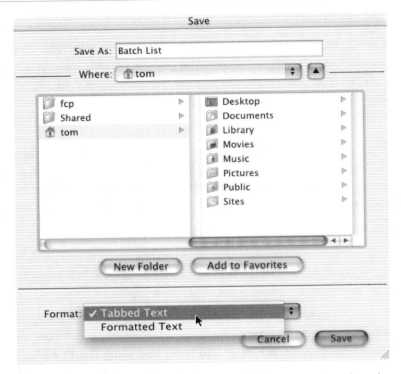

The exported Batch List will contain everything displayed in the List view columns, and not what's in the selected columns. If you don't want some information in the Batch List, simply use the contextual menu in the bin header to hide the column. Choosing either **Tabbed** or **Formatted**, the list can be opened either in a word processing application or in a spreadsheet application such as Excel, where it is ready to print out (Figure 13.24).

Batch Lists are really useful for long-form projects. After you have all your material captured and diced into subclips with notes and comments added, printing out a Batch List gives you a hard copy of your bins. You can look it over in those spare moments while you're rendering or waiting for the coffee to brew.

What's great about batch lists is that they work both ways. Because they are just tab-delineated files, you can create them in Word, Excel, or other applications. This way you can log material outside of FCP, such as when you're on the road. Then you can use your list in FCP as a Batch Capture List. Because tab-delineated files are common to many applications, you can move logging lists from one application to another.

Batch List

	A	B	C	D	E	F	G	H
1	Name	Duration	In	Out	Tracks	Frame Size	Vid Rate	Compressor
2	Stairs1	00:00:08:16	00:00:00:00	00:00:08:15	1V, 1A	320 × 240	29.97 fps	Photo - JPEG
3	Stairs2	00:00:08:29	00:00:08:16	00:00:17:14	1V, 1A	320 × 240	29.97 fps	Photo - JPEG
4	StoneBasin	00:00:05:08	00:00:17:15	00:00:22:22	1V, 1A	320 × 240	29.97 fps	Photo - JPEG
5	Temple	00:00:05:00	00:00:32:11	00:00:37:10	1V, 1A	320 × 240	29.97 fps	Photo - JPEG
6	Dance1	00:00:08:16	00:00:49:05	00:00:57:20	1V, 1A	320 × 240	29.97 fps	Photo - JPEG
7	Dance2	00:00:17:07	00:00:57:21	00:01:14:27	1V, 1A	320 × 240	29.97 fps	Photo - JPEG
8	Dance3	00:00:05:00	00:01:15:18	00:01:20:17	1V, 1A	320 × 240	29.97 fps	Photo - JPEG
9	Food1	00:00:06:04	00:01:32:04	00:01:38:07	1V, 1A	320 × 240	29.97 fps	Photo - JPEG
10	Food2	00:00:12:27	00:01:38:08	00:01:51:04	1V, 1A	320 × 240	29.97 fps	Photo - JPEG
11	Food3	00:00:05:00	00:01:51:05	00:01:56:04	1V, 1A	320 × 240	29.97 fps	Photo - JPEG
12	Food4	00:00:02:29	00:02:07:13	00:02:10:11	1V, 1A	320 × 240	29.97 fps	Photo - JPEG
13	Food5	00:00:15:10	00:02:10:22	00:02:26:01	1V, 1A	320 × 240	29.97 fps	Photo - JPEG
14	Food6	00:00:05:00	00:02:26:15	00:02:31:14	1V, 1A	320 × 240	29.97 fps	Photo - JPEG
15	Food7	00:00:03:00	00:02:34:01	00:02:37:00	1V, 1A	320 × 240	29.97 fps	Photo - JPEG
16	Food8	00:00:06:06	00:02:37:03	00:02:43:08	1V, 1A	320 × 240	29.97 fps	Photo - JPEG
17	Ceremony1	00:00:05:00	00:02:43:09	00:02:48:08	1V, 1A	320 × 240	29.97 fps	Photo - JPEG
18	Ceremony2	00:00:37:23	00:03:12:14	00:03:50:06	1V, 1A	320 × 240	29.97 fps	Photo - JPEG
19	Ceremony3	00:00:10:21	00:03:50:07	00:04:00:27	1V, 1A	320 × 240	29.97 fps	Photo - JPEG
20	Ceremony4	00:00:11:01	00:04:01:02	00:04:12:02	1V, 1A	320 × 240	29.97 fps	Photo - JPEG
21	Ceremony5	00:00:45:00	00:04:12:03	00:04:57:02	1V, 1A	320 × 240	29.97 fps	Photo - JPEG
22	Ceremony6	00:00:21:10	00:04:57:03	00:05:18:12	1V, 1A	320 × 240	29.97 fps	Photo - JPEG
23	Ceremony7	00:00:05:00	00:05:18:13	00:05:23:12	1V, 1A	320 × 240	29.97 fps	Photo - JPEG
24	Ceremony8	00:00:17:01	00:05:39:02	00:05:56:02	1V, 1A	320 × 240	29.97 fps	Photo - JPEG
25	Ceremony9	00:00:21:27	00:05:56:03	00:06:17:29	1V, 1A	320 × 240	29.97 fps	Photo - JPEG
26	Village1	00:00:07:18	00:06:18:00	00:06:25:17	1V, 1A	320 × 240	29.97 fps	Photo - JPEG
27	Village2	00:00:08:18	00:06:25:18	00:06:34:05	1V, 1A	320 × 240	29.97 fps	Photo - JPEG
28	Village3	00:00:16:22	00:06:34:06	00:06:50:27	1V, 1A	320 × 240	29.97 fps	Photo - JPEG
29	Bamboo1	00:00:05:00	00:06:54:19	00:06:59:18	1V, 1A	320 × 240	29.97 fps	Photo - JPEG
30	Bamboo2	00:00:16:25	00:07:06:24	00:07:23:18	1V, 1A	320 × 240	29.97 fps	Photo - JPEG
31								

Figure 13.24 Batch List in Excel

EDL

Final Cut Pro can export an Edit Decision List in a variety of common formats (Figure 13.25). CMX3600 is probably the most common carrier, but other systems use other formats. Because an

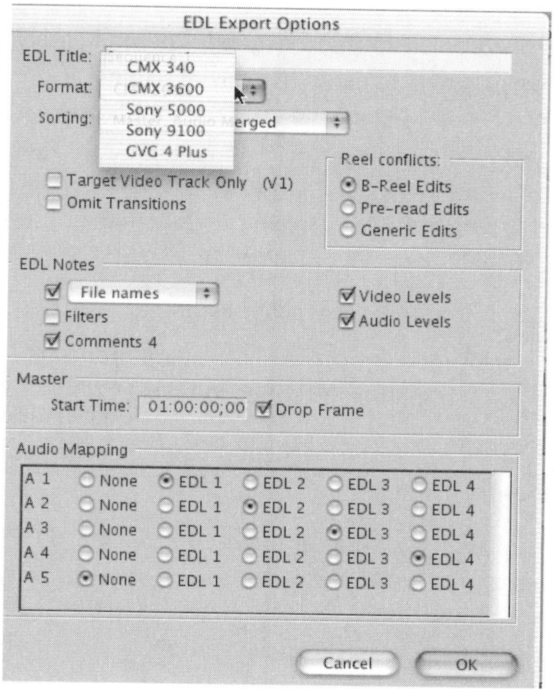

Figure 13.25 EDL Export Dialog (Left)

Figure 13.26 EDL Import Options (Below)

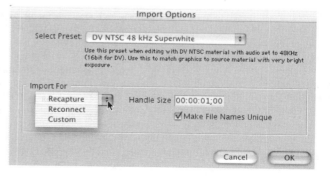

EDL is a text file, you can readily, if laboriously, edit it in any word-processing application. EDLs are great tools for moving between projects and sequences, between different types of edit systems, from offline to online, from nonlinear to linear. Remember however that an EDL is a fairly arcane format and limited to the types and numbers of tracks it can move, to the types of transitions it will understand, often only dissolves and simple wipes.

EDLs normally export only one video track. Any additional tracks should be output as separate EDLs. Only a limited number of audio tracks are allowed, usually no more than four. Split audio edits do not work correctly. No effects information and no motion information translate into EDLs. Titles do not export. Nested sequences do not export properly either. All in all, EDL export is a very limited format.

Remember also that FCP can not only export EDLs, it can also import them from the **File>Import>EDL** menu. This will bring an EDL into the application and lay it out as a sequence ready for batch capture or reconnect (Figure 13.26).

🦎 Note

QuickTime Warning: QuickTime export should not be used if you are exporting to the same format as your sequence settings as it will force the video to be recompressed. Use **Export To Final Cut Pro Movie** instead.

Batch Export

Batch Export is automation at its best, a good, comprehensive interface that allows you to trim media. It provides some of the same type of functionality as **Media Manager**, but specifically for exporting and trimming clips to another file format. You can select a bin, a group of shots, or even a sequence to batch export. Once you've selected **Batch Export** from the **File** menu, the **Export Queue** window will open (Figure 13.27).

It's like a bin window, but with special features, mainly the buttons at the bottom. Pressing the **Settings** button brings up an **Export** dialog box (Figure 13.28). Here you have all the usual settings options, like those in the Final Cut Pro and QuickTime **Export** windows. To trim video during batch export, check the box for **Use Item In/Out**.

The only two buttons that are slightly different from the FCP Movie and QT Exports are the **Set Destination** button at the top and the **Set Naming Options** button in the middle. **Set Destination** is pretty self-explanatory; it opens up navigation services and

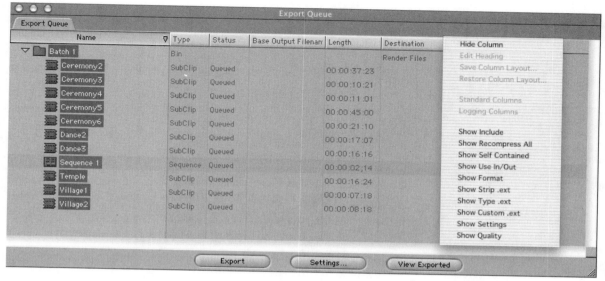

Figure 13.27 Export Queue

lets you pick a location on your hard drives for your material. **Set Naming Options** opens the dialog box in Figure 13.29.

Here you can remove any suffixes or add your own, as well as define the file type. When that's done, just press the **Export** button. Everything queued will be exported as specified in your settings. If

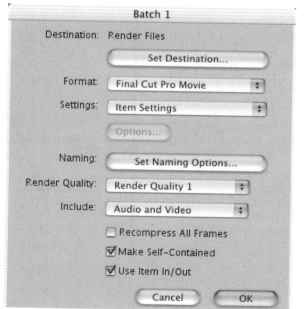

Figure 13.28 Batch Export Settings Options

Figure 13.29 Set Naming Options

your naming convention duplicates with an existing file name, you'll get the error dialog box, which allows you to rename the file you're exporting.

After exporting, clicking the **View Exported** button will open the clips in separate viewers within FCP.

Summary

We've now gone through the whole cycle of work in Final Cut Pro, starting from tape raw material, either analog or digital, capturing, editing, transitions, titling, special effects, compositing, and finally we have returned our finished project to tape. It's been a long journey, taking us into high places and rarefied air, but I hope an exciting, interesting, and rewarding one. It's the kind of journey that sometimes seems best undertaken by yak, maybe the one that's hidden in Final Cut Pro (Figure 13.30).

Figure 13.30 Yak

Index

Symbols

μLaw 562

Numerics

12-bit 81, 86
16:9 37, 77–78, 84, 351–352
16-bit 81, 273
180° rule 299
1-axis method 218
24fps 38
256MB 2
25fps 38
29.97fps 158
2-axis method 218
2-pop 229, 297, 497
300dpi 358
320x240 75–76, 108, 110, 348,
     378, 459, 533–534, 537,
     541, 547
32kHz 33, 81, 86, 564
3D 203, 209, 287, 312, 384, 483–
     484, 545
3D Simulation 201–204
4:3 464, 534
44.1kHz 33, 81, 86, 273, 564–565
48kHz 33, 74, 81, 273, 564–565
7.5IRE 97, 320, 410, 417
720x480 76, 350–353, 357–358,
     459
720x534 350, 352–353
720x540 350–351, 562
72dpi 318, 357, 382, 562

A

ABC xiii
Abort capture on dropped frames
     62
Abort capture on timecode break
     62
Abort on Dropped Frame 86

About This Mac 10–11
Acceleration 207
Access Denied 21
action 282
Adams, Ansel 309
Additive Dissolve 204
administrator's password 4, 6, 18,
     21
Adobe xvii, 22, 435
After Effects 6, 22–23, 78, 287, 435,
     443, 509, 517, 557, 560
AIFF 32–33, 86, 562–563, 565
AJA Kona 7, 84
alpha channel 37, 48, 225–226,
     319, 354–356, 446, 478,
     487, 523, 560
     reversing 37
Analyze Movie File 103
anamorphic 37, 78, 352
anchor point 374–375, 384
animation 322, 324–325, 363–400,
     452, 470, 523, 525, 545
Animation codec 80, 560
antialiasing 203, 227, 322, 332,
     344, 355, 493
Apple 1–3, 16, 22, 25, 33, 75, 87,
     190, 296, 397, 452, 519
Apple menu 10–12, 16, 89
Apple Software Restore 5
Apple System Profiler 18
AppleTalk 12, 89
Application menu 27
Application Support 15, 72–73, 313
Applications 15, 18–19, 57, 73
Arabic 342
Arrange
     Custom 29
     Restore Layout 273, 324, 365
     Save Layout 29
     Standard 28
     Wide 28–29, 110
arrays 6–7

Arrow keys
     Down 45, 123
     Left 45
     Right 45
     Up 45, 123, 258
Aspect 322
aspect ratio 377
     16:9 37, 77–78, 84, 351–352
     3:2 76
     4:3 76–78, 528, 534, 562
     pixel 37, 76–77, 352, 562
     widescreen 77
assemble edit 551–553, 555
ATI Radeon 25, 190
ATTO ExpressStripe 7
Attributes
     Paste 270–271, 387, 394, 444,
          468, 501, 546
     Remove 403
Audio 81, 559
     Levels 52, 266, 268
     Meters 27
     Pan 268
     Playback Quality 60
     Render Files 71, 110
     Settings 71–73, 81, 86
     Spread 268
     Stereo Pair 268
     tab 257–258, 266, 268, 304–
          305
     Waveform 66
audio 241–277
     crossfade 188, 197, 563
     digital 95
     fade out 267, 270–271
     format 37
     levels 52, 95, 265–277, 366
     meters 274
     mixdown 60, 95, 190, 557
     paired tracks 66
     pan 30